Collins

BESTSELLING BILINGUAL DICTIONARIES

Spurrell
Welsh
Dictionary

Collins

HarperCollins Publishers
Westerhill Road
Bishopbriggs
Glasgow
G64 2QT
Great Britain

Fourth Edition 2009

Reprint 10 9 8 7 6 5 4 3 2

© William Collins sons & Co. Ltd. 1960
© HarperCollins Publishers 1991, 2006,
2009

ISBN 978-0-00-729874-7

Collins® is a registered trademark of
HarperCollins Publishers Limited

www.collinslanguage.com

A catalogue record for this book is
available from the British Library

Typeset by Davidson Pre-Press,
Glasgow

Printed in Italy by LEGO Spa,
Lavis (Trento)

When you buy a Collins dictionary
or thesaurus and register on
www.collinslanguage.com for the free
online and digital services, you will not
be charged by HarperCollins for access
to Collins free Online Dictionary
content or Collins free Online Thesaurus
content on that website. However, your
operator's charges for using the internet
on your computer will apply. Costs vary
from operator to operator. HarperCollins
is not responsible for any charges levied
by online service providers for accessing
Collins free Online Dictionary or
Collins free Online Thesaurus on
www.collinslanguage.com using
these services.

HarperCollins does not warrant that
the functions contained in
www.collinslanguage.com content
will be uninterrupted or error free,
that defects will be corrected, or that
www.collinslanguage.com or the server
that makes it available are free from viruses
or bugs. HarperCollins is not responsible
for any access difficulties that may be
experienced due to problems with network,
web, online or mobile phone connections.

Acknowledgements
We would like to thank those authors
and publishers who kindly gave
permission for copyright material to be
used in the Collins Word Web. We would
also like to thank Times Newspapers Ltd
for providing valuable data.

Entered words that we have reason to
believe constitute trademarks have been
designated as such. However, neither the
presence nor absence of such designation
should be regarded as affecting the legal
status of any trademark.

In collaboration with the
Department of Welsh, University of
Wales Lampeter

Mewn cydweithrediad ag Adran y
Gymraeg, Prifysgol Cymru Llanbedr
Pont Steffan

MANAGING EDITOR/
GOLYGYDD RHEOLAETHOL
Gaëlle Amiot-Cadey

EDITOR/GOLYGYDD
Maggie Seaton

CONTRIBUTORS/CYFRANWYR
Eurwen Booth
Harry Campbell
Non Jenkins

SERIES EDITOR/GOLYGYDD Y GYFRES
Rob Scriven

CONTENTS

Notes on Pronunciation of Welsh   vi–viii
Abbreviations   ix

WELSH-ENGLISH   1–202

Language in Action   i–xv

ENGLISH-WELSH   203–422

INTRODUCTION

The first Spurrell Welsh-English dictionary appeared in 1848 published by William Spurrell (1813–89) the Carmarthen printer and publisher. One of his sons, Walter Spurrell (1858–1934), joined his father in the business and the family firm published a series of distinguished Welsh-English, English-Welsh dictionaries and influential Welsh grammars during the latter part of last century and the first half of the present century. William Spurrell was advised by and well-acquainted with Daniel Silvan Evans (1818–1903), one of the father figures of Welsh lexicography, sometime lecturer in Welsh at St David's University College, Lampeter and the first professor of Welsh to be appointed by the University of Wales.

The Collins-Spurrell Welsh Dictionary was first published in 1960 and quickly became an essential tool of general reference for Welsh learners as well as those anxious to interpret literature. It was edited by Henry Lewis, Professor of Welsh Language and Literature at University College, Swansea. The staff of the Department of Welsh Language and Literature at St David's University College, Lampeter are happy to cooperate with the editorial staff at Collins to produce this latest edition of a famous dictionary.

D A THORNE

NOTES ON THE PRONUNCIATION OF WELSH

VOWELS

They are sounded, long or short, as the vowels in the English words given.

A   p*a*lm, p*a*t.
E   g*a*te (without dipthongization), g*e*t.
I   f*ee*t, f*i*t.
O   m*o*re, n*o*t.
U (1) North Wales: like French *u* or German *ü* without rounding lips.
   (2) South Wales: as I.
W   c*oo*l, f*u*ll.
Y (1) In monosyllables generally, and in final syllables, as U (the 'clear' sound).
   (2) In all but final syllables, and in **y, yr** (the), **fy** (my), **dy** (thy), **yn, yng, ym** (in), the adverbial **yn**, the preverbal and relative particle **y, yr** (**y'm, y'th** etc), **syr** (sir), **nyrs** (nurse), as English f*u*n, (the 'obscure' sound).

DIPHTHONGS

1   Falling diphthongs, in which the second sound is consonantal: the two vowels have the sound noted above: **ae, oe, ai, oi,** the diphthong **ei** as English *by*, **aw, ew, iw, ow, uw, ŵy, yw.**

2   Rising diphthongs, in which the first sound is consonantal: **ia, ie, io, iw, iy,** ('obscure' y); **wa, we, wi, wo, wy,** ('clear' y), **wy,** ('obscure' y).

CONSONANTS

Only such as differ from English need be noted.

CH   (following C in the alphabet), as Scottish lo*ch*.
DD   (following D in the alphabet), as *th* in
        English *this*, breat*he*.
F   as English *v*.
FF   as English *f*.
G   always as in English *go*.
NG   (following G in the alphabet), as in English si*ng*.
        In some words (e.g. **dangos**), however, it is
        sounded *ng-g*, as in English lo*ng*er.
        Alphabetically this follows after N.
LL   produced by placing the tongue to pronounce *l*,
        then emitting breath without voice.
PH   (following P in the alphabet), as English *f*.
TH   always as th in English *thin*.

ACCENT

Welsh words are generally accented on the last syllable but one.
There are certain exceptions:

1   The reduplicated personal pronouns **myfi,
        tydi, efe, efô, hyhi, nyni, chwychwi,
        hwynt-hwy**, accented on the final syllable.
2   Verbs in **-(h)au**, **-(h)oi**, **-eu**, accented on the final syllable.
3   A few dissyllabic words beginning **y** + consonant,
        accented on the final syllable.
4   Certain polysyllabic words with a diphthong
        resulting in contraction in the final syllable,
        such as **Cymraeg**.
5   Some late borrowings accented as in the language
        of origin, generally English.

INITIAL MUTATIONS

Certain initial consonants are mutated under certain conditions, as shown in the following table. Only the radical form is given in the dictionary.

SOUNDS	EXAMPLES			
	Radical	Soft	Nasal	Spirant
p	pren	bren	mhren	phren
t	tad	dad	nhad	thad
c	cam	gam	ngham	cham
b	baich	faich	maich	
d	dyn	ddyn	nyn	
g	gŵr	-ŵr	ngŵr	
ll	llais	lais		
rh	rhes	res		
m	mam	fam		

ABBREVIATIONS		BYRFODDAU
abbreviation	*abbr*	byrfodd
adjective	*adj*	ansoddair
adverb	*adv*	adferf
collective noun	*coll n*	enw torfol
conjunction	*conj*	cysylltiad
contraction	*contr*	cywasgiad
demonstrative	*dem*	dangosol
emphatic	*emphat*	pwyslais
exclamation	*excl*	ebychiad
feminine	*f*	benywaidd
imperative	*imper*	gorchmynnol
masculine	*m*	gwrywaidd
noun	*n*	enw
noun dual	*nd*	enw deuol
plural	*pl*	luosog
pronoun	*pron*	rhagenw
preposition	*prep*	arddodiad
relative	*rel*	perthynol
singular	*sing*	unigol
verb	*vb*	berf
intransitive verb	*vi*	berf gyflawn
transitive verb	*vt*	berf anghyflawn

William Collins' dream of knowledge for all began with the publication of his first book in 1819. A self-educated mill worker, he not only enriched millions of lives, but also founded a flourising publishing house. Today, staying true to this spirit, Collins books are packed with inspiration, innovation, and practical expertise. They place you at the centre of a world of possibility and give you exactly what you need to explore it.

Language is the key to this exploration, and at the heart of Collins Dictionaries is language as it is really used. New words, phrases, and meanings spring up every day, and all of them are captured and analysed by the Collins Word Web. Constantly updated, and with over 2.5 billion entries, this living language resource is unique to our dictionaries.

Words are tools for life. And a Collins Dictionary makes them work for you.

Collins. Do more.

a

a *excl* ah, oh

a *interrogative particle, preverbal particle, rel pron* who, that, which

a, ac *conj* and

â, ag *conj* as

â, ag *prep* with

ab, ap *nm* son (*before name, in place of surname, like 'Mac', and 'Fitz'*)

abad (**-au**) *nm* abbot

abadaeth (**-au**) *nf* abbacy, abbotship

abades (**-au**) *nf* abbess

abatir (**-oedd**) *nm* abbey-land

abaty (**abatai**) *nm* abbey

aber (**-oedd, ebyr**) *nm* confluence; mouth of river, estuary; brook, stream

aberfa (**-oedd**) *nf* mouth of river, estuary

abergofiant *nm* forgetfulness, oblivion

aberth (**-au, ebyrth**) *nm* sacrifice

aberthged *nf* oblation; offering of fruits

aberthol *adj* sacrificial

aberthu *vb* sacrifice

aberthwr (**-wyr**) *nm* sacrificer

aberu *vb* flow into, disembogue

abid *nm, nf* apparel; dress of religious order

abiéc *nm, nf* alphabet

abl *adj* able; well-off

abladol *adj* ablative

abledd *nm* ability; plenty

abrwysg *adj* clumsy, drunken

absen *nm* absence; slander

absennol *adj* absent

absennu *vb* backbite, slander

absennwr (**absenwyr**) *nm* backbiter

absenoldeb *nm* absence

absenoli *vb* absent

absenoliaeth (**-au**) *nm* absenteeism

abwyd, abwydyn (**abwydod**) *nm* worm; fishing-bait

ac, a *conj* and

academaidd *adj* academic

academi (**-ïau**) *nm* academy

acen (**-ion**) *nf* accent

aceniad *nm* accentuation

acennod *nf* accent mark

acennu *vb* accent, stress

acenyddiaeth *nf* accentuation

acer (**-i**) *nf* acre

aciwbigiad (**-au**) *nm* acupuncture

acne *nm* acne

acrilig *adj* acrylic

act (**-au**) *nf* act

actio *vb* act

actor (**-ion**) *nm* actor

actores (**-au**) *nf* actress

acw *adv* there, yonder

ach *excl* ugh

ach (-au, -oedd) nf degree of kinship; (pl) pedigree, ancestry

aches nm tide, flood; eloquence

achfre n see **achwre**

achlân adv wholly, entirely

achles (-oedd) nf succour, protection; manure

achlesol adj succouring

achlesu vb succour, cherish; manure

achlod nm shame, disgrace

achlust nm rumour ▷ adj attentive

achlysur (-on) nm occasion

achlysuro vb occasion

achlysurol adj occasional

achos (-ion) nm cause, case

achos conj because, for

achosi vb cause

achres (-i, -au) nf genealogical table

achub vb seize, snatch; save, rescue; **achub y blaen** forestall; **achub y cyfle** seize the opportunity

achubiaeth nf salvation

achubol adj saving

achubwr (-wyr), achubydd (-ion) nm saviour, rescuer

achul adj thin, emaciated

achwre, achfre n under-thatch, protection; covering, garment

achwyn vb complain ▷ nm (-ion) complaint, plaint

achwyngar adj querulous

achwyniad (-au) nm complaint, accusation

achwynwr (-wyr) nm complainer; complainant, plaintiff

achwynyddes (-au) nf complainant

achydd (-ion) nm genealogist

achyddiaeth nf genealogy

achyddol adj genealogical

ad- prefix very; second; bad, re-

adail nf building, edifice, structure

adain, aden (adenydd) nf wing; fin; spoke

adamant nm adamant, diamond

adamantaidd adj adamantine

adar npl (nm **aderyn**) birds, fowls; **adar drudwy, adar yr eira** starlings; **adar y to** sparrows

adara vb catch birds, fowl

adardy (-dai) nm aviary

adareg nf ornithology

adargi (-gwn) nm retriever, setter, spaniel

adargraffiad (-au) nm reprint

adarwr (-wyr) nm fowler

adarwriaeth nf fowling

adarydd (-ion) nm ornithologist

adarydda n birdwatching ▷ vb go birdwatching

adaryddiaeth nf ornithology

ad-dalu vb repay, requite

ad-drefnu vb rearrange

adeg (-au) nf time, occasion, opportunity

adeilad (-au) nm, nf building, edifice

adeiladaeth nf building; edification, construction

adeiladol adj edifying, constructive

adeiladu vb build, edify

adeiladwr (-wyr), adeiladydd (-ion) nm builder

adeiledd nm structure

adeiniog adj winged

aden (-ydd, edyn) nf wing; see also **adain**

adenedigaeth nf regeneration

adeni vb regenerate

adennill vb regain, recover

aderyn (adar) nm bird

adfach (-au) nm barb; liver-fluke

adfail (-feilion) nm ruin

adfeddiannu vb repossess

adfeiliad nm decay, ruin

adfeiliedig adj decayed, in ruins

adfeilio vb decay, moulder

Adfent nm Advent

adfer, adferu, adferyd *vb* restore

adferf (-au) *nf* adverb

adferfol *adj* adverbial

adferiad *nm* restoration

adferol *adj* restorative; remedial

adferwr (-wyr) *nm* restorer

adflas *nm* after-taste, bad taste

adfyd *nm* adversity

adfydus *adj* adverse, miserable

adfynach *nm* renegade monk

adfyw *adj* half alive, half dead

adfywhau *vb* revive, reanimate

adfywiad (-au) *nm* revival

adfywio *vb* revive, resuscitate

adfywiol *adj* refreshing

adg- *see* **atg-**

adiad *nm* drake

adio *nm* addition ▷ *vb* add

adiolyn (adiolion) *nm* additive

adladd, adlodd *nm* aftermath

adlais (-leisiau) *nm* echo

adlam (-au) *nm* home; rebound; **cic adlam** drop-kick

adlamu *vb* rebound

adleisio *vb* resound

adlewyrch, adlewyrchiad (adlewyrchiadau) *nm* reflection

adlewyrchu *vb* reflect

adlewyrchydd (-ion) *nm* reflector

adlog (-au) *nm* compound interest

adloniadol *adj* of or for entertainment

adloniant *nm* recreation, entertainment

adlonni *vb* entertain, refresh

adlunio *vb* remodel, reconstruct

adnabod *vb* know, recognize

adnabyddiaeth *nf* knowledge, acquaintance

adnabyddus *adj* known, familiar; well-known

adnabyddwr *nm* knower

adnau (adneuon) *nm* deposit,

pledge; **ar adnau** on deposit

adneuo *vb* deposit

adneuol *adj* depositing

adneuwr (-wyr) *nm* depositor

adnewyddiad (-au) *nm* renewal, renovation

adnewyddu *vb* renew, renovate

adnewyddwr (-wyr) *nm* renewer, renovator

adnod (-au) *nf* verse

adnoddau *npl* resources

adolygiad (-au) *nm* review

adolygu *vb* review

adolygydd (-ion) *nm* reviewer

adran (-nau) *nf* division, section, department

adref *adv* homewards, home

Adriatig *nm*: **yr Adriatig** the Adriatic (Sea)

adrodd *vb* relate, recite

adroddgan (-au) *nf* recitative

adroddiad (-au) *nm* report; recitation

adroddwr (-wyr) *nm* narrator, reciter

ads- *see* **ats-**

aduniad *nm* reunion

aduno *vb* reunite

adwaith (-weithiau) *nm* reaction

adweithiol *adj* reactionary

adweithydd (-ion) *nm* reactor

adwr *nm* coward, churl

adwy (-au, -on) *nf* gap, breach; pass

adwyth (-au) *nm* evil, misfortune, illness

adwythig *adj* cruel; evil, baneful; sore, sick; harmful

adyn (-od) *nm* wretch

adysgrif (-au) *nf* copy, transcript

adysgrifio *vb* copy, transcribe

addas *adj* suitable, proper

addasiad (-au) *nm* adjustment, adaptation

addasrwydd nm suitableness, fitness

addasu vb suit, adapt, fit

addawol adj promising

addef vb acknowledge, own, admit

addefiad nm admission, confession

addewid (-ion) nf promise

addfain adj slender, shapely

addfed see **aeddfed**

addfwyn adj gentle, meek, mild

addfwynder nm gentleness, meekness

addien adj fair, beautiful

addo vb promise

addod nm: **wy addod** nest-egg

addoed nm death, hurt

addoedi vb delay, postpone, prorogue

addoediad nm prorogation

addoer adj sad, cruel; chilling

addoldy (-dai) nm place of worship

addolgar adj devout, reverent

addolgarwch nm devoutness, reverence

addoli vb worship, adore

addoliad nm worship

addolwr (-wyr) nm worshipper

adduned (-au) nf vow

addunedu vb vow

addurn (-au, -iadau) nm ornament, adornment

addurnedig adj decorated

addurniad nm ornamentation

addurno vb adorn, ornament

addurnol adj ornamental, decorative

addurnwr (-wyr) nm decorator

addysg nf education, instruction; **addysg gorfforol** PE; **addysg uwch** higher education

addysgiadol adj instructive, educational

addysgiaeth nf instruction, training

addysgol adj educational

addysgu vb educate, instruct

addysgwr (-wyr), **addysgydd (-ion)** nm educator, instructor, tutor

aeddfed adj ripe, mature

aeddfedrwydd nm ripeness, maturity

aeddfedu vb ripen; mature

ael (-iau) nf brow

aele adj sad, wretched

aelgerth, aelgeth see **elgeth**

aelod (-au) nm member, limb; **Aelod Seneddol** Member of Parliament

aelodaeth nf membership

aelodi vb become a member; enrol

aelwyd (-ydd) nf hearth, fireside

aer (-ion) nm heir

aer nm air

aerdymheru n air conditioning

aeres (-au) nf heiress

aerfa nf slaughter, battle

aerglo nm air-lock

aerobeg nm aerobics

aeron npl fruit, fruits, berries

aerwy (-au, -on) nm collar, torque; neck-chain

aes nf shield

aestheteg nf aesthetics

aesthetig adj aesthetic

aeth nm pain, grief, fear, shock

aethnen nf aspen, poplar

aethus adj poignant, grievous, severe

afal (-au) nm apple

afaleua vb gather apples

afallen (-nau) nf apple-tree

afan npl (nf **-en**) raspberries

afanc (-od) nm beaver

afiach adj unwell, unhealthy, morbid

afiachus adj sickly; unwholesome

afiaith nm zest, mirth, glee

afiechyd (-on) nm disease, malady

afieithus *adj* mirthful, gleeful
aflafar *adj* harsh, unmelodious
aflan *adj* unclean, polluted, foul
aflawen *adj* fierce; sad, cheerless, dismal; awful
aflednais *adj* immodest, indelicate
afledneisrwydd *nm* immodesty, indelicacy
aflem *adj* obtuse
aflendid *nm* uncleanness; pollution
aflêr *adj* untidy, slovenly
aflerwch *nm* untidiness, slovenliness
afles *nm* disadvantage, hurt
aflesol *adj* disadvantageous, unprofitable
afliwiog *adj* pale, colourless
aflonydd *adj* unquiet, restless
aflonyddu *vb* disquiet, disturb, molest
aflonyddwch *nm* disturbance, unrest
aflonyddwr (-wyr) *nm* disturber
afloyw *adj* turbid; opaque
afluniaidd *adj* mis-shapen, deformed
aflunio *vb* disfigure, deform
aflwydd *nm* misfortune, calamity
aflwyddiannus *adj* unsuccessful
aflwyddiant *nm* failure
aflwyddo *vb* fail
aflywodraeth *nf* misrule, anarchy
aflywodraethus *adj* ungovernable, uncontrollable
afocado (-s) *nm* avocado
afon (-ydd) *nf* river
afonig *nf* rivulet, streamlet, brook
afradlon *adj* wasteful, prodigal
afradlonedd *nm* prodigality
afradloni, afradu *vb* waste, lavish, squander
afraid *adj* unnecessary, needless
afrasol *adj* graceless, impious

afrealaidd, afrealistig *adj* unrealistic
afreidiau *nm* superfluity
afreidiol *adj* needless, superfluous
afreol *nf* misrule, disorder
afreolaidd *adj* irregular; disorderly
afreoleidd-dra *nm* irregularity
afreolus *adj* unruly, disorderly
afreswm *nm* absurdity
afresymol *adj* unreasonable
afresymoldeb *nm* unreasonableness
afrifed *adj* innumerable
afrllad (-au), afrlladen (-nau) *nf* wafer
afrosgo *adj* clumsy, unwieldy
afrwydd *adj* difficult, stiff, awkward
afrwyddineb *nm* difficulty
afrwyddo *vb* obstruct, hinder
afrywiog *adj* perverse, cross-grained, improper
afrywiogrwydd *nm* churlishness, roughness
afu *nm, nf* liver; **afu (g)las** gizzard
afwyn (-au) *nf* rein
affeithiad *nm* affection (in grammar)
Affganistan *nf* Afghanistan
afflau *nm* grip, hug, embrace
affliw *nm* shred, particle
Affrica *nf* Africa
Affricanaidd *adj* African
Affricanwr (-wyr) *nm* African
affwysol *nm* abysmal
ag *conj* as ▷ *prep* with; *see* **â**
agen (-nau) *nf* cleft, chink, fissure
agendor *nm, nf* gulf, abyss
agennu *vb* split, crack
ager, agerdd *nm* steam, vapour
agerfad (-au) *nm* steamboat
agerlong (-au) *nf* steamship, steamer
ageru *vb* steam, evaporate

agerw *adj* bitter, fierce
agor, agoryd *vb* open, expand
agorawd (-au) *nf* overture
agored *adj* open; liable
agorfa (-oedd) *nf* opening, orifice
agoriad (-au) *nm* opening; key
agoriadol *adj* opening, inaugural
agorwr (-wyr), agorydd (-ion) *nm* opener; **agorwr tuniau** can-opener
agos *adj* near, nigh
agosaol *adj* approaching
agosatrwydd *nm* intimacy
agosáu *vb* draw near, approach
agosrwydd *nm* nearness, proximity
agwedd (-au) *nf* form; aspect; attitude
agweddi *nm* dowry, marriage gift
agwrdd *adj* strong, mighty
angall *adj* unwise, foolish
angau *nm, nf* death
angel (angylion, engyl) *nm* angel
angen (anghenion) *nm* need, want; **anghenion arbennig** special needs
angenrheidiol *adj* necessary, needful
angenrheidrwydd *nm* necessity
angerdd *nm* heat; passion; force
angerddol *adj* ardent, intense, passionate
angerddoldeb *nm* vehemence, intensity
anghaffael *nm* mishap; defect, flaw
anghallineb *nm* unwisdom, imprudence
angharedig *adj* unkind
angharedigrwydd *nm* unkindness
anghelfydd *adj* unskilful, clumsy
anghenfil (angenfilod) *nm* monster
anghenraid (angenrheidiau) *nm* necessity
anghenus *adj* needy, necessitous, indigent

angheuol *adj* deadly, mortal, fatal
anghlod *nm* dispraise, dishonour
anghoelio *vb* disbelieve
anghofiedig *adj* forgotten
anghofio *vb* forget
anghofrwydd *nm* forgetfulness
anghofus *adj* forgetful, oblivious
anghred *nf* unbelief, infidelity
anghredadun (anghredinwyr) *nm* unbeliever
anghrediniaeth *nf* unbelief, infidelity
anghrediniol *adj* unbelieving
anghredu *vb* disbelieve
anghrefyddol *adj* irreligious
anghrist (-iau) *nm* antichrist
anghryno *adj* incompact, prolix
anghwrtais *adj* discourteous
anghwrteisi *nm* discourtesy
anghydbwysedd *nm* imbalance
anghydfod *nm* disagreement, discord
Anghydffurfiaeth *nf* Nonconformity
Anghydffurfiwr (-wyr) *nm* Nonconformist
anghydnaws *adj* uncongenial
anghydsynio *vb* dissent, disagree
anghydweddol *adj* incompatible
anghyfaddas *adj* unsuitable, unfit
anghyfaddasu *vb* unfit, disqualify
anghyfamodol *adj* uncovenanted
anghyfanhedd-dra *nm* desolation
anghyfanheddle (-aneddleoedd) *nm* desolate place
anghyfanheddol *adj* desolating; desert
anghyfannedd *adj* uninhabited, desert
anghyfansoddiadol *adj* unconstitutional
anghyfartal *adj* unequal, uneven
anghyfartaledd *nm* disparity

anghyfarwydd *adj* unfamiliar, unskilled

anghyfeillgar *adj* unfriendly

anghyfiaith *adj* foreign, alien

anghyfiawn *adj* unjust, unrighteous

anghyfiawnder *nm* injustice

anghyflawn *adj* incomplete

anghyfleus *adj* inconvenient

anghyfleustra (-terau) *nm* inconvenience

anghyflogaeth *nm* unemployment

anghyfnewidiol *adj* immutable

anghyfraith *nf* transgression, crime

anghyfranogol *adj* incommunicable

anghyfreithlon *adj* unlawful, illegal, illegitimate

anghyfrifol *adj* irresponsible

anghyffredin *adj* uncommon, rare

anghyffwrdd *adj* intangible

anghyffyrddus *adj* uncomfortable

anghymedrol *adj* immoderate

anghymen *adj* rash, coarse, untidy

anghymeradwy *adj* unacceptable

anghymeradwyo *vb* disapprove

anghymesur *adj* inordinate

anghymharol *adj* incomparable

anghymharus *adj* ill-matched

anghymhendod *nm* foolishness, indelicacy, untidiness

anghymhwyso *vb* unfit, disqualify

anghymhwyster *nm* incapacity, disqualification

anghymodlon *adj* implacable

anghymwys *adj* unfit, unsuitable

anghynefin *adj* unfamiliar

anghynefindra *nm* unfamiliarity

anghynhyrchiol *adj* unproductive

anghynnes *adj* odious, loathsome

anghysbell *adj* out-of-the-way; remote

anghyson *adj* inconsistent

anghysondeb (-au), **anghysonder (-au)** *nm* inconsistency

anghysur (-on) *nm* discomfort

anghysuro *vb* discomfort

anghysurus *adj* uncomfortable

anghytbwys *adj* unbalanced, lopsided

anghytgord (-iau) *nm* discord, dissension

anghytûn *adj* not agreeing, discordant

anghytundeb *nm* disagreement

anghytuno *vb* disagree

anghywair *adj* ill-equipped; discordant ▷ *nm* disrepair

anghyweithas *adj* uncivil

anghywir *adj* incorrect, inaccurate, false

anghywirdeb (-au) *nm* inaccuracy, falseness

anghywrain *adj* unskilful; slovenly

angladd (-au) *nm*, *nf* burial, funeral

angladdol *adj* funereal

angof *nm* forgetfulness, oblivion

angor (-au, -ion) *nm* anchor

angorfa (-oedd, -feydd) *nf* anchorage

angori *vb* anchor

angylaidd *adj* angelic

angyles (-au) *nf* female angel

ai *adv* is it? what?; **ai e?** is it so?

ai *conj* or; either; if

AID *nm* AIDS, Afiechyd Imiwnedd Diffygiol

aidd *nm* zeal, ardour, zest

Aifft *nf*: **yr Aifft** Egypt

aig, eigiau *nf* host, shoal

aig *nf* sea, ocean

ail *adj* second ▷ *adv* a second time, again

ailadrodd *vb* repeat

ailadroddiad (-au) *nm* repetition

ailarholiad (**-au**) *nm* resit
ailbriodi *vb* remarry
aildrydanu *vb* recharge
ailenedigaeth *nf* rebirth
aileni *vb* bear again, regenerate
Ailfedyddiwr (**-wyr**) *nm* Anabaptist
ailgylchu *vb* recycle ▷ *n* recycling
ailgynnig (**ailgynigion**) *nm* resit
ail-law *adj* second-hand
ail-lenwi *vb* top up, refill
ailsefyll *vb* resit
aillt *nm* vassal, villain, slave
ais *npl* (*nf* **eisen**) laths; ribs
à la carte *adv* à la carte
alaeth *nm* wailing, lamentation, grief
alaethu *vb* lament
alaethus *adj* mournful, lamentable
alarch (**-od, elyrch**) *nm* swan
alaru *vb* surfeit; loathe
alaw (**-on**) *nf* lily; air, melody, tune
Alban *nf*: **yr Alban** Scotland
Albanwr (**-wyr**) *nm* Scot
alcali (**-ïau**) *nm* alkali
alcam *nm* tin
alcohol *nm* alcohol
alch (**-au, eilch**) *nf* grate, grill
ale (**-au, -on**) *nf* aisle; gangway; alley
algebra *nm* algebra
Algeraidd *adj* Algerian
Algeria *nf* Algeria
Algeriad (**-iaid**) *nm, nf* Algerian
Almaen *nf*: **yr Almaen** Germany
Almaeneg *nf* German
Almaenwr (**-wyr**) *nm* German
almon *nm* almond
aloi (**aloeon**) *nm* alloy
Alpau *npl*: **yr Alpau** the Alps
Alzheimer *nm*: **clefyd Alzheimer** Alzheimer's (disease)
allan *adv* out
allanol *adj* outward, external

allblyg *adj* extrovert
allbrint (**-iau**) *nm* printout
allforio *vb* export
allfro *nm* foreigner; foreign land
allfudwr (**-wyr**) *nm* emigrant
allgarwch *nm* altruism
allgofnodi *vb* log off, log out
allor (**-au**) *nf* altar
allt (**elltydd**) *nf* hill; cliff; wood
alltud (**-ion**) *nm* alien; exile
alltudiaeth *nf* banishment, exile
alltudio *vb* banish, exile
allwedd (**-au, -i**) *nf* key, clef (in music)
am *prep* round, about; for; at; on ▷ *conj* for, because; so long as
am *see* **ym**
amaeth *nm* husbandman; agriculture
amaethdy (**-dai**) *nm* farm-house
amaethu *vb* farm, till
amaethwr (**-wyr**) *nm* farmer
amaethwraig *nf* farm-wife
amaethyddiaeth *nf* agriculture
amaethyddol *adj* agricultural
amarch *nm* disrespect, dishonour
amau *vb* doubt, suspect ▷ *nm* (**-heuon**) doubt
ambell *adj* occasional; **ambell waith** sometimes
amcan (**-ion**) *nm* purpose, aim; guess; **ar amcan** at random, approximately, at a guess
amcangyfrif *vb* estimate ▷ *nm* (**-on**) estimate
amcanu *vb* purpose; aim; guess
amdo (**-oeau**) *nm* shroud, winding-sheet
amdoi *vb* shroud, enshroud
amdorch (**-dyrch**) *nf* chaplet, wreath
amddifad *adj* destitute, orphan
amddifadrwydd *nm* destitution, privation

amddifadu *vb* bereave, deprive
amddifaty (-tai) *nm* orphanage
amddifedi *nm* destitution, privation
amddiffyn *vb* defend, protect,
  shield ▷ *nm* (**addiffynion**) defence
amddiffynfa (-feydd) *nf* fortress
amddiffyniad *nm* protection,
  defence
amddiffynnwr (-wyr),
  amddiffynnydd (-ion) *nm*
  defender, protector
amddyfrwys *adj* mighty, rugged;
  marshy
America Ladin *nf* Latin America
Amerig *nf*: **yr Amerig** America
amfesur (-au) *nm* perimeter
amgáu *vb* enclose, shut in
amgen *adj, adv* other, else,
  otherwise; different; **nid amgen**
  that is to say, namely
amgenach *adj, adv* otherwise;
  better
amgueddfa (-feydd) *nf* museum
amgyffred *vb* comprehend,
  comprise ▷ *nm* (**-ion**)
  comprehension
amgyffrediad *nm* comprehension
amgylch (-oedd) *nm* circuit;
  environs, surroundings; **o (oddi)**
  amgylch round about, about
amgylchedd *nm* circumference;
  environment
amgylcheddol *adj* environmental;
  yn amgylcheddol environmentally;
  amgylcheddol garedig
  environmentally friendly
amgylchfyd *nm* environment
amgylchiad (-au) *nm*
  circumstance; occasion
amgylchiadol *adj* circumstantial
amgylchu *vb* surround
amgylchynol *adj* surrounding
amgylchynu *vb* surround

amharchu *vb* dishonour, disrespect
amharchus *adj* disrespectful,
  disreputable
amhariad *nm* impairment, damage
amharod *adj* unprepared, unready
amharodrwydd *nm* unreadiness
amharu *vb* impair, harm, injure,
  damage
amhendant *adj* indefinite, vague
amhenderfynol *adj* irresolute
amhenodol *adj* indefinite
amherchi *vb* dishonour, insult
amherffaith *adj* imperfect
amherffeithrwydd *nm* imperfection
amhersonol *adj* impersonal
amherthnasol, amherthynasol
  adj irrelevant
amheuaeth *nf* doubt, scepticism
amheugar *adj* suspicious; sceptical
amheuol *adj* doubting, doubtful
amheus *adj* doubting, doubtful,
  dubious
amheuthun *adj* dainty, savoury
  ▷ *nm* (**-ion**) dainty, delicacy, treat
amheuwr (-wyr) *nm* doubter,
  sceptic
amhlantadwy *adj* childless,
  barren
amhleidiol, amhleitgar *adj*
  impartial
amhoblog *adj* sparsely populated
amhoblogaidd *adj* unpopular
amhosibl *adj* impossible
amhriodol *adj* improper
amhrisiadwy *adj* priceless
amhrofiadol *adj* inexperienced
amhrydlon *adj* unpunctual
amhûr *adj* impure, foul
amhwrpasol *adj* irrelevant
amhwyllo *vb* lose one's senses,
  go mad
aml *adj* frequent, abundant ▷ *adv*
  often

amlder, amldra *nm* abundance
amldduwiad (-iaid) *nm* polytheist
amldduwiaeth *nf* polytheism
amleiriog *adj* wordy, verbose, prolix
amlen (-ni) *nf* envelope, wrapper
amlhad *nm* increasing, increase
amlhau *vb* increase, multiply
amlinelliad (-au) *nm* outline
aml-lawr *adj* multi-storey
amlochrog *adj* many-sided
amlosgfa *nf* crematorium
amlosgi *vb* cremate
amlwg *adj* plain, clear, manifest, evident, prominent
amlwreigiaeth *nf* polygamy
amlwreigiwr (-wyr) *nm* polygamist
amlygiad (-au) *nm* manifestation
amlygrwydd *nm* prominence, limelight
amlygu *vb* manifest, reveal, evince
amnaid (-neidiau) *nf* beck, nod
amneidio *vb* beckon, nod
amnest (-au) *nm* amnesty
amod (-au) *nm, nf* condition
amodi *vb* covenant, stipulate
amodol *adj* conditional
amp (-au) *nm* amp
amrant (-au, -rannau) *nm* eyelid
amrantiad *nm* wink, twinkling, second
amreiniol *adj* not privileged
amrwd *adj* uncooked, raw, crude
amryddawn *adj* versatile
amryfal *adj* sundry, manifold
amryfus *adj* erroneous, inadvertent
amryfusedd (-au) *nm* error, oversight
amryliw *adj* variegated; multicoloured
amryw *adj* several, sundry, various
amrywiad (-au) *nm* variant
amrywiaeth *nm* variety, diversity
amrywio *vb* vary, differ

amrywiol *adj* sundry
amser (-oedd, -au) *nm, nf* time; **amser sbâr** spare time
amseriad (-au) *nm* timing, dating, date
amserlen (-ni) *nf* time-table
amserol *adj* timely; temporal
amseru *vb* time, date
amserydd (-ion) *nm* chronologist
amseryddiaeth *nf* chronology
amseryddol *adj* chronological
amwisg (-oedd) *nf* covering, shroud
amwisgo *vb* enwrap, shroud
amwys *adj* ambiguous
amwysedd *nm* ambiguity
amyn *conj, prep* unless, except, but
amynedd *nm* patience
amyneddgar *adj* patient
an- *prefix* un-, in-, de-, dis-
anabl *adj* disabled
anabledd *nm* disability
anad *adj*: **yn anad** above all, more than
anadferadwy *adj* irreparable
anadl (-au, -on) *nf, nm* breath
anadliad *nm* breath, breathing
anadlu *vb* breathe
anadlydd (-ion) *nm* inhaler
anadnabyddus *adj* unknown
anaddas *adj* unfit, unsuitable
anaddasu *vb* unfit, disqualify
anaeddfed, anaddfed *adj* unripe, immature
anaeddfedrwydd *nm* unripeness, immaturity
anaele *adj* awful, direful; incurable
anaesthetig *adj* anaesthetic
anaf (-au) *nm* blemish, defect; wound
anafu *vb* blemish, maim, hurt
anafus *adj* maimed, disabled
anair (-eiriau) *nm* ill report, slander
anallu *nm* inability

analluog *adj* unable
analluogi *vb* disenable; disable
anaml *adj* infrequent, rare ▷ *adv* rarely, seldom
anamlwg *adj* obscure, inconspicuous
anamserol *adj* untimely, mistimed
anap (anhapon) *nm, nf* mischance, mishap
anarchiaeth *nm* anarchy
anarchydd (-ion) *nm* anarchist
anarferol *adj* unusual, extraordinary
anarfog *adj* unarmed
anchwiliadwy *adj* unsearchable
ancr *nm, nf* anchorite, anchoress
ancwyn (-ion) *nm* dinner, supper; delicacy
andras *nm* curse; devil, deuce
andwyo *vb* spoil, ruin, undo
andwyol *adj* harmful, ruinous
anedifeiriol *adj* impenitent
aneddfa *see* **anheddfa**
aneffeithiol *adj* ineffectual
aneglur *adj* indistinct; illegible
aneirif *adj* innumerable
anelu *vb* bend, aim
anenwog *adj* unrenowned, ignoble, mean
anerchiad (-au) *nm* salutation, address
anesboniadwy *adj* inexplicable
anesgusodol *adj* inexcusable
anesmwyth *adj* uneasy, restless
anesmwythder, anesmwythdra *nm* uneasiness, unrest
anesmwytho *vb* be or make uneasy
anesmwythyd *nm* uneasiness, disquiet
anewyllysgar *adj* unwilling
anfad *adj* wicked, nefarious
anfadrwydd *nm* wickedness, villainy
anfadwaith *nm* villainy; crime

anfadwr (-wyr) *nm* villain, scoundrel
anfaddeugar *adj* unforgiving
anfaddeuol *adj* unpardonable
anfantais (-teision) *nf* disadvantage
anfanteisiol *adj* disadvantageous
anfarwol *adj* undying, immortal
anfarwoldeb *nm* immortality
anfedrus *adj* unskilful
anfedrusrwydd *nm* unskilfulness
anfeidrol *adj* infinite
anfeidroldeb *nm* infinity
anferth *adj* huge, monstrous
anferthedd *nm* hugeness, monstrosity
anfodlon *adj* unwilling
anfodloni *vb* discontent, dissatisfy
anfodlonrwydd *nm* discontent
anfodd *nm* unwillingness, displeasure
anfoddio *vb* displease, disoblige
anfoddlon *see* **anfodlon**
anfoddog *adj* discontented, dissatisfied
anfoddogrwydd *nm* discontentment
anfoesgar *adj* unmannerly, rude
anfoesgarwch *nm* rudeness, incivility
anfoesol *adj* immoral
anfoesoldeb *nm* immorality
anfon *vb* send, transmit, dispatch
anfoneddigaidd *adj* ungentlemanly
anfonheddig *adj* ignoble, discourteous
anfoniad *nm* sending, transmission
anfri *nm* disrespect, dishonour
anfucheddol *adj* immoral
anfuddiol *adj* unprofitable
anfwriadol *adj* unintentional
anfwyn *adj* unkind, uncivil

anfynych adj infrequent, seldom, rare

anffaeledig adj infallible

anffaeledigrwydd nm infallibility

anffafriol adj unfavourable

anffawd (-ffodion) nf misfortune

anffodus, anffortunus adj unfortunate

anffrwythlon adj unfruitful, barren

anffurfio vb disfigure, deform

anffurfiol adj informal

anffyddiaeth nf atheism

anffyddiwr (-wyr) nm infidel, atheist

anffyddlon adj unfaithful

anhaeddiannol adj unmerited, undeserved

anhaeddiant nm demerit, unworthiness

anhapus adj unhappy, unlucky

anhardd adj unhandsome, unseemly, ugly

anhawdd adj hard, difficult

anhawddgar adj unamiable, unlovely

anhawster (anawsterau) nm difficulty

anheddfa (aneddfaoedd) nf, **anheddle (aneddleoedd)** nm dwelling-place

anhepgor (-ion) nm essential

anhepgorol adj indispensable

anhoffter nm hatred, dislike

anhraethadwy adj unutterable

anhraethol adj unspeakable, ineffable

anhrefn nm disorder, confusion

anhrefnu vb disorder, disarrange

anhrefnus adj disorderly, untidy

anhreiddiol adj impervious, impenetrable

anhreuliedig adj undigested; unspent

anhrugarog adj unmerciful, merciless

anhuddo vb cover (a fire)

anhunedd nm wakefulness, disquiet

anhwyldeb nm disorder, complaint, illness

anhwylustod nm inconvenience

anhyblyg adj inflexible, stiff, rigid

anhydawdd adj insoluble

anhyder nm distrust, diffidence

anhyderus adj diffident

anhydrin adj unmanageable

anhydyn adj intractable, obstinate

anhyddysg adj unversed, ignorant

anhyfryd adj unpleasant

anhyfrydwch nm unpleasantness

anhygar adj unpleasant, unamiable

anhygoel adj incredible

anhygyrch adj inaccessible

anhylaw adj unhandy, unwieldy

anhynod adj indistinctive; uncertain

anhysbys adj unknown; unversed

anhywaith adj intractable, refractory

anial adj desert, wild ▷ nm wilderness

anialwch nm wilderness

anian (-au) nf nature, instinct, genius

anianawd nm temperament, disposition

anianol adj natural

anianyddol adj physical

anifail (-feiliaid) nm animal, beast

anifeilaidd adj beastly, brutish

anifeileiddio vb animalize, brutalize

anlwc nm bad luck, misfortune

anlwcus adj unlucky

anllad adj wanton, lascivious, lewd

anlladrwydd nm wantonness, lewdness

anlladu *vb* wanton
anllygredig *adj* incorrupt, incorruptible
anllygredigaeth *nf* incorruption
anllythrennog *adj* illiterate
anllywodraeth *nf* misrule, anarchy
annaearol *adj* unearthly, weird
annatodol *adj* indissoluble, that cannot be undone
annaturiol *adj* unnatural
annealladwy *adj* unintelligible
anneallus *adj* unintelligent
annedwydd *adj* unhappy, miserable
annedwyddwch *nm* unhappiness
annedd (anheddau) *nf* dwelling
anneddfol *adj* lawless
annefnyddiol *adj* useless; immaterial
annel (anelau) *nm, nf* trap; purpose, aim
annelwig *adj* shapeless, unformed; vague
anner (aneirod, -i, -au) *nf* heifer
annerbyniol *adj* unacceptable
annerch *vb* salute, greet, address ▷ *nm* **(anerchion)** salutation, greeting
annewisol *adj* ineligible, undesirable, unwelcome
annhebyg *adj* unlike, dissimilar
annhebygol *adj* unlikely, improbable
annhebygolrwydd *nm* improbability
annhebygrwydd *nm* unlikeness, unlikelihood
annheg *adj* unfair
annhegwch *nm* unfairness
annheilwng *adj* unworthy
annheilyngdod *nm* unworthiness
annherfynol *adj* endless; infinitive, infinite
annhirion *adj* cruel

annhosturiol *adj* pitiless, ruthless
annhuedd *nf* disinclination
annhueddol *adj* disinclined, indisposed
anniben *adj* untidy, slovenly
annibendod *nm* untidiness
annibyniaeth *nf* independence
annibynnol *adj* independent
Annibynnwr (-wyr) *nm* Independent
annichellgar *adj* guileless, simple
annichon, annichonadwy *adj* impossible
anniddan *adj* comfortless, miserable
anniddig *adj* peevish, irritable, fretful
anniddigrwydd *nm* peevishness
anniddos *adj* leaky, comfortless
annifeiriol *adj* innumerable, countless
anniflanedig *adj* unfading, imperishable
annifyr *adj* miserable, wretched
annifyrrwch *nm* misery
anniffoddadwy *adj* unquenchable
annigonedd *nm* insufficiency
annigonol *adj* insufficient, inadequate
annigonolrwydd *nm* inadequacy
annileadwy *adj* indelible, ineffaceable
annilys *adj* unauthentic, spurious, insincere
annillyn *adj* inelegant, clumsy
annioddefol *adj* unbearable, intolerable
anniogel *adj* unsafe, insecure
anniolchgar *adj* unthankful, ungrateful
anniolchgarwch *nm* ingratitude
annirnadwy *adj* incomprehensible
annisgrifiadwy *adj* indescribable

annisgwyliadwy *adj* unexpected

anniwair *adj* unchaste, incontinent, lewd

anniwall *adj* insatiable

anniweirdeb *nm* unchastity, incontinence

anniwylliedig *adj* uncultured

annoeth *adj* unwise, imprudent

annoethineb *nm* unwisdom, folly

annog *vb* incite, urge; exhort

annormal *adj* abnormal

annos *vb* incite, set (a dog) on

annosbarthus *adj* unruly, disorderly

annuw, annuwiad (annuwiaid) *nm* atheist

annuwiaeth *nf* atheism

annuwiol *adj* ungodly, godless

annuwioldeb *nm* ungodliness

annwn, annwfn *nm* the underworld; hell

annwyd (anwydau, -on) *nm* cold

annwyl *adj* dear, beloved

annyledus *adj* undue, wrongful

annymunol *adj* unpleasant, disagreeable

annynol *adj* inhuman, cruel

annysgedig *adj* unlearned

anobaith *nm* despair

anobeithio *vb* despair

anobeithiol *adj* hopeless

anochel, anocheladwy *adj* unavoidable, inevitable

anodd *adj* hard, difficult

anoddefgar *adj* impatient, intolerant

anogaeth (-au) *nf* exhortation

anolrheinadwy *adj* untraceable

anolygus *adj* unsightly

anonest *adj* dishonest

anonestrwydd *nm* dishonesty

anorchfygol *adj* irresistible; unconquerable

anorecsig *adj* anorexic

anorfod *adj* insuperable; unavoidable

anorffen *adj* endless, unending

anorffenedig *adj* incomplete, unfinished

anorthrech *adj* invincible

anrasol *adj* graceless

anrhaith (-rheithiau) *nf* prey, spoil, booty

anrheg (-ion) *nf* present, gift

anrhegu *vb* present, give

anrheithio *vb* prey, spoil, plunder

anrheithiwr (-wyr) *nm* spoiler, pillager

anrhydedd (-au) *nm* honour

anrhydeddu *vb* honour

anrhydeddus *adj* honourable

anrhydeddwr (-wyr) *nm* honourer

ansad *adj* unsteady, unstable

ansadrwydd *nm* instability

ansafadwy *adj* unstable; fickle

ansathredig *adj* untrodden, unfrequented

ansawdd (-soddau) *nm, nf* quality, state

ansefydlog *adj* unsettled, unstable; fickle

ansefydlogi *vb* unsettle

ansicr *adj* uncertain, doubtful

ansicrwydd *nm* uncertainty, doubt

ansoddair (-eiriau) *nm* adjective

ansoddeiriol *adj* adjectival

ansyber *adj* untidy, slovenly

Antarctig *nf*: **yr Antarctig** the Antarctic

anterliwt (-iau) *nm, nf* interlude

anterth *nm* meridian, zenith, prime

antur (-iau) *nm* attempt, venture; adventure; enterprise; **ar antur** at random

anturiaeth (-au) *nf* adventure, enterprise

anturiaethus *adj* adventurous, enterprising
anturiaethwr (-wyr) *nm* adventurer
anturio *vb* venture, adventure
anturus *adj* adventurous
anthem (-au) *nf* anthem
anudon (-au) *nm* false oath, perjury
anudoniaeth *nf* perjury
anudonwr (-wyr) *nm* perjurer
anufudd *adj* disobedient
anufudd-dod *nm* disobedience
anufuddhau *vb* disobey
anundeb *nm* disunion
anunion *adj* crooked; unjust
anuniondeb *nm* injustice, iniquity
anurddo *vb* spoil, mar, disfigure
anwadal *adj* unstable, fickle, changeable
anwadalu *vb* waver, vacillate
anwadalwch *nm* fickleness
anwar *adj* wild, barbarous, savage
anwaraidd *adj* uncivilized, barbarous
anwarddyn (-wariaid) *nm* barbarian, savage
anwareidd-dra *nm* barbarity
anwastad *adj* uneven, unstable, fickle
anwe (-oedd) *nf* woof
anwedd *nm* vapour, steam
anweddaidd *adj* unseemly, indecent
anweddus *adj* improper, indecent
anweledig *adj* unseen, invisible
anwes *nm* indulgence; caress
anwesog *adj* pampered, affectionate
anwesu *vb* fondle, caress, pamper, indulge
anwir *adj* untrue, lying, false; wicked
anwiredd (-au) *nm* untruth; iniquity

anwireddu *vb* falsify
anwireddus *adj* untruthful, false, lying
anwr (-wyr) *nm* wretch, coward
anwybod *nm* ignorance
anwybodaeth *nf* ignorance
anwybodus *adj* ignorant
anwybyddu *vb* ignore
anwydog *adj* cold, chilly; having a cold
anwydwst *nf* influenza
anwyldeb *nm* belovedness, dearness
anwyliaid *npl* beloved ones, favourites
anwylo *vb* cherish, fondle, caress
anwylyd (-iaid) *nm* beloved
anwylyn *nm* favourite
anwythiad *nm* induction
anwytho *vb* induce
anwythol *adj* inductive
anymarferol *adj* impractical, impracticable
anymddiried *vb, nm* mistrust, distrust
anymwybodol *adj* unconscious
anymwybyddiaeth *nf* unconsciousness
anynad *adj* peevish, petulant; brawling
anysgrifenedig *adj* unwritten
anysgrythurol *adj* unscriptural
anystwyth *adj* stiff, rigid
anystwytho *vb* stiffen
anystyriaeth *nf* heedlessness, rashness
anystyriol *adj* heedless, reckless, rash
anystywallt, anystywell *adj* unmanageable
apêl (apelion) *nm, nf*, **apeliad (-au)** *nm* appeal
apelio *vb* appeal
apostol (-ion) *nm* apostle

apostolaidd, apostolig *adj* apostolic
apostoliaeth *nf* apostleship
apwyntiad (-au) *nm* appointment
apwyntio *vb* appoint
ar *prep* on, upon, over; **ar gau** closed
âr *nm* ploughed land, tilth; ground
Arab (-iaid) *nm, nf* Arab
arab *adj* facetious, merry, pleasant
Arabaidd *adj* Arab
arabedd *nm* facetiousness, wit
arabus *adj* witty
aradr (erydr) *nm* plough
araf *adj* slow, soft, gentle, still
arafu *vb* slow; quiet; moderate
arafwch *nm* slowness; moderation
arail *vb* guard, care for, foster ▷ *adj*
   attending, careful
araith (areithiau) *nf* speech
arall (eraill) *adj, pron* another, other;
   else
aralleg (-au) *nf, nm* allegory
aralleiriad (-au) *nm* paraphrase
aralleirio *vb* paraphrase
araul *adj* sunny, sunlit; serene
arawd *nf* speech, oration
arbed *vb* spare, save
arbediad (-au) *nm* save, salvage
arbedol *adj* sparing, saving
arbedwr (-wyr) *nm:* **arbedwr sgrin**
   screen saver
arbenigaeth *nf* expertise;
   specialisation
arbenigo *vb* specialise
arbenigrwydd *nm* speciality,
   prominence
arbenigwr (-wyr) *nm* specialist
arbennig *adj* special
arbrawf (arbrofion) *nm* experiment
arbrofi *vb* experiment
arbrofol *adj* experimental
Arctig *nf:* **yr Arctig** the Arctic
arch (eirchion) *nf* request, petition;
   bidding

arch (eirch) *nf* ark, coffin; trunk,
   waist
archaeoleg *nf* archaeology
archangel (-ylion) *nm* archangel
archddiacon (-iaid) *nm* archdeacon
archeb (-ion) *nf* order
archebu *vb* order
archen *nf*, **archenad** *nm* shoe;
   clothing
archesgob (-ion) *nm* archbishop
archesgobaeth (-au) *nf*
   archbishopric
archfarchnad (-oedd) *nf*
   supermarket
archiad *nm* bidding
archif (-au) *nm* archive
archifdy (-dai) *nm* record office
archifydd (-ion) *nm* archivist
archoffeiriad (-iaid) *nm* high priest
archoll (-ion) *nf* wound
archolli *vb* wound
archwaeth *nm* taste, appetite
archwaethu *vb* taste, savour
archwiliad (-au) *nm* audit;
   checkup; inspection, examination;
   exploration
archwilio *vb* examine, audit;
   explore
archwiliwr (-wyr) *nm* examiner,
   auditor; explorer
ardal (-oedd) *nf* region, district
ardalydd (-ion) *nm* marquis
ardreth (-i) *nf* rent
ardrethu *vb* rent
ardystiad (-au) *nm* pledge,
   attestation
ardystio *vb* pledge, attest
arddangos *vb* show, exhibit,
   indicate
arddangosfa (-feydd) *nf* show,
   exhibition
arddegol *adj* teenage
arddel *vb* avow, own

arddeliad *nm* claim, avowal; unction

ardderchog *adj* excellent, noble, splendid

ardderchowgrwydd *nm* excellency

arddodi *vb* prefix; impose

arddodiad (-iaid) *nm* preposition

arddu *vb* plough

arddull (-iau) *nf* style

arddulleg *nf* stylistics

ardduniant *nm* sublimity

arddunol *adj* sublime

arddwr (-wyr) *nm* ploughman

arddwrn (-ddyrnau) *nm* wrist

arddywediad (-au) *nm* dictation

aredig *vb* plough

areitheg *nf* rhetoric

areithio *vb* speak, make a speech

areithiwr (-wyr) *nm* speaker, orator

areithyddiaeth *nf* oratory; elocution

arel *nm* laurel

aren (-nau) *nf* kidney; (*pl*) reins

arestio *vb* arrest

arf (-au) *nm, nf* weapon; (*pl*) arms; tool

arfaeth (-au) *nf* purpose; decree

arfaethu *vb* purpose, intend

arfbais (-beisiau) *nf* coat of arms

arfdy (-dai) *nm* armoury

arfer *vb* use, accustom ▷ *nf, nm* (**-ion**) use, custom, habit

arferiad *nm, nf* use, custom, habit

arferol *adj* usual, customary

arfod *nf* stroke of a weapon, fight; armour; opportunity

arfog *adj* armed

arfogaeth *nf* armour

arfogi *vb* arm

arfoll (-au) *nm* pledge, oath

arfordir (-oedd) *nm* coast

arforol *adj* maritime

arffed (-au) *nf* lap

argae (-au) *nm* dam, embankment; enclosed place

argeisio *vb* seek

argel *nm, nf* concealment, refuge ▷ *adj* hidden, occult

arglwydd (-i) *nm* lord

arglwyddaidd *adj* lordly

arglwyddes (-au) *nf* lady

arglwyddiaeth (-au) *nf* lordship, dominion

arglwyddiaethu *vb* have dominion

argoed (-ydd) *nm* enclosure of trees

argoel (-ion) *nf* sign, token, omen

argoeli *vb* betoken, portend, augur

argoelus *adj* ominous

argraff (-ion, -au) *nf* print, impression

argraffdy (-dai) *nm* printer's, printing-house

argraffiad (-au) *nm* impression; edition

argraffu *vb* print, impress

argraffwaith *nm* print, typography

argraffwasg *nf* printing-press

argraffwr (-wyr), argraffydd (-ion) *nm* printer

argraffydd (-ion) *nm* printer

argrwm, argrwn *adj* convex

argyfwng (-yngau, -yngoedd) *nm* crisis

argyhoeddi *vb* reprove; convince, convict

argyhoeddiad (-au) *nm* conviction

argyhoeddiadol *adj* convincing

argymell *vb* urge, recommend

argymhelliad *nm* recommendation

arholi *vb* examine

arholiad (-au) *nm* examination; **arholiad mynediad** entrance examination

arholwr (-wyr) *nm* examiner

arhosfa *nf* stop; **arhosfa bws, arhosfa bysiau** bus stop

arhosfan (**-nau**) *nm* = **arhosfa**
arhosiad *nm* staying, stay
arhosol *adj* abiding, permanent
arial *nm*, *nf* vigour, mettle
arian *nm* silver ▷ *coll n* money, cash;
  arian breiniol currency; **arian byw**
  mercury; **arian gleision** silver; **arian**
  parod cash; **arian pen** exact money;
  arian treigl current money
ariandy (**-dai**) *nm* bank
ariangar *adj* fond of money,
  avaricious
ariangarwch *nm* love of money,
  avarice
ariannaid *adj* silver, silvern
ariannaidd *adj* silvery
arianneg *nm*, *nf* finance
Ariannin *nf* Argentina
ariannog *adj* moneyed, wealthy,
  rich
ariannol *adj* financial, monetary
ariannu *vb* silver; finance/fund
ariannydd (**arianyddion**) *nm*
  banker, investor, financier
arlais (**-leisiau**) *nf* temple
arlein, ar-lein *adj*, *adv* online
arloesi *vb* clear, prepare the way,
  pioneer
arloesydd (**-wyr**) *nm* pioneer
arluniaeth *nf* portraiture, painting
arlunio *vb* draw, paint, portray
arlunydd (**-wyr**) *nm* artist
arlwy (**-au, -on**) *nm*, *nf* provision,
  feast, menu
arlwyaeth (**-au**) *nf* catering
arlwyo *vb* prepare, provide; cook
arlywydd (**-ion**) *nm* president
arlywyddiaeth *nf* presidency
arlywyddol *adj* presidential
arlliw (**-iau**) *nm* varnish, tint, shade,
  trace
arlliwio *vb* colour, tint, paint
arllwys *vb* pour out, empty

arllwysfa *nf* outfall, outlet, vent
armel *nm* second milk
armes *nf* prophecy; calamity
arobryn *adj* worthy, prize-winning
arofun *vb* intend, purpose
arogl (**-au**), **aroglau** (**-euon**) *nm*
  scent, smell
arogl-darth *nm* incense
arogldarthu *vb* burn incense
arogli, arogleuo *vb* scent; smell
arogliad *nm* smelling, sense of
  smell
aroleuadau *npl*: **aroleuadau**
  gwallt highlights
aroleuydd (**-ion**) *nm* highlighter
  (pen)
arolwg *nm* survey
arolygiad (**-au**) *nm* inspection
arolygiaeth *nf* superintendency
arolygu *vb* superintend
arolygwr (**-wyr**), **arolygydd** (**-ion**)
  nm superintendent, inspector;
  supervisor
aros *vb* wait, await, stay, stop, tarry,
  abide, remain; **aros ar ôl** stay
  behind; **aros gartref** stay in
arswyd *nm* dread, terror, horror
arswydo *vb* dread; shudder
arswydus *adj* fearful, terrible,
  dreadful
arsyllfa (**-feydd**) *nf* observatory
arsylwi *vb* observe
artaith (**-teithiau**) *nf* torture,
  torment, pang
arteithio *vb* torture, rack
arteithiol *adj* racking, excruciating
arth (**eirth**) *nm*, *nf* bear
arthes (**-au**) *nf* she-bear
arthio, arthu *vb* bark, growl
artisiog (**-au**) *nm* artichoke
artistig *adj* artistic
aruchel *adj* lofty, sublime
arucheledd *nm* loftiness, sublimity

aruthr *adj* marvellous, strange
aruthredd *nm* amazement, horror
aruthrol *adj* huge, prodigious
arwahanrwydd *nm* uniqueness, individuality
arwain *vb* conduct, lead, guide, carry
arwedd (-au, -ion) *nf* bearing, aspect
arweddu *vb* bear
arweddwr (-wyr) *nm* bearer
arweiniad *nm* guidance; introduction
arweiniol *adj* leading, introductory
arweinydd (-ion) *nm* guide, leader; conductor
arweinyddiaeth *nf* leadership
arwerthiant (-iannau) *nm* auction
arwerthu *vb* sell by auction
arwerthwr (-wyr) *nm* auctioneer
arwisgiad *nm* investiture
arwisgo *vb* enrobe, array, invest
arwr (-wyr) *nm* hero
arwraidd *adj* heroic, epic
arwres (-au) *nf* heroine
arwrgerdd (-i) *nf* epic poem
arwriaeth *nf* heroism
arwrol *adj* heroic, gallant
arwybod *nm* awareness
arwydd (-ion) *nm*, *nf* sign, signal; ensign; **arwydd ffordd** road sign
arwyddair (-eiriau) *nm* motto
arwyddlun (-iau) *nm* emblem, symbol
arwyddluniol *adj* emblematic, symbolic
arwyddnod (-au) *nm* mark, token
arwyddo *vb* sign; signify
arwyddocâd *nm* signification, significance
arwyddocaol *adj* significant
arwyddocáu *vb* signify, denote
arwyl (-ion) *nf* funeral, funeral rites

arwylo *vb* mourn over the dead
arwynebedd *nm* surface, superficies
arwynebol *adj* superficial
arwyrain *nm*, *nf* praise, panegyric ▷ *vb* rise, extol
arwystlo *vb* pledge, mortgage
arysgrif (-au), **arysgrifen (-nau)** *nf* inscription, epigraph
asb (-iaid) *nf* asp
asbri *nm* animation, vivacity, spirits
aseiniad (-au) *nm* assignment
asen (-nau) *nf* rib
asen (-nod) *nf* she-ass
asesiad *nm*: **asesiad parhaus** continuous assessment
asesu *vb* assess; **asesu parhaus** continuous assessment
aseth *nf* stake, spar, lath
asgell (esgyll) *nf* wing, fin; **asgell fraith** chaffinch
asgellog *adj* winged
asgellwr (-wyr) *nm* wing, outside-forward
asglod, asglodion *npl* chips
asgre *nf* bosom, heart
asgwrn (esgyrn) *nm* bone
Asia *nf* Asia
Asiad (Asiaid) *nm*, *nf* Asian
asiad (-au) *nm* joint, weld
Asiaidd *adj* Asian
asiant (-au) *nm* agent
asio *vb* join, weld; solder; cement
astell (estyll, ystyllod) *nf* plank, shelf
astroleg *nf* astrology
astrus *adj* abstruse, difficult
astud *adj* attentive
astudiaeth (-au) *nf* study; **astudiaethau cyfrifiadurol** computer studies
astudio *vb* study
astudrwydd *nm* attentiveness

aswy *adj* left
asyn (**-nod**) *nm* he-ass
asynnaidd *adj* asinine
at *prep* to, towards; for; at; by
atafaeliad *nm* confiscation, distraint
atafaelu *vb* distrain, confiscate
atal *vb* stop, hinder, withhold ▷ *nm* (**-ion**) hindrance, impediment; **atal dweud** stammering
ataleb (**-au**) *nf* injunction
atalfa (**-feydd**) *nf* check; stoppage
ataliad (**-au**) *nm* stoppage
ataliol *adj* preventive
atalnod (**-au**) *nf* stop, point
atalnodi *vb* point, punctuate
atblygol *adj* reflexive
ateb *vb* answer, reply ▷ *nm* (**-ion**) answer
atebol *adj* answerable, responsible
ateg (**-ion**) *nf* prop, stay, support
ategiad (**-au**) *nm* affirmation
ategol *adj* confirming; auxiliary
ategu *vb* support
atgas *adj* odious, hateful
atgasedd *nm* hatred
atgasrwydd *nm* odiousness, hatefulness
atgenhedliad *nm* regeneration
atgenhedlu *vb* regenerate
atgno (**-oeau, -oeon**) *nm* remorse
atgof (**-ion**) *nm* remembrance, reminiscence
atgofio *vb* recollect, remember, remind
atgofus *adj* reminiscent
atgoffa *vb* recall, remind
atgyfnerthion *npl* reinforcements
atgyfnerthu *vb* reinforce
atgyfodi *vb* rise, raise again
atgyfodiad *nm* resurrection
atgynhyrchu *vb* reproduce
atgyweiriad (**-au**) *nm* repair

atgyweirio *vb* repair, mend
atgyweiriwr (**-wyr**) *nm* repairer, mender
atig (**-au**) *nm, nf* attic
Atlantaidd *adj* Atlantic
Atlantig *adj* Atlantic
atodi *vb* add, append, affix
atodiad (**-au**) *nm* addition, appendix
atodlen (**-ni**) *nf* supplement; schedule
atodol *adj* supplementary
atolwg, atolygu *vb* pray, beseech
atom (**-au**) *nm, nf* atom
atomfa (**-feydd**) *nf* nuclear power station
atomig *adj* atomic
atsain (**-seiniau**) *nf* echo
atseinio *vb* resound, echo
atwf (**atyfion**) *nm* second growth
atyniad (**-au**) *nm* attraction
atyniadol *adj* attractive
atynnu *vb* attract
Athen *nf* Athens
athletau *npl* athletics
athrawes (**-au**) *nf* teacher, governess
athrawiaeth (**-au**) *nf* doctrine
athrawiaethol *adj* doctrinal
athrist *adj* very sad, pensive, sorrowful
athro (**athrawon**) *nm* teacher, master
athrod (**-ion**) *nm* slander, libel
athrodwr (**-wyr**) *nm* slanderer, libeller
athrofa (**-feydd**) *nf* college, academy, institute
athrofaol *adj* academic
athroniaeth *nf* philosophy
athronydd (**-ion, -wyr**) *nm* philosopher
athronyddol *adj* philosophical
athronyddu *vb* philosophize
athrylith (**-oedd**) *nf* genius

athrylithgar *adj* of genius, talented
athrywyn *nm* mediation, intervention ▷ *vb* mediate, arbitrate
au pair (-s) *nf* au pair
aur *nm* gold
awch *nm* edge; ardour, zest; relish, appetite
awchlym *adj* sharp, keen, acute
awchlymu *vb* sharpen, whet
awchus *adj* sharp, keen; eager; greedy
awdl (-au, odlau) *nf* ode
awdur (-on, -iaid) *nm* author
awdurdod (-au) *nm, nf* authority
awdurdodedig *adj* authorised
awdurdodi *vb* authorize
awdurdodol *adj* authoritative
awdures (-au) *nf* authoress
awduriaeth *nf* authorship
awel (-on) *nf* breeze, wind
awelog *adj* breezy, windy
awen (-au) *nf* muse
awen (-au) *nf* rein
awenydd (-ion) *nm* poet
awenyddiaeth *nf* poetry, poesy
awenyddol *adj* poetical
awenyddu *vb* poetize
awgrym (-au, -iadau) *nm* hint, suggestion
awgrymiadol *adj* suggestive
awgrymog *adj* suggestive
awgrymu *vb* hint, suggest
awr (oriau) *nf* hour; **oriau hamdden** spare time, leisure; **oriau hyblyg** flexitime; **oriau ychwanegol** overtime
Awst *nm* August
Awstralia *nf* Australia
Awstria *nf* Austria
awtistig *adj* autistic
awydd (-au) *nm* desire, eagerness
awyddfryd *nm* vehement desire, zeal

awyddu *vb* desire
awyddus *adj* desirous, eager, zealous
awyr *nf* air, sky
awyrdrom (-au) *nf* aerodrome
awyren (-nau, -ni) *nf* balloon, aeroplane
awyrendy (-dai) *nm* hangar
awyrgylch (-au, -oedd) *nm, nf* atmosphere
awyriad *nm* ventilation
awyrlong (-au) *nf* airship
awyru *vb* air, ventilate

baban (-od) *adj* baby
babanaidd *adj* babyish
babandod *nm* babyhood, infancy
babi *nm, nf* baby
bacas (bacs(i)au) *nf* footless
  stocking; hair on horse's fetlocks
baco *nm* tobacco
bacwn *nm* bacon
bach (-au) *nm* hook; **bachau
  petryal** square brackets
bach *adj* little, small
bachell (-au, -ion) *nf* nook, corner;
  snare
bachgen (bechgyn) *nm* boy
bachgendod *nm* boyhood
bachgennaidd *adj* boyish
bachgennyn (bechgynnos) *nm*
  little boy
bachigyn (bachigion) *nm* little bit,
  diminutive
bachog *adj* hooked

bachu *vb* hook, grapple
bachwr (-wyr) *nm* hooker (in rugby)
bad (-au) *nm* boat; **bad achub**
  lifeboat
badwr (-wyr) *nm* boatman
badd (-au), baddon (-au) *nm* bath
bae (-au) *nm* bay
baedd (-od) *nm* boar
baeddu *vb* beat, buffet; soil
baetio *vb* bait, maltreat
bag (-iau) *nm* bag; **bag aer, bag
  awyr** airbag
bagad (-au) *nm* cluster; troop,
  multitude
bagl (-au) *nf* crook; crutch; leg
baglor (-ion) *nf* bachelor
bagloriaeth *nf* bachelorship
baglu *vb* entangle, ensnare, trip
bai (beiau) *nm* fault, vice; defect;
  blame
baich (beichiau) *nm* burden,
  load
bais *nm* bottom, ford; walking
bala *nm* efflux of river from lake
balch *adj* proud; glad; delighted
balchder *nm* pride
balchdra *nm* joy, gladness
balchïo *vb* pride
baldordd *nm* babble, balderdash
baldorddi *vb* babble
bale *nm* ballet
baled (-i) *nf* ballad
baledwr (-wyr) *nm* ballad-monger
balm *nm* balm
balmaidd *adj* balmy
balog (-au, -ion) *nf* fly, cod-piece;
  flap
balleg *nf* hamper, net, purse
ballegrwyd (-au) *nf* drag-net
ban (-nau) *nm, nf* peak; horn;
  corner; stanza
banadl *npl (nf -badlen)* broom
banc (-iau) *nm* bank

banc (**bencydd**) *nm* bank, mound, hill

bancaw (**-iau**) *nm* band, tuft

band (**-iau**) *nm* band; **band eang, band llydan** broadband

baner (**-au, -i**) *nf* banner, flag

banerog *adj* with banners, bannered

banerwr (**-wyr**) *nm* standard-bearer; ensign

banffagl (**-au**) *nf* bonfire, blaze

bangaw *adj* eloquent, melodious, skilful

Bangladesh *nf* Bangladesh

bangor (**-au, bangyr**) *nf, nm* upper row of rods in wattle fence; monastery

baniar (**-ieri**) *nm, nf* shout; banner

banllawr (**-lloriau**) *nm* platform

banllef (**-au**) *nf* loud shout

bannod (**banodau**) *nf* article

bannog *adj* elevated, conspicuous; horned

bar (**-rau**) *nm* bar

bâr *nm* fury, greed

bara *nm* bread

barbaraidd *adj* barbarous

barbareidd-dra *nm* barbarity

barbareiddio *vb* barbarize

barbariad (**-iaid**) *nm* barbarian

barbariaeth *nm* barbarism

barbwr (**-wyr**) *nm* barber

barcer (**-iaid**) *nm* tanner

barclod (**-iau**) *nm* apron

barcud (**-iaid**), **barcutan** (**-od**) *nm* kite

bardd (**beirdd**) *nm* bard, poet

barddas *nm, nf* bardism

barddol *adj* bardic

barddoni *vb* compose poetry, poetize

barddoniaeth *nf* poetry, verse

barddonol *adj* poetic, poetical

barf (**-au**) *nf* beard, whiskers

barfog *adj* bearded

bargeinio, bargenna *vb* bargain

bargen (**-einion**) *nf* bargain

bargod (**-ion**) *nm* eaves

bargyfreithiwr (**-wyr**) *nm* barrister

bariaeth *nf, nm* evil, grief, wrath; greed

baril (**-au**) *nf* barrel

barilaid (**-eidiau**) *nf* barrelful

bario *vb* bar, bolt

barlad *nm* drake

barlys *nm* barley

barn (**-au**) *nf* judgment; opinion; sentence

barnais *nf* varnish

barnedigaeth (**-au**) *nf* judgment

barneisio *vb* varnish

barnol *adj* judicial, condemnatory, annoying

barnu *vb* judge

barnwr (**-wyr**) *nm* judge

baromedr *nm* barometer

barrug *nm* hoar-frost

barugo *vb* cast hoar-frost

barugog *adj* white with hoar-frost

barus *adj* voracious, greedy

barwn (**-iaid**) *nm* baron

barwnes (**-au**) *nf* baroness

barwniaeth (**-au**) *nf* barony

barwnig (**-iaid**) *nm* baronet

bas *adj* shallow ▷ *npl* (**bais, beis**) shallows

bas *adj, nm* bass

basged (**-i, -au**) *nf* basket

basgedaid (**-eidiau**) *nf* basketful

basgedwr (**-wyr**) *nm* basket-maker

basil *nm* basil

basn (**-au, -ys**) *nm* basin

bastard (**-iaid**) *nm* bastard

bastardiaeth *nf* bastardy

batri *nm* battery

bath (**-au**) *nm* kind, sort; stamp; coin

bathdy (**-dai**) *nm* mint

b

bathodyn (**-odau**) *nm* medal, badge
bathol *adj* coin, coined
bathu *vb* coin
baw *nm* dirt, mire, dung, filth
bawaidd *adj* dirty, vile; sordid, mean
bawd (**bodiau**) *nf* thumb, toe
bechan *adj f of* **bychan**
bechgynnos *npl* little boys, youngsters
bedw *npl* (*nf*-**en**) birch
bedydd *nm* baptism
bedyddfa (**-fâu, -feydd**) *nf* baptistry
bedyddfaen (**-feini**) *nm* font
bedyddio *vb* baptize
bedyddiol *adj* baptismal; baptized
Bedyddiwr (**-wyr**) *nm* Baptist
bedd (**-au**) *nm* grave, tomb, sepulchre
beddargraff (**-iadau**) *nm* epitaph
beddfaen (**-feini**) *nm* tombstone
beddgell (**-oedd**) *nf* vault, catacomb
beddrod (**-au**) *nm* tomb, sepulchre
Beibl (**-au**) *nm* Bible
Beiblaidd *adj* Biblical
beic (**-iau**) *nm* bike; **beic modur** motorbike; **beic mynydd** mountain bike
beichio *vb* burden; low; sob
beichiog *adj* pregnant
beichiogi *vb* conceive
beichus *adj* burdensome, oppressive
beicio *vb* cycle
beiciwr, beicwr (**-wyr**) *nm* cyclist; **beiciwr modur** motorcyclist
beiddgar *adj* daring, audacious; outrageous
beiddgarwch *nm* daring, audacity
beiddio *vb* dare, presume
beili (**beiliaid**) *nm* bailiff
beio *vb* blame, censure
beirniad (**-iaid**) *nm* adjudicator; critic

beirniadaeth (**-au**) *nf* adjudication; criticism
beirniadol *adj* critical
beirniadu *vb* adjudicate; criticize
beisgawn (**-au**) *nf* stack, heap of corn sheaves
beiston *nf* sea-shore, beach; surf
beius *adj* faulty; blameworthy
bellach *adv* now, at length
bendigaid, bendigedig *adj* blessed
bendigedigrwydd *nm* blessedness
bendith (**-ion**) *nf* blessing, benediction
bendithio *vb* bless
bendithiol *adj* conferring blessings
benthyca, benthycio *vb* borrow, lend
benthyciwr (**-wyr**) *nm* borrower, lender
benthyg *nm* loan
benyw *adj* female ▷ *nf* (**-od**) female, woman
benywaidd *adj* feminine; effeminate
benywol *adj* feminine, female
ber *adj f of* **byr**
bêr (**berau, -i**) *nm* spear; roasting-spit
bera *nf, nm* rick; pyramid
berdys *npl* (*nm*-**yn**, *nf*-**en**) shrimps
berf (**-au**) *nf* verb; **berf anghyflawn** transitive verb; **berf gyflawn** intransitive verb
berfa (**-fâu, -feydd**) *nf* barrow
Berlin *nf* Berlin
berth *adj* beautiful, valuable
berthog *adj* wealthy, fair
berw *nm, adj* boiling, seething, ebullition
berwedig *adj* boiling
berwedydd (**-ion**) *nm* boiler
berwedd-dy (**-dai**) *nm* brewery
berweddu *vb* brew

berwi *vb* boil, seethe, effervesce
berwr *coll n* cress
betgwn *nm, nf* nightgown
betws *nm* oratory, chapel; birch grove
beudy (-dai) *nm* cow-house, byre
beunoeth, beunos *adv* nightly, every night
beunydd *adv* daily, every day, always
beunyddiol *adj* daily, quotidian
bidog (-au) *nf* dagger; bayonet
bil (-iau) *nm* bill
bilidowcar *nm* cormorant
bilwg (-ygau) *nm* billhook
bin (-iau) *nm, nf*: **bin sbwriel** litter bin
bing (-oedd) *nm* alley, bin
biocemeg *nm, nf* biochemistry
bir (-oedd) *nm* beer
biswail *nm* dung
blaen *adj* fore, foremost, first; front ▷ *nm* (**-au, -ion**) point, end, top, tip; front, van, priority, precedence; edge
blaenasgellwr (-wyr) *nm* wing-forward
blaenbrawf (-brofion) *nm* foretaste
blaendal *nm* prepayment, deposit
blaenddu *vb* sprout
blaenddalen (-nau) *nf* title page
blaenddodi *vb* prefix
blaenddodiad (-iaid) *nm* prefix
blaenffrwyth *nm* first-fruits
blaengar *adj* prominent, progressive
blaengroen (-grwyn) *nm* foreskin
blaenllaw *adj* forward, prominent
blaenllym *adj* sharp, keen
blaenllymu *adj* sharpen, whet
blaenor (-iaid) *nm* leader; elder
blaenori *vb* lead, precede
blaenoriaeth *nf* preference; precedence
blaenorol *adj* previous, antecedent
blaenu *vb* point; outrun; precede

blaenwr (-wyr) *nm* leader; forward
blagur *coll n* sprouts, buds, shoots
blaguro *vb* sprout, bud; flourish
blaguryn *nm* sprout, bud, shoot
blaidd (bleiddiaid, bleiddiau) *nm* wolf
blas *nm* taste, savour, relish
blasio, blasu *vb* taste
blasus *adj* tasty, savoury, delicious
blawd (blodion, -iau) *nm* flour, meal
blêr *adj* untidy, slovenly
blerwm *nm* blabberer; blab-blab
blew *npl* (*nm* **-yn**) hairs; hair; fur
blewog *adj* hairy, shaggy
bliant *nm* lawn, fine linen
blif (-iau) *nm* catapult
blingo *vb* skin, flay
blin *adj* tired, weary; peevish, irritable
blinder (-au) *nm* weariness; trouble
blinderog, blinderus *adj* wearisome
blinfyd *nm* tribulation
blino *vb* tire, weary; trouble, vex
blith (-ion) *nm* milk ▷ *adj* milch
blith draphlith *adv* helter-skelter
bloc (-iau) *nm*: **bloc swyddfeydd** office block
blodeugerdd (-i) *nf* anthology
blodeuglwm *nm* bunch, nosegay
blodeuo *vb* flower, bloom, flourish
blodeuog *adj* flowery; flourishing
blodeuyn, blodyn (blodau) *nm* flower
blodiog *adj* floury, mealy
bloddest *nf* rejoicing, acclamation
bloedd (-iau, -iadau) *nf* shout
bloeddio, bloeddian *vb* shout, cry
bloeddiwr (-wyr) *nm* shouter
bloesg *adj* lisping, faltering, indistinct
bloesgi *vb* lisp, falter, speak indistinctly

blog (**-iau**) *nm* blog
blogio *vb* to blog
blogiwr (**-wyr**) *nm* blogger
bloneg *nm*, **blonegen** *nf* lard, grease
blwch (**blychau**) *nm* box; **blwch postio** mailbox
blwng *adj* angry, sullen, cheerless ▷ *nm* anger
blwydd (**-au, -i**) *nf*, *adj* year of age; year-old
blwydd-dal *nm* annuity, pension
blwyddiad (**-iaid**) *nm* yearling, annual
blwyddiadur (**-on**) *nm* yearbook, annual
blwyddyn (**blynyddoedd**) *nf* year; **blwyddyn bwlch** gap year
blychaid (**-eidiau**) *nm* boxful
blynedd *npl* years (*after numerals*)
blynyddol *adj* annual, yearly
blys (**-iau**) *nm* craving, lust
blysig *adj* greedy, lustful
blysigrwydd *nm* greediness
blysio *vb* crave, lust
bocs (**-ys**) *nm* box
bocsach *nm* vaunt, boast, brag
bocsio *vb* box
bocsiwr (**-wyr**) *nm* boxer
boch (**-au**) *nf* check
bochgoch *adj* rosy-cheeked
bod *vb* be, exist ▷ *nm* (**-au**) being, existence; **Y Bod Mawr** God
boda *nm*, *nf* buzzard
bodio *vb* thumb, finger
bodlon *adj* content, willing
bodloni *vb* satisfy, content; be content
bodlonrwydd *nm* contentment
bodolaeth *nf* existence
bodoli *vb* exist
bodd *nm* pleasure, will, consent
boddfa *nf* flood, drenching

boddhad *nm* pleasure, satisfaction
boddhaol *adj* pleasing, satisfactory
boddhau *vb* please, satisfy
boddhaus *adj* pleased
boddi *vb* drown; flood
boddio *vb* please, satisfy
boddlon *see* **bodlon**
bogail (**-eiliau**) *nm*, *nf* navel; boss, hub
boglwm (**boglymau**), **boglyn** (**-nau**) *nm* boss, knob, stud, bud, bubble
bol, bola (**boliau**) *nm* belly
bolaid (**-eidiau**) *nm* bellyful
bolera *vb* gorge, guzzle; sponge
bolerwr (**-wyr**) *nm* sponge, parasite
bolgi (**-gwn**) *nm* gourmand, glutton
bolgno *nm*, **bolgfa** *nf* gripes, colic
bolheulo *vb* bask in the sun
bolio *vb* belly, gorge
boliog *adj* big-bellied, corpulent
boloch *nm* pain, anxiety, destruction
bolrwth *adj* gluttonous, greedy
bolrwym *adj* costive, constipated
bolsothach, bolysothach *nm* hotchpotch; jargon
bollt (**-au, -ydd, byllt**) *nf* bolt
bolwst *nf*, *nm* gripes, colic
bom (**-iau**) *nm*, *nf* bomb
bomio *vb* bomb
bomiwr (**-wyr**) *nm* bomber; **bomiwr hunanleiddiol** suicide bomber
bôn (**bonau, bonion**) *nm* bottom; stump; **yn y bôn** basically
boncath (**-od**) *nm* buzzard
bonclust (**-iau**) *nm* box on the ear
boncyff (**-ion**) *nm* stump, trunk, stock
bondigrybwyll *adv* forsooth ▷ *adj* hardly mentionable
bondo *nm* eaves
bonedd *nm* gentility, nobility

boneddigaidd *adj* noble; gentlemanly

boneddigeiddrwydd *nm* gentlemanliness

boneddiges (**-au**) *nf* lady

bonesig *nf* lady; Miss

bonet (**-i**) *nf* bonnet

bongam *adj* bandy-legged

bonheddig *adj* noble, gentle, gentlemanly

bonheddwr (**-wyr**) *nm* gentleman

bonllef (**-au**) *nf* shout

bonllwm *adj* bare-bottomed; bare-backed

Bonn *nf* Bonn

bonyn (**bonion**) *nm* stump

bord (**-ydd, -au**) *nf* table, board

bordhwylio *n* windsurfing

bore (**-au**) *nm* morning ▷ *adj* early

boreddydd *nm* day-break, morning

borefwyd *nm* breakfast

boreol *adj* morning

bors *nf* hernia

bos *nf* palm of the hand, fist

Bosnia *nf* Bosnia

bost (**-iau**) *nm* boast, brag

bostio *vb* boast, brag

botas, en (**-asau**) *nf* boot

botwm (**-ymau**) *nm* button

botymog *adj* buttoned

botymu *vb* button

both (**-au**) *nf* nave of wheel; boss

brac *adj* free, frank, talkative

bracso *vb* wade, paddle

bracty (**-tai**) *nm* malt-house, brewery

brad (**-au**) *nm* treason; plot

bradfwriadu *vb* plot, conspire

bradlofrudd (**-ion**) *nm* assassin

bradlofruddiaeth (**-au**) *nf* assassination

bradlofruddio *vb* assassinate

bradwr (**-wyr**) *nm* traitor

bradwriaeth (**-au**) *nf* treason, treachery

bradwrus *adj* traitorous, treacherous

bradychu *vb* betray

braen *adj* rotten, corrupt

braenar (**-au**) *nm* fallow

braenaru *vb* fallow, pioneer

braenu *vb* rot, putrify

braf *adj* fine

brag *nm* malt

bragad *nf* army, battle; offspring

bragaldian *vb* jabber, gabble, prate

bragio *vb* brag, boast

bragiwr (**-wyr**) *nm* bragger, boaster

bragod (**-au, -ydd**) *nm* bragget

bragu *vb* malt, brew

bragwair *nm* moorland hay, coarse grass

bragwr (**-wyr**) *nm* maltster, brewer

braich (**breichiau**) *nf* arm; branch, handle; headland

braidd *adv* rather, somewhat

braint (**breintiau**) *nf* privilege

braisg *adj* gross, thick, large; pregnant

braith *adj f of* **brith**

brân (**brain**) *nf* crow, rook, raven

bras (**breision**) *adj* fat; coarse; rich; luxuriant

brasáu *vb* grow fat or gross

brasbwytho *vb* baste, tack

brasgamu *vb* stride

Brasil *nf* Brazil

braslun (**-iau**) *nm* sketch, outline

braslun bywyd *nm* curriculum vitae

braslunio *vb* sketch, outline

brasnaddu *vb* rough-hew

braster *nm* fat

brasterog *adj* fat, greasy

brat (**-iau**) *nm* rag, clout; pinafore

bratiaith *nf* debased language

bratiog adj ragged, tattered
brath (-au) nm stab, wound; sting; bite
brathog adj that bites; biting
brathu vb stab, wound; sting; bite
brau adj brittle, frail, fragile; kindly; prompt
braw (-iau) nm terror, dread, fright
brawd (brodyr) nm brother; friar; **brawd yng nghyfraith** brother-in-law
brawd (brodiau) nf judgment
brawdgarwch nm brotherly love
brawdle (-oedd) nf, nm judgement-seat
brawdlys (-oedd) nf, nm assize-court
brawdmaeth nm foster-brother
brawdol adj brotherly, fraternal
brawdoliaeth (-au) nf brotherhood, fraternity
brawddeg (-au) nf sentence
brawddegu vb construct sentences
brawl nm boast, brag; gabble, tattle
brawychu vb frighten, terrify
brawychus adj frightful, terrible
bre (-on, -oedd) nf hill, highland
brebwl (-yliaid) nm blockhead; prattler
breci nm wort; spree
brecwast (-au) nm, nf breakfast
brecwasta vb breakfast
brech nf eruption, pox; **brech yr ieir** chickenpox
brech adj f of **brych**
brechdan (-au) nf slice of bread and butter
brechiad (-au) nm inoculation, vaccination
brechu vb vaccinate, inoculate
bredych (-au, -ion) nm betrayal; fear; rascal
bref (-iadau) nf lowing; bleat; bray

breferad (-au) nm bellowing
brefiad (-au) nm lowing; bleating
brefu vb low; bleat; bray
breg nm guile, blemish, breach ▷ adj fragile, faulty
bregliach vb jabber
bregus adj frail, brittle, rickety
breichled (-au) nf bracelet
breichrwy, breichrwyf (-au) nm, nf bracelet
breinio vb privilege, enfranchise
breiniol adj privileged, free
breinlen (-ni) nf charter
breintal nm bonus; royalty
breintiedig adj patented, patent
breintio vb privilege, favour
brenhinaidd adj kingly, regal
brenhindod nm royalty
brenhindref (-i) nf royal city
brenhindy (-dai) nm royal palace
brenhines (breninesau) nf queen
brenhinfainc nf throne
brenhiniaeth (breniniaethau) nf kingdom
brenhinllys nm basil
brenhinol adj royal, regal
brenin (-hinoedd) nm king
brest (-iau) nf breast, chest
bresych npl (nf-**en**) cabbages
brethyn (-nau) nm cloth
brethynnwr (-ynwyr) nm clothier; cloth-worker
breuan (-au) nf quern; print of butter
breuder nm brittleness, frailty
breuddwyd (-ion) nm, nf dream; **breuddwyd gwrach** wishful thinking
breuddwydio vb dream
breuddwydiol adj dreaming, dreamy
breuddwydiwr (-wyr) nm dreamer
brëyr, brehyr (brehyrion, -iaid) nm nobleman, chief, baron

bri nm honour, renown, distinction
briallu npl (nf **briallen**) primroses
bribys npl fragments, scraps
brifo vb hurt
brig (**-au**) nm top; (pl) twigs
brigâd (**-au**) nf brigade; **brigâd dân** fire-brigade
briger (**-au**) nm hair of head; top
brigo vb top; branch
brigog adj branching; flourishing
brigwyn adj white-topped, white-crested
brigyn (**brigau**) nm twig
brith (f **braith**) adj mottled, speckled
britho vb mottle, speckle; dazzle
Brithwr (**-wyr**) nm Pict
brithyll (**-od, -iaid**) nm trout
briw adj broken, bruised, sore ▷ nm (**-iau**) wound, sore
briwfwyd nm crumbs, mince
briwlaw nm drizzling rain
briwlio vb broil
briwo vb wound, hurt
briwsion npl (nm **-yn**) crumbs, fragments
briwsioni vb crumble
briwsyn (**briwsion**) nm crumb, morsel
bro (**-ydd**) nf land; region; vale
broch nm badger
broch nm froth, anger, tumult
brochi vb chafe, fume; bluster
brochus adj fuming; blustering
brodio vb embroider; darn
brodor (**-ion**) nm native; fellow countryman
brodorol adj native, indigenous
broga (**-od**) nm frog
brol nf boast, brag
brolio vb boast, brag, vaunt
broliwr (**-wyr**) nm boaster, braggart
bron (**-nau, -nydd**) nf breast; hillside

bron adv almost, nearly, practically; **o'r bron** completely, in succession
bronfraith (**-freithod**) nf thrush
brongoch (**-iaid**) nf, nm robin redbreast
bronwen nf weasel
bru nm womb
brud (**-iau**) nm chronicle; divination
brudio vb prognosticate, divine
brudiwr (**-wyr**) nm wizard, soothsayer
brwd adj hot, fervent ▷ nm boil, heat
brwdfrydedd nm ardour, enthusiasm
brwdfrydig adj ardent, enthusiastic
brwmstan nm brimstone, sulphur
brwmstanaidd adj sulphury
brwnt (f **bront**) adj foul, nasty, dirty; harsh
brwyd (**-au**) nm embroidering frame; skewer
brwyd adj variegated; bloodstained; shattered
brwydo vb embroider; tear, consume
brwydr (**-au**) nf battle, combat
brwydro vb battle, combat
brwydrwr (**-wyr**) nm fighter, combatant
brwydwaith nm embroidery
brwylio vb broil
brwyn nm grief, sadness
brwynen (**brwyn**) nf rush
brwynog adj rushy
brwysg adj drunk; vigorous
brycan, brecan (**-au**) nf, nm blanket, rug
brych (f **brech**) adj mottled, brindled, freckled ▷ nm the after-birth of a cow
brychau npl (nm **-euyn**) spots, freckles
brycheulyd adj spotted, brindled

brychni nm spots, freckles
brychu vb spot, freckle
bryd nm mind, heart, will
brydio vb burn, inflame, boil, throb
brygawthan vb jabber, prate, rant
bryn (**-iau**) nm hill
bryncyn (**-nau**) nm hillock
bryniog adj hilly
brynti, bryntni nm filthiness, filth
brys nm haste, hurry
brysio vb hasten, hurry
brysiog adj hurried, hasty
bryslythyr (**-au**) nm dispatch
brysneges (**-au**) nf telegram
brytheirio vb belch; utter oaths,
  threats etc
Brython (**-iaid**) nm Briton,
  Welshman
Brythoneg nf British language,
  Welsh
brythwch nm storm, tumult; groan
bryweddu vb brew
brywes nm brewis
bual (**buail**) nm buffalo, drinking
  horn
buan adj fast, quick, swift, fleet;
  soon
buander, buandra nm swiftness,
  speed
buandroed adj swift-footed
buarth (**-au**) nm yard
buchdraeth (**-au**) nf biography,
  memoir
buchedd (**-au**) nf life, conduct
bucheddol adj right-living, virtuous
bucheddu vb live, flourish
buches (**-au**) nf herd of cows
buchfrechu vb vaccinate
budr adj dirty, filthy, foul, vile
budreddi nm filthiness, filth
budro vb dirty, soil, foul
budd (**-ion**) nm benefit, profit, gain
buddai (**-eiau**) nf churn

buddel (**-wydd**) nm, nf cow-house
  post, pillar
buddiant (**-iannau**) nm interest
buddio vb profit, avail
buddiol adj profitable, beneficial,
  useful
buddioldeb nm profitableness,
  expediency
buddsodd (**-ion**), **buddsoddiad**
  (**-au**) nm investment
buddsoddi vb invest
buddugol adj winning, victorious
buddugoliaeth (**-au**) nf victory
buddugoliaethus adj victorious,
  triumphant
buddugwr (**-wyr**) nm winner, victor
bugail (**-eiliaid**) nm shepherd;
  pastor
bugeiles (**-au**) nf shepherdess
bugeiliaeth (**-au**) nf pastorate
bugeilio, bugeilia vb watch,
  shepherd
bugeiliol adj pastoral
bugunad nm bellowing, roar
bun nf maid, maiden
burgyn (**-nod, iaid**) nm carcass,
  carrion
burman, burum nm barm, yeast
busnes (**-ion**) nm, nf business
busnesa vb interfere, meddle
busnesgar, busneslyd adj
  meddlesome
bustach (**-tych**) nm bullock, steer
bustachu vb buffet about, bungle
bustl nm gall, bile
bustlaidd adj like gall; bitter as gall
buwch (**buchod**) nf cow; **buwch
  goch gota** ladybird
bwa (**bwâu**) nm bow; arch
bwaog adj arched, vaulted
bwbach (**-od**) nm bugbear, bogey,
  scarecrow
bwced (**-i**) nm, nf bucket

bwci (**-ïod**) nm bugbear, bogey, ghost

bwcl (**byclau**) nm buckle

bwcled (**-au**) nf buckler

bwch (**bychod**) nm buck; **bwch dihangol** scapegoat; **bwch gafr** he-goat

bwgan (**-od**) nm bogey, ghost, scarecrow

bwgwl (**bygylau**) nm threat, menace

bwgwth see **bygwth, bygythio**

bwhwman vb beat about; vacillate

bŵl (**bylau**) nm globe, ball, knob

bwlch (**bylchau**) nm gap; pass; notch

bwled (**-i**) nf bullet

Bwlgaria nf Bulgaria

bwn (**bynnoedd, byniaid**) nm bittern

bwndel (**-i**) nm bundle

bwngler (**-iaid**) nm bungler

bwnglera vb bungle

bwngleraidd adj bungling, clumsy

bwnglerwaith nm bungle, botch

bwnglerwch nm clumsiness

bwr (**byr**) adj fat, big, strong

bwrdais (**-deisiaid**) nm burgess

bwrdeistref (**-i**) nm borough

bwrdd (**byrddau**) nm table; deck; board; **bwrdd du** black-board

bwriad (**-au**) nm purpose, intention

bwriadol adj intentional

bwriadu vb purpose, intend

bwrlwm (**byrlymau**) nm bubble; gurgling

bwrn (**byrnau**) nm burden, incubus; bale

bwrw vb cast, shed; strike; imagine, suppose; spend ▷ nm cast, throw; woof

bws (**bysiau, bysys**) nm bus; **bws mini** minibus

bwtler (**-iaid**) nm butler

bwtri nm buttery, pantry, dairy

bwth (**bythod**) nm hut, booth, cot

bwthyn (**bythynnod**) nm cottage, cabin, hut

bwyall (**bwyeill**), **bwyell** (**bwyeill**) nf axe

bwyd (**-ydd**) nm food; **bwyd sothach** junk food; **bwyd sydyn** fast food

bwyda, bwydo vb feed

bwyd-offrwm (**-ymau**) nm meat-offering

bwydwr (**-wyr**) nm feeder

bwygilydd adv (from one) to the other

bwylltid (**-au**) nm swivel

bwyllwr, bwyllwrw (**-yriau**) nm provisions for journey

bwysel (**-au, -i**) nm bushel

bwystfil (**-od**) nm (wild) beast

bwystfilaidd adj beastly, brutish

bwystfiles (**-au**) nf beast

bwyta vb eat; corrode

bwytadwy adj eatable, edible

bwytawr (**-wyr**) nm eater

bwyteig adj greedy, voracious

bwyty (**-tai, -tyau**) nm restaurant

bychan (f **bechan**) adj little, small

bychander, bychandra nm littleness, smallness

bychanu vb belittle, minimize

bychanus adj derogatory

byd (**-oedd**) nm world; state; life

bydaf (**-au**) nm, nf beehive

bydio vb live, fare

bydol adj worldly, secular

bydolddyn (**-ion**) nm worldling

bydolrwydd nm worldliness

bydwraig (**-wragedd**) nf midwife

bydwreigiaeth nf midwifery

bydysawd nm universe

byddag (**-au**) nf running knot, noose

byddar adj deaf ▷ nm (**-iaid, byddair**) deaf person
byddardod nm deafness
byddarol adj deafening
byddaru vb deafen, stun
byddin (**-oedd**) nf army, host
byddino vb set army in array, embattle
byddinog adj with armies
bygwth vb threaten, menace ▷ nm (**-ythion, -ythiau**) threat, menace
bygythiad (**-au**) nm threat; **bygythiad bom** bomb scare
bygythio vb threaten, menace
bygythiol adj threatening, menacing
byl (**-au**) nm, nf edge, brim (of vessel); **hyd y fyl** to the brim
bylb (**-au**) nm bulb
bylchog adj gapped, gappy; notched
bylchu vb make a gap, breach; notch
byngalo (**-s, -au**) nm bungalow
bynnag pron -ever, -soever
byr (f **ber**) adj short, brief
byrbryd (**-iau**) nm luncheon, snack
byrbwyll adj impulsive, rash
byrbwylltra nm impulsiveness
byrder, byrdra nm shortness, brevity
byrdwn nm burden, refrain, chorus
byrddaid (**-eidiau**) nm tableful
byrddio vb board
byrddiwr (**-wyr**) nm boarder
byrfyfyr adj impromptu
byrgorn adj shorthorn
byrhau vb shorten, abridge
byrhoedlog adj short-lived
byrlymu vb bubble, gurgle
byrllysg (**-au**) nm, nf mace
byrnio (**-u**) vb bale, bundle
byrnwr (**-wyr**) nm baler
bys (**-edd**) nm finger; toe; hand of dial, latch
bysaid (**-eidiau**) nm pinch

byseddu vb finger
bysled, bysledr (**-au**) nm finger-stall
byth adv ever, for ever ▷ nm eternity
bytheiad (**-aid**) nm hound
bytheirio vb belch, threaten
bythgofiadwy adj memorable
bythol adj everlasting, eternal, perpetual
bytholi vb perpetuate
bytholwyrdd (**-ion**) adj, nm evergreen
bythynnwr (**-ynwyr**) nm cottager
byw vb live ▷ adj alive, living, quick ▷ nm life
bywad, bywiad nm soft part of bread
bywgraffiad (**-au**) nm biography
bywgraffiadol adj biographical
bywgraffiadur (**-on**) nm biographical dictionary
bywgraffydd (**-ion**) nm biographer
bywgraffyddol adj biographical
bywhau, bywiocáu vb animate, vivify, quicken
bywiad nm see **bywad**
bywiog adj lively, animated, vivacious
bywiogi vb enliven, animate
bywiol adj living, animate
bywoliaeth (**-iolaethau**) nf living
bywyd (**-au**) nm life
bywydeg nf biology
bywydegwr (**-wyr**) nm biologist
bywydfad (**-au**) nm lifeboat
bywydol adj of life, vital
bywyn (**-nau**) nm pith, core

C

cabaets npl (nf **cabaetsen**) cabbage
caban (**-au**) nm cabin
cabidwl nm consistory, chapter
cabl (**-au**) nm blasphemy, reviling
cabledd (**-au**) nm blasphemy
cableddus adj blasphemous
cablu vb blaspheme, revile
cablwr (**-wyr**), **cablydd** (**-ion**) nm blasphemer
caboli vb polish
cacamwci nm burdock
cacen (**-nau, -ni**) nf cake
cacwn npl (nf **cacynen**) wasps; wild bees
cachfa (**-feydd**) nf excretion; closet
cachgi (**-gwn**) nm coward; sneak
cachiad nm excretion, jiffy; coward
cachlyd adj befouled, dirty
cachu vb defecate
cachwr (**-wyr**) nm coward; sneak; one who excretes

cad (**-au, -oedd**) nf battle; army, host
cadach (**-au**) nm cloth, kerchief, clout
cadair (**-eiriau**) nf chair, seat; cradle; udder
cadarn (**cedyrn**) adj strong, mighty; firm
cadarnhad nm affirmation, confirmation
cadarnhaol adj affirmative
cadarnhau vb strengthen, confirm
cadeirfardd (**-feirdd**) nm chaired bard
cadeirio vb chair
cadeiriog adj chaired
cadeiriol adj pertaining to a chair, cathedral
cadeirydd (**-ion**) nm chairman
cadernid nm strength; stability
cadfarch (**-feirch**) nm war-horse
cadfridog (**-ion**) nm general
cadfwyall (**-eill, -yll**) nf battle-axe
cadlas (**-lesydd**) nf close, enclosure
cadlong (**-au**) nf warship, battleship
cadlys (**-oedd**) nf camp, headquarters
cadno (**cadnoid, cadnawon**) nm fox
cadnöes, cadnawes (**-au**) nf vixen
cadoediad (**-au**) nm armistice, truce
cadofydd (**-ion**) nm tactician, strategist
cadofyddiaeth nf tactics, strategy
cadofyddol adj tactical, strategic
cadw vb keep, preserve, save; hold; **cadw'n heini** keep-fit
cadwedig adj saved
cadwedigaeth nf salvation
cadw-mi-gei nm money-box
cadwraeth nf keeping; observance; conservation
cadwyn (**-au, -i**) nf chain

cadwyno vb chain
cadwynog adj chained, in chains
caddug nm darkness; mist, fog
caddugo vb darken, obscure
cae (**-au**) nm field; fence, hedge;
  brooch
caead (**-au**) nm cover, lid ▷ adj shut,
  closed
caeadle (**-oedd**) nm enclosure
caeëdig adj closed, fenced
cael vb have; get; find
caen (**-au**) nf surface; peel; coating
caenen (**-nau**) nf layer, film, flake
caentach (**-au**) nf wrangle,
  grumbling ▷ vb wrangle, grumble
caenu vb coat, finish
caer (**-au, ceyrydd**) nf wall; castle;
  city
Caerdydd nf Cardiff
Caeredin nf Edinburgh
caeriwrch nm roebuck
caerog adj walled, fortified;
  brocaded
Caersalem nf Jerusalem
caeth adj bound, captive, confined;
  caeth i gyffuriau addicted to drugs
  ▷ nm (**-ion**) bondman, slave
caethder nm strictness; restraint;
  asthma
caethfab (**-feibion**) nm slave
caethfasnach nf slave-trade
caethferch (**-ed**) nf slave
caethforwyn (**-forynion**) nf slave
caethglud nf captivity
caethgludiad (**-au**) nm captivity
caethgludo vb lead captive
caethiwed nm slavery, bondage,
  captivity, detention
caethiwo vb bind, confine, enslave
caethiwus adj confining; confined,
  tied
caethlong (**-au**) nf slave-ship
caethwas (**-weision**) nm slave

caethwasanaeth,
  caethwasiaeth nm slavery
cafell (**-au**) nf cell; sanctuary, oracle
cafn (**-au**) nm trough, gutter
cafnedd nm concavity
cafnio, cafnu vb hollow out, scoop,
  gouge
cafod see **cawod**
caffael vb get, obtain
caffaeledd nm availability;
  acquisitiveness
caffaeliad (**-au**) nm acquisition,
  asset; prey, spoil
caffe (**-s**), **caffi** (**-s**) nm café,
  restaurant; **caffe rhyngrwyd**
  internet café, cybercafé
caffio vb snatch, grapple
cafflo vb cheat; entangle
cagl nm clotted dirt
caglu vb befoul, bedraggle
cangell (**-hellau**) nf chancel
cangelloriaeth nf chancellorship
cangen (**-hennau**) nf branch, bough
canghellor (**cangellorion**) nm
  chancellor
canghennog adj branching
canghennu vb branch, ramify
caib (**ceibiau**) nf pickaxe, mattock
cail (**ceiliau**) nf sheepfold, flock of
  sheep
caill (**ceilliau**) nf testicle
cain adj fair, fine, elegant
cainc (**cangau, ceinciau**) nf branch;
  strand; strain
cais (**ceisiadau**) nm application;
  attempt; try
cal, cala (**-iau**) nf penis
calan (**-nau**) nm first day of month;
  Dydd Calan New Year's Day
calch nm lime
calchaidd adj calcareous
calchbibonwy nm stalactite
calchbost (**-byst**) nm stalagmite

calchen *nf* limestone; lump of lime
calchfaen (**-feini**) *nm* limestone
calcho, calchu *vb* lime
calcwlws (**calcwli**) *nm* calculus
caled *adj* hard; severe; harsh; dry
caledfwrdd *nm* hardboard
caledi *nm* hardness; hardship
caledu *vb* harden, dry
caledwch *nm* hardness
calen (**-nau, -ni**) *nf* whetstone; bar
calendr *nm* calendar
calennig *nm, nf* New Year's gift
calon (**-nau**) *nf* heart
calondid *nm* encouragement
calon-dyner *adj* tender-hearted
calon-galed *adj* hard-hearted
calon-galedwch *nm*
  hard-heartedness
calonnog *adj* hearty; high-spirited
calonogi *vb* hearten, encourage
call *adj* wise, sensible, rational
callestr (**cellystr**) *nf* flint
callineb *nm* wisdom, sense
calori (**-ïau**) *nm* calorie
calsiwm *nm* calcium
cam (**-au**) *nm* step
cam *adj* crooked, wry; wrong ▷ *nm*
  (**-au**) injury, wrong
cam- *prefix* wrong, mis-
camarfer *vb* misuse, abuse ▷ *nm, nf*
  (**-ion**) misuse, malpractice
camargraff *nf, nm* wrong impression
camarwain *vb* mislead
camarweiniol *adj* misleading
Cambodia *nf* Cambodia
cambren (**-ni**) *nm* swingletree
camchwarae *nm* foul play
camdafliad (**-au**) *nm* foul throw
camdaflu *vb* foul throw
camder, camdra *nm* crookedness
cam-drefn *nf* disorder
camdreuliad *nm* indigestion
camdreulio *vb* mis-spend

cam-drin *vb* ill-treat, abuse
camdriniaeth (**-au**) *nf* ill-treatment
camdystiolaeth (**-au**) *nf* false
  witness
camdystiolaethu *vb* bear false
  witness
camddeall *vb* misunderstand
camddealltwriaeth *nm*
  misunderstanding
camddefnydd *nm* misuse
camddefnyddio *vb* misuse
camedd *nm* bend, curvature;
  camedd y droed instep; **camedd y
  gar** knee-joint
cameg (**-au, cemyg**) *nf* felloe
camel (**-od**) *nm* camel
camenw (**-au**) *nm* misnomer
camenwi *vb* misname
camera (**camerâu**) *nm* camera;
  camera digidol digital camera;
  camera fideo video camera
camfa (**-feydd**) *nf* stile
camfarnu *vb* misjudge
camgred (**-oau, -au**) *nf* misbelief,
  heresy
camgredu *vb* misbelieve
camgredwr (**-wyr**) *nm* heretic
camgwl *nm* penalty, fine; blame
camgyfrif *vb* miscalculate
camgyhuddiad (**-au**) *nm* false
  accusation
camgyhuddo *vb* accuse falsely
camgymeriad (**-au**) *nm* mistake
camgymryd *vb* mistake, err
camlas (**-lesi, -lesydd**) *nf, nm* canal
camliwio *vb* misrepresent
camochri *vb* be offside
camog (**-au**) *nf* felloe
camp (**-au**) *nf* feat, exploit; game;
  prize
campfa (**-feydd**) *nf* gymnasium
campus *adj* excellent, splendid,
  grand

campwaith (**-weithiau**) *nm* masterpiece, feat

campwr (**-wyr**) *nm* champion

camre *nm* walk, footstep(s)

camsyniad (**-au**) *nm* mistake

camsynied *vb* mistake

camsyniol *adj* mistaken

camu *vb* bow, bend, stoop

camu *vb* step, stride

camwedd (**-au**) *nm* iniquity, transgression

camweddu *vb* transgress

camwri *nm* injury, wrong

camymddwyn *vb* misbehave

camymddygiad (**-au**) *nm* misconduct

can *adj* white ▷ *nm* flour

cân (**caniadau, caneuon**) *nf* song

canabis *nm* cannabis

Canada *nf* Canada

cancr *nm* canker; cancer

cancro *vb* canker, corrode

candryll *adj* shattered, wrecked

canfasio *vb* canvass

canfed *adj* hundredth

canfod *vb* see, perceive, behold

canfyddadwy *adj* perceptible

canfyddiad *nm* perception

canhwyllbren (**canwyllbrenni, -au**) *nm, nf* candlestick

canhwyllwr (**canhwyllwyr**) *nm* chandler

caniad *nm* singing; ringing; crowing

caniad (**-au**) *nf* song, poem

caniadaeth *nf* singing, psalmody

caniatâd *nm* leave, permission, consent

caniataol *adj* permissive; granted

caniatáu *vb* permit, allow

caniedydd (**-ion**) *nm* singer, songster; song-book

canlyn *vb* follow, pursue

canlyniad (**-au**) *nm* consequence, result

canlynol *adj* following, consequent

canlynwr (**-wyr**) *nm* follower

canllaw (**-iau**) *nf, nm* hand-rail, parapet, aid

canmlwyddiant *nm* centenary

canmol *vb* praise, commend

canmoladwy *adj* praiseworthy

canmoliaeth (**-au**) *nf* praise, commendation

canmoliaethus *adj* eulogistic, complimentary

cannaid *adj* white, bright, luminous

cannu *vb* whiten, bleach

cannwr (**canwyr**) *nm* bleacher

cannwyll (**canhwyllau**) *nf* candle

canol *adj, nm* (**-au**) middle, centre, midst; **canol y ddinas** city centre

canolbarth (**-au**) *nm* middle part, midland

canolbwynt (**-iau**) *nm* centre, focus

canolbwyntio *vb* centre, concentrate

canoldir (**-oedd**) *nm* inland region

canolddydd *nm* mid-day, noon

canolfan (**-nau**) *nm, nf* centre; **canolfan chwaraeon** sports centre; **canolfan galwadau** call centre; **canolfan iechyd** health centre; **canolfan ymwelwyr** visitor centre

canoli *vb* centre; arbitrate; centralize

canolig *adj* middling

canoloesol *adj* mediaeval

canolog *adj* central

canolradd (**-ol**) *adj* intermediate

canolwr (**-wyr**) *nm* mediator, referee; centre half, centre; **canolwr blaen** centre forward

canon (**-au**) *nf, nm* canon (*music*)

canon (**-iaid**) *nm* canon (*priest*)

canonaidd *adj* canonical

canoneiddio *vb* canonize
canoniaeth (-au) *nf* canonry
canonwr (-wyr) *nm* canon, canonist
canradd (-au) *adj, nf* centigrade, percentile
canran (-nau) *nm* percentage
canrif (-oedd) *nf* century
cansen (-ni) *nf* cane
canser *nm* cancer
canslo *vb* cancel
cant (-au) *nm* circle, ring, rim; tyre
cant (cannoedd) *nm* hundred
cantel (-au) *nm* rim, brim
cantîn (cantinoedd) *nf* canteen
cantor (-ion) *nm* singer
cantores (-au) *nf* songstress, singer
cantref (-i, -ydd) *nm* hundred
cantwr (-orion) *nm* singer, songster
cantwraig *nf* songstress, singer
canu *vb* sing, chant; play; crow; ring; **canu gwlad** country music
canŵ (-od) *nm* canoe
canŵa *vb* canoe, go canoeing ▷ *n* canoeing
canŵo *vb* canoe
canwr (-wyr) *nm* singer
canwriad (-iaid) *nm* centurion
canwyr (-au, -ion) *nm* plane (*in carpentry*)
canys *conj* because, for
cap (-iau) *nm* cap
capan (-au) *nm* cap; lintel
capel (-i, -ydd, -au) *nm* chapel
capelwr (-wyr) *nm* chapel-goer
caplan (-iaid) *nm* chaplain
caplaniaeth (-au) *nf* chaplaincy
capteiniaeth *nf* captaincy
capten (-einiaid) *nm* captain
car (ceir) *nm* car; **car campau** sports car; **car cefn codi** hatchback; **car llog** hire car
câr (ceraint) *nm* friend; relation
carafán (-au) *nf* caravan

carbohydrad (-au) *nm* carbohydrate
carbon (-au) *adj, nm* carbon
carbwl *adj* clumsy, awkward
carco *vb* take care
carcus *adj* solicitous, anxious, careful
carchar (-au) *nm* prison; restraint
carchardy (-dai) *nm* prison-house
carchariad *nm* imprisonment
carcharor (-ion) *nm* prisoner
carcharu *vb* imprison
carden (cardiau) *nf* card
cardigan (-au) *nf* cardigan
cardod (-au) *nf* charity, alms, dole
cardota *vb* beg
cardotyn (-wyr) *nm* beggar
cardydwyn, cardodwyn *nm* weakest of brood or litter
caredig *adj* kind
caredigrwydd *nm* kindness
caregog *adj* stony
caregu *vb* stone; petrify; gather stones
carennydd *nm* friendship; kinship
caretsen (carets) *nf* carrot
carfaglog *adj* clumsy
carfan (-au) *nf* beam; swath; party, faction
cariad (-au) *nm* love
cariad (-au, -on) *nm, nf* lover, sweetheart
cariadfab *nm* lover, sweetheart
cariadferch *nf* sweetheart, mistress
cariadlawn *adj* full of love, loving
cariadus *adj* loving, beloved, dear
caridým (-s) *nm* ragamuffin
cario *vb* carry, bear
carismatig *adj* charismatic
cariwr *nm* carrier; **y Cariwr Dŵr** Aquarius
carlam (-au) *nm* prance, gallop
carlamu *vb* prance, gallop

carlwm (**-lymod**) *nm* ermine, stoat
carn (**-au**) *nm* hoof; hilt, haft, handle
carn (**-au**), **carnedd** (**-au**) *nf* cairn
cárnifal *nm* carnival
carniforus *adj* carnivorous
carnog, carnol *adj* hoofed
carol (**-au**) *nm, nf* carol
carp (**-iau**) *nm* clout, rag
carped (**-au, -i**) *nm* carpet
carpiog *adj* ragged, tattered
carrai (**careiau**) *nf* lace, thong
carreg (**cerrig**) *nf* stone
cart (**ceirt**) *nm, nf* cart
cartaid, certaid (**-eidiau**) *nm* cartful
cartilag (**-au**) *nm* cartilage
cartref (**-i, -ydd**) *nm* home, abode; **cartref henoed** old people's home; **cartref symudol** mobile home ▷ *adj* home-made
cartrefle (**-oedd**) *nm* abode
cartreflu *nm* militia
cartrefol *adj* homely, domestic, home; civil
cartrefu *vb* make one's home, settle
cartŵn (**cartwnau**) *nm* cartoon
cartwnydd (**-ion**) *nm* cartoonist
carth (**-ion**) *nm* tow, oakum; off-scouring
carthen (**-ni, -nau**) *nf* Welsh blanket, coverlet; **carthen blu** duvet
carthffos (**-ydd**) *nf* sewer
carthffosaeth *nf* sewage
carthu *vb* cleanse, purge, scavenge
caru *vb* love; like; court
caruaidd *adj* loving, kind
carw (**ceirw**) *nm* stag, deer
carwden (**-ni**) *nf* back-chain; tall awkward fellow
carwr (**-wyr**) *nm* lover, wooer
carwriaeth (**-au**) *nf* courtship

cas *adj* hateful, odious; nasty, disagreeable ▷ *nm* hatred, aversion
cas (**caseion**) *nm* hater, foe, enemy
casáu *vb* hate, detest, abhor
casbeth (**-au**) *nm* aversion, nuisance
caseg (**cesig**) *nf* mare
casét (**-iau**) *nm* cassette
casgen (**-ni, casgiau**) *nf* cask
casgl *nf, nm* collection
casgliad (**-au**) *nm* collection; gathering
casglu *vb* collect, gather; infer
casglwr (**-wyr**), **casglydd** (**-ion**) *nm* collector
casineb *nm* hatred
cast (**-iau**) *nm* vice, knack
castan (**-au**) *nf* chestnut
castanwydd *npl* (*nf*-**en**) chestnut-trees
castell (**cestyll**) *nm* castle
castellog *adj* castled, castellated
castellu *vb* castle, encamp
castio *vb* trick, cheat; cast, calculate
castiog *adj* full of tricks, tricky
casul (**-(i)au**) *nm, nf* chasuble, cassock
caswir *nm* unpalatable truth
casyn (**casiau**) *nm* case, casing
cat (**-iau**) *nm* bit, piece, fragment; pipe
catalog (**-au**) *nm* catalogue
catalogio *vb* catalogue
catalydd (**-ion**) *nm* catalyst
categori (**-ïau**) *nm* category
catel *coll n* chattels; cattle
catgor (**-(i)au**) *nm* ember day(s)
catrawd (**-rodau**) *nf* regiment
cath (**-od, -au**) *nf* cat
cathl (**-au**) *nf* melody, hymn, lay
cathlu *vb* sing, hymn
cathod (**-au**) *nf* cathode
catholig *adj* catholic
Catholigiaeth *nf* Catholicism

catholigrwydd nm catholicity
cau adj hollow, concave
cau vb shut, close, enclose
caul (ceulion) nm maw; rennet; curd
caw (-(i)au) nm band, swaddling-clothes
cawdel nm hotchpotch, mess
cawell (cewyll) nm hamper, basket, cradle
cawellaid (-eidiau) nm hamperful
cawellwr (-wyr) nm basket-maker
cawg (-iau) nm basin, bowl, pitcher
cawl nm broth, soup; hotchpotch
cawn npl (nf-**en**) reeds
cawod (-ydd) nf shower
cawodi vb shower
cawodog adj showery
cawr (cewri) nm giant
cawraidd adj gigantic
cawres (-au) nf giantess
caws nm cheese; curd
cawsai, cawsi nf, nm causeway
cawsaidd adj cheesy, caseous
cawsellt (-ydd, -i, -au) nm cheese-vat
cawsio vb curd, curdle
cawsiog adj curdled
CC adv BC
CD (-s, -au) nm CD
cecian vb stammer
cecren (-nod) nf shrew, scold, cantankerous woman
cecru vb wrangle, bicker
cecrus adj cantankerous, quarrelsome
cecryn (-nod) nm wrangler, brawler
cedor nm, nf pubic hair
cedrwydd npl (nf-**en**) cedars
cefn (-au) nm back; support
cefndedyn nm mesentery; diaphragm, pancreas
cefnder (-dyr) nm first cousin

cefndir (-oedd) nm background
cefnen (-nau) nf ridge
cefnfor (-oedd) nm main sea, ocean
cefngrwm adj hump-backed
cefnog adj well-off, well-to-do
cefnogaeth nf encouragement, support
cefnogi vb encourage, support
cefnogol adj encouraging
cefnu vb back, turn the back, forsake
cefnwlad (-wledydd) nf hinterland
cefnwr (-wyr) nm back, full-back
ceffyl (-au) nm horse
ceg (-au) nf mouth
cega vb mouth, prate
cegaid (-eidiau) nf mouthful
cegen (-nau) nf gullet, windpipe
cegid, cegiden (cegidau) nf green woodpecker, jay
cegin (-au) nf kitchen
cegrwth adj gaping
cegyr npl hemlock
cengl (-au) nf band; girth; hank
cenglu vb hank; girth; wind
cei (-au) nm quay
ceibio vb pick with pickaxe
ceidwad (-aid) nm keeper, saviour
ceidwadaeth nf conservatism; conservancy
ceidwadol adj conservative
Ceidwadwr (-wyr) nm Conservative
ceiliagwydd (-au) nm gander
ceiliog (-od) nm cock; **ceiliog rhedyn** grasshopper
ceinach (-od) nf hare
ceincio vb branch out, ramify
ceinciog adj branched, branching
ceinder nm elegance, beauty
ceiniog (-au) nf penny
ceiniogwerth (-au, -i) nf pennyworth
ceinion npl beauties, gems

ceintach vb grumble, croak
ceintachlyd adj querulous
ceintachwr (-wyr) nm grumbler, croaker
ceirch (nf **-en**) coll n oats
ceirios npl (nf **-en**) cherries
ceisbwl (-byliaid) nm catchpole, bailiff
ceisio vb seek; ask; try, attempt, endeavour; fetch, get
cêl adj hidden, concealed ▷ nm concealment ▷ npl kale
celain (celanedd) nf dead body
celanedd coll n carnage, slaughter
celc nm, nf concealment; hoard
celf (-au) nf art, craft
celfi npl (nm **-cyn**) tools, gear; furniture
celfydd adj skilled, skilful
celfyddgar adj ingenious; artistic
celfyddwr (-wyr) nm artificer, artist
celfyddyd (-au) nf art, craft; skill; **celfyddydau graffig** graphic arts
celfyddydol adj relating to art/the Arts
celu vb hide, conceal
celwrn (-yrnau) nm tub, bucket, pail
celwydd (-au) nm lie, falsehood, untruth
celwyddog adj lying, mendacious; false
celwyddwr (-wyr) nm liar
celyn npl (nf **-nen**) holly
cell (-oedd, -au) nf cell, chamber; **celloedd cenhedlu** germ cells; **enyniad y celloedd** cellulitis
celli (cellïau, -ïoedd) nf grove
cellog adj cellular
cellwair vb jest, trifle ▷ nm fun
cellweiriwr (-wyr) nm jester, trifler
cellwirus adj playful, jocular
cemeg nm chemistry
cemegol adj chemical

cemegwr (-wyr), cemegydd (-ion) nm chemist
cemegyn (cemegau) nm chemical
cen coll n skin, peel, scales, scurf, film, lichen
cenadwri nf message
cenau (cenawon) nm cub, whelp; rascal
cenedl (-hedloedd) nf nation; gender
cenedlaethol adj national
cenedlaetholdeb nm nationalism
cenedlaetholi vb nationalize
cenedlaetholwr (-wyr) nm nationalist
cenedl-ddyn (-ion) nm gentile
cenfaint (-feiniau) nf herd
cenfigen (-nau) nf envy, jealousy
cenfigennu vb envy
cenfigennus, cenfigenllyd adj envious, jealous
cenhadaeth (cenadaethau) nf mission
cenhadol adj missionary
cenhadu vb permit; propagate, conduct a mission
cenhadwr (-hadon) nm missionary
cenhedlaeth (cenedlaethau) nf generation
cenhedlig adj gentile, pagan
cenhedlu vb beget, generate
Cenia nf Kenya
cenllif nm flood, torrent, deluge
cenllysg coll n hailstones, hail
cennad (-hadau, -hadon) nf leave; messenger
cennin npl (nf **-hinen**) leeks
cennog adj scaly, scurfy
cennu vb scale, scurf
centimedr (-au) nm centimetre
cêr nf gear, tools, trappings
cerameg nm, nf ceramics
ceramig adj ceramic
cerbyd (-au) nm chariot, coach, car

cerbydwr (-wyr) nm coachman
cerdyn (cardiau) nm card; **cerdyn adnabod** identity card; **cerdyn cof** memory card; **cerdyn crafu** scratch card; **cerdyn credyd** credit card; **cerdyn debyd** debit card; **cerdyn sweip** swipe card
cerdd (-i) nf song, poem; music, poetry
cerddbrenni npl woodwinds
cerddbresi npl brass section (orchestra)
cerdded vb walk; go; travel
cerddediad nm walking, going; pace
cerddgar adj harmonious, musical
cerddin, cerdin npl (nf-**en**) rowan
cerddor (-ion) nm singer, musician
cerddorfa (-feydd) nf orchestra
cerddorfaol adj orchestral
cerddoriaeth nf music
cerddorol adj musical
cerddwr (-wyr) nm walker
cerfddelw (-au) nf graven image, statue
cerfio vb carve
cerflun (-iau) nm statue; engraving
cerfluniaeth nf sculpture
cerflunydd (-lunwyr) nm sculptor
cerfwaith nm carving, sculpture
cern (-au) nf cheek, jaw
cernod (-iau) nf buffet
cernodio vb buffet, clout
cerpyn (carpiau) nm clout, rag
cerrynt nm, nf course, road; current
cert (-i) nf cart
certiwr (-wyr) nm carter
certh adj right; awful
cerub, ceriwb (-iaid) nm cherub
cerwyn (-i) nf tub; vat; winepress
cerydd (-on) nm correction, chastisement; rebuke, reproof, censure
ceryddol adj chastising, chastening

ceryddu vb correct, chastise; rebuke
ceryddwr (-wyr) nm chastiser; rebuker
cesail (-eiliau) nf arm-pit; bosom
cesair npl, coll n hailstones, hail
cest (-au) nf belly, paunch
cestog adj corpulent
cetyn (catiau) nm piece, bit; pipe
cethin adj dark, fierce, ugly
ceubren (-nau) nm hollow tree
ceubwll (-byllau) nm pit
ceudod nm cavity; abdomen; thought, heart
ceuffordd (-ffyrdd) nf tunnel
ceuffos (-ydd) nf drain, ditch
ceugrwm adj concave
ceulan (-nau, -lennydd) nf bank, brink
ceulo vb curdle, coagulate
ceunant (-nentydd) nm ravine, gorge
cewyn (-nau, cawiau) nm napkin
ci (cŵn) nm dog, hound
cïaidd adj dog-like, brutal
cib (-au) nm pod, husk
cibddall adj purblind
cibo vb frown, scowl
cibog adj scowling
cibws, cibwst nf kibes, chilblains
cibwts (-au) nm kibbutz
cibyn (-nau) nm shell; husk; half a bushel
cic (-iau) nm, nf kick; **cic gychwyn** kick-off
cicio vb kick
ciciwr (-wyr) nm kicker
cidwm (-ymiaid, -ymod) nm wolf; rascal
cieidd-dra nm brutality
cig (-oedd) nm flesh, meat
cigfran (-frain) nf raven
cignoeth adj touching to the quick, caustic

cigog *adj* fleshy
cigwain (**-weiniau**) *nf* flesh-hook
cigydd (**-ion**) *nm* butcher
cigyddiaeth *nf* butchery
cigysol *adj* carnivorous
cigysydd (**-ion**) *nm* carnivore
cil (**-iau, -ion**) *nm* back; retreat; corner
cilagor *vb* open partly
cilagored *adj* ajar
cilbost (**cilbyst**) *nm* gate-post
cilchwyrn *npl* (*nf*-**en,** *nm* -**au,** *nm* -**od**) glands
cildrem (**-iau**) *nf* leer
cildremio *vb* leer
cildroi *vb* reverse
cildwrn *nm* tip, bribe
cildyn *adj* obstinate, stubborn
cildynnu *vb* be obstinate
cildynnus *adj* obstinate, stubborn
cildynrwydd *nm* obstinacy
cilddant (**-ddannedd**) *nm* molar
cilfach (**-au**) *nf* nook; creek, bay
cilfilyn (**-filod**) *nf* ruminant
cilgnoi *vb* chew the cud, ruminate
cilgwthio *vb* push, shove, jostle
cilgynnyrch (**-gynhyrchion**) *nm* by-product
cilio *vb* retreat, recede, swerve
cilocalori (**-ïau**) *nm* kilocalorie
cilogram (**-au**) *nm* kilogram
cilomedr (**-au**) *nm* kilometre
cilwen (**-au**) *nf* half smile
cilwenu *vb* simper, smile, leer
cilwg (**-ygon**) *nm* frown, scowl
cilydd (**-ion**) *nm* fellow, companion
cilyddol *adj* reciprocal
cimwch (**-ychiaid**) *nm* lobster
ciniawa *vb* dine
cinio (**ciniawau**) *nm* dinner; **cinio gwadd** dinner party
cip (**-ion**) *nm* pluck, snatch; glimpse

cipdrem (**-iau**) *nf, nm* glance, glimpse
cipedrych *vb* glance, glimpse
cipio *vb* snatch
cipiwr (**-wyr**) *nm* snatcher
cipolwg *nm, nf* glance, glimpse
ciprys *vb, nm* scramble
cis (**-iau**) *nm, nf* buffet; slap, touch
cist (**-iau**) *nf* chest, coffer, box; bin
ciw (**-iau**) *nm* cue, queue
ciwb *nm* cube
ciwed *coll n* rabble, mob, crew
ciwrad (**-iaid**) *nm* curate
ciwt *adj* cute, clever, ingenious
claddedigaeth (**-au**) *nf, nm* burial
claddfa (**-feydd**) *nf* burial-ground, cemetery
claddu *vb* bury
claear *adj* lukewarm, tepid; mild; cool
claearineb *nm* lukewarmness
claearu *vb* make mild or tepid; soothe
claer *adj* clear, bright, shining
claerder *nm* clearness, brightness
claf (**cleifion**) *adj* sick, ill ▷ *nm* sick person, patient
clafdy (**-dai**) *nm* hospital, infirmary
clafr *nm* itch, mange
clafrllyd *adj* mangy
clafychu *vb* sicken, fall ill
clai (**cleiau**) *nm* clay
clais (**cleisiau**) *nm* stripe; bruise
clamp (**-iau**) *nm* mass, lump; monster
clap (**-iau**) *nm* lump
clapgi (**-gwn**) *nm* telltale
clapio *vb* lump; strike; gossip
clapiog *adj* lumpy
clas *nm* monastic community, cloister, college
clasur (**-on**) *nm* classic
clasurol *adj* classical

clau *adj* quick, swift, soon; true; audible

clawdd (cloddiau) *nm* hedge; dyke, embankment

clawr (cloriau) *nm* face, surface; cover, lid; board

clebar, cleber *nf, nm* idle talk, gossip, tattle

clebran *vb* chatter, gossip, tattle

clebryn *nm*, **clebren** *nf* tattler

clec (-iau, -s) *nf* click; clack; crack; gossip

cleci (-cwn) *nm* telltale

clecian *vb* click; clack; crack, snap

clecyn *nm*, **clecen** *nf* gossip, telltale

cledr (-au) *nf* pole; rail; palm (of hand)

cledren (-nau, -ni) *nf* pale, pole, rail

cleddyf, cleddau, cledd (cleddyfau) *nm* sword; brace

cleddyfwr (-wyr) *nm* swordsman

clefyd (-au) *nm* disease; fever; **clefyd melys** diabetes; **clefyd y galon** heart disease; **clefyd y gwair** hay fever

clegar *vb* clack, cluck, cackle

clegyr, clegr *nm* rock; cairn, stony place

cleiog *adj* clayey

cleiriach *nm* decrepit one

cleisio *vb* bruise

cleisiog *adj* bruised

clem (-iau) *nf* notion, idea; look, gaze ▷ *pl* grimaces

clep (-iau) *nf* clack, clap; gossip

clepgi (-gwn) *nm* babbler; telltale

clepian *vb* clap; slam; blab

clêr *coll n* itinerant minstrels; bards

clêr *npl* (*nf* **cleren**) flies

clera *vb* stroll as minstrels

clerc (-od) *nm* clerk

clercio *vb* serve as clerk

clerigol *adj* clerical

clerigwr (-wyr) *nm* clergyman

clerwr (-wyr) *nm* itinerant minstrel

clerwriaeth *nf* minstrelsy

clewt (-iau) *nm* clout

clewtian *vb* clout

clic (cliciau) *nm* clique

clicied (-au) *nf* clicker; trigger

cliciedu *vb* latch, fasten

clicio *vb* click; **clicio dwywaith** double-click

clindarddach *vb* crackle ▷ *nm* crackling

clinig (-au) *nm* clinic

clir *adj* clear

clirio *vb* clear

clo (cloeau, cloeon) *nm* lock, conclusion

clobyn *nm*, **cloben** *nf* monster

cloc (-iau) *nm* clock; **cloc larwm** alarm clock

clocian *vb* cluck

clocsiau *npl* (*nf* **clocsen**) clog

cloch (clych, clychau) *nf* bell; **o'r/ar gloch** o'clock

clochaidd *adj* sonorous, noisy

clochdar *vb* cluck, cackle

clochdy (-dai) *nm* belfry, steeple

clochydd (-ion) *nm* bell-man; sexton

clod (-ydd) *nm, nf* praise, fame, renown

clodfori *vb* praise, extol

clodwiw *adj* commendable, praiseworthy

cloddfa (-feydd) *nf* quarry, mine

cloddio *vb* dig, delve; quarry, mine

cloddiwr (-wyr) *nm* digger, navvy

cloëdig *adj* locked, closed

cloer (-(i)au) *nm, nf* locker; niche, embrasure; pigeon-hole

cloff *adj* lame

cloffi *vb* lame, halt ▷ *nm* lameness

cloffni *nm* lameness

cloffrwym (-au) *nm* fetter, hobble;
**cloffrwym y cythraul, cloffrwym
y mwci** great bindweed
clog (-au) *nm, nf* cloak
clog (-au) *nf* rock, precipice
clogfaen (-feini) *nm* boulder
clogwyn (-i) *nm* cliff, crag, precipice
clogwynog *adj* craggy, precipitous
clogyn (-nau) *nm* cloak, cape
clogyrnaidd *adj* rough, rugged,
clumsy
cloi *vb* lock
clonc *nf* clank; gossip ▷ *adj* addled
clopa (-âu) *nf, nm* noddle; knob;
club
cloren (-nau) *nf* rump, tail
clorian (-nau) *nm, nf* pair of scales
cloriannu *vb* weigh, balance
clorin *nm* chlorine
clorinio, clorinadu *vb* chlorinate
clos (-ydd) *nm* yard
clos (closau) *nm* pair of breeches
clòs *adj* close
closio *vb* close, near
cludadwy *adj* portable
cludair (-eiriau) *nf* heap, load,
wood-pile
cludiad *nm* carriage
cludiant (-nnau) *nm* transport,
haulage
cludo *vb* carry, convey
cludwr (-wyr), cludydd (-ion) *nm*
porter
clul (-iau) *nm* knell
clun (-iau) *nf* hip, haunch, thigh, leg;
moor
cluro *vb* rub, smear
clust (-iau) *nf, nm* ear; handle
clustfeinio *vb* prick up the ears;
eavesdrop
clustfys *nm* little finger
clustffôn (-ffonau) *nm* earphone
clustlws (-lysau) *nm* earring

clustnod (-au) *nm* earmark
clustog (-au) *nf, nm* cushion, pillow
clwb (clybiau) *nm* club
clwc *adj* addled
clwcian *vb* cluck
clwm (clymau) *nm* knot, tie
clwpa (-od) *nm* knob, boss; club;
dolt
clws (*f* clos) *adj* pretty, nice
clwstwr (clystyrau) *nm* cluster
clwt (clytiau) *nm* patch, clout, rag
clwyd (-au, -i, -ydd) *nf* hurdle; gate;
roost
clwydo *vb* roost
clwyf (-au) *nm* wound; disease
clwyfo *vb* wound
clwyfus *adj* wounded; sore; sick
clybodeg *nf* acoustics
clybodig *adj* acoustic
clyd *adj* warm, sheltered, snug, cosy
clydwch, clydwr *nm* warmth,
shelter
clyfar *adj* clever; pleasant, agreeable
clymblaid (-bleidiau) *nf* clique,
cabal
clymog *adj* knotty, entangled
clymu *vb* knot, tie
clytio *vb* patch, piece
clytiog *adj* patched; ragged
clytwaith (-weithiau) *nm*
patchwork
clyw *nm* sense of hearing
clywadwy *adj* audible
clywed *vb* hear; feel; taste; smell
clywedigaeth *nf* hearing
clywedol *adj* aural
clywedydd (-ion) *nm* hearer,
auditor
clyweled *adj* audio-visual
cnaf (-on, -iaid) *nm* knave, rascal
cnafaidd *adj* knavish, rascally
cnaif (cneifion) *nm* shearing, fleece
cnap (-iau) *nm* lump, knob, boss

cnapan (-au) nm ball, bowl, kind of ball game
cnapiog adj lumpy
cnau npl (nf **cneuen**) nuts
cnawd nm flesh
cnawdol adj carnal, fleshly, fleshy
cneifio vb shear, fleece
cneifiwr (-wyr) nm shearer
cneua vb nut
cneuen (cnau) nf nut
cnewyllyn (cnewyll) nm kernel, nucleus
cnith (-iau, -ion) nm slight touch, blow; pluck
cno nm bite, chewing, gnawing
cnoc (-iau) nm, nf knock
cnocio vb knock
cnofa (-feydd) nf gnawing, pang
cnofil (-od) nm rodent
cnoi vb gnaw, chew, bite; ache
cnot (-iau) nm knot, bunch
cnu (-au), cnuf (-iau) nm fleece
cnud (-oedd) nf pack
cnùl, cnul (-iau) nm knell
cnwd (cnydau) nm crop; covering
cnydfawr adj fruitful, productive
cnydio vb crop, yield increase
cnydiog adj fruitful, productive
cob (cobau) nf coat, cloak, robe
còb (-iau) nm embankment; miser; wag; cob
coban (-au) nf: **coban nos** nightshirt
coblyn (-nod) nm sprite, goblin, imp
cocos npl cogs; **olwyn gocos** cog-wheel
cocos, cocs npl (nf **cocsen**) cockles
coch adj, nm red
coch-gam nf robin
cochi vb redden, blush
cochni, cochder nm redness
cochl (-au) nm, nf mantle, cloak
cod (-au) nf bag, pouch

codaid (-eidiau) nf bagful
codi vb rise, get up; raise, lift; erect
codiad (-au) nm rise, rising; erection
codog adj baggy ▷ nm, nf (-ion) rich man; miser
codwm (codymau) nm fall, tumble
codwr (-wyr) nm riser; raiser; lifter; **codwr canu** precentor
codymu vb wrestle
codymwr (-wyr) nm wrestler
codded nm anger; grief
coddi vb anger, offend
coed (-ydd) coll n wood, timber, trees
coeden (coed) nf tree
coedio vb timber
coediog adj wooded, woody
coedwig (-oedd) nf wood, forest
coedwigaeth nf forestry
coedwigwr (-wyr) nm woodman, forester
coedd adj public
coeg adj empty, vain; one-eyed, blind
coegddyn (-ion) nm fop, coxcomb, fool
coegedd nm emptiness, silliness
coegen (-nod) nf minx, coquette
coegennaidd adj coquettish
coegfalch adj vain, foppish
coegi vb jeer at, mock
coeglyd adj vain, sarcastic
coegni nm vanity; spite; sarcasm
coegwr (-wyr) nm fool
coegwych adj gaudy, garish, tawdry
coegyn (-nod) nm coxcomb
coel (-ion) nf belief, trust, credit
coelbren (-nau, -ni) nm lot
coelcerth (-i) nf bonfire, blaze
coelgrefydd (-au) nf superstition
coelgrefyddol adj superstitious
coelio vb believe, credit, trust
coes (-au) nf leg, shank ▷ nm, nf handle; stem, stalk

coetgae *nm* hedge; enclosure
coetmon (**-myn**) *nm* lumberjack
coetref *nf* woodland, homestead
coeth *adj* fine, refined; elegant
coethder *nm* refinement, elegance
coethi *vb* refine; chastise; babble
coethwr (**-wyr**) *nm* refiner
cof (**-ion**) *nm* memory; remembrance
cofadail (**-eiladau**) *nf* monument
cofbin (**-nau**) *nm* memory stick, pen drive
cofeb (**-ion**) *nf* memorandum; memorial
cof-gerdyn (**cof-gardiau**) *nm* memory card
cofgolofn (**-au**) *nf* monument
cofiadur (**-on, -iaid**) *nm* recorder
cofiadwy *adj* memorable
cofiannydd (**-anyddion**) *nm* biographer
cofiant (**-iannau**) *nm* memoir, biography
cofio *vb* remember, recollect
cofl (**-au**) *nf* embrace; bosom
coflaid (**-eidiau**) *nf* armful; bundle
coflech (**-au**) *nf* memorial tablet
cofleidio *vb* embrace, hug
coflyfr (**-au**) *nm* record, chronicle
cofnod (**-ion**) *nm* memorandum, minute
cofnodi *vb* record, register
cofrestr (**-au**) *nf* register, roll
cofrestrfa *nf* registry
cofrestru *vb* register
cofrestrydd (**-ion**) *nm* registrar
cofus *adj* mindful
cofweini *vb* prompt
cofweinydd (**-ion**) *nm* prompter
coffa *vb* remember ▷ *nm* remembrance
coffâd *nm* remembrance
coffadwriaeth *nf* remembrance, memory

coffadwriaethol *adj* memorial
coffáu *vb* remember; remind; commemorate
coffi *nm* coffee
coffr (**-au**) *nm* coffer, trunk, chest
cog (**-au**) *nf* cuckoo
cog (**-au**) *nm* cook
coginiaeth *nf* cookery
coginio *vb* cook
cogio *vb* cog; sham, feign, pretend
cogiwr (**-wyr**) *nm* pretender, swindler
cogor *vb* chatter, caw, croak ▷ *nm* chattering
cogwrn (**-yrnau, cegyrn**) *nm* knob, cone; cock (of corn); shell
cogydd (**-ion**) *nm*, **cogyddes** (**-au**) *nf* cook
cogyddiaeth *nf* cookery
congl (**-au**) *nf* corner
col (**-ion**) *nm* awn, beard
côl *nf* bosom, embrace
coladu *vb* collate
coledd, coleddu *vb* cherish, foster
coleddwr (**-wyr**) *nm* cherisher, fosterer, patron, supporter
coleg (**-au**) *nm* college; **coleg chweched dosbarth** sixth-form college; **coleg technoleg dinasol** city technology college
colegol *adj* collegiate
colegwr (**-wyr**) *nm* collegian
coler (**-i**) *nf*, *nm* collar
colfen (**-nau, -ni**) *nf* bough, branch; tree
colofn (**-au**) *nf* column, pillar
colomen (**-nod**) *nf* dove, pigeon
colomendy (**-dai**) *nm* dove-cot
colomennaidd *adj* dove-like
coluddion *npl* (*nm* **-yn**) bowels
colur (**-au**) *nm* make-up, colour
coluro *vb* make-up, paint; conceal
colwyn (**-od**) *nm* puppy

colyn (-nau) *nm* pivot; sting; tail
colynnog *adj* stinging; hinged
colynnu *vb* sting
coll (-iadau) *nm* loss; failing, defect
colladwy *adj* perishable
collddail *adj* deciduous
colled (-ion) *nm, nf* loss
colledig *adj* lost, damned
colledigaeth *nf* perdition
colledu *vb* occasion loss
colledus *adj* fraught with loss
colledwr (-wyr) *nm* loser
collen (cyll) *nf* hazel
collfarn (-au) *nf* doom, condemnation
collfarnu *vb* condemn
colli *vb* lose; be lost, perish; spill, shed
collnod (-au) *nm* apostrophe
collwr (-wyr) *nm* loser
coma (-s) *nm* comma
côma (comâu) *nm* coma
comed (-au) *nf* comet
comedi (-ïau) *nf, nm* comedy
comig *adj* comic, comical ▷ *nm* comic (paper)
comisiwn (-iynau) *nm* commission
comisiynu *vb* commission
comiwnydd (-ion) *nm* communist
comiwnyddiaeth *nf* communism
comiwnyddol *adj* communist
conach *vb* grumble
conclaf *nm* conclave
concro *vb* conquer
concwerwr (-wyr) *nm* conqueror
concwest (-au) *nf* conquest, victory
condemniad *nm* condemnation
condemnio *vb* condemn
confensiwn (-iynau) *nm* convention
conffederasiwn (-asiynau) *nm* confederation
conffirmasiwn *nm* confirmation
conffirmio *vb* confirm
conifferaidd *adj* coniferous
cono *nm* rascal; wag; old fogey
consesiwn (-iynau) *nm* concession
consol (-au) *nm*: **consol gêmau** games console
consuriaeth *nf* conjuring
consurio *vb* conjure
consuriwr (-wyr) *nm* conjurer
conwydd *npl* (*nf* **-en**) coniferous trees
cop, copyn (-nod, -nau) *nm* spider
copa (-âu) *nf* top, crest; head
copi (-ïau) *nm* copy; copy-book
copïo *vb* copy, transcribe
copïwr (-wyr) *nm* copyist, transcriber
copr *nm* copper
cor (-rod) *nm* dwarf; spider
côr (corau) *nm* choir; stall, pew; **côr feistr** choirmaster
corachaidd *adj* dwarfish, stunted
corawl *adj* choral
corbwll (-byllau) *nm* whirlpool; puddle
corcyn (cyrc) *nm* cork
cord (-iau) *nm* cord; chord
cordeddu *vb* twist, twine
corddi *vb* churn; turn; agitate
corddiad (-au) *nm* churning
corddwr (-wyr) *nm* churner
Corea *nf* Korea
cored (-au) *nf* weir, dam
coreograffiaeth *nf* choreography
corfan (-nau) *nm* metrical foot
corff (cyrff) *nm* body
corfflu (-oedd) *nm* corps
corffol *adj* corpulent; physical
corffolaeth *nf* bodily form; stature
corfforaeth (-au) *nf* corporation
corffori *vb* embody, incorporate
corfforiad (-au) *nm* embodiment**

corfforol adj bodily, corporeal, corporal

corgan (-au), **côr-gân** (**côr-ganau**) nf chant

corganu vb chant

corgi (-gwn) nm cur, corgi

corgimwch (-ychiaid) nm prawn

corhwyad (-aid) nf teal; moorhen

corlan (-nau) nf fold

corlannu vb fold

corn (cyrn) nm horn; pipe, tube; roll; corn; stethoscope; **corn gwddw(f)**, **corn gwynt** windpipe; **corn siarad** loudspeaker

cornant (-nentydd) nm brook, rill

cornboer nm phlegm

cornchwiglen (-chwiglod) nf lapwing

cornel (-i, -au) nf, nm corner

cornelu vb corner

cornicyll (-od) nm lapwing, plover, peewit

cornio vb horn, butt; examine with a stethoscope

corniog adj horned

cornwyd (-ydd) nm boil, abscess, sore

coron (-au) nf crown

coroni vb crown ▷ nm coronation

coroniad nm coronation

coronog adj crowned

corrach (corachod) nm dwarf, pygmy

corryn (corynnod) nm spider

cors (-ydd) nf bog, swamp

corsen (-nau, cyrs) nf reed; stem, stalk; cane

cortyn (-nau) nm cord, rope

corun (-au) nm crown of the head; tonsure

corwg, corwgl (-yg(l)au) nm coracle

corws nm chorus

corwynt (-oedd) nm whirlwind

cosb (-au) nf punishment, penalty; **cosb ddihenydd** capital punishment

cosbadwy adj punishable

cosbedigaeth nf punishment

cosbi vb punish

cosbol adj punitive, penal

cosbwr (-wyr) nm punisher

cosfa (-feydd) nf itch, itching; thrashing

cosi vb scratch, itch ▷ nm itching

cosmetigau npl cosmetics

cosmig adj cosmic

Cosofo nf Kosovo

cost (-au) nf cost, expense

costiad (-au) nm costing

costio vb cost

costiwm (-tiymau) nm, nf costume

costog (-ion) nm mastiff; cur ▷ adj surly

costowci (-cwn) nm mastiff, mongrel

costrel (-au, -i) nf bottle

costrelaid (-eidiau) nf bottleful

costrelu vb bottle

costus adj costly, expensive

cosyn (-nau, -nod) nm a cheese

côt, cot (cotiau) nf coat

cotwm nm cotton

Coweit nf Kuwait

cowlas (-au) nm, nf bay of building; hay-mow

cownter (-au, -i) nm counter

cowntio vb count, account, esteem

crac (-iau) nm crack

cracio vb crack

craciog adj cracked

crach npl scabs ▷ adj scabby; petty

crachach npl snobs

crachboer nm phlegm

crachen nf scab

crachfardd (-feirdd) nm poetaster

crachfeddyg (-on) nm quack doctor
crachfonheddwr (-wyr) nm snob
crafangio, crafangu vb claw, grab
crafanc (-angau) nf claw; talon; clutch
crafiad (-au) nm scratch
crafog adj cutting, sarcastic
crafu vb scrape; scratch ▷ nm itch
crafwr (-wyr) nm scraper
craff adj close; keen; sagacious ▷ nm hold, grip
craffter nm keenness, sagacity
craffu vb look closely, observe intently
craffus adj keen, sagacious
cragen (cregyn) nf shell
crai adj new, fresh, raw
craidd (creiddiau) nm middle, centre
craig (creigiau) nf rock
crair (creiriau) nm relic
craith (creithiau) nf scar
cramen (-nau) nf crust, scab
cranc (-od) nm crab; **y Cranc** Cancer
crand adj grand
crandrwydd nm grandeur, finery
crap (-iau) nm hold; smattering
crapio vb grapple; pick up
cras (creision) adj parched, dry; harsh
crasiad nm baking
craslyd adj harsh, grating
craster nm dryness; harshness
crasu vb parch, scorch; bake
crau (creuau) nm hole, eye, socket
crau nm, nf blood, gore
crau (creuau) nm sty; stockade
crawcian, crawcio vb croak, caw
crawen (-nau) nf crust
crawn nm matter, pus
crawni vb gather, suppurate
crawnllyd adj purulent
cread nm creation

creadigaeth (-au) nf creation
creadigol adj creative
creadur (-iaid) nm creature; animal
creadures (-au) nf female creature
creawdwr (-wyr) nm creator
crebach adj shrunk, withered
crebachlyd adj crabbed, wrinkled
crebachu vb shrink, shrivel, wrinkle, pucker
crebwyll (-ion) nm invention, understanding, fancy
crecian vb cluck; crackle
crechwen nf loud laughter, guffaw
crechwenu vb laugh loud, guffaw
cred (-au) nf belief; trust; pledge, troth
credadun (credinwyr) nm believer
credadwy adj credible
crediniaeth nf belief
crediniol adj believing
credo (-au) nm, nf creed, belief
credu vb believe
credwr (-wyr) nm believer
credyd (-on) nm credit
credydu vb credit
cref adj f of **cryf**
crefu vb crave, beg, implore
crefydd (-au) nf religion
crefydda vb profess or practise religion
crefyddol adj religious, pious
crefyddolder nm religiousness, piety
crefyddwr (-wyr) nm religionist
crefft (-au) nf handicraft, trade; **crefftau'r cartref** DIY, do-it-yourself
crefftus adj skilled, workmanlike
crefftwaith nm craftwork
crefftwr (-wyr) nm craftsman
cregyn npl (nf **cragen**) shells
creider nm freshness
creifion npl scrapings

creigiog *adj* rocky
creigiwr (**-wyr**) *nm* quarryman
creigle (**-oedd**) *nm* rocky place
creinio *vb* wallow, lie or fall down; cringe
creision *npl* flakes, crisps
crempog (**-au**) *nf* pancake
crensio *vb* grind (the teeth)
crepach *adj* numb ▷ *nf* numbness
crest *nm* crust, scurf
Creta *nf* Crete
creu *vb* create
creulon *adj* cruel
creulondeb (**-derau**) *nm* cruelty
crëwr (**crewyr**) *nm* creator
crëyr (**crehyrod**) *nm* heron
cri (**-au**) *nm* cry, clamour
cri *adj* new, fresh, raw; unleavened
criafol, criafolen *nf* mountain ash
crib (**-au**) *nf, nm* comb, crest; ridge
cribddeilio *vb* grab, extort
cribddeiliwr (**-wyr**) *nm* extortioner; speculator
cribin (**-iau**) *nf, nm* rake; skinflint
cribinio *vb* rake
cribo *vb* comb; card
criced *nm* cricket
cricedwr (**-wyr**) *nm* cricketer
crimog (**-au**) *nf*, **crimp** (**-(i)au**) *nm* shin
crin *adj* withered, sear, dry
crino *vb* wither, dry up
crintach, crintachlyd *adj* niggardly, stingy
crintachrwydd *nm* niggardliness
crintachu *vb* scrimp, skimp, stint
crio *vb* cry, weep
cripio *vb* scratch; climb, creep
cris-groes *nf* criss-cross
crisial (**-au**) *nm, adj* crystal
crisialu *vb* crystallise
Cristion (**-ogion**), **Cristnogion** *nm* Christian

Cristionogaeth *nf* Christianity
Cristionogol *adj* Christian
criw (**-iau**) *nm* crew
crïwr (**-wyr**) *nm* crier
Croatia *nf* Croatia
crocbont (**-ydd**) *nf* suspension bridge
crocbren (**-ni**) *nm, nf* gallows, gibbet
crocbris (**-iau**) *nm* exorbitant price
croch *adj* loud, vehement
crochan (**-au**) *nm* pot, cauldron
crochanaid (**-eidiau**) *nm* potful
crochenwaith (**-weithiau**) *nm* pottery
crochenydd (**-ion**) *nm* potter
croen (**crwyn**) *nm* skin; hide; peel, rind
croendenau *adj* thin-skinned
croeni, croenio *vb* form skin, skin over
croes (**-au**) *nf* cross ▷ *nm* transept
croes (**-ion**) *adj* cross, contrary
croesair (**-eiriau**) *nm* crossword
croesawgar *adj* hospitable
croesawiad *nm* welcome, reception
croesawu *vb* welcome
croesawus *adj* hospitable
croesbren (**-nau**) *nm, nf* cross
croesddweud *vb* contradict
croesfan (**-nau**) *nf* crossing;
  croesfan sebra zebra crossing
croesffordd (**-ffyrdd**) *nf* crossroad
croesgad (**-au**) *nf* crusade
croesgadwr (**-wyr**) *nm* crusader
croeshoeliad *nm* crucifixion
croeshoelio *vb* crucify
croesholi *vb* cross-examine
croesholiad (**-au**) *nm* cross-examination
croesi *vb* cross
croeso *nm* welcome
croesymgroes *adj* criss-cross; vice-versa

crofen (**-nau, -ni**) *nf* rind, crust

crog (**-au**) *nf* cross, rood ▷ *adj* hanging

crogi *vb* hang, suspend

croglath (**-au**) *nf* springe, snare, gibbet

Croglith *nm, nf*: **Dydd Gwener y Groglith** Good Friday

croglofft (**-ydd, -au**) *nf* garret; rood-loft

crogwr (**-wyr**) *nm* hangman

cronglwyd (**-ydd**) *nf*: **tan fy nghronglwyd** under my roof

crombil (**-iau**) *nf* crop; gizzard; bowels

cromen (**-ni, -nau**) *nf* dome

cromfach (**-au**) *nf* bracket, parenthesis

cromlech (**-au, -i**) *nf* cromlech

cromosom (**-au**) *nm* chromosome

cron *adj f of* **crwn**

cronfa (**-feydd**) *nf* reservoir; fund; **cronfa ddata** database

cronicl (**-au**) *nm* chronicle

cronicli *vb* chronicle

cronnell (**cronellau**) *nf* sphere, globe

cronni *vb* collect, hoard; dam

cronolegol *adj* chronological

cropian *vb* creep, crawl, grope

crosiet (**-au, -i**) *nm* crotchet

croth (**-au**) *nf* womb; calf (*of leg*)

croyw *adj* clear, plain, distinct; fresh

croywder *nm* clearness; freshness

croywi *vb* clear; freshen

crud (**-au**) *nm* cradle

crug (**-iau**) *nm* hillock; tumulus; heap; multitude; abscess, blister

cruglwyth (**-i**) *nm* heap, pile

cruglwytho *vb* heap, pile up; overload

crugo *vb* fester, vex, plague

crwban (**-od**) *nm* tortoise, turtle

crwca *adj* crooked, bowed, bent

crwm (*f* **crom**) *adj* convex, curved, bowed

crwn (*f* **cron**) *adj* round; complete

crwner (**-iaid**) *nm* coroner

crwsâd (**-adau**) *nm, nf* crusade

crwst (**crystiau**) *nm* crust

crwt (**cryts**) *nm* boy, lad

crwth (**crythau**) *nm* crowd, fiddle; purring; hump

crwybr *nm* honeycomb; mist; hoarfrost

crwydr *nm* wandering; **ar grwydr** astray

crwydro *vb* wander, stray, roam

crwydrol, crwydrus *adj* wandering

crwydrwr (**-wyr**) *nm* rambler; wanderer, rover

crwydryn (**-riaid**) *nm* vagrant, tramp

crwys *nf, npl* cross, crucifix; **dan ei grwys** laid out for burial

crybwyll *vb* mention ▷ *nm* (**-ion**) mention

crybwylliad *nm* mention, notice

crych *adj* rippling; curly; quavering ▷ *nm* (**-au**) crease, ripple, wrinkle

crychlais (**-leisiau**) *nm* trill, tremolo

crychlyd *adj* wrinkled, puckered

crychnaid (**-neidiau**) *nf* leap, gambol

crychneidio *vb* skip, frisk

crychni *nm* curliness; wrinkle

crychu *vb* wrinkle, pucker; ruffle, ripple

cryd (**-iau**) *nm* shivering; fever; ague

crydd (**-ion**) *nm* cobbler, shoemaker

crydda *vb* cobble

cryf (*f* **cref**) *adj* strong

cryfder, cryfdwr *nm* strength

cryfhaol *adj* strengthening

cryfhau *vb* strengthen; grow strong

cryg (*f* **creg**) *adj* hoarse

cryglyd *adj* hoarse, raucous
crygni *nm* hoarseness
crygu *vb* hoarsen
cryman (-au) *nm* reaping-hook, sickle
crymanwr (-wyr) *nm* reaper
crymu *vb* bow, bend, stoop
cryn *adj* considerable, much
crŷn, cryn *nm, adj* shivering
crynder *nm* roundness
cryndod *nm* trembling, shivering
crynedig *adj* trembling, tremulous
crynfa (-feydd) *nf* tremble, tremor
crynhoad (-noadau) *nm* collection, digest
crynhoi *vb* gather together, collect
cryno *adj* compact; neat, tidy
cryno ddisg (-iau) *nm* CD, compact disc
crynodeb (-au) *nm* summary
crynswth *nm* mass, bulk, whole
crynu *vb* shiver, tremble, quake
Crynwr (-wyr) *nm* Quaker
crys (-au) *nm* shirt; **crys chwys** sweatshirt
crysbaid (-beisiau) *nf* jacket, jerkin
crystyn (crystiau) *nm* crust
crythor (-ion) *nm* fiddler, violinist
cryw (-iau) *nm* creel; weir
cu *adj* dear, fond, kind
cuchio *vb* scowl, frown
cuchiog *adj* scowling, frowning
cudyll (-od) *nm* hawk
cudyn (-nau) *nm* lock (of hair), tuft
cudd *adj* hidden, concealed
cuddfa (-feydd) *nf* hiding-place; hoard
cuddiad *nm* hiding
cuddiedig *adj* hidden, concealed
cuddio *vb* hide, conceal
cufydd (-au) *nm* cubit
cul (-ion) *adj* narrow, lean
culfor (-oedd) *nm* strait

culhau *vb* narrow; grow lean
culni *nm* narrowness
cun *adj* dear, beloved; lovely
cunnog (cunogau) *nf* pail
cur *nm* throb, ache, pain; care, trouble
curad (-iaid) *nm* curate
curadiaeth (-au) *nf* curacy
curfa (-feydd) *nf* beating, flogging
curiad (-au) *nm* beat, throb, pulse
curio *vb* pine, waste
curlaw *nm* pelting rain
curn (-au), curnen (-nau) *nf* mound, core, rick
curnennu *vb* heap, stack
curo *vb* beat, strike, knock; throb; clap
curwr (-wyr) *nm* beater
curyll (-od) *nm* hawk
cusan (-au) *nf, nm* kiss
cusanu *vb* kiss
cut (-iau) *nm* hovel, shed, sty
cuwch (cuchiau) *nm* scowl, frown
CV (-s) *nm* CV
cwafrio *vb* quaver, trill
cwar (-rau) *nm* quarry
cwb (cybiau) *nm* kennel, coop, sty
cwbl *adj, nm* all, whole, total
cwblhad *nm* fulfilment
cwblhau *vb* fulfil, complete, finish
cwcer (-au) *nm* cooker
cwcw *nf* cuckoo
cwcwallt (-iaid) *nm* cuckold
cwcwalltu *vb* cuckold
cwcwll (cycyllau) *nm* hood, cowl
cwch (cychod) *nm* boat; hive; **cwch gwyllt** speed boat
cwd (cydau) *nm* pouch, bag
cweir (-iau) *nm* thrashing, hiding
cweryl (-on) *nm* quarrel
cweryla *vb* quarrel
cwerylgar *adj* quarrelsome
cwest (-au) *nm* inquest
cwestiwn (-iynau) *nm* question

cwestiynu *vb* question

cwffio *vb* fight, box

cwgn (**cygnau**) *nm* knot; knuckle; joint

cwilt (**-iau**) *nm* quilt

cwlbren (**-ni**) *nm* bludgeon

cwlff (**cylffiau**), **cwlffyn** (**cylffiau**) *nm* chunk

cwlwm *see* **clwm**

cwlltwr (**cylltyrau**) *nm* coulter

cwm (**cymau, cymoedd**) *nm* valley

cwman *nm* rump; stoop; churn

cwmanu *vb* stoop

cwmni (**-ïau, -ïoedd**) *nm* company

cwmnïaeth *nf* companionship

cwmpas (**-oedd**) *nm* round; **wmpasgwmpas** about

cwmpasog *adj* round about, circuitous

cwmpasu *vb* round, wind, surround

cwmpawd (**-odau**) *nm* compass

cwmpeini, cwmpni *nm* company

cwmwd (**cymydau**) *nm* commot

cwmwl (**cymylau**) *nm* cloud

cŵn *see* **ci**

cwndid (**-au**) *nm* song, carol

cwningen (**-ingod**) *nf* rabbit

cwnsel (**-au, -oedd, -i**) *nm* council; counsel, advice, secret

cwnsela *vb* counsel

cwnsler (**-iaid**) *nm* counsellor

cwnstabl (**-iaid**) *nm* constable; **cwnstabl heddlu** PC, police constable; **prif gwnstabl** chief constable

cworwm *nm* quorum

cwota (**-au**) *nm* quota

cwpan (**-au**) *nm, nf* cup, goblet; chalice

cwpanaid (**-eidiau**) *nm, nf* cupful

cwpl (**cyplau**) *nm* couple; tie beam

cwplâd, cwplâu *see* **cwblhad, cwblhau**

cwpled (**-i, -au**) *nm* couplet

cwplws (**cyplysau**) *nm* coupling; brace

cwpwrdd (**cypyrddau**) *nm* cupboard; **cwpwrdd ffeilio** filing cabinet

cwr (**cyrrau**) *nm* edge, border, skirt

cwrcwd *nm* stooping; squatting

cwrdd (**cyrddau**) *nm* meeting

cwrdd, cwrddyd *vb* meet, touch

cwrel *nm* coral

cwricwlwm (**cwricwla**) *nm* curriculum

cwrlid (**-au**) *nm* coverlet

cwrs (**cyrsiau**) *nm* course; fit; **prif gwrs** main course; **cwrs hyfforddiant** training course

cwrt (**cyrtiau**) *nm* court

cwrtais *adj* courteous

cwrteisi, cwrteisrwydd *nm* courtesy

cwrw (**cyrfau**) *nm* ale, beer

cwrwg, cwrwgl *see* **corwg**

cwsg *nm* sleep

cwsmer (**-iaid**) *nm* customer

cwsmeriaeth *nf* custom

cwstard (**-iau**) *nm* custard

cwstwm (**cystymau**) *nm* custom, patronage

cwt (**cytiau**) *nf, nm* tail, skirt, queue

cwt (**cytiau**) *nm* hut, sty

cwta *adj* short, curt

cwter (**-i, -ydd**) *nf* gutter, channel

cwtogi *vb* shorten, curtail

cwthr (**cythrau**) *nm* anus, rectum

cwthwm (**cythymau**) *nm* puff of wind, storm

cwymp (**-au**) *nm* fall, tumble

cwympo *vb* fall; fell

cwyn (**-ion**) *nm, nf* complaint, plaint

cwynfan *vb* complain, lament

cwynfanllyd *adj* querulous

cwynfanus *adj* plaintive, mournful

cwyno vb complain, lament
cwyr nm wax
cwyro vb wax
cwys (-au, -i) nf furrow-slice, furrow
cybôl nm nonsense, rubbish
cybolfa nf hotchpotch, medley
cyboli vb muddle; talk nonsense;
  mess, bother
cybydd (-ion) nm miser, niggard
cybydda vb stint, hoard
cybydd-dod, cybydd-dra nm
  miserliness
cybyddlyd adj miserly
cycyllog adj hooded, cowled
cychaid (-eidiau) nm boatful;
  hiveful
cychwr (-wyr) nm boatman
cychwyn vb rise, stir, start; switch
  on
cychwynfa nf start, starting-point
cychwyniad (-au) nm start,
  beginning
cyd adj joint, united, common;
  fellow ▷ prefix together
cydadrodd vb to recite together
cydaid (-eidiau) nm bagful
cydbwysedd nm balance
cyd-destun (-au) nm context
cydfod nm agreement, concord
cydfodolaeth nf coexistence
cydfyned vb go with, concur, agree
cydfyw vb cohabit
cydffurfio vb conform
cydgordio vb agree, harmonize
cydgwmni (-ïau) nm consortium
cydiedig adj adjoined
cydio vb join; bite; take hold
cydletywr (-wyr) nm roommate,
  flatmate, housemate
cydnabod vb acknowledge ▷ nm
  acquaintance
cydnabyddiaeth nf acquaintance;
  recognition

cydnabyddus adj acquainted;
  familiar
cydnaws adj congenial
cydnerth adj well set
cydol nf, nm, adj whole
cydradd adj equal
cydraddoldeb nm equality
cyd-rhwng prep between
cydsyniad nm consent
cydsynio vb consent
cydwastad adj level (with), even
cydweddog adj conjugal
cydweddu vb accord, agree
cydweithfa (-feydd) nf co-operative
cydweithrediad nm co-operation
cydweithredol adj co-operative
cydweithredu vb co-operate
cydweled vb agree
cydwladol adj international
cyd-wladwr (-wyr) nm compatriot
cydwybod (-au) nf conscience
cydwybodol adj conscientious
cydwybodolrwydd nm
  conscientiousness
cydymaith (cymdeithion) nm
  companion
cydymdeimlad nm sympathy
cydymdeimlo vb sympathize
cydymffurfiad nm conformity
cydymffurfio vb conform
cydymgais nm competition, rivalry,
  joint effort
cydymgeisydd (-wyr) nm rival
cyddwysiad (-au) nm condensation
cyfadran (-nau) nf faculty (in
  college), period (in music)
cyfaddas adj fit, suitable,
  convenient
cyfaddasiad (-au) nm adaptation
cyfaddasrwydd nm fitness, suitability
cyfaddasu vb fit, adapt
cyfaddawd (-odau) nm
  compromise

cyfaddawdu vb compromise

cyfaddef vb confess, own, admit

cyfaddefiad (-au) nm confession, admission

cyfaenad nm, adj harmonious song

cyfagos adj near, adjacent, neighbouring

cyfaill (-eillion) nm friend

cyfair (-eiriau) nm acre

cyfair, cyfer nm direction; **ar gyfair** opposite for

cyfalaf nm capital

cyfalafiaeth nf capitalism

cyfalafol adj capitalistic

cyfalafwr (-wyr) nm capitalist

cyfamod (-au) nm covenant

cyfamodi vb covenant

cyfamodol adj federal; covenanted

cyfamodwr (-wyr) nm covenanter

cyfamser nm meantime

cyfamserol adj timely; synchronous

cyfan adj, nm whole

cyfandir (-oedd) nm continent

cyfandirol adj continental

cyfanfor (-oedd) nm main sea, ocean

cyfanfyd nm whole world, universe

cyfangorff nm whole, bulk, mass

cyfan gwbl adj: **yn gyfan gwbl** altogether, completely

cyfanheddol adj habitable, inhabited

cyfanheddu vb dwell, inhabit

cyfannedd adj inhabited ▷ nf (**-anheddau**) inhabited place, habitation

cyfannol adj integrated, integral

cyfannu vb make whole, complete

cyfanrwydd nm wholeness, entirety

cyfansawdd adj composite, compound

cyfansoddi vb compose, constitute

cyfansoddiad (-au) nm composition; constitution

cyfansoddiadol adj constitutional

cyfansoddwr (-wyr) nm composer

cyfansoddyn (-ion) nm constituent, compound

cyfanswm (-symiau) nm total

cyfantoledd (-au) nm equilibrium

cyfanwaith (-weithiau) nm complete composition, whole

cyfarch vb greet, salute, address

cyfarchiad (-au) nm greeting, salutation

cyfaredd (-ion) nf charm, spell

cyfareddol adj enchanting

cyfareddu vb charm, enchant

cyfarfod vb meet ▷ nm (**-ydd**) meeting

cyfarfyddiad (-au) nm meeting

cyfarpar nm provision, equipment; diet; **cyfarpar rhyfel** munitions of war

cyfarparu vb equip

cyfartal adj equal, even

cyfartaledd nm proportion, average

cyfartalu vb proportion, equalize

cyfarth vb, nm bark

cyfarwydd adj skilled; familiar ▷ nm (**-iaid**) storyteller

cyfarwyddo vb direct; become familiar

cyfarwyddwr (-wyr) nm director

cyfarwyddyd (-iadau) nm direction, instruction

cyfatal adj unsettled, hindering

cyfateb vb correspond, agree, tally

cyfatebiaeth (-au) nf correspondence, analogy

cyfatebol adj corresponding, proportionate

cyfathrach (-au) nf affinity; intercourse

cyfathrachu vb have intercourse
cyfathrachwr (-wyr) nm kinsman
cyfathreb (-au) nm communication
cyfathrebu vb communicate
cyfddydd nm day-break, dawn
cyfeb, cyfebr adj pregnant (of mare, ewe)
cyfebol adj in foal
cyfeddach (-au) nf carousal
cyfeddachwr (-wyr) nm carouser
cyfeiliant nm musical accompaniment
cyfeilio vb accompany
cyfeiliorn nm error; wandering, lost (person etc); **ar gyfeiliorn** astray
cyfeiliornad (-au) nm error, heresy
cyfeiliorni vb err, stray
cyfeiliornus adj erroneous, mistaken
cyfeilydd (-ion) nm accompanist
cyfeillach (-au) nf fellowship; fellowship-meeting
cyfeillachu vb associate
cyfeilles (-au) nf female friend
cyfeillgar adj friendly
cyfeillgarwch nm friendship
cyfeiriad (-au) nm direction; reference; (postal) address; **cyfeiriad ebost** email address; **cyfeiriad gwe** web address
cyfeiriannu nm orienteering
cyfeirio vb point; direct; refer; address (letter)
cyfeirnod (-au) nm mark of reference; aim; direct (in music)
cyfeirydd (-ion) nm indicator, guide
cyfenw (-au) nm surname; namesake
cyfenwi vb surname
cyfer nm: **ar gyfer** opposite for
cyferbyn adj opposite
cyferbyniad (-au) nm contrast

cyferbyniol adj opposing, opposite, contrasting
cyferbynnu vb contrast, compare
cyfethol vb co-opt
cyfiaith adj of the same language
cyfiawn adj just, righteous
cyfiawnder (-au) nm justice, righteousness
cyfiawnhad nm justification
cyfiawnhau vb justify
cyfieithiad (-au) nm translation, version
cyfieithu vb translate, interpret
cyfieithydd (-wyr) nm translator, interpreter
cyfisol adj of the present month, instant
cyflafan (-au) nf outrage; massacre
cyflafareddiad nm arbitration
cyflafareddu vb arbitrate
cyflafareddwr (-wyr) nm arbitrator
cyflaith nm toffee
cyflawn adj full, complete
cyflawnder nm fullness; abundance
cyflawni vb fulfil, perform, commit
cyflawniad (-au) nm fulfilment, performance
cyfle (-oedd) nm place; chance, opportunity
cyfled adj as broad as
cyflegr (-au) nm gun, cannon, battery
cyflegru vb bombard
cyflenwad (-au) nm supply
cyflenwi vb supply
cyfleu vb place, set; convey
cyfleus adj convenient
cyfleustra (-terau) nm opportunity, convenience
cyflin adj parallel
cyfliw adj of the same colour
cyflo adj in calf

cyflog (**-au**) nm, nf hire, wage, wages

cyflogaeth nf employment

cyflogedig (**-ion**) nm employee

cyflogi vb hire; engage in service

cyflogwr (**-wyr**) nm hirer, employer

cyflwr (**-lyrau**) nm condition; case

cyflwyniad nm presentation; dedication

cyflwyno vb present; dedicate

cyflwynydd (**-ion**) nm compère, presenter

cyflychwr, cyflychwyr nm evening twilight, dusk

cyflym adj quick, fast, swift

cyflymder, cyflymdra nm swiftness, speed

cyflymu vb speed, accelerate

cyflynu vb stick together

cyflyru vb condition

cyflythreniad (**-au**) nm alliteration

cyfnerthu vb confirm; aid, help

cyfnerthydd (**-ion, -wyr**) nm strengthener, booster

cyfnesaf (**-iaid, -eifiaid**) nm, nf next of kin, kinsman ▷ adj next, nearest

cyfnewid vb change, exchange

cyfnewidfa (**-oedd, -feydd**) nf exchange

cyfnewidiad (**-au**) nm change, alteration

cyfnewidiol adj changeable

cyfnewidiwr (**-wyr**) nm changer, trader

cyfnither (**-oedd**) nf female cousin

cyfnod (**-au**) nm period; **cyfnod prawf** trial period

cyfnodol adj periodic(al)

cyfnodolyn (**-ion**) nm periodical publication

cyfnos nm evening twilight, dusk

cyfochredd nm parallelism

cyfochrog adj parallel

cyfodi vb rise, arise; raise

cyfodiad nm rise, rising

cyfoed adj contemporary, of the same age ▷ nm (**-ion**) contemporaries

cyfoes adj contemporary, up-to-date

cyfoesi vb be contemporary

cyfoeswr (**-wyr**) nm contemporary

cyfoeth nm power; riches, wealth

cyfoethog adj powerful; rich, wealthy

cyfoethogi vb make or grow rich

cyfog nm sickness

cyfogi vb vomit

cyfor nm flood, abundance; rim, brim, edge ▷ adj entire, brim-full

cyforiog adj brim-full, overflowing

cyfosodiad nm apposition

cyfradd (**-au**) nf rate ▷ adj of equal rank; **cyfradd llog** rate of interest

cyfraid (**-reidiau**) nm necessity

cyfraith (**-reithiau**) nf law

cyfran (**-nau**) nf part, portion, share

cyfranc (**-rangau**) nf, nm meeting; combat; incident; story, tale

cyfranddaliad (**-au**) nm share

cyfranddaliwr (**-wyr**) nm shareholder

cyfraniad (**-au**) nm contribution

cyfrannog adj participating, partaking

cyfrannol adj contributing

cyfrannu vb contribute; impart

cyfrannwr (**-anwyr**) nm contributor

cyfranogi vb participate, partake

cyfranogwr (**-wyr**) nm partaker

cyfredol adj current, concurrent

cyfreithio vb go to law, litigate

cyfreithiol adj legal

cyfreithiwr (**-wyr**) nm lawyer

cyfreithlon adj lawful, legitimate

cyfreithlondeb *nm* lawfulness
cyfreithloni *vb* legalize; justify
cyfreithus *adj* legitimate
cyfres (-i) *nf* series
cyfresol *adj* serial
cyfresu *vb* serialise
cyfresymiad (-au) *nm* syllogism
cyfresymu *vb* syllogise
cyfrgolli *vb* lose utterly; damn
cyfrif *vb* count, reckon; account;
impute ▷ *nm* **(-on)** account,
reckoning; **cyfrif banc** bank account
cyfrifeg *nm, nf* accountancy
cyfrifiad (-au) *nm* counting; census
cyfrifiadur (-on) *nm* computer;
cyfrifiadur personol PC, personal
computer
cyfrifiadureg *nf* computer science
cyfrifiaduro *n* computing
cyfrifianell *nf* calculator
cyfrifol *adj* of repute; responsible
cyfrifoldeb (-au) *nm* responsibility
cyfrifydd (-ion) *nm* statistician,
accountant
cyfrin *adj* secret, subtle
cyfrinach (-au) *nf* secret
cyfrinachol *adj* secret, private,
confidential
cyfrinair (-eiriau) *nm* password
cyfrinfa *nf* lodge of friendly society
or trade union
cyfrin-gyngor (-nghorau) *nm* privy
council
cyfriniaeth *nf* mystery; mysticism
cyfriniol *adj* mysterious, mystic
cyfriniwr (-wyr) *nm* mystic
cyfrodedd *adj* twisted, twined
cyfrodeddu *vb* twist, twine
cyfrol (-au) *nf* volume
cyfrwng (-ryngau) *nm* medium,
means
cyfrwy (-au) *nm* saddle
cyfrwyo *vb* saddle

cyfrwys *adj* cunning
cyfrwystra *nm* cunning
cyfrwywr (-wyr) *nm* saddler
cyfryngdod *nm* mediation,
intercession; mediatorship
cyfryngiad *nm* mediation;
intervention
cyfryngol *adj* mediatorial
cyfryngu *vb* mediate; intervene
cyfryngwr (-wyr) *nm* mediator
cyfryngwriaeth *nf* mediatorship
cyfryw *adj* like, such
cyfuchlinedd (-au) *nm* contour
cyfuchliniau *npl* contours
cyfundeb (-au) *nm* union;
connexion
cyfundebol *adj* connexional;
denominational
cyfundrefn (-au) *nf* system
cyfundrefnol *adj* systematic
cyfundrefnu *vb* systematize
cyfuniad (-au) *nm* combination
cyfuno *vb* unite, combine
cyfunol *adj* united
cyfunrywiol *adj* homosexual
cyfuwch *adj* as high
cyfweld *vb* interview
cyfweliad (-au) *nm* interview
cyfwelydd (-wyr) *nm* interviewer
cyfwerth *adj* equivalent
cyfwng (-yngau) *nm* space; interval
cyfwrdd *vb* meet
cyfyng *adj* narrow, confined
cyfyngder (-au) *nm* trouble,
distress
cyfyngdra *nm* narrowness; distress
cyfyngedig *adj* confined, restricted,
limited
cyfyng-gyngor *nm* perplexity
cyfyngu *vb* narrow, confine, limit
cyfyl *nm* neighbourhood; **ar ei gyfyl**
near him
cyfyrder (-dyr) *nm* second cousin

cyfystlys *adj* side by side
cyfystyr *adj* synonymous
cyfystyron *npl* synonyms
cyff (-ion) *nm* stock
cyffaith (-ffeithiau) *nm* confection
cyffelyb *adj* like, similar
cyffelybiaeth (-au) *nf* likeness, similitude
cyffelybiaethol *adj* figurative
cyffelybrwydd *nm* likeness, similarity
cyffelybu *vb* liken, compare
cyffes (-ion) *nf* confession
cyffesgell (-oedd) *nf* confessional
cyffesu *vb* confess
cyffeswr (-wyr), **cyfessydd (-ion)** *nm* confessor
cyffin (-iau, -ydd) *nf, nm* border, confine
cyffindir (-oedd) *nm* frontier, march
cyffio *vb* stiffen; fetter, shackle; beat
cyffion *npl* stocks
cyffordd (-ffyrdd) *nf* junction
cyffredin *adj* common; general
cyffredinedd *nm* mediocrity, banality
cyffredinol *adj* general, universal
cyffredinoli *vb* universalize, generalize
cyffredinolrwydd *nm* universality
cyffredinwch *nm* commonness
cyffro (-adau) *nm* motion, stir; excitement
cyffroi *vb* move, excite; provoke
cyffrous *adj* exciting; excited
cyffur (-iau) *nm, nf* ingredient, drug
cyffuriwr (-wyr) *nm* apothecary, druggist
cyffwrdd *vb* meet, touch
cyffylog (-od) *nm* woodcock
cyffyrddiad (-au) *nm* touch, contact
cyffyrddus *adj* comfortable

cygnog *adj* knotted, gnarled
cyngaf, cyngaw *nm* burdock; burs
cyngan *adj* suitable, harmonious
cynganeddol *adj* in *cynghanedd*
cynganeddu *vb* form *cynghanedd*; harmonize
cynganeddwr (-wyr) *nm* writer of *cynghanedd*
cyngaws (cynghawsau, -ion) *nm* lawsuit, action; trial; battle
cyngerdd (-ngherddau) *nm, nf* concert
cynghanedd (cynganeddion) *nf* music, harmony; Welsh metrical alliteration
cynghori *vb* counsel, advise; exhort
cynghorwr (-wyr) *nm* councillor; counsellor; exhorter
cynghrair (-eiriau) *nm, nf* alliance, league
cynghreiriad (-iaid) *nm* confederate, ally
cynghreirio *vb* league, confederate
cynghreiriwr (-wyr) *nm* confederate, ally
cyngor (-nghorion) *nm* counsel, advice ▷ *nm* (**-nghorau**) council; **Cyngor Bro** Community Council; **Cyngor Tref** Town Council; **Cyngor Sir** County Council
cyngres (-au, -i) *nf* congress
cyngresydd (-wyr) *nm* congressman
cyngwystl (-(i)on) *nm, nf* wager, pledge
cyhoedd *adj, nm* public
cyhoeddi *vb* publish, announce
cyhoeddiad (-au) *nm* publication; announcement; (preaching) engagement
cyhoeddus *adj* public
cyhoeddusrwydd *nm* publicity
cyhoeddwr (-wyr) *nm* publisher

cyhuddiad (-au) *nm* accusation, charge

cyhuddo *vb* accuse, charge

cyhuddwr (-wyr) *nm* accuser

cyhwfan *vb* wave, heave

cyhyd *adj* as long, so long

cyhydedd *nm* equator

cyhydeddol *adj* equatorial, equinoctial

cyhyr (-au) *nm* flesh, muscle

cyhyrog *adj* muscular

cylch (-au, oedd) *nm* round, circle, sphere, hoop

cylchdaith (-deithiau) *nf* circuit

cylchdro (-eon, -adau) *nm* orbit

cylchdroi *vb* rotate, revolve

cylched (-au) *nm* coverlet, blanket

cylchedd (-au) *nm, nf* compass, circle, circuit

cylchgrawn (-gronau) *nm* magazine

cylchlythyr (-au) *nm* circular

cylchredeg *vb* circulate

cylchrediad *nm* circulation

cylchres (-i) *nf* round, rota

cylchwyl (-iau) *nf* anniversary, festival

cylchynol *adj* surrounding

cylchynu *vb* surround, encompass

cylion *npl* (*nm -yn, nf -en*) flies, gnats

cylymu *vb* knot, tie

cyll *npl* (*nf* **collen**) hazel-trees

cylla (-on) *nm* stomach

cyllell (-yll) *nf* knife

cyllid (-au) *nm* revenue, income

cyllideb (-au) *nf* budget

cyllidol *adj* financial, fiscal

cyllidwr (-wyr), cyllidydd (-ion) *nm* tax gatherer, revenue or excise officer, financier

cymaint *adj* as big, as much, as many; so big *etc*

cymal (-au) *nm* joint; clause

cymalwst *nf* rheumatism

cymanfa (-oedd) *nf* assembly; festival

cymantoledd (-au) *nm* equilibrium

cymanwlad *nf* commonwealth

cymar (-heiriaid) *nm* fellow, partner

cymathiad *nm* assimilation

cymathu *vb* assimilate

cymdeithas (-au) *nf* society, association; **Cymdeithas yr Iaith Gymraeg** The Welsh Language Society

cymdeithaseg *nf, nm* sociology

cymdeithasegol *adj* sociological

cymdeithasgar *adj* sociable

cymdeithasol *adj* social

cymdeithasu *vb* associate; socialize

cymdogaeth (-au) *nf* neighbourhood

cymdogol *adj* neighbourly

cymedr (-au) *nm* mean (*in maths*), average

cymedrol *adj* moderate, temperate

cymedroldeb *nm* moderation, temperance

cymedroli *vb* moderate

cymedrolwr (-wyr) *nm* moderator; moderate drinker

cymell *vb* urge, press, persuade, induce; motivate

cymen *adj* wise, skilful, neat, becoming

cymer (-au) *nm* confluence

cymeradwy *adj* acceptable, approved, commendable

cymeradwyaeth *nf* approval; applause; recommendation

cymeradwyo *vb* approve; recommend

cymeradwyol *adj* commendatory

cymeriad (-au) *nm* character, reputation

cymesur *adj* proportionate, symmetrical
cymesuredd *nm* proportion, symmetry
cymesurol *adj* commensurate, proportionate
cymhareb (**cymarebau**) *nf* ratio
cymhariaeth (**cymariaethau**) *nf* comparison
cymharol *adj* comparative
cymharu *vb* pair; compare
cymhathu *vb* assimilate
cymhelliad (**-hellion**) *nm* motive, inducement
cymhelliant (**-nnau**) *nm* motivation
cymhendod *nm* knowledge; proficiency; tidiness; eloquence; affection
cymhennu *vb* put in order, trim; scold, reprove
cymhercyn *adj* limping, infirm ▷ *nm* valetudinarian
cymhleth (**-au**) *adj* complex, complicated
cymhlethdod (**-au**) *nm* complexity
cymhlethu *vb* complicate
cymhorthdal (**cymorthdaloedd**) *nm* subsidy, grant
cymhwysiad *nm* application, adjustment
cymhwyso *vb* apply, adjust
cymhwyster (**cymwysterau**) *nm* fitness, suitability; (*pl*) qualifications
cymod *nm* reconciliation
cymodi *vb* reconcile; be reconciled
cymodol *adj* reconciliatory, propitiatory
cymodwr (**-wyr**) *nm* reconciler
cymon *adj* orderly, tidy; seemly
cymorth *vb* assist, aid, help ▷ *nm* assistance, aid, help
Cymraeg *nf, nm, adj* Welsh

Cymraes *nf* Welshwoman
cymrawd (**-odyr**) *nm* comrade, fellow
Cymreictod *nm* Welshness
Cymreig *adj* Welsh
Cymreiges (**-au**) *nf* Welshwoman
Cymreigio *vb* translate into Welsh
Cymreigiwr (**-wyr**) *nm* one versed or skilled in Welsh; Welsh-speaking Welshman
Cymro (**Cymry**) *nm* Welshman
cymrodedd *nm* arbitration; compromise
cymrodeddu *vb* compromise, reconcile
cymrodor (**-ion**) *nm* consociate, fellow
cymrodoriaeth *nf* fellowship
Cymru *nf* Wales
cymrwd *nm* mortar, plaster
Cymry *see* **Cymro**
cymryd *vb* take, accept; **cymryd ar** pretend
cymun, cynumdeb *nm* communion, fellowship
cymuned *nf* community; **y Gymuned Ewropeaidd** the European Community
cymunedol *adj* community
cymuno *vb* commune
cymunwr (**-wyr**) *nm* communicant
cymwy (**-au**) *nm* affliction
cymwynas (**-au**) *nf* kindness, favour
cymwynasgar *adj* obliging, kind
cymwynasgarwch *nm* obligingness, kindness
cymwynaswr (**-wyr**) *nm* benefactor
cymwys *adj* fit, proper, suitable; exact
cymwysedig *adj* applied
cymwysiadol *adj* applicable

cymydog (**cymdogion**, *f* **cymdoges**) *nm* neighbour
cymylog *adj* cloudy, clouded
cymylu *vb* cloud, dim, obscure
cymyndod *nm* committal
cymynnu *vb* bequeath
cymynrodd (**-ion**) *nf* legacy, bequest
cymynroddi *vb* bequeath
cymynu *vb* hew, fell
cymynwr (**-wyr**) *nm* hewer, feller
cymysg *adj* mixed
cymysgedd *nm*, *nf* mixture
cymysgfa *nf* mixture, medley, hotchpotch
cymysgliw *adj* motley
cymysglyd *adj* muddled, confused
cymysgryw *adj* mongrel; heterogeneous
cymysgu *vb* mix, blend; confuse
cymysgwch *nm* mixture, jumble
cymysgwr (**-wyr**) *nm* mixer, blender
cyn *prefix* before, previous, first, former, pre-, ex-; **Cyn Crist** Before Christ, BC
cyn *adv*: **cyn gynted (â phosib)** as soon as possible; **cyn wynned â** as white as
cŷn (**cynion**) *nm* wedge, chisel
cynadledda *vb* meet in conference
cynaeafa, cynhaeafa *vb* dry in the sun
cynaeafu, cynhaeafu *vb* harvest
cynaeafwr, cynhaeafwr (**-wyr**) *nm* harvester
cynamserol *adj* premature, untimely
cynaniad *nm* pronunciation
cynanu *vb* pronounce
cyndad (**-au**) *nm* forefather, ancestor
cynderfynol *adj* semi-final
cyndyn *adj* stubborn, obstinate

cyndynnu *vb* be obstinate
cyndynrwydd *nm* stubbornness, obstinacy
cynddaredd *nf* madness; rabies
cynddeiriog *adj* mad, rabid
cynddeiriogi *vb* madden, enrage
cynddeiriogrwydd *nm* rage, fury
cynddrwg *adj* as bad
cynddydd *nm* day-break, dawn
cynefin *adj* acquainted, accustomed, familiar ▷ *nm* haunt, habitat
cynefindra *nm* use, familiarity
cynefino *vb* get used, become accustomed
cynefinol *adj* usual, accustomed
cynfas (**-au**) *nf*, *nm* (bed) sheet; canvas
cynfyd *nm* primitive world, antiquity
cynffon (**-nau**) *nf* tail; tang
cynffonna *vb* fawn, toady, cringe
cynffonnwr (**-onwyr**) *nm* toady, sycophant; sneak
cyn-geni *adj* antenatal
cynhadledd (**cynadleddau**) *nf* conference
cynhaeaf (**cynaeafau**) *nm* harvest
cynhaeafa *vb see* **cynaeafa**
cynhaeafu *vb see* **cynaeafu**
cynhaeafwr *nm see* **cynaeafwr**
cynhaliaeth *nf* maintenance, support
cynhaliol *adj* sustaining
cynhaliwr (**-wyr**) *nm* supporter, sustainer
cynhanesiol *adj* prehistoric
cynhebrwng (**-yngau**) *nm* funeral
cynhenid *adj* innate
cynhennu *vb* contend, quarrel
cynhennus *adj* contentious, quarrelsome
cynhennwr (**-henwyr**) *nm* wrangler

cynhesol *adj* agreeable, amiable
cynhesrwydd *nm* warmth
cynhesu *vb* warm, get warm;
cynhesu byd-eang global warming
cynhorthwy (**cynorthwyon**) *nm*
help, aid
cynhwynol *adj* natural, congenital,
innate
cynhwysedd (**cynwyseddau**) *nm*
capacity, capacitance
cynhwysfawr *adj* comprehensive
cynhwysiad *nm* contents
cynhyrchiad (**-au**) *nm* production
cynhyrchiol *adj* productive
cynhyrchu *vb* produce
cynhyrchydd (**-ion, cynhyrchwyr**)
nm producer, generator
cynhyrfiad (**cynyrfiadau**) *nm*
stirring, agitation
cynhyrfiol *adj* stirring, thrilling
cynhyrfu *vb* stir, agitate
cynhyrfus *adj* agitated; exciting
cynhyrfwr (**-wyr**) *nm* agitator,
disturber
cynhysgaeth *nf* dower, portion,
fortune
cyni *nm* anguish, distress, adversity
cynifer *adj, nm* as many, so many
cynigiad (**-au**) *nm* proposal, motion
cynigiwr (**-wyr**), **cynigydd** (**-ion**)
nm proposer, mover
cynildeb *nm* frugality, economy
cynilion *npl* savings
cynilo *vb* save, economise
cynio *vb* chisel, gouge
cyniwair *vb* go to and fro, frequent
cyniweirfa (**-feydd**) *nf* resort,
haunt
cyniweirydd *nm* wayfarer
cynllun (**-iau**) *nm* pattern; plan
cynllunio *vb* plan, design
cynllunydd (**-ion, -wyr**) *nm*
designer

cynllwyn *vb* plot, conspire ▷ *nm*
(**-ion**) plot
cynllwynio *vb* conspire, plot
cynllwynwr (**-wyr**) *nm* conspirator
cynnal *vb* hold, uphold, support,
sustain
cynnar *adj* early
cynnau *vb* kindle, light
cynneddf (**cyneddfau**) *nf* quality,
faculty
cynnen (**cynhennau**) *nf*
contention, strife; **asgwrn y
gynnen** bone of contention
cynnes *adj* warm
cynnig *vb* offer; attempt; propose,
move; bid; apply ▷ *nm* (**cynigion**)
offer; attempt; motion
cynnil *adj* economical; delicate
cynnor (**cynorau**) *nf* door-post
cynnud *nm* firewood, fuel
cynnull *vb* collect, gather, assemble
cynnwrf *nm* stir, commotion,
agitation
cynnwys *vb* contain, include,
comprise, comprehend ▷ *nm*
content(s)
cynnydd *nm* increase, growth,
progress
cynnyrch (**cynhyrchion**) *nm*
produce, product; (*pl*) productions
cynoesol *adj* primeval
cynorthwyo *vb* help, assist
cynorthwyol *adj* auxiliary;
assistant
cynorthwywr (**-wyr**) *nm* helper,
assistant
cynorthwy-ydd (**-ion**) *nf:*
cynorthwy-ydd dosbarth
classroom assistant
cynradd *adj* primary
cynrhon *npl* (*nm* **-yn**) maggots
cynrhoni *vb* breed maggots
cynrhonllyd *adj* maggoty

cynrychioladol *adj* representative
cynrychiolaeth *nf* representation
cynrychioli *vb* represent
cynrychiolwr (**-wyr**),
   cynrychiolydd (**-ion**) *nm*
   representative, delegate
cynt *adj* earlier, sooner, quicker ▷ *adv*
   see **gynt**
cyntaf *adj*, *adv* first
cyntedd (**-au**) *nm* court; porch,
   foyer
cyntefig *adj* prime, primitive
cyntun *nm* nap
cynulleidfa (**-oedd**) *nf*
   congregation
cynulleidfaol *adj* congregational
cynulliad (**-au**) *nm* gathering
cynuta *vb* gather fuel
cynyddol *adj* increasing, growing
cynyddu *vb* increase
cynysgaeddu *vb* endow, endue
cyplad *nm* copula
cypladu *vb* copulate
cyplu, cyplysu *vb* couple
cyraeddadwy *adj* attainable
cyraeddiadau *npl* attainments
cyrbibion *npl* atoms, smithereens
cyrcydu *vb* squat, cower
cyrch (**-au**) *nm* attack
cyrchfa (**-feydd**) *nf* resort
cyrchu *vb* go, resort, repair
cyrchwr (**-wyr**) *nm* cursor
cyrhaeddgar *adj* telling, incisive
cyrhaeddiad (**cyraeddiadau**) *nm*
   reach, attainment
cyrliog *adj* curly
cyrraedd *vb* reach, attain; arrive;
   get back
cyrren *npl* (*nf* **cyrensen**) currants
cyrydiad *nm* corrosion
cyrydu *vb* corrode
cysawd (**-odau**) *nm* system;
   constellation

cysefin *adj* original, primordial
cysegr (**-au**, **-oedd**) *nm* sanctuary
cysegredig *adj* consecrated, sacred
cysegredigrwydd *nm* sacredness
cysegriad (**-au**) *nm* consecration
cysegr-ladrad *nm* sacrilege
cysegr-lân *adj* holy
cysegru *vb* consecrate, dedicate,
   devote
cyseinedd *nm* alliteration
cysetlyd *adj* fastidious
cysgadrwydd *nm* sleepiness,
   drowsiness
cysgadur (**-iaid**) *nm* sleeper
cysglyd *adj* sleepy
cysgod (**-au**, **-ion**) *nm* shade,
   shadow; shelter; type
cysgodi *vb* shadow, shade; shelter
cysgodol *adj* shady, sheltered
cysgu *vb* sleep
cysgwr (**-wyr**) *nm* sleeper
cysidro *vb* consider
cysodi *vb* set type, compose
cysodydd (**-ion**, **-wyr**) *nm*
   compositor
cyson *adj* consistent, constant
cysondeb *nm* consistency; regularity
cysoni *vb* harmonize; reconcile
cysonwr (**-wyr**), **cysonydd** (**-ion**)
   nm harmonist
cystadleuaeth (**-au**) *nf*
   competition
cystadleuol *adj* competitive
cystadleuwr (**-wyr**),
   cystadleuydd *nm* competitor
cystadlu *vb* compete; compare
cystal *adj* as good, so good ▷ *adv* as
   well, so well
cystrawen (**-nau**) *nf* construction,
   syntax
cystudd (**-iau**) *nm* affliction; illness
cystuddiedig *adj* afflicted, contrite
cystuddio *vb* afflict, trouble

cystuddiol *adj* afflicted
cystuddiwr (-wyr) *nm* oppressor
cystwyo *vb* tell off, chastise
cysur (-on) *nm* comfort, consolation
cysuro *vb* comfort, console
cysurus *adj* comfortable
cysurwr (-wyr) *nm* comforter
cyswllt (-ylltiadau) *nm* joint, junction
cysylltiad (-au) *nm* conjunction; joining, connexion; **cysylltiadau cyhoeddus** public relations
cysylltiol *adj* connecting; connected
cysylltnod (-au) *nm* ligature, hyphen
cysylltu *vb* join, connect
cysylltydd (-ion) *nm* connector, contact
cysyniad (-au) *nm* concept
cytbell *adj* equidistant
cytbwys *adj* of equal weight
cytbwysedd *nm* balance
cytew *nm* batter
cytgan (-au) *nm, nf* chorus
cytgord *nm* concord
cytir (-oedd) *nm* common
cytras *adj* allied, related; cognate
cytsain (-seiniaid) *nf* consonant
cytûn *adj* agreed, of one accord, unanimous
cytundeb (-au) *nm* agreement, consent
cytuno *vb* agree, consent
cythlwng *nm* fasting, fast, hunger
cythraul (-euliaid) *nm* devil, demon
cythreuldeb *nm* devilment
cythreulig *adj* devilish, fiendish
cythru *vb* snatch, rush
cythruddo *vb* annoy, provoke, irritate
cythrwfl *nm* uproar, tumult
cythryblu *vb* trouble, agitate
cythryblus *adj* troubled, agitated

cyw (-ion) *nm* young bird, chick, chicken; baby
cywain *vb* convey, carry; garner
cywair (-eiriau) *nm* order; key; tune
cywaith (-weithiau) *nm* collective work, project
cywarch *nm* hemp
cywasg, cywasgedig *adj* diminished
cywasgiad (-au) *nm* contraction, compression
cywasgu *vb* contract, compress
cywasgydd (-ion) *nm* compressor
cyweiriad (-au) *nm* repair
cyweiriadur (-on) *nm* modulator
cyweirio *vb* set in order; prepare, dress
cyweirnod (-au) *nm* key-note
cywen (-nod) *nf* pullet, young hen
cywerth *adj* equivalent
cywilydd *nm* shame; shyness
cywilydd-dra *nm* shamefulness
cywilyddgar *adj* bashful, shy
cywilyddio *vb* shame; be ashamed
cywilyddus *adj* shameful, disgraceful; outrageous
cywir *adj* correct, accurate, true, faithful
cywirdeb *nm* correctness; integrity
cywiriad (-au) *nm* correction
cywiro *vb* correct; make good; perform
cywirwr (-wyr) *nm* corrector
cywladu *vb* naturalize
cywrain *adj* skilful; curious
cywreinbeth (-au, -einion) *nm* curiosity
cywreindeb *nm* skill, ingenuity
cywreinrwydd *nm* skill; curiosity
cywydd (-au) *nm* alliterative Welsh poem
cywyddwr (-wyr) *nm* composer of *cywyddau*

ch

Chechnya *nf* Chechnya
Chile *nf* Chile
China *nf* China
chwa (-on) *nf* puff, gust, breeze
chwaer (chwiorydd) *nf* sister
chwaeroliaeth *nf* sisterhood
chwaeth (-au, -oedd) *nf* taste
chwaethu *vb* taste
chwaethus *adj* tasteful; decent
chwaith *adv* nor either, neither
chwâl *adj* scattered, loose
chwalfa (-feydd) *nf* upset, rout
chwalu *vb* scatter, spread
chwalwr (-wyr) *nm* scatterer,
  demolisher
chwaneg *adj, nm* more
chwanegiad (-au) *nm* addition
chwanegol *adj* additional
chwanegu *vb* add, augment,
  increase
chwannen (chwain) *nf* flea

chwannog *adj* desirous; addicted;
  prone
chwant (-au) *nm* desire, craving, lust
chwantu *vb* desire, lust
chwap *nm* sudden blow, moment
  ▷ *adv* instantly
chwarae, chware *vb* play ▷ *nm*
  play; **chwaraeon y gaeaf** winter
  sports
chwaraedy (-dai) *nm* playhouse,
  theatre
chwaraefa (-feydd) *nf* pitch,
  playground
chwaraegar *adj* playful, sportive
chwaraewr (-wyr) *nm* player, actor,
  performer; **chwaraewr
  cryno-ddisgiau** CD player;
  chwaraewr DVD DVD player
chwaraeydd (-ion) *nm* actor
chwarddiad (-au) *nm* laugh
chwarel (-au, -i, -ydd) *nf* quarry
chwarelwr (-wyr) *nm* quarryman
chwareus *adj* playful
chwarren (-arennau) *nf* gland;
  kernel
chwart (-iau) *nm* quart
chwarter (-i, -au) *nm* quarter
chwarterol *adj* quarterly
chwarterolyn (-olion) *nm*
  quarterly (magazine)
chwarteru *vb* quarter
chwe *adj* six *(before a noun)*
chweban (-nau) *nm* sestet, sextain
chwech (-au) *adj, nm* six
chwechawd (-au) *nm* sextet
chweched *adj* sixth; **chweched
  dosbarth** sixth form
chwedl (-au) *nf* story, tale
chwedleua *vb* talk, gossip
chwedleuwr (-wyr) *nm* story-teller
chwedloniaeth *nf* mythology
chwedlonol *adj* mythical,
  mythological

chwedlonydd (**-wyr**) *nm* mythologist
chwedyn *adv*: **na chynt na chhwedyn** neither before nor after
Chwefror, Chwefrol *nm* February
chwennych, chwenychu *vb* covet, desire
chwenychiad (**-au**) *nm* desire
chweongl (**-au**) *nm* hexagon
chwephlyg *adj* sixfold
chwerthin *vb* laugh ▷ *nm* laughter
chwerthiniad (**-au**) *nm* laugh
chwerthinllyd *adj* laughable, ridiculous
chwerthinog *adj* laughing, merry
chwerw *adj* bitter
chwerwder, chwerwdod *nm* bitterness
chwerwedd *nm* bitterness
chwerwi *vb* grow bitter, embitter
chwi *pron* you
chwib (**-iau**) *nm* whistle
chwiban *vb, nm* whistle
chwibaniad *nm* whistling, whistle
chwibanogl (**-au**) *nf* whistle, flute
chwibanu *vb* whistle
chwibon (**-iaid**) *nm* curlew, stork
chwifio *vb* wave, flourish, brandish
chwiff (**-iau**) *nf* whiff, puff
chwiffiad *nm* whiff, jiffy
chwil (**-od**) *nm, nf* beetle, chafer
chwil *adj* whirling, reeling
chwilboeth *adj* scorching, piping hot
chwildroi *vb* whirl, spin
chwilen (**chwilod**) *nf* beetle
chwilenna *vb* rummage; pry; pilfer
chwiler (**-od**) *nm* chrysalis, pupa
chwilfriw *adj* smashed to atoms
chwilfriwio *vb* smash, shatter
chwilfrydedd *nm* curiosity
chwilfrydig *adj* curious, inquisitive
chwilgar *adj* curious, inquisitive
chwilgarwch *nm* inquisitiveness
chwiliad (**-au**) *nm* search, scrutiny

chwiliadur (**-on**) *nm* search engine
chwilibawa, chwilibawan *vb* dawdle, trifle
chwilio *vb* search; examine
chwiliwr (**-wyr**) *nm* searcher
chwil-lys *nm* inquisition
chwilmantan *vb* pry, rummage
chwilolau (**-oleuadau**) *nm* searchlight
chwilota *vb* rummage, pry
chwilotwr (**-wyr**) *nm* searcher, rummager
chwim *adj* nimble, quick, agile
chwimder, chwimdra *nm* nimbleness
chwimio *vb* move, stir, accelerate
chwimwth *adj* nimble, brisk
chwinc *nm* wink
chwinciad *nm* twinkling, trice
chwiorydd *see* **chwaer**
chwip (**-iau**) *nf* whip; whipping
chwipiad (**-au**) *nm* whipping
chwipio *vb* whip
chwipyn *adv* instantly
chwirligwgan *nf* whirligig
chwisgi *nm* whisky
chwisl (**-au**) *nm* whistle
chwistrell (**-au, -i**) *nf* squirt, syringe
chwistrelliad (**-au**) *nm* injection
chwistrellu *vb* squirt, syringe, inject
chwit-chwat *adj* fickle, inconstant
chwith *adj* left; wrong; sad; strange
chwithau *pron* you (on your part), you also
chwithdod, chwithdra *nm* strangeness
chwithig *adj* strange, wrong, awkward
chwithigrwydd *nm* awkwardness
chwiw (**-iau**) *nf* fit, attack, malady
chwiwgar *adj* fickle
chwychwi *pron* you yourselves
chwŷd, chwydiad *nm* vomit

ch

chwydu *vb* vomit, spew

chwydd, chwyddi *nm* swelling

chwyddiant (-nnau) *nm* inflation; inflammation

chwyddo *vb* swell, increase, magnify

chwyddwydr (-au) *nm* microscope

chwŷl (chwylion) *nm, nf* turn, rotation

chwyldro (-ion) *nm* rotation; orbit

chwyldroad (-au) *nm* revolution

chwyldroadol *adj* revolutionary

chwyldroadwr (-wyr) *nm* revolutionary

chwyldroi *vb* whirl, revolve, rotate

chwyldrowr *see* **chwyldroadwr**

chwylolwyn (-ion) *nf* flywheel

chwyn *(nm* **chwynnyn)** *coll n, npl* weeds

chwynladdwr *nm* weed-killer

chwynnu *vb* weed

chwyrligwgan (-od) *nm* spinning top, whirligig

chwyrlïo *vb* whirl, spin, speed

chwyrlwynt (-oedd) *nm* whirlwind

chwyrn *adj* rapid, swift

chwyrnellu *vb* whirl, whiz

chwyrnu *vb* hum; snore; snarl

chwyrnwr (-wyr) *nm* snorer; snarler

chwys *nm* sweat, perspiration

chwysfa (-feydd) *nf* sweating

chwysiant *nm* exudation

chwysigen (-igod) *nf* blister, vesicle

chwyslyd *adj* sweaty

chwystyllau *npl* pores

chwysu *vb* sweat, perspire; exude

chwyswr (-wyr) *nm* sweater

chwyth, chwythad *nm* breath

chwythbib (-au) *nf* blowpipe

chwythbrenni *npl* woodwinds

chwythell (-i) *nf* jet

chwythiad (-au) *nm* blow, blast

chwythu *vb* blow, blast; breathe; hiss

chwythwr (-wyr) *nm* blower

d

da *adj* good, well ▷ *nm* **(-oedd)** good; goods; stock, cattle

dacw *adv* there is, are; behold there

dad-, dat- *prefix* un-, dis-, re-, back

da-da *nm* sweets

dadansoddi *vb* analyse

dadansoddiad (-au) *nm* analysis

dadansoddol *adj* analytic(al)

dadansoddwr (-wyr) *nm* analyst

dadansoddydd (-wyr) *nm* analyser

dadchwyddiant (-nnau) *nm* deflation

dad-ddyfrio *vb* dehydrate

dadebriad *nm* resuscitation

dadebru *vb* resuscitate, revive

dadelfeniad (-au) *nm* decomposition

dadelfennu *vb* decompose; refine

dadeni *vb* regenerate, reanimate ▷ *nm* rebirth, renascence, renaissance

dadfachu *vb* unhook
dadfathiad *nm* dissimulation
dadfeiliad *nm* decay
dadfeilio *vb* fall to ruin, decay
dadflino *vb* rest (after exertion)
dadl (**-euon**) *nf* debate; doubt; plea
dadlaith *vb* thaw; dissolve
dadlau *vb* argue, debate; plead
dadleniad (**-au**) *nm* disclosure, exposure
dadlennol *adj* revealing, disclosing, exposing
dadlennu *vb* disclose, expose
dadleoli *vb* dislocate
dadleoliad (**-au**) *nm* dislocation
dadleuaeth *nf* polemics, controversy
dadleugar *adj* argumentative
dadleuol *adj* controversial, polemical
dadleuwr (**-wyr**), **dadleuydd** (**-ion**) *nm* debater, controversialist; advocate
dadluddedu *vb* rest (after exertion)
dadlwytho *vb* unload, unburden; download
dadlygru *vb* decontaminate
dadmer *vb* thaw; dissolve
dadnitreiddiad *nm* denitrification
dadolwch *nm* propitiation ▷ *vb* worship, seek forgiveness
dadorchuddio *vb* unveil, uncover
dadreolaeth *nf* decontrol
dadrewlifiant *nm* deglaciation
dadrithiad (**-au**) *nm* disillusionment
dadrithio *vb* disillusion
dadsefydlu *vb* disestablish
dadwaddoli *vb* disendow
dadwaddoliad *nm* disendowment
dadwneuthur, dadwneud *vb* undo, unmake
dadwrdd *nm* noise, uproar, hubbub
dadymchwel, dadymchwelyd *vb* overturn, overthrow

daear (**-oedd**) *nf* earth, ground, soil
daeardy (**-dai**) *nm* dungeon
daeareg *nf* geology
daearegol *adj* geological
daearegwr (**-wyr**), **daearegydd** (**-ion**) *nm* geologist
daearen *nf* the earth; land, country
daearfochyn (**-foch**) *nm* badger
daeargell (**-oedd**) *nf* dungeon, vault
daeargi (**-gwn**) *nm* terrier
daeargryd (**-iau**) *nm* earth tremor
daeargryn (**-fâu**) *nm, nf* earthquake
daearol *adj* terrestrial, earthly, earthy
daearu *vb* earth; inter
daearyddiaeth *nf* geography
daearyddol *adj* geographical
daearyddwr (**-wyr**) *nm* geographer
dafad (**defaid**) *nf* sheep; wart
dafaden (**-ennau**) *nf* wart
dafn (**-au**) *nm* drop
dafnu *vb* trickle
dagr (**-au**) *nm* dagger, bayonet, dirk
dagrau *npl* (*nm* **deigryn**) tears
dagreuol *adj* tearful, sad
dail *npl* (*nf* **dalen**, *nf* **deilen**) leaves
daioni *nm* goodness, good
daionus *adj* good; beneficial; beneficent
dal, dala *vb* hold; catch; arrest; last; **dal ati!** carry on!, don't give up!
dalen (**-nau, dail**) *nf* leaf
dalfa (**-feydd**) *nf* hold; arrest, custody; prison
dalgylch (**-oedd**) *nm* catchment area
daliad (**-au**) *nm* holding; tenet; spell
daliwr (**-wyr**) *nm* jig, catcher
dall (**deillion**) *adj* blind
dallbleidiaeth *nf* bigotry
dallbleidiol *adj* bigoted
dallbleidiwr (**-wyr**) *nm* bigot
dallineb *nm* blindness

dallu vb blind; dazzle
damcaniaeth (-au) nf theory
damcaniaethol adj theoretical
damcaniaethwr (-wyr) nm theorist
damcanu vb theorize, speculate
dameg (-hegion) nf parable
damhegol adj parabolic(al), allegorical
damhegwr (-wyr) nm allegorist
damnedig adj damned, damnable
damnedigaeth nf damnation, condemnation
damnio vb damn
damniol adj damning, damnatory
damsang vb tread, trample
damwain (-weiniau) nf accident, chance, fate
damweinio vb befall, happen
damweiniol adj accidental, casual
dan see **tan**
danadl npl (nf **danhadlen**) nettles
danas coll n deer; **bwch danas** buck
danfon vb send, convey; escort
dangos vb show
dangoseg (-ion) nf index; indication
dangosol adj indicative, demonstrative
danheddog adj jagged, serrated, toothed
dannod vb reproach, upbraid, taunt, twit
dannoedd nf toothache
dansoddol adj abstract
dant (dannedd) nm tooth
danteithfwyd (-teithion) nm dainty
danteithiol adj dainty, delicious
danteithion npl delicacies
darbodus adj provident, thrifty
darbwyllo vb persuade, convince
darfod vb finish, end; perish; happen
darfodadwy adj transitory, perishable

darfodedig adj perishable, transient
darfodedigaeth nm consumption
darfudiad (-au) nm convection
darfudol adj convectional
darganfod vb discover, find out
darganfyddiad (-au) nm discovery
darganfyddwr (-wyr) nm discoverer
dargludedd nm conductivity
dargludo vb conduct
dargludydd (-ion) nm conductor
dargyfeiredd nm divergence
dargyfeirio vb diverge, divert
darlith (-iau, -oedd) nf lecture
darlithfa (-feydd) nf lecture room, lecture theatre
darlithio vb lecture
darlithiwr (-wyr), darlithydd (-ion) nm lecturer
darlun (-iau) nm picture
darluniad (-au) nm portrayal, description
darluniadol adj pictorial, illustrated
darluniaeth nf imagery
darlunio vb portray, depict, describe
darluniol adj pictorial
darllediad (-au) nm broadcast
darlledu vb broadcast
darlledwr (-wyr) nm broadcaster
darllen vb read
darllenadwy adj readable, legible
darllenfa (-feydd) nf reading room; reading-desk; lectern
darllengar adj fond of reading, studious
darlleniad (-au) nm reading
darllenwr (-wyr), darllenydd (-ion) nm reader
darn (-au) nm piece, fragment, part
darnguddio vb conceal or withhold a part
darniad (-au) nm fragmentation
darnio vb cut up, hack

darn-ladd *vb* beat mercilessly
darogan *vb* predict, foretell,
forebode ▷ *nf* (**-au**) prediction,
foreboding
daroganu *vb* predict, foretell
daroganwr (**-wyr**) *nm* predictor,
prophet, soothsayer, forecaster
darostwng *vb* lower; subdue;
subject, humiliate
darostyngiad *nm* humiliation;
subjection
darpar (**-ion, -iadau**) *nm*
preparation, provision ▷ *adj*
intended, elect
darpariaeth (**-au**) *nf* preparation,
provision
darparu *vb* prepare, provide
darparwr (**-wyr**) *nm* provider
darwden *nf* ringworm
das (**-au, deisi**) *nf* rick, stack
dat- *prefix see* **dad-**
data *nm* data
datblygiad (**-au**) *nm* development,
evolution
datblygol *adj* nascent, developing
datblygu *vb* develop, evolve
datblygus *adj* developmental
datblygydd (**-ion**) *nm* developer
datchwyddiant *nm* deflation
datgan *vb* declare; recount; render
datganiad (**-au**) *nm* declaration;
rendering
datganoli *vb* devolve, decentralize
▷ *nm* devolution
datganoliad *nm* devolution
datganu *vb* declare; sing, render
datgeliad (**-au**) *nm* detection;
revelation
datgelu *vb* detect; reveal
datgloi *vb* unlock
datglymu *vb* unhitch, undo
datgorffori *vb* dissolve (*parliament*)
datgorfforiad *nm* dissolution

datguddiad (**-au**) *nm* revelation,
disclosure
datguddio *vb* reveal, disclose
datgyffesiad *nm* recantation
datgyffesu *vb* recant
datgymalu *vb* dislocate, dismember
datgysylltiad *nm* disestablishment
datgysylltu *vb* disconnect;
disestablish
datod *vb* undo, untie, dissolve
datrannu *vb* dissect
datro *vb* change; undo
datru *vb* de-code
datrys *vb* solve
datrysiad (**-au**) *nm* solution,
resolution
datseinio *vb* resound, reverberate
datsgwar (**-au**) *nm* square root
datysen (**datys**) *nf* date
dathliad (**-au**) *nm* celebration
dathlu *vb* celebrate
dau (*f* **dwy**) *adj, nm* two
dau-, deu- *prefix* two, bi-
dauddyblyg *adj* twofold, double
daufiniog *adj* double-edged
dauwynebog *adj* two-faced
dawn (**doniau**) *nm, nf* gift, talent
dawns (**-iau**) *nf* dance
dawnsio *vb* dance
dawnsiwr (**-wyr**) *nm* dancer
dawnus *adj* gifted, talented
de *adj, nm* right; south
De Affrica *nf* South Africa
deall *vb* understand ▷ *nm*
understanding, intellect,
intelligence
dealladwy *adj* intelligible
deallgar *adj* intelligent
deallol *adj* intellectual
dealltwriaeth (**-au**) *nf*
understanding, intelligence
deallus *adj* understanding,
intelligent

deallusion *npl* intelligentsia
deallusrwydd *nm* intelligence
deau *adj, nm* right; south
debentur (-on) *nm* debenture
debyd (-au) *nm* debit
debydu *vb* debit
dec (-iau, -s) *nm* deck
decilitr (-au) *nm* decilitre
decimetr (-au) *nm* decimetre
decstros *nm* dextrose
dectant *nm* ten-stringed
  instrument, psaltery
dechrau *vb* begin ▷ *nm* beginning
dechreuad (-au) *nm* beginning
dechreunos *nf* nightfall, dusk
dechreuol *adj* initial
dechreuwr (-wyr) *nm* beginner
dedfryd (-au) *nf* verdict; sentence
dedfrydu *vb* sentence
dedlein (-s) *nf* deadline
dedwydd *adj* happy, blessed
dedwyddwch, dedwyddyd *nm*
  happiness, bliss
deddf (-au) *nf* law, statute, act
deddfeg *nf* jurisprudence
deddfegwr (-wyr) *nm* jurist
deddfol *adj* legal, lawful
deddfu *vb* legislate, enact
deddfwr (-wyr) *nm* legislator
deddfwriaeth *nf* legislation,
  legislature
deddfwriaethol *adj* legislative
deddlyfr (-au) *nm* statute book
defni *vb* drip, trickle
defnydd (-iau) *nm* material, stuff;
  use
defnyddio *vb* use, utilize, employ;
  **defnyddio'r cwbl o, defnyddio'r
  cyfan o** use up
defnyddiol *adj* useful
defnyddioldeb *nm* usefulness, utility
defnyddiwr (-wyr) *nm* user,
  consumer

defnyn (-nau) *nm* drop
defnynnu *vb* drop, drip, dribble, distil
defod (-au) *nf* custom; rite,
  ceremony
defodaeth *nf* ritualism
defodol *adj* ritualistic
defosiwn (-ynau) *nm* devotion
defosiynol *adj* devotional, devout
deffiniad, deffinio *see* **diff-**
deffro, deffroi *vb* rouse; wake
deffroad (-au) *nm* awakening
deg *adj* ten ▷ *nm* **(-au)** ten
degaidd *adj* denary
degawd (-au) *nm* decade
degiad (-au) *nm* decimal
degol (-ion) *nm, adj* decimal
degoli *vb* decimalise
degoliad *nm* decimalisation
degolyn (degolion) *nm* decimal
degwm (-ymau) *nm* tenth, tithe
degymu *vb* tithe
deng *adj* ten (*before certain words*)
dehau, deheu *see* **deau**
deheubarth, deheudir *nm*
  southern region, south
deheuig *adj* dexterous, skilful
deheulaw *nf* right hand
deheuol *adj* southern
deheurwydd *nm* dexterity, skill
deheuwr (-wyr) *nm* southerner
deheuwynt *nm* south wind
dehongli *vb* interpret
dehongliad (-au) *nm* interpretation
**dehonglwr (-wyr), dehonglydd
  (-ion)** *nm* interpreter
dehydrad (-au) *nm* dehydration
dehydru *vb* dehydrate
deial (-au) *nm* dial
deialog (-au) *nm, nf* dialogue
deialu *vb* dial
deifio *vb* singe, scorch; blast; dive
deifiol *adj* scorching, scathing
deifiwr (-wyr) *nm* diver

deigryn (**dagrau**) *nm* tear
deilbridd *nm* humus
deildy (**-dai**) *nm* bower, arbour
deilen (**dail**) *nf* leaf
deilgoll *adj* deciduous
deiliad (**-on, deiliaid**) *nm* tenant;
    subject
deiliant (**-nnau**) *nm* foliage
deilio *vb* leaf
deiliog *adj* leafy
deillio *vb* proceed, emanate, issue
deinameg *nf, nm* dynamics
deinamig *adj* dynamic
deinamo (**-s, -au**) *nm* dynamo
deincod *nm* teeth on edge
deincryd *nm* chattering or gnashing
    of teeth
deintio *vb* nibble
deintrod (**-au**) *nf* cog
deintydd (**-ion**) *nm* dentist
deintyddiaeth *nf* dentistry
deintyddol *adj* dental
deiseb (**-au**) *nf* petition
deisebu *vb* petition
deisebwr (**-wyr**), **deisebydd** (**-ion**)
    nm petitioner
deisyf, deisyfu *vb* desire, wish;
    beseech, entreat
deisyfiad (**-au**) *nm* request, petition
del *adj* pretty, neat
delfryd (**-au**) *nm* ideal
delfrydiaeth *nf* idealism
delfrydol *adj* ideal
delfrydwr (**-wyr**) *nm* idealist
delff *nm* churl, oaf, dolt, rascal
delio *vb* deal
delw (**-au**) *nf* image; form, mode,
    manner
delwedd (**-au**) *nf* image
delweddaeth *nf* imagery
delweddu *vb* portray
delwi *vb* be wool-gathering; pale,
    be paralysed with fright.

dellni *nm* blindness
dellt *npl* (*nf* **-en**) laths, lattice,
    splinters
democratiaeth (**-au**) *nf* democracy
democratig *adj* democratic
demograffeg *nf* demography
demograffig *adj* demographic
dengar *adj* attractive
dengarwch *nm* attractiveness
deniadau *npl* attractions,
    allurements
deniadol *adj* attractive
denims *npl* denims
Denmarc *nf* Denmark
denu *vb* attract, allure, entice
deon (**-iaid**) *nm* dean
deondy (**-dai**) *nm* deanery
deoniaeth (**-au**) *nf* deanery
deor *vb* brood, hatch, incubate
deorfa (**-fâu, -feydd**) *nf* hatchery
deorydd (**-ion**) *nf* incubator
derbyn *vb* receive; accept; admit
derbyniad (**-au**) *nm* receipt;
    reception
derbyniadwy *adj* admissible
derbyniol *adj* acceptable
derbyniwr (**derbynwyr**)
    = **derbynnydd**
derbynneb (**-ynebau, -ynebion**) *nf*
    receipt, voucher
derbynnydd (**-ynyddion**) *nm*
    receiver
deri *npl* (*nf* **dâr**) oak-trees, oak
dernyn (**-nau**) *nm* piece, scrap
derwen (**derw, deri**) *nf* oak-tree,
    oak
derwydd (**-on**) *nm* druid
derwyddiaeth *nf* druidism
derwyddol *adj* druidic(al)
desg (**-iau**) *nf* desk; **desg dalu**
    checkout
desgant (**-au**) *nm* descant
desibel (**-au**) *nm* decibel

destlus *adj* neat
destlusrwydd *nm* neatness
detector (**-au**) *nm* detector
dethol *vb* select, pick, choose ▷ *adj* select
detholedd *nm* selectivity
detholiad (**-au, detholion**) *nm* selection, anthology
deu- *see* **dau-**
deuawd (**-au**) *nm, nf* duet
deublyg *adj* double, twofold
deuddeg *adj, nm* twelve
deufin *adj* two-edged
deuffocal *adj* bifocal
deugain *adj, nm* forty
deugraff *nm* digraph
deunaw *adj, nm* eighteen
deunydd (**-iau**) *nm* stuff, material; **deunydd lapio** packaging
deuocsid *nm* dioxide
deuod (**-au**) *nm* diode, binary
deuol *adj* dual
deuoliaeth *nf* dualism, duality
deuparth *nd* two-thirds
deuris *adj* two-tier
deurudd *nd* the cheeks
deuryw *adj* bisexual
deusain *nd* diphthong
deutu *nd*: **o ddeutu** about
dewin (**-iaid**) *nm* diviner, magician, wizard
dewines (**-au**) *nf* witch, sorceress
dewiniaeth *nf* divination, witchcraft
dewinio *vb* divine
dewiniol, dewinol *adj* prophetic, divinatory
dewis *vb* choose, select ▷ *nm* choice
dewisiad *nm* choice, option
dewisol *adj* choice, desirable; optional
dewr *adj* brave ▷ *nm* (**-ion**) brave man, hero
dewrder *nm* bravery, valour

di- *neg prefix* without, not, un-, non-, -less
diabetig *adj, nm, nf* diabetic
diacon (**-iaid**) *nm* deacon
diacones (**-au**) *nf* deaconess
diaconiaeth *nf* diaconate
diadell (**-au, -oedd**) *nf* flock
diaddurn *adj* unadorned, plain, rude
diaelodi *vb* dismember; expel a member
diafael *adj* slippery, careless
diafol (**diefyl, dieifl**) *nm* devil
diaffram (**-au**) *nm* diaphragm
diagnosis *nm* diagnosis
diangen *adj* unnecessary, free from want
dianghenraid *adj* unnecessary, needless
di-ail *adj* unequalled, unrivalled
dial *vb* avenge, revenge ▷ *nm* vengeance, revenge
dialedd (**-au**) *nm* vengeance, nemesis
dialgar *adj* revengeful, vindictive
dialgarwch *nm* vindictiveness
di-alw-amdano *adj* redundant, uncalled for
dialwr (**-wyr**), **dialydd** (**-ion**) *nm* avenger
diamau *adj* doubtless
diamcan *adj* aimless, purposeless
diamedr (**-au**) *nm* diameter
diamedral *adj* diametral
diamheuol *adj* undoubted, indisputable
diamod *adj* unconditional, absolute
diamodol *adj* unconditional, unqualified
diamwys *adj* unambiguous
diamynedd *adj* impatient
dianc *vb* escape
dianwadal *adj* unwavering, immutable

dianwadalwch *nm* immutability
diarddel *vb* expel, excommunicate
diarddeliad *nm* expulsion,
excommunication
diarfogi *vb* disarm
diarfogiad *nm* disarmament
diarffordd *adj* out of the way,
inaccessible
diargyhoedd *adj* blameless
diaroglydd (**-ion**) *nm* deodorant
diarhebol *adj* proverbial
diarwybod *adj* unawares
diasbad *nf* cry, scream
diasbedain *vb* resound, ring
diatreg *adj* immediate
diau *adj* true, certain; doubtless
diawl (**-iaid**) *nm* devil
diawledig *adj* devilish
di-baid, dibaid *adj* unceasing,
ceaseless
di-ball, diball *adj* unfailing,
infallible, sure
diben (**-ion**) *nm* end, purpose, aim
di-ben-draw *adj* endless
dibeniad (**-au**) *nm* ending,
conclusion, predicate
di-benllanw *adj* off-peak
dibennu *vb* end, conclude, finish
diberfeddu *vb* disembowel,
eviscerate
dibetrus *adj* unhesitating
dibl (**-au**) *nm* border, edge
dibloblogaeth *nf* depopulation
diboblogi *vb* depopulate
dibrin *adj* abundant, plentiful
dibriod *adj* unmarried, single
dibris *adj* reckless, contemptuous
dibrisio *vb* depreciate, despise
dibristod *nm* depreciation,
contempt
dibwys *adj* trivial, unimportant
dibwysiant (**-nnau**) *nm* depression
dibyn (**-nau**) *nm* steep, precipice

dibynadwy *adj* reliable
dibynadwyedd *nm* reliability
dibyniad *nm* dependence
dibyniant *nm* dependence
dibynnedd *nm* reliability
dibynnol *adj* depending;
subjunctive
dibynnu *vb* depend, rely
dibynnydd (**dibynyddion**) *nm*
dependant
dicllon *adj* wrathful, angry
dicllonrwydd *nm* wrath, indignation
dicotomi (**-ïau**) *nm* dichotomy
dicra *adj* squeamish, fastidious, slow
dicter *nm* anger, wrath, displeasure
dichell (**-ion**) *nf* wile, craft, guile
dichellgar *adj* wily, crafty, cunning
dichlyn *vb* choose, pick ▷ *adj* careful,
circumspect, exact
dichon *vb* be able; it may be
di-dact *adj* tactless
didactig *adj* didactic
didaro *adj* unaffected, unconcerned,
cool
di-daw *adj* ceaseless, clamant
diden (**-nau**) *nf* nipple, teat
diderfyn *adj* unlimited
didoli *vb* separate, segregate
didoliad *nm* separation, segregation
didolnod (**-au**) *nm, nf* diæresis
di-dor, didor *adj* unbroken,
uninterrupted
didoreth *adj* shiftless, silly, fickle
didoriad *adj* unbroken, untamed,
rough
di-drais, didrais *adj* non-violent,
meek
diduedd *adj* impartial, unbiassed
didwyll *adj* guileless, sincere
didwylledd *nm* guilelessness,
sincerity
di-ddadl *adj* unquestionable,
indisputable

diddan *adj* amusing, diverting, pleasant

diddanion *npl* pleasantries, jokes

diddanu *vb* amuse, divert; comfort

diddanwch *nm* comfort, consolation

diddanwr (-wyr), diddanydd (-ion) *nm* comforter

diddarbod *adj* shiftless

di-dderbyn-wyneb *adj* outspoken

diddig *adj* contented, pleased

diddigrwydd *nm* contentment, placidity

diddim *adj, nm* void

diddordeb *nm* interest

diddori *vb* interest

diddorol *adj* interesting

diddos *adj* watertight, sheltered; snug

diddosi *vb* shelter

diddosrwydd *nm* shelter, safety

di-dduw, didduw *adj* ungodly ▷ *nm* atheist

di-ddweud *adj* taciturn, stubborn

diddwythiad *nm* deduction

diddwytho *vb* deduce

diddyfnu *vb* wean

diddymdra *nm* nothingness, void

diddymiad, diddymiant *nm* annihilation

diddymu *vb* annihilate, abolish

dieflig *adj* devilish, diabolical, fiendish

diegwyddor *adj* unprincipled

dieisiau *adj* unnecessary, needless

dieithr *adj* strange, alien, foreign ▷ *nm* (**-iaid**) stranger

dieithrio *vb* estrange, alienate

dieithrwch *nm* strangeness

dienaid *adj* soulless, senseless

dienyddiad (-au) *nm* execution

dienyddio *vb* put to death, execute

dienyddiwr (-wyr) *nm* executioner

dieuog *adj* guiltless, innocent

difa *vb* consume, destroy, devour

di-fai, difai *adj* blameless, faultless

difalch *adj* humble

difancoll *nf* total loss, perdition

difaol *adj* consuming, devouring

difater *adj* indifferent, unconcerned

difaterwch *nm* indifference, apathy

difeddiannu *vb* dispossess, deprive

di-feind *adj* heedless

difenwad (-au) *nm* defamation

difenwi *vb* revile, abuse, belittle

diferlif *nm* stream, issue

diferol *adj* dripping, dropping

diferu *vb* drip, drop, dribble, distil

diferyn (-nau, diferion) *nm* drop

difesur *adj* huge, immeasurable, unstinted

di-feth, difeth *adj* infallible, certain

difetha *vb* destroy, spoil, waste

difethwr (-wyr) *nm* destroyer

Difiau *nm* Thursday

difidend (-au) *nm* dividend

diflanbwynt *nm* vanishing point

diflanedig *adj* evanescent, fleeting

diflannu *vb* vanish, disappear

di-flas *adj* tasteless

diflas *adj* insipid, dull, wearisome

diflastod *nm* disgust

diflasu *vb* disgust; weary, surfeit

diflin, diflino *adj* untiring, indefatigable

difodi *vb* annihilate, exterminate

difodiad, difodiant *nm* annihilation

di-foes, difoes *adj* rude, unmannerly

difreiniad *nm* disfranchisement

difreinio *vb* disfranchise, deprive

difrïaeth *nf* abuse, calumny

difrif *nm* seriousness, earnestness

difrifddwys *adj* solemn

difrifol *adj* serious, earnest, solemn, grave

difrifoldeb *see* **difrifwch**
difrifoli *vb* sober, solemnize
difrifwch *nm* seriousness, earnestness, solemnity
difrïo *vb* scold, abuse, malign
difrod *nm* waste, havoc, damage
difrodi *vb* waste, spoil, ravage
difrodol *adj* destructive
difrodwr (-wyr) *nm* spoiler, devastator
difrycheulyd *adj* spotless, immaculate
di-fudd, difudd *adj* unprofitable, useless, futile
di-fwlch, difwlch *adj* without a break, continuous
difwyniad (-au) *nm* adulteration, pollution
difwyniant *nm* defilement
difwyno *vb* mar, soil, sully, defile
difyfyr *adj* impromptu
difynio *vb* dissect, vivisect
difyr *adj* pleasant, diverting, amusing
difyrion *npl* diversions, amusements
difyrru *vb* divert, amuse, beguile
difyrrus *adj* diverting, amusing
difyrrwch *nm* diversion, amusement, fun
difyrrwr (-yrwyr) *nm* entertainer
difyrwaith (-weithiau) *nm* hobby
difwyd *adj* inert
diffaith *adj* waste, desert; base, mean ▷ *nm* **(-ffeithydd)** wilderness, desert
diffeithdra *nm* dereliction
diffeithio *vb* lay waste
diffeithwch (-ychau) *nm* desert, wilderness
diffiniad (-au) *nm* definition
diffinio *vb* define
diffodd, diffoddi *vb* put out, quench, extinguish; switch off

diffoddiad *nm* quenching, extinction
diffoddwr (-wyr), diffoddydd (-ion) *nm* quencher
diffrwyth *adj* barren; numb, paralysed
diffrwythder, diffrwythdra *nm* barrenness; numbness
diffrwytho *vb* make barren; paralyse
diffuant *adj* unfeigned, sincere, genuine; **yn ddiffuant** sincerely
diffuantrwydd *nm* genuineness
di-ffurf *adj* amorphous
diffwys *adj* wild, waste; high, steep; huge, awful
diffyg (-ion) *nm* defect, want, lack; eclipse
diffygiant *nm* deficiency
diffygio *vb* fail; faint, weary
diffygiol *adj* defective; faint, weary
diffyndoll (-au) *nf* tariff
diffyndollaeth *nf* protectionism
diffynnydd (-ynyddion) *nm* defendant
dig *adj* angry, wrathful ▷ *nm* anger, wrath
digalon *adj* disheartened, depressed, dejected, sad
digalondid *nm* depression, dejection
digalonni *vb* dishearten, discourage, put off
digamsyniol *adj* unmistakable
digasedd *nm* hatred, enmity
digid (-au) *nm* digit
digidiad (-au) *nm* digitation
digidol *adj* digital
digio *vb* anger, offend; take offence
di-glem *adj* inept
digllon *see* **dicllon**
digofaint *nm* anger, wrath, indignation

digofus *adj* angry, indignant
digolledu *vb* indemnify, compensate
digon *nm, adj, adv* enough; done (*of cooking*)
digonedd *nm* abundance, plenty
digoni *vb* suffice; satisfy; cook
digonol *adj* satisfying; sufficient, adequate; satisfied
digonolrwydd *nm* sufficiency, abundance
digornio *vb* dehorn
di-gred *adj* infidel
di-grefft, digrefft *adj* unskilled
digrif, digrifol *adj* mirthful, funny
digriflun (-iau) *nm* caricature, cartoon
digrifwas (-weision) *nm* clown, buffoon
digrifwch *nm* mirth, fun
digroeso *adj* inhospitable
digwydd *vb* befall, happen, occur
digwyddiad (-au) *nm* happening, occurrence, event
digyfnewid *adj* unchangeable
digyffelyb *adj* incomparable
digymysg *adj* unmixed
digyswllt *adj* incoherent
digywilydd *adj* impudent
digywilydd-dra *nm* impudence
dihafal *adj* unequalled, peerless
dihangfa (diangfâu) *nf* escape
dihangol *adj* escaped, safe
dihareb (diarhebion) *nf* proverb
dihatru *vb* strip, undress
dihefelydd *adj* unequalled
diheintio *vb* disinfect
diheintydd (-ion) *nm* disinfectant, sterilizer
di-hid, di-hidio *adj* heedless, indifferent, reckless
dihidlo *vb* drop, distil; shed
dihidrwydd *nm* indifference, recklessness

dihiryn (-hirod) *nm* rascal, scoundrel
dihoeni *vb* languish, pine
dihuno *vb* wake, rouse
di-hwyl *adj* out of sorts
dihyder *adj* lacking confidence
dihydradu *vb* dehydrate
dihysbydd *adj* inexhaustible
dihysbyddu *vb* empty, exhaust
dil (-iau) *nm*: **dil mêl** honeycomb
dilead *nm* abolition, deletion
dilechdid *nm* dialectic
diledryw *adj* pure, genuine
dileu *vb* delete, rub out; blot out; abolish
dilewyrch *adj* dismal; not prosperous
dilorni *vb* abuse, revile
di-lun *adj* slovenly
diluw *see* **dilyw**
dilyffethair *adj* unencumbered, unfettered
dilyn *vb* follow, pursue; imitate
dilyniad *nm* following; imitation
dilyniant (-nnau) *nm* sequence, progression
dilynol *adj* following; consequent
dilynwr (-wyr) *nm* follower; imitator
dilys *adj* sure, certain; genuine
dilysiant (-nnau) *nm* validation
dilysnod (-au) *nm* hallmark
dilysrwydd *nm* genuineness
dilysu *vb* certify, warrant, guarantee
dilyw *nm* flood, deluge
dillad (*nm* dilledyn) *npl* clothes, clothing; **dillad isaf** underwear
dilladu *vb* clothe
dilledydd *nm* clothier
dilledyn *nm* garment
dim *adj* any (*with negative understood*); no ▷ *nm* anything; none, nothing
dimensiwn (-iynau) *nm* dimension

dimensiynol *adj* dimensional
di-nam, dinam *adj* faultless
dinas (-oedd) *nf* city
dinasol *adj* municipal
dinasyddiaeth *nf* citizenship
dincod *see* **deincod**
dinesig *adj* civil, civic
dinesydd (dinasyddion) *nm* citizen
dinistr *nm* destruction
dinistrio *vb* destroy
dinistriol *adj* destroying, destructive
dinistriwr (-wyr) *nm* destroyer
dinistrydd (-ion) *nm* destroyer
diniwed *adj* harmless, innocent
diniweidrwydd *nm* innocence
di-nod, dinod *adj* insignificant,
  obscure
dinodedd *nm* insignificance,
  obscurity
dinoethi *vb* bare, denude, expose
diod (-ydd) *nf* drink, beverage
diodi *vb* give drink
dioddef *vb* suffer, bear; wait ▷ *nm*
  (-iadau) suffering
dioddefaint *nm* suffering, passion
dioddefgar, dioddefus *adj* patient
dioddefgarwch *nm* patience
dioddefwr (-wyr), dioddefydd
  (-ion) *nm* sufferer, patient
di-oed, dioed *adj* without delay,
  immediate
diofal *adj* careless
diofalwch *nm* carelessness
diog *adj* slothful, indolent, lazy
diogel *adj* safe, secure; sure, certain
diogelu *vb* make safe, secure
diogelwch *nm* safety, security
diogi *vb* be lazy, idle ▷ *nm* laziness
dioglyd *adj* lazy, sluggish, indolent
diogyn *nm* lazy one, idler, sluggard
diolch *vb* thank, give thanks ▷ *nm*
  (-iadau) thanks, thanksgiving
diolchgar *adj* thankful, grateful

diolchgarwch *nm* thankfulness,
  gratitude, thanksgiving
diolwg *adj* ugly
diorseddu *vb* dethrone, depose
di-os *adj* without doubt
diosg *vb* undress, put off, strip, divest
diota *vb* tipple
diotwr (-wyr) *nm* boozer, drunkard
dioty (-tai) *nm* ale-house,
  public-house
diploma (-âu) *nm, nf* diploma
diplomateg *nf* diplomacy
diplomydd (-ion) *nm* diplomat
diplomyddol *adj* diplomatic
dipton (-au) *nf* diphthong
dir *adj* certain, necessary
diraddiad (-au) *nm* degradation
diraddio *vb* degrade
diraddiol *adj* degrading
di-raen *adj* shabby, dull
dirboeni *vb* torture, excruciate
dirdyniad (-au) *nm* convulsion
dirdynnol *adj* excruciating
dirdynnu *vb* rack, torture
direidi *nm* mischievousness,
  mischief
direidus *adj* mischievous
direol *adj* unruly, disorderly
direwydd *nm* defroster
direwyn *nm* antifreeze
dirfawr *adj* vast, huge, immense,
  enormous
dirgel *adj* secret ▷ *nm* **(-ion)** secret
dirgeledig *adj* hidden, secret;
  mystical
dirgeledigaeth (-au) *nm, nf* mystery
dirgelu *vb* secrete, conceal, hide
dirgelwch *nm* secrecy, mystery,
  secret
dirgryniad (-au) *nm* tremor,
  vibration
dirgrynol *adj* vibrating
dirgrynu *vb* tremble, vibrate

d

diriaethol *adj* concrete

dirlawn *adj* saturated

dirmyg *nm* contempt, scorn

dirmygu *vb* despise, scorn

dirmygus *adj* contemptuous; contemptible

dirnad *vb* discern, comprehend

dirnadaeth *nf* discernment, comprehension

dirnadwy *adj* discernible

dirprwy (-on) *nm* deputy; delegate

dirprwyaeth (-au) *nf* commission; deputation

dirprwyo *vb* deputise, delegate

dirprwyol *adj* vicarious

dirprwywr (-wyr) *nm* commissioner

dirwasgiad (-au) *nm* depression

dirwest *nm, nf* abstinence, temperance

dirwestol *adj* temperate

dirwestwr (-wyr) *nm* abstainer

dirwy (-on) *nf* fine

dirwyn *vb* wind, twist, twine

dirwynwr (-wyr) *nm* winder

dirwyo *vb* fine

di-rym *adj* powerless, void

dirymu *vb* nullify, annul, cancel

diryw *adj* neuter

dirywiad *nm* degeneration, deterioration

dirywiaeth *nf* degeneracy

dirywiedig *adj* degenerate

dirywio *vb* degenerate, deteriorate

dirywiol *adj* decadent, retrograde

dis (-iau) *nm* die, dice

di-sail *adj* groundless, baseless

disbaddu *vb* castrate, geld, spay

disbaddwr (-wyr) *nm* castrator

disberod *nm:* **ar ddisberod** wandering, astray

disbyddedig *adj* exhausted

disbyddu *vb* empty, exhaust

disbyddwr *nm* exhaust

disco (-au) *nm* disco

diserch *adj* sullen, sulky, loveless

disg (-iau) *nm* disk, record; **disg caled** hard disk

disgen (disgiau) *nf* discus; **disgen galed** hard disk

disglair *adj* bright, brilliant

disgleirdeb, disgleirder *nm* brightness, brilliance

disgleirio *vb* shine, glitter

disgloff *adj* free from lameness

disgownt (-iau, -s) *nm* discount

disgrifiad (-au) *nm* description

disgrifiadol *adj* descriptive

disgrifio *vb* describe

disgwyl *vb* look, expect, wait

disgwylfa (-feydd) *nf* watch-tower

disgwylgar *adj* watchful, expectant

disgwyliad (-au) *nm* expectation

disgybl (-ion) *nm* disciple, pupil

disgyblaeth *nf* discipline

disgyblu *vb* discipline

disgyblwr (-wyr) *nm* disciplinarian

disgyn *vb* descend, get off; fall, drop; let down

disgynfa (-feydd) *nf* descent, declivity; landing place

disgyniad (-au) *nm* descent

disgynnol *adj* descending

disgynnydd (-ynyddion) *nm* descendant

disgyrchedd *nm* gravitation

disgyrchiad, disgyrchiant *nm* gravity; **craidd** centre of gravity

disgyrchu *vb* gravitate

di-sigl *adj* unshaken, steadfast, firm

disiog *adj* diced

disodli *vb* trip up, supplant

dist (-iau) *nm* joist, beam

distadl *adj* insignificant, low, base, mean

distadledd nm insignificance, obscurity

distain (-einiaid) nm steward

distaw adj silent, quiet

distawrwydd nm silence, quiet

distewi vb silence; calm, quiet

distryw nm destruction

distrywgar adj destructive, wasteful

distrywio vb destroy

distrywiwr (-wyr) nm destroyer

distyll nm ebb, distillation

distyllio vb distil

di-sut adj unwell; small

diswta adj sudden, abrupt

diswyddiad (-au) nm dismissal

diswyddo vb dismiss from office, discharge

disychedu vb quench thirst

di-syfl adj immovable, impregnable

disyfyd adj sudden, instantaneous

disyml adj simple, artless, ingenuous

disymwth adj sudden, instantaneous

disynnwyr adj senseless

ditectif (-s) nm detective

diwahân adj inseparable, indiscriminate

diwair adj chaste; celibate

di-waith, diwaith adj unemployed, idle

diwall adj satisfied, full, perfect

diwallu vb satisfy, supply

diwarafun adj unforbidden, ungrudging

diwasgedd (-au) nm depression (*weather*)

diwedydd (-iau) nm evening, eventide

diwedd nm end, conclusion

diweddar adj late, modern

diweddaru vb modernize

diweddarwch nm lateness

diweddeb nf cadence

diweddglo nm conclusion

diweddu vb end, finish, conclude

diweirdeb nm chastity

diweithdra nm unemployment

diwelfa (-feydd) nf watershed

diwethaf adj last

di-wifr adj wireless; **rhwydwaith di-wifr** wireless network

diwinydd (-ion) nm divine, theologian

diwinyddiaeth nf divinity, theology

diwinyddol adj theological

diwreiddio vb uproot, eradicate

diwrnod (-iau) nm day

diwrthdro adj inexorable

diwyd adj diligent, industrious, hard-working

diwydianfa nf industrial estate

diwydiannaeth nf industrialization, industrialism

diwydiannol adj industrial

diwydiannwr (-ianwyr) nm industrialist

diwydiant (-iannau) nm industry

diwydrwydd nm diligence, industry

diwyg nm form, dress, garb

diwygiad (-au) nm reform, reformation; revival

diwygiadol adj reformatory; revivalistic

diwygiedig adj reformed; revised

diwygio vb amend, reform, revise

diwygiol adj reformatory

diwygiwr (-wyr) nm reformer; revivalist

diwylliadol adj cultural

diwylliannol adj cultural

diwylliant (-nnau) nm culture

diwylliedig adj cultured

diwyllio vb cultivate

diymadferth *adj* helpless
diymadferthedd *nm* helplessness
diymdroi *adj* without delay
diymhongar *adj* unassuming
diymod *adj* steadfast, immovable
diymwad *adj* undeniable, indisputable
diysgog *adj* steadfast, firm, stable
diystyr *adj* contemptuous; contemptible; meaningless
diystyrllyd *adj* contemptuous, disdainful
diystyru *vb* disregard, despise
diystyrwch *nm* contempt, disdain, scorn
do *adv* yes (*to questions in preterite tense*)
doc (**-iau**) *nm* dock
docfa (**-feydd**) *nf* berth
docio *vb* shorten; dock, berth
doctor (**-iaid**) *nm* doctor
doctora *vb* doctor
dod *vb* come; become; **dod i mewn** come in; **dod yn ôl** come back
dodi *vb* put, place; give; switch on
dodrefn *npl* (*nm* **-yn**) furniture
dodrefnu *vb* furnish
dodrefnwr (**-wyr**) *nm* furnisher
dodwy *vb* lay eggs
doe *adv* yesterday
doeth (**-ion**) *adj* wise
doethineb *nm*, *nf* wisdom
doethinebu *vb* discourse wisely, pontificate
doethor (**-iaid**) *nm* doctor (*of university*)
doethur (**-iaid**) *nm* doctor (*of university*)
doethuriaeth (**-au**) *nf* doctorate
dof *adj* tame, domesticated; garden
dofednod *npl* fowls, poultry
dofi *vb* tame, domesticate; assuage
dofn *adj* f of **dwfn**

Dofydd *nm* God
dogfen (**-ni, -nau**) *nf* document
dogfennaeth *nf* documentation
dogfennen (**-ennau**) *nf* documentary
dogfennol *adj* documentary
dogn (**-au**) *nm* share, portion; dose
dogni *vb* ration
doili *nm* doyley
dol (**-iau**) *nf* doll
dôl *nm* dole
dôl (**dolydd, dolau**) *nf* meadow
dolbridd (**-oedd**) *nm* alluvium, meadow soil
doldir (**-oedd**) *nm* meadow-land
dolef (**-au**) *nf* cry
dolefain *vb* cry out
dolefus *adj* wailing, plaintive
dolen (**-nau**) *nf* loop, link, ring, bow
dolennog *adj* ringed, looped; winding
dolennu *vb* loop; wind, meander
doler (**-i**) *nf* dollar
dolffin *nm* dolphin
dolur (**-iau**) *nm* sore; ailment; grief
dolurio *vb* hurt, wound; grieve
dolurus *adj* sore
dominyddu *vb* dominate
donio *vb* endow, gift
doniol *adj* gifted; witty, humorous
donioldeb, doniolwch *nm* wit, humour
dôr (**dorau**) *nf* door
dos (**-ys, -au**) *nf* dose
dosbarth (**au, -iadau**) *nm* reason; class; district
dosbarthiad *nm* distribution
dosbarthu *vb* class, classify; distribute
dosbarthwr (**-wyr**) *nm* distributor
dosio *vb* dose
dosran (**-nau**) *nf* division, section
dosrannu *vb* separate, analyse

dot (**-iau**) *nm*, *nf* dot

dot *nf* giddiness, vertigo

dotio *vb* dote

drachefn *adv* again

dracht (**-iau**) *nm* draught (*of liquor*)

drachtio *vb* drink deep

draen (**draeniau**) *nf* drain

draen, draenen (**drain**) *nf* thorn

draeniad (**-au**) *nm* drainage

draenio *vb* drain

draenog (**-od**) *nm* hedgehog

drafft (**-iau**) *nm* draft, draught

draffts *npl* draughts

dragio *vb* drag, tear, mangle

draig (**dreigiau**) *nf* dragon

drain *see* **draen, draenen**

drama (**dramâu**) *nf* drama

dramateiddio *vb* dramatize

dramatig *adj* dramatic

dramodiad (**-au**) *nm* dramatization

dramodwr (**-wyr**) *nm* dramatist

draw *adv* yonder, away

dreflan *vb* dribble

dreng *adj* morose, surly, sullen, harsh

dresel (**dreseli, dreselydd**), **dreser** *nm* dresser

drewdod *nm* stink, stench

drewi *vb*, *nm* stink

drewllyd *adj* stinking

driblo *vb* dribble

drifft (**-iau**) *nm* drift

dril (**-iau**) *nm* drill

drilio *vb* drill

dringad *vb*, *nm* climb

dringfa (**-feydd**) *nf* climb, ascent

dringo *vb* climb

dringwr (**-wyr**) *nm* climber

dripsych *adj* drip-dry

drôr (**drors**) *nm* drawer

dros *see* **tros**

drud *adj* dear, precious, costly; reckless

drudfawr *adj* costly, expensive

drudwen *nf*, **drudwy** *nm* starling

drwg *adj* evil, bad, naughty, wicked ▷ *nm* (**drygau**) evil, harm, hurt

drwgdybiaeth (**-au**) *nf* suspicion

drwgdybio *vb* suspect

drwgdybus *adj* suspicious

drwglosgiad *nm* arson

drwgweithredwr (**-wyr**) *nm* evildoer

drwm (**drymiau**) *nm* drum

drws (**drysau**) *nm* door

drwy *see* **trwy**

drycin (**-oedd**) *nf* foul weather

drycinog *adj* stormy

drych (**-au**) *nm* spectacle; mirror; object, pattern

drychfeddwl (**-yliau**) *nm* idea

drychiolaeth (**-au**) *nf* apparition, phantom

drygair *nm* ill report; scandal

dryganadl *nm* halitosis

drygfyd *nm* adversity

drygioni *nm* badness, wickedness

drygionus *adj* bad, wicked

drygu *vb* hurt, harm, injure

dryll (**-iau**) *nm* piece; part ▷ *nm*, *nf* gun, rifle

drylliad (**-au**) *nm* breaking; wreck

drylliedig *adj* broken, shattered

dryllio *vb* break in pieces, shatter

drylliog *adj* broken, contrite

drymiwr (**-wyr**) *nm* drummer

drysi *npl* (*nf*-**ïen**) thorns, briers

dryslwyn (**-i**) *nm* thicket

dryslyd *adj* perplexing; confused

drysu *vb* tangle; perplex; be confused

dryswch *nm* tangle; perplexity; confusion

dryw (**-od**) *nm*, *nf* wren

DU *nf* UK

du *adj*, *nm* black

duc, dug (**-iaid**) *nm* duke

dugiaeth nf duchy
dull (-iau) nm form, manner, mode
dullwedd (-au) nm mannerism
Dulyn nf Dublin
duo vb black, blacken
dur nm steel
duw (-iau) nm god; **Duw** God
düwch nm blackness
duwdod nm godhead, divinity, deity
duwies (-au) nf goddess
duwiol (-ion) adj godly, pious
duwioldeb nm godliness, piety
duwiolfrydedd nm godliness, piety
duwiolfrydig adj god-fearing, pious
DVD (-s) n DVD
dwbio vb daub, plaster
dwbl adj double
dweud, dweyd see **dywedyd**
dwfn (f **dofn**) adj deep, profound
dwfr, dŵr (dyfroedd) nm water
dwl adj dull, stupid, foolish
dwlu vb dote
dwmbwr-dambar adv helter-skelter
dwndwr nm din, babble, hubbub
dwnsiwn (-iynau) nm dungeon
dŵr see **dwfr**
dwrdio vb scold
dwrn (dyrnau) nm fist; knob, handle, hilt
dwsin (-inau) nm dozen
dwst nm dust, powder
dwster (-i) nm duster
dwthwn nm day
dwy see **dau**
dwyfol adj divine
dwyfoldeb nm divinity, deity
dwyfoli vb deify
dwyfron (-nau) nf breast, chest
dwyfronneg nf breastplate
dwyieithedd nm bilingualism
dwyieitheg nf study of bilingualism
dwyieithog adj bilingual, duoglot

dwyieithrwydd nm bilingualism
dwylaw, dwylo nd, pl two hands, hands
dwyn vb bear; bring; steal
dwyochredd nm bilateralism
dwyochrol adj bilateral
dwyradd adj quadratic, two-tier
dwyrain nm, adj east; **Dwyrain yr Almaen** East Germany
dwyraniad nm dichotomy
dwyrannu vb bisect
dwyreiniol adj easterly, eastern, oriental
dwyreiniwr (-wyr) nm easterner, oriental
dwys adj dense, grave, deep, intense
dwysáu vb deepen, intensify
dwysbigo vb prick, sting
dwysedd (-au) nm density
dwyster nm gravity, solemnity
dwythell (-au) nf duct
dwywaith adv twice
dy pron thy, thine
dyblu vb double; repeat
dyblyg adj twofold, double
dyblygiad (-au) nm duplication, duplicate
dyblygu vb double, fold
dyblygydd (-ion) nm duplicator
dybryd adj sore, dire; flagrant
dychan (-au) nf lampoon, satire
dychangerdd (-i) nf satirical poem, satire
dychanol adj satirical
dychanu vb lampoon, satirize, revile
dychanwr (-wyr) nm satirist
dychmygadwy adj imaginable
dychmygol adj imaginary
dychmygu vb imagine
dychmygus adj imaginative, inventive
dychryn (-iadau) nm fright, terror
▷ vb frighten

dychrynllyd adj frightful, terrible
dychrynu vb frighten, be frightened
dychweledig adj returned
dychweliad (**-au**) nm return;
conversion
dychwelyd vb return, come back
dychymyg (**dychmygion**) nm
imagination, fancy; riddle, device
dydd (**-iau**) nm day; **dyddiau cŵn**
silly season; **Dydd Sant Folant**
Valentine's Day
dyddfu vb flag, pine, faint
dyddiad (**-au**) nm date
dyddiadur (**-on**) nm diary, journal
dyddiedig adj dated
dyddio vb become day, dawn; date
dyddiol adj daily
dyddlyfr (**-au**) nm diary, journal
dyddodyn (**-odion**) nm deposit
dyfais (**-feisiau**) nf device, invention
dyfal adj diligent
dyfalbarhad nm perseverance
dyfalbarhau vb persevere
dyfaliad (**-au**) nm guess, conjecture
dyfalu vb guess, conjecture
dyfalwch nm diligence, assiduity
dyfarniad (**-au**) nm decision, verdict
dyfarnu vb adjudge; referee
dyfarnwr (**-wyr**) nm judge, umpire,
referee
dyfeisio vb make up, devise, invent,
imagine; guess
dyfeisiwr (**-wyr**) nm inventor
dyfnant (**-nentydd**) nf ravine
dyfnder (**-au, -oedd**) nm deep,
depth
dyfnhau vb deepen
dyfod vb come; become
dyfodfa nf access, entrance
dyfodiad nm coming, arrival,
advent
dyfodiad (**-iaid**) nm incomer,
stranger

dyfodol adj coming, future ▷ nm
future
dyfradwy adj watered; watering
dyfredig adj irrigated
dyfrffos (**-ydd**) nm canal,
watercourse
dyfrgi (**-gwn**) nm otter
dyfrhad nm irrigation
dyfrhau, dyfrio vb water
dyfrllyd adj watery
dyfrwr n waterman, water-carrier;
y Dyfrwr Aquarius
dyfyniad (**-au**) nm citation,
quotation
dyfynnod (**-ynodau**) nm quotation
mark
dyfynnol adj citatory, summoned
dyfynnu vb cite, quote; summon
dyffryn (**-noedd**) nm valley
dyffryndir (**-oedd**) nm low country;
vale
dygn adj hard, severe, grievous, dire
dygnu vb strive, persevere
dygnwch nm perseverance,
assiduity
dygwyl nm holiday, feast day
dygymod vb agree (with), put up
(with)
dyhead (**-au**) nm aspiration
dyheu vb pant; long, yearn, aspire
dyhiryn see **dihiryn**
dyladwy adj due
dylanwad (**-au**) nm influence
dylanwadol adj influential
dylanwadu vb influence
dyled (**-ion**) nf debt, obligation
dyledog adj in debt, indebted
dyledus adj due
dyledwr (**-wyr**) nm debtor
dyletswydd (**-au**) nf duty,
obligation
dylif nm flood, deluge ▷ nf warp
dylifo vb flow, stream, pour

d

dylni *nm* stupidity, dullness
dyluniad (-au) *nm* design, drawing
dylunio *vb* design
dylunydd (-ion) *nm* designer
dylyfu gên *vb* yawn, gape
dylluan *see* **tylluan**
dyma *adv* here is, here are; this is, these are
dymchweliad *nm* overthrow
dymchwelyd *vb* overthrow, upset, subvert
dymuniad (-au) *nm* wish, desire
dymuno *vb* wish, desire
dymunol *adj* desirable, agreeable, pleasant
dyn (-ion) *nm* man, person
dyna *adv* there is, there are; that is, those are
dynad *npl* nettles
dyndod *nm* manhood, humanity
dyneiddiaeth *nf* humanism
dyneiddiol *adj* humanistic
dyneiddiwr (-wyr) *nm* humanist
dynes *nf* woman
dynesiad *nm* approach
dynesu *vb* draw near, approach
dyngar *adj* humane
dyngarol *adj* philanthropic
dyngarwch *nm* philanthropy
dyngarwr (-wyr) *nm* philanthropist
dyniawed (-iewaid) *nm* yearling, steer
dyn-laddiad *nm* manslaughter
dynodi *vb* denote, signify
dynodiad (-au) *nm* denotation
dynol *adj* human; man-like; manly
dynoliaeth *nf* humanity
dynoliaethau *npl* humanities
dynolryw *coll n* mankind
dynwared *vb* imitate, mimic
dynwarededd *nm* mimicry
dynwarediad (-au) *nm* imitation, mimicry

dynwaredol *adj* imitative
dynwaredwr (-wyr) *nm* imitator, mimic
dyraddiant *nm* degradation
dyraniad (-au) *nm* allocation
dyrchafael *vb* rise, ascend ▷ *nm* ascension
dyrchafedig *adj* exalted
dyrchafiad *nm* elevation, promotion
dyrchafol *adj* elevating
dyrchafu *vb* raise, elevate; rise, ascend
dyri (-ïau), dyrif (-au) *nf* ballad, lyric
dyrnaid (-eidiau) *nm* handful
dyrnio *vb* punch
dyrnod (-iau) *nm, nf* blow, stroke
dyrnu *vb* thump; thresh
dyrnwr (-wyr) *nm* thresher
dyrnwr medi *nm* combine harvester
dyrys *adj* tangled; difficult; perplexing
dyryslyd, dyrysu, dyryswch *see* **dryslyd, drysu, dryswch**
dysg *nm, nf* learning
dysgedig (-ion) *adj* learned
dysgeidiaeth *nf* teaching, doctrine
dysgl (-au) *nf* dish; **dysgl loeren** satellite dish
dysglaid (-eidiau) *nf* dishful, dish
dysgu *vb* learn, teach
dysgwr (-wyr) *nm* learner, teacher
dyslecsig *adj* dyslexic
dywalgi (-gwn) *nm* tiger
dywediad (-au) *nm* saying
dywedwst *adj* taciturn ▷ *nm* taciturnity
dywedyd *vb* say, speak, tell
dyweddi (-ïau) *nf* betrothal, fiancé(e) ▷ *coll n* betrothed
dyweddïad *nm* betrothal
dyweddïo *vb* betroth

e

eang *adj* wide, broad, immense
eangder, eangu *see* **ehangder, ehangu**
eangfrydedd *nm* magnanimity
eangfrydig *adj* broad-minded, magnanimous
eb, ebe, ebr *vb* said, quoth
ebargofiant *nm* oblivion
ebill (-ion) *nm* auger, borer; peg
ebillio *vb* bore
ebol (-ion) *nm* colt, foal
eboles (-au) *nf* foal, filly
eboni *nm* ebony
ebost (ebyst) *nm* email
ebostio *vb* email
ebran (-nau) *nm* provender, fodder
Ebrill *nm* April
ebrwydd *adj* quick, swift, soon
ebwch (-ychau) *nm* gasp
ebychiad (-au) *nm* interjection, ejaculation

ebychu *vb* gasp, interject, ejaculate
eciwmenaidd *adj* ecumenical
ecliptig *adj, nm* ecliptic
ecoleg (-au) *nf, nm* ecology
ecolegol *adj* ecological
ecolegwr (-wyr) *nm* ecologist
economaidd *adj* economic
economeg *nf* economics
economegol *adj* economic
economegwr (-wyr) *nm* economist
economegydd (-ion) *nm* economist
economi (-ïau) *nm* economy
economydd *nm* economist
ecsbloetio *vb* exploit
ecsbloetiwr (-wyr) *nm* exploiter
ecseis *nm* excise
ecseismon (-myn) *nm* exciseman
ecsema *nm* eczema
ecsentredd (-au) *nm* eccentricity
ecsentrig *adj* eccentric (*in maths*)
ecstasi *nm* ecstasy
ecstatig *adj* ecstatic
echblyg *adj* explicit, outward
echblygol *adj* extrovert
echdoe *adv* day before yesterday
echdoriad (-au) *nm* eruption
echel (-au) *nf* axle, axletree; axis
echelin (-au) *nm* axis
echnos *adv* night before last
echrydus *adj* fearful, frightful, shocking
echwyn (-ion) *nm* loan
echwynna *vb* borrow, lend
echwynnwr (-wynwyr) *nm* lender, creditor
edau (edafedd) *nf* thread; (*pl*) yarn, wool
edfryd *vb* restore
e-diced (-i) *nm* e-ticket
edifar *adj* penitent, sorry
edifarhau, edifaru *vb* repent, be sorry

edifarus, edifeiriol *adj* repentant, penitent

edifeirwch *nm* repentance, penitence

edliw *vb* upbraid, reproach, taunt

edmygedd *nm* admiration

edmygol *adj* admiring

edmygu *vb* admire

edmygwr, edmygydd (edmygwyr) *nm* admirer

edrych *vb* look, examine; **edrych ar** look at

edrychiad *nm* look

edrychwr (-wyr) *nm* beholder, spectator

edwi, edwino *vb* fade, wither, decay

eddi *npl* thrums; fringe, nap

ef, efe *pron* he, him; it

efallai *adv* perhaps, peradventure

e-fasnach (-au) *nf* e-commerce

efengyl (-au) *nf* gospel

efengylaidd *adj* evangelical

efengyleiddio *vb* evangelize

efengyles (-au) *nf* female evangelist

efengylu *vb* evangelize

efengylwr, efengylydd (efengylwyr) *nm* evangelist

efelychiad (-au) *nm* imitation

efelychiadol *adj* imitative

efelychu *vb* imitate

efelychwr (-wyr) *nm* imitator

efelychydd (-ion) *nm* simulator

eferw *adj* effervescent

eferwad (-au) *nm* effervescence

eferwi *vb* effervesce

efo *prep* with

efô *pron* he, him; it

efrau *npl* tares

Efrog Newydd *nf* New York

efrydiaeth (-au) *nf* study

efrydu *vb* study

efrydydd (-ion, -wyr) *nm* student

efydd *nm* bronze, copper, brass

effaith (-eithiau) *nf* effect; **effeithiau arbennig** special effects

effeithio *vb* effect, affect

effeithiol *adj* effectual, effective, efficient

effeithioli *vb* render effectual

effeithiolrwydd *nm* efficacy

effeithlon *adj* efficient

effeithlonedd *nm* efficiency (of machines etc)

effeithlonrwydd *nm* efficiency

effro *adj* awake, vigilant

eger (-au) *nm* bore, eagre

egin *npl* (*nm* **-yn**) germs, sprouts

eginhad, eginiad (-au) *nm* germination, sprouting

egino *vb* germinate, shoot, sprout

eginol *adj* germinal, shooting

eginyn (egin) *nm* sprout

eglur *adj* clear, plain, evident

eglurdeb, eglurder *nm* clearness

eglureb (-au) *nf* illustration

eglurhad *nm* explanation, demonstration

eglurhaol *adj* explanatory

egluro *vb* make clear, explain

eglwys (-i, -ydd) *nf* church

eglwysig *adj* church, ecclesiastical

eglwyswr (-wyr) *nm* churchman

eglwyswraig (-wragedd) *nf* churchwoman

egni (-ïon) *nm* effort, might, energy

egnïo *vb* endeavour, make an effort

egnïol *adj* energetic

egnioli *vb* energise

ego *nm* ego

egoistiaeth *nm* egoism

egosentrig *adj* egocentric

egöydd *nm* egoist

egr *adj* sharp; sour; severe; savage; cheeky

egroes *npl* (*nf* **-en**) hips

egwan *adj* weak, feeble

egwyd (-ydd) nf fetlock; fetter
egwyddor (-ion, -au) nf rudiment; principle; alphabet
egwyddorol adj high-principled
egwyl nf lull, respite; opportunity
enghraifft (-eifftiau) nf example, instance
enghreifftiol adj exemplary, illustrative
englyn (-ion) nm Welsh alliterative stanza
englyna, englynu vb compose englynion
englynwr (-wyr) nm composer of englynion
engyl see **angel**
ehangder (eangderau) nm breadth, immensity
ehangu vb enlarge, extend
ehedeg vb fly; run to seed
ehedfa (-feydd) nf flight
ehedfan vb hover, fly
ehediad (-au) nm flight
ehediad (-iaid) nm fowl, bird
ehedog adj flying
ehedydd (-ion) nm lark
ehofndra nm fearlessness, boldness
ei pron his, hers; its
eicon (-au) nm icon
eich pron your
Eidal nf: **yr Eidal** Italy
eidion (-nau) nm ox
eiddew coll n ivy
eiddgar adj zealous, ardent
eiddgarwch nm zeal, ardour
eiddigedd nm jealousy; zeal
eiddigeddu vb be jealous, envy; have zeal
eiddigeddus adj jealous, envious
eiddigus adj jealous; zealous
eiddil adj slender, feeble
eiddilwch nm slenderness, feebleness

eiddiorwg coll n ivy
eiddo nm property, possessions
  ▷ pron his etc
eidduno vb desire, wish, pray
Eifftaidd adj Egyptian
Eifftiwr (-wyr), Eifftiad (-iaid) nm Egyptian
eigion nm depth, ocean
eigioneg nf, nm oceanography
eigionol adj pelagic
eingion (-au) nf anvil
Eingl npl Angles, Englishmen
Eingl-Gymro (-Gymry) nm Anglo-Welshman
Eingl-Sais (-Saeson) nm Anglo-Saxon
Eingl-Seisnig adj Anglo-Saxon
eil- prefix second
eilchwyl adv again
eiliad (-au) nm, nf second, moment
eiliadur (-on) nm alternator
eilio vb weave, plait; sing; second
eiliwr (-wyr) nm seconder
eilradd (-ol) adj secondary, inferior
eilrif (-au) nm even number
eilun (-od) nm image, idol
eilunaddolgar adj idolatrous
eilunaddoli vb worship idols
eilunaddolwr (-wyr) nm idolator
eilwaith adv again
eilydd (-ion) nm seconder, reserve
eillio vb shave
eilliwr (-wyr) nm shaver, barber
ein pron our
einioes nf life, lifetime
einion (-au) nf anvil
eira nm snow
eirchion see **arch**
eirias adj burning, glowing, fiery
eirin npl (nf **-en**) plums; **eirin gwlanog** peaches; **eirin duon** damsons; **eirin duon bach** sloes; **eirin Mair** gooseberries

eiriol vb plead, pray, intercede
eiriolaeth nf intercession
eiriolwr (-wyr) nm intercessor, mediator
eirlaw nm sleet
eirlin (-iau) nm snow line
eirlithrad (-au) nm avalanche
eirlys (-iau) nm snowdrop
eironi nm irony
eisen (ais) nf rib; lath
eisglwyf nm pleurisy
eisiau nm want, need, lack
eisin coll n bran, husk
eising nm icing
eisio vb ice
eisoes adv already
eistedd vb sit, seat
eisteddfa (-oedd, -fâu) nf seat
eisteddfod (-au) nf session; eisteddfod
eisteddfodol adj eisteddfodic
eisteddfodwr (-wyr) nm frequenter of eisteddfodau
eisteddfota vb frequent eisteddfodau
eisteddiad (-au) nm sitting, session
eisteddle (-oedd) nm seat, sitting, pew
eitem (-au) nf item
eithaf (-ion) adj, nm extreme; superlative ▷ adv very, quite
eithafbwynt (-iau) nm extremity; apogee
eithafiaeth nf extremism
eithafion npl extremes, extremities
eithafol adj extreme; extremist
eithafwr (-wyr) nm extremist
eithin npl (nf **-en**) furze, gorse
eithinog adj furzy
eithr prep except; besides ▷ conj but
eithriad (-au) nm exception
eithriadol adj exceptional
eithrio vb except, exclude
elastig adj, nm elastic

elastigedd nm elasticity
electromagneteg nf, nm electromagnetism
electromedr (-au) nm electrometer
electron (-au) nm electron
electroneg nf, nm electronics
electronig adj electronic
elegeiog adj elegiac, mournful
eleni adv this year
elfen (-nau) nf element
elfennig adj elemental
elfennol adj elementary
eli (elïoedd) nm ointment, salve
elifiant (-nnau) nm effluence
elifyn (elifion) nm effluent
eliffant (-od, -iaid) nm elephant
eliffantaidd adj elephantine
elin (-au, -oedd) nf elbow; angle, bend
elips (-au) nm ellipse
eliptig adj elliptical
elor (-au) nf bier
elusen (-nau) nf alms
elusendy (-dai) nm almshouse
elusengar adj charitable, benevolent
elusengarwch nm charity, benevolence
elusennol adj eleemosynary
elusennwr (-enwyr) nm almoner
elw nm possession, gain, profit
elwa vb gain, profit
elwlen (-wlod) nf kidney
ellyll (-on) nm fiend; goblin
ellyllaidd adj fiendish; elfish
ellylles (-au) nf fury, she-goblin
ellyn (-au, -od) nm razor
embryo nm embryo
embryoleg nf embryology
emosiwn (-iynau) nm emotion
emosiynol adj emotional
empeiraeth nf empiricism
empeiraidd adj empirical

empirig *adj* empirical
emrallt *nm* emerald
emyn (-au) *nm* hymn
emyn-dôn (-au) *nf* hymn-tune
emyniadur (-on) *nm* hymnal
emynwr (-wyr) *nm* hymnist
emynydd (-ion, -wyr) hymnist
emynyddiaeth *nf* hymnody, hymnology
enaid (eneidiau) *nm* life, soul
enamel (-au) *nm* enamel
enamlio *vb* enamel
enbyd, enbydus *adj* dangerous, perilous
enbydrwydd *nm* peril, danger, jeopardy
encil (-ion) *nm* retreat, flight
encilfa (-feydd) *nf* retreat
enciliad (-au) *nm* retreat; desertion
encilio *vb* retreat; desert
enciliwr (-wyr) *nm* retreater; deserter
enclitig *adj* enclitic
encôr *nm* encore
encyd *nm* space; while
enchwythu *vb* inflate
endemig *adj* endemic
endid *nm* entity, existence
endothermig *adj* endothermic
eneidiog *adj* animate
eneidiol *adj* animate, living
eneiniad (-au) *nm* anointing, unction
eneinio *vb* anoint
Eneiniog *nm* The Messiah, Christ
eneiniog *adj, nm* anointed
enfawr *adj* enormous, huge, immense
enfys (-au) *nf* rainbow
engiriol *adj* nefarious, cruel, terrible
engrafiad (-au) *nm* engraving
engrafu *vb* engrave
enhuddo *see* **anhuddo**

enigma *nm* enigma
enigmatig *adj* enigmatic
enillfawr *adj* lucrative, remunerative
enillgar *adj* gainful; winsome
enillion *npl* profits, earnings
enillwr, enillydd (enillwyr) *nm* gainer, winner
enllib (-ion, -iau) *nm* slander, libel
enllibaidd *adj* slanderous, libellous
enllibio *vb* slander, libel
enllibiwr (-wyr) *nm* slanderer, libeller
enllibus *adj* slanderous, libellous
enllyn *nm* relish eaten with bread
ennaint (eneiniau) *nm* ointment
ennill *vb* gain, win; earn ▷ *nm* **(enillion)** gain, profit; (*pl*) earnings; **ennill pwysau** put on weight
ennyd *nm, nf* while, moment
ennyn *vb* kindle, burn, inflame; excite
ensyniad (-au) *nm* insinuation
ensynio *vb* insinuate
entrych (-ion) *nm* firmament, height, zenith
enw (-au) *nm* name; noun; **enw bedydd** first name, Christian name
enwad (-au) *nm* denomination, sect
enwadaeth *nf* sectarianism
enwadol *adj* sectarian; nominative
enwadwr (-wyr) *nm* sectarian, sectary
enwaediad *nm* circumcision
enwaedu *vb* circumcise
enwebai (-eion) *nm* nominee
enwebiad (-au) *nm* nomination
enwebu *vb* nominate
enwedig *adj:* **yn enwedig** particularly, especially
enwi *vb* name
enwog (-ion) *adj* famous, renowned, noted
enwogi *vb* make famous

enwogrwydd *nm* fame, renown
enwol *adj* nominal, nominative
enwyn *nm*: **llaeth enwyn**
buttermilk
enynfa *nf* inflammation; itching
enyniad (-au) *nm* inflammation
enynnol *adj* inflammatory;
inflamed
eofn *adj* fearless, bold
eog (-iaid) *nm* salmon
eos (-au) *nf* nightingale
eosaidd *adj* like a nightingale
epa (-od) *nm* ape, monkey
epidemig *adj*, *nm* epidemic
epig *nf* epic
epiglotis (-au) *nm* epiglottis
epigram (-au) *nm* epigram
epil *nm* offspring, brood
epilepsi *nm* epilepsy
epilgar *adj* prolific, teeming
epiliad (-au) *nm* reproduction
epilio *vb* bring forth, teem, breed
epilog *nm* epilogue
episeicloid (-au) *nm* epicycloid
epistol (-au) *nm* epistle
eples *nm* leaven, ferment
eplesiad *nm* fermentation
eplesu *vb* leaven, ferment
er *prep* for, in order to; since ▷ *conj*
though
eraill *see* **arall**
erbyn *vb* receive, meet ▷ *prep*
against, by
erch *adj* speckled; frightful
erchi *vb* ask, pray, command,
demand
erchwyn (-ion) *nm* side, bed-side
erchyll *adj* hideous, horrible
erchyllter (-au) *nm* atrocity
erchylltod, erchylltra *nm*
hideousness, horror
eres *adj* wonderful, strange
erestyn *nm* minstrel, buffoon

erfin *npl* (*nf*-**en**) turnips
erfyn *vb* beg, pray, implore, expect
erfyniad (-au) *nm* prayer, petition
ergyd (-ion) *nm*, *nf* blow, stroke;
shot; cast
ergydio *vb* strike; throw, cast
ergydiwr (-wyr) *nm* striker
erial (-au) *nm* aerial
erioed *adv* ever
erledigaeth (-au) *nf* persecution
erlid *vb* persecute ▷ *nm* (**-iau**)
persecution
erlidiwr (-wyr) *nm* persecutor
erlyn *vb* pursue, prosecute
erlyniad *nm* prosecution
erlynydd (-ion) *nm* prosecutor
ern, ernes (-au) *nf* earnest, pledge,
deposit
ers *prep* since
erthwch *nm* grunt, pant
erthygl (-au) *nf* article
erthyl (-od) *nm* abortion
erthylaidd *adj* abortive
erthyliad (-au) *nm* abortion,
miscarriage
erthylu *vb* abort, miscarry
erw (-au) *nf* acre
erwain *npl* meadow-sweet
erwydd *npl* stave (*in music*)
erydiad (-au) *nm* erosion
erydol *adj* erosive
erydu *vb* erode
erydydd (-ion) *nm* erosive agent
eryr (-od) *nm* eagle; shingles
eryraidd *adj* eagle-like, aquiline
esblygiad (-au) *nm* evolution
esblygiadaeth *nf* evolutionism
esboniad (-au) *nm* explanation;
commentary
esboniadaeth *nf* exposition,
exegesis
esboniadol *adj* expository,
explanatory

esbonio vb explain, expound
esboniwr (-wyr) nm expositor, commentator
esbonydd (-ion) nm exponent
esbonyddol adj exponential
escaladur (-on) nm escalator
esgair (-eiriau) nf shank, leg; ridge
esgeirlwm adj exposed, wind-swept
esgeulus adj neglectful, negligent
esgeuluso vb neglect
esgeulustod, esgeulustra nm negligence
esgid (-iau) nf boot, shoe; **esgidiau ymarfer** trainers
esgob (-ion) nm bishop
esgobaeth (-au) nf bishopric, see, diocese
esgobyddiaeth nf episcopalianism
esgoli vb escalate
esgor vb bring forth, bear
esgud adj quick, swift, active
esgus (-ion, -odion) nm excuse, pretext
esgusodi vb excuse
esgusodol adj excusable, excused
esgymun adj execrable, excommunicate
esgymuno vb excommunicate
esgyn vb ascend, rise; take off
esgynbren (-nau) nm perch
esgynfa (-feydd) nf ascent, rise
esgynfaen nm horse-block
esgyniad nm ascension
esgynneb (esgynebau) nf climax
esgynnol adj ascending
esgyrn see **asgwrn**
esgyrnog adj bony
esiampl (-au) nf example
esmwyth adj soft, smooth; easy
esmwythâd nm ease, relief
esmwytháu vb soothe, ease
esmwythder, esmwuthdra nm ease

esmwytho, esmwytháu vb ease, soothe, soften
esmwythyd nm ease, luxury
estron (-iaid) nm foreigner, alien
estron adj foreign, strange, alien
estrones (-au) nf alien woman
estronol adj strange, foreign, alien
estrys (-od) nm, nf ostrich
estyll npl (nf **-en**) planks, boards
estyn vb extend, reach; stretch; prolong
estynadwy adj extensible
estyniad nm extension, prolongation
estheteg nm, nf aesthetics
esthetig adj aesthetic
etifedd (-ion) nm heir, inheritor
etifeddeg nm, nf heredity
etifeddes (-au) nf heiress
etifeddiaeth (-au) nf inheritance
etifeddol adj hereditary
etifeddu vb inherit
eto conj yet, still ▷ adv again; yet, still
ether nm ether
ethnig nm ethnic
ethnoleg nf ethnology
ethol vb elect
etholaeth (-au) nf constituency
etholedig (-ion) adj elect
etholedigaeth nf election (theology)
etholiad (-au) nm election
etholiadol adj electoral, elective
etholwr (-wyr) nm elector, voter
ethos nm ethos
eu pron their
euog adj guilty
euogrwydd nm guiltiness, guilt
euraid, euraidd adj golden, (of) gold
euro vb apply or bestow gold; gild
eurych (-od) nm goldsmith
ewig (-od) nf hind

ewin (**-edd**) *nm, nf* nail, talon, claw; hoof
ewino *vb* claw
ewinog *adj* having nails or claws
ewinrhew *nf* frost-bite
ewro (**-aid, -s**) *nm* euro
Ewrop *nf* Europe
Ewropead (**-aid**) *nm* European
Ewropeaidd *adj* European
ewyllys (**-iau**) *nf* will
ewyllysio *vb* will, wish
ewyn *nm* foam, froth, surf
ewynnog *adj* foaming, foamy, frothy
ewynnu *vb* foam, froth
ewythr (**-edd**) *nm* uncle

fagddu *nf*: **y fagddu** gross darkness
falf (**-iau**) *nf* valve
fan (**-iau**) *nf* van
fandal (**-iaid**) *nm* vandal
fandaleiddio *vb* vandalize
fandaliaeth *nf* vandalism
farnais (**-eisiau**) *nm* varnish
farneisio *vb* varnish
fe *pron* he, him ▷ preverbal particle
feallai *adv* perhaps, peradventure
fegan (**-iaid**) *nm, nf* vegan
feganaidd *adj* vegan
fel *adv, conj, prep* so, as, that, thus, like; how; **fel arall** otherwise; **fel arfer, fel rheol** usually
felly *adv* so, thus
festri (**-ïoedd**) *nf* vestry
ficer (**-iaid**) *nm* vicar
ficerdy (**-dai**) *nm* vicarage
fideo (**-s**) *nm, nf* video; **gêm fideo** video game

figan (**-iaid**) *nm, nf* vegan
figanaidd *adj* vegan
finegr *nm* vinegar
fiola (**-s**) *nf* viola
firws (**-au, fira**) *nm* virus
fitamin (**-au**) *nm* vitamin
folt (**-iau**) *nf* volt
foltamedr (**-au**) *nm* voltameter
foltedd (**-au**) *nm* voltage
foltmedr (**-au**) *nm* voltmeter
fortais (**-eisiau**) *nm* vortex
fory (**yfory**) *adv* tomorrow
fry *adv* above, aloft
fwltur (**-iaid**) *nm* vulture
fy *pron* my
fyny *adv* up, upwards

ff

ffa *npl* (*nf* **ffäen**, *nf* **ffeuen**) beans; **ffa'r gors** buckbeans; **ffa pob** baked beans
ffabrigo *vb* fabricate
ffacbys *npl* fitches, vetches
ffacbysen (**ffacbys**) *nf* chickpea
ffactor (**-au**) *nm, nf* factor; **fffactor cyffredin mwyaf** highest common factor; **fffactor cysefin** prime factor
ffactori, -o *vb* factorize
ffactri (**-ïoedd**) *nf* factory, mill
ffaeledig *adj* fallible, ailing
ffaeledigrwydd *nm* fallibility
ffaeledd (**-au**) *nm* failing, defect
ffaelu *vb* fail
ffafr (**-au**) *nf* favour
ffafraeth *nf* favouritism
ffafrio *vb* favour
ffafriol *adj* favourable
ffagl (**-au**) *nf* blaze, flame; torch
ffair (**ffeiriau**) *nf* fair, exchange; **ffair sborion** jumble sale

ffaith (**ffeithiau**) *nf* fact
ffald (**-au**) *nf* fold; pound
ffals (**ffeilsion**) *adj* false, deceitful
ffalsedd *nm* falsehood, deceit
ffalster *nm* deceitfulness, cunning
ffalwm *nm* whitlow
ffan (**-nau**) *nf* fan
ffanatig *nm* fanatic
ffanatigiaeth *nf* fanaticism
ffansi *nf* fancy
ffansïo *vb* fancy
ffansïol *adj* fanciful
ffantasi, ffantasia (**-ïau**) *nf, nm* fantasy
ffarm (**ffermydd**) *nf* farm
ffarmio *vb* farm
ffarmwr (**ffermwyr**) *nm* farmer
ffarmwraig (**-wragedd**) *nf* farmer
ffârs (**-iau**) *nf* farce
ffarwél *nf* farewell
ffarwelio *vb* bid farewell
ffas (**-ys, -au**) *nf* face, coal-face
ffasâd (**ffasadau**) *nm* facade
ffasiwn (**-iynau**) *nm* fashion
ffasiynol *adj* fashionable
ffasner (**-i**) *nm* fastener
ffasnin (**-au**) *nm* fastening
ffasno *vb* fasten
ffasnydd (**-ion**) *nm* fastener
ffatri (**-ïoedd**) *nf* factory, mill
ffatrïaeth *nf* manufacturing
ffau (**ffeuau**) *nf* den
ffawd (**ffodion**) *nf* fortune, fate
ffawdheglu *vb* hitch-hike
ffawdheglwr (**-wyr**) *nm* hitch-hiker
ffawna *nf* fauna
ffawydd *npl* (*nf*-**en**) beech trees
ffederal *adj* federal
ffederaliaeth *nf* federalism
ffederasiwn (**-iynau**) *nm* federation
ffedereiddio, ffedreiddio *vb* federate
ffefryn (**-nau**) *nm* favourite

ffeil *nf* file; **ffeil sip** zip file
ffein, ffeind *adj* fine
ffeirio *vb* barter, exchange
ffelt *nm* felt
ffelwm *nm* whitlow
ffemwr (**ffemora**) *nm* femur
ffendir *nm* fenland
ffenestr (**-i**) *nf* window; **ffenestri dwbl** double glazing
ffenigl *nm* fennel
ffenomen (**-au**) *nf* phenomenon
ffens (**-ys**) *nf* fence
ffensio *vb* fence
ffêr (**fferau**) *nf* ankle
fferdod *nm* numbness
fferi (**-ïau**) *nf* ferry
fferins *npl* sweets
fferm (**-ydd**) *nf* farm
ffermdy (**-dai**) *nm* farm-house
ffermio *vb* farm
ffermwr (**-wyr**) *nm* farmer
fferru *vb* congeal, freeze; perish with cold
fferyllfa (**-feydd**) *nf* dispensary
fferylliaeth *nf* pharmacy
fferyllol *adj* chemical, pharmaceutical
fferyllydd (**-wyr**) *nm* chemist, pharmacist
ffesant (**-s, -au**) *nm* pheasant
ffest *adj* fast
ffest *nf* feast
ffetan (**-au**) *nf* sack, bag
ffi (**-oedd**) *nf* fee
ffiaidd *adj* loathsome, abominable
ffibr (**-au**) *nm* fibre
ffibrog, -us *adj* fibrous
Ffichtiad (**-iaid**) *nm* Pict
ffidil (**ffidlau**) *nf* fiddle
ffidlan *vb* fiddle, dawdle
ffidler (**-iaid**) *nm* fiddler
ffidlo *vb* fiddle
ffieiddbeth (**-au**) *nm* abomination

ffieidd-dra *nm* abomination
ffieiddio *vb* loathe, abominate, abhor
ffigur (-au) *nf* figure, type
ffigurol *adj* figurative
ffigys *npl (nf-***en)** figs
ffigysbren (-nau) *nm* fig-tree
ffiled (-au, -i) *nf* fillet
ffilharmonig *adj* philharmonic
ffilm (-iau) *nf* film
ffilmio *vb* film
ffiloreg *nf* rigmarole, nonsense
ffilter (-au, -i) *nm* filter
ffin (-iau) *nf* boundary, limit
Ffindir *nf*: **y Ffindir** Finland
ffindir (-oedd) *nm* borderland
ffinio *vb* border (upon), abut
ffiniol *adj* bordering
ffiol (-au) *nf* vial; cup
ffiseg *nm* physics
ffisegol *adj* physical
ffisegwr (-wyr) *nm* physicist
ffisig *nm* physic, medicine
ffisigwr (-wyr) *nm* physician
ffisigwriaeth *nm* physic, medicine
ffisioleg *nf, nm* physiology
ffit *adj* fit ▷ *nf* **(-iau)** fit, paroxysm
ffit-ffatio *vb* flip-flop
ffitrwydd *nm* fitness
ffiwdal *adj* feudal
ffiwg (-iau) *nf* fugue
ffiws (-iau) *nm* fuse
ffiwsio *vb* fuse
fflach (-iau) *nf*, **fflachiad (-au)** *nm* flash
fflachio *vb* flash
fflachiog *adj* flashing
fflag (-iau) *nf* flag
fflagen (-ni) *nf* flagon, flag-stone
fflangell (-au) *nf* scourge
fflangelliad (-au) *nm* flagellation
fflangellu *vb* scourge, whip, flog
fflam (-au) *nf* flame
fflamadwy *adj* (in)flammable

fflamio *vb* flame, blaze
fflamllyd *adj* flaming, blazing
fflan (-iau) *nm* flan
fflap (-iau) *nm* flap
fflasg (-iau) *nf* flask, basket
fflat *adj* flat ▷ *nm* **(-iau)** flat-iron ▷ *nf* **(-au, -iau)** a flat
fflatio *vb* flat, flatten
fflatwadn *adj* flatfooted
fflecs (-ys) *nm* flex
fflêm, fflem *nf* phlegm
fflint *nm* flint
ffliwt (-iau) *nf* flute
ffloch (-au) *nm* floe; **ffloch iâ** ice floe
fflodiad, -iart *nf* floodgate
ffo *nm* flight
ffoadur (-iaid) *nm* fugitive, refugee
ffodus *adj* fortunate, lucky
fföedigaeth *nf* flight
ffoi *vb* flee, run away
ffôl *adj* foolish, silly ▷ *nf* **(ffols)** fall (in a slate quarry)
ffoledd *nm* foolishness, folly, fatuity
ffolen (-nau) *nf* buttock
ffoli *vb* infatuate, dote; fool
ffolineb *nm* foolishness, folly
ffon (ffyn) *nf* stick, staff
ffôn (ffonau) *nm* phone; **ffonau clust** headphones; **ffôn camera** camera phone; **ffôn symudol** mobile phone
ffonnod (ffonodiau) *nf* stroke, blow, stripe
ffonodio *vb* cudgel, beat
fforc (ffyrc) *nf* (table) fork
fforch (-au, ffyrch) *nf* fork
fforchi *vb* fork
fforchog *adj* forked, cleft, cloven
ffordd (ffyrdd) *nf* way, road; distance
fforddio *vb* afford
fforddol (-ion) *nm* wayfarer, passer-by

fforest (**-ydd, -au**) *nf* forest; **fforest law** rainforest

fforffedu *vb* forfeit

ffortiwn (**-iynau**), **-un** (**-au**) *nf* fortune

fforwm (**-ymau**) *nm* forum

ffos (**-ydd**) *nf* ditch, trench

ffosffad (**-au**) *nm* phosphate

ffosil (**-au**) *nm* fossil

ffracsiwn (**-iynau**) *nm* fraction

ffrae (**-au**) *nf* quarrel

ffraeo *vb* quarrel

ffraeth *adj* fluent; witty, facetious

ffraetheb (**-ion**) *nf* joke, witticism

ffraethineb *nm* wit, facetiousness

Ffrangeg *nf* French (language)

Ffrainc *nf* France

ffrâm (**fframiau**) *nf* frame

fframio *vb* frame

fframwaith *nm* framework

Ffrances (**-au**) *nf* Frenchwoman

Ffrancwr (**-wyr, Ffrancod**) *nm* Frenchman

Ffrengig *adj* French; **llygod fffrengig** rats

ffres *adj* fresh

ffresgo (**-au**) *nm* fresco

ffresni *nm* freshness

ffretwaith *nm* fretwork

ffreutur *nf* refectory

ffrewyll (**-au**) *nf* whip, scourge

ffridd (**-oedd**) *nf* mountain pasture

ffrimpan (**-au**) *nf* frying pan

ffrind (**-iau**) *nm* friend

ffrio *vb* fry; hiss

ffrîs (**-iau**) *nf* frieze

ffrit (**-iau**) *nm* frit, flop ▷ *adj* worthless, unsubstantial

ffrith (**-oedd**) *nf* mountain pasture

ffrithiant (**-nnau**) *nm* friction

ffroch, ffrochwyllt *adj* furious

ffroen (**-au**) *nf* nostril; muzzle (of gun)

ffroenell (**-au**) *nf* nozzle

ffroeni *vb* snort, snuff, sniff

ffroenuchel *adj* haughty, disdainful

ffroes *npl* (*nf*-**en**) pancakes

ffrog (**-iau**) *nf* frock

ffrom *adj* angry, irascible, testy, touchy

ffromi *vb* fume, chafe, rage

ffrostgar *adj* boastful

ffrwd (**ffrydiau**) *nf* stream, torrent

ffrwgwd (**ffrygydau**) *nm* squabble

ffrwst *nm* hurry, haste, bustle

ffrwtian *vb* splutter

ffrwydriad (**-au**) *nm* explosion

ffrwydro *vb* explode

ffrwydrol *adj* explosive

ffrwydryn (**-nau, ffrwydron**) *nm* mine, explosive

ffrwyn (**-au**) *nf* bridle

ffrwyno *vb* bridle, curb

ffrwyth (**-au, -ydd**) *nm* fruit; vigour, use

ffrwythlon *adj* fruitful, fertile

ffrwythlondeb, -der *nm* fruitfulness, fertility

ffrwythloni *vb* become fruitful; fertilize

ffrwytho *vb* bear fruit

ffrydio *vb* stream, gush

ffrydlif *nm, nf* stream, flood, torrent

ffug *adj* fictitious, false, sham ▷ *nm* (**-ion**) fiction, sham

ffug-bas (**-ys**) *nf* dummy (pass)

ffugbasio *vb* dummy

ffugenw (**-au**) *nm* pseudonym

ffugiad (**-au**) *nm* forgery

ffugio *vb* feign; forge

ffugiwr (**-wyr**) *nm* impostor; forger

ffuglen *nf* fiction; **ffuglen wyddonol** science fiction

ffugliw (**-iau**) *nm* camouflage

ffugliwio *vb* camouflage

ffunud *nm* form, manner; **yr un ffunud â** exactly like

ffured (-au) *nf* ferret
ffureta *vb* ferret
ffurf (-iau) *nf* form, shape
ffurfafen *nf* firmament, sky
ffurfdro (-eon) *nm* inflection
ffurfeb (-au) *nf* formula
ffurfiad (-au) *nm* formation
ffurfiant (-nnau) *nm* accidence; formation
ffurfio *vb* form
ffurfiol *adj* formal
ffurfiolaeth *nf* formalism
ffurfioldeb *nm* formality, formalism
ffurflen (-ni) *nf* form (to fill); **ffurflen gais** application form
ffurflin (-iau) *nm* formline
ffurfwasanaeth (-au) *nm* liturgy
ffurfwedd (-au) *nf* configuration
ffust (-iau) *nf* flail
ffustio, -o *vb* beat
ffwdan *nf* fuss, bustle, flurry
ffwdanllyd *adj* fussy, bustling
ffwdanu *vb* fuss, bustle
ffwdanus *adj* fussy, fidgety, flurried
ffwng (ffyngoedd, ffyngau) *nm* fungus
ffwngleiddiad (-au) *nm* fungicide
ffŵl (ffyliaid) *nm* fool
ffwlbart (-iaid) *nm* polecat
ffwlbri *nm* fudge, nonsense, tomfoolery
ffwlcyn *nm* fool, nincompoop
ffwndro *vb* founder, become confused
ffwndrus *adj* confused, bewildered
ffwndwr *nm* confusion, hurly-burly
ffwr *nm* fur
ffwrdd *nm* way; **i ffwrdd** away
ffwrn (ffyrnau) *nf* furnace, oven
ffwrnais (-eisiau) *nf* furnace
ffwrwm (ffyrymau) *nf* form, bench
ffydd *nf* faith
ffyddiog *adj* strong in faith, trustful

ffyddlon *adj* faithful
ffyddlondeb *nm* faithfulness, fidelity
ffyddloniaid *npl* faithful ones
ffynhonnell (ffynonellau) *nf* fount, source
ffyniannus *adj* prosperous
ffyniant *nm* prosperity
ffynidwydd *npl* (*nf*-**en**) fir-trees, pine-trees
ffynnon (ffynhonnau) *nf* fountain, well, spring
ffynnu *vb* prosper, thrive
ffyrf (fffferf) *adj* thick, stout
ffyrfder *nm* thickness, stoutness
ffyrling (-au, -od) *nf* farthing
ffyrnig *adj* fierce, savage, ferocious
ffyrnigo *vb* grow fierce; enrage
ffyrnigrwydd *nm* fierceness, ferocity

ff

g

gadael, gadu *vb* leave, forsake; let, allow

gaeaf (-au, -oedd) *nm* winter

gaeafaidd, gaeafol *adj* wintry

gaeafu *vb* winter, hibernate

gafael, gafaelyd *vb* hold, grasp ▷ *nf* (gafaelion) hold, grasp

gafaelgar *adj* gripping, tenacious

gafl (-au, geifl) *nf* fork, groin

gafr (geifr) *nf* goat; yr Afr Capricorn

gafrewig (-od) *nf* gazelle, antelope

gagendor *see* agendor

gaing (geingau) *nf* chisel; gaing gau gouge

gair (geiriau) *nm* word

galanas (-au) *nf* murder, massacre

galanastra *nm* slaughter; mess

galar *nm* mourning, grief, sorrow

galarnad (-au) *nf* lamentation

galarnadu *vb* bewail, lament

galaru *vb* mourn, grieve, lament

galarus *adj* mournful, lamentable, sad

galarwr (-wyr) *nm* mourner

galw *vb* call ▷ *nm* call, demand

galwad (-au) *nm, nf* call, demand

galwedigaeth (-au) *nf* occupation, vocation, calling

galwedigaethol *adj* vocational

galwyn (-i) *nm* gallon

gallt (gelltydd) *nf* wooded slope; hill, rise

gallu *vb* be able ▷ *nm* (-oedd) power, ability

galluog *adj* able, powerful, mighty

galluogi *vb* enable, empower

gan *prep* with, by; of, from

gar (-rau) *nf, nm* thigh, shank

garan (-od) *nf* heron, crane

Garawys *nm* Lent

gardas, gardys (gardysau) *nm, nf* garter

gardd (gerddi) *nf* garden; garth, yard

garddio *vb* garden ▷ *nm* gardening

garddwr (-wyr) *nm* gardener

garddwriaeth *nf* horticulture

gargam *adj* knock-kneed

garlant (-au) *nm* garland

garlleg *npl* (*nf*-en) garlic

gartref *adv* at home (*mutation of* cartref)

garth *nm* hill; enclosure

garw (geirwon) *adj* coarse, rough, harsh

garwedd *nm* roughness

garwhau *vb* roughen; ruffle

gast (geist) *nf* bitch

gau *adj* false; hollow

gefail (-eiliau) *nf* smithy

gefel (-eiliau) *nf* tongs, pincers

gefell (-eilliaid) *n* twin; yr Efeilliaid Gemini

gefelldref (-i) *nf* twinned town

gefyn (-nau) *nm* fetter, shackle
gefynnu *vb* fetter, shackle
geingio *vb* chisel, gouge
geilwad (-waid) *nm* caller
geirbrosesu *n* word processing
geirfa (-oedd) *nf* vocabulary, glossary
geiriad *nm* wording, phraseology
geiriadur (-on) *nm* dictionary, lexicon
geiriadurol *adj* lexicographical
geiriadurwr (-wyr) *nm* lexicographer
geirio *vb* word, phrase
geirlyfr (-au) *nm* word-book, dictionary
geirwir *adj* truthful, truth-speaking
geirwiredd *nm* truthfulness
gel (-iau) *nm*, *nf* gel; **gel cawod** shower gel
gelau, gelen (gelod) *nf* leech
gelyn (-ion) *nm* foe, enemy
gelyniaeth *nf* enmity, hostility
gelyniaethus *adj* hostile, inimical
gelynol *adj* hostile, adverse
gellyg *npl* (*nf*-**en**) pears
gem (-au) *nf* gem, jewel
gêm (gêmau, gemau) *nf* game; **gêm cyfrifiadur** computer game; **gêm fideo** video game
gemog *adj* gemmed, jewelled
gemydd (-ion) *nm* jeweller
gên *nf* jaw, chin
genau (-euau) *nm* mouth, orifice
genau-goeg, geneuoeg (-ion) *nf* lizard; newt
genedigaeth (-au) *nf* birth
genedigol *adj* native
Genefa *nf* Geneva
geneth (-od) *nf* girl
genethaidd *adj* girlish
genethig *nf* little girl, maiden
geni *vb* be born
genni *vb* be contained

genwair (-eiriau) *nf* fishing-rod
genweirio *vb* angle, fish
genweiriwr (-wyr) *nm* angler
genyn (-nau) *nm* gene
ger *prep* by, near
gêr *coll n* gear, tackle
gerbron *prep* before (*place*); in the presence of
gerfydd *prep* by
geri *nm* bile, gall; **geri marwol** cholera
geriach *coll n* gear, odds and ends
gerllaw *prep* near ▷ *adv* at hand
gerwin *adj* rough, severe, harsh
gerwindeb, gerwinder *nm* roughness, severity
gerwino *vb* roughen
gewyn (-nau, giau) *nm* sinew, tendon
gewynnog *adj* sinewy
Ghana *nf* Ghana
gïach (-od) *nm* snipe
Gibraltar *n* Gibraltar
gieuwst *nf* neuralgia
gig (-iau) *nm* gig (*concert*)
gildio *vb* yield; gild
gilydd *nm*: **ei gilydd** each other **gyda'i gilydd** together
gimbill *nf* gimlet
gitarydd (-ion) *nm*, *nf* guitarist
glafoerio *vb* drivel, slobber
glafoerion *npl* drivel, slobber
glaif, gleifiau *nm* lance, sword, glaive
glain (gleiniau) *nm* gem, jewel; bead
glan (-nau, glennydd) *nf* bank, shore
glân *adj* clean; holy; fair, beautiful
glanhad *nm* cleansing, purification
glanhaol *adj* cleansing, purging
glanhau *vb* cleanse, purify
glaniad *nm* landing, disembarkation

g

glanio vb land, disembark
glanwaith adj clean, tidy
glanweithdra nm cleanliness
glas (gleision) adj blue, green, grey, silver ▷ nm blue
glasgoch adj, nm purple
glaslanc (-iau) nm youth, stripling
glasog (-au) nf crop, gizzard
glastwr nm milk and water
glastwraidd adj watered down, feeble; muddled
glasu vb become blue, green or grey; turn pale
glaswellt coll n grass
glaswelltyn nm blade of grass; tigridia
glaw (-ogydd) nm rain
glawiad (-au) nm rainfall
glawio vb rain
glawlen (-ni) nf umbrella
glawog adj rainy
gleisiad (-iaid) nm sewin
gleision npl whey
glendid nm cleanness; fairness; beauty
glesni nm blueness, verdure
glew (-ion) adj brave, daring; astute
glewdra, glewder nm courage, resource
glin (-iau) nm knee
gliniadur (-on) nm laptop, laptop computer
glo nm coal
globaleiddio nm globalization
gloddest (-au) nm carousal, revelling
gloddesta vb carouse, revel
gloddestwr (-wyr) nm reveller
gloes (-au, -ion) nf pang; qualm
glofa (-feydd) nf colliery
glöwr (-wyr) nm collier
glowty (-tai) nm cow-house, shippon

glöyn nm coal; **glöyn byw** butterfly
gloyw (-on) adj bright, clear; shiny, glossy
gloywder nm brightness, clearness
gloywi vb brighten, polish
glud (-ion) nm glue; bird-lime
gludio vb glue
gludiog adj sticky
glwth (glythau) nm couch
glwth (glythion) adj gluttonous ▷ nm glutton
glwys adj fair; holy
glyn (-noedd) nm glen, valley
glynu vb stick, adhere, cleave
glythineb, glythni nm gluttony
glythinebu, glythu vb glut, gormandize
go adv rather, somewhat
goachul adj lean; puny; sickly, poorly
gobaith (-eithion) nm hope
gobeithio vb hope
gobeithiol adj hopeful
gobeithlu (-oedd) nm Band of Hope
gobennydd (-enyddiau) nm bolster, pillow
goblygu vb fold, wrap
gochel see **gochelyd**
gocheladwy adj avoidable
gochelgar adj wary, cautious
gocheliad nm avoidance; **ar ei ocheliad** on his guard
gochelyd vb avoid, shun
godidog adj excellent, splendid
godidowgrwydd nm excellence
godineb nm adultery
godinebu vb commit adultery
godinebus adj adulterous
godinebwr (-wyr) nm adulterer
godre (-on) nm skirt, border, edge
godriad (-au) nm milking
godro vb milk
goddaith (-eithiau) nf fire, bonfire

goddef *vb* bear, suffer, allow, permit
goddefgar *adj* forbearing, tolerant
goddefgarwch *nm* forbearance, tolerance
goddefiad (-au) *nm* licence; toleration
goddefol *adj* tolerable; passive
goddiweddyd, goddiwes *vb* over-take
goddrych *nm* subject (*in grammar*)
goddrychol *adj* subjective
gof (-aint) *nm* smith
gofal (-on) *nm* care, charge
gofalu *vb* care, mind, take care; **gofalu am** look after
gofalus *adj* careful; **yn ofalus** carefully
gofaniaeth *nf* smith's craft
gofer (-oedd, -ydd) *nm* overflow of well; rill
gofid (-iau) *nm* grief, sorrow, trouble
gofidio *vb* afflict, grieve, vex
gofidus *adj* grievous, sad
gofod *nm* space; **llong ofod** spaceship
gofodwr (-wyr) *nm* astronaut
gofyn *vb* ask, demand, require ▷ *nm* **(-ion)** demand, requirement
gofyniad (-au) *nm* question, query
gofynnod (-ynodau) *nm* note of interrogation, question-mark
gofynnol *adj* necessary, requisite; interrogative (*pronoun etc*)
gogan *nf* defamation, satire
goganu *vb* defame, satirize, lampoon
goganwr (-wyr) *nm* satirist
goglais *vb, nm* tickle
gogledd *nm, adj* north
Gogledd Iwerddon *nf* Northern Ireland
gogleddol *adj* northern
gogleddwynt *nm* north wind
gogleddwr (-wyr) *nm* northerner; North Walian
gogleisio *vb* tickle
gogleisiol *adj* tickling, titillating, amusing
gogoneddu *vb* glorify
gogoneddus *adj* glorious
gogoniant *nm* glory
gogor (-ion) *nf* fodder, provender
gogr (-au) *nm* sieve, riddle
gogri, gogrwn, gogryn *vb* sift, riddle
gogwydd *nm* slant, inclination, bent
gogwyddiad (-au) *nm* inclination
gogwyddo *vb* incline, slope, lean
gogyfer *adj* opposite; for, by
gogyfuwch *adj, prep* of equal height
gogyhyd *adj* of equal length
gogymaint *adj* equal in size
gohebiaeth (-au) *nf* correspondence
gohebol *adj* corresponding
gohebu *vb* correspond (*by letter etc*); reply
gohebydd (-wyr) *nm* correspondent, reporter
gohiriad (-au) *nm* postponement
gohirio *vb* delay, postpone, defer, put off
golau *adj, nm, vb* light
golau-leuad *nm* moonlight
golch (-ion) *nm* wash; coating; lye
golchdy (-dai) *nm* wash-house, laundry
golchfa *nf* wash; lathering
golchi *vb* wash; coat
golchiad (-au) *nm* washing; plating, coating
golchion *npl* slops; suds
golchwr (-wyr), golchydd (-ion) *nm* washer
golchwraig (-wragedd) *nf* washerwoman

g

golchyddes (-au) nf laundress

goledd, goleddf nm slant, slope

goleddu, goleddfu vb slant, slope

goleuad (-au) nm light, luminary

goleudy (-dai) nm lighthouse

goleuni nm light

goleuo vb light, enlighten, illuminate

golosg nm coke, charcoal

golud (-oedd) nm wealth, riches

goludog adj wealthy, rich

golwg (-ygon) nf, nm sight, look; (pl) eyes

golwr (-wyr) nm goalkeeper

golwyth (-ion) nm chop, slice, cut

golygfa (-feydd) nf scene, view; (pl) scenery

golygiad (-au) nm view

golygu vb view; mean; edit

golygus adj comely, handsome

golygwedd (-au) nf feature, aspect

golygydd (-ion, -wyr) nm editor

golygyddiaeth nf editorship

golygyddol adj editorial

gollwng vb drop, release, let go; discharge; dismiss; leak; let down

gollyngdod nm release; absolution

gollyngiadau npl emissions

gomedd vb refuse

gomeddiad nm refusal, omission

gonest, onest adj honest

gonestrwydd nm honesty

gôr nm pus

gor- prefix over-, super-

goramser nm overtime

gorau (-euon) adj best; **o'r gorau** very well

gorawen nf joy, ecstasy

gorblu npl immature feathers

gorboblogi vb overpopulate

gorbwyso vb outweigh, overweigh

gorchest (-ion) nf feat, exploit

gorchestol adj excellent, masterly

gorchfygu vb overcome, conquer

gorchfygwr (-wyr) nm victor; conqueror

gorchudd (-ion) nm cover, covering, veil

gorchuddio vb cover

gorchwyl (-ion) nm task, undertaking

gorchymyn vb command ▷ nm **(gorchmynion)** command, commandment

gor-dewdra nm obesity

gordoi vb overspread, cover

gordyfu vb overgrow

gordd (gyrdd) nf sledge-hammer, mallet

gordderch (-adon) nf concubine; lover; bastard

gor-ddogn (-au) nm overdose

goresgyn vb overrun, invade; conquer

goresgyniad nm invasion; conquest

goresgynnydd nm invader; conqueror

goreuro vb gild

gorfod vb be obliged ▷ nm obligation, necessity

gorfodaeth nf obligation, compulsion

gorfodi vb oblige, compel

gorfodol adj obligatory, compulsory

gorfoledd nm joy, rejoicing, triumph

gorfoleddu vb rejoice, triumph

gorfoleddus adj jubilant, triumphant

gorffen vb finish, complete, conclude

gorffeniad nm finishing, finish

Gorffennaf nm July

gorffennol adj, nm past

gorffwyll adj mad, frenzied

gorffwyllo vb rave

gorffwyllog adj mad, insane
gorffwylltra nm madness, insanity
gorffwys vb, nm rest, repose
gorffwysfa (-oedd) nf resting-place, rest
gorffwysiad (-au) nm rest, pause
gorffwyso, gorffwystra see **gorffwys**
gorhendaid nm great-great-grandfather
gorhennain nf great-great-grandmother
gori vb hatch
gorifyny nm ascent, hill, steep climb
goris prep below, beneath, under
goriwaered nm descent, declivity
gorlawn adj superabundant; packed
gorlenwi vb overfill
gorliwio vb colour too highly, exaggerate
gorllewin nm west; **Gorllewin yr Almaen** West Germany
gorllewinol adj westerly, western
gorllewinwr (-wyr) nm westerner
gormes nm oppression, tyranny
gormesol adj oppressive, tyrannical
gormesu vb oppress, tyrannize
gormeswr (-wyr), gormesydd (-ion) nm oppressor, tyrant
gormod (-ion) nm too much, excess
gormodedd nm excess, superfluity
gormodiaith nf hyperbole, exaggeration
gormodol adj excessive
gormwyth nm catarrh
gornest, ornest (-au) contest, match
goroesi vb outlive, survive
goroesiad (-au) nm survival
goroeswr (-wyr) nm survivor
goror (-au) nm border, coast, frontier

gorsaf (-oedd) nf station; **gorsaf dân** fire station; **gorsaf fws, gorsaf fysian** bus station
gorsedd (-au) nf, **gorseddfa (-oedd)** nf, **gorseddfainc (-feinciau)** nf throne
gorseddu vb throne, enthrone, install
gorsin, gorsing (-au) nf door-post
gorthrech nm oppression; coercion
gorthrechu vb oppress; coerce
gorthrwm nm oppression
gorthrymder nm oppression, tribulation
gorthrymedig adj oppressed
gorthrymu vb oppress
gorthrymus adj oppressive
gorthrymwr (-wyr), gorthrymydd nm oppressor
goruchaf adj most high, supreme
goruchafiaeth nf supremacy; triumph
goruchel adj high, exalted
goruchwyliaeth (-au) nf over-sight, supervision; dispensation
goruchwylio vb oversee, supervise
goruchwyliwr (-wyr) nm supervisor, steward
goruwch prep above, over
goruwchnaturiol adj supernatural
goruwchreoli vb overrule
gorwedd vb lie; **gorwedd i lawr** lie down
gorweddfa (-oedd), gorweddfan (-au) nf bed, couch
gorweddian vb lounge, loll
gorweiddiog adj bedridden
gorwel (-ion) nm horizon
gorwych adj gorgeous
gorwyr (-ion) nm great-grandson
gorwyres (-au) nf great-grand-daughter

g

gorymdaith (-deithiau) *nf*
procession

gorymdeithio *vb* walk in
procession

gorynys (-oedd) *nf* peninsula

goryrru *vb* drive too fast ▷ *n*
speeding

gosber (-au) *nm* vespers

gosgedd (-au) *nm* form, figure

gosgeiddig *adj* comely, graceful

gosgordd (-ion) *nf* retinue, train,
escort

gosgorddlu (-oedd) *nm* body-guard

goslef (-au) *nf* tone, intonation

gosod *vb* put, place, set; let ▷ *adj*
false, artificial

gosodiad (-au) *nm* proposition,
statement

gosteg (-ion) *nf* silence; (*pl*) banns

gostegu *vb* silence, still, quell

gostwng *vb* lower, reduce; bow; put
down, humble

gostyngedig *adj* humble

gostyngeiddrwydd *nm* humility

gostyngiad *nm* reduction;
humiliation

gowt *nm* gout

gradell (-gredyll) *nf* griddle

gradd (-au) *nm, nf* grade, degree,
stage

graddedigion *npl* graduates

graddfa (-feydd) *nf* scale

graddio *vb* graduate

graddol *adj* gradual

graddoli *vb* grade, graduate

graean *coll n*, **greyenyn** *nm* gravel

graeanu *vb* granulate

graeanwst *nf* gravel (*complaint*)

graen *nm* grain, gloss, lustre

graenus *adj* of good grain, glossy,
sleek

graff (-iau) *nm* graph

gramadeg (-au) *nm* grammar

gramadegol *adj* grammatical

gramadegwr (-wyr),
gramadegydd *nm* grammarian

gran (-nau) *nm* cheek

gras (-au, -usau) *nm* grace

graslawn, graslon *adj* full of grace,
gracious

graslonrwydd *nm* graciousness,
grace

grasol, grasusol *adj* gracious

grât (gratiau) *nm* grate

grawn *npl* (*nm* **gronyn**) grain;
grapes; roe

grawnfwyd (-ydd) *coll n* cereal

grawnwin *npl* grapes

Grawys *nm* Lent

gre (-oedd) *nf* stud, flock

greddf (-au) *nf* instinct, intuition

greddfol *adj* instinctive, intuitive,
rooted

greddfu *vb* become ingrained

grefi *nm* gravy

gresyn *nm* pity

gresyni, gresyndod *nm* misery,
wretchedness

gresynu *vb* commiserate, pity

gresynus *adj* miserable, wretched

gridyll (-au) *nm, nf* griddle

griddfan *vb* groan, moan ▷ *nm*
(**-nau**) groan

grillian, grillio *vb* squeak, creak;
chirp; crunch

gris (-iau) *nm* step, stair

grisial *nm* crystal

grisialaidd *adj* crystal, crystalline

gro *coll n* (*nm* **grôyn**) gravel, pebbles

Groeg *nf* Greek language; Greece
▷ *adj* Greek

Groegaidd *adj* Grecian, Greek

Groeges (-au) *nf* Greek woman

Groegwr (-wyr, -iaid) *nm* Greek

gronell (-au) *nf* roe

Grønland *nf* Greenland

gronyn (-nau) *nm* grain, particle; while

grot (-iau) *nm* groat, fourpence

grual *nm* gruel

grud *nm* grit

grudd (-iau) *nf* cheek

gruddfan *see* **griddfan**

grug *nm* heather

grugiar (-ieir) *nf* moor-hen, grouse

grugog *adj* heathery

grwgnach *vb* grumble, murmur

grwgnachlyd *adj* given to grumbling

grwgnachwr (-wyr) *nm* grumbler

grwn (grynnau) *nm* ridge (*in* ploughing)

grŵn, grwndi *nm* purr

grwnan *vb* croon, purr

grwndwal (-au) *nm* foundation

grydian *vb* murmur; grunt

grym (-oedd) *nm* force, power, might

grymial *vb* mutter, murmur, grumble

grymus *adj* strong, powerful, mighty

grymuso *vb* strengthen

grymuster, grymustra *nm* power, might

gwacáu *vb* empty

gwacsaw *adj* trivial, frivolous

gwacsawrwydd *nm* levity, vanity

gwacter *nm* emptiness, vacuity

gwachul *see* **goachul**

gwad, gwadiad *nm* denial, disavowal

gwadn (-au) *nm* sole

gwadnu *vb* sole; foot it

gwadu *vb* deny, disown; renounce, forsake

gwadwr (-wyr) *nm* denier

gwadd (-od) *nf* mole

gwadd *see* **gwahodd**

gwaddod (-ion) *nm* sediment, lees, dregs

gwaddodi *vb* deposit sediment

gwaddol (-ion, -iadau) *nm* endowment; dowry

gwaddoli *vb* endow

gwae (-au) *nm, nf* woe

gwaed *nm* blood

gwaedlif, gwaedlyn *nm* hæmorrhage, dysentery

gwaedlyd *adj* bloody, sanguinary

gwaedoliaeth *nf* blood, consanguinity

gwaedu *vb* bleed

gwaedd (-au) *nf* cry, shout

gwaeddi *see* **gweiddi**

gwaeg (gwaegau) *nf* buckle, clasp

gwael *adj* poor, vile; poorly, ill

gwaelder, gwaeldra *nm* poorness, vileness

gwaeledd *nm* illness

gwaelod (-ion) *nm* bottom; (*pl*) sediment

gwaelodi *vb* settle, deposit sediment

gwaelu *vb* sicken

gwaell (gwëyll, gweill) *nf* knitting-needle

gwaered *nm* descent; **i waered** down

gwaeth *adj* worse

gwaethwaeth *adj* worse and worse

gwaethygu *vb* worsen

gwaew *see* **gwayw**

gwag (gweigion) *adj* empty, vacant, vain

gwagedd *nm* vanity

gwagelog *adj* wary, circumspect

gwagen (-i) *nf* waggon

gwagenwr (-wyr) *nm* waggoner

gwagfa (-feydd) *nf* vacuum

gwagle (-oedd) *nm* space, void

gwagu *vb* empty

gwahadden (gwahaddod) *nf* mole

gwahan, gwahân *nm*: **ar wahan** apart, separately

gwahangleifion *npl* lepers

gwahanglwyf *nm* leprosy

gwahanglwyfus *adj* leprous ▷ *nm* leper

gwahaniaeth (-au) *nm* difference

gwahaniaethol *adj* distinguishing

gwahaniaethu *vb* differ; distinguish

gwahanol *adj* different

gwahanu *vb* divide, part, separate

gwahardd *vb* forbid, prohibit

gwaharddiad (-au) *nm* prohibition, veto

gwahodd *vb* invite

gwahoddedigion *npl* guests

gwahoddiad (-au) *nm* invitation

gwahoddwr (-wyr) *nm* inviter, host

gwain (gweiniau) *nf* sheath, scabbard

gwair (gweiriau) *nm* hay

gwaith (gweithiau) *nm* work

gwaith (gweithiau) *nf* time, turn

gwal (-iau, gwelydd) *nf* wall

gwâl (gwalau) *nf* couch, bed; lair

gwala *nf* enough, plenty

gwalch (gweilch) *nm* hawk; rogue, rascal

gwaled (-au) *nf* wallet

gwalio *vb* wall, fence

gwall (-au) *nm* defect, want; mistake, error

gwallgof *adj* mad, insane

gwallgofdy (-dai) *nm* madhouse, lunatic asylum

gwallgofddyn (-gofiaid) *nm* madman

gwallgofi *vb* go mad, rave

gwallgofrwydd *nm* madness, insanity

gwallt (-iau) *nm*, *coll n* hair of the head

gwalltog *adj* hairy

gwallus *adj* faulty, incorrect, inaccurate

gwamal *adj* fickle, frivolous

gwamalio, gwamalu *vb* waver; behave frivolously

gwamalrwydd *nm* frivolity, levity

gwan (gweiniaid, gweinion) *adj* weak, feeble

gwanaf (-au) *nf* layer; row, swath

gwanc *nm* greed, voracity

gwancus *adj* greedy, voracious

gwaneg (-au, gwenyg) *nf* wave, billow

gwangalon *adj* faint-hearted

gwangalonni *vb* lose heart

gwanhau *vb* weaken, enfeeble

gwanllyd, gwannaidd *adj* weakly, delicate

gwant *nm* caesura; division

gwantan *adj* unsteady, fickle; feeble, poor

gwanu *vb* pierce, stab

gwanwyn (-au) *nm* spring

gwanwynol *adj* vernal, spring-like

gwanychu *vb* weaken, enfeeble

gwar (-rau) *nm*, *nf* (nape of) neck

gwâr *adj* civilised, tame, gentle

gwaradwydd (-iadau) *nm* shame, disgrace

gwaradwyddo *vb* shame, disgrace

gwaradwyddus *adj* shameful, disgraceful

gwarafun *vb* forbid, refuse, grudge

gwaraidd *adj* gentle, civilized

gwarant (-au) *nf* warrant

gwarantu *vb* warrant, guarantee

gwarchae *vb* besiege ▷ *nm* siege

gwarcheidiol *adj* guardian, tutelary

gwarcheidwad (-waid) *nm* guardian

gwarchod *vb* watch, look after, ward, mind; **gwarchod plant** baby-sit, do baby-sitting

gwarchodaeth *nf* ward, custody
gwarchodfa (-feydd) *nf*:
  gwarchodfa natur nature reserve
gwarchodlu (-oedd) *nm* garrison,
  guards
gwarchodwr (-wyr) *nm* custodian;
  security guard; babysitter, child
  minder
gward (-iau) *nm, nf* ward
gwarden (-deiniaid) *nm* warden
gwared *vb* rid; deliver, redeem
gwaredigaeth (-au) *nf* deliverance
gwaredigion *npl* redeemed,
  ransomed
gwaredu *vb* save, deliver, redeem; rid
gwaredwr (-wyr), **gwaredydd
  (-ion)** *nm* saviour
gwaredd *nm* mildness, gentleness
gwareiddiad (-au) *nf* civilization
gwareiddiedig *adj* civilized
gwareiddio *vb* civilize
gwargaled *adj* stiff-necked,
  stubborn
gwargaledwch *nm* stubbornness
gwargam *adj* stooping
gwargamu *vb* stoop
gwarged *nm* remains
gwargrwm *adj* round-shouldered
gwargrymu *vb* stoop
gwario *vb* spend
gwarogaeth *see* **gwrogaeth**
gwarth *nm* shame, disgrace
gwarthaf *nm* top, summit; **ar
  warthaf** on top of, upon
gwarthafl (-au) *nf* stirrup
gwartheg *npl* cows, cattle
gwarthnod (-au) *nm* stigma
gwarthnodi *vb* stigmatize
gwarthol (-ion) *nf* stirrup
gwarthrudd *nm* shame, disgrace
gwarthruddo *vb* shame, disgrace
gwarthus *adj* shameful, disgraceful,
  outrageous

gwas (gweision) *nm* lad; servant
gwasaidd *adj* servile, slavish
gwasanaeth (-au) *nm* service
gwasanaethferch (-ed) *nf*
  handmaid
gwasanaethgar *adj* serviceable;
  obliging
gwasanaethu *vb* serve, minister
gwasanaethwr (-wyr) *nm*
  manservant, servant
gwasanaethwraig (-wragedd) *nf*
  maidservant
gwasanaethydd (-ion) *nm* servant
gwasanaethyddes (-au) *nf*
  handmaid
gwaseidd-dra *nm* servility
gwasg (-au, -oedd, gweisg) *nf*
  press ▷ *nm* waist; bodice
gwasgar *nm* dispersion; **ar wasgar**
  scattered, dispersed
gwasgaredig (-ion) *adj* scattered
gwasgarog *adj* scattered; divided
gwasgaru *vb* scatter, disperse;
  spread
gwasgarwr (-wyr) *nm* scatterer;
  spreader
gwasgfa (-feydd, -feuon) *nf*
  squeeze; fit
gwasgod (-au) *nf* waistcoat
gwasgu *vb* press, squeeze, crush,
  wring
gwasod *adj* in heat (*of a cow*)
gwastad *adj* level, flat; even;
  constant, continual
gwastadedd (-au) *nm* plain
gwastadol *adj* continual, perpetual
gwastadrwydd *nm* evenness
gwastatáu *vb* make even, level;
  settle
gwastatir (-oedd) *nm* level ground,
  plain
gwastraff *nm* waste, extravagance
gwastraffu *vb* waste, squander

g

gwastraffus *adj* wasteful, extravagant

gwastrawd (-odion) *nm* groom, ostler

gwastrodaeth *nf* grooming; discipline

gwastrodaeth, gwastrodi *vb* discipline

gwatwar *vb* mock; mimic ▷ *nm* mockery

gwatwareg *nf* sarcasm, satire, irony

gwatwarus *adj* mocking, scoffing

gwatwarwr (-wyr) *nm* mocker, scoffer

gwau *vb* knit, weave

gwaun (gweunydd) *nf* moor, meadow

gwawch (-iau) *nf* scream, yell

gwawchio *vb* scream, yell

gwawd *nm* scoff, scorn, ridicule

gwawdiaeth *nf* ridicule

gwawdio *vb* mock, scoff, jeer, ridicule

gwawdiwr (-wyr) *nm* mocker, scoffer

gwawdlyd *adj* mocking, jeering, sneering

gwawl *nm* light

gwawn *nm* gossamer

gwawr *nf* dawn, day-break; hue, nuance

gwawrio *vb* dawn

gwayw (gwewyr) *nm* pang, pain, stitch

gwaywffon (-ffyn) *nf* spear

gwden (-ni, gwdyn) *nf* withe

gwdihŵ *nm* owl

gwddf (gyddfau) *nm* neck, throat

gwe (-oedd) *nf* web; texture; **y We (Fyd-Eang)** the (World-Wide) Web

gwead *nm* weaving, knitting; texture

gwedd (-au) *nf* aspect, form; appearance

gwedd (-oedd) *nf* yoke; team

gweddaidd *adj* seemly, decent

gweddeidd-dra *nm* seemliness, decency

gwedder (gweddrod) *nm* wether; **cig gwedder** mutton

gweddgar *adj* plump, sleek

gweddi (-ïau) *nm* prayer

gweddigar *adj* prayerful

gweddill (-ion) *nm* remnant, remainder, rest; (*pl*) remains

gweddillio *vb* leave spare, leave a remnant

gweddïo *vb* pray

gweddïwr (-ïwyr) *nm* one who prays

gweddol *adj* fair, fairly

gweddu *vb* suit, become, befit

gweddus *adj* seemly, decent, proper

gweddustra *nm* decency, propriety

gweddw *adj* single; widow, widowed ▷ *nf* (**-on**) widow; **gŵr gweddw** widower

gweddwdod *nm* widowhood

gweddwi *vb* widow

gwefan (-nau) *nm, nf* website

gwefl (-au) *nf* lip (*usu. of animal*)

gwefr *nm* thrill, excitement; charge

gwefreiddio *vb* electrify, thrill

gwefreiddiol *adj* thrilling

gwefus (-au) *nf* (human) lip

gwefusol *adj* of the lip, labial

gwe-gamera (gwe-gamerâu) *nm* webcam

gwegi *nm* vanity, levity

gwegian *vb* sway, totter

gwegil *nm* back of head

gwehelyth *nm, nf* lineage, pedigree

gwehilion *npl* refuse, trash, riffraff

gwehydd (-ion) *nm* weaver

gwehyddu *vb* weave

gwehynnu *vb* draw, pour, empty

gweiddi *vb* cry, shout

gweilgi *nf* sea, torrent
gweili *adj* empty, idle
gweini *vb* serve, minister; be in service
gweinidog (-ion) *nm* minister, servant
gweinidogaeth (-au) *nf* ministry, service
gweinidogaethol *adj* ministerial
gweinidogaethu *vb* minister
gweinio *vb* sheathe
gweinydd (-ion) *nm* waiter; server
gweinyddes (-au) *nf* attendant, nurse; waitress
gweinyddiaeth (-au) *nf* administration
gweinyddol *adj* administrative
gweinyddu *vb* administer, officiate
gweinyddwr (-wyr) *nm* administrator
gweirglodd (iau) *nf* meadow
gweitied, gweitio *vb* wait
gweithdy (-dai) *nm* workshop
gweithfa (-oedd, -feydd) *nf* works
gweithfaol *adj* industrial
gweithgar *adj* hard-working, industrious
gweithgaredd (-au), gweithgarwch *nm* activity
gweithio *vb* work; ferment; purge
gweithiwr (-wyr) *nm* workman, worker; **gweithiwr cymdeithasol** social worker
gweithred (-oedd) *nf* act, deed, work
gweithrediad (-au) *nm* action, operation
gweithredol *adj* active, actual, virtual
gweithredu *vb* act, work, operate
gweithredwr (-wyr) *nm* doer
gweithredydd (-ion) *nm* doer, factor, agent

gweladwy *adj* perceptible, visible
gweled, gweld *vb* see, perceive
gwelediad *nm* sight, appearance
gw.eledig *adj* seen, visible
gweledigaeth (-au) *nf* vision
gweledydd (-ion) *nm* seer
gwelw *adj* pale
gwelwi *vb* pale
gwely (-au, gwelâu) *nm* bed; river basin; sea bed; stratum; flat surface; **gwely haul** sunbed
gwell *adj* better, superior
gwella *vb* better, mend, improve, recover
gwellau, gwellaif (-eifiau) *nm* shears
gwellen (gweill) *nf* knitting-needle
gwellhad *nm* recovery, improvement
gwellhau *vb* better, improve
gwelliant (-iannau) *nm* amendment, improvement
gwellt *coll n* grass; sward; straw
gwelltglas *nm* grass, greensward
gwelltog *adj* grassy, green
gwelltyn *nm* blade of grass; a straw
gwellwell *adv* better and better
gwen *adj f of* **gwyn**
gwên (gwenau) *nf* smile
gwenci (-ïod) *nf* stoat, weasel
gwendid (-au) *nm* weakness, frailty
Gwener *nf* Venus; **dydd Gwener** Friday
gwenerol *adj* venereal
gwenfflam *adj* blazing, ablaze
gweniaith *nf* flattery
gwenieithio *vb* flatter
gwenieithiwr (-wyr) *nm* flatterer
gwenieithus *adj* flattering
gwenith *npl (nf -en)* wheat
gwenithfaen *nm* granite
gwennol (gwenoliaid) *nf* swallow, martin; shuttle

gwenu vb smile

gwenwisg (-oedd) nf surplice

gwenwyn nm poison, venom; jealousy

gwenwynig, gwenwynol adj poisonous, venomous

gwenwynllyd adj peevish; jealous

gwenwyno vb poison; fret; be jealous

gwenyn npl (nf-**en**) bees

gwep nf visage, grimace

gwêr nm tallow, suet etc

gŵer nm shade

gwerchyr nm cover, lid, valve

gwerdd adj f of **gwyrdd**

gwerin coll n men, people; democracy; crew

gweriniaeth (-au) nf democracy; republic; **Gweriniaeth Tsiec** Czech Republic; **Gweriniaeth Iwerddon** Irish Republic

gwerinlywodraeth (-au) nf republic

gwerinol adj plebian, vulgar

gwerinos coll n rabble, mob

gwerinwr (-wyr) nm democrat

gwern (-i, -ydd) nf swamp, meadow; alder-grove

gwern npl (nf-**en**) alder-trees

gwerog adj tallowy, suety

gwers (-i) nf verse; lesson; **gwers yrru** driving lesson

gwersyll (-oedd) nm camp, encampment

gwersylla, gwersyllu vb camp; encamp

gwerth nm worth, value; **ar werth** for sale

gwerthfawr adj valuable, precious

gwerthfawredd nm preciousness

gwerthfawrogi vb appreciate

gwerthfawrogiad nm appreciation

gwerthu vb sell

gwerthwr (-wyr) nm seller; **gwerthwr cyffuriau** drug dealer; **gwerthwr eiddo** estate agent

gwerthyd (-au) nf spindle, axle

gweryd (-au) nm earth, soil; sward ▷ nf groin

gweryriad nm neighing

gweryru vb neigh

gwestai (-eion) nm guest

gwesty (-au, -tai) nm inn, hotel

gweu vb weave, knit

gwewyr nm anguish

gwg nm frown, scowl; disapproval

gwgu vb frown, scowl, lower

gwialen (gwiail) nf rod, switch

gwialennod (-enodiau) nf stroke, stripe

gwialenodio vb beat with a rod

gwib nf wandering, jaunt ▷ adj wandering

gwibdaith (-deithiau) nf excursion

gwiber (-od) nf viper

gwibio vb flash, flit, dart, wander

gwibiog adj flitting, darting, wandering

gwiblong (-au) nf cruiser

gwich nf squeak; creak; wheeze, wheezing

gwichiad (-iaid) nm periwinkle

gwichian vb squeak, squeal; creak; wheeze

gwichlyd adj creaking; wheezy

gwiddon (-od) nf witch

gwiddon npl mites

gwif (-iau) nm lever, crowbar

gwig (-oedd) nf wood

gwingo vb wriggle, fidget; writhe; kick, struggle

gwin (-oedd) nm wine

gwinau adj bay, brown, auburn

gwinc (-od) nf chaffinch

gwinegr nm vinegar

gwinllan (-noedd, -nau) nf vine-yard

gwinllannwr, gwinllanydd nm vine-dresser

gwinwryf (-oedd) nm wine-press

gwinwydd npl (nf **-en**) vines

gwir adj true ▷ nm truth

gwireb (-au, -ion) nf truism, axiom

gwireddu vb verify, substantiate

gwirfodd nm goodwill; own accord

gwirfoddol adj voluntary, spontaneous

gwirfoddolwr (-wyr) nm volunteer

gwirio vb verify

gwirion (-iaid) adj innocent; silly

gwiriondeb nm innocence; silliness

gwirionedd (-au) nm truth, verity, reality

gwironeddol adj true, real, genuine

gwirioni vb infatuate, dote

gwirionyn nm simpleton

gwiriwr (-wyr) nm verifier; **gwiriwr sillafu** spellchecker

gwirod (-ydd) nm liquor, spirits

gwisg (-oedd) nf dress, garment, robe

gwisgi adj brisk, lively, nimble; ripe

gwisgo vb dress; wear; put on

gwisgwr (-wyr) nm wearer

gwiw adj fit, meet; worthy

gwiwer (-od) nf squirrel

gwlad (gwledydd) nf country, land

gwladaidd adj countrified, rustic

Gwlad Belg nf Belgium

gwladfa (-oedd) nf colony, settlement

gwladgar see **gwlatgar**

gwladgarol adj patriotic

gwladgarwch nm patriotism

gwladgarwr (-wyr) nm patriot

gwladol adj of a country, civil, state

gwladoli vb nationalize

Gwlad Thai nf Thailand

gwladweiniaeth nf statesmanship

gwladweinydd (-ion, -wyr) nm statesman

gwladwr (-wyr) nm countryman, peasant

gwladwriaeth (-au) nf state

gwladwriaethol adj state, political

gwladychfa (-oedd) nf settlement, colony

gwladychu vb inhabit, settle, colonize; rule

gwladychwr (-wyr) nm settler, colonist

Gwlad yr Iâ nf Iceland

gwlân (gwlanoedd) nm wool

gwlana vb gather wool

gwlanen (-ni) nf flannel

gwlanog adj woolly

gwlatgar adj patriotic

gwlaw see **glaw**

gwledig adj countrified, country, rural

gwledd (-oedd) nf feast, banquet

gwledda vb feast

gwleddwr (-wyr) nm feaster

gwleidydd (-ion) nm politician, statesman

gwleidyddiaeth nf politics

gwleidyddol adj political

gwleidyddol-gywir adj politically correct

gwleidyddwr (-wyr) nm politician

gwlith (-oedd) nm dew

gwlitho vb dew, bedew

gwlithog adj dewy; inspiring

gwlithyn nm dewdrop

gwlyb (-ion) adj wet, fluid, liquid ▷ nm fluid, liquid

gwlybaniaeth nm wet, moisture

gwlybwr nm wet, moisture, liquid, fluid

gwlybyrog adj wet, damp, rainy

gwlych nm wet; **rhoi yng ngwlych** steep

gwlychu vb wet, moisten; get wet; dip

gwlydd npl, coll n (nm **-yn**) haulm

gwn (**gynnau**) nm gun

gŵn (**gynau**) nm gown

gwndwn see **gwyndwn**

gwneud, gwneuthur vb do, make; make up

gwneuthuriad nm make, making

gwneuthurwr (**-wyr**) nm maker, doer, manufacturer

gwnïad nm sewing, stitching, seam

gwniadur (**-iau, on**) nm, nf thimble

gwniadwraig nf stitcher, seamstress

gwniadyddes (**-au**) nf seamstress

gwnïo vb sew, stitch

gwnïyddes (**-au**) nf seamstress

gwobr (**-au**) nf, nm, **gwobrwy** (**-au, -on**) nm reward, prize

gwobrwyo vb reward

gwobrwywr (**-wyr**) nm rewarder

gŵr (**gwŷr**) nm man; husband

gwra vb seek or marry a husband

gwrach (**-ïod, -od**) nf hag, witch; **breuddwyd gwrach** wishful thinking

gwrachïaidd adj old-womanish

gwraidd (**gwreiddiau**) coll n roots

gwraig (**gwragedd**) nf woman; wife

gwrandaw see **gwrando**

gwrandawiad nm listening, hearing

gwrandawr (**-wyr**) nm listener, hearer

gwrando vb listen, hearken

gwrcath (**-od**) nm tom-cat

gwrddni nm greenness, verdure

gwregys (**-au**) nm girdle, belt, truss; zone

gwregysu vb girdle, gird

gwrêng nm, coll n (one of the) common people

gwreica vb seek or marry a wife

gwreichion npl (nf **-en**) sparks

gwreichioni vb emit sparks, sparkle

gwreiddio vb root

gwreiddiol adj radical, rooted; original

gwreiddioldeb nm originality

gwreiddyn (**gwreiddiau**) nm root

gwres nm heat, warmth

gwresfesurydd (**-ion**) nm thermometer

gwresog adj warm, hot; fervent

gwresogi vb warm, heat

gwrhyd (**-oedd**), **gwryd** nm fathom

gwrhydri nm exploit; valour

gwrid nm blush, flush

gwrido vb blush, flush

gwridog, gwritgoch adj rosy-cheeked, ruddy

gwrogaeth nf homage

gwrogi vb do homage

gwrol adj brave, courageous

gwroldeb nm bravery, courage

gwroli vb hearten

gwron (**-iaid**) nm hero

gwroniaeth nf heroism

gwrtaith (**-teithiau**) nm manure, fertiliser

gwrteithiad nm cultivation, culture

gwrteithio vb manure; cultivate, culture

gwrth- prefix counter-, contra-, anti-

gwrthban (**-au**) nm blanket

gwrthblaid nf (party in) opposition

gwrthbrofi vb disprove, refute

gwrthbwynt nm counterpoint

gwrthdaro vb clash, collide

gwrthdrawiad (**-au**) nm collision

gwrthdystiad (**-au**) nm protest

gwrthdystio vb protest

gwrthddadl (**-euon**) nf objection

gwrthddadlau vb object, controvert

gwrthddywediad (-au) *nm* contradiction

gwrthddywedyd *vb* contradict

gwrthgiliad (-au) *nm* backsliding

gwrthgilio *vb* backslide, secede

gwrthgiliwr (-wr) *nm* backslider, seceder

gwrthglawdd (-gloddiau) *nm* rampart

gwrthglocwedd *adj* anticlockwise

gwrthgyferbyniad (-au) *nm* contrast, antithesis

gwrthgyferbynnu *vb* contrast

gwrthnaws *nm* antipathy ▷ *adj* repugnant

gwrthnysig *adj* obstinate, stubborn

gwrthod *vb* refuse, reject

gwrthodedig *adj* rejected, reprobate

gwrthodiad *nm* refusal, rejection

gwrthodwr (-wyr) *nm* refuser, rejecter

gwrthol *nm, adv* back; **ôl a gwrthol** to and fro

gwrthrych (-au) *nm* object; subject (*of biography*)

gwrthrychol *adj* objective

gwrthryfel (-oedd) *nm* rebellion, mutiny

gwrthryfela *vb* rebel

gwrthryfelgar *adj* rebellious, mutinous

gwrthryfelwr (-wyr) *nm* rebel, mutineer

gwrthsafiad *nm* resistance

gwrthsefyll *vb* withstand, resist

gwrthun *adj* repugnant, odious, absurd

gwrthuni *nm* odiousness, absurdity

gwrthuno *vb* mar, deform, disfigure

gwrthweithio *vb* counteract

gwrthwyneb *nm* opposite, contrary

gwrthwynebiad (-au) *nm* objection

gwrthwynebol *adj* opposed

gwrthwynebu *vb* resist, oppose

gwrthwynebus *adj* repugnant; antagonistic

gwrthwynebwr (-wyr), **gwrthwynebydd** *nm* opponent, adversary

gwrych (-oedd) *nm* hedge

gwrych *npl, coll n* (*nm* **-yn**) bristles

gwryd *see* **gwrhyd**

gwryf (-oedd) *nm* press

gwrym (-iau) *nm* seam; wale

gwrysg *npl* (*nf* **-en**) stalks, haulm

gwryw *adj* male ▷ *nm* (**-od**) male

gwrywaidd, gwrywol *adj* masculine

gwrywgydiaeth *nm* homosexuality

gwrywgydiol *adj* homosexual

gwrywgydiwr (-wyr) *nm* homosexual

gwth *nm* push, thrust, shove; gust

gwthio *vb* push, thrust, shove

gwthiwr (-wyr) *nm* pusher

gwyar *nm* gore, blood

gwybed *npl* (*nm* **-yn**) flies

gwybod *vb* know ▷ *nm* (**-au**) knowledge; **gwybodau** studies

gwybodaeth (-au) *nf* knowledge

gwybodeg *nm* epistemology

gwybodus *adj* knowing, well-informed

gwybyddus *adj* known, aware of

gwych *adj* fine, splendid, brilliant

gwychder *nm* splendour, pomp

gwŷd (gwydiau) *nm* vice

gwydn *adj* tough

gwydnwch *nm* toughness

gwydr (-au) *nm* glass

gwydraid (-eidiau) *nm* glassful, glass

gwydro *vb* glaze; **gwydro dwbl** double glazing

gwydrwr (-wyr) nm glazier
gwydryn (gwydrau) nm
drinking-glass
gwŷdd (gwehyddion, gwyddion)
nm loom; plough
gwŷdd npl (nf **gwydden**) trees
gŵydd nm presence
gŵydd (gwyddau) nm goose
gwyddbwyll nf chess
Gwyddel (-od, Gwyddyl) nm
Irishman
Gwyddeleg nf Irish language
Gwyddeles (-au) nf Irishwoman
Gwyddelig adj Irish
gwyddfa nf tumulus, grave
gwyddfid nm honeysuckle
gwyddfod nm presence
gwyddoniadur (-on) nm
encyclopædia
gwyddoniaeth nf science
gwyddonol adj scientific
gwyddonydd (-wyr) nm scientist
gwyddor (-ion) nf rudiment;
science; **yr wyddor** the alphabet
gwyddori vb instruct, ground
gwyfyn (-od) nm moth
gwŷg coll n vetch
gwygbysen (gwygbys) nf chickpea
gŵyl adj bashful, modest
gŵyl (-iau) nf holiday, feast, festival
gwylaidd adj bashful, modest
gwylan (-od) nf sea-gull
gwylder nm bashfulness, modesty
gwyleidd-dra nm bashfulness,
modesty
gwylfa (-fâu, -feydd) nf watch;
lookout
gwyliadwriaeth nm watchfulness,
caution ▷ nf (**-au**) watch; guard
gwyliadwrus adj watchful,
cautious
gwyliedydd (-ion) nm watchman,
sentinel

gwylio vb watch, mind, beware
gwyliwr (-wyr) nm watchman,
sentinel
gwylmabsant (-au) nf wake
gwylnos (-au) nf watch-night,
wake, vigil
gwyll nm darkness, gloom
gwylliad (-iaid) nm robber, bandit
gwyllt adj wild, savage, mad; rapid;
bywyd gwyllt wildlife ▷ nm (**-oedd**)
wild
gwylltineb nm wildness; rage, fury
gwylltio, gwylltu vb frighten; fly
into a passion
gwymon nm seaweed
gwyn (f gwen) adj white; blessed
gwŷn (gwyniau) nm, nf ache, smart;
lust
gwynder, gwyndra nm whiteness
gwyndwn nm unploughed land
gwyneb see **wyneb**
gwynegon nm rheumatism
gwynegu vb throb, ache
gwynfa nf paradise
gwynfyd (-au) nm blessedness,
bliss; (pl) beatitudes
gwynfydedig adj blessed, happy,
beatific
gwyngalch nm whitewash
gwyngalchog adj whitewashed
gwyngalchu vb whitewash
gwyniad (-iaid) nm whiting
gwynias adj white-hot
gwyniedyn nm sewin
gwynio vb throb, ache
gwynnu vb whiten, bleach
gwynnwy nm white of egg
gwynt (-oedd) nm wind; breath;
smell
gwyntell (-i) nf round basket
without handle
gwyntio vb smell
gwyntog adj windy

gwyntyll (-au) nf fan
gwyntylliad nm ventilation
gwyntyllio, gwyntyllu vb ventilate, winnow
gwŷr see **gŵr**
gŵyr adj crooked, oblique, sloping
gwyrdraws adj perverse
gwyrdro (-ion) nm perversion
gwyrdroi vb pervert, distort
gwyrdd (-ion) adj, nm green
gwyrddlas adj green, verdant
gwyrddlesni nm verdure
gwyrgam adj crooked
gwyrni nm crookedness, perverseness
gwyro vb swerve; slope; stoop; tilt; deviate
gwyrth (-iau) nf miracle
gwyrthiol adj miraculous
gwyry, gwyryf (gwyryfon) nf virgin; **y Wyryf** Virgo
gwyryfdod nm virginity
gwyryfol adj virgin
gwŷs (gwysion) nf summons
gwysio vb summon
gwystl (-on) nm pledge; hostage
gwystlo vb pledge, pawn
gwystno vb dry, wither, flag
gwythïen (gwythi, gwythiennau) nf vein, blood vessel, artery; **cwlwm gwythi** cramp
gwyw adj withered, faded, sere
gwywo vb wither, fade
gyda, gydag prefix with
gyddfol adj guttural
gyferbyn prefix over against, opposite
gylfin (-od) nm bill, beak
gylfinir nm curlew
gynfad (-au) nm gunboat
gynnau adv a little while ago, just now
gynt adv formerly, of yore

gyr (-roedd) nm drove
gyrfa (-oedd, -feydd) nf race; course; career
gyrfaol adj vocational
gyriant (gyriannau) nm drive; **gyriant disg** disk drive
gyriedydd (-ion) nm driver
gyrru vb drive; send; work, forge; **gyrru tra'n feddw** drink-driving
gyrrwr (gyrwyr) nm driver; sender
gyrwynt (-oedd) nm hurricane, tornado
gysb nm staggers

g

h

ha *excl* ha
hac (-iau) *nf* cut, notch, hack
hacio *vb* hack
haciwr (-wyr) *nm* hacker
had (-au) *nm, coll n (nm* **hedyn**) seed
hadlif *nm* seminal fluid
hadog *nm* haddock
hadu *vb* seed
hadyd *coll n* seed-corn
haearn (heyrn) *nm* iron; **haearn bwrw** cast iron; **haearn gyr** wrought iron
haearnaidd *adj* like iron
haeddiannol *adj* meritorious; merited
haeddiant (-iannau) *nm* merit, desert
haeddu *vb* deserve, merit
hael *adj* generous, liberal
haelfrydedd *nm* liberality
haelfrydig *adj* generous, free

haelioni *nm* generosity
haelionus *adj* generous, liberal
haen (-au) *nf* layer, stratum; seam; **haen osôn** ozone layer
haenen (-nau) *nf* layer, film
haenu *vb* stratify
haeriad (-au) *nm* assertion
haerllug *adj* importunate; impudent
haerllugrwydd *nm* importunity; impudence
haeru *vb* affirm, assert
haf (-au) *nm* summer
hafaidd *adj* summer-like, summery
hafal *adj* like, equal
hafaliad *nm* equation
hafan *nf* haven
hafn (-au) *nf* hollow, gorge, ravine
hafod (-ydd) *nf* summer dwelling, upland farm
hafog *nm* havoc
hafoty (-tai) *nm* summer residence
hagr *adj* ugly
hagru *vb* mar, disfigure
hagrwch *nm* ugliness
haid (heidiau) *nf* swarm, drove, horde
haidd (heiddiau) *nm, coll n (nf* **heidden**) barley
haig (heigiau) *nf* shoal
haint (heintiau) *nm, nf* pestilence; faint
hala *vb* send, spend
halen *nm* salt, brine
halog, halogedig *adj* defiled, polluted
halogi *vb* defile, profane, pollute
halogrwydd *nm* defilement, pollution
halogwr (-wyr) *nm* defiler, profaner
hallt *adj* salt, salty; severe
halltedd, halltrwydd *nm* saltness, saltiness

halltu vb salt
halltwr (**-wyr**) nm salter
hambwrdd (**-byrddau**) nm tray
hamdden nf leisure, respite
hamddenol adj leisurely
hanerob (**-au**) nf flitch of bacon
haneru vb halve
hanes (**-ion**) nm history, story, account
hanesydd (**-wyr**) nm historian
hanesyddol adj historical
hanesyn (**-nau**) nm anecdote
hanfod vb descend from, issue ▷ nm essence
hanfodol adj essential
haniad nm derivation, descent
haniaeth nf abstraction
haniaethol adj abstract
hanner (**hanerau, haneri**) nm, adj, adv half; **hanner ffordd (i)** halfway (to); **hanner pris** half fare; **hanner tymor** half term
hanner-sgim adj semi-skimmed
hanu vb proceed, be derived, be descended
hapus adj happy
hapusrwydd nm happiness
hardd adj beautiful, handsome
harddu vb beautify, embellish, adorn
harddwch nm beauty
harnais (**-eisiau**) nm harness
harneisio vb harness
hatling (**-au, -od**) nf mite, half a farthing
hau vb sow, disseminate
haul (**heuliau**) nm sun
hawdd adj easy; **hawdd ei drin** user-friendly
hawddamor nm, excl good luck, welcome
hawddfyd nm ease, prosperity
hawddgar adj amiable; comely
hawddgarwch nm amiability

hawl (**-iau**) nf claim; right; **hawl ac ateb** question and answer
hawlio vb claim, demand
hawlydd (**-ion**) nm claimant, plaintiff
haws adj easier
heb prep without; **heb afael** hands-free
heblaw prep beside(s)
hebog (**-au**) nm hawk, falcon
Hebraeg nf, adj Hebrew (language)
Hebreaidd, Hebreig adj Hebrew, Hebraic
Hebrees (**-au**) nf Hebrew woman
Hebreigydd (**-ion**) nm Hebraist
Hebrëwr (**-wyr**) nm a Hebrew
hebrwng vb accompany, conduct, convey, escort
hebryngydd (**-ion**) nm conductor, guide
hedeg vb fly; run to seed
hedegog adj flying; high-flown
hedfa (**-feydd**) nf flight
hedfan vb fly, hover
hedydd (**-ion**) nm lark
hedyn (**hadau**) nm seed, germ
hedd nm peace, tranquillity
heddgeidwad (**-waid**) nm policeman
heddiw adv today
heddlu nm police force
heddwas (**-weision**) nm policeman; **yr Heddwas Elwyn Jones** PC Elwyn Jones
heddwch nm peace, quiet, tranquillity
heddychiaeth nf pacifism
heddychlon adj peaceful, peaceable
heddychol adj peaceable, pacific
heddychu vb pacify, appease
heddychwr (**-wyr**) nm pacifist, peace-maker
heddyw see **heddiw**

h

hefelydd *adj* similar
hefyd *adv* also, besides
heffer (**heffrod**) *nf* heifer
hegl (**-au**) *nf* leg, shank
heglog *adj* leggy, long-legged
heglu *vb* foot it, 'hook it'
heibio *adv* past
heidio *vb* swarm, throng, flock
heidden *nf* grain of barley
heigio *vb* shoal, teem
heini *adj* active, lively, nimble, brisk
heintio *vb* infect
heintus *adj* infectious, contagious
heislan (**-od**) *nf* hackle
heislanu *vb* hackle flax
hel *vb* gather, collect; drive, chase
hela *vb* hunt, spend (*money, time*);
 cŵn hela hounds
helaeth *adj* ample, abundant,
 extensive
helaethrwydd *nm* abundance
helaethu *vb* enlarge, extend,
 amplify
helaethwych *adj* sumptuous
helbul (**-on**) *nm* trouble
helbulus *adj* troubled, troublous
helcyd *vb* hunt ▷ *nm* worry, trouble
helfa (**-fâu, -feydd**) *nf* hunt, catch
helfarch (**-feirch**) *nm* hunter (*horse*)
helgi (**-gwn**) *nm* hound
heli *nm* salt water, brine
heliwr (**-wyr**) *nm* hunter, huntsman
helm (**-au**) *nf* helm, helmet, stack
help *nm* help, aid, assistance
helpio, helpu *vb* help, aid, assist
helwriaeth *nf* game, hunting;
 chase
helyg *npl* (*nf*-**en**) willows
helynt (**-ion**) *nf* trouble, fuss, bother,
 hassle
helltni *nm* saltiness, saltness
hem *nm* rivet
hem (**-iau**) *nf* hem, border

hen *adj* old, aged, ancient, of old
henadur (**-iaid**) *nm* alderman
henaduriad (**-iaid**) *nm*
 Presbyterian, elder
henaduriaeth (**-au**) *nf* presbytery
henafgwr, henafol *see* **hy-**
henaint *nm* old age
hendaid (**-deidiau**) *nm*
 great-grandfather
hender *nm* oldness
hendref (**-i, -ydd**) *nf* winter
 dwelling, lowland farm
heneb (**-ion**) *nf* ancient monument
heneiddio *vb* grow old, age
henfam *nf* grandmother
henffasiwn *adj* old-fashioned
hennain (**heneiniau**) *nf*
 great-grandmother
heno *adv* tonight
henoed *coll n* elderly people, the
 aged
henuriad (**-iaid**) *nm* elder, presbyter
heol (**-ydd**) *nf* road
hepgor *vb* spare, dispense with ▷ *nm*
 (**-ion**) what may be dispensed with
hepian *vb* slumber, doze
her (**-iau**) *nf* challenge
herc (**-iau**) *nf* hop; limp
hercian *vb* hop, hobble, limp
heresi (**-ïau**) *nf* heresy
heretic (**-iaid**) *nm* heretic
hereticaidd *adj* heretical
herfeiddio *vb* dare, brave, defy
herfeiddiol *adj* daring, defiant
hergwd *nm* push, thrust, shove
herio *vb* challenge, dare, brave, defy
heroin *nm* heroin
herw *nm* raid; outlawry
herwa *vb* scout, prowl, raid
herwgipio *vb* kidnap
herwgipiwr (**-wyr**) *nm* kidnapper;
 hijacker
herwhela *vb* poach (*game*)

herwr (**-wyr**) nm scout, raider; outlaw

herwydd see **oherwydd**

hesb adj f of **hysb**

hesben (**-nau**) nf hasp

hesbin (**-od**) nf yearling ewe

hesbio vb dry up

hesbwrn (**-yrniaid**) nm young ram

hesg npl (nf **-en**) sedge, rushes

het (**-iau**) nf hat

heulo vb shine (as the sun); sun

heulog adj sunny

heulwen nf sunshine

heuwr (**-wyr**) nm sower

hi pron she, her; it

hidio vb heed

hidl adj: **wylo yn hidl** weep abundantly

hidl (**-au**) nf strainer, sieve

hidlen (**-ni**) nf strainer, sieve

hidlo vb distil, run; strain, filter

hil nf race, lineage, posterity

hilio vb bring forth, teem, breed

hiliogaeth nf offspring, issue, posterity

hiliol adj racist

hiliwr (**-wyr**) nm racist

hilydd (**-ion**) nm racist

hilyddiaeth nf racism

hin nf weather

Hindw (**-iaid**) nm Hindu

hinfynegydd (**-ion**) nm barometer

hiniog (**-au**) nf threshold, door-frame

hinon nf fair weather

hinsawdd (**-soddau**) nf climate

hinsoddol adj climatic

hir (**hirion**) adj, prefix long

hiraeth nm longing, nostalgia, grief; homesickness

hiraethu vb long, yearn, sorrow

hiraethus adj longing; homesick

hirbell adj: **o hirbell** from afar

hirben adj long-headed, shrewd

hirhoedledd nm longevity

hirhoedlog adj long-lived

hirymarhous adj long-suffering

hirymaros nm long-suffering

hithau pron she (on her part), she also

HIV n HIV; **HIV negyddol/positif** HIV negative/positive

hobaid (**-eidiau**) nf peck

hobi (**hobïau**) nm hobby

hoced (**-ion**) nf deceit, fraud

hocedu vb cheat, deceive, defraud

hocedwr (**-wyr**) nm cheat, fraud

hoci nm hockey

hocys npl mallows

hodi vb shoot, ear, run to seed

hoe nf spell, rest

hoeden (**-nau**) nf hoyden

hoedl (**-au**) nf lifetime, life

hoel, hoelen (**heolion**) nf nail

hoelio vb nail

hoeliwr (**-wyr**) nm nailer

hoen nf joy, gladness; vigour

hoenus adj joyous, blithesome, gay

hoenusrwydd nm liveliness, sprightliness

hoenyn (**-nau**) nm snare

hoew see **hoyw**

hofran vb hover

hoff adj dear, fond; favourite

hoffi vb like, love

hoffter nm fondness; delight

hoffus adj lovable, amiable, affectionate

hogen (**-nod**) nf girl

hogennaidd adj girlish

hogfaen (**-feini**) nm whetstone, hone

hogi vb sharpen, whet

hogyn (**hogiau**) nm boy, lad

hongiad (**-au**) nm suspension

hongian vb hang, dangle

h

holgar *adj* inquisitive, curious
holi *vb* ask, question, inquire
holiad (-au) *nm* interrogation, question
holiadur (-on) *nm* questionnaire
holwr (-wyr) *nm* questioner, interrogator; catechist, question-master
holwyddoreg (-au) *nf* catechism
holwyddori *vb* catechize
holl *adj* all, whole
hollalluog *adj* almighty, omnipotent
hollalluowgrwydd *nm* omnipotence
hollbresennol *adj* omnipresent
hollbresenoldeb *nm* omnipresence
hollfyd *nm* universe
hollgyfoethog *adj* almighty
holliach *adj* whole, sound
hollol *adj* quite
hollt (-au) *nf* split, slit, cleft
hollti *vb* split, cleave, slit
hollwybodaeth *nf* omniscience
hollwybodol *adj* omniscient
homeopatheg *nf* homeopathy
homili (-ïau) *nf* homily
hon *pron f of* **hwn**
honcian *vb* waggle; jolt; limp
honedig *adj* alleged
honiad (-au) *nm* claim, assertion, allegation
honni *vb* assert, allege, profess, pretend
honno *pron f of* **hwnnw**
hopran (-au) *nf* mill-hopper; mouth
hosan (-au) *nf* stocking
hoyw *adj* alert, sprightly, lively, gay
hoywdeb, hoywder *nm* sprightliness
hoywi *vb* brighten, smarten
hual (-au) *nm* fetter, shackle
hualu *vb* fetter, shackle
huan *nf* the sun

huawdl *adj* eloquent
hud *nm* magic, illusion, charm, enchantment
hudlath (-au) *nf* magic wand
hudo *vb* charm, allure, beguile
hudol *adj* enchanting ▷ *nm* (**-ion**) enchanter
hudoles (-au) *nf* enchantress, sorceress
hudoliaeth (-au) *nf* enchantment, allurement
hudolus *adj* enchanting, alluring
hudwr (-wyr) *nm* enticer, allurer
huddygl *nm* soot
hufen *nm* cream; **hufen iâ** ice cream
hugan (-au) *nf* cloak, covering; rug
hulio *vb* cover, spread
hun (-au) *nf* sleep, slumber
hun *pron* self; **ei dŷ ei hun** his own house
hunan (-ain) *pron* self ▷ *prefix* self-
hunan-dyb *nm* self-conceit
hunangar *adj* self-loving, selfish
hunanhyderus *adj* self-confident
hunaniaeth *nf* identity
hunanladdiad *nm* self-murder, suicide
hunanol *adj* selfish, conceited
hunanoldeb *nm* selfishness; conceit
hunanymwadiad *nm* self-denial
hunanymwadu *vb* deny oneself
hunell (-au) *nf* wink (of sleep)
hunllef (-au) *nf* nightmare
huno *vb* sleep
huodledd *nm* eloquence
hur (-iau) *nm* hire, wage
hurbwrcas *nm* hire purchase
hurio *vb* hire
huriwr (-wyr) *nm* hirer; hireling
hurt *adj* stunned, stupid
hurtio *vb* stun, stupefy
hurtrwydd *nm* stupidity

hurtyn (**-nod**) *nm* stupid, blockhead

hwb (**hybiau**) *nm* push; effort; lift

hwde (**hwdiwch**) *vb imper* take, accept

hwdi (**-s**) *nm* hoodie

Hwngari *nf* Hungary

hwn (*f* **hon**) *adj, pron* this (one)

hwnnw (*f* **honno**) *adj, pron* that one (*absent*)

hwnt *adv* beyond, away, aside; **tu hwnt** beyond

hwp *nm* push

hwpio, hwpo *vb* push

hwrdd (**hyrddod**) *nm* ram; **yr Hwrdd** Aries

hwrdd (**hyrddiau**) *nm* impulse, stroke

hwre *vb see* **hwde**

hwsmon (**-myn**) *nm* farm-bailiff

hwtio *vb* hoot, hiss

hwy *pron* they, them

hwyad, hwyaden (**hwyaid**) *nf* duck

hwyhau *vb* lengthen, elongate

hwyl (**-iau**) *nf* sail; humour; religious fervour

hwylbren (**-nau, -ni**) *nm* mast

hwylio *vb* sail; prepare, order

hwyliog *adj* fervent, eloquent

hwylus *adj* easy, convenient, comfortable

hwyluso *vb* facilitate

hwylustod *nm* ease, facility, convenience

hwynt *pron* them, they

hwynt-hwy *pron* they, they themselves

hwyr *adj* late ▷ *nm* evening

hwyrach *adv* perhaps ▷ *adj* later

hwyrdrwm *adj* sluggish, drowsy, dull

hwyrfrydig *adj* slow, tardy, reluctant

hwyrfrydigrwydd *nm* tardiness, reluctance

hwyrhau *vb* get late

hwyrol *adj* evening

hwythau *pron* they (on their part), they also

hy *adj* bold

hybarch *adj* venerable

hyblyg *adj* flexible, pliant, pliable

hyblygrwydd *nm* flexibility, pliancy

hybu *vb* improve in health; promote

hyd (**-au, -oedd**) *nm* length ▷ *prep* to, till, as far as

hyder *nm* confidence, trust

hyderu *vb* confide, rely, trust

hyderus *adj* confident

hydred (**-ion**) *nm* longitude

hydredol *adj* longitudinal

hydref (**-au**) *nm* autumn; **Hydref** October

hydrefol *adj* autumnal

hydrin *adj* tractable, docile

hydwyll *adj* gullible

hydwylledd *nm* gullibility

hydwyth *adj* supple, elastic

hydwythedd *nm* elasticity

hydyn *adj* tractable, docile

hydd (**-od**) *nm* stag

hyddysg *adj* well versed, learned

hyf *see* **hy**

hyfder, hyfdra *nm* boldness

hyfedr *adj* expert, skilful, clever

hyfryd *adj* pleasant, delightful, agreeable

hyfrydu *vb* delight

hyfrydwch *nm* delight, pleasure

hyfwyn *adj* kindly, genial

hyfforddedig *adj* trainee

hyfforddi *vb* direct, instruct, train

hyfforddiadol *adj* training

hyfforddiant *nm* instruction, training; **cwrs hyfforddiant** training course

h

hyfforddwr (-wyr) nm guide, instructor; **hyfforddwr gyrru** driving instructor

hygar adj amiable

hygarwch nm amiability

hyglod adj celebrated, renowned, famous

hyglyw adj audible

hygoel adj credible

hygoeledd nm credibility; credulity

hygoelus adj credulous, gullible

hygyrch adj accessible

hyhi pron she, her; herself

hylaw adj handy, convenient; dexterous

hylif (-au) nm, adj fluid, liquid

hylithr adj slippery, fluent

hylosg adj combustible, inflammable

hylwydd adj prosperous

hyll adj ugly, hideous

hylltra nm ugliness

hyllu vb mar, disfigure

hyn adj, pron this; these; that

hynafgwr (-gwyr) nm old man, elder

hynafiad (-iaid) nm ancestor

hynafiaeth (-au) nf antiquity

hynafiaethol adj antiquarian

hynafiaethwr (-wyr), **hynafiaethydd** nm antiquary

hynafol adj ancient

hynaws adj kind, genial

hynawsedd nm kindness, geniality

hynny adj, pron that; those

hynod adj noted, notable, remarkable

hynodi vb distinguish, characterize

hynodion npl peculiarities

hynodrwydd nm peculiarity

hynt (-iau, -oedd) nf way, course

hyrddio, hyrddu vb hurl, impel

hyrddwynt (-oedd) nm hurricane

hyrwyddiad nm promotion

hyrwyddo vb facilitate, promote

hyrwyddwr (-wyr) nm sponsor, promoter

hysb (f **hesb**) adj dry, barren

hysbio vb dry

hysbyddu vb exhaust, drain

hysbys adj known, evident; **dyn hysbys** wise man, sorcerer; **tra hysbys** well-known

hysbyseb (-ion) nf advertisement

hysbysebu vb advertise

hysbysebwr (-wyr) nm advertiser

hysbysiad (-au) nm announcement, advertisement

hysbysrwydd nm information

hysbysu vb inform, announce

hysbyswr (-wyr) nm informant, informer

hysian, hysio vb hiss; set on, incite

hytrach adv rather

hywaith adj industrious, dexterous

hywedd adj trained, tractable

i *prep* to, into
i *pron* I, me
iâ *nm* ice
iach *adj* healthy, well
iachâd *nm* healing
iacháu *vb* heal; save
iachawdwr (-wyr) *nm* saviour
iachawdwriaeth *nf* salvation
iachawr (-wyr) *nm* healer
iachus, iachol *adj* healthy,
 healthful, wholesome
iad (-au) *nf* pate, cranium
iaith (ieithoedd) *nf* language; **yr
 iaith fain** English
iâr (ieir) *nf* hen
iard (ierdydd) *nf* yard
iarll (ieirll) *nm* earl
iarllaeth (-au) *nf* earldom
iarlles (-au) *nf* countess
ias (-au) *nf* shiver; thrill
Iau *nm* Jupiter; **dydd Iau** Thursday

iau (ieuau) *nm* liver
iau (ieuau, ieuoedd) *nf* yoke
iawn *adj* right ▷ *nm* right;
 atonement ▷ *adv* very; **yn iawn** all
 right
iawndal *nm* compensation
iawnder (-au) *nm* right, equity
iawnol *adj* atoning, expiatory
idealaeth *nf* idealism
ideoleg (-au) *nf* ideology
idiom (-au) *nm* idiom
Iddew (-on) *nm* Jew
Iddewes (-au) *nf* Jewess
Iddewiaeth *nf* Judaism
Iddewig *adj* Jewish
iddwf *nm*: **tân iddwf** erysipelas
ie *adv* yes, yea
iechyd *nm* health
iechydaeth *nf* hygiene, sanitation
iechydol *adj* hygienic, sanitary
iechydwriaeth *nf* salvation
ieitheg *nf* philology
ieithegydd (-ion, -wyr) *nm*
 philologist
ieithwedd (-au, -ion) *nf* diction,
 (literary) style
ieithydd (-ion) *nm* linguist
ieithyddiaeth *nf* linguistics,
 philology
ieithyddol *adj* linguistic,
 philological
iet (-au, -iau) *nf* gate
ieuanc (-ainc) *adj* young
ieuenctid *nm* youth
ieuo *vb* yoke
ifanc (-ainc) *adj* young
ifori *nm* ivory
ig (-ion) *nm* hiccup
igam-ogam *adj* zigzag
igian *vb* hiccup
ing (-oedd) *nm* agony, anguish
ingol *adj* agonizing, agonized
ildio *vb* give in, give way

ill *pron* they; **ill dau** they both
impio *vb* sprout, shoot; bud, graft
impyn *nm* graft; scion
inc *nm* ink
incil (**-iau**) *nm* tape
incwm *nm* income
India *nf* India
India'r Gorllewin *npl* West Indies
Indonesia *nf* Indonesia
iod *nm* iota, jot
ioga *nm*, *nf* yoga
Iôn *nm* the Lord
Ionawr *nm* January
Iôr *nm* the Lord
Iorddonen *nf* Jordan
iorwg *nm* ivy
ir *adj* fresh, green, raw
irai *nm* ox-goad
iraid (**ireidiau**) *nm* grease
iraidd *adj* fresh, succulent, luxuriant
Iran *nf* Iran
Iraq *nf* Iraq
irder *nm* freshness, greenness
ireidd-dra *nm* freshness, vigour
ireiddio *vb* freshen
iriad (**-au**) *nm* lubrication, greasing
iro *vb* grease, smear, rub, anoint
irwr (**-wyr**) *nm* greaser
is *adj* inferior, lower ▷ *prep* below,
under ▷ *prefix* under-, sub-, vice-
isadran (**-nau**) *nf* subsection
Isalmaen *nf* Holland
is-deitl (**-au**) *nm* subtitle
isel *adj* low; base; humble;
depressed
iselder (**-au**) *nm* lowness, depth;
depression
iseldir (**-oedd**) *nm* lowland
Iseldiroedd *npl*: **yr Iseldiroedd** the
Netherlands
iselfryd *adj* humble-minded
iselfrydedd *nm* humility,
condescension

iselhau *vb* lower, abase, degrade
isetholiad (**-au**) *nm* by-election
is-gadeirydd *nm* vice-chairman
is-ganghellor *nm* vice-chancellor
is-gapten (**-iaid, -einiaid**) *nm*
lieutenant
isgell *nm* broth, stock
isiarll (**-ieirll**) *nm* viscount
Islamaidd *adj* Islamic
islaw *prep* below, beneath
isod *adv* below, beneath
isop *nm* hyssop
isosod *vb* sublet
isradd (**-iaid**) *nm* inferior,
subordinate
israddol *adj* inferior
israddoldeb *nm* inferiority
Israel *nf* Israel
iswasanaethgar *adj* subservient
isymwybod *nm* subconscious
isymwybyddiaeth *nf*
subconsciousness
ithfaen *nm* granite
Iwerddon *nf* Ireland
Iwerddon Rydd *nf* Eire
Iwerydd *nm*: **yr Iwerydd** the
Atlantic (Ocean)
Iwganda *nf* Uganda
Iwgoslavia *nf* Yugoslavia
iwrch (**iyrchod**) *nm* roebuck

jac codi baw *nm* JCB
jac-y-do *nm* jackdaw
jam *nm* jam
Jamaica *nf* Jamaica
jamio *vb* preserve
jar (-iau) *nf* jar, hot water bottle
jel *n* gel
jersi (-s) *nf* jersey
jest *adv* just, almost
jeti (-iau) *nm* jetty
jetlif *nm* jet stream
jet-sgi (-sgïau) *nf* jet-ski
jet-sgïo *vb* jet-ski
ji-binc (-od) *nf* chaffinch
jîns *npl* jeans
job (-sys) *nf* job
jobyn *nm* job
jôc *nf* joke
jocan *vb* joke
joci (-s) *nm* jockey
jwg (jygiau) *nf* jug
jyngl (-oedd) *nm* jungle

label (-i) *nf* label
labelu *vb* label
labordy (-dai) *nm* laboratory
labro *vb* labour
labrwr (-wyr) *nm* labourer
lafant *nm* lavender
lamp (-au) *nf* lamp
lamplen (-ni) *nf* lampshade
lapio *vb* lap, wrap
larwm *nm* alarm; **larwm lladron** burglar alarm; **larwm mwg, larwm fwg** smoke alarm
lasagne *nm* lasagne
laser (-au, -i) *nm* laser
lawnt (-iau) *nf* lawn
lawrlwytho *vb* download
lefain *nm* leaven
lefeinio *vb* leaven
lefeinllyd *adj* leavened
lefel (-au) *nf* level; **Lefel A** A level
leicio *vb* like

lein (**-iau**) *nf* clothes line, line-out (*rugby*)
lesbiad (**-iaid**) *nf* lesbian
lesbiaidd *adj* lesbian
letys *npl* (*nf* **-en**) lettuce
Libanus *nf* Lebanon
libart *nm* back-yard
Libya *nf* Libya
lifft (**-iau**) *nm* lift
lifrai *nm, nf* livery
lili *nf* lily
limwsîn (**-s, -au**) *nm* limousine
lindys *npl* (*nm* **-yn**) caterpillars
locust (**-iaid**) *nm* locust
lodes *see* **herlodes**
loetran *vb* loiter
lol *nf* nonsense
lolfa (**-feydd**) *nf* lounge, sitting room; **lolfa ymadael** departure lounge
lolian *vb* talk nonsense
lôn (**lonydd**) *nf* lane
loncian *vb* jog
lonciwr (**-wyr**) *nm* jogger
lori (**-ïau**) *nf* lorry
losin *npl* (*nf* **-en**) sweets
lot (**-iau**) *nf* lot
Luxembourg *nf* Luxembourg
lŵans, lwfans *nm* allowance
lwc *nf* luck
lwcus *adj* lucky
lwmp (**lympiau**) *nm* lump

llabed (**-au**) *nf* lappet, lapel, flap
llabwst (**-ystiau**) *nm* lubber, lout
llabyddio *vb* stone
llac *adj* slack, loose, lax
llacio *vb* slacken, loosen, relax
llacrwydd *nm* slackness, laxity
llacs *nm* mud, dirt
llacsog *adj* muddy, dirty
llach (**-iau**) *nf* lash, slash
llachar *adj* bright, brilliant, flashing
llachio *vb* lash, slash
Lladin *nf* Latin
lladmerydd (**-ion**) *nm* interpreter
lladrad (**-au**) *nm* theft, robbery
lladradaidd *adj* stealthy, furtive
lladrata *vb* thieve, steal
lladron *see* **lleidr**
lladrones (**-au**) *nf* female thief
lladronllyd *adj* thievish, pilfering
lladd *vb* cut; kill, slay, slaughter
lladd-dy (**-dai**) *nm* slaughter-house
lladdedig (**-ion**) *adj* killed, slain

lladdedigaeth (-au), lladdfa, lladdwr (-wyr) nm killer, slayer
llaes adj long, loose; **treiglad llaes** spirant mutation
llaesod, llaesodr nf litter (for animals)
llaesu vb slacken, loosen, relax, droop, flag
llaeth nm milk
llaetha vb yield milk
llaethdy (-dai) nm milk-house, dairy
llaethog adj rich in milk; milky
llafar nm utterance, speech ▷ adj vocal; loud
llafariad (-iaid) nf vowel
llafn (-au) nm blade
llafrwyn npl (nf-**en**) bulrushes
llafur (-iau) nm labour; corn
llafurfawr adj elaborate; laborious
llafurio vb labour, toil; till
llafurlu (-oedd) nm manpower, labour force, workforce
llafurus adj laborious, toilsome, painstaking
llafurwr (-wyr) nm labourer, husbandman
llai adj smaller
llaid nm mud, mire
llain (lleiniau) nf patch, piece, narrow strip
llais (lleisiau) nm voice, vote
llaith adj damp, moist
llall (lleill) pron other, another
llam (-au) nm stride, leap, jump, bound
llamhidydd (llamidyddion) nm porpoise
llamsachus adj prancing, frisky
llamu vb stride, leap, bound
llan (-nau) nf church; village
llanast, llanastr nm confusion, mess
llanc (-iau) nm young man, youth, lad

llances (-au, -i) nf young woman, lass
llannerch (llennyrch), llanerchau (-i, -ydd) nf spot, patch, glade
llanw nm flow (of tide) ▷ vb flow, fill
llaprwth nm lout
llariaidd adj mild, meek, gentle
llarieidd-dra nm meekness, gentleness
llarieiddio vb soothe, mollify
llarp (-iau) nm shred, clout
llarpio vb rend, tear, mangle, maul
llarpiog adj tattered, ragged
llaswyr (-au) nm psalter
llatai (-eion) coll n love-messenger
llath (-au) nf yard, wand
llathen (-ni) nf yard
llathr adj bright, glossy, smooth
llathraidd adj smooth; of fine growth
llathru vb polish
llau npl (nf **lleuen**) lice
llaw (dwylaw, dwylo) nf hand
llawcio vb gulp, gorge, gobble
llawchwith adj left-handed
llawdde adj dexterous
llawddryll (-iau) nm pistol, revolver
llawen adj merry, joyful, glad, cheerful
llawenhau vb rejoice, gladden
llawenychu vb rejoice
llawenydd nm joy, gladness, mirth
llawer (-oedd) nm, adj, adv many, much
llawes (llewys) nf sleeve
llawfaeth adj reared by hand
llawfeddyg (-on) nm surgeon
llawfeddygaeth nf surgery
llawfeddygol adj surgical
llaw-fer nf shorthand
llawfom (-iau) nf grenade
llawforwyn (-forynion) nf handmaid

llawn *adj* full ▷ *adv* quite
llawnder, llawndra *nm* fullness, abundance
llawr (lloriau) *nm* floor, ground, earth
llawrydd *adj* freelance
llawryf (-oedd) *nm* laurel, bay
llawryfog, llawryfol *adj* laureate
llawysgrif (-au) *nf* manuscript
llawysgrifen *nf* handwriting
lle (-oedd, llefydd) *nm* place
llecyn (-nau) *nm* place, spot
llech (-au, -i) *nf* slab, flag, slate
llechgi (-gwn) *nm* sneak
llechres (-i) *nf* table, catalogue, list
llechu *vb* hide, shelter; lurk, skulk
llechwedd (-au, -i) *nf* slope, hillside
llechwraidd *adj* stealthy, underhand, insidious
lled (-au) *nm* breadth, width
lled *adv* partly, rather
lledaenu *vb* spread, disseminate, circulate
lleden (lledod) *nf* flat-fish
llediaith *nf, nm* foreign accent
llednais *adj* modest, delicate; meek
llednant (-nentydd) *nf* tributary
lledneisrwydd *nm* modesty, delicacy
lled-orwedd *vb* recline, lounge, loll
lledr (-au) *nm* leather; **lledr y gwefusau** gums
lledred (-ion) *nm* latitude
lledrith *nm* magic, illusion, phantasm
lledrithio *vb* appear, haunt
lledrithiol *adj* illusory, illusive
lledrwr (-wyr) *nm* leather-merchant
lledryw *adj* degenerate
lledu *vb* widen, broaden, expand, spread
lleddf *adj* slanting; flat, minor; plaintive

lleddfolyn (-olion) *nm* sedative
lleddfu *vb* flatten; soften, soothe, allay
llef (-au) *nf* voice, cry
llefain *vb* cry
llefareg *nf* speech training
llefaru *vb* speak, utter
llefarwr (llefarwyr), llefarydd (-ion) *nm* speaker
lleferydd *nm, nf* utterance, voice, speech
llefn *adj of* **llyfn**
llefrith *nm* sweet milk, new milk, milk
llegach *adj* weak, feeble, infirm, decrepit
lleng (-oedd) *nf* legion
lleiaf *adj* least, smallest
lleiafrif (-au) *nm* minority
lleian (-od) *nf* nun
lleiandy (-dai) *nm* nunnery, convent
lleibio *vb* lap, lick
lleidiog *adj* miry
lleidr (lladron) *nm* thief, robber
lleiddiad (-iaid) *nm* assassin
lleihad *nm* diminution, decrease
lleihau *vb* lessen, diminish, decrease
lleill *see* **llall**
lleisio *vb* sound, utter, voice
lleisiol *adj* vocal
lleisiwr (-wyr) *nm* vocalist
lleithder, lleithdra *nm* damp, moisture
lleithig *nf* couch; footstool
lleitho *vb* damp, moisten
llem *adj of* **llym**
llen (-ni) *nf* sheet; veil, curtain
llên *nf* literature, lore, learning
llencyn *nm* stripling, lad
llencyndod *nm* adolescence
llengar *adj* literary, learned
llengig *nf* diaphragm, midriff; **tor llengig** rupture
llên-ladrad (-au) *nm* plagiarism

llenor (**-ion**) *nm* literary man
llenwi *vb* fill; fill in; flow in
llenydda *vb* practise literature
llenyddiaeth (**-au**) *nf* literature
llenyddol *adj* literary
lleol *adj* local
lleoli *vb* locate; localize
lleoliad *nm* location; localization
llercian *vb* lurk, loiter
lles *nm* benefit, profit, good, advantage; **y wladwriaeth les** the welfare state
llesâd *nm* advantage, profit, benefit
llesáu *vb* benefit, advantage
llesg *adj* feeble, faint; languid, sluggish
llesgáu *vb* weaken, languish, faint
llesgedd *nm* weakness, languor, debility
llesmair (**-meiriau**) *nm* faint, swoon
llesmeirio *vb* faint, swoon
llesol *adj* advantageous, profitable, beneficial
llestair, llesteirio *vb* hinder, impede, baulk
llestr (**-i**) *nm* vessel
llesyddiaeth *nf* utilitarianism
lletbai *adj* askew, awry; oblique
lletchwith *adj* awkward, clumsy
lletem (**-au**) *nf* wedge, stud, rivet
lletraws *adj* diagonal
lletwad (**-au**) *nf* ladle
llety (**-au**) *nm* lodging(s)
lletya *vb* lodge
lletygar *adj* hospitable
lletygarwch *nm* hospitality
lletywr (**-wyr**) *nm* lodger; host
lletywraig (**-wragedd**) *nf* landlady
llethol *adj* oppressive, overpowering
llethr (**-au**) *nf* slope, declivity
llethrog *adj* sloping, steep, declining
llethu *vb* overlie; smother; oppress, overpower, overwhelm

lleuad (**-au**) *nf* moon
lleuog *adj* lousy
llew (**-od**) *nm* lion; **dant y llew** dandelion; **y Llew** Leo
llewaidd *adj* lionlike, leonine
llewes (**-au**) *nf* lioness
llewpart (**-pardiaid**) *nm* leopard
llewych *nm* light, brightness
llewyg (**-on**) *nm* faint, swoon
llewygu *vb* faint, swoon
llewyrch *nm* brightness, radiance, gleam
llewyrchu *vb* shine
llewyrchus *adj* flourishing, prosperous
lleyg (**-ion**) *adj* lay
lleygwr (**-wyr**) *nm* layman
lliain (**-einiau**) *nm* linen; cloth; towel
lliaws *nm* host, multitude
llibin *adj* limp, feeble; awkward, clumsy
llid *nm* wrath; irritation, inflammation
llidiart (**-ardau**) *nm* gate
llidio *vb* be angry, chafe, inflame
llidiog *adj* angry, wrathful; inflamed
llidiowgrwydd *nm* wrath, indignation
llidus *adj* inflamed
llieiniwr (**-wyr**) *nm* linen-draper
llif (**-iau**) *nf* saw
llif (**-ogydd**) *nm* stream, flood, current
llifbridd *nm* alluvium
llifddor (**-au**) *nf* floodgate
llifddwfr (**-ddyfroedd**) *nm* flood, torrent
llifeiriant (**-iaint**) *nm* flood
llifeirio *vb* flow, stream
llifeiriol *adj* streaming, overflowing
llifio *vb* saw
llifiwr (**-wyr**) *nm* sawyer

llifo vb flow, stream
llifo vb grind (tool)
llifo vb dye
llifogydd npl flooding
llifolau (-euadau) nm floodlight
llifwr (-wyr) nm dyer
llifyn (-nau, -ion) nm dye
llilinio vb streamline
llin nm flax; **had llin** linseed
llinach (-au) nf lineage, pedigree
llindagu vb strangle, throttle, choke
llinell (-au) nf line; **llinell gais** try
  line; **llinell gymorth** helpline
llinelliad (-au) nm lineation,
  drawing
llinellog adj lined, ruled
llinellol adj lineal
llinglwm nm: **cwlwm llinglwm**
  tight knot
lliniaru vb ease, soothe, allay
llinorog adj eruptive; purulent,
  suppurating
llinos (-od) nf linnet
llinyn (-nau) nm line, string, twine
llinynnu vb string
llipa adj limp, weak
llipryn (-nod) nm hobbledehoy,
  weakling
lliprynnaidd adj limp, flabby
llith (-iau, -oedd) nf lesson, lecture;
  bait, mash
llithio vb entice, allure, seduce; feed
llithren (-nau) nf chute
llithriad (-au) nm slip, glide
llithrig adj slippery, glib, fluent
llithrgrwydd nm slipperiness,
  glibness
llithro vb slip, glide, slide
lliw (-iau) nm colour, hue, dye
lliwio vb colour, dye
lliwiog adj coloured
llo (lloi) nm calf
lloc (-iau) nm fold, pen

lloches (-au) nf refuge, shelter, den
llochesu vb harbour, shelter
llochi vb stroke, caress, fondle
llodig adj in heat (of a sow)
llodrau npl trousers, breeches
Lloegr nf England
lloer (-au) nf moon
lloeren (-ni, -nau) nf satellite
lloerig adj lunatic
llofnod (-au), **llofnodiad** nm
  signature
llofnodi vb sign
llofrudd (-ion) nm murderer;
  llofrudd cyfresol serial killer
llofruddiaeth (-au) nf murder
llofruddio vb murder
llofruddiog adj guilty of murder
lloffa vb glean
lloffion npl gleanings
llofft (-ydd) nf loft, bedroom, gallery
lloffwr (-wyr) nm gleaner
lloffyn nm bundle of gleanings
llog (-au) nm interest
llogi vb hire
llogwr (-wyr) nm hirer
llong (-au) nf ship; **llong ofod**
  spaceship
llongddrylliad (-au) nm shipwreck
llongwr (-wyr) nm sailor
llongwriaeth nf seamanship
llom adj f of **llwm**
llon adj glad, merry
llonaid, llond nm full
llonder nm gladness, joy
llongyfarch vb congratulate
llongyfarchiad (-au, -archion) nm
  congratulation
lloniant nm joy, cheer
llonni vb cheer, gladden
llonydd adj quiet, still ▷ nm quiet,
  calm
llonyddu vb quiet, still, calm
llonyddwch nm quietness, quiet

llorgynllun (-iau) *nm* ground plan
llorio *vb* floor; ground (*rugby*)
llorwedd *adj* horizontal
llosg *nm, adj* burning
llosgach *nm* incest
llosgadwy *adj* combustible
llosgfa (-fâu, -feydd) *nf* burning, inflammation
llosgfynydd (-oedd) *nm* volcano
llosgi *vb* burn, scorch; smart
llosgwrn (-yrnau) *nm* tail
llosgydd (-ion) *nm* incinerator
llu (-oedd) *nm* host
lluched *npl* (*nf*-**en**) lightning
lluchfa (-feydd) *nf* snowdrift
lluchio *vb* throw, fling, pelt; throw away
lluchiwr (-wyr) *nm* thrower
lludlyd *adj* ashy
lludu, lludw *nm* ashes, ash
lludded *nm* weariness, fatigue
lluddedig *adj* wearied, tired, fatigued
lluddedu *vb* tire, weary
lluddias, lluddio *vb* hinder; forbid
lluest (-au) *nm* tent, booth
lluestfa (-feydd) *nf* encampment
lluestu *vb* encamp
lluesty (-tai) *nm* tent, booth
llugoer *adj* lukewarm
lluman (-au) *nm* banner, standard, ensign
llumanwr (-wyr) *nm* linesman
llumon *nm* chimney stack, peak
Llun, dydd Llun *nm* Monday
llun (-iau) *nm* form, image, picture
Llundain *nf* London
lluniad (-au) *nm* drawing
lluniadaeth (-au) *nf* draughtsmanship
lluniaeth *nm* food, nourishment
lluniaethu *vb* order, ordain, decree
lluniaidd *adj* shapely

lluniedydd *nm* draughtsman
llunio *vb* form, shape, fashion
lluniwr (-wyr) *nm* former, maker
llun-recordydd (-ion) *nm* video-tape recorder
lluosflwydd *adj* perennial
lluosi *vb* multiply
lluosiad *nm* multiplication
lluosill, lluosillafog *adj* polysyllabic
lluosog *adj* numerous; plural
lluosogi *vb* multiply
lluosogiad *nm* multiplication
lluoswm *nm* product (*in maths*)
lluosydd *nm* multiplier
llurgunio *vb* mangle, mutilate
llurguniwr (-wyr) *nm* mangler, mutilator
llurig (-au) *nf* coat of mail, cuirass
llurigog *adj* mail-clad
llus *npl* (*nf*-**en**) bilberries, whinberries
llusern (-au) *nf* lantern, lamp
llusg (-ion) *nm* draught; drag
llusgfad (-au) *nm* tugboat
llusgo *vb* drag; trail; crawl; drawl
llusgwr (-wyr) *nm* dragger, slowcoach
llutrod *nm* mire, ashes, debris
lluwch *nm* dust; spray; snowdrift
lluydd *nm* host, army
lluyddu *vb* mobilise
llw (-on) *nm* oath
llwch *nm* dust, powder
llwdn (llydnod) *nm* young of animals
llwfr *adj* timid, cowardly
llwfrdra *nm* cowardice
llwfrddyn, llwfrgi *nm* coward
llwfrhau *vb* faint
llwglyd *adj* hungry, famished
llwgr *nm* corruption ▷ *adj* corrupt
llwgrwobrwy (-on) *nm* bribe

llwgrwobrwyo vb bribe
llwgu vb starve, famish
llwm(f **llom**) adj bare; destitute, poor
llwnc nm gulp, swallow; gullet
llwncdestun nm toast (health)
llwr, llwrw nm track; **llwr ei ben** headlong; **llwr ei gefn** backwards
llwy (-au) nf spoon, ladle
llwyaid (-eidiau) nf spoonful
llwybr (-au) nm path, track
llwybreiddio vb direct, forward
llwybro vb walk
llwyd adj brown; grey; pale; hoary
llwydaidd adj greyish, palish
llwydi, llwydni nm greyness; mould, mildew
llwydnos nf dusk, twilight
llwydo vb turn grey; become mouldy
llwydrew nm hoar-frost
llwydrewi vb cast hoar-frost
llwydd, -iant nm success, prosperity
llwyddiannus adj successful, prosperous
llwyddo vb succeed, prosper
llwyfan (-nau) nm, nf platform, stage
llwyfandir (-oedd) nm plateau
llwyfannu vb stage
llwyfen (llwyf) nf elm
llwyn (-i) nm grove; bush
llwyn (-au) nf loin
llwynog (-od) nm fox
llwynoges (-au) nf vixen
llwynwst nf lumbago
llwyo vb use a spoon; ladle
llwyr adj entire, complete, total ▷ adv entirely, altogether ▷ prefix total
llwyredd nm entireness, completeness
llwyrymatal, llwyrymwrthod vb abstain totally

llwyrymwrthodwr (-wyr) nm teetotaller
llwyth (-au) nm tribe, clan
llwyth (-i) nm load, burden
llwytho vb load, burden
llwythog adj laden, burdened
llychlyd adj dusty
Llychlyn nf Scandinavia
llychwino vb spot, tarnish, soil, sully
llychyn nm particle of dust, mote
llydan adj broad, wide
Llydaw nf Brittany
llydnu vb bring forth, foal
llyfn(f **llefn**) adj smooth, sleek
llyfnder, -dra nm smoothness, sleekness
llyfndew adj plump, sleek
llyfnhau vb smooth, level
llyfnu vb smooth, level; harrow
llyfr (-au) nm book; **llyfr nodiadau** notebook
llyfrbryf (-ed) nm bookworm
llyfrfa nf (-feydd) library; book room; official publishing house of religious denomination, government etc
llyfrgell (-oedd) nf library
llyfrgellydd (-ion) nm librarian
llyfrifeg nm, nf book-keeping
llyfrnod (-au) nm bookmark
llyfrwerthwr (-wyr) nm bookseller
llyfrydd (-ion) nm bibliographer, transcriber of books
llyfryddiaeth nf bibliography
llyfryn (-nau) nm booklet, pamphlet
llyfu vb lick
llyffant (-od, llyffaint) nm frog, toad
llyffethair (-eiriau) nf fetter, shackle
llyffetheirio vb fetter, shackle
llyg (-od) nm, nf shrew(-mouse)
llygad (llygaid) nm eye; **llygad y dydd** daisy

llygad-dynnu vb bewitch
llygadog adj eyed, sharp-eyed
llygadrwth adj wide-eyed, staring
llygadrythu vb stare
llygadu vb eye
llygatgraff adj keen-eyed, sharp-sighted
llygedyn nm ray of light
llygeidiog adj eyed
llygoden (llygod) nf mouse; **llygoden fawr, llygoden ffrengig** rat
llygota vb catch mice
llygotwr (-wyr, f **llygotwraig)** nm mouser, ratter
llygradwy adj corruptible
llygredig adj corrupt, depraved, degraded
llygredigaeth (-au) nf corruption
llygredd nm corruptness, depravity
llygriad (-au) nm corruption, adulteration
llygru vb corrupt, adulterate
llygrwr (-wyr) nm corrupter, adulterator
llynges (-au) nf fleet, navy
llyngeswr (-wyr) nm navy-man
llyngesydd (-ion) nm admiral
llyngyr npl (nf **-en)** (intestinal) worms
llym (f **llem)** adj sharp, keen, severe
llymaid (-eidiau) nm sip, drink
llymarch (llymeirch) nm oyster
llymder nm sharpness, keenness, severity
llymder, llymdra nm bareness, poverty
llymeitian, llymeitio vb sip, tipple
llymeitiwr (-wyr) nm tippler, sot
llymhau vb make bare
llymhau vb sharpen
llymrïaid npl (nf **-ïen)** sand-eels
llymru nm flummery

llymsur adj acrid
llymu vb sharpen, whet
llyn (-noedd) nm lake, pond, pool
llynciad (-au) nm draught, gulp
llyncu vb swallow, gulp, absorb
llyncwr (-wyr) nm swallower, guzzler
llynedd nf last year
llyo vb lick
llys (-oedd) nm court, hall, palace
llysaidd adj courtly, polite
llysblant npl step-children
llyschwaer nf step-sister
llysenw (-au) nm nickname
llysenwi vb nickname
llysfab nm step-son
llysfam nf step-mother
llysferch nf step-daughter
llysfrawd nm step-brother
llysgenhadaeth nf embassy, legation
llysgenhadol adj ambassadorial
llysgennad (-genhadon) nm ambassador
llysiau npl (nm **-ieuyn)** herbs, vegetables
llysieuol adj herbal, vegetable
llysieuydd (-ion, -wyr) nm botanist; vegetarian
llysnafedd nm snivel, slime
llystad nm step-father
llyswenwyn nm herbicide
llysysol adj herbivorous
llyswen (llyswyod) nf eel
llysywenna vb catch eels
llythrennol adj literal
llythyr (-au) nm letter, epistle
llythyrdy (-dai) nm post-office
llythyren (llythrennau) nf letter, type
llythyrwr (-wyr) nm letter-writer
llyw (-iau) nm ruler; rudder, helm
llywaeth adj hand-fed, tame, pet

ll

llywiawdwr (-wyr) *nm* ruler, governor

llywio *vb* rule, govern, direct, steer

llywiwr (-wyr) *nm* steersman, helmsman

llywodraeth (-au) *nf* government

llywodraethol *adj* governing, dominant

llywodraethu *vb* govern, rule

llywodraethwr (-wyr) *nm* governor, ruler

llywydd (-ion) *nm* president

llywyddiaeth (-au) *nf* presidency

llywyddol *adj* presidential

llywyddu *vb* preside

mab (meibion) *nm* boy, son; man, male

mabaidd *adj* filial

maban (-od) *nm* babe, baby

mabandod *nm* childhood, infancy

mabinogi *nm* tale, story

mablygad *nm* eyeball

mabmaeth (-au, -od) *nm* foster-son

maboed *nm* childhood, infancy, youth

mabolaeth *nf* sonship; boyhood, youth

mabolaidd *adj* youthful, boyish

mabolgamp (-au) *nf* game, sport, feat

mabsant *nm* patron saint

mabwysiad *nm* adoption

mabwysiadol *adj* adoptive; adopted

mabwysiadu *vb* adopt

macrell (**mecryll**) *nf, nm* mackerel

macsu *vb* to brew

macwy (**-aid**) *nm* youth, page

machlud, machludo *vb* set, go down; **haul** sunset

machludiad *nm* setting, going down

machnïydd *nm* mediator

madarch *npl* (*nf*-**en**) mushrooms

madfall (**-od**) *nm* lizard

madrondod *nm* giddiness, stupefaction

madroni *vb* make or become giddy

madru *vb* putrefy, fester, rot

madruddyn *nm* cartilage; **madruddyn y cefn** spinal cord

maddau *vb* pardon, forgive, remit

maddeuant *nm* pardon, forgiveness

maddeugar *adj* of a forgiving disposition

maddeuol *adj* pardoning, forgiving

maddeuwr (**-wyr**) *nm* pardoner

mae *vb* is, are; there is, there are

maeden *nf* slut, jade

maeddu *see* **baeddu**

maen (**meini**) *nm* stone

maenol, maenor (**-au**) *nf* manor

maentumio *vb* maintain

maer (**-od, meiri**) *nm* mayor

maeres (**-au**) *nf* mayoress

maerol *adj* mayoral

maeryddiaeth *nf* mayoralty

maes (**meysydd**) *nm* field ▷ *adj* free-range; **i maes** out; **maes glanio** airport

maesglaf (**-gleifion**) *nm* outpatient

maeslywydd (**-ion**) *nm* field-marshal

maestir (**-oedd**) *nm* open country, plain

maestref (**-i, -ydd**) *nf* suburb

maeth *nm* nourishment, nutriment

maethlon *adj* nourishing, nutritious

maethu *vb* nourish, nurture

maethydd (**-ion**) *nm* nourisher

maethyn (**-nau**) *nm* nutrient; suckling

mafon *npl* (*nf*-**en**) raspberries

magl (**-au**) *nf* snare; mesh

maglu *vb* snare, mesh, trip

magnel (**-au**) *nf* gun, cannon

magnelaeth *nf* artillery

magnelwr (**-wyr**) *nm* gunner

magnesiwm *nm* magnesium

magnetedd *nm, nf* magnetism

magneteiddio *vb* magnetise

magu *vb* breed, rear, nurse; gain, acquire

magwraeth *nf* nourishment, nurture

magwyr (**-ydd**) *nf* wall

maharen (**meheryn**) *nm* ram; wether

Mai *nm* May

mai *conj* that it is

maidd *nm* whey

main (**meinion**) *adj* fine, slender, thin; **main y cefn** small of the back

mainc (**meinciau**) *nf* bench, form, seat

maint *nm* size, quantity, number

maintioli *nm* size, stature

Maiorca *nf* Majorca

maip *npl* (*nf* **meipen**) turnips

maith (**meithion**) *adj* long, tedious

mâl *adj* ground

malais *nm* malice

maldod *nm* dalliance, affection

maldodi *vb* pet, pamper, indulge

Maleisia *nf* Malaysia

maleisus *adj* malicious

maleithiau *npl* chilblains

malio *vb* care, mind, heed

Malta *nf* Malta

malu *vb* grind, mince, chop, smash

malurio *vb* pound; crumble, moulder

m

malurion *npl* fragments, debris

malwod *npl* (*nf* **-en,** *nf* **malwen**) snails

malwr (**-wyr**) *nm* grinder

mall *nf* blight; **y fall** Belial, perdition

malltod *nm* rot, blight, blast

mallu *vb* rot, blast

mam (**-au**) *nf* mother, mum; **mam-gu** grandmother

mamaeth (**-od**) *nf* nurse

mamal (**-iaid**) *nm* mammal

mamiaith (**-ieithoedd**) *nf* mother-tongue

mamog (**-iaid**) *nf* dam, sheep with young

mamolaeth (**-au**) *nf* maternity

mamwlad (**-wledydd**) *nf* motherland

man (**-nau**) *nm, nf* place, spot; blemish

mân *adj* small, fine, petty

mandyllog *adj* porous

maneg (**menig**) *nf* glove, gauntlet

mangre *nf* place, spot

manion *npl* scraps, trifles, minutiæ

mantais (**-eision**) *nf* advantage

manteisio *vb* take advantage, profit

manteisiol *adj* advantageous; profitable

mantell (**-oedd, mentyll**) *nf* mantle

mantellog *adj* mantled

mantol (**-ion**) *nf* balance; **y Fantol** Libra

mantolen (**-ni**) *nf* balance-sheet

mantoli *vb* turn scale, balance, weigh

manŵaidd *adj* delicate, fine

mân-werthu *vb* retail

manwl *adj* exact, precise, strict, particular

manwl-gywir *adj* precise

manylion *npl* particulars, details

manylrwydd *nm* exactness, precision

manylu *vb* go into detail, particularize

manylwch *nm* exactness, precision

map (**-iau**) *nm* map

mapio *vb* map

mapiwr (**-wyr**) *nm* cartographer

marathon (**-au**) *nm, nf* marathon

marblen (**marblys**) *nf* marble

marc (**-iau**) *nm* mark

marcio *vb* mark

march (**meirch**) *nm* horse, stallion

marchlu (**-oedd**) *nm* cavalry

marchnad (**-oedd**) *nf* market

marchnadfa (**-oedd**) *nf* marketplace

marchnata *vb* market, trade

marchnatwr (**-wyr**) *nm* merchant

marchnerth (**-oedd**) *nm* horsepower

marchocáu *vb* ride a horse

marchog (**-ion**) *nm* horseman, rider; knight

marchogaeth *vb* ride

marchogwr (**-wyr**) *nm* rider, horseman

marchredyn *npl* (*nf* **-en**) polypody fern

marchwellt *nm* tall, coarse grass

marian *nm* holm, strand, moraine

marlad *nm* drake

marmalêd (**-au**) *nm* marmalade

marmor *nm* marble

marsialydd (**-ion**) *nm* marshal

marsiandïaeth *nf* merchandise

marsiandïwr (**-wyr**) *nm* merchant

marsipan *nm* marzipan

marw *vb* die

marw (**meirw, meirwon**) *n, adj* dead

marwaidd *adj* lifeless, sluggish, moribund

marwdon *nf* dandruff

marweidd-dra *nm* deadness, sluggishness

marweiddio vb deaden, mortify
marwhad nm mortification
marwhau vb deaden, mortify
marwnad (-au) nf lament, elegy
marwol adj deadly, mortal, fatal
marwolaeth (-au) nf death
marwoldeb nm mortality
marwolion npl mortals
marwor npl (nm **-yn**) embers; charcoal
marwydos npl embers
masarnen (masarn) nf sycamore
masgl (-au) nf shell, pod
masglo, masglu vb shell; interlace
masnach (-au) nf trade, traffic, commerce; **masnach deg** fair trade
masnachol adj commercial, business
masnachu vb do business, trade, traffic
masnachwr (-wyr) nm dealer, merchant
masw adj wanton
maswedd nm wantonness, ribaldry
masweddol adj wanton, ribald
maswr (-wyr) nm outside half
mat (-iau) nm mat
mater (-ion) nm matter
materol adj material; materialistic
materoliaeth nf materialism
matog (-au) nf mattock
matras (-resi) nm mattress
matrics (-au) nm matrix
matsien (matsys) nf match
math (-au) nm sort, kind
mathemateg nm mathematics, maths
mathru vb trample, tread
mathrwr (-wyr) nm trampler
mawl nm praise
mawn coll n (nf **-en**) peat
mawnog adj peaty ▷ nf peat-bog
mawr (-ion) adj big, great, large

mawredd nm greatness, grandeur, majesty
mawreddog adj grand, majestic; grandiose
mawrfrydig adj magnanimous
mawrfrydigrwydd nm magnanimity
mawrhau vb magnify, enlarge
mawrhydi nm majesty
Mawrth nm Mars; March; **dydd Mawrth** Tuesday
mawrygu vb magnify, extol
mebyd nm childhood, infancy, youth
mecaneg nf mechanics
mecanwaith (-weithiau) nm mechanism
mecanyddol adj mechanical
Mecsico nf Mexico
mechnïaeth nf surety, bail
mechnïo vb go bail, become surety
mechnïol adj vicarious
mechnïydd (-ion) nm surety, bail
medel (-au) nf reaping; reaping party
medelwr (-wyr) nm reaper
Medi nm September
medi vb reap
medr nm skill, ability
medru vb know, be able
medrus adj clever, skilful
medrusrwydd nm cleverness, skilfulness, skill
medrydd (-ion) nm gauge
medd nm mead
medd vb says
meddal adj soft, tender
meddalhau, meddalu vb soften
meddalwch nm softness
meddalwedd nm software
meddiannol adj possessing, possessive
meddiannu vb possess, occupy
meddiant (-iannau) nm possession

m

meddu *vb* possess, own

meddw (-on) *adj* drunk, intoxicated

meddwdod *nm* drunkenness, intoxication

meddwi *vb* get drunk, intoxicate, inebriate

meddwl *vb* think; mean ▷ *nm* (**meddyliau**) thought; meaning; opinion

meddwol *adj* intoxicating

meddwyn (-won) *nm* drunkard, inebriate

meddyg (-on) *nm* physician, doctor; **meddyg teulu** GP, general practitioner

meddygaeth *nf* medicine

meddygfa (-feydd) *nf* surgery

meddyginiaeth (-au) *nf* medicine, remedy, medication

meddyginiaethol *adj* medicinal, remedial

meddyginiaethu *vb* cure, remedy, heal

meddygol *adj* medicinal; medical

meddylfryd *nm* mind, affection, bent

meddylgar *adj* thoughtful

meddylgarwch *nm* thoughtfulness

meddyliol *adj* mental, intellectual

meddyliwr (-wyr) *nm* thinker

mefus *npl* (*nf*-**en**) strawberries

megin (-au) *nf* bellows

megino *vb* work bellows, blow

megis *conj*, *prep* as, so as, like a

Mehefin *nm* June

meicrobioleg *nm*, *nf* microbiology

meicro-brosesydd *nm* micro-processor

meicroffon (-au) *nm* microphone

meicro-sglodyn (-ion) *nm* microchip

meicrosgop (-au) *nm* microscope

meichiad (-iaid) *nm* swineherd

meichiau (-iafon) *nm* surety, bail

meidrol *adj* finite

meidroldeb *nm* finiteness

meiddio *vb* dare, venture

meiddion *npl* curds and whey

meiddlyd *adj* wheyey, curdled

meigryn *nm* migraine

meilart *nm* drake

meillion *npl* (*nf*-**en**) clover

meim (-iau) *nm*, *nf* mime

meimio *vb* mime

meinder *nm* fineness, slenderness

meindio *vb* mind, care

meinedd *nm* slender part, small

meingefn *nm* small of the back

meinhau *vb* grow slender, taper

meini *see* **maen**

meinllais *nm* shrill voice, treble

meintoli *vb* quantify

meintoliad *nm* quantification

meinwe (-bledd) *nf* tissue

meipen (maip) *nf* turnip

meirch *see* **march**

meirioli *vb* thaw

meirw *see* **marw**

meistr (-iaid, -i, -adoedd) *nm* master

meistres (-i) *nf* mistress

meistrolaeth *nf* mastery

meistrolgar *adj* masterful, masterly

meistroli *vb* master

meitin *nm*: **ers meitin** some time since

meitr (-au) *nm* mitre

meithder *nm* length

meithrin *vb* nurture, rear, foster

meithrinfa (-oedd) *nf* nursery

mêl *nm* honey

mela *vb* gather honey

melan *nf* melancholy

melen *adj f of* **melyn**

melfaréd *nm* corduroy

melfed *nm* velvet

melin (-au) *nf* mill

melinydd (-ion) *nm* miller
melodaidd *adj* melodious
melodi *nm* melody
melyn (*f* **melen**) *adj* yellow ▷ *nm* yellow; **melyn wy** yolk of egg; **y clefyd melyn** jaundice
melynaidd *adj* yellowish, tawny
melynder, melyndra *nm* yellowness
melynddu *adj* tawny, swarthy
melyngoch *adj* yellowish red, orange
melyni *nm* yellowness; jaundice
melynu *vb* yellow
melynwyn *adj* yellowish white, cream
melys *adj* sweet ▷ *npl* (**-ion**) sweets
melyster, melystra *nm* sweetness
melysu *vb* sweeten
mellt *npl* (*nf* **-en**) lightning
melltennu *vb* flash lightning
melltigaid, melltigedig *adj* accursed, cursed
melltith (-ion) *nf* curse
melltithio *vb* curse
memorandwm (-anda) *nm* memorandum
memrwn (-rynau) *nm* parchment, vellum
men (-ni) *nf* wain, waggon, cart
mên *adj* mean
mendio *vb* mend, heal, recover
menestr *nm* cup-bearer
menig *see* **maneg**
mentr *nf* venture, hazard
mentro *vb* venture, hazard
mentrus *adj* adventurous
mentrwr (-wyr) *nm* entrepreneur
menyw (-od) *nf* woman
mêr (merion) *nm* marrow
mercwri *nm* mercury
merch (-ed) *nf* daughter, woman
Mercher *nm* Mercury; **dydd Mercher** Wednesday

mercheta *vb* womanise
merchetaidd *adj* effeminate
merddwr (-ddyfroedd) *nm* stagnant water
merf, merfaidd *adj* insipid, tasteless, flat
merfdra, merfeidd-dra *nm* insipidity
merlota *vb* pony-trek
merlyn (-nod, merlod, *f* **merlen)** *nm* pony
merllyd *adj* insipid
merthyr (-on, -i) *nm* martyr
merthyrdod *nm* martyrdom
merthyru *vb* martyr
merwindod *nm* numbness, tingling
merwino *vb* benumb, tingle, smart
meryw *npl* (*nf* **-en**) juniper trees
mes *npl* (*nf* **-en**) acorns
mesa *vb* gather acorns
mesur (-au) *nm* measure; metre; tune; bill
mesur, mesuro *vb* measure, mete
mesureg *nf* mensuration
mesuriad (-au) *nm* measurement
mesurwr (-wyr) *nm* measurer; surveyor
mesurydd (-ion) *nm* measurer, meter
metamorffedd *nm* metamorphism
metel (-oedd) *nm* metal; mettle
metelaidd *adj* metallic
metelydd (-ion) *nm* metallurgist
metelyddiaeth *nf* metallurgy
metr (-au) *nm* metre
metrig *adj* metric
metrigeiddio *vb* metricate
meth (-ion) *nm* miss, failure
methdaliad (-au) *nm* bankruptcy
methdalwr (-wyr) *nm* bankrupt
methedig (-ion) *adj* decrepit, infirm, disabled
methiannus *adj* failing, decayed

m

methiant *nm* failure
methodoleg *nf* methodology
methu *vb* fail, miss
meudwy (-aid, -od) *nm* hermit, recluse
meudwyaidd *adj* hermit-like, retiring
meudwyol *adj* eremitic
mewian *vb* mew
mewn *prep* in, within
mewnadlu *vb* inhale
mewnforio *vb* import ▷ *npl* **(-ion)** imports
mewnfudwr (-wyr) *nm* immigrant
mewngofnodi *vb* log in, log on
mewnol *adj* inward, internal; subjective
mewnrwyd (-i, -au) *nf* intranet
mewnwr (-wyr) *nm* scrum-half
mewnyn (mewnion) *nm* filling
mi *pron* I, me
mieri *npl* (*nf* **miaren**) brambles
mig *nf*: **chwarae mig** play bo-peep
mign, mignen *nf* bog, quagmire
migwrn (-yrnau) *nm* knuckle; ankle
mil (-od) *nm* animal
mil (-oedd) *nf* thousand
milain *adj* angry, fierce, savage, cruel
mileindra *nm* savageness, ferocity
mileinig *adj* savage, ferocious, malignant
milfed *adj* thousandth
milfeddyg (-on) *nm* veterinary surgeon
milfil *nf* million, an indefinite number
milflwyddiant *nm* millennium
milgi (-gwn) *nm* greyhound
miliast (-ieist) *nf* greyhound bitch
militariaeth *nf* militarism
militarydd *nm* militarist
miliwn (-iynau) *nf* million
miliynydd (-ion) *nm* millionaire
milodfa (-oedd, -feydd) *nf* menagerie

milwr (-wyr) *nm* soldier
milwraidd *adj* soldierly
milwriad (-iaid) *nm* colonel
milwriaeth *nf* warfare
milwriaethus *adj* militant
milwrio *vb* militate
milwrol *adj* military
milltir (-oedd) *nf* mile
min (-ion) *nm* edge; brink; lip
mindlws *adj* simpering, affected, precious
mingamu *vb* grimace
minibws (-bysiau, -bysys) *nm* minibus
minio *vb* edge, sharpen; make impression
miniog *adj* sharp, keen, cutting
minlliw (-iau) *nm* lipstick
minnau *pron* I (on my part), I also
mintai (-eioedd) *nf* band, troop
mintys *nm* mint
mirain *adj* fair, beautiful, comely
mireinder *nm* beauty, comeliness
miri *nm* merriment, fun, festivity
mis (-oedd) *nm* month
misio *vb* miss, fail
misol (-ion) *adj* monthly
misolyn (-olion) *nm* monthly (magazine)
mitsio *vb* mitch, play truant
miwsig *nm* music
mo *contr. of* **dim o**; **nid oes mo'i debyg** there is none like him
moch *npl* (*nm* **-yn**) swine, pigs, hogs
mocha *vb* pig, litter
mochaidd *adj* swinish, hoggish
mochynnaidd *adj* piggish, swinish
modfedd (-i) *nf* inch
modiwl (-au) *nm* module
modrwy (-au) *nf* ring
modrwyo *vb* ring
modrwyog *adj* ringed
modryb (-edd) *nf* aunt

modur (-on) nm motor
modurdy (-dai) nm garage
modurwr (-wyr) nm motorist
modylu vb modulate
modylydd (-ion) nm modulator
modd (-ion, -au) nm mode, manner; means; mood
moddion npl means; medicine
moddol adj modal
moel (-ion) adj bare, bald; hornless, polled
moel (-ydd) nf hill
moeli (-ydd) vb make or become bald; hang (ears)
moelni nm bareness, baldness
moelyn nm bald-head
moes vb imper give, bring hither
moes (-au) nf morality; (pl) manners, morals
moeseg nf ethics
Moesenaidd adj Mosaic
moesgar adj mannerly, polite
moesgarwch nm politeness
moesol adj moral, ethical
moesoldeb nm morality
moesoli vb moralize
moesolwr (-wyr) nm moralist
moeswers (-i) nf moral
moesymgrymu vb bow
moeth (-au) nm luxury, indulgence
moethi vb pamper, indulge
moethlyd adj pampered, spoilt
moethus adj luxurious, pampered
moethusrwydd nm luxuriousness, luxury
molawd nm, nf eulogy, panegyric
molecwl (-cylau) nm molecule
molecwlar adj molecular
moled (-au) nf kerchief; muffler
moli, moliannu vb praise, laud
moliannus adj praised, praiseworthy
moliant (-iannau) nm praise

mollt (myllt) nm wether
molltgig nm mutton
moment (-au) nf moment
momentwm (momenta) nm momentum
monarchiaeth nf monarchy
monarchydd (-ion) nm monarchist
monni vb sulk, pout
monocsid (-au) nm monoxide
monópoli (-ïau) nm monopoly
mor adv how, so, as
môr (moroedd) nm sea, ocean; **Môr Adria** the Adriatic; **y Môr Canoldir, Môr y Canoldir** the Mediterranean; **Môr Hafren** the Bristol Channel; **Môr y Gogledd** the North Sea; **Môr Iwerddon** the Irish Sea; **Môr Coch** the Red Sea; **y Môr Iwerydd** the Atlantic; **y Môr Tawel** the Pacific; **y Môr Udd** the English Channel
moratoriwm (-atoria) nm moratorium
mordaith (-deithiau) nf voyage
mordeithiwr (-wyr) nm voyager
mordwyaeth nf navigation
mordwyo vb go by sea, voyage, sail
mordwywr (-wyr) nm mariner, sailor
morddwyd (-ydd) nf, nm thigh
morfa (-feydd) nm moor, fen, marsh
morfil (-od) nm whale
môr-forwyn (-forynion) nf mermaid
morfran (-frain) nf cormorant
morffoleg nm, nf morphology
morffolegol adj morphological
morgainc (-geinciau) nf gulf
morgais (-geisiau) nm mortgage
morgeisî nm mortgagee
morgeisio vb mortgage
môr-gerwyn nf whirlpool, vortex, abyss

m

morglawdd (-gloddiau) nm embankment, mole
morgrug npl (nm -**yn**) ants
morio vb voyage, sail
môr-ladrad (-au) nm piracy
môr-leidr (-ladron) nm pirate
morlen (-ni) nm chart
morlo (-loi) nm sea-calf, seal
morllyn (-noedd) nf, nm lagoon
Moroco nf Morocco
morol adj maritime
moron npl (nf -**en**) carrots
mortais (-eisiau) nf mortise
morteisio vb mortise
morter (-au) nm mortar
morthwyl (-ion) nm hammer
morthwylio vb hammer
morthwyliwr (-wyr) nm hammerer
morwr (-wyr) nm seaman, sailor, mariner
morwriaeth nf seamanship, navigation
morwydd npl (nf -**en**) mulberry-trees
morwyn (-ynion) nf maid, virgin; **y Forwyn** Virgo
morwyndod nm virginity
morwynol adj virgin, maiden
moryd (-iau) nf estuary
moryn (-nau) nm billow, breaker
mosaig (-au) nm, adj mosaic
Moscow nf Moscow
Moslem nm, nf Moslem
Moslemaidd adj Moslem, Muslim
motif (-au) nm motive
motiff (-au) nm motif
MP3 n MP3; **peiriant MP3** MP3 player
muchudd nm jet
mud adj dumb, mute; dull
mudan (-od) nm mute
mudandod nm muteness
mudanes (-au) nf dumb woman
mudferwi vb simmer

mudiad (-au) nm removal; movement
mudo vb move, remove
mudol adj mobile, moving, migratory
mudwr (-wyr) nm remover
mul (-od) nm mule; donkey
mulaidd adj mulish, asinine
mules (-au) nf she-mule, she-ass
mulfran (-frain) nf cormorant
mun see **bun**
munud (-au) nm, nf minute, moment
munud (-iau) nm sign, gesture; nod
munudio vb make gestures, gesticulate
mur (-iau) nm wall
murddun (-od) nm ruin, ruins
murio vb wall
murlun (-iau) nm mural
murmur vb murmur ▷ nm (-**on**) murmur
mursen (-nod) nf coquette; prude
mursendod nm prudery, affectation
mursennaidd adj prudish, affected
mursennu vb coquette, mince
musgrell adj feeble, decrepit
musgrellni nm feebleness, debility
mwd nm mud
mwdwl (mydylau) nm cock (of hay)
mwg nm smoke
mwgwd (mygydau) nm blind mask
mwng (myngau) nm mane
mwngial vb mumble
mwlsyn nm nincompoop; mule
mwlwg nm refuse, sweepings, chaff
mwll adj close, warm, sultry
mwmian vb hum, mumble
mŵn see **mwyn**
mwnci (-ïod) nm monkey
mwncïaidd adj monkeyish, apish
mwnglawdd = **mwynglawdd**
mwnwgl (mynyglau) nm neck

mwnws *coll n* small particles, dust, debris

mwrdro *vb* murder

mwrllwch *nm* fog, mist, vapour

mwrn *adj* sultry, close, warm

mwrndra *nm* sultriness

mwrthwl (**myrthylau**) *nm* hammer

mws *adj* stale, rank, stinking

mwsg *nm* musk

mwsged (**-i**) *nm, nf* musket

Mwslim *nm, nf* = **Moslem**

Mwslimaidd *adj* = **Moslemaidd**

mwsogl, mwswgl *nm* moss

mwstard, mwstart *nm* mustard

mwstro *vb* fidget, hurry

mwstwr *nm* muster; bustle, commotion

mwy *adj* more, bigger ▷ *adv* more, again

mwyach *adv* any more, henceforth

mwyafrif (**-au**) *nm* majority

mwyalch, mwyalchen (**mwyalchod**) *nf* blackbird

mwyar *npl* (*nf*-**en**) blackberries

mwyara *vb* gather blackberries

mwydion *npl* crumb; pith, pulp

mwydo *vb* moisten, soak, steep

mwydro *vb* moider, bewilder

mwydyn (**mwydod**) *nm* worm

mwyfwy *adv* more and more

mwyhau *vb* increase, enlarge, magnify

mwyn *nm* sake

mwyn, mŵn (**-au**) *nm* ore, mineral

mwyn *adj* kind, gentle, mild; dear

mwynder (**-au**) *nm* gentleness; (*pl*) delights

mwyndoddi *vb* refine

mwyneidd-dra *nm* kindness, gentleness

mwynglawdd (**-gloddiau**) *nm* mine

mwyngloddio *vb* mine

mwynhad *nm* enjoyment, pleasure

mwynhau *vb* enjoy

mwyniant (**-iannau**) *nm* pleasure

mwynofydd (**-ion**) *nm* mineralogist

mwynoleg *nf* mineralogy

mwynwr (**-wyr**) *nm* miner

mwys *adj* ambiguous, equivocal

mwythau *npl* indulgence, caresses

mwytho *vb* pet, fondle, pamper

mwythus *adj* pampered

myctod *nm* asphyxia

mydr (**-au**) *nm* metre, verse

mydryddiaeth *nf* versification

mydryddol *adj* metrical

mydryddu, mydru *vb* versify

mydylu *vb* cock

myfi *pron* I, me, myself

myfïaeth *nf* egotism

myfïol *adj* egotistic

myfyrdod (**-au**) *nm* meditation

myfyrgar *adj* studious, contemplative

myfyrgell (**-oedd**) *nf* study

myfyrio *vb* meditate, study

myfyriol *adj* meditative

myfyriwr (**-wyr**) *nm* student; **myfyriwr hŷn** mature student

mygedol *adj* honorary

mygfa (**-feydd**) *nf* suffocation

myglyd *adj* smoky; close; asthmatic

myglys *nm* tobacco

mygu *vb* smoke; suffocate, stifle, smother

mygydu *vb* blindfold

mygyn *nm* a smoke

myngial *vb* mumble, mutter

myngog *adj* maned

myngus *adj* indistinct, mumbling

myllni *nm* sultriness

mympwy (**-on**) *nm* whim, caprice, fad

mympwyol *adj* arbitrary, capricious

mymryn (**-nau**) *nm* particle, bit,

mite

myn *prep* by (*in swearing*)

myn (-nod) *nm* kid

mynach (-aich, -od) *nm* monk

mynachaeth *nf* monasticism

mynachdy (-dai) *nm* monastery, convent

mynachlog (-ydd) *nf* monastery, abbey

mynawyd (-au) *nm* awl

mynci (-ïau) *nm* hame(s)

myned, mynd *vb* go, proceed

mynedfa (-oedd, -feydd) *nf* entrance, passage

mynediad *nm* going; access, admission

mynegai (-eion) *nm* index, exponent

mynegair (-eiriau) *nm* concordance

mynegfys (-edd) *nm* forefinger, index

mynegi *vb* tell, express, relate, declare

mynegiad (-au) *nm* statement, declaration

mynegiant *nm* expression

mynnu *vb* will, wish; insist; get, obtain

mynor (-ion) *nm* marble

mynwent (-au, -ydd) *nf* churchyard, graveyard

mynwes (-au) *nf* breast, bosom

mynwesol *adj* bosom

mynwesu *vb* cherish

mynych *adj* frequent, often

mynychiad *nm* frequenting; repetition

mynychu *vb* frequent, attend; repeat

mynydd (-oedd) *nm* mountain

mynydda *n* mountaineering ▷ *vb* go mountaineering

mynydd-dir *nm* hill-country

mynyddig *adj* mountainous, hilly

mynyddwr (-wyr) *nm* mountaineer

myrdd, myrddiwn (myrddiynau) *nm* myriad

myrndra *nm* sultriness

myrr *nm* myrrh

myrtwydd *npl* (*nf*-**en**) myrtles

mysg *nm* middle, midst; **ymysg** among

mysgu *vb* loose, undo

myswynog (-ydd) *nf* barren cow

mysyglog *adj* mossy

mytholeg *nf* mythology

mytholegol *adj* mythological

n

na *conj* nor, neither; than ▷ *adv* no, not

nac *adv* no, not ▷ *conj* nor, neither

nacâd *nm* refusal, denial

nacaol *adj* negative

nacâu *vb* refuse, deny

nad *adv* not

nâd (nadau) *nf* cry, howl; clamour

Nadolig *nm* Christmas

Nadoligaidd *adj* Christmassy

nadu *vb* cry (out), howl

nadu *vb* stop, hinder

nadd *adj* hewn, wrought

naddion *npl* chips; shreds; lint

naddo *adv* no (*to questions in preterite tense*)

naddu *vb* hew, chip, whittle

Naf *nm* Lord

nag *conj* than

nage *adv* not so, no

nai (neiaint) *nm* nephew

naid (neidiau) *nf* jump, leap, bound

naïf *adj* naïve

naïfder *nm* naïveté

naill *dem pron* the one ▷ *conj* either

nain (neiniau) *nf* grandmother

nam (-au) *nm* mark, blemish, flaw

namyn *pron* except, but, save

nant (nentydd) *nf* brook; gorge, ravine

napcyn (-au) *nm* napkin

narcotig *nm, adj* narcotic

natur *nf* nature; temper

naturiaeth (-au) *nf* nature

naturiaethwr (-wyr) *nm* naturalist

naturiol *adj* natural

naturioldeb *nm* naturalness

naturus *adj* angry, quick-tempered

naw *adj, nm* nine

nawdd *nm* protection; patronage

nawddogaeth *nf* patronage, protection

nawfed *adj* ninth

nawn *nm* noon

naws *nf* nature, disposition; essence, tincture

nawseiddio *vb* temper, soften

neb *nm* any one (*with negative understood*); no one

nedd *npl* (**nf-en**) nits

neddau, neddyf (neddyfau) *nf* adze

nef (-oedd) *nf* heaven

nefi-blw *n, adj* navy blue

nefol, nefolaidd *adj* heavenly, celestial

nefoli *vb* make or become heavenly

nefrosis *nm* neurosis

neges (-au, -euau) *nf* errand, message; **neges destun** text message; **neges lais** voicemail

negesa, negeseua *vb* run errands; trade

negeseuwr (-wyr) *nm* messenger

negodi *vb* negotiate

negyddiaeth *nf* negativism

negyddol adj negative
neidio vb leap, jump; throb
neidiwr (-wyr) nm leaper, jumper
neidr (nadroedd, nadredd) nf snake
neiedd nm nepotism
neillog (-ion) nm alternative
neilltu nm one side; **o'r neilltu** aside, apart
neilltuad nm separation
neilltuaeth nf separation, privacy, seclusion
neilltuedig adj separated, secluded
neilltuo vb set apart, separate
neilltuol adj particular, peculiar, special
neilltuolion npl peculiarities
neilltuolrwydd nm peculiarity, distinction
neis adj nice
neisied (-i) nf kerchief
neithdar nm nectar
neithior (-au) nf marriage feast
neithiwr adv last night
nemor adj few; **nid nemor** hardly any
nen (-nau, -noedd) nf ceiling; heaven; **nen tŷ** house-top
nenbren nm roof-tree
nenfwd (-fydau) nm ceiling
nepell adv far; **nid nepell** not far
nerf (-au) nf nerve
nerfwst nm neurasthenia
nerth (-oedd) nm might, power, strength
nerthol adj strong, powerful, mighty
nerthu vb strengthen
nes adj nearer; **yn nes ymlaen** further on
nes adv till, until
nesaf adj nearest, next
nesáu vb draw near, approach
nesnes adv nearer and nearer
nesu vb draw near; **nesu draw** move away

neu conj or
neuadd (-au) nf hall
newid vb change, alter ▷ nm change; **newid hinsawdd** climate change
newidiant nm variability
newidiol adj changeable, variable
newidydd (-ion) nm transformer
newidyn (-nau) nm variable
newydd adj new, novel; fresh ▷ nm (-ion) news
newyddbeth (-au) nm novelty
newydd-deb, newydd-der nm newness, novelty
newyddiadur (-on) nm newspaper
newyddiaduriaeth nf journalism
newyddiadurwr (-wyr) nm journalist
newyddian (-od) coll n novice, neophyte
newyn nm hunger, famine
newynog adj hungry, starving
newynu vb starve, famish
ni pron we, us
ni, nid adv not
nifer (-oedd, -i) nm, nf number
nifwl nm mist, fog; nebula
Nigeria nf Nigeria
Nihon nf Japan
ninnau pron we (on our part), we also
nionyn (nionod) nm onion
nis adv not … it; **nis cafodd** he did not find it
nitrad (-au) nm nitrate
nith (-oedd) nf niece
nithio vb sift, winnow
nithiwr (-wyr) nm sifter, winnower
nithlen (-ni) nf winnowing-sheet
niwclear adj nuclear
niwed (-eidiau) nm harm, injury
niweidio vb harm, hurt, injure, damage
niweidiol adj harmful, injurious
niwl (-oedd) nm, **niwlen** nf mist, fog, haze

niwliog, niwlog *adj* misty, foggy, hazy

niwmatig *adj* pneumatic

niwmonia *nm* pneumonia

niwtral *adj* neutral

niwtraleiddio *vb* neutralise

niwtraliaeth *nf* neutrality

nobyn (**nobiau**) *nm* knob

nod (**-au**) *nm, nf* note; mark, token

nodachfa (**-feydd**) *nf* bazaar

nodedig *adj* appointed, set; remarkable

nodi *vb* mark, note, appoint, state

nodiad (**-au**) *nm* note

nodiadur (**-on**) *nm* notebook

nodiant *nm* notation

nodlyfr (**-au**) *nm* notebook

nodwedd (**-ion**) *nf* character, characteristic, feature

nodweddiadol *adj* characteristic

nodweddu *vb* characterize

nodwydd (**-au**) *nf* needle

nodwyddiad *nm* acupuncture

nodyn (**-nau, nodau, nodion**) *nm* note

nodd (**-ion**) *nm* moisture; juice, sap

nodded *nm* refuge, protection

noddfa (**-fâu, -feydd**) *nf* refuge

noddi *vb* protect

noddlyd *adj* juicy, sappy

noddwr (**-wyr**) *nm* protector; patron

noe (**-au**) *nf* dish; kneading-trough

noeth *adj* naked, bare, exposed, raw

noethder *nm* bareness, nakedness

noethi *vb* bare, denude

noethlymun *adj* nude

noethlymunwr (**-wyr**) *nm* streaker

noethlymunwraig *nf* stripper

noethni *nm* nakedness, nudity

noethwr (**-wyr**) *nm* nudist

nofel (**-au**) *nf* novel

nofelwr (**-wyr**), **nofelydd** *nm* novelist

nofiadwy *adj* swimmable

nofiedydd (**-ion**) *nm* swimmer

nofio *vb* swim; float

nofiwr (**-wyr**) *nm* swimmer

nogio *vb* jib

noglyd *adj* jibbing

nôl *vb* fetch, bring

Norwy *nf* Norway

nos (**-au, nosweithiau**) *nf* night; **Nos Galan** New Year's Eve

nosi *vb* become night

noson, noswaith (**nosweithiau**) *nf* night, evening; **noson stag** stag night

noswyl (**-iau**) *nf* eve of festival, vigil; **Noswyl Nadolig** Christmas Eve

noswylio *vb* cease work at eve

nudden *nf* fog, mist, haze

nwy (**-on**) *nm* gas; **nwy tŷ gwydr** greenhouse gas

nwyd (**-au**) *nm* passion; emotion

nwydd (**-au**) *nm* substance, article; (*pl*) goods

nwyf *nm* vivacity, energy, vigour

nwyfiant *nm* vivacity, vigour

nwyfus *adj* sprightly, spirited, lively

nwyol *adj* gaseous

nychdod *nm* feebleness, infirmity

nychlyd *adj* sickly, feeble

nychu *vb* sicken, pine, languish

nydd-dro (**-droeau, -droeon**) *nm* twist

nydd-droi *vb* twist, screw

nyddu *vb* spin, twist

nyddwr (**-wyr**) *nm* spinner

nyf *coll n* snow

nyni *pron* we, us

nyrs (**-ys**) *nm, nf* nurse

nyrsio *adj* nurse

nytmeg *nm* nutmeg

nyth (**-od**) *nm, nf* nest

nythu *vb* nest, nestle

o *prep* from; of, out of; by
o *excl* oh!, O!
oblegid *conj, prep* because, for
obry *adv* beneath, below
obstetreg *nm* obstetrics
obstetregydd (-wyr) *nm* obstetrician
ocsid (-iau) *nm* oxide
ocsidiad *nm* oxidisation
ocsidio *vb* oxidise
ocsidydd (-ion) *nm* oxidising agent
ocsigen *nm* oxygen
och *excl* oh, alas, woe
ochenaid (-eidiau) *nf* sigh
ocheneidio, ochneidio *vb* sigh
ochr (-au) *nf* side
ochrgamu *vb* sidestep
ochri *vb* side
od *adj* odd, remarkable
ôd *nm* snow
odiaeth *adj* excellent, exquisite
  ▷ *adv* very, most, extremely

odid *adv* perchance, peradventure
odl (-au) *nf* rhyme; ode, song
odli *vb* rhyme
odrif (-au) *nm* odd number
odrwydd *nm* oddity
odyn (-au) *nf* kiln
oddeutu *prep* about
oddi *prep* out of, from
oddieithr, oddigerth *prep* except,
  unless
oed (-au) *nm* age; time
oed-dâl (-iadau) *nm*
  superannuation
oedfa (-on, -feuon) *nf* meeting,
  service
oedi *vb* delay; postpone, defer
oediad (-au) *nm* delay
oedolyn (-ion) *nm* grown-up
oedran *nm* age, full age
oedrannus *adj* aged
oedd *vb* was, were
oen (ŵyn) *nm* lamb
oena *vb* lamb, yean
oenig *nf* ewe-lamb
oer *adj* cold, chill, frigid; sad
oeraidd *adj* cool, chilly
oerddrws (-ddrysau) *nm* wind gap
oerfel *nm* cold
oergell (-oedd) *nf* refrigerator
oeri *vb* cool, chill
oerllyd *adj* chilly, frigid; cool
oernad (-au) *nf* howl, wail,
  lamentation
oernadu *vb* howl, wail, lament
oerni *nm* cold, coldness, chillness
oes (-oedd, -au) *nf* age, lifetime; **yn
  oes oesoedd** for ever and ever
oes *vb* there is, there are; is there?
oesoffagws *nm* oesophagus
oesol *adj* age-long, perpetual
ofer *adj* vain, idle; prodigal;
  dissipated; waste
ofera *vb* waste, squander, idle

oferedd nm vanity, dissipation

ofergoel (-ion) nf superstition

ofergoeledd, ofergoeliaeth nm superstition

ofergoelus adj superstitious

oferwr (-wyr) nm idler, waster

ofn (-au) nm fear, dread

ofnadwy adj awful, terrible, dreadful

ofnadwyaeth nf awe, terror, dread

ofni vb fear, dread

ofnog adj fearful, timorous

ofnus adj timid, nervous, frightened

ofnusrwydd nm timidity, nervousness

ofwl (-au) nm ovule

ofydd (-ion) nm ovate

offeiriad (-iaid) nm priest, clergyman

offeiriadaeth nf priesthood

offeiriades (-au) nf priestess

offeiriadol adj priestly, sacerdotal

offeiriadu vb officiate, minister

offer npl implements, tools, gear

offeren (-nau) nf mass

offeryn (-nau, offer) nm instrument, tool; **offeryn cerdd** musical instrument

offerynnol adj instrumental

offerynoliaeth nf instrumentality

offrwm (-ymau) nm offering, oblation

offrymu vb offer, sacrifice

offrymwr (-wyr) nm offerer, sacrificer

offthalmia nm ophthalmia

offthalmosgop (-au) nm ophthalmoscope

og (-au), oged (-au, -i) nf harrow

ogof (-au, -fâu, -feydd) nf cave, cavern; den

ogylch prep about

ongl (-au) nf angle, corner

onglog adj angled, angular

oherwydd conj, prep because, for, owing to

ôl adj back, hind, hindmost ▷ nm **(olion)** mark, print, trace, track; **yn ôl** ago; according to

ôl-dâl (-oedd) nm back-pay

ôl-ddodiad (-iaid) nm suffix

ôl-ddyddio vb post-date

ôl-ddyled (-ion) nf arrears

olew (-au) nm oil

olewydd npl (nf **-en**) olive-trees

olifaid npl olive-berries

olrhain vb trace

ôl-troed (olion traed) nm footprint; **ôl-troed carbon** carbon footprint

olwr (-wyr) nm back (in rugby)

olwyn (-ion) nf wheel

olwyno vb wheel, cycle

olwynog adj wheeled

Olympaidd adj Olympic

olyniaeth nf succession, sequence

olynol adj successive, consecutive

olynu vb succeed (to)

olynwr (-wyr), olynydd (-ion) nm successor

ôlysgrif (-au) nf postscript

oll adv all, wholly; ever, at all

ombwdsman (-myn) nm ombudsman

omlet (-i) nm omelette

ond conj but, only ▷ prep except, save, but

onest adj honest

onestrwydd nm honesty

oni, onid adv not?, is it not? ▷ conj if not, unless ▷ prep except, save, but

onid e adv otherwise, else; is it not?

onis conj if it is not; **onis caiff** if he does not get it

onnen (onn, ynn) nf ash

opiniwn (-ynau) nm opinion

o

opiniynllyd, opiniynus *adj*
  opinionated
optimistaeth *nf* optimism
optimistaidd *adj* optimistic
optimwm (-tima) *nm* optimum
oracl (-au) *nm* oracle
oraclaidd *adj* oracular
oraens *nm* orange
ordeiniad (-au) *nm* ordination,
  ordinance
ordeinio *vb* ordain
ordinhad (-au) *nf* ordinance,
  sacrament
oren (-nau) *nm, nf* orange
organ (-au) *nf, nm* organ
organaidd *adj* organic
organeb (-au) *nf* organism
organig *adj* organic
organydd (-ion) *nm* organist
orgraff (-au) *nf* orthography
orgraffyddol *adj* orthographical
oriawr (oriorau) *nf* watch
oriel (-au) *nf* gallery
orig *nf* little while
oriog *adj* fickle, changeable,
  inconstant
os *conj* if
osgo *nm* slant, slope, inclination
osgoi *vb* swerve, avoid, evade, shirk
oslef *nf* tone, voice
osôn *nm* ozone
ow *excl* oh!, alas!

p

pa *adj* what, which
pab (-au) *nm* pope
pabaeth *nf* papacy
pabaidd *adj* papal, popish
pabell (pebyll) *nf* tent, tabernacle
pabellu *vb* tent, tabernacle, encamp
pabi *nm* poppy
pabwyr *npl* (*nf* **-en,** *nm* **-yn**) rushes
pabwyr *nm* wick, candle-wick
pabydd (-ion) *nm* Roman Catholic
pabyddiaeth *nf* Roman Catholicism
pabyddol *adj* Roman Catholic
pac (-iau) *nm* pack, bundle
pacio *vb* pack
Pacistan *nf* Pakistan
padell (-au, -i, pedyll) *nf* pan, bowl
padellaid (-eidiau) *nf* panful
pader (-au) *nm* paternoster, Lord's
  Prayer
padera *vb* repeat prayers, patter
pae *nm* pay, wage

paediatreg nm paediatrics
paediatregydd nm paediatrician
paent nm paint
paentiad (-au) nm painting
pafiliwn nm pavilion
paffio vb box, fight
paffiwr (-wyr) nm boxer
pagan (-iaid) nm pagan, heathen
paganaidd adj pagan, heathen
paganiaeth nf paganism, heathenism
pang (-au) nm, **pangfa (-feydd)** nf pang, fit
paham adv why, wherefore
paill nm flour; pollen
pair (peiriau) nm cauldron, furnace
pais (peisiau) nf coat, petticoat
paith (peithiau) nm prairie
pâl (palau) nf spade
paladr (pelydr) nm ray, beam; staff; stem
palaeolithig adj palaeolithic
palas (-au) nm palace
Palestina nf Palestine
palf (-au) nf palm, hand; paw
palfais (-eisiau) nf shoulder
palfalu vb feel, grope
palfod (-au) nf smack, slap, buffet
palff nm fine, well-built man
pali nm silk brocade
palis (-au) nm pale, partition, wainscot
palmant (-mentydd) nm pavement
palmantu vb pave
palmwydd npl (nf **-en**) palm-trees
palu vb dig, delve
palwr (-wyr) nm digger
pall (-au) nm mantle; tent
pall nm fail, failing; lack; lapse
pallu vb fail, cease; neglect; refuse
pam adv why, wherefore
pamffled, pamffledyn (pamffledi, pamffledau) nm pamphlet

pan conj when
pandy (-dai) nm fulling-mill
pannas npl (nf **panasen**) parsnips
pannu vb full cloth
pannwl (panylau) nm dimple, hollow
pannwr (panwyr) nm fuller
pant (-iau) nm hollow, valley
pantio vb depress, dent, sink
pantiog adj hollow, sunken; dimpled
papur (-au) nm paper
papuro vb paper
papurwr (-wyr) nm paperer, paperhanger
papuryn nm scrap of paper
pâr (parau) nm pair; suit
pâr (peri) nm spear, lance
para vb last, endure, continue
parabl (-au) nm speech, discourse
parablu vb speak
paradeim (-au) nm paradigm
paradwys nf paradise
parafeddyg (-on) nm paramedic
paragraff (-au) nm paragraph
paratoad (-au) nm preparation
paratoawl adj preparatory
paratoi vb prepare, get ready
parc (-iau) nm park, field; **parc cenedlaethol** national park
parch nm respect, reverence
parchedig (-ion) adj reverend; reverent
parchedigaeth nf reverence
parchu vb respect, revere, reverence
parchus adj respectful; respectable
parchusrwydd nm respectability
pardwn (-ynau) nm pardon
pardynu vb pardon
parddu nm fire-black, smut; soot
pardduo vb blacken, vilify, defame
pared (parwydydd) nm partition wall, wall

p

paredd *nm* parity
parhad *nm* continuance, continuation
parhaol *adj* lasting, perpetual
parhau *vb* last, continue; persevere
parhaus *adj* lasting; continual, perpetual
Paris *nf* Paris
parlwr (**-yrau**) *nm* sitting room; parlour
parlys *nm* paralysis, palsy
parlysu *vb* paralyse
parod *adj* ready, prepared; prompt
parodrwydd *nm* readiness, willingness
parôl (**-ion**) *nm* parole
parsel (**-i, -ydd**) *nm* parcel
parti (**-ïon**) *nm* party
partïaeth *nf* partisanship
partïol *adj* partial, biassed, partisan
parth (**-au**) *nm* part, region; floor
parthed *prefix* about, concerning
parthu *vb* part, divide
parwyden (**-nau**) *nf* wall, side; breast
pas *nm* whooping-cough
Pasg *nm* Passover, Easter
pasgedig (**-ion**) *adj* fatted, fattened, fat
pasiant (**-iannau**) *nm* pageant
pasio *vb* pass
past *nm* paste
pastai (**-eiod**) *nf* pasty, pie
pastio *vb* paste
pasturedig *adj* pasteurised
pasturo *vb* pasteurise
pastwn (**-ynau**) *nm* baton, club, cudgel
pastynu *vb* club, cudgel, bludgeon
patriarch (**-iaid, patrieirch**) *nm* patriarch
patriarchaeth (**-au**) *nf* patriarchate

patriarchaidd *adj* patriarchal
patrwm (**-ymau**) *nm* pattern
patrymlun (**-iau**) *nm* template
pathew (**-od**) *nm* dormouse
patholeg *nf* pathology
patholegol *adj* pathological
patholegydd (**-egwyr**) *nm* pathologist
pau *nf* country
paun (**peunod**) *nm* peacock
pawb *pron* everybody, all
pawen (**-nau**) *nf* paw
pawl (**polion**) *nm* pole, stake
pe *conj* if
pebyll *see* **pabell**
Pecing *nf* Peking
pecyn (**-nau**) *nm* packet, package
pech-aberth (**-au**) *nm* sin-offering
pechadur (**-iaid**) *nm* sinner, offender
pechadures (**-au**) *nf* woman sinner
pechadurus *adj* sinful, wicked
pechadurusrwydd *nm* sinfulness
pechod (**-au**) *nm* sin, offence
pechu *vb* sin, offend
ped *conj* if
pedair *adj f of* **pedwar**
pedeirongl *adj* foursquare
pedi *vb* worry, grieve
pedoffeil (**-s**), **pedoffilydd** (**-ion**) *nm* paedophile
pedol (**-au**) *nf* horseshoe
pedoli *vb* shoe
pedrain *nf* haunches, crupper
pedrongl *adj* square ▷ *nf* (**-au**) square
pedronglog *adj* quadrangular
pedryfwrdd (**-fyrddau**) *nm* quarter-deck
pedwar (*f* **pedair**) *adj* four
pedwarawd *nm* quartette
pedwarcarnol (**-ion**) *adj* four-footed, quadruped

pedwaredd adj f of **pedwerydd**
pedwarplyg adj fourfold, quarto
pedwerydd (f **pedwaredd**) adj fourth
peddestr nm pedestrian
peddestrig nm walking; pedestrian
pefr adj radiant, bright, beautiful
pefrio vb radiate, sparkle
peg (**-iau**) nm peg
pegio vb peg
pegor (**-au**) nm manikin; dwarf; imp
pegwn (**-ynau**) nm pivot, pole, axis
Pegwn y Gogledd nm North Pole
pegynol adj axial, polar
peidio vb cease, stop, desist
peilon (**-au**) nm pylon
peilot (**-iaid**) nm pilot
peillio vb bolt, sift
peint (**-iau**) nm pint
peintiad (**-au**) nm painting
peintio vb paint
peintiwr (**-wyr**) nm painter
peipen (**peipiau**) nf pipe
peirianneg nf engineering
peiriannol adj mechanical
peiriannydd (**-ianyddion**) nm engineer
peiriant (**-iannau**) nm machine, engine; **peiriant arian** ATM, cash machine; **peiriant chwilio** search engine; **peiriant golchi** washing machine; **peiriant MP3/DVD** MP3/DVD player
peirianwaith nm mechanism
peiswyn nm chaff
peithyn (**-au**) nm ridge-tile
pêl (**pelau, peli**) nf ball
pelawd (**-au**) nf over (in cricket)
pêl-droed nf football
pêl-fasged nf basketball
pelferyn (**-nau**) nm ball-bearing
pêl-foli nf volley-ball
pêl-rwyd nf netball

pelten (**pelts**) nf blow
pelydr (**-au**) nm ray, beam
pelydru vb beam, gleam, radiate
pelydryn nm ray, beam
pell adj far, distant, remote, long
pellen (**-nau, -ni**) nf ball (of yarn)
pellennig adj far, distant, remote
pellhau vb put or remove far off
pellter (**-au, -oedd**) nm distance
pen (**-nau**) nm head; chief; end; top
pen adj head, chief, supreme
penadur (**-iaid**) nm sovereign
penaduriaeth nf sovereignty
penagored adj open, indefinite, undecided
penarglwyddiaeth nf sovereignty
penbaladr adj general, universal
penben adv at loggerheads
penbleth nf perplexity, quandary
pen-blwydd (**-i**) nm birthday
penboeth adj hot-headed, fanatical
penboethni nm fanaticism
penboethyn (**-boethiaid**) nm fanatic
penbwl (**-byliaid**) nm blockhead; tadpole
pencadlys nm head-quarters
pencampwr (**-wyr**) nm champion
pencampwriaeth (**-au**) nf championship
pencerdd (**-ceirddiaid**) nm chief musician
penchwiban adj giddy, flighty
pendant adj positive, emphatic
pendantrwydd nm positiveness
pendefig (**-ion**) nm prince, peer, noble
pendefigaeth nf aristocracy, peerage
pendefigaidd adj noble, aristocratic
pendefiges (**-au**) nf peeress
penderfyniad (**-au**) nm determination, resolution

p

penderfynol adj determined, resolute

penderfynu vb determine, resolve

pendew adj thick-headed, stupid

pendifaddau adj: **yn bendifaddau** especially

pendil (-iau) nm pendulum

pendramwnwgl adj topsy-turvy; headlong

pendraphen adj helter-skelter, confused

pendro nf giddiness, vertigo; staggers

pendroni vb perplex oneself, worry over

pendrwm adj top-heavy; drowsy

pendrymu vb drowse, droop

pendwmpian vb nod, doze, slumber

penddaredd nm giddiness

penddaru vb make or become giddy

pendduyn (-nod) nm botch, boil

penelin (-oedd) nm, nf elbow

penelino vb elbow

penffest (-au) nm headgear

penffol adj silly, idiotic

penffrwyn (-au) nm, nf head-stall, halter

pengaled adj headstrong ▷ nf knapweed

pengaledwch nm stubbornness

pengam adj wrong-headed, perverse

pen-glin (-iau) nf knee

penglog (-au) nf skull

pengryf adj headstrong, stubborn

pengryniad (-iaid) nm roundhead

peniad (-au) nm header

penigamp adj excellent, splendid

penisel adj downcast, crestfallen

penlinio vb kneel

penllwyd adj grey-headed

penllwydni nm grey hair, white hair

penllywydd (-ion) nm sovereign

penllywyddiaeth nf sovereignty

pennaeth (penaethiaid) nm chief

pennaf adj chief, principal

pennawd (penawdau) nm heading; headline

pennill (penillion) nm verse, stanza

pennod (penodau) nf chapter

pennoeth adj bare-headed

pennog (penwaig) nm herring

pennu vb specify, appoint, determine

penodi vb appoint

penodiad (-au) nm appointment

penodol adj particular, specific

penrhydd adj unbridled, loose

penrhyddid nm licence, licentiousness

penrhyn (-noedd, -nau) nm cape, foreland

pensaer (-seiri) nm architect

pensaernïaeth nf architecture

pensil (-iau) nm pencil

pensiwn (-iynau) nm pension

pen-swyddog (-ion) nm chief officer

pensyfrdan adj stunned, dazed

pensyfrdandod nm giddiness, dizziness

pensyfrdanu vb stun, daze

pensyth adj perpendicular

pentan (-au) nm hob

penteulu (pennau teuluoedd) nm head of family

pentewyn (-ion) nm firebrand

pentir (-oedd) nm headland

pentis nm penthouse

pentref (-i, -ydd) nm village; homestead

pentrefan (-nau) nm hamlet

pentrefol adj village

pentrefwr (-wyr) nm villager

pentwr (-tyrrau) nm heap, pile

penty (**-tai**) nm cottage, shed
pentyrru vb heap, pile, accumulate
penuchel adj proud, haughty
penwan adj weak-minded
penwyn adj white-headed
penwynni nm white hair, grey hair
penyd (**-iau**) nm penance,
　punishment
penyd-wasanaeth nm penal
　servitude
penysgafn adj light-headed, giddy,
　dizzy
penysgafnder nm giddiness,
　dizziness
pêr adj sweet, delicious, luscious
peraidd adj sweet, mellow
perarogl (**-au**) nm perfume,
　fragrance
perarogli vb perfume; embalm
peraroglus adj fragrant, scented
percoladur (**-on**) nm percolator
perchen, perchennog
　(**perchenogion**) nm owner
perchenogaeth nf ownership
perchenogi vb possess, own
perchentywr (**-wyr**) nm
　householder
pereidd-dra nm sweetness
pereiddio vb sweeten
pererin (**-ion**) nm pilgrim
pererindod (**-au**) nm, nf pilgrimage
pererinol adj pilgrim
perfedd (**-ion**) nm guts, bowels
perfeddwlad (**-wledydd**) nf
　interior, heartland
perffaith adj perfect
perffeithio vb perfect
perffeithrwydd nm perfection
perffeithydd (**-ion**) nm perfecter
perfformiad (**-au**) nm performance
perfformio vb perform
perfformiwr (**-wyr**) nm performer
peri vb cause, bid

perl (**-au**) nm pearl
perlewyg (**-on**) nm ecstasy, trance
perlysiau npl aromatic herbs; spices
perllan (**-nau**) nf orchard
perocsid (**-au**) nm peroxide
peroriaeth nf melody, music
persain adj euphonious, melodious
　▷ nf (**-seiniau**) euphony
persawr (**-au**) nm fragrance;
　persawr eillio aftershave (lotion)
perseiniol adj melodious
persli nm parsley
person (**-au**) nm person
person (**-iaid**) nm parson, clergyman
personadu vb impersonate
personadwr (**-wyr**) nm
　impersonator
persondy (**-dai**) nm parsonage
personol adj personal
personoli vb personify
personoliad (**-au**) nm
　personification
personoliaeth (**-au**) nf personality
perswâd nm persuasion
perswadio vb persuade
pert adj quaint, pretty; pert
perth (**-i**) nf bush, hedge
perthnasedd (**-au**) nm relativity,
　relevance
perthnasiad (**-au**) nm affiliation
perthnasol adj relevant
perthyn vb belong, pertain, be
　related
perthynas (**-au**) nf relation;
　relationship
perthynol adj relative
perwyl nm purpose, effect
perygl (**-on**) nm danger, peril, risk
peryglu vb endanger, imperil
peryglus adj dangerous, perilous
pes conj if … it; **pes adwaenasent**
　had they known him
pesgi vb feed, fatten

p

pesimist (**-iaid**) *nm* pessimist
pesimistaidd *adj* pessimistic
pesimistiaeth *nf* pessimism
pestl (**-au**) *nm* pestle
peswch *nm* cough
pesychiad (**-au**) *nm* cough
pesychu *vb* cough
petris *npl* (*nf*-**en**) partridges
petrocemegolau (*nm* -**yn**) *npl*
   petrochemicals
petrol (**-au**) *nm* petrol
petroleg *nm*, *nf* petrology
petrus *adj* hesitating; doubtful
petruso *vb* hesitate, doubt
petruster *nm* hesitation, doubt
petryal *nm*, *adj* square
peth (**-au**) *nm* thing; part, some
petheuach *npl* odds and ends,
   trifles
peunes (**-od**) *nf* peahen
pianydd (**-ion**) *nm* pianist
piau *vb* own, possess
pib (**-au**) *nf* pipe, tube; diarrhœa
pibell (**-au, -i**) *nf* pipe, tube
pibgorn (**-gyrn**) *nm* recorder (music)
pibo *vb* pipe; squirt
pibonwy (*nf*-**en**) *npl* icicles
pibydd (**-ion**) *nm* piper
picell (**-au**) *nf* dart, javelin, spear
picellu *vb* spear, stab
picfforch (**-ffyrch**) *nf* pitchfork
picil *nm* pickle, trouble
picio *vb* dart, hie
piclo *vb* pickle
pictiwr (**-tiyrau**) *nm* picture
picwns (*nf*-**nen**) *npl* wasps
piff (**-iau**) *nm* puff, sudden blast
piffian *vb* snigger, giggle
pig (**-au**) *nf* point, spike; beak; spout
pigan *vb* drizzle
pigdwr (**-dyrau**) *nm* spire, steeple
pigiad (**-au**) *nm* prick, sting;
   injection

pigion *npl* pickings, selections
pigo *vb* pick; peck; prick; sting
pigog *adj* prickly
pigyn *nm* thorn, prickle
pilcod *npl* (*nm*-**yn**) minnows
pilen (**-nau**) *nf* membrane, film;
   cataract
piler (**-au, -i**) *nm* pillar
pilio *vb* peel, pare
pili-pala *nm* butterfly
Pilipinas *npl* the Philippines
pilsen (**pils**) *nf* pill
pilyn *nm* garment, rag, clout
pin (**-nau**) *nm*, *nf* pin ▷ *nm* pen; **pin
   blaen ffelt** felt-tip pen
pîn *nm* pine, fir
pinacl (**-au**) *nm* pinnacle
pinaclog *adj* pinnacled
pinafal (**-au**) *nf* pineapple
pinbwyntio *vb* pinpoint
pinc (**-od**) *nm* finch, chaffinch
pincio *vb* pink; **parlwr pincio** beauty
   parlour
pincws (**-cysau**) *nm* pincushion
pindwll (**-dyllau**) *nm* pinhole
pinsiad (**-au**) *nm* pinch
pinsio *vb* pinch
pioden (**pïod**) *nf* magpie
piser (**-au, -i**) *nm* pitcher, jug, can
pistyll (**-oedd**) *nm* spout; cataract
pistyllio *vb* spout, gush
pisyn (**-nau, pisiau**) *nm* piece
piti *nm* pity
pitw *adj* petty, puny, paltry
piw (**-od**) *nm* dug, udder
Piwritan (**-iaid**) *nm* Puritan
piwritanaidd *adj* puritan,
   puritanical
piwritaniaeth *nf* puritanism
pla (**plâu**) *nm*, *nf* plague, pestilence;
   nuisance
pladur (**-iau**) *nf* scythe
pladurwr (**-wyr**) *nm* mower

plaen *adj* plain, clear
plaen (**-au**) *nm* plane
plaenio *vb* plane
plagio *vb* plague, tease, torment
plagus *adj* annoying, troublesome
plaid (**pleidiau**) *nf* side, party; **Plaid Cymru** the Welsh Nationalist Party
planced (**-i**) *nf* blanket
planed (**-au**) *nf* planet
planhigfa (**-feydd**) *nf* plantation
planhigyn (**-higion**) *nm* plant; **planhigyn wy** aubergine
plannu *vb* plant; dive
plannwr (**planwyr**) *nm* planter
plant *npl* (*nm* **plentyn**) children
planta *vb* beget or bear children
plantos *npl* (little) children
plas (**-au**) *nm* hall, mansion, palace
plasaidd *adj* palatial
plastr (**-au**) *nm* plaster
plastro *vb* plaster
plastrwr (**-wyr**) *nm* plasterer
plât, plat (**-iau**) *nm* plate
platŵn (**-tynau**) *nm* platoon
platwydr *nm* plate-glass
ple *nm* plea
pledio *vb* plead, argue
pledren (**-nau, -ni**) *nf* bladder
pleidgarwch *nm* partisanship
pleidio *vb* side with, support
pleidiol *adj* favourable, partial
pleidiwr (**-wyr**) *nm* partisan, supporter
pleidlais (**-leisiau**) *nf* vote, suffrage
pleidleisio *vb* vote
pleidleisiwr (**-wyr**) *nm* voter
plencyn (**planciau**) *nm* plank
plentyn (**plant**) *nm* child, infant
plentyndod *nm* childhood, infancy
plentyneiddiwch *nm* childishness
plentynnaidd *adj* childish, puerile
plentynrwydd *nm* childishness
pleser (**-au**) *nm* pleasure

pleserdaith (**-deithiau**) *nf* trip, excursion
pleserus *adj* pleasurable, pleasant
plesio *vb* please
plet, pleten (**pletiau**) *nf* pleat
pletio *vb* pleat
pletiog *adj* pleated
pleth (**-au**) *nf* plait
plethdorch (**-au**) *nf* wreath
plethu *vb* plait, weave, fold
plewra (**-e**) *nm* pleura
plicio *vb* pluck, peel, strip
plisg *coll n* (*nm* **-yn**) shells, husks, pods
plisgo *vb* shell, husk
plisman, plismon (**plismyn**) *nm* policeman
plismones (**-au**) *nf* policewoman
plith *nm* midst
pliwrisi *nm* pleurisy
plocyn (**plociau**) *nm* block
plod *adj, nm* plaid, tartan
ploryn (**-nod**) *nm* pimple
plorynnod *npl* acne
pluen (**plu**) *nf* feather; **plu eira** snow-flakes
plufyn (**pluf**) *nm* = **pluen**
pluo, plufio *vb* pluck, deplume; plume
pluog *adj* feathered, fledged
plwc (**plyciau**) *nm* pluck; space, while
plwg (**plygiau**) *nm* plug
plwm *nm* lead
plws *nm* plus
plwtonium *nm* plutonium
plwyf (**-i, -ydd**) *nm* parish
plwyfol *adj* parochial
plwyfolion *npl* parishioners
plycio *vb* pluck
plyg (**-ion**) *nm* fold, double; hollow
plygain *nm* cock-crow, dawn; matins
plygeiniol *adj* dawning; very early
plygell (**-au**) *nm* folder

p

plygiad (**-au**) *nm* folding, fold

plygu *vb* fold; bend, stoop; bow

plymen *nf* plummet

plymio *vb* plumb, sound

plymwr (**-wyr**) *nm* plumber

po *particle used before superlative:*
  gorau po gyntaf the sooner the
  better

pob *adj* each, every; all

pobi *vb* bake; roast; toast

pobiad (**-au**) *nm* baking, batch

pobl (**-oedd**) *nf* people

poblog *adj* populous

poblogaeth (**-au**) *nf* population

poblogaidd *adj* popular

poblogeiddio *vb* popularize

poblogi *vb* people, populate

poblogrwydd *nm* popularity

pobwr (**-wyr**), **pobydd** (**-ion**) *nm*
  baker

poced (**-i**) *nf* pocket

pocedu *vb* pocket

pocer (**-i, -au**) *nm* poker

poen (**-au**) *nm*, *nf* pain, torment

poenedigaeth *nf* torment

poeni *vb* pain, torment; worry, grieve

poenus *adj* painful

poenwr (**-wyr**) *nm* tormentor,
  torturer

poenydio *vb* torment, torture; fret,
  vex

poenydiwr (**-wyr**) *nm* tormentor

poer (**-ion**) *nm* spittle, saliva

poeri *vb* spit, expectorate

poeryn *nm* spittle

poeth *adj* hot; burning; **dŵr poeth**
  heart-burn

poethder, poethni *nm* hotness,
  heat

poethdon (**-nau**) *nf* heat wave

poethi *vb* heat

pôl (**polau**) *nm* poll

polaredd *nm* polarity

polareiddiad *nm* polarisation

polareiddio *vb* polarise

polymorff *nm* polymorph

polymorffedd *nm* polymorphism

polyn (**polion**) *nm* pole

pomgranad (**-au**) *nm* pomegranate

pompiwn (**-iynau**) *nm* pumpkin,
  gourd

pompren *nf* plank bridge, footbridge

ponc, poncen (**ponciau**) *nf*,
  poncyn *nm* hillock, tump; bank

pont (**-ydd**) *nf* bridge, arch

pontffordd (**-ffyrdd**) *nf* fly-over,
  viaduct

pontio *vb* bridge

popeth *nm* everything

poplys *npl* (*nf*-**en**) poplar-trees

popty (**-tai**) *nm* bakehouse; oven;
  popty ping microwave (oven)

porc *nm* pork

porchell (**perchyll**) *nm* little pig

porfa (**-feydd**) *nf* pasture, grass

porffor *adj*, *nm* purple

pori *vb* graze, browse; eat

pornograffi *nm*, **pornograffiaeth**
  nf pornography

Portiwgal *nf* Portugal

portread (**-au**) *nm* portrayal,
  pattern

portreadu *vb* portray

porth *nm* aid, help, succour

porth (**pyrth**) *nm* gate, gateway;
  porch door; **porth awyr** airport

porthfa (**-feydd**) *nf* port, harbour;
  ferry

porthi *vb* feed

porthiannus *adj* well-fed,
  high-spirited

porthiant *nm* food, sustenance,
  support

porthladd (**-oedd**) *nm* port,
  harbour, haven

porthmon (**-myn**) *nm* cattle-dealer

porthor (**-ion**) nm porter, door-keeper, commissionaire

pôs (**-au**) nm riddle, conundrum, puzzle

posib, posibl adj possible

posibilrwydd nm possibility

positif adj positive

positifiaeth nf positivism

post (**pyst**) nm post; pillar; **post sothach** junk mail

poster (**-i**) nm poster

postfarc (**-iau**) nm postmark

postio vb post

postman, postmon (**postmyn**) nm postman

postyn (**pyst**) nm post

pot (**-iau**) nm pot

potel (**-i**) nf bottle

potelaid (**-eidiau**) nf bottleful

potelu vb bottle

poten (**-ni**) nf paunch; pudding

potensial (**-au**) nm, adj potential

potes nm pottage, broth, soup

potio vb pot; tipple

potsiar (**-s**) nm poacher

potsio vb poach

pothell (**-au, -i**) nf blister

powdr (**-au**) nm powder

powl, powlen (**powliau**) nf bowl, basin

powlio vb roll; wheel, trundle

powltis (**-au**) nm poultice

practis nm practice

praff adj thick, stout

praffter nm thickness, stoutness, girth

pragmatiaeth nf pragmatism

praidd (**preiddiau**) nm flock

pranc (**-iau**) nm frolic, prank

prancio vb caper, prance

pratio vb pat, stroke, caress

praw, prawf (**profion**) nm test, trial, proof; **prawf gyrru** driving test

preblan vb chatter, babble

pregeth (**-au**) nf sermon, discourse

pregethu vb preach

pregethwr (**-wyr**) nm preacher

pregethwrol adj preacher-like

pregowtha vb jabber, rant

preifat adj private

preifatrwydd nm privacy

preimin nm ploughing match

prelad (**-iaid**) nm prelate

preladiaeth nf prelacy

preliwd (**-au**) nm prelude

premiwm (**-iymau**) nm premium

pren (**-nau**) nm tree, timber; wood

prentis (**-iaid**) nm apprentice

prentisiaeth nf apprenticeship

prentisio vb apprentice

prepian vb babble, blab

pres nm brass; bronze; copper; money

preseb (**-au**) nm crib, stall

presennol adj, nm present

presenoldeb nm presence; attendance

presenoli vb be present (reflexive)

presgripsiwn (**-iynau**) nm prescription

preswyl nm, **preswylfa** (**preswylfeydd**) nf, **preswylfod** nm abode, dwelling

preswylio vb dwell, reside, inhabit

preswylydd (**-ion, -wyr**) nm dweller, inhabitant

pric (**-iau**) nm stick, chip

prid adj dear, costly ▷ nm price, value

pridwerth nm ransom

pridd nm mould, earth, soil, ground

priddell (**-au, -i**) nf clod

priddglai nm loam

priddio, priddo vb earth

priddlech (**-au, -i**) nf tile

priddlestr (**-i**) nm earthenware vessel

P

priddlyd *adj* earthy
priddo *vb see* **priddio**
priddyn *nm* earth, soil, mould
prif *adj* prime, principal, chief; **prif gwrs** main course
prifardd (-feirdd) *nm* chief bard
prifathro (-athrawon) *nm* headmaster, principal
prifddinas (-oedd) *nf* metropolis, capital
prifiant *nm* growth
prifio *vb* grow
prifodl (-au) *nf* chief rhyme
prifysgol (-ion) *nf* university
priffordd (-ffyrdd) *nf* highway
prin *adj* scarce, rare ▷ *adv* scarcely
prinder, prindra *nm* scarceness, scarcity
prinhau *vb* make or grow scarce, diminish
print (-iau) *nm* print
printiedig *adj* printed
printio *vb* print
printiwr (-wyr) *nm* printer
priod *adj* own; proper; married ▷ *n* husband or wife, spouse
priodas (-au) *nf* marriage, wedding
priodasfab (-feibion) *nm* bridegroom
priodasferch (-ed) *nf* bride
priodasol *adj* matrimonial
priod-ddull (-iau) *nm* idiom
priodfab (-feibion) *nm* bridegroom
priodferch (-ed) *nf* bride
priodi *vb* marry
priodol *adj* proper, appropriate
priodoldeb (-au) *nm* propriety
priodoledd (-au) *nf* attribute
priodoli *vb* attribute
prior (-iaid) *nm* prior
priordy (-dai) *nm* priory
pris (-iau) *nm* price, value
prisiad, prisiant *nm* valuation

prisio *vb* price, value; prize
prisiwr (-wyr) *nm* valuer
problem (-au) *nm, nf* problem
proc (-iau) *nm* poke
procer (-au, -i) *nm* poker
procio *vb* poke; throb
procsi *nm* proxy
prodin (-au) *nm* protein
profedig *adj* approved, tried
profedigaeth (-au) *nf* trouble, tribulation
profedigaethus *adj* beset with trials
profi *vb* prove; taste; try; experience
profiad (-au) *nm* experience; **profiad gwaith** work experience
profiadol *adj* experienced
profiannaeth (-au) *nf* probation
proflen (-ni) *nf* proof-sheet
profocio *vb* provoke, tease
profoclyd *adj* provoking, provocative
profwr (-wyr) *nm* taster, tester
proffes (-au) *nf* profession
proffesiwn (-iynau) *nm* profession
proffesu *vb* profess
proffid *nf* profit
proffidio *vb* profit, benefit
proffidiol *adj* profitable
proffwyd (-i) *nm* prophet
proffwydes (-au) *nf* prophetess
proffwydo *vb* prophesy
proffwydol *adj* prophetic
proffwydoliaeth (-au) *nf* prophecy
project (-au) *nm* project
proses (-au) *nm, nf* process
prosesu *vb* process
prosesydd *nm* processor; **prosesydd geiriau** word processor
protest (-au) *nf* protest
Protestannaidd *adj* Protestant
Protestant (-aniaid) *nm* Protestant
protestio *vb* protest

protestiwr (-wyr) *nm* protestor
prudd *adj* grave, serious, sad; wise
pruddaidd *adj* sad, gloomy, mournful
prudd-der *nm* sadness, gloom
pruddglwyf *nm* depression, melancholy
pruddglwyfus *adj* depressed, melancholy
pruddhau *vb* sadden, depress
Prwsia *nf* Prussia
pryd (-iau) *nm* time; season ▷ *nm* **(-au)** meal
pryd *adv* while, when, since
pryd *nm* form, aspect; complexion
Prydain *nf* Britain; **Prydain Fawr** Great Britain
Prydeindod *nm* Britishness
Prydeinig *adj* British
Prydeiniwr (-wyr) *nm* Britisher
pryder (-on) *nm* anxiety, solicitude
pryderu *vb* be anxious
pryderus *adj* anxious, solicitous
prydferth *adj* beautiful, handsome
prydferthu *vb* beautify
prydferthwch *nm* beauty
prydles (-au, -i) *nf* lease
prydlon *adj* timely, punctual
prydlondeb *nm* punctuality
prydydd (-ion) *nm* poet
prydyddu *vb* compose poetry, poetize
pryddest (-au) *nf* poem in free metre
pryf (-ed) *nm* insect; worm; vermin
pryfedog *adj* verminous
pryfleiddiad (-au) *nm* insecticide
pryfyn *nm* worm
prŷn *adj* bought, purchased
prynedigaeth *nf, nm* redemption
prynhawn (-au) *nm* afternoon
prynhawnol *adj* afternoon, evening
pryniad *nm* purchase

prynu *vb* buy, purchase; redeem
prynwr (-wyr) *nm* buyer; redeemer
prysg *nm* bush, wood
prysgwydd *npl* brushwood
prysur *adj* busy, hasty; diligent; serious
prysurdeb *nm* haste, hurry; busyness
prysuro *vb* hurry, hasten
publican (-od) *nm* publican (New Test.)
pulpud (-au) *nm* pulpit
pulsau *npl* pulses
pum, pump *adj* five
pumawd (-au) *nm* quintet
pumed *adj* fifth
pumongl (-au) *nm* pentagon
punt (punnoedd, punnau) *nf* pound (money)
pupur *nm* pepper
pur *adj* pure, sincere ▷ *adv* very, fairly
purdan *nm* purgatory
purdeb *nm* purity, sincerity
puredigaeth *nf* purification
puredd *nm* purity, innocence
purfa (-feydd) *nf* refinery
purion *adj* very well; right enough
puro *vb* purify, cleanse
puror *nm* harpist
purwr (-wyr) *nm* purifier, refiner
purydd (-ion) *nm* purist
putain (-einiaid) *nf* prostitute
puteindra *nm* prostitution
puteinio *vb* commit fornication
puteiniwr (-wyr) *nm* fornicator
pw *excl* pooh
pwbig *adj* pubic
pwdin *nm* pudding, dessert
pwdlyd *adj* sulking
pwdr *adj* rotten, corrupt, putrid
pwdu *vb* pout, sulk
pŵer (-au) *nm* power
pwerus *adj* powerful

pwff (**pyffiau**) *nm* puff, blast
pwffian *vb* puff
pwl (**pyliau**) *nm* fit, attack, paroxysm
pŵl *adj* blunt, obtuse; dull, dim
pwll (**pyllau**) *nm* pit, pool, pond;
  pwll glo coal pit; **pwll tro** whirlpool
pwmp (**pympiau**) *nm* pump
pwn (**pynnau**) *nm* pack, burden
pwnc (**pynciau**) *nm* point, subject,
  question
pwniad (**-au**) *nm* nudge, dig
pwnio *vb* nudge; beat, thump, wallop
pwrcas (**-au**) *nm* purchase
pwrcasu *vb* purchase
pwrffil *nm* purfle, train
pwrpas (**-au**) *nm* purpose
pwrpasol *adj* suitable
pwrpasu *vb* purpose, intend
pwrs (**pyrsau**) *nm* purse, bag;
  udder; scrotum
pwt (**pytiau**) *nm* anything short;
  stump
pwt, pwtian *vb* prod, poke
pwti *nm* putty
pwy *pron* who
Pŵyl *nf* Poland
pwyll *nm* sense, discretion
pwyllgor (**-au**) *nm* committee
pwyllgorwr (**-wyr**) *nm*
  committee-man
pwyllo *vb* pause, consider, reflect
pwyllog *adj* discreet, prudent,
  deliberate
pwynt (**-iau**) *nm* point
pwyntil *nm* tab, tag; pencil
pwyntio *vb* point; fatten
pwyo *vb* beat, batter, pound
pwys (**-au, -i**) *nm* weight, burden,
  pressure; pound (lb.); importance
pwysau *nm* weight
pwysedd *nm* pressure
pwysi (**-ïau**) *nm* posy
pwysig *adj* important

pwysigrwydd *nm* importance
pwyslais (**-leisiau**) *nm* emphasis
pwysleisio *vb* emphasize, highlight
pwyso *vb* weigh, press; lean, rest; rely
pwyswr (**-wyr**) *nm* weigher
pwyth (**-au**) *nm* stitch; **talu'r pwyth**
  requite
pwytho *vb* stitch
pwythwr (**-wyr**) *nm* stitcher
pybyr *adj* strong, stout, staunch,
  valiant
pybyrwch *nm* stoutness, vigour,
  valour
pydew (**-au**) *nm* well, pit
pydredig *adj* rotten, putrid
pydredd *nm* rottenness, putridity, rot
pydru *vb* rot, putrefy
pyg *nm* pitch, bitumen
pygddu *adj* pitch-black
pygu *vb* pitch
pyngad, pyngu *vb* cluster
pylni *nm* bluntness, dullness
pylor *nm* dust, powder
pylu *vb* blunt, dull
pyllog *adj* full of pits
pyllu *vb* pit
pymtheg *adj, nm* fifteen
pymthegfed *adj* fifteenth
pyncio *vb* sing, play, make melody
pynfarch (**-feirch**) *nm* pack-horse;
  mill-race
pynio *vb* burden, load
pys *npl* (*nf* **-en**) peas
pysgod *npl* (*nm* **pysgodyn**) fish,
  fishes; **pysgod a sglodion** fish and
  chips; **sglodion pysgod** fish fingers;
  y Pysgod Pisces
pysgodfa (**-feydd**) *nf* fishery
pysgota *vb* fish
pysgotwr (**-wyr**) *nm* fisherman
pystylad *vb* stamp with the feet
pytaten (**-tws**) *nf* potato
pythefnos (**-au**) *nm, nf* fortnight

ph r

Pharisead (-aid) *nm* Pharisee
Phariseaeth *nf* Pharisaism
Phariseaidd *adj* Pharisaic(al)
Philistiad (-iaid) *nm* Philistine
Philistiaeth *nf* Philistinism

rabi (-niaid) *nm* rabbi
rabinaidd *adj* rabbinical
radio *nm* radio
radioleg *nf* radiology
radiws *nm* radius
ras (-ys) *nf* race
rasal, raser (-elydd, -erydd) *nf*
   razor
realaidd *adj*, **realistig** *adj* realistic
record (-iau) *nf*, *nm* record
recordiad (-au) *nm* recording
reiat *nf* row, riot
reis *nm* rice
reit *adv* right, very, quite
ridens *nf* fringe, nap
riwl *nf* ruler
robin goch *nm* robin
robin y gyrrwr *nm* gadfly
roced (-i) *nf* rocket
România *nf* Romania
ruban (-au) *nm* ribbon

rŵan *adv* now
rwbel *nm* rubble, rubbish
rwber *nm* rubber
rwdins *npl* (*nf* **rwden**) swedes
Rwmania *nf* Rumania
Rwsia *nf* Russia
Rwsiad (**Rwsiaid**) *nm* Russian
  (citizen)
Rwsieg *nm* Russian (language)

rhaca (**-nau**) *nf* rake
rhacanu *vb* rake
rhacs (*nm* **rhecsyn**) *npl* rags
rhad *adj* free; cheap
rhad (**-au**) *nm* grace, favour,
  blessing
rhadlon *adj* gracious, kind; genial
rhadlondeb, rhadlonrwydd *nm*
  graciousness, cheapness
rhadus *adj* economical
rhaeadr (**-au**) *nf* cataract, waterfall
rhaeadru *vb* pour, gush
rhaff (**-au**) *nf* rope, cord
rhaffo, rhaffu *vb* rope
rhag *prep* before, against; from; lest
  ▷ *prefix* pre-, fore-, ante-
rhagafon (**-ydd**) *nf* tributary
rhagair (**-au**) *nm* preface
rhagarfaethiad *nm* predestination
rhagarfaethu *vb* predestine
rhagarweiniad *nm* introduction

rhagarweiniol adj introductory, preliminary

rhagarwyddo vb foretoken, portend

rhagbaratoawl adj preparatory

rhagbrawf (-brofion) nm foretaste; preliminary test

rhagdraeth (-au) nm preface, introduction

rhag-dyb (-ion) nm presupposition

rhagdybied, rhagdybio vb presuppose

rhagddodiad (-iaid) nm prefix

rhagddywedyd, rhagddweud vb foretell

rhagenw (-au) nm pronoun

rhagenwol adj pronominal

rhagfarn (-au) nf prejudice

rhagfarnllyd adj prejudiced

rhagferf (-au) nf adverb

rhagflaenor (-iaid) nm forerunner

rhagflaenu vb precede, anticipate, forestall

rhagflaenydd (-ion, -wyr) nm predecessor, precursor

rhagflas nm foretaste

rhagfur (-iau) nm bulwark

rhagfyfyrio vb premeditate

rhagfynegi vb foretell

Rhagfyr nm December

rhaglaw (-iaid, -lofiaid) nm prefect, viceroy, governor

rhaglawiaeth nf prefecture, governorship

rhaglen (-ni) nf program(me); **rhaglen gyfrifiadur** computer program

rhaglennu vb program(me)

rhaglennydd (rhaglenwyr) nm programmer

rhagluniaeth (-au) nf providence

rhagluniaethol adj providential

rhaglunio vb predestine, predestinate

rhagod vb ambush, hinder, waylay

rhagofnau npl forebodings

rhagolwg (-ygon) nm prospect, outlook; **rhagolygon y tywydd** weather forecast

rhagor (-au, -ion) nm difference; more

rhagorfraint (-freintiau) nf privilege

rhagori vb exceed, excel, surpass

rhagoriaeth (-au) nf superiority; excellence

rhagorol adj excellent, splendid

rhagoroldeb nm excellence

rhagorsaf (-oedd) nf out-station; outpost

rhagredegydd (-ion) nm forerunner

rhagrith (-ion) nm hypocrisy

rhagrithio vb practise hypocrisy

rhagrithiol adj hypocritical

rhagrithiwr (-wyr) nm hypocrite

rhagrybuddio vb forewarn

rhagweld vb foresee

rhagwelediad nm foresight, prescience

rhagwybod vb foreknow

rhagwybodaeth nf foreknowledge

rhagymadrodd (-ion) nm introduction

rhai pron ones ▷ adj some

rhaib nm rapacity, greed; spell

rhaid (rheidiau) nm need, necessity

rhaidd (rheiddiau) nf antler

rhain pron these

rhamant (-au) nf romance

rhamantus adj romantic

rhan (-nau) nf part, portion; fate

rhanbarth (-au) nm division, district

rhandir (-oedd) nm, nf division, district

rhangymeriad (-iaid) nm participle

rhaniad (**-au**) *nm* division
rhannu *vb* divide, share, distribute
rhannwr (**rhanwyr**) *nm* divider,
sharer
rhanrif *nm* fraction
rhathell (**-au**) *nf* rasp
rhathiad *nm* friction, chafing
rhathu *vb* rub, rasp, file
rhaw (**-iau, rhofiau**) *nf* spade,
shovel
rhawd *nf* course, career
rhawg *adv* for a long time (to come)
rhawio, rhofio *vb* shovel
rhawn *coll n* coarse long hair,
horse-hair
rhech *nf* fart
rhechain *vb* fart
rhedeg *vb* run; flow; **rhedeg allan
(o)** run out (of); **rhedeg i ffwrdd,
rhedeg ymaeth** run away
rhedegfa (**-feydd**) *nf* racecourse,
race
rhedegog *adj* running, flowing
rhedegydd (**-ion, -wyr**) *nm* runner
rhedfa *nf* running, course, race
rhediad *nm* running, trend; slope
rhedweli (**-ïau**) *nf* artery
rhedyn *npl* (*nf* **-en**) fern
rheffyn (**-nau**) *nm* cord; string,
rigmarole
rheg (**-au, -feydd**) *nf* curse;
swearword
rhegen yr ŷd, rhegen ryg *nf*
corncrake
rhegi *vb* curse
rheglyd *adj* given to cursing, profane
rheng (**-au, -oedd**) *nf* row, rank
rheibio *vb* raven, ravage, ravish
rheibus *adj* rapacious, of prey
rheidiol *adj* necessary, needful
rheidrwydd *nm* necessity, need
rheidus *adj* necessitous, needy
rheilffordd (**-ffyrdd**) *nf* railway

rheini *pron* those
rheitheg *nf* rhetoric
rheithfarn (**-au**) *nf* verdict
rheithgor (**rheithwyr**) *nm* jury
rheithiwr (**-wyr**) *nm* juryman, juror
rheithor (**-ion, -iad**) *nm* rector
rhelyw *nm* residue, rest, remainder
rhemp *nf* excess; defect
rhent (**-i**) *nm* rent
rhentu *vb* rent
rheol (**-au**) *nf* rule, regulation
rheolaeth *nf* rule, management,
control; **rheolaeth bell** remote
control
rheolaidd *adj* regular; **yn rheolaidd**
regularly
rheoleiddio *vb* regulate; regularize
rheoli *vb* rule, govern, control
rheoliadur (**-on**) *nm*: **rheoliadur
calon, rheoliadur y galon**
pacemaker
rheolwr (**-wyr**) *nm* ruler, controller
rhes (**-i**) *nf* line, stripe; row, rank
rhesen (**rhesi**) *nf* line, parting,
streak, stripe
rhesin (**-au, -ingau**) *nm* raisin
rhesog *adj* striped; ribbed
rhestl (**-au**) *nf* rack
rhestr (**-au, -i**) *nf* list; row
rhestru *vb* list
rheswm (**-ymau**) *nm* reason
rhesymeg *nf* logic
rhesymegol *adj* logical
rhesymol *adj* reasonable, rational
rhesymoldeb *nm* reasonableness
rhesymolwr (**-wyr**) *nm* rationalist
rhesymu *vb* reason
rhetoreg, rhethreg *nf* rhetoric
rhew (**-oedd, -ogydd**) *nm* frost, ice
rhewfryn (**-iau**) *nm* iceberg
rhewgell (**-oedd**) *nf* freezer
rhewi *vb* freeze
rhewllyd *adj* icy, frosty, frigid

rhewyn (-au) nm ditch, stream
rhewynt (-oedd) nm freezing wind
rhi nm king, lord
rhiain (rhianedd) nf maiden
rhialtwch nm pomp; festivity, jollity
rhiant (rhieni) nm, nf parent; **rhiant sengl** single parent
rhibidirês nf rigmarole
rhibin nm streak
rhic (-iau) nm notch, nick; groove
rhiciog adj notched; grooved; ribbed
rhidyll (-iau) nm riddle, sieve
rhidyllio, rhidyllu vb riddle, sift
rhieingerdd (-i) nf love-poem
rhieni npl parents
rhif (-au) nm, **rhifedi** nm number
rhifo vb number, count, reckon
rhifol (-ion) nm numeral
rhifyddeg, rhifyddiaeth nf arithmetic
rhifyddwr (-wyr) nm arithmetician
rhifyn (-nau) nm number
rhigol (-au, -ydd) nf rut, groove
rhigwm (-ymau) nm rigmarole; rhyme
rhigymu vb rhyme, versify
rhigymwr (-wyr) nm rhymester
rhingyll (-iaid) nm sergeant, bailiff
rhimyn (-nau) nm strip, string
rhin (-iau) nf virtue, essence
rhincian vb creak; gnash
rhiniog (-au) nm threshold
rhinwedd (-au) nm, nf virtue
rhinweddol adj virtuous
rhip nm strickle
rhisgl nm bark
rhith (-iau) nm form, guise, appearance, image; foetus
rhithio vb appear
rhithyn nm atom, particle, scintilla
rhiw (-iau) nf hill, acclivity
rhoch nf grunt, groan; death rattle
rhochain, rhochian vb grunt

rhod (-au) nf wheel, orb; ecliptic
rhodfa (-feydd) nf walk, promenade, avenue
rhodiad nm walk
rhodianna vb stroll
rhodio vb walk, stroll
rhodres nm ostentation, affectation
rhodresa vb behave ostentatiously
rhodresgar adj ostentatious, affected
rhodreswr (-wyr) nm swaggerer
rhodd (-ion) nf gift, present
rhoddi vb give, bestow, yield; put
rhoddwr (-wyr) nm giver, donor
rhoi vb give, bestow, yield; put; **rhoi yn ôl, rhoi nôl** put back
rhol, rhôl (-iau) nf roll
rholbren (-ni) nm rolling-pin
rholen (rholiau) nf roll; roller
rholio vb roll
rholyn (rholion) nm roll; roller; **rholyn bara, rholyn o fara** bread roll; **rholyn tŷ bach, rholyn toiled** toilet roll
rhombws (rhombi) nm rhombus
rhonc adj rank, stark, out-and-out
rhos (-ydd) nf moor, heath; plain
rhos npl (nm **-yn**) roses
rhost adj roast, roasted
rhostio vb roast
rhosyn (-nau) nm rose
rhuad (-au) nm roaring, roar
rhuadwy adj roaring
rhuchen (rhuchion) nf husk; film, pellicle
rhudd adj red, crimson
rhuddell nf rubric
rhuddem (-au) nf ruby
rhuddin nm heart of timber
rhuddion npl bran
rhuddygl nm radish
Rhufain nf Rome
Rhufeinaidd adj Roman

rh

Rhufeiniad (**-iaid**), **Rhufeiniwr**
(**-wyr**) *nm* Roman
Rhufeinig *adj* Roman
rhugl *adj* free, fluent, glib
rhuglen (**-ni**) *nf* rattle
rhuglo *vb* rattle
rhuo *vb* roar, bellow, bluster
rhusio *vb* start, scare, take fright
rhuthr (**-au**) *nm* rush; attack; sally
rhuthro *vb* rush; attack, assault
rhwbio *vb* rub, chafe; **rhwbio allan**
rub out
rhwd *nm* rust
rhwng *prep* between, among
rhwnc *nm* snort, snore; death-rattle
rhwth *adj* gaping, distended
rhwyd (**-au, -i**) *nf* net, snare
rhwydo *vb* net, ensnare
rhwydog *adj* reticulated, netted
rhwydwaith (**-weithiau**) *nm*
network
rhwydweithio *vb* network ▷ *nm*
networking; **rhwydweithio**
cymdeithasol social networking
rhwydd *adj* easy, expeditious,
prosperous
rhwyddhau *vb* facilitate
rhwyddineb *nm* ease, facility
rhwyf (**-au**) *nf* oar
rhwyflong (**-au**) *nf* galley
rhwyfo *vb* row; sway; toss about
rhwyfus *adj* restless
rhwyfwr (**-wyr**) *nm* rower, oarsman
rhwyg (**-iadau**) *nf* rent, rupture;
schism
rhwygo *vb* rend, tear
rhwyll (**-au**) *nf*, **rhwyllyn** *nm*
buttonhole, aperture; lattice
rhwyllwaith *nm* fretwork,
lattice-work
rhwym *adj* bound ▷ *nm* (**-au**) bond,
tie; obligation
rhwymedig *adj* bound, obliged

rhwymedigaeth (**-au**) *nf* bond,
obligation
rhwymedd *nm* constipation
rhwymiad (**-au**) *nm* binding
rhwymo *vb* bind, tie; constipate
rhwymwr (**-wyr**) *nm* binder
rhwymyn (**-nau**) *nm* band, bond,
bandage
rhwysg (**-au**) *nm* sway; pomp
rhwysgfawr *adj* pompous,
ostentatious
rhwystr (**-au**) *nm* hindrance,
obstacle
rhwystro *vb* hinder, prevent,
obstruct
rhwystrus *adj* embarrassed,
confused
rhy *adv* too
rhybedio *vb* rivet
rhybudd (**-ion**) *nm* notice, warning
rhybuddio *vb* warn, admonish,
caution
rhybuddiwr (**-wyr**) *nm* warner
rhych (**-au**) *nm*, *nf* furrow, rut,
groove
rhychog *adj* furrowed, seamed
rhychwant (**-au**) *nm* span
rhychwantu *vb* span
rhyd (**-au, -iau**) *nf* ford
rhydio *vb* ford
rhydlyd *adj* rusty
rhydu *vb* rust
rhydd *adj* free; loose; liberal
Rhyddfrydiaeth *nf* Liberalism
rhyddfrydig *adj* liberal, generous
Rhyddfrydol *adj* liberal (*in politics*)
Rhyddfrydwr (**-wyr**) *nm* Liberal,
Radical
rhyddhad *nm* liberation,
emancipation
rhyddhau *vb* free, release, liberate
rhyddhawr (**-wyr**) *nm* liberator
rhyddiaith *nf* prose

rhyddid *nm* freedom, liberty
rhyddieithol *adj* prose, prosaic
rhyddni *nm* looseness, diarrhœa
rhyfedd *adj* strange, queer,
  wonderful
rhyfeddnod (-au) *nm* note of
  exclamation
rhyfeddod (-au) *nm, nf* wonder,
  marvel
rhyfeddol *adj* wonderful, marvellous
rhyfeddu *vb* wonder, marvel
rhyfel (-oedd) *nm, nf* war, warfare
rhyfela *vb* wage war, war
rhyfelgar *adj* warlike, bellicose
rhyfelgri *nm* war-cry, battle-cry
rhyfelgyrch (-oedd) *nm* campaign
rhyfelwr (-wyr) *nm* warrior
rhyferthwy *nm* torrent, inundation
rhyfon *npl* currants
rhyfyg *nm* presumption,
  foolhardiness
rhyfygu *vb* presume, dare
rhyfygus *adj* presumptuous;
  foolhardy
rhyg *nm* rye
rhyglyddu *vb* deserve, merit
rhygnu *vb* rub, grate, jar; harp
rhygyngu *vb* amble; caper, mince
rhyngrwyd *nf* internet
rhyngu *vb*: **rhyngu bodd** please
rhyngweithiol *adj* interactive
rhyngwladol *adj* international
rhyndod *nm* shivering, chill
rhynion *npl* grits, groats
rhynllyd *adj* shivering, chilly
rhynnu *vb* starve with cold
rhysedd *nm* abundance, excess
rhython *npl* cockles
rhythu *vb* gape; stare
rhyw *adj* some, certain ▷ *nf, nm*
  (-iau) sort; sex
rhywbeth *nm* something
rhywfaint *nm* some amount

rhywfodd, rhywsut *adv* somehow
rhywiaeth *nf* sexism
rhywiaethol *adj* sexist
rhywiog *adj* kindly, genial; fine;
  tender
rhywiol *adj* sexual
rhywle *adv* somewhere, anywhere
rhywogaeth (-au) *nf* species, sort,
  kind
rhywun (rhywrai) *nm* someone,
  anyone

S

Sabath, Saboth (-au) *nm* Sabbath
Sabothol *adj* Sabbath, sabbatic(al)
sacrament (-au) *nm, nf* sacrament
sacramentaidd *adj* sacramental
sach (-au) *nf, nm* sack
sachaid (-eidiau) *nf* sackful
sachlen *nf*, **sachliain** *nm* sack-cloth
sachu *vb* sack, bag
sad *adj* firm, steady, solid; sober
sadio *vb* firm, steady
sadistiaeth *nf* sadism
sadrwydd *nm* firmness, steadiness
Sadwrn (-yrnau) *nm* Saturn; **dydd Sadwrn** Saturday
saer (seiri) *nm* wright, mason, carpenter
saernïaeth *nf* workmanship, construction
saernïo *vb* fashion, construct
Saesneg *nf, adj* English
Saesnes (-au) *nf* Englishwoman

saets *nm* sage
saeth (-au) *nf* arrow, dart
saethiad (-au) *nm* shooting
saethu *vb* shoot, dart; blast
saethwr (-wyr) *nm* shooter, shot
saethydd (-ion) *nm* shooter, archer; **y Saethydd** Sagittarius
saethyddiaeth *nf* archery
saethyn (-nau) *nm* projectile
safadwy *adj* stable
safanna *nm* savannah
safbwynt (-iau) *nm* standpoint
safiad *nm* standing; stature; stand
safio *vb* save
safle (-oedd) *nm* position, station, situation; **safle gwe** website
safn (-au) *nf* mouth, jaws
safnrhwth *adj* open-mouthed, gaping
safnrhythu *vb* gape, stare
safon (-au) *nf* standard, criterion; **safon byw** standard of living
safoni *vb* standardise
safonol *adj* standard
saffir *nm* sapphire
saffrwm, saffron *nm* crocus
sagrafen (-nau) *nf* sacrament
sang (-au) *nf* pressure, tread
sangu, sengi *vb* tread, trample
saib (seibiau) *nm* leisure; pause, rest
saig (seigiau) *nf* meal, dish
sail (seiliau) *nf* base, foundation
saim (seimiau) *nm* grease
sain (seiniau) *nf* sound, tone
Sais (Saeson) *nm* Saxon, Englishman
saith *adj, nm* seven
sâl *adj* poor; poorly, ill; **sâl môr** seasick
salad (-au) *nm* salad
saldra *nm* poorness; illness
salm (-au) *nf* psalm
salmydd (-ion) *nm* psalmist
salw *adj* poor, mean, vile; ugly
salwch *nm* illness

Sallwyr *nm* Psalter
sampl (-au) *nf* sample
samplu *vb* sample
Sanct *nm* the Holy One
sanctaidd *adj* holy
sancteiddio *vb* sanctify, hallow
sancteiddrwydd *nm* holiness, sanctity
sandal (-au) *nm* sandal
sant (saint, seintiau) *nm* saint
santes (-au) *nf* female saint
sarff (seirff) *nf* serpent
sarhad (-au) *nm* insult, disgrace, injury
sarhau *vb* insult, affront, injure
sarhaus *adj* insulting, offensive, insolent
sarn (-au) *nf* causeway ▷ *nm* litter, ruin, destruction
sarnu *vb* trample; litter; spoil, ruin
sarrug *adj* gruff, surly, morose
sarugrwydd *nm* gruffness, surliness
sasiwn (-iynau) *nm* C.M. Association
satan (-iaid) *nm* satan
sathredig *adj* common, vulgar
sathru *vb* tread, trample
Saudi Arabia, Sawdi Arabia *nf* Saudi Arabia
sawdl (sodlau) *nm, nf* heel
sawl *pron* whoso, he that; **pa sawl** how many
sawr, sawyr *nm* savour
sawrio, sawru *vb* savour
sawrus *adj* savoury
saws *nm* sauce
sba (-on) *nm* spa
Sbaen *nf* Spain
sbageti *nm* spaghetti
sbam *nm* spam
sbamio *vb* spam
sbamiwr (-wyr) *nm* spammer
sbaner (-i) *nm* spanner
sbâr (sbarion) *nm* spare; (*pl*) leavings
sbario *vb* spare, save

sbectol *nf* spectacle(s)
sbeit *nf* spite
sbeitio *vb* spite
sbeitlyd *adj* spiteful
sbel (-iau) *nf* spell
sbon *adv*: **newydd sbon** brand-new
sbonc (-iau) *nm* leap, jerk
sboncen *nf* squash
sbort *nf* sport, fun, game
sbri *nm* spree, fun
sbring *nm* spring
sbwylio *vb* spoil
sebon (-au) *nm* soap
seboni *vb* soap, lather; soft-soap, flatter
sebonwr (-wyr) *nm* flatterer
secsist *adj* sexist
sect (-au) *nf* sect
sectyddiaeth *nf* sectarianism
sectyddol *adj* sectarian
sech *adj f of* **sych**
sedd (-au) *nf* seat, pew
sef *conj* that is to say, namely, to wit
sefnig *nm* pharynx
sefydledig *adj* established
sefydliad (-au) *nm* establishment, institution
sefydlog *adj* fixed, settled, stationary, stable
sefydlogrwydd, sefydlowgrwydd *nm* stability
sefydlu *vb* establish, found, settle
sefyll *vb* stand; stop; stay
sefyllfa (-oedd) *nf* situation, position
sefyllian *vb* stand about, loiter
sefyllwyr *npl* bystanders
segur *adj* idle
segura *vb* idle
segurdod *nm* idleness
segurwr (-wyr) *nm* idler
seguryd *nm* idleness
seguryn, segurwr (-wyr) *nm* idler

S

sengi *vb* tread, trample
sengl *adj* single
seiat (-adau) *nf* fellowship meeting, 'society'
seibiant *nm* leisure, respite;
 seibiant salwch sick leave
seibio *vb* pause
seiciatreg *nm* psychiatry
seiciatrydd *nm* psychiatrist
seicoleg *nf* psychology
seicolegydd (-wyr) *nm* psychologist
seidin *nm* sidings
seilio *vb* ground, found
seimio *vb* grease
seimllyd *adj* greasy
seinber *adj* melodious, euphonious
seindorf (-dyrf) *nf* band
seineg *nf* phonetics
seinfawr *adj* loud
seinfforch (-ffyrch) *nf* tuning-fork
seinio *vb* sound, resound; pronounce
seintio *vb* saint, canonize
seintwar *nf* sanctuary
seinyddol *adj* phonetic
Seisnig *adj* English
Seisnigaidd *adj* English, Anglicized
Seisnigeiddio, Seisnigo *vb* Anglicize
seithblyg *adj* sevenfold
seithfed *adj* seventh
seithongl (-au) *nf* heptagon
seithug *adj* futile, fruitless, bootless
sêl *nf* zeal
sêl (seliau) *nf* seal
sêl (-s) *nf* sale; **sêl cist car** car boot sale
Seland Newydd *nf* New Zealand
seld (-au) *nf* dresser, sideboard, bookcase
seler (-au, -i, -ydd) *nf* cellar
selio *vb* seal
selni *nm* illness
selog *adj* zealous, ardent
selsig (-od) *nf* black-pudding, sausage
semanteg *nf* semantics

seminar (-au) *nm, nf* seminar
seml *adj f of* **syml**
sen (-nau) *nf* reproof, rebuke, censure, snub
senedd (-au) *nf* senate; parliament
seneddol *adj* senatorial, parliamentary
seneddwr (-wyr) *nm* senator
sennu *vb* rebuke, censure
sentimentaleiddiwch *nm* sentimentality
sêr *see* **seren**
seraff (-iaid) *nm* seraph
Serbia *nf* Serbia
serch *conj, prep* although, notwithstanding
serch (-iadau) *nm* affection, love
serchog *adj* affectionate, loving
serchowgrwydd *nm* affection, love
serchu *vb* love
serchus *adj* loving, affectionate, pleasant
sêr-ddewin (-iaid) *nm* astrologer
sêr-ddewiniaeth *nf* astrology
seremoni (-ïau) *nf* ceremony
seremonïol *adj* ceremonial
seren (sêr) *nf* star; asterisk; **seren ffilmiau** film star
serennog *adj* starry
serennu *vb* sparkle, scintillate
serfyll *adj* unsteady
seri *nm* causeway, pavement
serio *vb* sear
sero (-au) *nm* zero
serth *adj* steep, precipitous; obscene
serthedd *nm* ribaldry, obscenity
serwm *nm* serum
seryddiaeth *nf* astronomy
seryddol *adj* astronomical
seryddwr (-wyr) *nm* astronomer
sesbin *nm* shoehorn
sesiwn (sesiynau) *nm* session; **sesiwn ymarfer** workout

set (**-iau**) *nf* set

sêt (**seti**) *nf* seat, pew; **sêt fawr** deacons' pew

setl (**-au**) *nf* settle

setlo *vb* settle

sethrydd (**-ion**) *nm* treader, trampler

sew (**-ion**) *nm* juice; pottage; delicacy

sffêr *nf* sphere

sg- *see also* **ysg-**

sgâm (**sgamiau**) *nf* scheme, dodge, scam

sgamio *vb* scheme, dodge

sgamiwr (**-wyr**) *nm* scammer

sganiwr (**-wyr**) *nm* scanner; **sganiwr feirws** virus scanner

sgaprwth *adj* uncouth, rough

sgarff (**-iau**) *nf* scarf

sgêri *adj* scary

sgil *nm* pillion; **sgil effaith** side effect

sgiw *nf* settle; **ar y sgiw** askew

sglefren *nf* slide

sglefrio *vb* skate, slide

sgolor (**-ion**) *nm* scholar

sgôr *nm* score

sgorpion (**-au**) *nm* scorpion; **y Sgorpion** Scorpio

sgrafell (**-i**) *nf* scraper

sgrechian *vb* shriek

sgrech y coed *nf* jay

sgrin (**-au**) *nf* screen

sgriw (**-iau**) *nf* screw

sgwâr (**-iau**) *nm* square

sgwd (**sgydiau**) *nf* cataract, waterfall

sgwrs (**sgyrsiau**) *nf* talk, chat, conversation

sgwrsio *vb* talk, chat

sgwter (**-i**) *nm* scooter

si *nm* whiz, buzz; rumour, murmur

siaced (**-i**) *nf* jacket, coat

siâd (**sidau**) *nf* pate

sialc *nm* chalk

sialens *nf* challenge

sialensio *vb* challenge

siambr *nf* chamber

sianel (**-i, -ydd**) *nf* channel

siant (**-au**) *nf* chant

siâr *nf* share

siarad *vb* talk, speak ▷ *nm* talk

siaradus *adj* talkative, garrulous

siaradwr (**-wyr**) *nm* talker, speaker

siario *vb* share

siars *nf* charge, command

siarsio *vb* charge, enjoin, warn

siart (**-iau**) *nm* chart

siartr (**-au**) *nf* charter

siasbi *nm* shoehorn

siawns *nf* chance

siawnsio *vb* chance

sibrwd *vb* whisper, murmur ▷ *nm* (**-ydion**) whisper, murmur

sicr *adj* sure, certain; secure

sicrhau *vb* assure, affirm, confirm; secure

sicrwydd *nm* certainty, assurance

sidan (**-au**) *nm* silk

sidanaidd *adj* silky

sidanbryf (**-ed**) *nm* silkworm

sied (**-au**) *nf* shed

siêd *nm* escheat, forfeit

siesbin *nm* shoehorn

siew *nf* show

siffrwd *vb* rustle, shuffle

sigâr *nf* cigar

sigaret (**sigaretau**) *nf* cigarette

sigledig *adj* shaky, rickety, unstable

siglen (**-nydd**) *nf* swing; bog, swamp

siglo *vb* shake, quake, rock, swing, wag

sil (**-od**) *nm* spawn, fry

silff (**-oedd**) *nf* shelf

silwair *nm* silage

sill (**-iau**), **sillaf** (**-au**) *nf* syllable

sillafiaeth *nf* spelling

sillafu *vb* spell

sillgoll (**-au**) *nf* apostrophe

simnai (**-neiau**) *nf* chimney

s

simsan *adj* unsteady, tottering, rickety
simsanu *vb* totter
sinach (-od) *nf* balk, waste ground; skinflint
sinc *nm* zinc
sinema (sinemâu) *nf* cinema
sinig *nm* cynic
sinigaidd *adj* cynical
sinsir *nm* ginger
sïo *vb* hiss, whiz; murmur, purl
sioe (-au) *nf* show; **sioe gêm, sioe gêmau** game show; **sioe sgwrsio** chat show
sïol (-au) *nf* skull, pate
sïôl (siolau) *nf* shawl
siom (-au) *nm* disappointment
siomedig *adj* disappointed, disappointing
siomedigaeth (-au) *nf* disappointment
siomi *vb* disappoint, let down; balk, thwart; deceive
siomiant *nm* disappointment
sionc *adj* brisk, nimble, agile, active
sioncio *vb* brisk
Siôn Corn *nm* Father Christmas
sioncrwydd *nm* briskness, agility
sioncyn y gwair *nm* grasshopper
siop (-au) *nf* shop; **dyn siop** shop assistant; **merch siop** shop assistant
siopladrad (-au) *nm* shoplifting
siopwr (-wyr) *nm* shopkeeper
sipian *vb* sip, sup, suck
sipio *vb* zip
siprys *nm* mixed corn (oats and barley)
sipsiwn *npl* gypsies
sir (-oedd) *nf* shire, county
siriol *adj* cheerful, bright, pleasant
sirioldeb *nm* cheerfulness
sirioli *vb* cheer, brighten
sirydd (-ion), siryf (-ion) *nm* sheriff
siryddiaeth *nf* shrievalty
sisial *vb* whisper

siswrn (-yrnau) *nm* scissors
siwgr *nm* sugar
siwmper (-i) *nf* jumper
siwr, siŵr *adj* sure, certain
siwrnai (-eiau) *nf* journey ▷ *adv* once
siwt (-iau) *nf* suit
slaf (slafiaid) *nm* slave, drudge
slei *adj* sly
sleifio *vb* slink
sleisen *nf* slice
slic *adj* slick
Slofacia *nf* Slovakia
Slofenia *nf* Slovenia
slotian *vb* paddle, dabble; tipple
slumyn *see* **ystlum**
slwt *nf* slut
smala *adj* droll
smalio *vb* joke
sment *nm* cement
smocio *vb* smoke (tobacco)
smociwr (-wyr) *nm* smoker
smotyn (smotiau) *nm* spot
smygu *see* **smocio**
snisin *nm* snuff
snwffian *vb* snuff, sniff; snuffle; whimper
sobr *adj* sober, serious
sobreiddio, sobri *vb* sober
sobrwydd *nm* sobriety, soberness
socas (-au) *nf* gaiter, legging
sodomiaeth *nf* sodomy
sodr *nm* solder
soddi *vb* submerge
soeg *nm* brewers' grains, draff
sofl *npl* (*nm* -**yn**) stubble
sofliar (-ieir) *nf* quail
sofraniaeth *nf* sovereignty
sofren (sofrod) *nf* sovereign (coin)
solas *nm* solace, joy
sol-ffa *nm* sol-fa
solffaeo *vb* sol-fa
sôn *vb, nm* talk, mention, rumour
soned (-au) *nf* sonnet

sonedwr (-wyr) nm composer of sonnets
soniarus adj melodious, tuneful; loud
soriant nm indignation, displeasure
sorod npl dross, dregs, refuse
sorri vb chafe, sulk, be displeased
sosban (-nau, -benni) nf saucepan
sosej (-ys) nf sausage
soser (-i) nf saucer; **soser lloeren** satellite dish
sosialaeth nf socialism
sothach coll n refuse, rubbish, trash
st- see also **yst-**
stac (-iau) nf stack
stad (-au) nf estate; state; **stad ddiwydiannol** industrial estate
staen (-au) nm stain
staenio vb stain
stafell (-oedd) nf room; **stafell sgwrsio** chat room
stâl (-au) nf stall
stamp (-iau) nm, nf stamp
stampio vb stamp
starts nm starch
steil (-iau) nf style; surname; **steil gwallt** hairdo
stên (stenau) nf pitcher
stesion (-au) nf station
sticil, sticill nf stile
stilio vb question
stiward (-iaid) nm steward
stiwdio nf studio
stoc (-au) nf stock
stomp nf bungle, mess, muddle
stompio vb beat, pound; bungle, mess
stompiwr (-wyr) nm bungler
stori (-ïau, -ïâu, straeon) nf story, tale
storm, storom (stormydd) nf storm
stormus adj stormy
storom nf see **storm**
straegar adj gossiping, gossipy
strancio vb play tricks
strategaeth nf strategy

strategol adj strategic
strategydd (-ion) nm strategist
streic (-iau) nf strike
strwythur nm structure
stryd (-oedd) nf street; **stryd fawr** high street
stwc (stycau) nm pail, bucket
stwff (styffiau) nm stuff
stwffio vb stuff, thrust
stwffwl (styffylau) nm post; staple
styffylydd (-ion) nm stapler
su nm buzz, murmur, hum
suad nm buzzing, lulling; hum
sucan nm gruel
sudd (-ion) nm juice, sap
suddgloch (-glychau) nf diving-bell
suddlong (-au) nf submarine
suddo vb sink, dive; invest (money)
sug (-ion) nm juice, sap
sugn nm suck; suction; sap
sugno vb suck, imbibe, absorb
Sul (-iau) nm: **dydd Sul** Sunday
Sulgwyn nm Whitsunday
suo vb buzz, hum; lull, hush
sur (-ion) adj sour, acid
surdoes nm leaven
surni nm sourness, staleness, tartness
suro vb sour
suryn nm acid
sut nm manner; plight; **(pa) sut?** how?; what sort of?
swalpio vb flounder, jump, bounce
swci adj tame, pet
swcro vb succour
swcwr nm succour
swch (sychau) nf ploughshare; tip; lips
Sweden nf Sweden
swil adj shy, bashful
swilder nm shyness, bashfulness
Swistir nf: **y Swistir** Switzerland
switsfwrdd (switsfyrddau) nm switchboard

S

swllt (**sylltau**) *nm* shilling
swm (**symiau**) *nm* sum, bulk
swmbwl (**symbylau**) *nm* goad
swmer (**-au**) *nm* beam; pack
swmp *nm* bulk
swmpus *adj* bulky
sŵn *nm* noise, sound
swnian *vb* murmur, grumble, nag
swnio *vb* sound, pronounce
swnllyd *adj* peevish, querulous
swnt *nm* sound, strait
sŵoleg *nf* zoology
swp (**sypiau**) *nm* mass, heap; cluster
swper (**-au**) *nm, nf* supper
swpera, swperu *vb* give or take
  supper
swrn (**syrnau**) *nf* fetlock, ankle ▷ *nm*
  good number
swrth *adj* heavy, sluggish; sullen
sws (**-ys**) *nf* kiss
swta *adj* abrupt, curt
swydd (**-au, -i**) *nf* office; county
swyddfa (**-feydd**) *nf* office
swyddog (**-ion**) *nm* officer, official
swyddogaeth *nf* office, function
swyddogol *adj* official
swyn (**-ion**) *nm* charm, fascination,
  spell, magic
swyngyfaredd (**-ion**) *nf* sorcery,
  witchcraft
swyngyfareddwr (**-wyr**) *nm* sorcerer
swyno *vb* charm, enchant, bewitch
swynol *adj* charming, fascinating
swynwr (**-wyr**) *nm* magician, wizard
swynwraig (**-wragedd**) *nf* sorceress
sy *see* **sydd**
syber *adj* sober, decent; clean, tidy
sych (*f* **sech**) *adj* dry
sychder *nm* dryness, drought
sychdir (**-oedd**) *nm* dry land
syched *nm* thirst
sychedig *adj* thirsty, parched, dry
sychedu *vb* thirst

sychin *nf* drought
sychlyd *adj* dry
sychu *vb* dry, dry up; wipe dry, wipe
sychydd *nm* dryer
sydyn *adj* sudden, abrupt
sydynrwydd *nm* suddenness
sydd *vb* is, are
syfi *npl* (*nf* **syfien**) strawberries
syflyd *vb* stir, move, budge
syfrdan *adj* giddy, dazed, stunned
syfrdandod *nm* giddiness, stupor
syfrdanol *adj* stunning
syfrdanu *vb* daze, bewilder, stupefy,
  stun
sylfaen (**-feini**) *nf* foundation
sylfaenol *adj* basic
sylfaenu *vb* found
sylfaenwr (**-wyr**), **sylfaenydd**
  (**-ion**) *nm* founder
sylw (**-adau**) *nm* notice, attention,
  remark
sylwadaeth *nf* observation
sylwebaeth *nf* commentary
sylwedydd (**-ion**) *nm* observer
sylwedd (**-au**) *nm* substance, reality
sylweddol *adj* substantial, real
sylweddoli *vb* realize
sylweddoliad *nm* realization
sylwi *vb* observe, regard, notice
syllu *vb* gaze
symbal (**-au**) *nm* cymbal
symbol *nm* symbol
symboliaeth *nf* symbolism
symbyliad *nm* stimulus,
  encouragement
symbylu *vb* goad, spur, stimulate
symbylydd (**-ion**) *nm* stimulant
symio *vb* sum
syml (*f* **seml**) *adj* simple
symledd *nm* simplicity
symleiddiad *nm* simplification
symleiddio *vb* simplify
symlrwydd *nm* simplicity

symol *adj* middling, fair

symud *vb* move, remove

symudiad (-au) *nm* movement, removal

symudol *adj* moving, movable, mobile

syn *adj* amazed; astonishing, surprising

synagog (-au) *nm* synagogue

synamon *nm* cinnamon

syndod *nm* marvel, amazement, surprise

syndrom (-au) *nm* syndrome; **syndrom Down** Down's syndrome

synfyfyrdod *nm* reverie

synfyfyrio *vb* muse

synhwyro *vb* sense

synhwyrol *adj* sensible

syniad (-au) *nm* notion, idea, view

syniadaeth *nf* conception

synied, synio *vb* think, believe, feel

synnu *vb* marvel, be amazed, surprise, be surprised

synnwyr (synhwyrau) *nm* sense; **synnwyr digrifwch** sense of humour

synwyroldeb *nm* sensibleness

synwyrusrwydd *nm* sensuousness

sypio *vb* pack, heap, bundle

sypyn (-nau) *nm* package, packet

syr *nm* sir

syrcas *nf* circus

syrffed *nm* surfeit

syrffedu *vb* surfeit

Syria *nf* Syria

syrthiedig *adj* fallen

syrthio *vb* fall, tumble

syrthni *nm* listlessness, sloth; inertia

system *nm*, *nf* system

systematig *adj* systematic

syth *adj* stiff; straight

sythu *vb* stiffen, straighten; starve with cold

sythwelediad *nm* intuition

tabernacl (-au) *nm* tabernacle

tabl (-au) *nm* table

tablen *nf* ale, beer

tabŵ *nm* taboo

tabwrdd (-yrddau) *nm* drum

tabyrddu *vb* drum, thrum

taclau *npl* (*nm* **teclyn**) tackle, gear

taclo *vb* tackle

taclu *vb* put in order, trim

taclus *adj* neat, trim, tidy

tacluso *vb* trim, tidy

taclusrwydd *nm* tidiness

tacsi (-s) *nm* taxi; **gyrrwr tacsi** taxi driver

tacteg (-au) *nf* tactic

Tachwedd *nm* November

tad (-au) *nm* father; **tad-cu** grandfather

tadmaeth (-au, -od) *nm* foster father

tadogaeth *nf* paternity; derivation

tadogi *vb* father
tadol *adj* fatherly, paternal
taenelliad *nm* sprinkling, affusion
taenellu *vb* sprinkle
taenellwr (-wyr) *nm* sprinkler
taenlen (-ni) *nf* spreadsheet
taenu *vb* spread, expand, stretch
taenwr (-wyr) *nm* spreader,
  disseminator
taeog *adj* churlish, blunt ▷ *nm* **(-au,
  -ion)** churl
taeogaidd *adj* churlish, rude
taer *adj* earnest, importunate,
  urgent
taerineb, taerni *nm* earnestness,
  importunity
taeru *vb* insist, maintain; contend,
  wrangle
tafarn (-au) *nf, nm* tavern, inn,
  public-house
tafarndy (-dai) *nm* public-house
tafarnwr (-wyr) *nm* inn-keeper,
  publican
tafell (-au, -i, tefyll) *nf* slice
tafl (-au) *nf* cast; scale; **ffon dafl**
  sling
tafledigion *npl* projectiles
taflegryn (taflegrau) *nm* missile
tafleisiaeth *nf* ventriloquism
tafleisydd (-ion, -wyr) *nm*
  ventriloquist
taflen (-nau, -ni) *nf* table, list,
  leaflet; **taflen waith** worksheet
taflennu *vb* tabulate
tafliad (-au) *nm* throw; set-back
taflod (-ydd) *nf* loft; **taflod y genau**
  palate
taflodol *adj* palatal
taflu *vb* throw, fling, cast, hurl;
  throw away
tafluniad *nm* projection
taflunio *vb* project
taflunydd *nm* projector

tafod (-au) *nm* tongue
tafodi *vb* berate, scold
tafodiaith (-ieithoedd) *nf* speech,
  language, dialect
tafod-leferydd *nm* speech,
  utterance; **ar dafod-leferydd** by
  rote
tafol *nf* scales, balance
tafol *coll n* dock
tafoli *vb* weigh up, assess
tafotrwg *adj* foul-mouthed, abusive
tafotrydd *adj* garrulous, flippant
tagell (-au, tegyll) *nf* gill; wattle;
  dewlap; double chin
tagellog *adj* wattled; double-
  chinned
tagfa (-feydd) *nf* choking,
  strangling
tagu *vb* choke, stifle; strangle
tangnefedd *nm, nf* peace
tangnefeddu *vb* make peace;
  appease
tangnefeddus *adj* peaceable,
  peaceful
tangnefeddwr (-wyr) *nm*
  peacemaker
tai *see* **tŷ**
taid (teidiau) *nm* grandfather
tail *nm* dung, manure
tair *adj f of* **tri**
taith (teithiau) *nf* journey, voyage,
  progress
tal *adj* tall, high, lofty
tâl (talau, taloedd) *nm* end, forehead
tâl (taliadau) *nm* pay, payment;
  taloedd rates
talaith (-eithiau) *nf* diadem;
  province, state
talar (-au) *nf* headland in field
talcen (-nau, -ni) *nm* forehead;
  gable
taldra *nm* tallness, loftiness, stature
taleb (-au, -ion) *nf* receipt, voucher

taledigaeth *nf* payment, recompense

taleithiol *adj* provincial

talent (-au) *nf* talent

talentog *adj* talented

talfyriad (-au) *nm* abbreviation, abridgement

talfyrru *vb* abbreviate, abridge

talgryf *adj* sturdy, robust; impudent

taliad (-au) *nm* payment

talm *nm* space, while; quantity, number; **er ys talm** long ago

talog *adj* jaunty

talp (-au, -iau) *nm* mass, lump

talpiog *adj* lumpy

talu *vb* pay, render; answer, suit; be worth

talu-wrth-ddefnyddio *adj* pay-as-you-go

talwr (-wyr) *nm* payer

talwrn *nm* threshing floor; poetic contest

tamaid (-eidiau) *nm* morsel, bit, bite

tan *prep* to, till, until, as far; under

tân (tanau) *nm* fire

tanbaid *adj* fiery, hot, fervent; brilliant

tanbeidrwydd *nm* fierce heat, ardour

tanchwa (-oedd) *nf* fire-damp; explosion

tanddaearol *adj* underground, subterranean

tanforol *adj* submarine

taniad *nm* ignition, firing

tanio *vb* fire, stoke

taniwr (-wyr) *nm* firer, fireman, stoker

tanlinellu *vb* underline

tanlwybr *nm* subway

tanlli *adj*: **newydd sbon danlli** brand new

tanllwyth (-i) *nm* blazing fire

tanllyd *adj* fiery

tannu *vb* adjust, spread, make (bed)

tanodd *adv* below, beneath

tanosodiad (-au) *nm* understatement

Tansanïa *nf* Tanzania

tant (tannau) *nm* chord, string

tanwent *nm* fuel

tanwydd *coll n* firewood, fuel

tanysgrifiad (-au) *nm* subscription

tanysgrifio *vb* subscribe

tanysgrifiwr (-wyr) *nm* subscriber

taradr (terydr) *nm* auger; **taradr y coed** woodpecker

taran (-au) *nf* (peal of) thunder

taranfollt (-au) *nf* thunderbolt

taranu *vb* thunder

tarddell *nf* source, spring

tarddiad (-au) *nm* source, derivation

tarddle (-oedd) *nm* source

tarddu *vb* sprout, spring; derive, be derived

tarfu *vb* scare, scatter

targed (-au) *nm* target

tarian (-au) *nf* shield

tario *vb* tarry

taro *vb* strike, smite, hit, knock; tap; stick; hot; suit

tarren (tarenni, -ydd) *nf* knoll, rock

tarth (-oedd) *nm* mist, vapour

tarw (teirw) *nm* bull; **y Tarw** Taurus

tarwden *nf* ringworm

tas (teisi) *nf* rick, stack

tasel *nm* tassel

tasg (-au) *nf* task

tasgu *vb* task; start, jump; splash, spirt

tato, tatws *npl* (*nf* **taten,** *nf* **tatysen**) potatoes

taw *nm* silence; **rhoi taw ar** silence

taw *conj* that

tawch *nm* vapour, haze, mist, fog
tawdd *adj* melted, molten, dissolved
tawedog *adj* silent, taciturn
tawedogrwydd *nm* taciturnity
tawel *adj* calm, quiet, still, tranquil
tawelu *vb* calm; grow calm
tawelwch *nm* calm, quiet, tranquillity
tawelydd *nm* silencer
tawlbwrdd *nm* draughtboard, backgammon
tawtologiaeth *nf* tautology
te *nm* tea; **te llysieuol** herbal tea
tebot (-au) *nm* teapot
tebyg *adj* similar, like, likely
tebygol *adj* likely, probable
tebygolrwydd *nm* likelihood, probability
tebygrwydd *nm* likeness, resemblance
tebygu *vb* liken, resemble; suppose
tecáu *vb* beautify, adorn, embellish
teclyn (taclau) *nm* tool, instrument; **teclyn heb afael** hands-free kit
tecstio *vb* text
techneg *nf* technique
technegol *adj* technical
technoleg (-au) *nf* technology; **technoleg gwybodaeth** information technology, IT
teg *adj* fair, beautiful, fine
tegan (-au) *nm* plaything, toy, bauble
tegell (-au, -i) *nm* kettle, teakettle
tegwch *nm* fairness, beauty
tei *nm, nf* tie
teiar *nm* tyre
teigr (-od) *nm* tiger
teilchion *npl* fragments, atoms, shivers
teiliwr (-eilwriaid) *nm* tailor
teilo *vb* dung, manure
teilwng *adj* worthy; deserved

teilwra *vb* tailor
teilwres (-au) *nf* tailoress
teilwriaeth *nf* tailoring
teilyngdod *nm* worthiness, merit
teilyngu *vb* deserve, merit; deign
teim *nm* thyme
teimlad (-au) *nm* feel, feeling, sensation, emotion
teimladol *adj* emotional
teimladrwydd *nm* feelingness, sensibility
teimladwy *adj* feeling; sensitive
teimlo *vb* feel, touch, handle, manipulate
teimlydd (-ion) *nm* feeler, antenna, tentacle
teios *npl* cottages
teip (-iau) *nm* type
teipiadur (-ion) *nm* typewriter
teipio *vb* type
teipydd (-ion) *nm* typist
teisen (-nau) *nf* cake
teitl (-au) *nm* title
teithi *coll n* traits, characteristics, qualities
teithio *vb* travel, journey
teithiol *adj* travelling, itinerant
teithiwr (-wyr) *nm* traveller, passenger
telathrebiaeth *nf* telecommunication
teledu *nm* television ▷ *vb* televise; **teledu cylch cyfyng** CCTV
teleffon (-au) *nm* telephone
teler (-au) *nm* term, condition
teligraff *nm* telegraph
telm (-au) *nf* snare
telori *vb* warble; quaver
telyn (-au) *nf* harp
telyneg (-ion) *nf* lyric
telynegol *adj* lyrical
telynegwr *nm* lyric poet
telynor (-ion) *nm* harpist

telynores *nf* female harpist
teml (-au) *nf* temple
tempro *vb* temper
temtasiwn (-iynau) *nm, nf* temptation
temtio *vb* tempt
temtiwr (-wyr) *nm* tempter
tenant (-iaid) *nm* tenant
tenantiaeth *nf* tenancy
tenau *adj* thin, lean; slender; rarified; sensitive
tendio *vb* tend, mind
teneuad *nm* dilution
teneuo *vb* thin, become thin, dilute
teneuwch *nm* thinness, leanness; tenuity
tenewyn (-nau) *nm* flank
tenis *nm* tennis
tenlli, tenllif *nm* lining
tennyn (tenynnau) *nm* cord, rope, halter
têr *adj* clear, refined, pure, fine
teras (-au) *nm* terrace
terfyn (-au) *nm* end, extremity, bound
terfyniad (-au) *nm* ending, termination
terfynol *adj* final; conclusive
terfynu *vb* end, terminate, determine
terfysg (-oedd) *nm* tumult, riot
terfysgaeth *nf* terrorism
terfysgaidd, terfysglyd *adj* riotous, turbulent
terfysgu *vb* riot, rage, surge
terfysgwr (-wyr) *nm* rioter, insurgent
term (-au) *nm* term
terminoleg *nf* terminology
tes *nm* sunshine, warmth, heat; haze
tesog *adj* sunny, hot, close, sultry
testament (-au) *nm* testament
testamentwr (-wyr) *nm* testator

testun (-au) *nm* text, theme, subject
testunio *vb* taunt, deride
tetanws *nm* tetanus
teth (-au) *nf* teat
teulu (-oedd) *nm* family; **teulu-yng-nghyfraith** in-laws
teuluaidd *adj* family, domestic
tew *adj* thick, fat, plump
tewdra, tewdwr *nm* thickness, fatness
tewhau *vb* thicken, fatten
tewi *vb* keep silence, be silent
tewychu *vb* thicken, fatten; condense
tewychydd *nm* condenser
tewyn (-ion) *nm* ember, brand
teyrn (-edd, -oedd) *nm* monarch, sovereign
teyrnas (-oedd) *nf* kingdom, realm; **y Deyrnas Gyfunol, y Deyrnas Unedig** the United Kingdom
teyrnasiad (-au) *nm* reign
teyrnasu *vb* reign
teyrnfradwr (-wyr) *nm* traitor
teyrnfradwriaeth *nf* (high) treason
teyrngar *adj* loyal
teyrngarwch *nm* loyalty
teyrnged (-au) *nf* tribute
teyrnwialen (-wiail) *nf* sceptre
TG *n* IT
ti *pron* you
ticed (-i) *nm, nf* ticket
tician *vb* tick
tid (-au) *nf* chain
tila *adj* feeble, puny, insignificant
tîm (timau) *nm* team
tin (-au) *nf* bottom; rump; tail
tinc (-iadau) *nm* clang, tinkle
tincian *vb* tinkle, chink, click, clank
tip (-iadau) *nm* tick (of clock)
tipian *vb* tick
tipyn (-nau, tipiau) *nm* bit

t

tir (**-oedd**) nm land, ground, territory
tirio vb land, ground
tiriog adj landed
tiriogaeth (**-au**) nf territory
tiriogaethol adj territorial
tirion adj kind, tender, gentle,
  gracious
tiriondeb nm kindness, tenderness
tirlun (**-iau**) nm landscape
tirol adj relating to land
tirwedd nf relief (*geographic*)
tisian vb sneeze
titw nf puss, pussy
tithau pron thou (on thy part), thou
  also
tiwmor nm tumour
tiwn (**-iau**) nf tune
tiwnio vb tune
tlawd (**tlodion**) adj poor
tlodaidd adj poorish, mean, dowdy
tlodi vb impoverish ▷ nm poverty
tlos adj f of **tlws**
tloty (**-ai**) nm poorhouse,
  workhouse
tlotyn (**tlodion**) nm pauper
tlws (f **tlos**) adj pretty
tlws (**tlysau**) nm jewel, gem; medal
tlysni nm prettiness
to (**toeau**) nm roof; generation
toc adv shortly, presently, soon
tocio vb clip, dock, prune
tocyn (**tociau**) nm pack, heap,
  hillock; slice of bread
tocyn (**-nau**) nm ticket
tocynnwr (**-ynwyr**) nm bus
  conductor
toddedig adj molten; melting
toddi vb melt, dissolve, thaw
toddiant (**-nnau**) nm solution
toddion npl dripping
toddwr (**-wyr**), **toddydd** (**-ion**) nm
  melter
toes nm dough

toi vb cover; roof; thatch
toili nm spectral funeral
tolach vb fondle
tolc (**-iau**) nm dent, dinge
tolcio vb dent, dinge
tolciog adj dented, dinged
tolchen (**-au**) nf clot
tolchennu vb clot
toll (**-au**) nf toll, custom
tolli vb take toll
tom nf dirt, mire, dung
tomen (**-nydd**) nf heap; dunghill
tomlyd adj dirty, miry
ton (**-nau**) nf wave, billow, breaker
ton (**-nau**) nm lay-land
tôn (**tonau**) nf tone; tune; **tôn ffôn**
  ring tone
tonc (**-iau**) nf tinkle, ring, clash
toncio, **-ian** vb tinkle, ring
tonfedd (**-i**) nf wavelength
tonig (**-iau**) adj tonic
tonnen (**tonennydd, -au**) nf skin;
  sward; bog
tonni vb wave, undulate
tonnog adj wavy, billowy
tonyddiaeth nf tone, intonation
topio vb plug, stop up
topyn nm plug, stopper
tor (**-ion**) nm break, interruption
tor (**-rau**) nf belly; palm (of hand)
torcalonnus adj heartbreaking
torch (**-au**) nf wreath; coil
torchi vb wreathe; coil; roll, tuck
torchog adj wreathed; coiled
tordyn adj tight-bellied; hectoring
toreithiog adj abundant, teeming
toreth nf abundance
torf (**-eydd**) nf crowd, multitude
torfynyglu vb break neck of; behead
torgoch (**-ion**) nm roach
torgwmwl nm cloudburst
torheulo vb bask, sunbathe
tori (**-ïaid**) nm tory

toriad (**-au**) *nm* cut, break; fraction
torïaeth *nf* toryism
torïaidd *adj* tory, conservative
torlan (**-nau, -lennydd**) *nf* river bank
torllengig *nm* rupture
torllwyth (**-i**), **torraid** *nf* litter
torogen (**-ogod**) *nf* tick (in cattle)
torri *vb* break, cut; dig; write, trace;
  torri i lawr break down
torrwr (**torwyr**) *nm* breaker, cutter
tors *nm, nf* torch
torsyth *adj* swaggering
torsythu *vb* strut, swagger
torth (**-au**) *nf* loaf
tost *adj* severe, sharp, sore; ill
tost *nm* toast
tosturi (**-aethau**) *nm* compassion, pity
tosturio *vb* be compassionate, pity
tosturiol *adj* compassionate
tosyn (**tosau**) *nm* pimple
töwr (**towyr**) *nm* tiler
tra *adv* over; very ▷ *conj* while, whilst
tra-arglwyddiaeth (**-au**) *nf* tyranny
tra-arglwyddiaethu *vb* tyrannize
tra-awdurdodi *vb* lord it over, domineer
trabludd *nm* trouble, tumult, turmoil
trac (**-iau**) *nm* track
tractor (**-s, -au**) *nm* tractor
trachefn *adv* again
trachwant (**-au**) *nm* lust, covetousness
trachwanta, trachwantu *vb* lust, covet
trachwantus *adj* covetous
tradwy *adv* three days hence
traddodi *vb* deliver; commit
traddodiad (**-au**) *nm* tradition; delivery

traddodiadol *adj* traditional
traddodwr (**-wyr**) *nm* deliverer
traean *nm* one third, the third part
traed *see* **troed**
traeth (**-au**) *nm* strand, shore, beach
traethawd (**-odau**) *nm* treatise, essay; tract
traethell (**-au**) *nf* strand, sandbank
traethiad (**-au**) *nm* predicate
traethodydd (**-ion**) *nm* essayist
traethu *vb* utter, declare; treat
trafael (**-ion**) *nf* travail, trouble
trafaelio *vb* travel
trafaeliwr (**-wyr**) *nm* traveller
trafaelu *vb* travel; travail
traflyncu *vb* guzzle, gulp, devour
trafnidiaeth *nf* traffic
trafod *vb* handle; discuss; transact
trafodaeth (**-au**) *nf* discussion, transaction
trafodion *npl* transactions
trafferth (**-ion**) *nf, nm* trouble
trafferthu *vb* trouble
trafferthus *adj* troublesome; troubled
tragwyddol *adj* everlasting, eternal
tragwyddoldeb *nm* eternity
tragywydd *adj* everlasting, eternal
traha *nm* arrogance, presumption
trahaus *adj* arrogant, haughty
trahauster *nm* arrogance, presumption
trai *nm* ebb
trais *nm* oppression, force, violence
trallod (**-ion, -au**) *nm* trouble, tribulation
tralloddi *vb* afflict, vex, trouble
trallodus *adj* troubled; troublous
trallodwr (**-wyr**) *nm* troubler
tramgwydd (**-iadau**) *nm* stumbling; offence
tramgwyddo *vb* stumble; offend; take offence

t

tramgwyddus *adj* scandalous; offensive

tramor *adj* foreign

tramorwr (-wyr) *nm* foreigner

trampolîn (trampolinau) *nm* trampoline

tramwy, tramwyo *vb* pass, traverse

tramwyfa (-feydd) *nf* passage, thoroughfare

tranc *nm* end, dissolution, death

trancedig *adj* deceased

trancedigaeth *nf* death, decease

trannoeth *adv* next day ▷ *nm* the morrow

trapio *vb* trap

traphlith *adv*: **blith draphlith** higgledy-piggledy

tras *nf* kindred, affinity

traserch *nm* great love, infatuation

trasiedi (trasiedïau) *nf* tragedy

traul (treuliau) *nf* wear; cost, expense; digestion

trawiad (-au) *nm* stroke, beat, flash

trawiadol *adj* striking, spectacular

traws *adj* cross; froward, perverse

trawsblannu *vb* transplant

trawsdoriad *nm* cross-section

trawsenwad *nm* metonymy

trawsfeddiannu *vb* usurp

trawsfudo *vb* transmigrate

trawsffurfio *vb* transform

trawsgludo *vb* transport, conduct

trawsgyweiriad *nm* transposition, modulation

trawsgyweirio *vb* transpose, change key

trawslif *nm* cross-saw

trawslythrennu *vb* transliterate

traws-sylweddiad *nm* transubstantiation

trawst (-iau) *nm* beam

trebl *nm*, *adj* treble

treblu *vb* treble

trech *adj* superior, stronger, mightier

trechu *vb* overpower, overcome, conquer

tref (-i, -ydd) *nf* home; town

trefedigaeth (-au) *nf* settlement, colony

trefgordd (-au) *nf* township

treflan (-nau) *nf* small town, townlet

trefn (-au) *nf* order, method, system

trefniad (-au) *nm* arrangement, ordering

trefniant *nm* arrangement, organization

trefnlen (-ni) *nf* schedule

trefnu *vb* order, arrange, dispose

trefnus *adj* orderly, methodical

trefnusrwydd *nm* orderliness

trefnydd (-ion) *nm* arranger; Methodist

trefol *adj* town, urban

treftadaeth *nf* patrimony, inheritance

trengi *vb* die, perish, expire

treial (-on) *nm* trial

treiddgar *adj* penetrating, keen

treiddgarwch *nm* penetration, acumen

treiddio *vb* pass, penetrate

treiddiol *adj* penetrating

treigl (-au) *nm* turn, revolution, course

treiglad, treigliad (-au) *nm* mutation; inflection

treiglo *vb* roll; mutate; inflect; decline

treio *vb* ebb

treio *vb* try

treisiad (-iedi) *nf* heifer

treisio *vb* force, ravish, violate, oppress, rape

treisiwr (-wyr) *nm* violator, oppressor; rapist

trem (**-iau**) *nf* sight, look, aspect
tremio *vb* look, gaze
trên (**trenau**) *nm* train
trenars, treners *npl* trainers
trennydd *adv* day after tomorrow
tres (**-i**) *nf* trace, chain; tress
tresbasu, tresmasu *vb* trespass
tresglen *nf* thrush
treth (**-i**) *nf* rate; tax; **treth ffordd** road tax; **treth y pen** poll tax
trethadwy *adj* rateable, taxable
trethdalwr (**-wyr**) *nm* ratepayer
trethu *vb* tax, rate, assess
trethwr (**-wyr**) *nm* taxer
treuliad *nm* digestion
treulio *vb* wear, consume; spend; digest
tri (*f* **tair**) *adj, nm* three
triagl *nm* treacle, balsam, balm
triawd (**-au**) *nm* trio
triban (**-nau**) *nm* triplet (*metre*); Plaid Cymru badge
tribiwnlys (**-oedd**) *nm* tribunal
tric (**-iau**) *nm* trick
tridiau *npl* three days
trigain *adj, nm* sixty
trigfa (**trigfeydd**), **trigfan** (**-nau**) *nf* dwelling-place, abode
trigiannol *adj* residentiary
trigiannu *vb* reside, dwell
trigiannydd (**-ianwyr**) *nm* resident
trigo *vb* stay, abide; dwell; die (*animals*)
trigolion *npl* inhabitants, dwellers
trimio *vb* trim
trin (**-oedd**) *nf* battle
trin *vb* handle; treat; dress; till; transact
trindod (**-au**) *nf* trinity
tringar *adj* skilful, tender
triniaeth (**-au**) *nf* treatment
trioedd *npl* triads
triongl (**-au**) *nm, nf* triangle

trionglog *adj* triangular
trist *adj* sad, sorrowful
tristáu *vb* sadden, grieve
tristwch *nm* sadness, sorrow
triw *adj* loyal, faithful
tro (**troeau, troeon**) *nm* turn, twist; conversion
troad (**-au**) *nm* bend, turning; figure of speech
trobwll (**-byllau**) *nm* whirlpool
trobwynt (**-iau**) *nm* turning-point
trochfa (**-feydd**) *nf* plunge, immersion
trochi *vb* dip, plunge, immerse; soil
trochion *npl* lather, suds, foam
trochioni *vb* lather, foam
trochwr (**-wyr**) *nm* immerser, immersionist
troed (**traed**) *nm, nf* foot, base; leg; handle
troedfainc (**-feinciau**) *nf* footstool
troedfedd (**-i**) *nf* foot (=12 inches)
troëdig *adj* turned, converted, perverse
tröedigaeth (**-au**) *nf* turning, conversion
troedio *vb* foot, tread, trudge
troednodyn *nm* footnote
troednoeth *adj* barefoot, barefooted
troedwst *nf* gout
troell (**-au**) *nf* wheel, spinning-wheel
troelli *vb* spin; twist, wind
troellog *adj* winding, tortuous
troellwr (**-wyr**) *nm* disc-jockey
troetffordd (**-ffyrdd**) *nf* footway, footpath
trofa (**-feydd**) *nf* turn; bend, turning
trofan (**-nau**) *nf* tropic
trofannol *adj* tropical
trofaus *adj* perverse
trofwrdd (**-fyrddau**) *nm* turntable
trogen *see* **torogen**
trogylch (**-au**) *nm* orbit

troi vb turn, revolve; convert; plough; **troi ymlaen** switch on
trol (**-iau**) nf cart
trolian, trolio vb roll
troliwr (**-wyr**) nm carter
trom adj f of **trwm**
trôns npl underpants; **trôns bocsiwr** boxer shorts
tros prep over, for, instead of, on behalf of
trosedd (**-au**) nm transgression, offence, crime
troseddol adj criminal
troseddu vb transgress, trespass, offend
troseddwr (**-wyr**) nm transgressor, trespasser, offender; criminal
trosgais (**trosgeisiau**) nm converted try
trosglwyddiad nm transference, transfer
trosglwyddo vb hand over, transfer
trosgynnol adj transcendental
trosi vb turn; translate; convert (a try)
trosiad (**-au**) nm translation; metaphor; conversion (in rugby)
trosodd adv over, beyond
trosol (**-ion**) nm lever, crow-bar, bar; staff
trostan (**-au**) nf pole
trotian vb trot
trothwy (**-au**) nm threshold
trowr (**-wyr**) nm ploughman
trowsus (**-au**) nm trousers; **trowsus nofio** swimming trunks
trowynt (**-oedd**) nm whirlwind, tornado
truan (**truain**, f **truanes**) adj poor, wretched, miserable ▷ nm (**trueiniaid**) wretch
trueni nm wretchedness; misery; pity

truenus adj wretched, miserable
trugaredd (**-au**) nf, nm mercy, compassion
trugarhau vb have mercy, take pity
trugarog adj merciful, compassionate
trugarowgrwydd nm mercifulness
trulliad (**-iaid**) nm butler, cupbearer
trum (**-au, -iau**) nm ridge
truth nm flattery; rigmarole
trwbl nm trouble
trwblo vb trouble
trwch nm thickness; **trwch y blewyn** hair's breadth
trwch adj broken; unfortunate; wicked
trwchus adj thick
trwm (**trymion**, f **trom**) adj heavy
trwnc (**trynciau**) nm trunk
trwodd adv through
trwsgl adj awkward, clumsy, bungling
trwsiad nm dress, attire
trwsiadus adj well-dressed, smart
trwsio vb dress, trim; mend, repair
trwsiwr (**-wyr**) nm mender, repairer
trwst nm noise, din, tumult
trwstan adj awkward, clumsy, untoward
trwstaneiddiwch nm awkwardness
trwy prep through, by, by means of
trwyadl adj thorough
trwydded (**-au**) nf leave, licence
trwyddedu vb license
trwyn (**-au**) nm nose, snout; point, cape
trwyno vb nose, nuzzle, sniff
trwynol adj nasal
trwynsur adj sour, morose
trwyth (**-i**) nm decoction, infusion, urine
trwytho vb steep, saturate, imbue

trybedd, trybed *nf* tripod, trivet
trybelid *adj* bright, brilliant
trybestod *nm* commotion, bustle, fuss
trybini *nm* trouble, misfortune, misery
tryblith *nm* muddle, chaos
trychfil (-od) *nm* insect, animalcule
trychiad (-au) *nm* cutting, fracture, section
trychineb (-au) *nm, nf* disaster, calamity
trychinebus *adj* disastrous, calamitous
trychu *vb* cut, hew, pierce, lop
trydan *nm* electric fluid, electricity
trydaneg *nm, nf* electrical engineering
trydaniaeth *nf* electricity; thrill
trydanol *adj* electric, electrical
trydanu *vb* electrify
trydar *nm, vb* chirp, chatter
trydydd (*f* **trydedd**) *adj* third
tryfer (-i) *nf* harpoon, trident
tryferu *vb* spear, harpoon
tryfesur *nm* diameter
tryfrith *adj* speckled; swarming, teeming
trylediad (-au) *nm* diffusion
tryledu *vb* diffuse
tryloyw *adj* pellucid, transparent
tryloywder *nm* transparency
trylwyr *adj* thorough
trylwyredd *nm* thoroughness
trymaidd *adj* heavy, close, oppressive
trymder *nm* heaviness, drowsiness
trymfryd *nm* sadness, sorrow
trymhau *vb* make or grow heavy
trymllyd *adj* heavy, close, oppressive
tryryw *adj* thoroughbred
trysor (-au) *nm* treasure
trysordy (-dai) *nm* treasure house

trysorfa (-feydd) *nf* treasury, fund
trysori *vb* treasure
trysorlys *nm* treasury, exchequer
trysorydd (-ion) *nm* treasurer
trystio *vb* make a noise; trust
trystiog *adj* noisy, rowdy
trythyll *adj* wanton, lascivious
trythyllwch *nm* lasciviousness
trywanu *vb* transfix, stab, pierce
trywel *nm* trowel
trywydd *nm* scent, trail
Tsiecoslofacia *nf* Czechoslovakia
Tseina *nf* China
Tsieinead (-eaid) *nm, nf* Chinese person
Tsieineaidd *adj* Chinese
tu *nm* side, part, direction
tua, tuag *prep* towards; about
tuchan *vb* grumble, groan, murmur
tudalen (-nau) *nm, nf* page; **tudalen cartref, tudalen gartref, tudalen hafan** home page; **tudalen we** web page
tudded (-i) *nf* covering; pillowcase
tuedd (-iadau) *nf* tendency, inclination
tuedd (-au) *nm* district, region
tueddfryd *nm* inclination, bent
tueddol *adj* inclined, apt
tueddu *vb* incline, tend, trend
tufewnol *adj* inward, internal
tulath (-au) *nf* beam, rafter
Tunisia *nf* Tunisia
tunnell (tunelli) *nf* ton; tun
turio *vb* root up, burrow, delve
turn *nm* lathe
turniwr (-wyr) *nm* turner
turtur (-od) *nf* turtle-dove
tusw (-au) *nm* wisp, bunch
tuth (-iau) *nm* trot
tuthio *vb* trot
twb (tybiau) *nm* tub
twca *nm* tuck-knife

t

twffyn (**twffiau**) *nm* tuft
twlc (**tylciau**) *nm* sty
twlcio *vb* horn, butt, gore
twlciog *adj* given to horning
twll (**tyllau**) *nm* hole
twmpath (**-au**) *nm* tump, hillock;
  bush; folk-dance
twndis (**-au**) *nm* funnel
twndra (**-âu**) *nm* tundra
twnffed (**-i**) *nm* funnel
twnnel (**twnelau, twneli**) *nm*
  tunnel; **Twnnel y Sianel** the
  Channel Tunnel
twp *adj* stupid, dull, obtuse
twpdra *nm* stupidity
twpsyn *nm* stupid person
twr (**tyrrau**) *nm* heap; group, crowd
tŵr (**tyrau**) *nm* tower
Twrc (**Tyrciaid**) *nm* Turk
Twrci *nf* Turkey
twrci (**-ïod**) *nm* turkey
twrch (**tyrchod**) *nm* hog; **twrch
  daear** mole
twrf (**tyrfau**) *nm* noise; (*pl*) thunder
twrnai (**-eiod**) *nm* attorney, lawyer
twrw *nm* noise
twt *excl* tut!
twt *adj* tidy, neat, smart
twtio *vb* tidy
twyll *nm* deceit, deception, fraud
twyllo *vb* deceive, cheat, swindle
twyllodrus *adj* deceitful, false
twyllresymeg *nf* sophism
twyllresymiad (**-au**) *nm* sophistry
twyllwr (**-wyr**) *nm* deceiver
twym *adj* warm, hot, sultry
twymder, twymdra *nm*
  warmness, warmth
twymgalon *adj* warm-hearted
twymo, twymno *vb* warm, heat
twymyn (**-au**) *nf* fever; **y dwymyn
  goch** scarlet fever; **y dwymyn
  doben** mumps

twyn (**-i**) *nm* hill, hillock, knoll; bush
twysged *nf* lot, quantity
tŷ (**tai, teiau**) *nm* house; **tŷ pâr**
  semidetached (house)
tyaid (**-eidiau**) *nm* houseful
tyb (**-iau**) *nm*, *nf* opinion, notion,
  surmise
tybaco *nm* tobacco
tybed *adv* I wonder; is that so?
tybiaeth (**-au**) *nf* supposition
tybied, tybio *vb* suppose, think,
  imagine
tybiedig *adj* supposed, putative
tycio *vb* prosper, succeed, avail
tydi *pron* thou, thyself
tyddyn (**-nod**) *nm* (small) farm,
  holding
tyddynnwr (**-ynwyr**) *nm*
  smallholder
tyfadwy *adj* growing
tyfiant *nm* growth
tyfu *vb* grow; **tyfu i fyny, tyfu lan**
  grow up
tyfwr (**-wyr**) *nm* grower
tynged *nf* destiny, fate
tyngedfennol *adj* fateful, fatal
tynghedu *vb* destine, fate; adjure
tyngu *vb* swear, vow
tyngwr (**-wyr**) *nm* swearer
tylath *see* **tulath**
tyle *nm* slope, hill
tylino *vb* knead; **tylino y corff**
  massage
tylinwr (**-wyr**) *nm* kneader, masseur
tylwyth (**-au**) *nm* household, family;
  tylwyth teg fairies
tyllog *adj* holey
tyllu *vb* hole, bore, perforate, pierce
tylluan (**-od**) *nf* owl
tyllwr (**-wyr**) *nm* borer
tymer (**-herau**) *nf* temper
tymestl (**-hestloedd**) *nf* tempest,
  storm

tymheredd *nm* temperature
tymherus *adj* temperate
tymhestlog *adj* tempestuous, stormy
tymhoraidd *adj* seasonable
tymhorol *adj* temporal
tymor (-horau) *nm* season; **tymor y gaeaf** wintertime
tymp *nm* (appointed) time, season
tympan (-au) *nf* drum; timbrel
tyn *adj* tight
tynder, tyndra *nm* tightness, tension
tyndro (tyndroeon) *nm* wrench
tyner *adj* tender, gentle
tyneru *vb* make tender, soften
tynerwch *nm* tenderness, gentleness
tynfa (-feydd) *nf* draw, attraction
tynfaen (-feini) *nm* loadstone, magnet
tynhau *vb* tighten, strain
tynnu *vb* draw, pull; take off, remove
tyno *nm* hollow; tenon
tyrchu *vb* root up, burrow
tyrchwr (-wyr) *nm* mole-catcher
tyrfa (-oedd) *nf* multitude, host, crowd
tyrfau *npl* thunder
tyrfedd (-au) *nm* turbulence, thunder
tyrfo, tyrfu *vb* make a noise or commotion
tyrpant *nm* turpentine
tyrpeg *nm* turnpike
tyrru *vb* heap, amass; crowd together
tyst (-ion) *nm* witness
tysteb (-au) *nf* testimonial
tystio *vb* testify, witness
tystiolaeth (-au) *nf* testimony, evidence
tystiolaethu *vb* bear witness, testify

tystlythyr (-au) *nm* testimonial
tystysgrif (-au) *nf* certificate
tywallt *vb* pour, shed, spill
tywalltiad (-au) *nm* outpouring
tywarchen (tywyrch) *nf* sod, turf
tywel (-ion) *nm* towel
tywod *nm* sand
tywodfaen *nm* sandstone
tywodlyd, tywodog *adj* sandy
tywodyn *nm* grain of sand
tywydd *nm* weather
tywyll *adj* dark, obscure; blind
tywyllu *vb* darken, obscure
tywyllwch *nm* darkness
tywyn (-au) *nm* sea-shore, strand
tywynnu *vb* shine
tywys *vb* lead, guide
tywysen (-nau, tywys) *nf* ear of corn
tywysog (-ion) *nm* prince
tywysogaeth (-au) *nf* principality
tywysogaidd *adj* princely
tywysoges (-au) *nf* princess
tywysydd (-ion) *nm* leader, guide

t

th u

theatr (-au) *nf* theatre
thema (themâu) *nf* theme
theorem (-au) *nf* theorem
theori (-ïau) *nf* theory
thermomedr *nm* thermometer
thesis (-au) *nm* thesis
thus *nm* frankincense

ubain *vb* howl, wail, moan; sob
uchaf *adj* uppermost, highest
uchafbwynt (-iau) *nm* climax; zenith
uchafiaeth *nf* supremacy; ascendancy
uchafion *npl* heights
uchafrif (-au) *nm* maximum
uchder *nm* height; top
uchel *adj* high, lofty; uppish; loud
uchelbwynt (-iau) *nm* highlight
uchelder (-au) *nm* highness, height
ucheldir (-oedd) *nm* highland
uchelfryd *adj* high-minded
uchelgais *nm, nf* ambition
uchelgeisiol *adj* ambitious
uchelion *npl* heights
uchelradd *adj* of high degree, superior
uchelseinydd (-ion) *nm* loudspeaker

uchelwr (**-wyr**) *nm* gentleman, nobleman
uchelwydd *coll n* mistletoe
uchgapten (**-teiniaid**) *nm* major
uchod *adv* above
UD *n* US
UDA *n* USA
udo *vb* howl
udd *nm* lord
UE *nf* EU
ufudd *adj* obedient, humble
ufudd-dod *nm* obedience, humility
ufuddhau *vb* obey
uffern *nf* hell
uffernol *adj* infernal, hellish
ugain (**ugeiniau**) *adj, nm* twenty, score
Uganda *nf* Uganda
Ulster *nf* Ulster
ulw *coll n* ashes, powder ▷ *adv* utterly
un *adj* one, only; same ▷ *coll n* (**-au**) one, unit
unawd (**-au**) *nm, nf* solo
unawdydd (**-wyr**) *nm* soloist
unben (**-iaid, unbyn**) *nm* sovereign lord, despot
unbenaethol *adj* despotic
unbennaeth *nf* sovereignty, despotism
undeb (**-au**) *nm* unity; union; **yr Undeb Ewropeaidd** the European Union; **yr Undeb Sofietaidd** the Soviet Union
undebaeth *nf* unionism
undebol *adj* united, union
undebwr (**-wyr**) *nm* unionist
undod (**-au**) *nm* unity; unit
Undodaidd *adj* Unitarian
Undodiaeth *nf* Unitarianism
Undodwr (**-wyr, -iaid**) *nm* Unitarian
undonedd *nm* monotony
undonog *adj* monotonous

uned (**-au**) *nf* unit
unfan *nm* same place
unfarn *adj* unanimous
unfryd, unfrydol *adj* unanimous
unfrydedd *nm* unanimity
unffurf *adj* uniform
unffurfiaeth *nf* uniformity
ungell *adj* monocellular
uniaith *adj* monoglot
uniawn *adj* straight; right, upright; just
unig *adj* sole, only; alone, lonely
unigedd *nm* loneliness, solitude
unigol *adj* singular; individual ▷ *nm* (**-ion**) individual
unigoliaeth *nf*, **unigolrwydd** *nm* individuality
unigrwydd *nm* loneliness, solitude
union *adj* straight, direct; just, exact
uniondeb *nm* straightness; rectitude
uniongred *adj* orthodox
uniongrededd *nm, nf* orthodoxy
uniongyrch, uniongyrchol *adj* immediate, direct
unioni *vb* straighten; rectify; make for
unionsgwar *adj* perpendicular
unionsyth *adj* straight, direct; erect
unllygeidiog *adj* one-eyed
unman *adv* anywhere
unnos *adj* of one night
uno *vb* join, unit, amalgamate
unochrog *adj* unilateral, biased
unodl *adj* of the same rhyme
unol *adj* united; **yr Unol Daleithiau** the United States
unoli *vb* unify
unoliaeth *nf* unity, oneness, identity
unplyg *adj* of one fold; folio; simple, ingenuous
unplygrwydd *nm* sincerity
unrhyw *adj* same; any

u

unrhywiol *adj* unisexual
unsain *adj* unison; **yn unsain** in unison
unsill *adj* monosyllabic
unswydd *adj* of one purpose
unwaith *adv* once
unwedd *adj* like ▷ *adv* likewise
urdd (-au) *nf* order; rank
urddas (-au) *nm* dignity, honour
urddasol *adj* dignified, noble
urddo *vb* ordain, confer degree or rank
us *coll n* chaff
ust *excl, nm* hush
ustus (-iaid) *nm* justice, magistrate
usuriaeth *nf* usury
utganu *vb* sound a trumpet
utganwr (-wyr) *nm* trumpeter
utgorn (-gyrn) *nm* trumpet
uwch *adj* higher ▷ *prep* above, over
uwchbridd (-oedd) *nm* topsoil
uwchgapten (-iaid) *nm* major
uwchradd *nm, adj* superior
uwchsonig *adj* ultrasonic, supersonic
uwd *nm* porridge

W

wadi (-iau) *nm* wadi
wagen (-ni) *nf* truck, waggon
waldio *vb* wallop, beat
warws (warysau) *nm* warehouse
wats (-iau) *nm* watch
wedi *prep* after ▷ *adv* afterwards
wedyn *adv* afterwards, then
weiren *nf* wire
weirio, weiro *vb* wire
weithian, weithion *adv* now, now at length
weithiau *adv* sometimes
wel *excl* well
wele *excl* behold, lo
wermod *nf* wormwood
wfft *excl* fie, for shame
wfftio *vb* cry fie, flout, scout
whado *vb* beat, thrash
wiced (-i) *nf* wicket
wicedwr (-wyr) *nm* wicket-keeper
widw *nf* widow

wlser (-au) *nm* ulcer
wmbredd *nm* abundance
wraniwm *nm* uranium
wrth *prep* by; with; to; because, since
wy (-au) *nm* egg
wybr (-au), wybren (-nau, -nydd) *nf* sky; cloud
wybrol *adj* ethereal
wyf *vb* I am
wygell (-oedd) *nf* ovary
wylo *vb* weep, cry
wylofain *vb* wail, weep ▷ *nm* wailing
wylofus *adj* wailing, doleful, tearful
ŵyn *see* **oen**
ŵyna *vb* lamb
wyneb (-au) *nm* face, surface; front
wyneb-ddalen *nf* title-page
wynebgaled *adj* barefaced, impudent
wyneblun (-iau) *nm* frontispiece
wynebu *vb* face, front
wynepryd *nm* countenance
wynwyn *npl* onions
ŵyr (wyrion) *coll n* grandchild, grandson
wysg *nm* track; **yn wysg ei gefn** backwards
wystrys *npl, coll n* oysters
wyth (-au) *adj, nm* eight
wythawd (-au, -odau) *nf* octave
wythblyg *adj* octavo
wythfed *adj* eighth
wythnos (-au) *nf* week
wythnosol (-ion) *adj* weekly
wythnosolyn (-olion) *nm* weekly paper
wythongl (-au) *nf* octagon
wythwr (-wyr) *nm* number eight (in rugby)

Y

y, yr, 'r *adj* the
y, yr *preverbal and relative particle*
ych (-en) *nm* ox
ychwaith *adv* (nor) either, neither
ychwaneg *nm* more
ychwanegiad (-au) *nm* addition
ychwanegol *adj* additional
ychwanegu *vb* add, augment, increase
ychydig *adj, adv, nm* little, few
ŷd (ydau) *nm* corn
ydlan (-nau) *nf* stack yard, rick yard
ydwyf *vb* I am
ydys *vb*: **yr ydys yn disgwyl** it is expected
ydyw *vb* is, are
yfed *vb* drink; absorb
yfory *adv* tomorrow
yfwr (-wyr) *nm* drinker
yfflon *npl (nm* **yfflyn)** shivers, pieces, bits ▷ *adj* highly annoyed

yng *prep* in (*mutation of* **yn**)

yngan, ynganu *vb* utter, speak

ynghyd *adv* together

ynghylch *prep* about, concerning

ynglŷn â *prep* in connection with

ym *prep* in (*mutation of* **yn**)

ym- *prefix usu. reflexive or reciprocal*

yma *adv* here, in this place; this

ymadael, ymadaw *vb* depart

ymadawedig *adj* departed, deceased

ymadawiad *nm* departure; decease

ymadawol *adj* farewell, valedictory

ymado *vb* depart

ymadrodd (-ion) *nm* speech, saying, expression

ymadroddus *adj* eloquent

ymaddasu *vb* adjust, adapt

ymaelodi *vb* become a member, join

ymaelyd, ymafael, ymaflyd *vb* take hold

ymageru *vb* evaporate

ymagor *vb* open, unfold, expand

ymagweddiad (-au) *nm* demeanour, attitude

ymaith *adv* away, hence

ymarfer *vb* practise, exercise ▷ *nf* (**-ion**) practice, exercise

ymarferiad (-au) *nm* exercise

ymarhous *adj* dilatory; long-suffering, patient

ymaros *vb* bear with, endure ▷ *nm* long-suffering, patience

ymarweddiad *nm* conduct, behaviour

ymatal *vb* forbear, refrain, abstain

ymateb *vb* answer, respond, correspond

ymbalfalu *vb* grope

ymbaratoi *vb* get oneself ready

ymbarél *nm* umbrella

ymbelydredd *nm* radiation

ymbelydrol *adj* radioactive

ymbellhau *vb* go further away

ymbil (-iau) *nm* supplication, entreaty

ymbil, ymbilio *vb* implore, beseech, entreat

ymboeni *vb* take pains

ymborth *nm* food, sustenance

ymbortheg *nf, nm* dietetics

ymborthi *vb* feed

ymbriodi *vb* marry; intermarry

ymbwyllo *vb* pause, reflect

ymchwelyd *vb* turn, return; overturn

ymchwil *nf* search, research, quest

ymchwiliad (-au) *nm* investigation

ymchwydd (-iadau) *nm* swelling, surge

ymchwyddo *vb* swell; surge

ymdaith *vb* journey, march ▷ *nf* (**-deithiau**) journey, march

ymdebygu *vb* grow like; resemble

ymdeimlad *nm* feeling, sense

ymdeimlo *vb* feel; be conscious of

ymdeithio *vb* travel, journey; sojourn

ymdoddi *vb* melt, become dissolved

ymdopi *vb* manage

ymdrech (-ion) *nm, nf* effort, endeavour, struggle

ymdrechgar *adj* striving, energetic

ymdrechu *vb* wrestle; strive, endeavour

ymdrin *vb* treat, deal with

ymdriniaeth *nf* treatment; discussion

ymdrochi *vb* bathe

ymdrochwr (-wyr) *nm* bather

ymdroi *vb* linger, loiter, dawdle

ymdrybaeddu *vb* wallow

ymdynghedu *vb* vow

ymddangos *vb* appear, seem

ymddangosiad (-au) *nm* appearance

ymddangosiadol *adj* seeming, apparent

ymddarostwng *vb* submit

ymddarostyngiad *nm* humiliation, submission

ymddatod *vb* dissolve

ymddeol *vb* resign, retire

ymddeoliad (-au) *nm* retirement; **ymddeoliad cynnar** early retirement

ymddiddan *vb* talk, converse ▷ *nm* **(-ion)** talk, conversation

ymddihatru *vb* divest, undress

ymddiheuriad (-au) *nm* apology

ymddiheuro *vb* apologize

ymddiosg *vb* strip, undress

ymddiried *vb* trust ▷ *nm* trust, confidence

ymddiriedaeth *nf* trust, confidence

ymddiriedolwr (-wyr) *nm* trustee

ymddiswyddo *vb* resign

ymddwyn *vb* behave, act

ymddygiad (-au) *nm* behaviour, conduct; (*pl*) actions

ymddyrchafu *vb* exalt oneself; rise, ascend

ymegnïo *vb* exert oneself

ymehangu *vb* become enlarged, expand

ymennydd (ymenyddiau) *nm* brain

ymenyn *nm* butter

ymerawdwr (-wyr) *nm* emperor

ymerodraeth (-au) *nf* empire

ymerodres (-au) *nf* empress

ymerodrol *adj* imperial

ymesgusodi *vb* excuse oneself, apologize

ymestyn *vb* stretch, extend, reach

ymestyniad (-au) *nm* extension

ymfalchïo *vb* pride oneself

ymfodloni *vb* acquiesce

ymfudo *vb* emigrate

ymfudwr (-wyr) *nm* emigrant

ymffrost *nm* boast

ymffrostio *vb* boast, vaunt

ymffrostiwr (-wyr) *nm* boaster

ymgadw *vb* keep oneself (from), forbear

ymgais *nm, nf* effort, attempt

ymgasglu *vb* gather together

ymgecru *vb* quarrel, wrangle

ymgeisio *vb* try, apply; aim at

ymgeisydd (-wyr) *nm* applicant, candidate

ymgeledd *nm* succour, care

ymgeleddu *vb* cherish, succour

ymgeleddwr (-wyr) *nm* succourer; tutor, guardian

ymgilio *vb* retreat, recede

ymgiprys *vb, nm* scramble

ymglymu *vb* involve, bind together

ymglywed *vb* feel (oneself), be inclined

ymgnawdoliad *nm* incarnation

ymgodymu *vb* wrestle, fight

ymgofleidio *vb* mutually embrace

ymgom (-ion) *nf* chat, conversation

ymgomio *vb* chat, converse

ymgorfforiad *nm* embodiment

ymgreinio *vb* prostrate oneself; grovel

ymgroesi *vb* cross oneself; beware

ymgryfhau *vb* strengthen oneself, be strong

ymgrymu *vb* bow down, stoop

ymguddfa *nf* shelter, hiding-place

ymguddio *vb* hide (oneself)

ymgydio *vb* copulate

ymgydnabod *vb* acquaint oneself

ymgyfathrachu *vb* have dealings with

ymgyfeillachu *vb* associate

ymgyfoethogi *vb* get rich

ymgynghori *vb* consult, confer

ymgynghoriad *nm* consultation

ymgymeriad (-au) *nm* undertaking

ymgymryd *vb* undertake

ymgynefino *vb* become familiar, get used to

ymgynnal *vb* bear up; support oneself; control oneself

ymgynnull *vb* assemble, congregate

ymgyrch (-oedd) *nm, nf* campaign, expedition

ymgyrraedd *vb* stretch, strive after

ymgysegriad *nm* devotion, consecration

ymgysegru *vb* devote oneself

ymhél *vb* meddle

ymhelaethu *vb* abound; enlarge

ymhell *adv* far, afar

ymhellach *adv* further, furthermore

ymherodr *see* **ymerawdwr**

ymhlith *prep* among

ymhlyg *adj* implicit

ymhoelyd *vb* overturn, topple

ymhoffi *vb* take delight; boast

ymholi *vb* inquire

ymholiad (-au) *nm* inquiry

ymhonni *vb* lay claim to, pretend

ymhonnwr (-honwyr) *nm* pretender

ymhŵedd *vb* beseech, implore, crave

ymhyfrydu *vb* delight (oneself)

ymiacháu *vb* become healed, get well

ymlacio *vb* relax

ymladd *vb* fight ▷ *nm* **(-au)** fighting

ymlâdd *vb* kill oneself (with exertion), tire oneself out; **wedi ymlâdd** dead beat

ymladdfa (-feydd) *nf* fight

ymladdgar *adj* pugnacious, warlike

ymladdwr (-wyr) *nm* fighter, combatant

ymlaen *adv* on, onward

ymlafnio *vb* toil, strive, struggle

ymlawenhau *vb* rejoice

ymledu *vb* spread, expand

ymlenwi *vb* fill oneself

ymlid *vb* pursue, chase

ymlidiwr (-wyr) *nm* pursuer

ymlonyddu *vb* grow calm or still

ymlosgiad *nm* combustion

ymlusgiad (-iaid) *nm* reptile

ymlusgo *vb* creep, crawl

ymlwybro *vb* make one's way

ymlyniad *nm* attachment

ymlynu *vb* attach, adhere, cleave (to)

ymlynwr (-wyr) *nm* adherent

Ymneilltuaeth *nf* Nonconformity

ymneilltuo *vb* retire

Ymneilltuol *adj* Nonconformist

Ymneilltuwr (-wyr) *nm* Nonconformist

ymnesáu *vb* approach, draw near

ymochel, ymochelyd *vb* shelter; beware

ymod, ymodi *vb* move, stir

ymofyn *vb* ask, inquire, seek ▷ *nm* **(-ion)** inquiry

ymofynnydd (-ofynwyr) *nm* inquirer

ymolchfa (-feydd) *nf* wash; lavatory

ymolchi *vb* wash oneself, bathe

ymollwng *vb* sink, drop, give way, collapse

ymorchestu *vb* strive, labour

ymorffwys *vb* rest, repose

ymorol *vb* seek; take care, attend to, see to it

ymosod *vb* attack, assail, assault

ymosodiad (-au) *nm* attack, assault

ymosodol *adj* aggressive, offensive, forward

ymosodwr (-wyr) *nm* attacker, assailant

ymostwng *vb* stoop; humble oneself; submit

ymostyngar *adj* submissive

ymostyngiad *nm* submission

ympryd (-ion) *nm* fast

ymprydio *vb* fast

ymprydiwr (-wyr) *nm* faster

ymrafael (-ion) *nm* quarrel, contention

ymrafaelgar *adj* quarrelsome, contentious

ymraniad (-au) nm division, schism
ymrannu vb part, divide, separate
ymrannwr (-ranwyr) nm separatist
ymreolaeth nf self-government, Home Rule
ymrestru vb enlist
ymresymiad (-au) nm reasoning, argument
ymresymu vb reason, argue
ymresymwr (-wyr) nm reasoner
ymrithio vb appear
ymroad nm application, devotion
ymroddedig adj devoted
ymroddgar adj of great application
ymroddi, ymroi vb apply or devote oneself; yield or resign oneself, surrender, do one's best
ymroddiad nm application, devotion
ymron adv nearly, almost
ymrous adj assiduous
ymrwyfo vb struggle, toss about
ymrwygo vb tear, burst
ymrwymiad (-au) nm engagement
ymrwymo vb bind or engage oneself
ymryson vb contend, strive ▷ nm (-au) contention, strife, rivalry
ymrysongar adj contentious
ymsefydlu vb establish oneself, settle
ymsefydlwr (-wyr) nm settler
ymserchu vb cherish, dote
ymson vb soliloquize ▷ nm (-au) soliloquy
ymsuddiant nm subsidence
ymswyno vb cross oneself; beware
ymsymud vb move
ymuno vb join, unite
ymwacâd nm kenosis
ymwacáu vb empty oneself
ymwadiad nm denial, abnegation
ymwadu vb deny (oneself); renounce
ymwahanu vb part, divide, separate

ymwahanwr (-wyr) nm separatist
ymwared nm deliverance
ymwasgu vb embrace, hug
ymweithydd (-ion) nm reactor
ymweld vb visit
ymweliad (-au) nm visit, visitation
ymwelwr, ymwelydd (ymwelwyr) nm visitor, visitant; **canolfan ymwelwyr** visitor centre
ymwrando vb hearken
ymwroli vb take heart, be of good courage
ymwrthod vb abstain; renounce
ymwrthodiad nm abstinence
ymwthgar adj pushing, obtrusive
ymwthio vb push oneself, obtrude
ymwthiol adj obtrusive, intrusive
ymwybodol adj conscious
ymwybyddiaeth nf consciousness
ymwylltio vb fly into a passion
ymyl (-au, -on) nm, nf edge, border, margin
ymylu vb border
ymylwe nf selvedge
ymyrgar adj meddlesome, officious
ymyrraeth, ymyrru, ymyrryd vb meddle, interfere
ymyrraeth nf interference
ymyrrwr (-yrwyr) nm meddler
ymysg prep among, amid
ymysgaroedd npl bowels
ymysgwyd vb bestir oneself
yn prep in, at, into; for (also introduces verb-nouns)
yn particle
yna adv there; then; thereupon; that
ynad (-on) nm judge, justice, magistrate
yn awr adv now, at present
yndeintiad (-au) nm indentation
ynfyd (-ion) adj foolish, rash
ynfydrwydd nm foolishness, folly
ynfydu vb rave, be mad

y

ynfytyn (**-fydion**) *nm* fool, madman
ynni *nm* energy, vigour **ynni'r haul**, **ynni haul** solar power
yno *adv* there
yntau *pron* he (on his part), he also
ynteu, ynte *conj* or, or else, otherwise; then
Ynyd *nm* Shrovetide
ynys (**-oedd**) *nf* island, river meadow; **Ynys Cyprus** Cyprus; **yr Ynysoedd Dedwydd** the Canary Islands
ynysfor (**-oedd**) *nm* archipelago
ynysol *adj* island, insular
ynyswr (**-wyr**) *nm* islander
ynysydd (**-ion**) *nm* insulator
yr *see* **y**
yrhawg *adv* for a long time (to come)
yrŵan *adv* now
ys *vb* it is ▷ *conj* as
ysbaddu *vb* castrate
ysbaid (**-beidiau**) *nm, nf* space (of time)
ysbail (**-beiliau**) *nf* spoil, plunder
ysbardun *nm, nf* spur
ysbarduno *vb* spur
ysbeidiol *adj* occasional, intermittent
ysbeilio *vb* spoil, plunder
ysbeiliwr (**-wyr**) *nm* spoiler, robber
ysbienddrych (**-au**) *nm* spying-glass
ysbïo *vb* spy, look
ysbïwr (**-wyr**) *nm* spy
ysblander *nm* splendour
ysblennydd *adj* splendid
ysbonc (**-iau**) *nf* jump, bound; spurt
ysboncio *vb* jump, bounce; spurt, splash
ysborion *npl* cast-offs
ysbrigyn *nm* sprig, twig
ysbryd (**-ion, -oedd**) *nm* spirit, ghost
ysbrydegaeth *nf* spiritualism
ysbrydegol *adj* spiritualistic

ysbrydegydd (**-ion**) *nm* spiritualist
ysbrydiaeth *nf* encouragement, inspiration
ysbrydol *adj* spiritual; high-spirited
ysbrydoli *vb* spiritualize; inspire; inspirit
ysbrydoliaeth *nf* inspiration
ysbwng *nm* sponge
ysbwrial, ysbwriel *nm* rubbish, refuse
ysbwylio *vb* spoil
ysbyty (**-tai**) *nm* hospital; hospice; **ysbyty'r meddwl** mental hospital
ysfa (**-feydd**) *nf* itching; hankering
ysg- *see* **sg-**
ysgadan *npl* (*nm* **-enyn**) herrings
ysgafala *adj* secure, careless, free
ysgafn *adj* light ▷ *nm* stack
ysgafnder *nm* lightness, levity
ysgafnhau, ysgafnu *vb* lighten
ysgafnu *vb* heap, pile
ysgall *npl* (*nf* **-en**) thistles
ysgariad *nm*, **ysgariadiaeth** *nf* separation, divorce
ysgarlad *nm* scarlet
ysgarmes (**-oedd, -au**) *nf* skirmish; punch-up
ysgaru *vb* part, separate, divorce
ysgatfydd *adv* perhaps, peradventure
ysgathru *vb* spread, scatter
ysgaw *coll n* (*nf* **-en**) elder
ysgeler *adj* wicked, villainous, infamous
ysgerbwd (**-bydau**) *nm* skeleton, carcase
ysgithr (**-edd**) *nm* tusk, fang
ysgithrog *adj* fanged, tusked; craggy, rugged
ysgiw (**-ion**) *nf* settle
ysglefrio *vb* slide (on ice); skate
ysglyfaeth (**-au**) *nf* prey, spoil; carrion, filth

ysglyfaethus *adj* of prey; rapacious
ysgogi *vb* move, stir; motivate
ysgogiad (-au) *nm* movement, motion
ysgol (-ion) *nf* school; schooling; **ysgol breswyl** boarding school; **ysgol fach** infant school; **ysgol feithrin** nursery school; **ysgol fonedd** public school; **ysgol ganolraddol** middle school
ysgol (-ion) *nf* ladder
ysgoldy (-dai) *nm* schoolhouse, schoolroom
ysgolfeistr (-i, -iaid) *nm* schoolmaster
ysgolfeistres (-i) *nf* schoolmistress
ysgolhaig (-heigion) *nm* scholar
ysgolheictod *nm* scholarship
ysgolheigaidd *adj* scholarly
ysgolor (-ion) *nm* scholar
ysgoloriaeth (-au) *nf* scholarship
ysgorpion (-au) *nm* scorpion
Ysgotyn (-gotiaid) *nm* Scot, Scotsman
ysgrafell (-od, -i) *nf* scraper; curry-comb
ysgrafellu *vb* scrape, curry
ysgraff (-au) *nf* boat, barge, ferry-boat
ysgraffinio *vb* scarify, graze, abrade
ysgrech (-feydd) *nf* scream, shriek
ysgrechian, ysgrechin *vb* scream, shriek
ysgrepan (-au) *nf* wallet, scrip
ysgrif (-au) *nf* writing, article, essay
ysgrifbin (-nau) *nm*, **ysgrifell (-au)** *nf* pen
ysgrifen, ysgrifeniad (ysgrifeniadau) *nf* writing
ysgrifennu *vb* write
ysgrifennwyr (-enwyr) *nm* writer
ysgrifennydd (-enyddion) *nm* scribe, secretary

ysgrifenyddiaeth *nf* secretaryship
ysgriw (-iau) *nf* screw
ysgriwio *vb* screw
ysgrwbio *vb* scrub
ysgryd *nm* shiver
ysgrythur (-au) *nf* scripture
ysgrythurol *adj* scriptural
ysgrythurwr (-wyr) *nm* scripturist
ysgub (-au) *nf* sheaf; broom
ysgubo *vb* sweep
ysgubol *adj* sweeping
ysgubor (-iau) *nf* barn, granary
ysgubwr (-wyr) *nm* sweeper, sweep
ysgutor (-ion) *nm* executor
ysguthan (-od) *nf* wood-pigeon; jade
ysgwâr *adj, nf* square
ysgwario *vb* square
ysgwfd *nm* jerk, toss, fling, shove
ysgwïer (-iaid) *nm* squire
ysgwrfa *nf* scouring, lathering
ysgwrio *vb* scour, scrub; lather
ysgwyd *vb* shake; flutter; wag
ysgwydd (-au) *nf* shoulder
ysgwyddo *vb* shoulder, jostle
ysgydwad *nm* shaking, shake
ysgyfaint *npl* lungs, lights
ysgyfarnog (-od) *nf* hare
ysgymun *adj* excommunicate, accursed
ysgymundod *nm* excommunication, ban
ysgymuno *vb* excommunicate
ysgyrion *npl* staves, splinters, shivers
ysgyrnygu *vb* grind the teeth, snarl
ysgytiad (-au) *nm* shock
ysgytio *vb* shake violently, shock
ysgythru *vb* cut, carve; prune
ysictod *nm* contusion; sprain
ysig *adj* bruised, sore, sprained
ysigo *vb* bruise, crush; sprain
yslotian *vb* dabble, tipple

ysmala *adj* droll, funny, amusing
ysmaldod *nm* fun, drollery
ysmalio *vb* joke, jest
ysmaliwr (**-wyr**) *nm* joker, wit
ysmotyn (**ysmotiau**) *nm* spot
ysmwddio *vb* iron
ysmygu *vb* smoke (tobacco)
ysmygwr (**-wyr**) *nm* smoker
ysol *adj* consuming, devouring; corrosive
yst- *see also* **st-**
ystabl (**-au**) *nf* stable
ystad (**-au**) *nf* state; estate; furlong
ystadegau *npl* statistics
ystadegol *adj* statistical
ystadegydd (**-ion**) *nm* statistician
ystafell (**-oedd**) *nf* chamber, room; **ystafell fyw** living room; **ystafell molchi** bathroom
ystalwyn (**-i**) *nm* stallion
ystanc (**-iau**) *nm* stake, bracket
ystarn (**-au**) *nf* stern
ystelcian *vb* skulk, loaf, loiter
ystelciwr (**-wyr**) *nm* loafer, loiterer
ystên (**-enau**) *nf* pitcher, ewer, milk-can
ystinos *nm* asbestos
ystiwart (**-wardiaid**) *nm* steward
ystlum (**-od**) *nm* bat
ystlys (**-au**) *nf* side, flank
ystlyswr (**-wyr**) *nm* linesman
ystod (**-ion**) *nf* course; swath; **Yn ystod** during
ystof *nm*, *nf* warp
ystofi *vb* warp; weave, plan
ystôl (**-olion**) *nf* stool, chair
ystôr (**-orau**) *nm* store, abundance
ystordy (**-dai**) *nm* storehouse, warehouse
ystorfa (**-feydd**) *nf* store, storehouse
ystorio *vb* store
ystorïwr (**-ïwyr**) *nm* storyteller

ystorm (**-ydd**) *nf* storm
ystormus *adj* stormy
ystrad (**-au**) *nm*, *nf* vale, flat
ystranc (**-iau**) *nf* trick
ystrancio *vb* play tricks; jib
ystrodur (**-iau**) *nf* cart-saddle
ystryd (**ystrydoedd**) *nf* street
ystrydebol *adj* stereotyped
ystryw (**-iau**) *nf* wile, craft, ruse
ystrywgar *adj* wily, crafty
ystum (**-iau**) *nm*, *nf* bend; form; posture; (*pl*) grimaces
ystumio *vb* bend, distort; pose
ystumog (**-au**) *nf* stomach
ystŵr *nm* stir, noise, bustle, fuss
Ystwyll *nm* Epiphany
ystwyrian *vb* stretch and yawn, stir
ystwyth *adj* flexible, pliant, supple
ystwythder *nm* flexibility, pliancy
ystwytho *vb* make flexible; bend, soften
ystyfnig *adj* obstinate, stubborn
ystyfnigo *vb* behave obstinately
ystyfnigrwydd *nm* obstinacy
ystyr (**-on**) *nf*, *nm* sense, meaning
ystyrgar *adj* thoughtful, meditative
ystyriaeth (**-au**) *nf* consideration, heed
ystyried *vb* consider, regard, heed
ystyriol *adj* mindful, heedful
ysu *vb* eat, consume; hanker; itch
yswain (**-weiniaid**) *nm* esquire
yswil *adj* shy, bashful, timid
yswildod *nm* shyness, bashfulness
yswiriant *nm* insurance
yswirio *vb* insure
yswaeth *adv* more's the pity
yw *npl*, *coll n* (*nf*-**en**) yew
yw *vb* is, are

LANGUAGE IN ACTION

CONTENTS

Correspondence   2

Letters   2

Curriculum vitae   8

Email   10

Telephone   12

Useful phrases   13

Numbers   14

CORRESPONDENCE

▶ PERSONAL LETTER

18 Slateford Ave
Leeds
L24 3PR

14 February 2008

Dear Gran and Grandad,

Thank you both very much for the CDs which you sent me for my birthday. They are two of my favourite groups and I'll really enjoy listening to them.

There's not much news here. I seem to be spending most of my time studying for my exams which start in two weeks. I'm hoping to pass all of them but I'm not looking forward to the maths exam as that's my worst subject.

Mum says that you're off to Crete on holiday next week, so I hope that you have a great time and come back with a good tan.

Love from

Kerry

STARTING A PERSONAL LETTER

Dear Katie	*Annwyl Cêt*
Thank you for your letter	*Diolch am dy lythyr* (sing)
	Diolch am eich llythyr (pl)
It was lovely to hear from you	*Roedd yn dda clywed oddi wrthyt* (sing)
	Roedd yn dda clywed oddi wrthych (pl)
I'm sorry I didn't write earlier	*Mae'n ddrwg gen i beidio ysgrifennu ynghynt*

CORRESPONDENCE

▶ PERSONAL LETTER

18 Slateford Avenue
LEEDS
L24 3PR
14 Chwefror 2008

Annwyl Taid a Nain

Diolch yn fawr i chi'ch dau am y CDau gefais i gennych ar fy mhenblwydd. Mae dau grwp, sy'n ffefrynnau gen i, arnyn nhw a chaf fwynhau yn fawr gwrando ar rhain.

Does dim llawer o newyddion yma. Rwy'n gwario rhan fwyaf fy amser yn astudio ar gyfer yr arholidau sy'n cychwyn ymhen pythefnos. Rwy'n gobeithio llwyddo ynddyn nhw i gyd, ond dydw i ddim yn edrych ymlaen at yr arholiad mathemateg am mai dyna fy mhwnc gwaethaf.

Mae Mam yn dweud eich bod yn mynd ar wyliau i Creta yr wythnos nesaf. Rwy'n gobeithio y cewch amser da ac y byddwch yn dod adre wedi cael lliw haul.

Gyda chariad oddi wrth

Ceri

ENDING A PERSONAL LETTER

Write soon!	*Ysgrifenna yn fuan!* (sing)
	Ysgrifennwch yn fuan! (pl)
Love to Mair	*Cariad at Mair*
Sam sends his best wishes	*Mae Sam yn danfon ei ddymuniadau gorau*
All the best	*Dymuniadau gorau*

CORRESPONDENCE

▶ BUSINESS LETTER

11 Rhianedd Way
Caernarfon
LL57 1MG

2 March 2008

Mr Brian Hywel
Human Resources Manager
DTL Thompson Ltd
30 Llwydcoed Street
GLANADDA
GL6 8AB

Dear Mr Hywel

I am 19 years old and a student of Economics at Bangor University. I would like to work in Wales. I would be grateful if you would let me know if your agency could offer me work for a period of about ten weeks from Easter.

Yours in anticipation,

STARTING A BUSINESS LETTER

Dear ...	Annwyl ...
Dear Sir	Annwyl Syr
Dear Sir or Madam	Annwyl Syr neu Fadam

4

CORRESPONDENCE

▶ **BUSINESS LETTER**

11 Ffordd Rhianedd
Caernarfon
LL57 1MG

2 Mawrth 2008

Bn Brian Hywel
Rheolwr Adnoddau Dynol
DTL Thompson Cyf
30 Stryd y Llwydcoed
GLANADDA
GL6 8AB

Annwyl Fonwr Hywel

Rwy'n 19 oed ac yn fyfyriwr Economeg ym Mhrifysgol Bangor. Hoffwn ddal i weithio yng Nghymru. Byddwn yn ddiolchgar pe gallech roi gwybod i mi a fedr eich asiantaeth gynnig gwaith i mi am gyfnod o tua deng mis wedi cyfnod y Pasg.

Yr eiddoch mewn gobaith,

ENDING A BUSINESS LETTER

Yours sincerely	*Yr eiddoch yn ddiffuant*
Yours faithfully	*Yr eiddoch yn gywir*

CORRESPONDENCE

▶ COVERING LETTER

Rosalind Bowen
11 North Street
BRODALAITH
BR7 2BT

Human Resources Department
Messrs J M Kenyon Ltd
House of Heat
CAEREFYDD
CR7 4NC

20 February 2008

Dear Sir or Madam

With reference to your advertisement in today's *Western Herald*, I wish to apply for the post of Human Resources Manager.

I enclose my *curriculum vitae*. Please do not hesitate to contact me if you require any further details.

Yours faithfully

Rosalind Bowen

Enc: CV with two references

Rosalind Bowen
11 Stryd y Gogledd
BRODALAITH
BR7 2BT

Adran Adnoddau Dynol
Mri J M Kenyon Cyf
Ty Gwresogi
CAEREFYDD
CR7 4NC

20 Chwefror 2008

Annwyl Syr neu Fadam

Gan gyfeirio at eich hysbyseb yn y *Western Herald* heddiw, hoffwn ymgeisio am swydd Rheolwr Adnoddau Dynol.

Rwy'n amgau fy *curriculum vitae*. Cysylltwch â mi ar unwaith os gwelwch yn dda os byddwch angen unrhyw fanylion pellach.

Yr eiddoch yn gywir,

Rosalind Bowen

Amg. CV a dau eirda.

▶ CURRICULUM VITAE

CURRICULUM VITAE

Name:	Rosalind Anna BOWEN
Address:	11 Deiniol Road, Bangor, Gwynedd LL57 2UP
Telephone:	01248 53431
Email:	rabowen78@gmail.com
Nationality:	British
Qualifications:	1994: GCSE 9 subjects 1996: A-levels: Welsh (A), English (B), French (B) 2000: BA Hons in Welsh, Cardiff University
Present Post:	Assistant Human Resources Officer, Cardiff Metal Company plc
Previous Employment:	Nov 2000– Jan 2001: Human Resources Trainee, Cardiff Metal Company plc Oct 1996– June 2000: Part-time job in Siop Lyfrau Eleri, Cardiff
Skills:	Fluent Welsh and English, good numeracy skills, clean driving licence
Interests:	Riding and sailing

Referees:
Ms Elisabeth Dodd, Human Resources Manager, Cardiff Metal Company plc, Cardiff CF7 4NC

Dr Rhys ap Tomos, Welsh Department, Cardiff University, Cardiff CF2 6XD

CURRICULUM VITAE

	Rosalind Anna BOWEN
Enw:	
Cyfeiriad:	11 Ffordd Deiniol, Bangor, Gwynedd LL57 2UP
Ffôn:	01248 53431
E-bost:	rabowen78@gmail.com
Cenedligrwydd:	Prydeinig
Cymwysterau:	1994: TGAU 9 pwnc
	1996: Lefel A: Cymraeg (A), Saesneg (B), Ffrangeg (B)
	2000: BA Anrhydedd Ail Ddosbarth mewn Cymraeg, Prifysgol Caerdydd
Swydd bresennol:	Swyddog Adnoddau Dynol, Cardiff Metal Company plc
Swyddi cynharach:	Tach 2000 – Ion 2001 Hyfforddai Adnoddau Dynol, Cardiff Metal Company plc
	Hyd 1996 – Mehef 2000 Swydd rhan amser yn Siop Lyfrau Eleri, Caerdydd
Medrau:	Rhygl yn y Gymraeg a'r Saesneg, medrau rhifyddol da, trwydded yrru lân
Diddordebau:	Marchogaeth a hwylio
Canolwyr:	Ms Elisabeth Dodd, Rheolwr Adnoddau Dynol, Cardiff Metal Company plc, Caerdydd CF7 4NC
	Dr Rhys ap Tomos, Adran y Gymraeg, Prifysgol Caerdydd, Caerdydd CF2 6XD

CORRESPONDENCE

▶ EMAIL

	New message
To:	anna@aol.com
From:	siôr@tiscali.com
Subject:	concert next week
cc:	siani@btconnect.com
bcc:	

| Attachment | | Send |

Hi guys

I've just bought the new album by the Manicurists, and it's brilliant! I've got two spare tickets to a concert they're giving in Caerdelyn next Wednesday evening, so I hope you can both make it.

See you soon!

Do you have email?	*Oes e-bost gennyt?* (sing informal)
	Oes e-bost gennych? (sing formal, pl)
What's your email address?	*Beth yw dy gyfeiriad e-bost* (sing informal)
	Beth yw eich cyfeiriad e-bost (sing formal, pl)
My email address is ...	*... yw fy nghyfeiriad e-bost*
I'll email you the details	*Wna' i e-bostio'r manylion atat* (sing informal)
	Wna' i e-bostio'r manylion atoch (sing formal, pl)

CORRESPONDENCE

► EMAIL

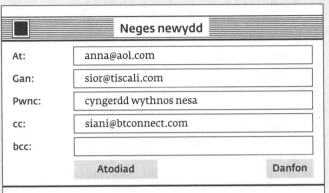

	Neges newydd
At:	anna@aol.com
Gan:	sior@tiscali.com
Pwnc:	cyngerdd wythnos nesa
cc:	siani@btconnect.com
bcc:	

Atodiad   **Danfon**

Helo bobol

Rwy' newydd brynu albwm newydd y Maniciwriaid ac mae e'n anhygoel!
Mae gen i ddau docyn sbâr i gyngerdd fyddan nhw'n perfformio ynddo nos Fercher nesa yng Nghaerdelyn, felly gobeithio gallwch ddod.

Wela i chi toc!

TELEPHONE

Hello!	Helo!
Who's speaking?	Pwy sy'n siarad?
It's Laura speaking	Lora sy'n siarad
Could I speak to ... please	Alla' i siarad â ... os gwelwch yn dda
My phone number is ...	Fy rhif ffôn yw ...
It's engaged	Mae'r ffôn yn brysur
There's no reply	Does dim ateb
Do you speak Welsh?	Ydych chi'n siarad Cymraeg?
Hold on please	Dal y lein os gweli di'n dda
Please hold the line	Daliwch y lein os gwelwch yn dda
Could you put me through to extension 3395?	Fedrwch chi 'nghysylltu i ag estyniad 3395?
Would you like to leave a message?	Hoffet ti adael neges? (*sing informal*)
	Hoffech chi adael neges? (*sing formal, pl*)
Could you tell him that I called?	Alli di ddweud wrtho mod i wedi galw? (*sing informal*)
	Allwch chi ddweud wrtho mod i wedi galw? (*sing formal, pl*)
I'll call back later.	Alwa' i nôl yn nes ymlaen.
I'm afraid you have the wrong number	Mae arna' i ofn bod y rhif anghywir gennyt (*sing informal*)
	Mae arna' i ofn bod y rhif anghywir gennych (*sing formal, pl*)

USEFUL PHRASES

Hello!	Helô!
Goodbye!	Hwyl!
Bye!	Hwyl!
Good morning	Bore da
Good afternoon	Prynhawn da
Good evening	Noswaith dda
Good night	Nos da
What's your name?	Beth yw d' enw di? (*informal*)
	Beth yw 'ch enw chi? (*formal*)
My name is ...	F' enw i yw ...
Where do you come from?	O ble dy'ch/da'ch chi'n dod?
I come from ...	(Ry)dw i'n dod o ...
Sorry, I don't understand	Mae'n ddrwg gen i, (dy)dw i ddim yn deall
Welcome!	Croeso!
How are you?	Sut wyt ti? (*sing informal*)
	Sut 'ych chi? (*sing formal, pl*)
I'm fine, thank you	Iawn, diolch
Pleased to meet you	Mae'n dda gen i gwrdd â chi
How's life?	Sut mae bywyd?
See you tomorrow!	Wela' i di fory! (*sing*)
	Wela' i chi fory! (*pl*)
See you later!	Wela' i di wedyn! (*sing*)
	Wela' i chi wedyn! (*pl*)
Good luck!	Pob lwc! Lwc dda!
Congratulations!	Llongyfarchiadau!
Have fun!	Mwynha! (*sing*)
	Mwynhewch! (*pl*)
Cheers!	Iechyd da!
Bless you!	Pob bendith!
Enjoy your meal	Mwynha dy bryd bwyd! (*sing informal*)
	Mwynhewch eich pryd bwyd! (*sing formal, pl*)
Happy Birthday!	Penblwydd Hapus!
Merry Christmas!	Nadolig Llawen!
Happy New Year!	Blwyddyn Newydd Dda!

NUMBERS

There are two forms of some cardinal numbers in Welsh. When using a form containing 'ar', the noun comes before 'ar', eg *seventeen days* can be translated as *dau ddydd ar bymtheg*.

Note that the numbers two, three and four change with the gender of the noun. Feminine form has been given at these main numbers but any other numbers containing these forms also change with the gender of the noun.

zero, nothing	0	sero, dim
one	1	un
two	2	dau (*m*), dwy (*f*)
three	3	tri (*m*), tair (*f*)
four	4	pedwar (*m*), pedair (*f*)
five	5	pump
six	6	chwech
seven	7	saith
eight	8	wyth
nine	9	naw
ten	10	deg
eleven	11	un deg un/un ar ddeg
twelve	12	un deg dau/deuddeg
thirteen	13	un deg tri/tri ar ddeg
fourteen	14	un deg pedwar/pedwar ar ddeg
fifteen	15	un deg pump/pymtheg
sixteen	16	un deg chwech/un ar bymtheg
seventeen	17	un deg saith/dau ar bymtheg
eighteen	18	un deg wyth/deunaw
nineteen	19	un deg naw/pedwar ar bymtheg
twenty	20	dau ddeg/ugain
twenty-one	21	dau ddeg un/un ar hugain
twenty-two	22	dau ddeg dau/dau ar hugain
thirty	30	tri deg/deg ar hugain
forty	40	pedwar deg/deugain
fifty	50	pum deg/hanner cant

NUMBERS

sixty	60	chwe deg/trigain
seventy	70	saith deg/deg a thrigain
eighty	80	wyth deg/pedwar ugain
ninety	90	naw deg/deg a phedwar ugain
a hundred	100	cant
a hundred and one	101	cant ac un
a hundred and thirty	130	cant tri deg
three hundred	300	tri chant
three hundred and one	301	tri chant ac un
a thousand	1,000	mil
ten thousand	10,000	deng mil
a hundred thousand	100,000	can mil
a million	1,000,000	miliwn

NUMBERS

first	1st	cyntaf
second	2nd	ail
third	3rd	trydydd (*m*), trydedd (*f*)
fourth	4th	pedwerydd (*m*), pedwaredd (*f*)
fifth	5th	pumed
sixth	6th	chweched
seventh	7th	seithfed
eighth	8th	wythfed
ninth	9th	nawfed
tenth	10th	degfed
eleventh	11th	unfed ar ddeg
twelfth	12th	deuddegfed
thirteenth	13th	trydydd ar ddeg
fourteenth	14th	pedwerydd ar ddeg
fifteenth	15th	pymthegfed
sixteenth	16th	unfed ar bymtheg
seventeenth	17th	ail ar bymtheg
eighteenth	18th	deunawfed
nineteenth	19th	pedwerydd ar bymtheg
twentieth	20th	ungeinfed
twenty first	21st	unfed ar hugain
twenty second	22nd	ail ar hugain
thirtieth	30th	degfed ar hugain
fortieth	40th	deugeinfed
fiftieth	50th	hanner canfed
sixtieth	60th	trigeinfed
seventieth	70th	degfed a thrigain
eightieth	80th	pedwar ugeinfed
ninetieth	90th	deg a phedwar ugeinfed
hundredth	100th	canfed
hundred and first	101st	canfed ac un
hundred and eleventh	111th	unfed ar ddeg a chant
thousandth	1,000th	milfed
millionth	1,000,000th	miliwnfed

16

a

a, an adj: **a man** dyn **an ass** asyn
aback adv yn ôl; **taken aback** wedi synnu
abandon vt rhoi'r gorau i, gadael
abandoned adj wedi ei adael, ofer, afradlon
abase vt darostwng, iselhau, gostwng
abash vt cywilyddio
abate vb gostwng, lleihau; gostegu
abattoir n lladd-dy
abbess n abades
abbey n abaty, mynachlog
abbot n abad
abbreviate vt byrhau, talfyrru
abbreviation n byrfodd
abdicate vb ymddeol, ymddiswyddo
abdomen n bol
abdominal adj perthynol i'r bol
abduct vt dwyn ymaith drwy drais, cipio

aberration n cyfeiliorn, gwyriad
abet vt cefnogi, cynorthwyo, ategu
abeyance n dirymedd dros dro, oediad
abhor vt ffieiddio, casáu
abhorrence n ffieidd-dod, atgasrwydd, atgasedd
abide vb aros, trigo; goddef
abiding adj arhosol, gwastadol
ability n gallu, medr
abject adj distadl, dirmygedig
ablative n abladol
ablaze adv ar dân, yn wenfflam
able adj abl, galluog
ablution n golchiad; puredigaeth
abnormal adj anghyffredin, annormal
aboard adv ar fwrdd (llong)
abode n annedd, trigfa, cartrefle
abolish vt diddymu, dileu
abominable adj ffiaidd
abomination n ffieidd-dra
aborigines npl cyn-drigolion
abort vb erthylu, atal
abortion n erthyliad; erthyl
abortive adj seithug, ofer
abound vi amlhau, heigio; ymhelaethu
about prep am, oddeutu, tua ▷ adv oddeutu, o gwmpas
above prep uwch, uwchlaw ▷ adv fry
abrasive adj yn peri traul; annymunol
abreast adj ochr yn ochr, cyfystlys
abridge vt talfyrru, cwtogi
abroad adv allan, ar led, ar daen, dros y dŵr
abrogate vt diddymu, dileu
abrupt adj disymwth, sydyn, swta; serth
abscess n cornwyd, casgliad, crynhofa
abscond vi rhedeg i ffwrdd, dianc

absence n absenoldeb
absent adj absennol ▷ vt absenoli
absenteeism n absenoliaeth
absent-minded adj anghofus
absolute adj cwbl, hollol; diamodol
  ▷ n diamod, absolwt
absolutely adv yn hollol
absolution n gollyngdod;
  maddeuant
absolve vt rhyddhau, gollwng;
  maddau
absorb vt yfed, llyncu, sugno, sychu
absorbent adj amsugnol ▷ n
  amsugnydd
absorption n llynciad, sychiad
abstain vb ymatal, ymgadw
abstemious adj cymedrol, sobr
abstention n ymataliad
abstinence n dirwest, ymataliad
abstinent adj cymedrol, sobr
abstract vt tynnu, haniaethu,
  crynhoi ▷ adj haniaethol ▷ n
  crynodeb
abstraction n haniaeth;
  synfyfyrdod
abstruse adj tywyll, dyrys, astrus
absurd adj gwrthun, afresymol
abundance n digonedd,
  helaethrwydd
abundant adj aml, helaeth, digonol
abuse vt camddefnyddio, cam-drin;
  difrïo
abuse n camddefnydd; difrïaeth
abusive adj sarhaus, gwatwarus
abysmal adj diwaelod, dwys, enbyd
abyss n y dyfnder, agendor
academic, academical adj
  athrofaol, academig
academy n ysgol, athrofa, academi
accede vi cytuno, cydsynio
accelerate vt cyflymu, chwimio
accelerator n ysbardun,
  chwimiadur

accent n acen; llediaith ▷ vt acennu
accentuate vt acennu; pwysleisio
accept vt derbyn (yn gymeradwy)
acceptable adj derbyniol,
  cymeradwy
acceptance n derbyniad
access n dyfodfa, dyfodiad,
  mynedfa, mynediad
accessary n cynorthwywr,
  cefnogydd
accessible adj hygyrch; hawdd dod
  ato
accession n esgyniad (i'r orsedd)
accessory adj cynorthwyol,
  cyfranogol; atodol
accidence n ffurfiant
accident n damwain, anap
accidental adj damweiniol
accidentally adv yn ddamweiniol
acclaim vt datgan cymeradwyaeth
acclamation n bloddest,
  cymeradwyaeth
accommodate vt cymhwyso;
  lletya
accommodating adj cyfaddasol
accommodation n lle, llety
accompaniment n cyfeiliant
accompanist n cyfeilydd
accompany vb hebrwng; cyfeilio
accomplice n cynorthwywr mewn
  trosedd
accomplish vt cyflawni, cwblhau
accomplished adj medrus
accomplishment n medr, dawn,
  camp
accord vb cytuno; cyflwyno ▷ n
  cydfod
accordance n: **in accordance with**
  yn unol â
according adv: **according to** yn ôl
accordingly adv felly, gan hynny
accordion n acordion
accost vt cyfarch

account vb cyfrif ▷ n cyfrif; hanes
accountable adj cyfrifol, atebol
accountancy n cyfrifyddiaeth
accountant n cyfrifydd
account number n rhif cyfrif
accredit vt coelio, credu; awdurdodi
accrue vt deillio, codi, digwydd
accumulate vb casglu, pentyrru, cronni
accumulator n cronadur
accuracy n cywirdeb
accurate adj cywir
accurately adv yn gywir
accursed adj melltigedig, melltigaid
accusation n cyhuddiad
accusative adj gwrthrychol; cyhuddol
accuse vt cyhuddo
accustom vt arfer, ymarfer, cynefino
accustomed adj cyfarwydd, cyffredin
ace n as; mymryn
ache vi poeni, gwynio ▷ n poen, cur
achieve vt cyflawni, gorffen, cwpláu, cwblhau
achievement n cyflawniad, camp
acid adj siarp, sur ▷ n suryn, asid
acidic adj asidig
acknowledge vt cydnabod, cyfaddef
acknowledgment n cydnabyddiaeth
acne n acne, plorynnod
acorn n mesen
acoustic adj clybodig
acoustics npl acwsteg
acquaint vt hysbysu, ymgydnabod
acquaintance n cydnabod, cydnabyddiaeth, adnabyddiaeth
acquainted adj cydnabyddus, cynefin, cyfarwydd
acquiesce vi dygymod, cydsynio
acquire vt cael, ennill

acquisition n caffaeliad
acquit vt rhyddhau
acre n erw, cyfair, acer
acrid adj chwerw, llymsur
acrimonious adj chwerw, sarrug, cecrus
acrobat n acrobat
across adv, prep yn groes, ar draws; trosodd
acrylic adj acrylig
act vb gweithredu, actio ▷ n act, gweithred, deddf
action n gweithred, gweithrediad
activate vb gweithredoli
active adj bywiog; gweithredol
activity n gweithgarwch, gweithgaredd
actor n actor, actiwr
actress n actores
actual adj gwir, gwirioneddol
actually adv mewn gwirionedd
actuary n ystadegydd, cyfrifydd
actuate vt ysgogi, cymell, cyffroi
acumen n treiddgarwch, craffter
acupuncture n nodwyddiad, aciwbigiad
acute adj llym, tost; craff
A.D. abbr O.C.
adage n dihareb, dywediad
adamant adj pendant, sicr
adapt vt cyfaddasu
adapter n adaptydd
add vb chwanegu, atodi; adio
adder n neidr, gwiber
addict vt ymroddi, gorddibynnu
addiction n ymroddiad, gorddibyniaeth, tueddiad
addition n ychwanegiad
additional adj ychwanegol
additive n adiolyn
address vb annerch; cyfeirio ▷ n anerchiad; cyfeiriad
adduce vt dwyn ymlaen; nodi**

adept n un cyfarwydd; campwr
adequate adj digonol
adhere vi ymlynu, glynu wrth
adhesion n glyniad, ymlyniad
adhesive adj glynol, ymlynol ▷ n adlyn, glud
adieu excl bydd wych! ffarwel!
adjacent adj cyfagos, gerllaw
adjective n ansoddair
adjoin vt cydio, cyffwrdd â
adjourn vt gohirio, oedi
adjudge vt dyfarnu, barnu
adjudicate vt beirniadu, barnu
adjudicator n beirniad
adjunct n atodiad, ychwanegiad
adjure vt tynghedu, tyngu
adjust vt cymhwyso, addasu, unioni
ad-lib adv yn rhydd, difyfyr
administer vt gweinyddu
administration n gweinyddiaeth
administrative adj gweinyddol
administrator n gweinyddwr
admirable adj rhagorol, campus
admiral n llyngesydd
admiralty n morlys
admiration n edmygedd
admire vt edmygu
admission n derbyniad; addefiad
admit vt derbyn; addef, cyfaddef
admittance n derbyniad; trwydded
admixture n cymysgiad, cymysgedd
admonish vt rhybuddio, ceryddu
admonition n rhybudd, cerydd
ad nauseam adv hyd syrffed
ado n helynt, heldrin, ffwdan
adolescence n llencyndod, adolesens
adolescent n adolesent, llencyn, llances
adopt vb mabwysiadu
adoption n mabwysiad
adore vt addoli
adorn vt addurno

Adriatic n: **the Adriatic (Sea)** Môr Adria, yr Adriatig
adrift adv yn rhydd, diangor
adroit adj medrus, deheuig, hyfedr
adulation n gweniaith, truth
adult n (un) mewn oed, oedolyn
adulterate vt llygru
adulterer n godinebwr
adulteress n godinebwraig
adultery n godineb
advance vb symud ymlaen; dyrchafu; rhoi benthyg ▷ n benthyg, echwyn
advanced adj ar y blaen
advancement n dyrchafiad; lles, budd
advancing adj cynyddol, ar gynnydd
advantage n mantais
advantageous adj manteisiol
advent n dyfodiad; yr Adfent
adventure n antur, anturiaeth
adverb n adferf
adversary n gwrthwynebydd
adverse adj adfydus, gwrthwynebus, croes
adversity n adfyd, drygfyd
advert n hysbyseb
advertise vt hysbysu, hysbysebu
advertisement n hysbysiad, hysbyseb
advertiser n hysbysydd
advertising adj hysbysebol
advice n cyngor, cyfarwyddyd
advisable adj doeth, buddiol
advise vt cynghori, annog; hysbysu
advisedly adv ar ôl ystyried, yn bwyllog
advisory adj ymgynghorol
advocate n eiriolwr, bargyfreithiwr ▷ vt eiriol, dadlau, cefnogi, pleidio
adze n neddau, neddyf
aerial adj awyrol, wybrol
aerobics n aerobeg

aeroplane n awyren
aerosol n erosol
aesthetic adj esthetig
aesthetics n estheteg
afar adv pell, hirbell
affable adj hynaws, caruaidd, clên
affair n achos; mater; helynt
affect vt effeithio; cymryd arno, ffugio
affectation n mursendod, rhodres, ffug
affection n serch, cariad; clefyd, haint; (in grammar) affeithiad
affectionate adj serchog, caruaidd
affiliate vt mabwysiadu, tadogi; uno
affinity n cyfathrach; tebygrwydd
affirm vb haeru, taeru; sicrhau, gwirio
affirmation n cadarnhad
affirmative adj cadarnhaol
affix vt sicrhau, gosod
afflict vt cystuddio
affliction n cystudd, adfyd
affluence n cyfoeth, digonedd
affluent adj goludog, cyfoethog, cefnog
afford vt rhoddi; fforddio
afforestation n coedwigaeth
affray n ymryson, ffrwgwd, ysgarmes
affront vt sarhau, tramgwyddo ▷ n sarhad
Afghanistan n Affganistan, Afghanistan
afield adv: **far afield** ymhell i ffwrdd
aflame adv ar dân
afloat adv yn nofio; ar daen, ar led
afoot adv ar droed
afraid adj ag ofn arno, ofnus
afresh adv o'r newydd, eilwaith
Africa n Affrica
African adj Affricanaidd ▷ n Affricanwr

after prep, conj wedi, ar ôl, yn ôl ▷ adv wedyn
aftercare n gofal wedyn, ôl-ofal
after-effects n ôl-effeithiau
afterlife n y byd a ddaw
aftermath n adladd, adlodd
afternoon n prynhawn
afters n y cwrs terfynol
aftershave, aftershave lotion n persawr eillio
aftersun, aftersun cream, aftersun lotion n hufen i drin llosg haul, hylif ar ôl haul
afterthought n syniad diweddar
afterwards adv wedi hynny, wedyn
again adv eilwaith, drachefn, eto
against prep erbyn, yn erbyn
age n oed, oedran; oes; henaint ▷ vb heneiddio
aged adj hen, oedrannus
agency n goruchwyliaeth, cyfrwng, asiantaeth
agenda n agenda
agent n goruchwyliwr; gweithredydd, cynrychiolydd
aggravate vt gwneuthur yn waeth
aggregate n cyfanswm, crynswth
aggression n ymosodiad, gormes
aggressive adj ymosodol, ymwthiol, gormesol
aggrieve vt blino, tramgwyddo
aghast adj syn, brawychedig
agile adj heini, sionc, gwisgi
agitate vt cynhyrfu, aflonyddu, cyffroi
agnostic n agnostig, anffyddiwr
ago adv yn ôl; **long ago** ers talm
agog adv yn awchus
agonizing adj mewn gwewyr meddwl
agony n ing, poen
agrarian adj tirol, gwledig

agree *vi* cytuno; dygymod; cyfateb
agreeable *adj* clên, dymunol, hyfryd
agreement *n* cytundeb
agricultural *adj* amaethyddol
agriculture *n* amaethyddiaeth
aground *adv* ar lawr, ar dir, i dir
ahead *adv* ymlaen, o flaen
aid *vt* cynorthwyo, helpu ▷ *n* cymorth, cynhorthwy
AIDS *n abbr* AID, afiechyd imiwnedd diffygiol
ail *vb* clafychu; blino, poeni
ailment *n* dolur, afiechyd, anhwyldeb
aim *vb* anelu, amcanu ▷ *n* amcan, nod
air *n* awyr; osgo; cainc, alaw ▷ *vt* awyru
airbag *n* bag awyr, bag aer
air conditioning *n* aerdymheru
aircraft *n* awyren
airforce *n* llu awyr
airline *n* cwmni hedfan
airlock *n* aerglo
air mail *n* post awyr
airport *n* maes glanio
airtight *adj* aerglos, aerdyn
aisle *n* ystlys eglwys; llwybr; eil
ajar *adv* cilagored
akin *adv, adj* perthynol, perthnasol
à la carte *adv* à la carte
alack *excl* och fi!
alacrity *n* bywiogrwydd, parodrwydd
alarm *vt* dychrynu ▷ *n* braw, dychryn; rhybudd; larwm
alarm clock *n* cloc larwm
alas *excl* och!
albeit *conj* er, er hynny, eto
album *n* albwm; record hir
alcohol *n* alcohol
alcoholic *adj, n* alcoholig, meddwyn
alcove *n* cilfach wely; hafdy, deildy, alcof

alder *n* gwernen
ale *n* cwrw
alert *adj* esgud, effro, gwyliadwrus
A level *n* Lefel A
algebra *n* algebra
Algeria *n* Algeria
Algerian *adj* Algeraidd ▷ *n* Algeriad
alias *adv* mewn modd, dan enw arall
alibi *n* dadlau bod mewn man arall
alien *adj* estronol ▷ *n* estron
alight *vi* disgyn
align *vb* cyfunioni
alike *adj* yr un fath ▷ *adv* yn gyffelyb
aliment *n* maeth, ymborth
alimony *n* alimoni
alive *adv, adj* yn fyw, byw
alkali *n* alcali
alkaline *adj* alcalïaidd
all *adj* holl; oll, i gyd ▷ *adv* yn hollol ▷ *n* y cwbl, y cyfan; pawb
allay *vt* lleddfu, lliniaru; tawelu
all clear *adv* yn glir
allege *vt* honni, haeru
allegedly *adv* yn honedig
allegiance *n* teyrngarwch, gwrogaeth
allegory *n* alegori
allergic *adj* alergig
allergy *n* alergedd
alleviate *vt* ysgafnhau, esmwytho
alley *n* llwybr, ale
alliance *n* cyfathrach, cynghrair
allied *adj* cynghreiriol
alliteration *n* cyflythreniad, cyseinedd
all-night *adv* drwy'r nos
allocate *vt* cyfleu, rhannu, dosbarthu
allot *vb* gosod, penodi
allotment *n* cyfran; rhandir
all-out *adv* yn llwyr, a'i holl egni
allow *vt* caniatáu, goddef

allowance n goddefiad; dogn; lwfans

alloy n aloi

all right adv yn iawn

allude vi cyfeirio, sôn

allure vb hudo, denu, llithio

allusion n crybwylliad, cyfeiriad (at)

alluvium n llifbridd, dolbridd

ally vt cynghreirio ▷ n cynghreiriad

almighty adj hollalluog, hollgyfoethog

almond n almon

almoner n elusennwr

almost adv bron, agos, braidd

alms n elusen, cardod

aloft adv yn uchel, fry, i fyny

alone adv, adj unig, ar ei ben ei hun

along adv ymlaen; ar hyd; **all along** o'r cychwyn

aloof adv, adj yn cadw draw; pell

aloud adv yn uchel, yn groch

alphabet n egwyddor, abiéc

alphabetical adj yn nhrefn yr wyddor

Alps npl: **the Alps** yr Alpau

already adv eisoes, yn barod

also adv hefyd

altar n allor

alter vb newid, altro

alteration n newid, cyfnewidiad

altercation n ymryson, ffrae

alternate adj bob yn ail ▷ vb digwydd bob yn ail; eilio

alternating adj bob yn ail

alternative n dewis arall

alternatively adv o ddewis arall

although conj er

altitude n uchder

alto n alto

altogether adv oll, i gyd, yn gyfan gwbl

aluminium n alwminiwm

always adv yn wastad(ol), bob amser

Alzheimer's, Alzheimer's disease n clefyd Alzheimer

a.m. abbr a.m.

amalgamate vb cymysgu, cyfuno, uno

amanuensis n ysgrifennydd dros arall

amass vt casglu, cronni, pentyrru

amateur n amatur

amateurish adj trwsgl, anfedrus, amaturaidd

amatory adj carwriaethol

amaze vt synnu, rhyfeddu, aruthro

amazement n syndod

amazing adj rhyfeddol

ambassador n llysgennad

amber n ambr

ambidextrous adj deheuig â'i ddwy law

ambiguity n amwysedd

ambiguous adj amwys

ambition n uchelgais

ambitious adj uchelgeisiol

amble vi rhygyngu ▷ n rhygyng

ambulance n ambiwlans

ambush n, vb cynllwyn, rhagod

ameliorate vt gwella, diwygio

amenable adj hydrin; atebol; cyfrifol

amend vb gwella, diwygio, cywiro

amendment n gwelliant

amends n iawn

amenity n hyfrydwch; hynawsedd

America n yr Amerig

American adj Americanaidd ▷ n Americanwr

amiable adj hawddgar, serchus

amicable adj cyfeillgar

amid, amidst prep ynghanol, ymhlith, ymysg

amiss adv ar fai, o'i le

amity n cyfeillgarwch

ammonia n amonia

ammunition n arlwy rhyfel; pylor etc

amnesty n maddeuant

amok adv yn wyllt, dilywodraeth

among, amongst prep ymhlith, ymysg, rhwng

amorous adj hoff o garu, carwriaethus

amorphous adj di-ffurf, amorffus

amount vi cyrraedd; codi ▷ n swm

amour n carwriaeth

amp n amp

ample adj helaeth, eang; cyflawn, digon

amplify vt helaethu, ehangu

amputate vt torri aelod, trychu

amulet n peth a wisgir fel swyn

amuse vt difyrru, diddanu

amusement n difyrrwch, digrifwch

an see **a**

anachronism n camamseriad

anaemia n diffyg gwaed

anaemic adj di-waed, diwryg

anaesthesia n dideimladrwydd

anaesthetic adj, n anesthetig

analogy n cyfatebiaeth, cydweddiad

analyse vt dadansoddi, dadelfennu

analysis (**-yses**) n dadansoddiad

analyst n dadansoddwr

analytical adj dadansoddol

anarchic, anarchical adj anarchol

anarchist n anarchydd, terfysgwr

anarchy n anhrefn, aflywodraeth, anarchaeth

anathema n anathema

anatomy n anatomeg

ancestor n cyndad, hynafiad

ancestry n ach, achau; hynafiaid

anchor n angor ▷ vb angori

anchoress, anchorite n meudwy, ancr

ancient adj hen, hynafol; oesol

ancillary adj ategol, cynorthwyol

and conj a, ac

anecdote n hanesyn, chwedl

anew adv o'r newydd

angel n angel

anger n dicter, llid ▷ vt digio, llidio

angle n ongl ▷ vi genweirio, pysgota

Anglican adj perthynol i Eglwys Loegr, Anglicanaidd

angling n pysgota

angry adj dig, llidiog

anguish n ing

angular adj onglog

animadvert vi beirniadu, ceryddu, sennu

animal n anifail, mil ▷ adj anifeilaidd

animate adj byw ▷ vt bywhau; ysgogi

animation n bywiogrwydd

animosity n gelyniaeth, digasedd

animus n drwgdeimlad, gelyniaeth

ankle n migwrn, ffêr, swrn

annals npl cofnodion blynyddol

annex vt cysylltu, cydio; meddiannu

annihilate vt diddymu, difodi

annihilation n diddymiant, difodiant

anniversary n pen blwydd; cylchwyl flynyddol

annotate vb gwneud nodiadau

announce vt datgan, cyhoeddi

announcement n cyhoeddiad, hysbysiad

announcer n cyhoeddwr

annoy vt poeni, blino, cythruddo

annoyance n blinder, poendod

annoying adj trafferthus, blinderus

annual adj blynyddol

annuity n blwydd-dal

annul vt diddymu, dileu, dirymu

anoint vt eneinio, iro

anomaly n peth croes i reol, afreoleidd-dra

anon adv yn union, toc, yn y man

anonymity n cyflwr dienw
anonymous adj dienw, anhysbys
anorak n anorac
anorexic adj anorecsig
another pron, n arall
answer vb ateb ▷ n ateb, atebiad
answerable adj atebol, cyfrifol
ant n morgrugyn
antagonism n gelyniaeth, gwrthwynebiaeth
antagonist n gwrthwynebydd
Antarctic n: **the Antarctic** yr Antarctig
antarctic adj o gylch y pegwn deheuol
ante- prefix cyn, o flaen, rhag- ▷ n rhagflaenydd
antecedent adj blaenorol
antediluvian adj cynddilywaidd
antelope n gafrewig, antelop
antenatal adj cyn-geni
anterior adj blaen, blaenorol, cyn-
anthem n anthem
anthology n blodeugerdd
anthracite n glo caled, glo carreg
anthropology n anthropoleg
anti-, ant- prefix gwrth-, yn erbyn
antibiotic n, adj gwrthfiotig
antichrist n anghrist
anticipate vt achub y blaen, disgwyl
anticlimax n disgynneb
anticlockwise adj o chwith, gwrthglocwedd ▷ adv yn gwrthglocwedd
antics npl munudiau, ystumiau, maldod, stranciau
antidote n gwrthwenwyn
antifreeze n, adj gwrthrew, direwyn
antipathy n gwrthnaws; casineb
antipodes npl pellafoedd byd, eithafoedd
antiquarian adj hynafiaethol ▷ n hynafiaethydd

antiquated adj hen a di-les
antique adj hen, hynafol, henffasiwn
antique n hen beth
antique shop n siop hen bethau
antiquity n hynafiaeth; y cynoesoedd
anti-Semitism n gwrth-Iddewiaeth
antiseptic adj, n antiseptig
antisocial adj gwrthgymdeithasol
antithesis (-es) n gwrthgyferbyniad
antler n cainc o gorn carw, rhaidd
anvil n eingion, einion
anxiety n pryder
anxious adj pryderus, awyddus
any adj un, unrhyw, rhyw, peth, dim
anybody pron unrhyw un, rhywun
anyone pron rhywun
anything pron dim, rhywbeth, rhywfaint
anywhere adv rhywle
apace adv ar garlam, ar ffrwst, ar frys
apart adv o'r neilltu, ar wahân
apartheid n aparteid
apartment n rhandy, llety
apathetic adj difraw, difater, didaro
apathy n difrawder, difaterwch
ape n epa ▷ vt dynwared
aperture n bwlch, twll, agorfa
apex n blaen, brig, pen, copa
aphis (aphides) n pryf gwyrdd
aphorism n gwireb, dihareb
apiece adv yr un, ar wahân, un bob un
apocalypse n datguddiad
apocryphal adj anghanonaidd, apocryffaidd
apologize vi ymddiheuro, ymesgusodi
apology n ymddiheuriad, esgusawd
apoplexy n parlys mud, strôc
apostasy n gwrthgiliad
apostate n gwrthgiliwr

apostle n apostol
apostolic, apostolical adj
apostolaidd
apostrophe n sillgoll, collnod (')
apothecary n apothecari, fferyllydd
appal vt brawychu, digalonni
appalling adj arswydus, gwarthus
apparatus n offer, aparatws
apparel n dillad, gwisg
apparent adj amlwg, eglur
apparently adv mae'n debyg
apparition n drychiolaeth, ysbryd
appeal vi apelio, erfyn ▷ n apêl
appear vi ymddangos, ymrithio
appearance n ymddangosiad
appease vt llonyddu, tawelu, dofi
appellation n enw, teitl
append vt atodi, ychwanegu
appendicitis n enyniad y coluddyn
crog, apendiseitis
appendix n atodiad, ychwanegiad
appertain vi perthyn
appetite n archwaeth, chwant,
awydd
appetizer n lluniaeth i greu blas,
blasyn
applaud vt cymeradwyo, curo dwylo
applause n cymeradwyaeth
apple n afal; **apple of the eye**
cannwyll llygad
appliance n offeryn, dyfais
applicant n ymgeisydd
application n cymhwysiad; cais;
ymroddiad
application form n ffurflen gais
applied adj cymwysedig
apply vb cymhwyso; ymroi; cynnig
(am), ymgeisio
appoint vb gosod, penodi, pennu
appointment n cyhoeddiad;
penodiad
apportion vt rhannu, dosbarthu
apposite adj addas, priodol

appraise vt prisio; tafoli
appreciate vt prisio, gwerthfawrogi
appreciation n gwerthfawrogiad
appreciative adj gwerthfawrogol
apprehend vt ymaflyd mewn;
dirnad; ofni
apprehension n dirnadaeth; ofn
apprehensive adj ofnus, pryderus
apprentice n prentis, dysgwr ▷ vt
prentisio
apprise vb hysbysu
approach vb nesáu, dynesu ▷ n
dyfodfa
approachable adj hawdd mynd ato
approbation n cymeradwyaeth
appropriate vt meddiannu ▷ adj
priodol, addas
approval n cymeradwyaeth
approve vt cymeradwyo; profi
approximate vi agosáu ▷ adj agos
approximately adv oddeutu, tua,
yn agos i
appurtenance n peth perthynol
apricot n bricyllen
April n Ebrill
apron n (ar)ffedog, barclod
apt adj tueddol; cymwys, parod
aquarium n pysgodlyn, pysgoty
Aquarius n y Cariwr Dŵr
aquatic adj dyfrol, dyfriog
aqueduct n dyfrffos
Arab n Arab ▷ adj Arabaidd
arable adj: **arable land** tir âr
arbiter n dyddiwr, brawdwr, beirniad
arbitrament n rhaith, dedfryd
arbitrary adj gormesol, mympwyol
arbitrate vb cyflafareddu, athrywyn
arbour n deildy
arc n bwa, arc
arcade n arcêd
arch n bwa, pont; nen ▷ vt pontio
arch- prefix arch-, carn-, prif-
archaeology n archaeoleg

archaic adj hynafol, henaidd
archangel n archangel
archbishop n archesgob
archdeacon n archddiacon, archddiagon
archdruid n archdderwydd
archer n saethydd, saethwr
archery n saethyddiaeth
archipelago n twr ynysoedd, ynysfor
architect n pensaer
architecture n pensaernïaeth
archive n archif
archway n ffordd fwaol
Arctic n: **the Arctic** yr Arctig
arctic adj gogleddol
ardent adj gwresog, poeth, angerddol
ardour n angerdd, aidd
arduous adj llafurus, blin, caled
area n arwynebedd, wyneb
Argentina n Ariannin
argue vb dadlau, ymresymu
argument n dadl, ymresymiad
arid adj sych, crin, cras, gwyw
Aries n yr Hwrdd
aright adv yn iawn, yn briodol
arise vi cyfodi, codi
aristocracy n pendefigaeth
aristocrat n pendefig, gŵr mawr
aristocratic adj pendefigaidd, bonheddig
arithmetic n rhifyddeg
arithmetician n rhifyddgwr
ark n arch
arm n braich; cainc
arm n arf ▷ vb arfogi
armament n offer rhyfel; arfogaeth
armchair n cadair freichiau
armed adj arfog
armful adj coflaid, ceseiliaid
armistice n cadoediad
armour n arfogaeth, arfwisg
armoured adj wedi ei amddiffyn

armoury n arfdy
armpit n cesail
armrest n man i orffwys braich
army n byddin
aroma n perarogl(au)
aromatic adj peraroglaidd, pêr, persawrus
around adv, prep am, o amgylch
arouse vt deffro(i), dihuno; cyffroi
arraign vt cyhuddo o flaen brawdle
arrange vb trefnu
arrangement n trefn, trefniad, trefniant
arrant adj dybryd, cywilyddus
array vt trefnu, cyfleu; gwisgo ▷ n trefn; gwisg
arrears npl ôl-ddyled
arrest vt atal; dal, dala, restio
arrival n dyfodiad, cyrhaeddiad
arrive vi cyrraedd, dyfod
arrogance n balchder, traha
arrogant adj balch, trahaus
arrogate vt hawlio, trawshawlio
arrow n saeth
arsenal n arfdy, ystordy neu ffatri arfau
arson n llosgiad, llosg
art n celfyddyd; ystryw
artefact n celflun
artery n rhedweli
artful adj ystrywgar, dichellgar, cyfrwys
art gallery n oriel gelf
arthritis n gwynegon, crydcymalau
artichoke n artisiog
article n erthygl; nwydd; bannod
articulate vb cymalu; cynanu ▷ adj â meddwl clir, trefnus
artifice n dyfais; ystryw, dichell
artificer n saer, crefftwr, celfyddydwr
artificial adj celfyddydol; gosod, dodi, ffug

artillery n offer rhyfel, magnelau
artisan n crefftwr
artist n celfyddydwr, arlunydd, artist
artistic adj celfydd, celfyddgar, artistig
as conj, adv megis, fel; cyn, mor; â, ag
a.s.a.p. abbr cyn gynted, cyn gynted â phosib
asbestos n ystinos, asbestos
ascend vb esgyn, dringo, dyrchafu
ascendancy n goruchafiaeth, uchafiaeth
ascension n esgyniad, dyrchafael
ascent n esgynfa, rhiw, gorifyny
ascertain vt cael gwybod, mynnu gwybod
ascetic n meudwy ▷ adj meudwyaidd, ymgosbol, asgetig
ascribe vt cyfrif i, priodoli, rhoddi
ash n onnen, onn
ash (-es) n lludw, ulw
ashamed adj ag arno gywilydd
ashore adv i'r lan, ar y lan
ashtray n plat lludw
Asia n Asia
Asian n Asiad ▷ adj Asiaidd
aside adv o'r neilltu
ask vb gofyn, holi; ceisio
askance adv yn llygatraws, yn gam
askew adv ar osgo, ar letraws
aslant adv ar ei ogwydd, ar oledd
asleep adv yng nghwsg, yn cysgu
asparagus n merllys, asbaragws
aspect n golwg, golygwedd, wyneb, agwedd
aspen n aethnen
asperity n gerwindeb, llymder
asperse vt taenellu; gwaradwyddo
aspersion n difriad, enllib
asphyxiate vt mygu, tagu
aspiration n dyhead
aspire vi dyheu
aspirin n asbrin

ass n asyn; asen
assail vt ymosod ar, rhuthro ar
assailant n ymosodwr
assassin n bradlofrudd, llofrudd
assassinate vt bradlofruddio
assault n ymosodiad ▷ vt ymosod
assay n praw(f) ▷ vb profi; cynnig, ceisio
assemble vb cynnull, ymgynnull
assembly n cynulliad, cymanfa
assent vi cydsynio ▷ n cydsyniad
assert vt haeru, honni, mynnu
assess vt trethu, prisio, asesu
assessment n asesiad
assessor n aseswr, cyfeisteddwr
asset n ased
assets npl eiddo, meddiannau
assiduous adj dyfal, diwyd
assign vt gosod, penodi; trosglwyddo
assignment n aseiniad
assimilate vb cymathu; tebygu
assist vb cynorthwyo, cymorth, helpu
assistance n cymorth
assistant n cynorthwyydd
assize n brawdlys
associate vb cymdeithasu, cyfeillachu, cysylltu ▷ n cydymaith
association n cymdeithas, cymdeithasfa
assort vb trefnu, dosbarthu
assorted adj amryfath
assortment n dosbarthiad, pigion
assuage vt llonyddu, lliniaru, lleddfu
assume vt cymryd ar; tybied; honni
assumption n tyb(iaeth), bwriant, honiad, dyrchafiad (Mair i'r nefoedd)
assurance n sicrwydd; hyder, hyfder
assure vt sicrhau; yswirio
asterisk n serennig, seren (*)
asthma n caethder, diffyg anadl, y fogfa

asthmatic adj byr ei wynt, caeth ei frest
astonish vt synnu
astound vt synnu, syfrdanu
astral adj serol
astray adv ar gyfeiliorn, ar grwydr
astride adv â'r traed ar led
astrologer n sêr-ddewin
astrology n sêr-ddewiniaeth
astronaut n gofodwr
astronomer n serydd, seryddwr
astronomy n seryddiaeth
astute adj craff, cyfrwys, call
asunder adv ar wahân, yn ddrylliau
asylum n noddfa; **lunatic asylum** gwallgofdy
at prep yn, wrth, ger, ar
atheist n anffyddiwr
Athens n Athen
athlete n mabolgampwr
athletics npl mabolgampau
Atlantic adj Atlantaidd, Atlantig ▷ n: **the Atlantic (Ocean)** yr Iwerydd, Môr Iwerydd
atlas n llyfr mapiau, atlas
ATM n abbr peiriant arian
atmosphere n awyrgylch
atom n mymryn, gronyn, atom
atomic adj atomig
atone vi gwneuthur iawn
atonement n iawn, cymod
atrocious adj erchyll, anfad, ysgeler
attach vb gosod, glynu; atafaelu
attachment n ymlyniad, serch
attack vt ymosod ar ▷ n ymosodiad
attain vt ennill; cyrraedd; cael gafael
attainment n cyrhaeddiad
attempt vt ceisio, cynnig ▷ n cynnig, ymgais
attend vb gweini; ystyried; dilyn, mynychu
attendance n gwasanaeth; presenoldeb

attendant n gweinydd ▷ adj yn dilyn, ynghlwm wrth
attention n sylw, ystyriaeth
attentive adj astud, ystyriol
attenuate vt teneuo, lleihau
attest vb tystio, gwirio; ardystio
attic n nenlofft, nenlawr
attire vt gwisgo ▷ n gwisg, dillad
attitude n ystum, agwedd, osgo
attorney n twrnai
attract vt tynnu, atynnu, denu, hudo
attraction n atyniad
attractive adj atyniadol
attribute n priodoledd
attribute vt priodoli, cyfrif i
attrition n rhathiad, treuliad, traul
attune vt hwylio, cyweirio
aubergine n planhigyn wy
auburn adj gwinau, browngoch
auction n arwerthiant, ocsiwn
auctioneer n arwerthwr
audacious adj hy, digywilydd, haerllug
audacity n hyfdra, ehofndra, beiddgarwch
audible adj hyglyw, clywadwy
audience n gwrandawyr, cynulleidfa
audio-visual adj clyweledol
audit vt archwilio cyfrifon ▷ n archwiliad
audition n clywelediad
auditor n gwrandawr; archwilydd
auger n taradr, ebill
augment vt ychwanegu, atodi
augur n dewin ▷ vb darogan; argoeli
August n Awst
august adj urddasol, mawreddog
aunt n modryb
au pair n au pair
aura n naws, awyrgylch
aural adj clywedol
auspices npl nawdd

auspicious *adj* yn argoeli'n dda, ffafriol

austere *adj* gerwin, llym, tost, caled

austerity *n* gerwindeb, llymder

Australia *n* Awstralia

Australian *n* Awstraliad ▷ *adj* Awstralaidd

Austria *n* Awstria

Austrian *n* Awstriad ▷ *adj* Awstriaidd

authentic *adj* dilys, gwir

author *n* awdur, awdwr

authoritarian *adj* awdurdodus

authoritative *adj* awdurdodol

authority *n* awdurdod

authorize *vt* awdurdodi

auto- *prefix* hunan-, ym-

autobiography *n* hunangofiant

autocracy *n* unbennaeth

autocrat *n* unben; dyn awdurdodol

autograph *n* llofnod

automatic *adj* hunanysgogol, awtomatig

automation *n* awtomasiwn

automobile *n* cerbyd, modur

autonomy *n* ymreolaeth

autumn *n* hydref

auxiliary *adj* cynorthwyol, ategol ▷ *n* cynorthwywr

avail *vb* llesáu, tycio ▷ *n* lles, budd

available *adj* ar gael

avalanche *n* syrthfa, cwymp (eira etc)

avarice *n* cybydd-dod, trachwant

avaricious *adj* cybyddlyd, ariangar

avenge *vt* dial cam

avenue *n* mynedfa, rhodfa

aver *vt* gwirio, haeru

average *n* canolbris; cyfartaledd; cyffredin

averse *adj* gwrthwynebol, gelynol; croesi

aversion *n* gwrthwynebiad; casbeth

avert *vt* troi heibio, gochel, osgoi

aviary *n* adardy

avidity *n* awydd, awch, gwanc

avocado *n* afocado

avocation *n* gorchwyl, galwedigaeth

avoid *vt* gochel, osgoi, arbed

avouch *vt* gwirio, haeru; arddelwi

avow *vt* addef; cydnabod

await *vt* disgwyl, aros

awake *vb* deffro, dihuno ▷ *adj* effro

award *vt* dyfarnu ▷ *n* dyfarniad

aware *adj* hysbys, ymwybodol

awareness *n* arwybod, ymwybyddiaeth

awash *adj* llawn, cyforiog

away *adv* ymaith, i ffwrdd

awe *n* (parchedig) ofn ▷ *vt* rhoi arswyd

awful *adj* ofnadwy, arswydus

awhile *adv* am ennyd, am dro

awkward *adj* trwsgl, lletchwith, anghyfleus

awl *n* mynawyd

awning *n* cysgodlen, adlen

axe *n* bwyall, bwyell

axiom *n* gwireb

axis (**axes**) *n* echel, pegwn

axle *n* echel

ay *adv* ie

aye *adv* yn wastad(ol), byth

azure *n* glas y ffurfafen, asur ▷ *adj* asur

b

babble *vb* baldordd, clebran ▷ *n* baldordd
babe *n* baban, plentyn bach
baby *n* baban, maban, babi
baby-sit *vi* gwarchod plant
babysitter *n* gwarchodwr babanod
bachelor *n* dyn dibriod, hen lanc; baglor
back *n* cefn ▷ *vb* cefnogi; bacio ▷ *adv* yn ôl
background *n* cefndir
backhander *n* tâl dirgel; ergyd â chefn y llaw
backpack *n* cefnbwn
backslide *vi* gwrthgilio
backward *adv* yn ôl, ar ôl ▷ *adj* hwyrfrydig; digynnydd; araf
backwater *n* dŵr disymud ar ymyl afon, lle o'r neilltu, dibwys, cwter gwsg
bacon *n* cig moch, bacwn

bad *adj* drwg, drygionus; gwael, sâl
badge *n* bathodyn
badger *n* mochyn daear, broch ▷ *vt* profocio, poeni
badminton *n* badminton
bad-tempered *adj* â thymer ddrwg
baffle *vt* drysu, siomi, trechu
bag *n* cwd, cod, bag
baggage *n* clud, celfi, pac
bagpipe *n* pibgod
bah *excl* pw!
bail *n* meichiau, gwystl ▷ *vt* mechnïo
bail, bale *vt* hysbyddu cwch
bailiff *n* beili; hwsmon, goruchwyliwr
bait *vt* abwydo; baeddu, eirthio ▷ *n* abwyd
bake *vb* pobi, crasu
baked potato *n* taten bob
baker *n* pobydd
bakery *n* popty
balance *n* clorian, mantol; gweddill ▷ *vt* mantoli; cydbwyso
balanced *adj* cytbwys, cymesur
balcony *n* oriel, balcon
bald *adj* moel, penfoel
bale *n* pwn, sypyn, bwrn
baleful *adj* alaethus, gresynol, galarus
baler *n* byrnwr
balk, baulk *n* balc; siom ▷ *vt* balcio; siomi
ball *n* pêl, pellen
ball *n* dawns, dawnsfa
ballad *n* baled
ballast *n* balast
ball bearings *npl* berynnau pêl, pelferynnau
ballerina *n* balerina
ballet *n* bale
balloon *n* balŵn
ballot *n* balot, tugel
balm *n* balm, triagl

bamboozle vb twyllo, llygad-dynnu
ban vt gwahardd, ysgymuno
banal adj cyffredin, sathredig
banana n banana
band n band, rhwymyn; mintai; seindorf
bandage n rhwymyn ▷ vb rhwymo, rhwymynnu
bandbox n bocs hetiau
bandit n herwr, ysbeiliwr
bandy vt taflu (pêl etc) yn ôl a blaen
bandy-legged adj coesgam
bane n dinistr, melltith
baneful adj dinistriol, andwyol
bang vb curo, dulio, clepian ▷ n ergyd, twrf
Bangladesh n Bangladesh
bangle n breichled
banish vt alltudio, deol
bank n mainc; rhes
bank n glan, torlan; traethell
bank n banc, ariandy ▷ vb bancio
bank account n cyfrif banc
banker n bancwr
bankrupt n methdalwr
bankruptcy n methdaliad
bank statement n datganiad banc, adroddiad banc
banner n baner, lluman
banns npl gostegion
banquet n gwledd ▷ vb gwledda
bantam n coriar, dandi
banter n ysmaldod, cellwair ▷ vb cellwair, profocio
baptism n bedydd
Baptist n Bedyddiwr
baptize vt bedyddio
bar n bar, bollt; rhwystr; traethell ▷ vt bario; eithrio
barb n barf; adfach
barbarian n barbariad, anwariad
barbaric adj barbaraidd
barbecue n rhostfa

barbed wire n weiar bigog
barber n barbwr
bard n bardd, prydydd
bare adj noeth, llwm, moel, prin ▷ vt dinoethi
barefooted adj troednoeth
barely adv prin, o'r braidd
bargain n bargen ▷ vb bargeinio
barge n bad mawr
bark n barc, llong, llestr
bark vi cyfarth, coethi ▷ n cyfarthiad
bark n rhisgl ▷ vt dirisglo, digroeni
barley n haidd, barlys
barm n burum, berem, berman
barmaid n barferch
barman n barmon
barn n ysgubor
barometer n hinfynegydd, baromedr
baron n barwn, arglwydd
baronet n barwnig
barrack n lluest, lluesty, gwersyllty
barrage n argae, clawdd
barrel n baril, casgen
barren adj diffrwyth; amhlantadwy
barricade n atalglawdd ▷ vt cau
barrier n atalfa, rhwystr, terfyn, ffin
barrister n bargyfreithiwr
barrow n berfa, whilber; crug
barter vb cyfnewid, ffeirio ▷ n cyfnewid
base adj isel, gwael, distadl, gau
base n sylfaen; bôn ▷ vt sylfaenu, seilio
baseball n pel-fâs
basement n islawr
bashful adj swil, gwylaidd
basic adj gwaelodol, sylfaenol
basics npl: **the basics** y bôn
basil n brenhinllys, basil
basin n basn, cawg, dysgl
basis (**bases**) n sail, sylfaen
bask vi ymheulo, torheulo

basket n basged, cawell
basketball n pêl-fasged
basketful n basgedaid
bass n bas, isalaw; bàs, draenogiad y môr
bastard n bastard, plentyn gordderch/siawns
baste vt iro, brasteru; ffusto, ffonodio
bat n ystlum
bat n bat ▷ vi batio
batch n pobiad, ffyrnaid; swp, sypyn
bath n ymolchfa, badd, baddon; bath
bathe vb ymdrochi, ymolchi, golchi
bathroom n ystafell ymolchi
baton n llawffon, baton, arweinffon
battalion n byddin, mintai, bataliwn
batter vt curo, pwyo ▷ n defnydd crempog, cytew
battery n magnelfa; batri
battle n brwydr, cad ▷ vi brwydro
battlefield n maes y gad
battlement n canllaw, murganllaw.
battleship n llongryfel
bauble n ffril, tegan
baulk see **balk**
bawdy adj anllad, anweddus
bawl vi gweiddi, crochlefain, bloeddio
bay n bae
bay vb, n cyfarth; **to hold at bay** rhoi cyfarth
bay n llawryf
bay adj gwinau, gwineugoch
bayonet n bidog ▷ vt bidogi
bazaar n basâr
BC abbr CC, Cyn Crist
be vi bod
beach n traeth, traethell ▷ vt gyrru ar y traeth
beacon n gwylfa, goleudy; coelcerth

bead n glain; **beads** npl paderau
beadle n rhingyll
beak n pig, gylfin, duryn
beaker n cwpan, diodlestr â phig, bicer
beam n trawst, paladr; pelydryn ▷ vi pelydru
bean n ffäen, ffeuen
bear n arth; arthes
bear vt dwyn, cludo; geni; dioddef, goddef
beard n barf; col ŷd
bearing n ymddygiad; traul
beast n bwystfil, anifail
beat vt curo ▷ n cur, curiad
beatitude n gwynfyd
beautiful adj prydferth, hardd, teg
beauty n prydferthwch, harddwch, tegwch; **beauty parlour** parlwr pincio
beaver n afanc, llostlydan
becalm vt tawelu, llonyddu
because adv, conj oherwydd, oblegid, o achos; gan, am
beck n amnaid, awgrym
beckon vb amneidio
become vb dyfod; gweddu
becoming adj gweddus
bed n gwely; cefn, pâm
bedding n dillad gwely
bedeck vt addurno, trwsio
bedew vt gwlitho, gwlychu
bedfellow n cywely
bedlam n bedlam
bedraggled adj wedi caglo, dwyno; aflêr
bedridden adj gorweiddiog
bedroom n ystafell wely, llofft
bedsitter n ystafell un gwely, ceginlofft
bedstead n pren neu haearn gwely
bee n gwenynen
beech n ffawydden

beef *n* eidion; cig eidion, biff
beehive *n* cwch gwenyn
beeline *n* llinell unionsyth, ddiwyro
beer *n* cwrw
beestings *npl* llaeth newydd, llaeth toro
beet *n* betys
beetle *n* chwilen
beetroot *n* betys
befall *vb* digwydd
befit *vb* gweddu
before *prep* o flaen, gerbron, cyn ▷ *adv* o'r blaen
beforehand *adv* ymlaen llaw
befriend *vt* ymgeleddu, bod yn gefn
beg *vb* erfyn, deisyf, ymbil; cardota
beget *vb* cenhedlu, creu, peri
beggar *n* cardotyn ▷ *vt* tlodi, llymhau
begin *vb* dechrau
beginner *n* dechreuwr
beginning *n* dechreuad
beguile *vt* hudo, twyllo; swyno, difyrru
behalf *n* plaid, rhan, achos, tu
behave *vb* ymddwyn
behaviour *n* ymddygiad
behead *vt* torri pen
behest *n* arch, archiad
behind *adv*, *prep* ar ôl, yn ôl, tu ôl, tu cefn
behold *vt* edrych, gweld ▷ *vb imper* wele
behove *vt* bod yn rhwymedig ar
beige *adj* beis
being *n* bod
belated *adj* diweddar; wedi ei ddal gan y nos
belch *vb* bytheirio
beleaguer *vt* gwarchae ar
belfry *n* clochdy
Belgium *n* Gwlad Belg
belie *vt* anwireddu, siomi

belief *n* cred, crediniaeth, coel
believe *vb* credu, coelio
believer *n* credwr, credadun
belittle *vt* bychanu
bell *n* cloch
belle *n* merch brydweddol, meinwen
bellicose *adj* rhyfelgar, ymladdgar
belligerent *adj* rhyfelog ▷ *n* rhyfelblaid
bellow *vb* rhuo, bugunad
bellows *npl* megin
belly *n* bol, bola; cest, tor ▷ *vb* bolio
belong *vi* perthyn
belongings *n* meddiannau, eiddo
beloved *adj* annwyl, cu ▷ *n* anwylyd
below *adv*, *prep* is, islaw, isod, obry, oddi tanodd
belt *n* gwregys
bemoan *vt* galaru am, arwylo
bemused *adj* syfrdan
bench *n* mainc
bend *vb* plygu, camu ▷ *n* tro, camedd
beneath *adv*, *prep* is, tan, oddi tanodd
benediction *n* bendith
benefactor *n* cymwynaswr, noddwr
benefice *n* bywoliaeth eglwysig
beneficent *adj* daionus, llesfawr
beneficial *adj* buddiol, llesol
benefit *n* budd, lles, elw ▷ *vb* llesáu, elwa
benevolent *adj* daionus, haelionus
benighted *adj* a ddaliwyd gan y nos; tywyll
benign *adj* tirion, mwyn
bent *n* tuedd, gogwydd
benumb *vt* merwino, fferru, diffrwytho
bequeath *vt* cymynnu, cymynroddi
bequest *n* cymynrodd
bereave *vt* difuddio, amddifadu
beret *n* bere

Berlin n Berlin
berry n aeronen, mwyaren
berserk adj gwyllt, aflywodraethus
berth n lle llong; gwely llongwr;
swydd
beseech vt atolygu, deisyf, erfyn
beseem vt gweddu
beset vt cynllwyn; amgylchynu
beside prep gerllaw, wrth, yn ymyl;
to be beside oneself o'i bwyll
besides adv, prep heblaw, gyda
besiege vt gwarchae ar
besmirch vt llychwino, pardduo
bespeak vt ymofyn ymlaen llaw
best adj, adv gorau
bestial adj bwystfilaidd
bestir vt cyffroi, ymysgwyd
bestow vt rhoddi, cyflwyno,
anrhegu
bestride vt eistedd neu gamu yn
groes i
bet n bet, cyngwystl ▷ vb betio, dal
am
betoken vt arwyddo, argoeli
betray vt bradychu
betrayal n brad
betroth vt dyweddïo
better adj gwell, rhagorach ▷ adv yn
well ▷ vt gwella
between, betwixt prep rhwng,
cydrhwng
beverage n diod
bewail vt cwyno, cwynfan, galaru
am
beware vi gochel, ymogelyd
bewilder vt drysu, mwydro,
pensyfrdanu
bewitch vt rheibio
beyond adv, prep tu hwnt
bi- prefix dau-, deu-
bias n tuedd, gogwydd, rhagfarn ▷ vt
tueddu
Bible n Beibl

bibliography n llyfryddiaeth
bibulous adj yfgar, llymeitgar
bicker vi ffraeo, ymrafaelio, ymgecru
bicycle n ceffyl haearn, deurod, beic
bid vb erchi; gwahodd; cynnig
bide vb aros, disgwyl
biennial adj dwyflynyddol
bier n elor
bifocals npl gwydrau deuffocal
big adj mawr; braisg
bigamy n dwywreigiaeth
bigheaded adj bras, mawreddog
bigot n penboethyn
bike n beic
bikini n bicini
bilberries npl llus
bile n bustl, geri
bilingual adj dwyieithog
bilingualism n dwyieithedd;
dwyieitheg
bill n bil; mesur; rhaglen; hysbyslen
bill n pig, gylfin, duryn
billet n llety (milwr) ▷ vt lletya
billiards n biliards
billion n biliwn
billow n ton, gwaneg, moryn ▷ vi
tonni
billy-goat n bwch gafr
bin n cist
bind vt rhwymo, caethiwo
binge n gloddest, sbri
bingo n bingo
binoculars n deulygadur
biography n bywgraffiad, cofiant
biological adj biolegol
biology n bywydeg, bioleg
birch n bedw, bedwen; gwialen fedw
▷ vt chwipio
bird n aderyn
birdwatching n adarydda, gwylio
adar
Biro® n biro
birth n genedigaeth

b

birthday n pen-blwydd
birthday card n carden pen-blwydd
birthmark n man geni
biscuit n bisgeden
bisect vt dwyrannu, rhannu
bisector n dwyrannydd
bisexual adj deurywiol
bishop n esgob
bishopric n esgobaeth
bison n ych gwyllt, bual
bit n tamaid; tipyn, dernyn; genfa, bit
bitch n gast
bite vb cnoi, brathu ▷ n cnoad, brath; tamaid
bitter adj chwerw, bustlaidd, tost
bittern n aderyn y bwn, bwmp y gors
bitterness n chwerwedd, chwerwder
bitumen n pyg
bituminous adj pyglyd
bizarre adj rhyfedd, od, chwithig
blab vb prepian, clepian ▷ n clepgi
black adj du ▷ n du, dyn du ▷ vt duo
blackberries npl mwyar duon
blackbird n aderyn du, mwyalchen
blackboard n bwrdd du
blackcurrant n cyrensen ddu ▷ adj cwrens du
blacken vt duo, pardduo; tywyllu
blackguard n dihiryn ▷ vt difrïo
black ice n iâ du
blackleg n bradwr
blackmail n arian bygwth, blacmel
blacksmith n gof
bladder n pledren, chwysigen
blade n llafn; eginyn, blewyn
blame vt beio ▷ n bai
blameless adj di-fai
blanch vt gwynnu, cannu
bland adj mwyn, tyner, tirion
blandish vt gwenieithio, truthio
blank adj gwag, syn; **blank verse** mesur di-odl

blank cheque n siec wag
blanket n blanced, gwrthban
blare vb canu utgorn ▷ n sain utgorn
blarney n gweniaith, truth
blaspheme vb cablu, difenwi
blasphemy n cabledd, cabl
blast n chwa, chwythiad, deifiad ▷ vt deifio; saethu; **blast furnace** ffwrnais chwythu
blatant adj stwrllyd, digywilydd, haerllug
blaze n fflam, ffagl ▷ vi fflamio, ffaglu
bleach vb cannu, gwynnu
bleak adj oer, digysgod, noeth, noethlwm
blear adj pŵl, dolurus, dyfriog
bleat vb brefu ▷ n bref
bleed vb gwaedu
blemish vt anafu, anurddo ▷ n anaf, bai, mefl
blend vb cymysgu ▷ n cymysgedd
bless vt bendithio
blessed adj bendigedig, gwyn ei fyd
blessing n bendith
blight n malltod ▷ vt mallu, deifio
blind adj dall, tywyll ▷ vt dallu ▷ n llen, bleind
blindness n dallineb
blink vb cau'r llygaid, ysmicio, amrantu
bliss n gwynfyd, dedwyddyd
blister n chwysigen, pothell ▷ vb pothellu
blithe adj llawen, llon, hoenus
blitz n blits
blizzard n ystorm erwin o wynt ac eira
bloat vb chwyddo, chwythu
blob n ysmotyn, bwrlwm
block n plocyn, cyff ▷ vt cau, rhwystro

blockade n gwarchae ▷ vb gwarchae ar

blockhead n penbwl, hurtyn

blog n blog

blogger n blogiwr

blonde adj o bryd golau

blood n gwaed; gwaedoliaeth

blood pressure n pwysedd gwaed

bloody adj gwaedlyd

bloom n blodeuyn; gwawr, gwrid ▷ vi blodeuo

blossom n blodeuyn ▷ vi blodeuo

blot n ysmotyn du, blot, mefl ▷ vb blotio

blotch n ysmotyn, blotyn, ystremp

blouse n blows

blow n dyrnod, ergyd

blow vb chwythu

blow-dry vb chwythu'n sych

bludgeon n pastwn

blue adj, n glas ▷ vt glasu

bluff adj garw, brochus

blunder n amryfusedd ▷ vb amryfuso

blunt adj pŵl, di-fin; plaen ▷ vt pylu

blur n ysmotyn, ystaen

blurb n broliant

blurt vt rhuthro dywedyd

blush vi cochi, gwrido ▷ n gwrid

bluster vi trystio, brochi ▷ n brawl, broch

blustery adj stormus, rhuadus

boar n baedd

board n bwrdd, bord; ymborth ▷ vb byrddio

boarding house n llety

boarding school n ysgol breswyl

boast n ymffrost ▷ vb ymffrostio

boat n bad, cwch

bobbin n gwerthyd

bobby n plismon

bode vt darogan, argoeli

body n corff

bog n cors, mignen, siglen

boggle vi petruso; rhusio, ffwndro

bogus adj ffug, gau, ffuantus

bogy, bogey n bwbach, bwci, bwgan

boil n cornwyd, casgliad

boil vb berwi

boiler n pair, crochan

boisterous adj terfysglyd, trystiog, brochus

bold adj hy, eofn; hyderus; eglur

bollard n bolard

bolster n gobennydd ▷ vt ategu

bolt n bollt ▷ vb bolltio; dianc; traflyncu

bomb n bom

bombast n chwyddiaith

bombastic n chwyddedig

bomb scare n bygythiad bom

bona fide adj o'r iawn ryw, dilys, didwyll

bond n rhwymyn; ysgrifrwym ▷ adj caeth

bondage n caethiwed

bone n asgwrn

bonfire n coelcerth, banffagl

Bonn n Bonn

bonnet n bonet

bonny adj braf, nobl

bonus n bonws, ychwanegiad

booby n hurtyn, penbwl

book n llyfr

booklet n llyfryn

boom n bŵm

boom vb trystio, utganu ▷ n trwst, swae

boon n ffafr, bendith, caffaeliad

boor n taeog

boost vb gwthio, hybu

boot n botasen, esgid

booth n bwth, lluest, lluesty, caban

booty n ysglyfaeth, anrhaith, ysbail

booze vi diota, meddwi ▷ n diod feddwol

border n ffin, goror, ymyl ▷ vb ymylu

bore vb tyllu, ebillio ▷ n twll

bore n pla, dyn diflas ▷ vt blino, diflasu, llethu

bored adj wedi syrffedu ar beth, wedi alaru

boring adj diflas, annifyr, llethol

born adj wedi ei eni

borough n bwrdeistref

borrow vt benthyca

Bosnia n Bosnia

bosom n mynwes, côl

boss n meistr

botany n llysieueg

botch n ystomp ▷ vb ystompio, bwnglera

both adj, pron, adv y ddau, ill dau

bother vb blino, trafferthu ▷ n helynt, trafferth

bottle n potel, costrel ▷ vt potelu, costrelu

bottle opener n agorwr poteli

bottom n gwaelod, godre, tin

bough n cainc, cangen

boulder n carreg fawr, clogfaen

bounce vb neidio, adlamu; bostio, ymffrostio

bound n terfyn, ffin, cyffin ▷ vt ffinio

bound vi llamu, neidio

boundary n ffin, terfyn

bounty n daioni, haelioni, ced

bouquet n blodeuglwm, pwysi

bout n sbel, term; ornest, ffrwgwd

bow n bwa; dolen

bow vb plygu, crymu, ymgrymu ▷ n moesymgrymiad

bow n pen blaen llong, bow

bowels npl ymysgaroedd, perfedd

bower n deildy

bowl n cawg, basn

bowler n het galed; bowliwr

box n bocs, pren bocs

box n bocs, blwch, cist; sedd, côr; bwth

box n bonclust ▷ vb taro bonclust; paffio

boxer n paffiwr, bocsiwr

boxer shorts npl trôns bocsiwr

boxing n (sport) paffio, bocsio

box office n swyddfa docynnau

boy n bachgen, hogyn, mab, gwas

boycott n, vb ymwrthod â pherthynas a chydweithrediad, boicot(io)

boyfriend n cariadfab, anwylyd

boyhood n bachgendod, mebyd

brace n rhwymyn; pâr ▷ vt tynhau, cryfhau

bracelet n breichled

bracken n rhedyn ungoes

bracket n braced, cromfach

brag n brol, ymffrost, bocsach ▷ vb brolio, ymffrostio

braid n pleth, brwyd ▷ vt plethu, brwydo

brain n ymennydd

brake n dryslwyn, prysglwyn

brake n brêc ▷ vt brecio

bramble n miaren

bran n eisin, bran, rhuddion

branch n cangen, cainc ▷ vi canghennu

brand n pentewyn; nod ▷ vt gwarthnodi

brandish vb ysgwyd, chwifio

brandy n brandi

brash adj byrbwyll, ehud

brass n pres, efydd

brassière n bronglwm

brat n crwt, crwtyn; croten

bravado n gwag-ymffrost, bocsach, gorchest

brave adj dewr, gwrol, glew ▷ vt herio

bravo excl da iawn! campus!

brawl vi ffraeo, terfysgu ▷ n ffrae, ffrwgwd

brawn n cnawd

bray vt pwyo, briwio, malurio

bray vi brefu (megis asyn), nadu

brazen adj haerllug, hy

Brazil n Brasil

breach n adwy, rhwyg, tor; trosedd

bread n bara

breadth n lled

break vb torri ▷ n toriad, tor

break down vi (car) torri i lawr

breakfast n brecwast ▷ vb brecwasta

breakwater n morglawdd

breast n bron, dwyfron, mynwes ▷ vt wynebu, ymladd â

breath n anadl, gwynt

Breathalyser® n anadlydd, anadliadur

breathe vb anadlu, chwythu

breathing n anadliad; anadlu

breech n tin, bôn

breeches npl llodrau, clos

breed vb magu; epilio; bridio ▷ n rhywogaeth, brid

breeze n awel, awelan, chwa

brethren npl brodyr (ffigurol yn bennaf)

brevity n byrder, byrdra

brew vt darllaw, bragu

brewer n darllawydd, bragwr

bribe n llwgrwobrwy ▷ vt llwgrwobrwyo

brick n bricsen, priddfaen ▷ vt bricio

bride n priodferch, priodasferch

bridegroom n priodfab

bridesmaid n morwyn briodas

bridge n pont ▷ vt pontio

bridle n ffrwyn ▷ vt ffrwyno

brief adj byr

brier, briar n miaren, drysïen

brigade n brigâd, mintai, torf

brigand n ysbeiliwr, carnleidr, herwr

bright adj disglair, claer, gloyw, hoyw

brilliance n disgleirdeb

brilliant adj disglair, llachar ▷ n gem

brim n ymyl, min, cyfor; cantel

brimstone n brwmstan

brindled adj brith, brych

brine n heli

bring vt dwyn, cyrchu, dyfod â, dod â

brink n min, ymyl, glan

brisk adj bywiog, heini, sionc

bristle n gwrychyn, gwrych ▷ vi codi gwrychyn

Britain n Prydain

British adj Prydeinig, Brytanaidd

Briton n Brython, Prydeiniwr

Brittany n Llydaw

brittle adj brau, bregus

broach vt agor baril, gollwng; agor ymddiddan

broad adj llydan; eang; bras

broadband n band llydan, band eang

broaden vb lledu, ehangu

broccoli n brocoli, math o fresych

brochure n llyfryn

brogue n llediaith (Gwyddelod)

broil vt briwlio

broken adj toredig, briw, drylliedig

broker n brocer, dyn canol

bronchitis n bronceitis

bronze n pres, efydd

brooch n tlws

brood n nythaid; hil, epil ▷ vi deor; synfyfyrio

brook n nant, cornant, afonig

broom n banadl; ysgub, ysgubell

broth n potes, cawl

brothel n puteindy

brother n brawd

brother-in-law n brawd yng nghyfraith

brotherly adj brawdol; **brotherly love** brawdgarwch
brow n ael, talcen; crib
brown adj brown, llwyd, gwinau
brown paper n papur llwyd
brown sugar n siwgr coch
browse vi brigbori, pori, blewynna
bruise vb cleisio, ysigo ▷ n clais
brunette n gwineuferch
brunt n pwys a gwres, ergyd
brush n brws ▷ vt brwsio, ysgubo
brushwood n manwydd, prysgwydd
brusque adj cwta, anfoesgar, taeog
Brussels sprouts npl ysgewyll Brwsel
brutal adj creulon, bwysfilaidd
brute n anifail, creadur (direswm)
bubble n bwrlwm ▷ vb byrlymu
buccaneer n môr-leidr, môr-herwr
buck n bwch; coegyn ▷ vb llamsachu
bucket n bwced, ystwc
buckle n bwcl, gwäeg ▷ vb byclu, gwaegu
bud n blaguryn, eginyn ▷ vb blaguro, egino
budge vb syflyd, chwimio
budget n cwd, coden; cyllideb
buff adj llwydfelyn
buffalo n bual
buffet n cernod ▷ vt cernodio, baeddu
buffoon n digrifwas, croesan, ysgentyn
bug n drewbryf, bwg
bugbear n bwgan, bwbach, bwci
bugle n corn, utgorn
build vt adeiladu ▷ n corffolaeth
builder n adeiladwr
building n adail, adeilad, adeiladaeth
bulb n bwlb
Bulgaria n Bwlgaria

bulge n chwydd ▷ vt chwyddo
bulk n swm, crynswth
bull n tarw
bulldozer n peiriant clirio ffordd, tarw dur
bullet n bwled, bwleden
bulletin n bwletin
bullfight n ymladd teirw
bullfinch n coch y berllan
bullion n aur neu arian clamp, bwliwn
bullock n bustach, eidion, ych
bull's eye n trawiad union
bully n gormeswr, bwli ▷ vt gormesu, erlid
bulrushes npl llafrwyn, hesg
bulwark n gwrthglawdd; canllaw
bumbailiff n bwmbeili
bumble-bee n cacynen
bump vb bwmpio, hergydio ▷ n bwmp, hergwd
bumper adj llawn, helaeth
bumpkin n lleban, llabwst, llelo
bumptious adj hunandybus, rhodresgar
bumpy adj aflonydd, anwadal, garw
bun n bynsen, bynnen, teisen
bunch n swp; cwlwm, pwysi ▷ vb sypio
bundle n bwndel, coflaid ▷ vt bwndelu
bungalow n tŷ unllawr, byngalo
bungle vb bwnglera, ystompio ▷ n bwnglerwaith
bunion n corn ar fys troed
bunker n bwncer
bunkum n lol, ffiloreg, truth
bunting n (defnydd) banerau
buoy n bwi ▷ vt cynnal, cadw rhag suddo
buoyant adj hynawf; calonnog
burden n baich ▷ vt beichio, llwytho
bureau n ysgrifgist; swyddfa

bureaucracy n biwrocratiaeth
burgess, burgher n dinesydd, bwrdais
burglar n bwrgler, lleidr
burglar alarm n larwm lladron
burial n claddedigaeth
burlesque n digrifwawd, gwatwargerdd
burly adj corffol, praff, mawr
burn vb llosgi, ysu ▷ n llosg, llosgiad
burnish vt caboli, llathru, gloywi
burrow n twll cwningen ▷ vb tyllu, tyrchu
bursar n bwrser, swyddog ariannol
bursary n amneriaeth, ysgoloriaeth
burst vb byrstio, ymrwygo, ymddryllio, torri ▷ n rhwyg
bury vt claddu
bus n bws
bush n perth, llwyn; prysgwydd, drysi
bushel n bwysel, mesur wyth galwyn
business n busnes, masnach, gwaith
businessman n gŵr fusnes
business trip n taith fusnes
businesswoman n gwraig fusnes
bus station n gorsaf fysiau, gorsaf bws
bus stop n arhosfan bysiau, arhosfan bws
bust n penddelw; mynwes
bustle vi trafferthu, ffwdanu ▷ n ffwdan
busy adj prysur
busybody n ymyrrwr, dyn busneslyd, trwyn
but conj, prep ond, eithr
butcher n cigydd ▷ vt cigyddio, lladd
butler n trulliad, bwtler
butt n nod, targed; cyff clêr
butt vt cornio, hyrddu, twlcio, hwylio

butt n casgen, baril
butter n ymenyn ▷ vt rhoi ymenyn ar
buttercup n blodyn yr ymenyn
butterfly n glöyn byw, iâr fach yr haf, pili-pala
buttermilk n llaeth enwyn
buttery n bwtri
buttock n ffolen
button n botwm ▷ vt botymu
buttress n ateg, gwanas ▷ vt ategu
buxom adj glandeg, gweddgar, nwyfus
buy vt prynu
buzz vb suo, sisial, mwmian ▷ n su, sŵn gwenyn
by prep gan, wrth, trwy, ger, gerllaw ▷ adv heibio, yn agos ▷ prefix rhag-, is-
bye-law n is-ddeddf
by-election n isetholiad
bygone n yr hyn a fu
bylaw n = **bye-law**
bypass n ffordd osgoi
by-product n isgynnyrch
bystander n un yn sefyll gerllaw
byword n ymadrodd cynefin, cyffredin

C

cab n cab
cabal n clymblaid, cabal ▷ vi clymbleidio
cabaret n cabare
cabbage n bresychen, bresych
cabin n caban ▷ vt cabanu, caethiwo
cabinet n cell, cist; cabinet
cable n rhaff fferf; cebl tanfor
cackle vi clegar
cactus n mwl ysgallen, cactws
cad n taeog, bryntyn, cenau
caddie n gwas golffwr
cadence n goslef, diweddeb
cadet n mab ieuengaf; cadlanc
café n tŷ bwyta, caffe
cage n cawell, caets ▷ vt cau, carcharu
cairn n carn, carnedd, crug
cajole vt twyllo drwy weniaith
cake n teisen, cacen ▷ vb torthi; caglu

calamity n adfyd, trallod, trychineb
calcine vb llosgi'n galch
calculate vb cyfrif, bwrw cyfrif, clandro
calculation n cyfrif
calculator n cyfrifiannell
calendar n calendr, almanac
calf (**calves**) n llo
calf n (of the leg) croth (coes)
calibre n calibr
call vb galw ▷ n galwad, galw; ymweliad
call back vb (telephone) galw yn ôl
call centre n canolfan galwadau
calling n galwedigaeth
callous adj croendew, dideimlad, caled
calm adj tawel ▷ n tawelwch ▷ vb tawelu
calorie n calori, uned gwres
calumny n anair, enllib, athrod, cabl
calve vi bwrw llo
Calvinism n Calfiniaeth
camber n camber
Cambodia n Cambodia
Cambrian adj Cymreig
camel n camel
cameo n cameo
camera n ystafell; teclyn tynnu lluniau, camera
camera phone n ffôn camera
camouflage n cuddliw, dull o ddieithrio ▷ vb dieithrio, cuddio
camp n gwersyll ▷ vi gwersyllu
campaign n ymgyrch, rhyfelgyrch
campbed n gwely plyg
camping n gwersylla; **to go camping** gwersyllu
campsite n maes gwersylla
campus n campws
can n tyn, piser, stên ▷ vb gallu
Canada n Canada

Canadian adj Canadaidd ▷ n Canadiad

canal n camlas; pibell

canary n caneri

Canary Islands npl: **the Canary Islands** yr Ynysoedd Dedwydd

cancel vt dileu, dirymu, diddymu

cancer n cancr; **Cancer** y Cranc

candid adj teg, onest, plaen

candidate n ymgeisydd

candle n cannwyll

candlestick n canhwyllbren

candour n onestrwydd, didwylledd

candy n candi

cane n corsen, cansen ▷ vt curo â chansen

canine adj perthynol i'r ci

canister n tun cadw te, bocs (te)

canker n cancr ▷ vb cancro

cannabis n canabis

canned adj ar gadw mewn can tun

cannibal n canibal

cannon n magnel

canny adj call, cyfrwys, ffel

canoe n ceufad, canŵ

canoeing n canŵa

canon n canon, rheol

can-opener n agorwr tuniau

canopy n gortho, nenlen

cant n ffugsancteiddrwydd, rhagrith ▷ vi rhagrithio

cantankerous adj cwerylgar, cynhennus

cantata n cantata, cantawd

canteen n cantîn

canter vi rhygyngu ▷ n rhygyng

canticle n cantigl, canig, cân, emyn

canto n cân, adran o gân

canton n rhandir, talaith

canvas n cynfas, lliain bras

canvass vb trafod; ymofyn pleidleisiau, canfasio

canyon n ceunant, canion

cap n cap, capan ▷ vt capio

capable adj galluog, cymwys, cyfaddas

capacity n gallu, cymhwyster; cynnwys

cape n penrhyn, pentir, trwyn

cape n mantell, cêp

caper n pranc ▷ vi prancio

capital adj prif, pen ▷ n priflythyren; prifddinas; cyfalaf

capitalism n cyfalafiaeth

capital punishment n y gosb eithaf

capitulate vi ymostwng ar amodau

caprice n mympwy, chwilen

Capricorn n yr Afr

capsize vb dymchwelyd, troi

capsule n capswl

captain n capten

caption n pennawd, teitl

captivate vt swyno, hudo, denu

captive adj caeth ▷ n carcharor

captivity n caethiwed; caethglud

captor n daliwr, deiliad

capture n daliad ▷ vt dal

car n car, cerbyd; **car wash** golchfa geir

caravan n carafán; men

caravan site n maes carafanau

carbine n dryll byr, byrddryll

carbohydrate n carbohydrad

carbohydrates npl carbohydradau

carbon n carbon; **carbon footprint** ôl-troed carbon

car boot sale n sêl cist car

carbuncle n carbwncl

carburettor n carburadur

carcass, carcase n celain, ysgerbwd

card n cerdyn, carden

card vt cribo gwlân

cardiac adj perthynol i'r galon

Cardiff n Caerdydd

cardigan n cardigan

cardinal *adj* prif, arbennig ▷ *n* cardinal

care *n* gofal, pryder ▷ *vi* gofalu, malio

career *n* gyrfa, hynt ▷ *vi* carlamu

careful *adj* gofalus, gwyliadwrus

carefully *adv* yn ofalus

careless *adj* diofal, esgeulus

caress *n* anwes, mwythau ▷ *vt* anwesu

caret *n* gwallnod, diffygnod (^)

caretaker *n* gofalwr

cargo *n* llwyth (llong), cargo

caricature *n* gwawdlun, digriflun

caring *adj* gofalus

carnage *n* galanastra, lladdfa

carnal *adj* cnawdol

carnation *n* blodyn cigliw

carnival *n* carnifal

carnivorous *adj* cigysol, rheibus

carol *n* carol ▷ *vi* caroli, canu

carouse *vi* gloddesta, cyfeddach

carp *vi* pigo beiau, cecru, cadw sŵn

car park *n* maes parcio

carpenter *n* saer coed

carpet *n* carped ▷ *vt* carpedu

carriage *n* cerbyd; cludiad; ymarweddiad

carrier *n* cariwr, cludydd

carrier bag *n* cludfag

carrion *n* burgyn, celain, ysgerbwd

carrot *n* moronen

carry *vb* cario, cludo, cywain

carry on *vi* mynd ymlaen, dal ati

cart *vb* men, trol, cert, cart, car

cartilage *n* madruddyn

carton *n* carton

cartoon *n* digriflun, cartŵn

cartridge *n* cetrisen

carve *vt* cerfio, naddu; torri cig

cascade *n* rhaeadr

case *n* achos, cyflwr; dadl

case *n* cas, gwain; cist wydr

casement *n* ffenestr adeiniog, casment

cash *n* arian parod

cash desk *n* safle talu

cashier *n* ariannwr, trysorydd

cashier *vt* diswyddo

cash point *n* peiriant arian

casing *n* plisgyn; casin

casino *n* casino

cask *n* casgen, baril

casket *n* cistan, prenfol, blwch

casserole *n* llestr coginio a dal bwyd

cassette *n* casét

cassock *n* llaeswisg ddu offeiriad, casog

cast *vb* bwrw, taflu ▷ *n* tafliad; **cast iron** haearn bwrw

caste *n* llwyth; gradd, braint; cast

castigate *vt* cystwyo

casting vote *n* pleidlais y cadeirydd

castle *n* castell ▷ *vi* castellu

castrate *vt* disbaddu

casual *adj* damweiniol, achlysurol

casualty *n* un wedi ei anafu

casuistry *n* achosionaeth

cat *n* cath

cataclysm *n* dilyw, dylif, rhyferthwy

catacomb *n* claddgell, claddogof

catalogue *n* catalog

catapult *n* blif, catapwlt

cataract *n* rhaeadr, sgwd; pilen

catarrh *n* llif annwyd, gormwyth

catastrophe *n* trychineb

catch *vt* dal ▷ *n* bach, clicied; dalfa

catching *adj* heintus

catchment area *n* dalgylch

catechism *n* holwyddoreg, catecism

category *n* trefn, dosbarth

cater *vi* arlwyo, darmerth, darparu

caterpillar *n* lindys

cathartic *n* carthlyn

cathedral *n* eglwys gadeiriol

catholic adj catholig; pabyddol ▷ n catholigydd; pabydd
catkins npl cenawon cyll, cywion gwyddau
cattle npl gwartheg, da
caucus n clymblaid
caudle n sucan
cauldron n crochan, pair, callor
cauliflower n blodfresychen
causality n achosiaeth
cause n achos ▷ vt achosi, peri
causeway n sarn, cawsai
caustic adj ysol, llosg, deifiol
cauterize vt serio
caution n pwyll, gwyliadwriaeth; rhybudd ▷ vt rhybuddio
cautious adj gwyliadwrus
cavalcade n mintai o farchogion
cavalier n marchog, marchfilwr
cavalry n gwŷr meirch
cave n ogof
cavern n ceudwll, ogof
caviar, caviare n grawn pysgod, cafiâr
cavil vi cecru
cavity n ceudod, gwagle
caw vi crawcian
CCTV n abbr teledu cylch cyfyng
CD n abbr CD, cryno-ddisg
CD player n chwaraewr cryno-ddisgiau
cease vb peidio, darfod
cedar n cedrwydden
cede vt rhoi i fyny, gildio, trosglwyddo
ceiling n nen, nenfwd
celebrate vt clodfori; dathlu; gweinyddu
celebrated adj clodfawr, enwog, hyglod
celebrity n bri, enwogrwydd; gŵr o fri
celery n seleri

celestial adj nefol, nefolaidd
celibate adj diwair
cell n cell
cellar n seler
cement n sment ▷ vt smentio; cadarnhau
cemetery n mynwent, claddfa
censer n thuser
censor n beirniad; sensor
censure n cerydd, sen ▷ vt ceryddu
census n cyfrifiad
cent n y ganfed ran o ddoler
centenarian n canmlwyddiad
centenary n canmlwyddiant
centigrade adj canradd, sentigred
centimetre n sentimedr
central adj canol, canolog
central heating n gwres canolog
centre n canol, canolfan, canolbwynt ▷ vb canolbwyntio
centre forward n canolwr blaen
centre threequarter n canolwr
centrifugal adj allgyrchol
centripetal adj mewngyrchol
centurion n canwriad
century n canrif
ceramic adj perthynol i grefft y crochenydd, ceramig
cereal n grawn, ŷd
cerebral adj ymenyddol
ceremony n seremoni, defod
certain adj sicr; neilltuol; rhyw, rhai
certainly adv yn sicr, yn siwr
certainty n sicrwydd
certificate n tystysgrif
certify vt hysbysu, tystio
cesspool n carthbwll
chafe vb rhwbio; llidio ▷ n llid, cythrudd
chaff n us, manus, mân us
chaffer vi edwica, bargeinio, bargenna

chaffinch n pinc, asgell fraith
chagrin n cythrudd, siom
chain n cadwyn ▷ vt cadwyno
chair n cadair ▷ vt cadeirio
chairman n cadeirydd
chalet n bwthyn (haf)
chalice n cwpan cymun, caregl
chalk n sialc ▷ vt sialcio
challenge n her, sialens ▷ vt herio, sialensio
chamber n ystafell, siambr
chamberlain n gwas ystafell, siambrlen
champ vt cnoi, dygnoi
champagne n gwin Champagne
champion n pencampwr; pleidiwr ▷ vt cymryd plaid
championship n pencampwriaeth
chance n damwain, siawns ▷ vt digwydd
chancel n cangell
chancellor n canghellor
chandelier n canhwyllyr
chandler n canhwyllydd, masnachydd
change vb newid, cyfnewid ▷ n newid
changing-room n ystafell newid
channel n sianel, gwely; rhigol
Channel Tunnel n: **the Channel Tunnel** Twnel y Sianel
chant vt corganu ▷ n corgan, salmdon
chaos n tryblith, anhrefn
chap vt agennu, torri (am ddwylo)
chapel n capel
chaplain n caplan
chapter n pennod; cabidwl
char vb golosgi, deifio
character n cymeriad; nod, arwydd
characteristic adj nodweddiadol ▷ n nodwedd
charcoal n marwor, golosg, sercol

charge vb siarsio; cyhuddo; rhuthro; codi; llwytho ▷ n siars; gofal; cyhuddiad; rhuthr; pris; ergyd
charger n march rhyfel, cadfarch
chariot n cerbyd
charity n cariad; cardod, elusen
charity shop n siop elusennol
charlatan n un yn honni gwybodaeth; cwac
charm n swyn, cyfaredd ▷ vt swyno
charming adj cyfareddol, swynol, cwrtais
chart n siart
charter n siarter, breinlen ▷ vt breinio; llogi
charter flight n hediad siartr
charwoman n morwyn wrth y dydd
chary adj gwagelog, gochelgar, gofalus
chase vt ymlid, erlid, hel ▷ n helwriaeth
chasm n hafn, ceunant, agendor
chaste adj diwair, pur, dillyn
chasten vt puro, coethi; ceryddu
chastise vb ceryddu, cosbi, cystwyo
chastity n diweirdeb, purdeb
chat vi sgwrsio, ymgomio ▷ n sgwrs, ymgom
chat room n (internet) stafell sgwrsio
chat show n sioe sgwrsio
chattel n catel
chatter vi trydar, cogor; clebran; rhincian
chatterbox n clebryn, clebren
chatty adj siaradus, parod am sgwrs
chauffeur n gyrrwr
cheap adj rhad, salw
cheat n twyll; twyllwr ▷ vt twyllo
Chechnya n Chechnya
check n rhwystr, atalfa ▷ vt atal, ffrwyno

checkout n (in supermarket) desg dalu
checkup n (medical) archwiliad
cheek n grudd, boch; digywilydd-dra
cheeky adj digywilydd, haerllug, eg(e)r
cheer n calondid, cysur; arlwy ▷ vb llonni, sirioli, sirio
cheerful adj llon, siriol
cheers! excl iechyd da!
cheese n caws
chef n prif gogydd
chemical adj cemegol ▷ n cyffur
chemise n crys merch
chemist n fferyllydd; cemegwr
chemistry n cemeg
cheque n archeb (ar fanc), siec
cheque book n llyfr siec, llyfr main
cheque card n carden siec
chequer vt amryliwio, britho
chequered adj brith, anwadal
cherish vt meithrin, coleddu, mynwesu
cherry n ceiriosen
cherub n ceriwb
chess n gwyddbwyll
chest n cist, coffr; brest
chestnut n castan
chevalier n marchog
chew vb cnoi; **to chew the cud** cnoi cil
chewing gum n gwm cnoi
chick, chicken n cyw (iâr)
chickenpox n brech yr ieir
chickpea n gwygbysen, ffacbysen
chide vt ceryddu, dwrdio
chief adj pen, pennaf, prif ▷ n pennaeth
chieftain n blaenor, pennaeth
chilblain n llosg eira, cibwst, malaith
child (-ren) n plentyn
childhood n plentyndod, mebyd
child minder n gwarchodwr

Chile n Chile
chill n oerni, annwyd ▷ adj oer, anwydog ▷ vb oeri, fferru, rhynnu
chilly adj (weather) oer; (manner) oeraidd
chime n sain cloch neu gloc ▷ vb canu (clychau)
chimera n anghenfil; bwgan, bwbach
chimney n corn mwg, simnai
chin n gên
China n China, Tseina
china n llestri te (tsieni)
Chinese adj Tsieineaidd ▷ n Tsieinead
chink n agen, hollt
chip vb hacio, naddu ▷ n asglodyn, pric
chips npl sglodion
chiropodist n troedfeddyg
chirp vi yswtitian, grillian, trydar
chisel n cŷn, gaing
chit n nodyn byr
chivalry n urddas marchog; sifalri
chives n cennin sifi
chocolate n siocl ed
choice n dewis, dewisiad ▷ adj dewisol, dethol
choir n côr; cafell
choke vb tagu; mygu; topio, cau
choler n geri, bustl; dicter, llid
cholera n y geri marwol, colera
choose vb dewis, dethol, ethol
chop vt torri ▷ n golwyth
choral adj corawl
chord n tant; cord
chore n y dwt
chorus n côr, cytgan, byrdwn, corws
Christ n Crist
christen vt bedyddio, enwi
Christendom n (gwledydd) Cred
Christian adj Cristnogol ▷ n Cristion
Christianity n Cristnogaeth
Christian name n enw bedydd

Christmas n Nadolig
Christmas Eve n Noswyl Nadolig
Christmassy adj Nadoligaidd
chrome n crôm
chronic adj parhaol (am anhwyldeb)
chronicle n cronicl ▷ vt croniclo
chronology n amseryddiaeth
chrysanthemum n ffarwel haf
chubby adj wynepgrwn, tew
chuck vt taro dan yr ên; taflu, lluchio
chuckle vi chwerthin yn nwrn dyn
chum n cyfaill mebyd ▷ vi cyfrinachu
chunk n tafell dew, toc
church n eglwys, llan ▷ vt eglwysa
churchyard n mynwent
churl n taeog, costog, cerlyn
churlish adj afrywiog, taeogaidd
churn n buddai ▷ vb corddi
chutney n picl cymysg
cider n seidr
cigar n sigâr
cigarette n sigarét
cincture n gwregys, rhwymyn
cinder n marworyn, colsyn
cine-camera n camera sine
cinema n sinema
cinnamon n sinamon
cipher n gwagnod (O); ysgrifen ddirgel ▷ vi cyfrif
circle n cylch ▷ vb cylchu
circuit n cylch; cylchdaith
circular adj crwn ▷ n cylchlythyr
circulate vb cylchredeg, lledaenu
circum- prefix cylch-, am-
circumcise vt enwaedu
circumference n cylchyn; cylchedd
circumflex n acen grom, to (^)
circumlocution n cylchymadrodd
circumscribe vt cyfyngu
circumspect adj gwyliadwrus, gofalus
circumstance n amgylchiad
circumstantial adj amgylchus

circumvent vb twyllo
circus n syrcas
cistern n dyfrgist, pydew, sistern
citadel n castell, amddiffynfa, caer
cite vt gwysio; dyfynnu
citizen n dinesydd
city n dinas
city centre n canol y ddinas
city technology college n coleg technoleg dinasol
civic adj dinesig
civil adj gwladol; moesgar
civilian n dinesydd (anfilwrol)
civilization n gwareiddiad
civilize vt gwareiddio
civil service n gwasanaeth sifil, gwasanaeth gwladol
civil war n rhyfel cartref
clack vi clecian, clepian, clegar
claim vt hawlio ▷ n hawl
clamber vi dringo, cribo
clammy adj gludiog, cleiog, toeslyd
clamour n gwaedd, dadwrdd ▷ vi crochlefain
clamp n ystyffwl, craff
clan n tylwyth, llwyth
clandestine adj lladradaidd
clang, clank vb cloncio ▷ n clonc
clap n twrf, trwst ▷ vb curo; taro; clepian
claret n claret
clarify vt gloywi, puro; egluro
clarinet n clarinet
clarion n utgorn
clash vb taro, gwrthdaro ▷ n gwrthdrawiad
clasp n gwâeg, bach, clesbyn ▷ vt gwaegu; cofleidio
class n dosbarth ▷ vt dosbarthu
classic n clasur, campwaith, llên goeth ▷ adj clasurol
classical adj clasurol
classics npl clasuron

classify vb dosbarthu
classroom n ystafell ddosbarth
classroom assistant n cynorthwy-ydd dosbarth
clatter vb clewtian, clepian, trystio ▷ n trwst
clause n adran, cymal
claw n crafanc, ewin ▷ vt crafangu, cripio
clay n clai
clean adj glân, glanwaith ▷ vt glanhau
cleaner n glanhawr, glanheydd
cleaning n glanhad, glanheuad
cleanly adv yn lân
cleanse vt glanhau
cleanser n glanhawr
clear adj clir, eglur, gloyw; croyw ▷ vt clirio
cleave vi glynu (wrth)
cleave vt hollti; fforchogi
clef n allwedd, cleff
cleft n hollt, agen
clement adj tyner, tirion, trugarog
clench vt cau yn dynn, clensio
clergy n offeiriaid
clergyman n clerigwr, offeiriad
clerical adj clerigol; perthynol i glerc
clerk n clerc
clever adj medrus, deheuig, clyfar
cleverness n medr, deheurwydd, clyfrwch
click vi clician, clepian ▷ n clic
client n cyflogydd cyfreithiwr, cwsmer
cliff n clogwyn, allt
climate n hinsawdd
climate change n newid hinsawdd
climax n uchafbwynt
climb vb dringo
climbing adj dringol
clinch vt clensio; cau, cloi
cling vi glynu, cydio
clinic n meddygfa, clinig

clinical adj clinigol
clink vi tincian
clip vt cneifio, tocio, clipio
clique n clic, clymblaid
cloak n mantell, clogyn, clog ▷ vt cuddio, celu
cloakroom n ystafell ddillad
clock n cloc
clod n tywarchen
clog n clocsen ▷ vt llesteirio; tagu; clocsio
cloister n clwysty
close vb cau; terfynu ▷ n diwedd, diweddglo
close adj agos, clòs; caeth, tyn
close n clas, clos, buarth, clwt, cae
closed adj ar gau
closed shop n gwaith cyfyngedig, gwaith i rai yn unig
closet n cell, ystafell; geudy
close-up n llun agos
closure n cau, gorffen, darfod
clot n tolchen ▷ vb tolchi, ceulo
cloth n brethyn, lliain
clothe vt dilladu, gwisgo
clothes npl dillad, gwisgoedd
clothes peg n bachyn dillad
clothier n brethynnwr, dilledydd
clothing n dillad
cloud n cwmwl ▷ vt cymylu
cloudy adj cymylog
clout n cernod, clewt; clwt ▷ vt clewtian; clytio
clover n meillion, clofer
clown n lleban; croesan, clown
club n pastwn; clwb ▷ vb pastynu; clybio
clue n pen llinyn, arwydd
clump n clwmp, clamp, cyff
clumsy adj trwsgl, anfedrus, lletchwith
cluster n clwstwr, swp ▷ vb casglu, tyrru

clutch n crafanc; gafael; hafflau
  ▷ vb crafangu
clutter n dadwrdd, helynt
co- prefix cyd-
coach n cerbyd; hyfforddwr ▷ vb
  hyfforddi
coagulate vb ceulo
coal n glöyn, glo
coalesce vi cyfuno, cyd-doddi
coalition n cyfuniad; cynghrair,
  clymblaid
coarse adj garw, aflednais; bras
coast n arfordir, glan ▷ vi hwylio
  gyda'r lan
coastal adj arfordirol
coastguard n gwyliwr y glannau
coastline n morlin
coat n cot
coat hanger n cambren (dillad)
coating n caen, golchiad
coat of arms n arfbais
coax vb hudo, denu, perswadio
cobble, cobblestone n carreg
  balmant
cobbler n crydd, cobler
cobweb n gwe pryf cop, gwe'r cor
cock n ceiliog; mwdwl; cliciad (dryll)
  ▷ vb mydylu; codi cliciad
cockerel n cyw ceiliog, ceiliogyn
cock-eyed adj â llygad tro
cockles npl cocos, cocs, rhython
cockpit n sedd peilot; ymladdfan
  ceiliogod
cockroach n chwilen ddu
cock-sure adj gorbendant,
  gorhyderus
cocktail n coctêl
cocoa n coco
coconut n cneuen goco, coconyt
cod n y penfras; cod
code n côd
coerce vb gorfodi, gorthrechu
coercion n gorfodaeth, gorthrech

coffee n coffi
coffin n arch, ysgrîn
cog n dant olwyn, còg
cogent adj cryf, grymus,
  argyhoeddiadol
cohabit vi cyd-fyw
cohere vb cydlynu
cohesion n cydlyniad
coil vb torchi ▷ n torch
coin n arian bath ▷ vb bathu
coincide vi cyd-ddigwydd, cyd-daro
coincidence n cyd-ddigwyddiad
coke n golosg
colander n hidl
cold adj oer ▷ n oerfel, oerni,
  annwyd; **to catch a cold** dal
  annwyd
colic n bolwst, colig
collapse vb disgyn, cwympo ▷ n
  cwymp, methiant
collapsible adj plygadwy
collar n coler ▷ vb coleru; **collar
  bone** pont yr ysgwydd
collateral adj cyfochrog, cyfystlys
colleague n cydweithiwr
collect n colect ▷ vb crynhoi, hel,
  ymgynnull, casglu
collection n casgliad
collector n casglwr
college n coleg
collide vb gwrthdaro
collie n ci defaid
collier n glöwr; llong lo
colliery n gwaith glo, pwll glo,
  glofa
collision n gwrthdrawiad
colloquial adj llafar, tafodieithol
colon n gorwahannod, colon (:);
  coluddyn mawr
colonel n cyrnol
colonial adj trefedigaethol
colony n trefedigaeth, gwladfa
colossal adj cawraidd, anferth

colour n lliw, baner ▷ vb lliwio;
cochi; **colour bar** gwahanfur lliw;
colour blind lliwddall
coloured adj lliw
colourful adj lliwgar
colouring n lliwiad
colourless adj di-liw
colt n ebol
column n colofn
columnist n newyddiadurwr,
colofnydd
coma n hunglwyf, côma
comb n crib ▷ vb cribo
combat n brwydr, gornest ▷ vb
brwydro
combination n cyfuniad
combine vb cyfuno; **combine
harvester** cynaeafydd, combein
come vi dod, dyfod; **to come to light**
dod i'r golwg; **to come to an end**
dod i ben; **to come to pass** digwydd
come across vt dod ar draws
come back vi dychwelyd, dod yn ôl
come by vt meddiannu
come in vi dod i mewn
comedian n comedïwr
comedy n comedi
comfort n cysur, diddanwch ▷ vt
cysuro, diddanu
comfortable adj cysurus, cyffyrddus
comfortably adv yn gysurus, yn
gyffyrddus
comic adj comic, digrif, ysmala
comma n rhagwahannod, atalnod,
coma
command vb gorchymyn ▷ n
gorchymyn, awdurdod
commandeer vb meddiannu
commander n cadlywydd,
comander
commandment n gorchymyn
commando n mintai (o filwyr), un
o'r fintai

commemorate vt coffáu, dathlu
commence vb dechrau
commend vt cymeradwyo, canmol
commensurate adj cymesur
comment vi sylwi, esbonio ▷ n sylw
commentary n sylwebaeth
commentator n esboniwr,
sylwebydd
commerce n masnach
commercial adj masnachol
commiserate vt cydymdeimlo â,
cyd-dosturio â
commission n comisiwn,
dirprwyaeth ▷ vb comisiynu
commissionaire n porthor
commissioner n comisiynydd
commit vt cyflawni; traddodi;
cyflwyno
commitment n ymrwymiad;
traddodiad
committee n pwyllgor
commodity n nwydd (masnachol)
common adj cyffredin ▷ n tir
cyffredin, cytir, comin; **the Common
Market** y Farchnad Gyffredin
commoner n cominwr, gwerinwr
commonplace adj dibwys,
cyffredin
commons npl y cyffredin; **House of
Commons** Tŷ'r Cyffredin
common sense n synnwyr cyffredin
commonwealth n cymanwlad
commotion n cyffro, terfysg
communal adj cymunol, cymunedol
commune vi ymddiddan; cymuno
▷ n cymundod; comun
communicate vb cyfathrebu;
cymuno
communication n cyfathrebiad,
cysylltiad, neges
communion n cymun, cymundeb
communism n comiwnyddiaeth
communist n comiwnydd

community n cymdeithas,
cymuned; **community centre**
canolfan gymuned
commute vt cymudo, pendilio
commuter n cymudwr, pendiliwr
compact n cytundeb, cyfamod; bag
bach, compact ▷ adj cryno ▷ vt
crynhoi
compact disc n cryno-ddisg, CD
companion n cydymaith
companionship n cwmnïaeth,
cyfeillach
company n cymdeithas, cwmni; **to
keep company with** cadw cwmni â
comparative adj cymharol
comparatively adv yn gymharol
compare vt cymharu, cyffelybu
comparison n cymhariaeth
compartment n adran, cerbydan
compass n cwmpawd; cwmpas ▷ vt
amgylchu
compassion n tosturi
compatible adj cydweddol, cyson
compatriot n cydwladwr
compel vt cymell, gorfodi
compendium n crynodeb, talfyriad
compensate vt talu iawn, digolledu
compensation n iawndal
compete vi cystadlu
competence n cymhwysedd
competent adj cymwys, digonol
competition n cystadleuaeth
competitive adj cystadleuol
competitor n cystadleuydd
complacency n ymfoddhad
complacent adj hunan-foddhaus,
digonol
complain vi cwyno, achwyn,
grwgnach
complaint n cwyn, achwyniad;
anhwyldeb
complement n cyflawnder,
cyflenwad

complementary adj cyflenwol
complete adj cyflawn ▷ vt cyflawni
completely adv yn llwyr
completion n cwblhad
complex adj cymhleth, dyrys
complexion n gwedd, pryd, gwawr
compliance n cydsyniad
complicate vt cymhlethu; drysu
complicated adj cymhleth, dyrys
complication n cymhlethdod
compliment n cyfarchiad;
canmoliaeth
comply vi cydsynio, ufuddhau
component n cydran, cyfansoddyn
compose vt cyfansoddi; cysodi;
tawelu
composed adj hunanfeddiannol
composer n cyfansoddwr
composition n cyfansoddiad,
traethawd
composure n tawelwch,
hunan-feddiant
compound adj cyfansawdd ▷ n
cymysg ▷ vb cymysgu
comprehend vt amgyffred, dirnad
comprehension n amgyffred,
dirnadaeth
comprehensive adj cynhwysfawr;
comprehensive school Ysgol Gyfun
compress vt gwasgu, crynhoi ▷ n
plastr
comprise vt amgyffred, cynnwys
compromise n cymrodedd,
cyfaddawd ▷ vb cymrodeddu,
cyfaddawdu
compulsion n gorfodaeth
compulsive adj trwy orfod, o anfodd
compulsory adj gorfodol
computer n cyfrifiadur
computer game n gêm cyfrifiadur
computer operator n cyfrifiadurwr
computer programmer n
rhaglennydd cyfrifiaduron

computer science n cyfrifanneg, cyfrifiadureg
computer studies npl astudiaethau cyfrifiadurol
computing n cyfrifiaduro
comrade n cydymaith
concave adj ceugrwm
conceal vb cuddio, celu, dirgelu
concede vt caniatáu, addef
conceit n tyb, mympwy; hunandyb, hunanoldeb, cysêt
conceited adj hunandybus, hunanol, balch
conceive vb dirnad; tybied, synied; beichiogi
concentrate vt crynodi, canolbwyntio
concentration n crynodiad, ymroddiad
concept n cysyniad
conception n syniad; beichiogiad
concern vt perthyn, ymwneud (â), gofalu (am), pryderu, bod a wnelo â
▷ n busnes, diddordeb; gofal, pryder
concerned adj yn teimlo pryder, pryderus, gofalus, yn ymboeni
concerning prep ynglŷn â, ynghylch
concert n cyngerdd ▷ vt cyd-drefnu
concerted adj cydunol, wedi ei gyd-drefnu
concertina n consertina
conclude vb diweddu; casglu, barnu
conclusion n diwedd; casgliad
conclusive adj terfynol
concoct vt llunio, dyfeisio
concoction n cymysgedd
concourse n tyrfa, torf
concrete adj diriaethol ▷ n concrit
concur vi cydredeg; cydgroesi; cytuno
concurrently adv yn gyfredol
concussion n cyd-drawiad, ysgytiad
condemn vb condemnio, collfarnu

condensation n cywasgiad, cyddwysedd
condense vb cywasgu, cyddwyso, cwtogi
condensed adj cyddwys
condition n cyflwr, ansawdd; amod ▷ vb cyflyru; amodi
conditional adj amodol
conditionally adv ar amod
conditioner n cyflyrydd
condole vt cydofidio, cydymdeimlo
condolence n cydymdeimlad
condom n condom
condominium n cydlywodraeth, condominiwm
condone vt maddau, esgusodi, cymeradwyo
conduce vi arwain, tueddu
conducive adj tueddol i, â thuedd i
conduct n ymddygiad, ymarweddiad, tywys
conduct vt arwain
conductor n arweinydd; tocynnwr
cone n pigwrn, côn
confection n cyffaith
confectioner n cyffeithiwr
confer vb ymgynghori, cyflwyno
conference n cynhadledd
confess vb cyffesu, cyfaddef
confession n cyffesiad, cyffes
confetti n conffeti
confide vb ymddiried
confidence n ymddiried, hyder; **self-confidence** hunanhyder
confident adj hyderus
confidential adj cyfrinachol
confine vt cyfyngu, carcharu, caethiwo
confined adj caeth, cyfyng
confinement n caethiwed, adeg geni
confirm vt cadarnhau; conffirmio
confirmation n cadarnhad; bedydd esgob, conffirmasiwn

confirmed adj cyson, arferol, gwastadol, wedi ei gadarnhau
confiscate vt atafaelu
conflict n gwrthdrawiad, ymryson
conflict vi anghytuno, gwrthdaro
conflicting adj anghyson
conform vb cydymffurfio; cydffurfio
confound vt cymysgu, drysu
confront vt wynebu
confrontation n gwrthdaro
confuse vt cymysgu, drysu
confused adj cymysg; didrefn; dyrys; tywyll
confusion n anhrefn
confute vt gwrthbrofi, dymchwelyd
congeal vb rhewi, fferru, tewychu, ceulo
congenial adj cydnaws, hynaws
congest vb cronni, gorlanw
congested adj gorlawn
congestion n gorlenwad, tagfa, crynhoad
congratulate vt llongyfarch
congratulations n llongyfarchiadau
congregate vb ymgynnull
congregation n cynulleidfa
congress n cyngres, cymanfa
conjunction n cysylltiad
conjunctivitis n llid yr amrant
conjure vb consurio
conjurer n consurwr
connect vb cysylltu, cydio
connected adj cysylltiedig, cysylltiol
connection n cysylltiad, perthynas; **in connection with** ynglŷn â
connive vi goddef, cau llygaid rhag
conquer vt gorchfygu, trechu
conqueror n gorchfygwr, concwerwr
conquest n buddugoliaeth, concwest
conscience n cydwybod
conscientious adj cydwybodol

conscious adj ymwybodol
consciousness n ymwybyddiaeth
conscript n gorfodog, gŵr rhif ▷ vb gorfodi
conscription n gorfodaeth filwrol
consecrate vt cysegru
consecutive adj olynol
consent vi cydsynio ▷ n cydsyniad, caniatâd
consequence n canlyniad
consequently adv o ganlyniad
conservation n cadwraeth, gwarchodaeth
conservative adj ceidwadol ▷ n ceidwadwr
conservatory n tŷ gwydr
conserve vt cadw, diogelu, amddiffyn
consider vb ystyried
considerable adj cryn
considerate adj ystyriol, tosturiol
consideration n ystyriaeth
considering prep ag ystyried
consign vt traddodi, trosglwyddo
consist vt cynnwys
consistency n cysondeb
consistent n cyson
consolation n cysur, diddanwch
console vt cysuro, diddanu
consonant adj cysain; cyson ▷ n cytsain
conspicuous adj amlwg
conspiracy n bradwriaeth, brad, cynllwyn
conspire vb bradfwriadu, cynllwynio
constable n cwnstabl, heddgeidwad
constant adj cyson
constantly adv yn gyson
constipate vt rhwymo
constipated adj rhwym
constipation n rhwymedd
constituency n etholaeth

constituent *adj* cyfansoddol ▷ *n* etholwr; cyfansoddyn
constitution *n* cyfansoddiad
constitutional *adj* cyfansoddiadol
constraint *n* cyfyngydd, cyfyngiad
construct *vt* ffurfio, llunio, adeiladu, saernïo
construction *n* adeiladwaith, lluniad; cystrawen
constructive *adj* ymarferol, adeiladol
construe *vt* cyfieithu; dehongli
consul *n* ynad, conswl; consul
consulate *n* consuliaeth
consult *vb* ymgynghori
consultant *n* ymgynghorwr
consume *vb* treulio, difa, ysu; nychu
consumer *n* prynwr, treuliwr, defnyddiwr
consummate *adj* perffaith, cyflawn
consummate *vt* perffeithio, cyflawni
consumption *n* traul; darfodedigaeth
contact *n* cyffyrddiad, cyswllt
contact lenses *npl* lensys cyffwrdd
contagious *adj* heintus
contain *vt* cynnwys, dal
container *n* cynhwysydd
contaminate *vt* halogi, llygru, heintio
contemplate *vb* ystyried, myfyrio; bwriadu
contemporary *adj* cyfoes(ol) ▷ *n* cyfoeswr
contempt *n* dirmyg, diystyrwch; **contempt of court** dirmyg llys
contemptuous *adj* dirmygus
contend *vb* ymryson, cystadlu
contender *n* cystadleuydd
content *adj* bodlon ▷ *vt* bodloni
content *n* cynnwys

contented *adj* bodlon
contention *n* cynnen, ymryson
contentment *n* bodlonrwydd
contents *npl* cynnwys, cynhwysiad
contest *n* cystadleuaeth, ymryson
contest *vb* amau, ymryson, ymladd
contestant *n* cystadleuydd
context *n* cyd-destun
continent *adj* cymedrol; diwair
continent *n* cyfandir
continental *adj* cyfandirol
contingency *n* damwain, digwyddiad
continual *adj* parhaus, gwastadol
continuation *n* parhad
continue *vb* parhau, para, dal (i)
continuous *adj* parhaol, di-fwlch, di-dor
continuous assessment *n* asesiad parhaus, asesu parhaus
contort *vt* gwyrdroi, dirdynnu
contour *n* amlinell, cyfuchlinedd
contra- *prefix* gwrth-, croes-
contraband *adj, n* (nwyddau) gwaharddedig
contraceptive *n* cyfarpar gwrth-genhedlu
contract *n* cytundeb, cyfamod
contract *vb* byrhau; cytuno, cyfamodi
contraction *n* talfyriad, cywasgiad
contractor *n* contractwr, adeiladydd
contradict *vt* gwrth-ddweud
contraption *n* dyfais
contrary *adj* gwrthwyneb, croes; **on the contrary** i'r gwrthwyneb
contrast *n* gwrthgyferbyniad ▷ *vb* gwrthgyferbynnu
contribute *vb* cyfrannu
contribution *n* cyfraniad
contributor *n* cyfrannwr
contrive *vb* dyfeisio, llwyddo, trefnu

control vt llywodraethu, rheoli ▷ n rheolaeth, awdurdod; **self control** hunan-reolaeth

controversial adj dadleuol

controversy n dadl

convalesce vi ymadfer, gwella

convene vt galw, gwysio, cynnull

convenience n cyfleustra, hwylustod

convenient adj cyfleus, gweddus, hwylus

convent n cwfaint, lleiandy

convention n confensiwn, cynhadledd

conventional adj confensiynol

conversant adj cyfarwydd, cynefin

conversation n ymddiddan, sgwrs

converse vi ymddiddan, ymgomio

converse adj, n gwrthwyneb, cyferbyniol

conversion n tröedigaeth, tro

convert vt troi, newid, trosi; **converted try** trosgais

convertible adj trosadwy

convex adj crwm

convey vt cludo; trosi, trosglwyddo; cyfleu

conveyor belt n cludfelt

convict vt barnu'n euog, euogfarnu; argyhoeddi

convict n troseddwr

conviction n euogfarn; argyhoeddiad

convince vt argyhoeddi

convincing adj argyhoeddiadol

convulse vt dirgrynu, dirdynnu

cook n cogydd, cogyddes ▷ vb coginio, gwneud bwyd

cooker n cwcer; **pressure cooker** gwascogydd, sosban wyllt

cookery n coginiaeth

cooking n coginiaeth

cool adj oeri, oeraidd; hunanfeddiannol ▷ vb oeri, claearu

coop n cawell, cut ieir ▷ vt cutio

co-operate vi cydweithio, cydweithredu

co-operation n cydweithrediad

co-operative n cydweithfa ▷ adj cydweithredol

co-opt vt cyfethol

co-ordinate n cyfesuryn ▷ vb cyfesur, cyd-drefnu

cop n plismon ▷ vt dal

cope n copa, crib

cope vi ymdaro â, ymdopi â

copious adj helaeth, dibrin

copper n copr, copor

copse n prysgwydd, prysglwyn

copy n copi ▷ vt copïo

copyright n hawlfraint

coracle n cwrwgl

coral n cwrel

cord n cortyn, rheffyn, tennyn ▷ vt rheffynnu

cordial adj o galon, calonnog ▷ n cordial, gwirod

cordon n rhes, cadwyn

corduroy n melfaréd, rib

core n calon, perfedd, craidd

cork n corc, corcyn ▷ vt corcio

corkscrew n corcsgriw

cormorant n mulfran, bilidowcar

corn n ŷd, llafur

corn n corn (ar droed)

corned beef n corn-bîff

corner n congl, cornel, cil ▷ vt cornelu; **corner kick** cic gornel

cornet n corned

cornflakes npl creision ŷd

cornflour n blawd corn

coronation n coroniad

coroner n crwner

coronet n coronig

corporal adj corfforol

corporate adj yn un corff, corfforedig

corporation n corfforaeth; cest
corporeal adj corfforol; materol
corps n corfflu
corpse n corff (marw), celain
corpuscle n corffilyn
correct adj cywir ▷ vt cywiro, ceryddu
correction n cywiriad; cerydd
correspond vi cyfateb; gohebu
correspondence n cyfatebiaeth; gohebiaeth
correspondent n gohebydd
corridor n coridor
corrode vb cyrydu, ysu, rhydu, treulio
corrugated adj rhychiog, gwrymiog
corrupt adj llygredig, pwdr ▷ vb llygru
corruption n llygredigaeth
corset n staes
cosmetic n cosmetig
cost vi costio ▷ n cost, traul
costly adj drudfawr, drud, prid
costume n gwisg, costiwm
cosy adj cysurus, clyd
cot n gwely bychan, cot
cottage n bwthyn
cotton n cotwm; edau; **cotton wool** gwlân cotwm
couch n glwth, soffa ▷ vb gorwedd
cough n peswch ▷ vb pesychu
council n cyngor; **council house** tŷ cyngor
councillor n cynghorwr
counsel n cyngor ▷ vt cynghori
counsellor n cynghorwr, cyfarwyddwr
count n cyfrif ▷ vb rhifo, cyfrif; **count the cost** bwrw'r draul
count n iarll
countenance n wynepryd; cefnogaeth ▷ vt cefnogi
counter n cownter

counter- prefix gwrth- ▷ adj croes ▷ adv yn erbyn, yn groes
counteract vt gwrthweithio
counterfeit n ffug, twyll ▷ adj gau, ffug ▷ vt ffugio
counterfoil n gwrthddalen
countermand vt gwrthorchymyn
counterpane n cwrlid, cwilt gwely
counterpart n rhan gyfatebol, cymar
countess n iarlles
countless adj aneirif, di-rif
country n gwlad, bro ▷ adj gwladaidd, gwledig; **country music** canu gwlad
countryman n gwladwr
countryside n cefn gwlad
county n sir, swydd
coup n ergyd, trawiad, dymchweliad, llwyddiannus
couple n cwpl ▷ vt cyplu, cyplysu
couplet n cwpled
coupon n cwpon
courage n gwroldeb, dewrder
courier n cennad; tywyswr
course n cwrs, hynt ▷ vt hela, ymlid; **of course** wrth gwrs; **in the course of** yn ystod; **in due course** yn ei bryd; **crash course** cwrs carlam
court n llys, cwrt; cyntedd ▷ vt caru
courteous adj cwrtais
courtesy n cwrteisrwydd, cwrteisi
courtier n gŵr llys, llyswr
courtly adj llysaidd, boneddigaidd
court-martial n cwrt-marsial ▷ vb dodi ar brawf
courtship n carwriaeth
courtyard n buarth, cwrt, clos, iard
cousin n cefnder; cyfnither
cove n cil, cilfach
covenant n cyfamod ▷ vb cyfamodi
cover vt gorchuddio, toi; amddiffyn ▷ n gorchudd, clawr; **book cover**

clawr llyfr; **to take cover** cuddio, cysgodi

cover charge n tâl am wasanaeth

covert adj cêl, cudd, dirgel

covert n lloches; prysglwyn

covet vt chwennych, chwenychu

cow n buwch; **barren cow** myswynog; **milking cow** buwch odro; **cow in calf** buwch gyflo

coward n llwfrddyn, llwfryn, llwfrgi

cowardice n llwfrdra

cowardly adj llwfr

cowboy n cowboi

cower vi swatio, cyrcydu

cowl n cwcwll, cwfl

cowpox n brech y fuwch

cowslip n briallu Mair

coxswain n llywydd cwch, cocs

coy adj swil, gwylaidd

crab n cranc

crab apple n afal sur, afal crabas

crack vb cracio, hollti ▷ n crac

cracker n cracer; bisgeden

crackle vi clindarddach

cradle n crud, cawell; cadair fagu

craft n crefft; cyfrwystra, dichell; llong, bad

craftsman n crefftwr

craftsmanship n crefftwriaeth

crafty adj cyfrwys, dichellgar

crag n craig, clegr, clogwyn

cram vb gorlenwi, stwffio, saco

cramp n cwlwm gwythi, cramp; creffyn ▷ vt caethiwo, gwasgu

cramped adj clòs

cranberries npl llugaeron

crane n garan, crëyr, crychydd, craen ▷ vt estyn (gwddf)

cranium (-ia) n penglog

crank n cranc; mympwywr ▷ vi cam-droi; troi

crankshaft n camwerthyd, cranciafft

cranny n agen, hollt, agennig

crape n crêp

crash vb gwrthdaro, cwympo ▷ n gwrthdrawiad, cwymp

crash helmet n helmed ddiogelwch

crate n cawell

crater n safn llosgfynydd; ceudod, cawg

cravat n cadach gwddf, crafat

crave vb crefu, deisyf, chwennych, dyheu

craving n blys, chwant

crawl vi ymlusgo, cropian; crafu

crayon n creon

craze n ysfa

crazy adj penwan, gorffwyll, o'i gof

creak vi gwichian

cream n hufen

creamery n hufenfa

creamy adj hufennog

crease n ôl plygiad, plyg ▷ vt crychu

create vt creu

creation n cread, creadigaeth

creative adj creadigol

creator n crëwr, creawdwr

creature n creadur

crêche n meithrinfa

credence n cred, coel, ffydd

credentials npl credlythyrau

credible adj credadwy, hygoel, hygred

credit n coel, cred; clod, credyd ▷ vt coelio

credit card n cerdyn credyd

creditor n credydwr

credulous adj hygoelus

creed n credo

creek n cilfach

creep vi ymlusgo, cropian

creeper n dringiedydd

creepy adj iasol

cremate vt amlosgi

crematorium n amlosgfa

crêpe n crêp
crescent n hanner lleuad; cilgant
  ▷ adj cynyddol
cress n berwr
crest n crib; mwng; arwydd ar arfbais
Crete n Creta
crevice n agen, hollt, rhigol
crew n criw, gwerin llong; haid
crib n preseb; caban; gwely plentyn
  ▷ vt copïo
cricket n criced; cricsyn
crime n trosedd
criminal adj troseddol ▷ n
  troseddwr
crimson adj, n rhuddgoch
cringe vi cynffonna, ymgreinio
crinkle vb crychu ▷ n crych, plyg
cripple n cloff, efrydd ▷ vt cloffi,
  efryddu
crisis (**crises**) n argyfwng
crisp adj cras, crych
crisps npl creision tatws
criterion (**-ia**) n maen prawf, safon
critic n beirniad
critical adj beirniadol; pryderus;
  peryglus
criticism n beirniadaeth
criticize vt beirniadu
croak vi crawcian ▷ n crawc
Croatia n Croatia
crochet vb crosio ▷ n crosiet, gwaith
  crosio
crockery n llestri
crocodile n crocodil
crocus n saffrwn, crocus
croft n tyddyn, crofft
crony n cyfaill agos, cydymaith
crook n crwca, bagl, ffon fugail;
  troseddwr
crooked adj crwca, cam
crop n cnwd, cynnyrch; crombil ▷ vt
  tocio, torri
cross n, adj croes ▷ vb croesi

cross-cut vb trawsdorri
cross-examine vb croesholi
crossing n croesfan
cross-road n croesffordd
cross-section n trawsdoriad
crosswise adv ar groes
crossword n croesair
crotchet n crosied
crouch vi cyrcydu ▷ n cwrcwd
crow n brân
crow vi canu fel ceiliog; ymffrostio
crow-bar n trosol, bar haearn
crowd n torf, tyrfa ▷ vb tyrru, heidio
crowded adj llawn o bobl
crown n coron; corun ▷ vt coroni
crucial adj hanfodol, terfynol
crucifix n croeslun
crucifixion n croeshoeliad
crucify vt croeshoelio
crude adj cri, crai; llymrig, amrwd
cruel adj creulon
cruelty n creulondeb
cruet n criwed
cruise vi morio ▷ n mordaith
cruiser n gwiblong
crumb n briwsionyn
crumble vb briwsioni, malurio ▷ n
  briwsiongrwst
crumbly adj briwsionllyd
crumpet n crymped; lefren
crumple vb crychu, gwasgu
crunch vb creinsio
crupper n pedrain, crwper, pen ôl
crusade n rhyfel y groes, croesgad
crush vb gwasgu, llethu ▷ n
  gwasgiad, torf
crust n crawen, crofen, crystyn
crutch n bagl, ffon fagl
crux n craidd
cry vb llefain, wylo, crio ▷ n llef,
  sgrech, cri
cryptic adj dirgel, cyfrin
crystal n grisial ▷ adj grisialaidd

crystallisation n crisialiad
cub n cenau
cube n ciwb ▷ vb ciwbio
cubic adj ciwbig; **cubic root** gwreiddyn ciwb
cubicle n cuddygl
cuckoo n cog, cwcw; gwirionyn
cucumber n cucumer
cud n cil
cuddle vb anwylo, anwesu, tolach
cue n awgrym; ciw
cuff n torch llawes
cuff vt cernodio ▷ n cernod, dyrnod
cul-de-sac n pen ffordd, heol hosan
cull vt dewis, pigo
culminate vi cyrraedd ei anterth, diweddu
culmination n anterth
culpable adj beius, camweddus
culprit n troseddwr, drwgweithredwr
cult n addoliad, cwlt
cultivate vt diwyllio, trin, meithrin
cultural adj diwylliannol
culture n diwylliant; gwrtaith
cultured adj diwylliedig, coeth
cumbersome adj afrosgo, beichus
cunning adj dichellgar, cyfrwys ▷ n cyfrwystra
cup n cwpan
cupboard n cwpwrdd
cup-tie n gornest gwpan
curate n curad
curator n curadur
curb n genfa, atalfa; cwrbyn ▷ vt ffrwyno
curd n caul, ceuled; caws
curdle vb ceulo, cawsio, cawsu
cure n iachâd, gwellhad; meddyginiaeth ▷ vb iacháu, gwella; halltu
curfew n hwyrgloch
curiosity n cywreinrwydd, chwilfrydedd

curious adj cywrain; chwilfrydig; hynod
curl n cwrl, cudyn ▷ vb cyrlio
curlew n gylfinir
curly adj cyrliog, crych
currants npl grawn Corinth, cwrens; **currant bread** bara brith
currency n arian breiniol
current adj rhedegol, cyfredol, cyfoes ▷ n ffrwd, llif; **current account** cyfrif cyfredol; **current affairs** materion cyfoes
currently adv ar hyn o bryd
curriculum n cwricwlwm; **National Curriculum** Cwricwlwm Cenedlaethol
curriculum vitae n braslun bywyd, manylion personol
curry vt trin lledr ▷ n cyrri; **to curry favour** cynffonna, ceisio ffafr
curse n melltith, rheg ▷ vb melltithio, rhegi
cursor n (computing) cyrchwr
cursory adj brysiog, diofal
curt adj cwta, byr, cryno
curtail vt cwtogi, talfyrru; prinhau
curtain n llen
curtsy n cyrtsi
curve vb camu, gwyro, troi ▷ n tro; cromlin
cushion n clustog
custard n cwstard
custodian n ceidwad
custody n dalfa, cadwraeth
custom n defod; cwsmeriaeth; toll
customary adj arferol
customer n cwsmer
customs npl y tollau
customs officer n swyddog tollau
cut vb torri ▷ n toriad, archoll, briw; **cut back** torri yn ôl; **cut in** torri ar draws; **cut out** torri allan; **cut through** torri trwodd

cute *adj* ciwt, cyfrwys
cuticle *n* croen, pilen, cwticl
cutlery *n* cwtleri
cutlet *n* golwyth, cydled
CV *n abbr* (= *curriculum vitae*) CV
cybercafé *n* caffi rhyngrwyd, caffe rhyngrwyd
cycle *n* cylch; cyfres; beic ▷ *vb* seiclo
cycling *n* beicio
cyclist *n* beiciwr
cyclone *n* trowynt
cygnet *n* cyw alarch, alarchen
cylinder *n* rhol; silindr
cymbal *n* symbal
cynic *n* gwawdiwr, sinig
cynical *adj* gwawdlyd, dirmygus
cynicism *n* coegni, gwawd
Cyprus *n* Ynys Cyprus
cyst *n* coden
cystitis *n* llid y bledren
Czech Republic *n*: **the Czech Republic** Gweriniaeth Tsiec

d

dab *vt* dabio ▷ *n* dab
dabble *vb* dablo
dad, dada, daddy *n* tad, tada, tyta, dada
daffodil *n* cenhinen Bedr
daft *adj* hurt, gwirion
dagger *n* dagr, bidog
daily *adj* dyddiol, beunyddiol ▷ *adv* beunydd, bob dydd
dainty *n* danteithfwyd, amheuthun ▷ *adj* danteithiol, dillyn, del
dairy *n* llaethdy; **dairy products** cynhyrchion llaeth
dais *n* esgynlawr, llwyfan
daisy *n* llygad y dydd
dale *n* dyffryn, glyn, dôl, cwm, bro
dam *n* argae, cronfa ▷ *vt* argáu, cronni
dam *n* mamog, mam (anifail)
damage *n* niwed, difrod ▷ *vt* niweidio, difrodi; **damages** *npl* iawn

damn vb damnio, rhegi, melltithio
damnation n damnedigaeth
damned adj colledig
damp adj llaith ▷ n lleithder ▷ vb lleitho
damson n eirinen ddu
dance vb dawnsio ▷ n dawns; **folk dance** dawns werin; **public folk dance** twmpath dawns
dancer n dawnsiwr
dandelion n dant y llew
dandruff n marwdon, cen
Dane n brodor o Ddenmarc, Daniad
danger n perygl, enbydrwydd
dangerous adj peryglus, enbyd
dangle vb hongian; siglo
dapper adj del, twt, sionc, heini
dare vb beiddio, mentro
dare-devil n un byrbwyll, un mentrus
daring adj beiddgar, mentrus ▷ n beiddgarwch
dark adj tywyll ▷ n tywyllwch, nos
darken vb tywyllu
darkness n tywyllwch
darling n anwylyd, cariad ▷ adj annwyl
darn vt cyweirio, trwsio ▷ n cyweiriad, trwsiad
dart n dart, picell, saeth ▷ vb dartio, rhuthro
dash vb rhuthro, chwalu, chwilfriwio ▷ n rhuthr; llinell (-)
dashboard n dashfwrdd
data npl data
database n cronfa ddata
date n dyddiad, amseriad; datysen (ffrwyth) ▷ vb dyddio; **out of date** henffasiwn, wedi dyddio; **up to date** hyd yn hyn, cyfoes
dated adj dyddiedig
daub vb dwbio, iro
daughter n merch; **daughter-in-law** merch yng nghyfraith

dawdle vi ymdroi, swmera
dawn vi gwawrio, dyddio ▷ n gwawr
day n diwrnod, dydd; **by day** liw dydd; **today** heddiw; **next day** trannoeth; **the day before yesterday** echdoe
day-break n gwawr, toriad dydd
day-dream vb pensynnu, synfyfyrio
daylight n golau dydd
day-time n y dydd
daze vt synnu, syfrdanu; dallu
dazzle vb disgleirio, pelydru; dallu
dazzling adj disglair, llachar
deacon n diacon, blaenor
dead adj marw, difywyd ▷ adv hollol; **the dead** y meirw; **dead centre** yn ei ganol; **dead tired** wedi blino 'n lân; **dead heat** cwbl gyfartal
deaden vb lleddfu, marweiddio
deadline n dedlein
deadlock n methu symud mlaen na nôl
deadly adj marwol, angheuol
Dead Sea n: **the Dead Sea** y Môr Marw
deaf adj byddar
deafen vb byddaru
deafness n byddardod
deal vb delio; trin ▷ n trafodaeth, dêl; **a great deal** llawer iawn; **to deal with** ymwneud â
dealer n masnachwr
dean n deon
dear adj annwyl, cu, hoff; drud ▷ n anwylyd, cariad; **dear me** o'r annwyl!
death n angau, marwolaeth, tranc; **Black Death** y Pla Du
deathly adj, adv fel angau, angheuol, marwol
death rate n cyfradd marw
debar vt atal, lluddias, cau allan

debase vt iselu, darostwng, llygru

debate vb dadlau, ymryson ▷ n dadl

debit n debyd

debit card n cerdyn debyd

debt n dyled

debtor n dyledwr

decade n degawd

decadence n dirywiad, adfeiliad

decapitate vt torri pen

decay vi dadfeilio, pydru ▷ n dadfeiliad

decease n tranc, marwolaeth ▷ vi marw, trengi

deceased n ymadawedig, trancedig

deceit n twyll, dichell, hoced

deceive vt twyllo, hocedu, siomi

December n Rhagfyr

decent adj gweddus, gweddaidd

deception n twyll, ffug, dichell

deceptive adj twyllodrus, dichellgar

decide vb penderfynu

decided adj pendant, penderfynol

decidedly adv yn siŵr, yn ddiau

deciduous adj collddail

decimal adj degol ▷ n degolyn; **decimal system** system ddegol; **decimal point** pwynt degol; **recurring decimal** degolyn cylchol

decipher vt datrys, dehongli

decision n penderfyniad

decisive adj penderfynol, pendant

deck vt trwsio, addurno

deck n bwrdd llong, dec

deck chair n cadair haul

declaration n datganiad; cau batiad

declare vb mynegi, datgan, cyhoeddi

decline vb dadfeilio; gwrthod ▷ n dadfeiliad; darfodedigaeth

decompose vb pydru, braenu; dadelfennu

decorate vt addurno, arwisgo

decoration n addurn, tlws

decorator n addurnwr, peintiwr tai

decoy n hud, magl ▷ vt hudo, llithio

decrease vb lleihau, gostwng ▷ n lleihad

decree n gorchymyn, dyfarniad ▷ vb gorchymyn, dyfarnu

dedicate vt cysegru, cyflwyno

dedication n cysegriad, cyflwyniad

deduce vt tynnu, casglu, diddwytho

deduct vt tynnu ymaith, didynnu

deduction n diddwythiad, didyniad

deed n gweithred

deem vt meddwl, ystyried, barnu

deep adj dwfn; dwys ▷ n dwfn, dyfnder

deep freeze n rhewgell

deepen vb dyfnhau, trymhau, dwysáu

deeply adv yn ddwys

deer (**deer**) n carw, hydd

deface vt difwyno, anurddo, hagru

default n diffyg, gwall, pall, meth ▷ vb methu, torri

defeat vt gorchfygu, trechu ▷ n gorchfygiad

defect n diffyg, nam

defective adj diffygiol

defence n amddiffyn, amddiffyniad

defenceless adj diamddiffyn

defend vt amddiffyn

defendant n diffynnydd

defender n amddiffynnwr

defer vb oedi, gohirio

defiance n her, herfeiddiad

defiant adj herfeiddiol

deficient adj diffygiol, prin, yn eisiau

deficit n diffyg

defile vi symud yn rhes ▷ n culffordd, bwlch, ceunant

defile vt halogi, difwyno

define vt diffinio

definite adj penodol, pendant

definitely adv yn bendant, heb os

definition n diffiniad
deflate vb dadchwythu
deflect vb gwyro, osgoi
deform vt anffurfio, hagru, aflunieiddio
deformed adj afluniaidd, anffurf
deformity n anffurfiad
defraud vt twyllo, hocedu; ysbeilio
defray vt talu (treuliau)
defrost vt (fridge) dadrewi
defroster n dadrewydd
deft adj medrus, hylaw, deheuig
defunct adj marw, trancedig
defy vt beiddio, herfeiddio, herio
degenerate vi dirywio ▷ adj dirywiedig
degrade vt diraddio, difreinio
degree n gradd
dehydrate vb dihydradu
dehydration n dihydrad
de-ice vb toddi
deign vb ymostwng, teilyngu
deity n duwdod; duw
deject vt digalonni
dejected adj digalon
delay vb oedi, gohirio ▷ n oediad
delectable adj hyfryd, hyfrydlon
delegate vt dirprwyo ▷ n dirprwy, cynrychiolydd
delete vt dileu
deliberate vb ystyried yn bwyllog ▷ adj pwyllog, bwriadol
deliberately adv yn fwriadol
delicacy n amheuthun, danteithfwyd; **delicacies** danteithion
delicate adj tyner; cain; gwanllyd
delicious adj danteithiol, blasus
delight vb difyrru; ymhyfrydu ▷ n hyfrydwch
delighted adj balch; **I'd be delighted to ...** Mi fyddai'n bleser gen i ...

delightful adj hyfryd, braf
delinquency n bai, trosedd
delinquent n troseddwr, tramgwyddwr ▷ adj troseddol, tramgwyddus
delirious adj wedi drysu, yn drysu, gwallgof
deliver vt traddodi; gwaredu, danfon; cludo
deliverance n gwaredigaeth
delivery n traddodiad; danfoniad
dell n glyn, pant, ceunant, cwm
delude vt twyllo, hudo
deluge n dilyw, dylif ▷ vt gorlifo
delusion n twyll, cyfeiliornad; lledrith
delve vb cloddio, palu, ymchwilio
demand vt gofyn, hawlio, mynnu ▷ n gofyn, hawl
demean vt ymddwyn
demeanour n ymddygiad
demented adj gwallgof, gorffwyll
demesne n treftadaeth, tiriogaeth; bro
demi- prefix hanner
demise n marwolaeth
democracy n gweriniaeth, democrat, democratiaeth
democrat n gwerinydd, gweriniaethwr
democratic adj gwerinol, democratig
demolish vt dymchwelyd, distrywio
demonstrate vb arddangos, profi; gwrthdystio
demonstration n arddangosiad; gwrthdystiad
demonstrator n arddangoswr; gwrthdystiwr
demote vb darostwng
demur vi codi gwrthwynebiad, petruso
demure adj swil, gwylaidd

den n ffau, gwâl, lloches
denial n gwadiad; nacâd, gwrthodiad; **self-denial** hunanymwadiad
denims npl denims
Denmark n Denmarc
denomination n enw, enwad
denote vt arwyddo, dynodi, hynodi
denounce vt lladd ar, cyhuddo, condemnio
dense adj tew, dwys; pendew, hurt
density n dwysedd, trwch
dent n tolc ▷ vt tolcio
dental adj deintiol
dentist n deintydd
dentistry n deintyddiaeth
dentures npl dannedd gosod/dodi
deny vt gwadu, gomedd, gwrthod
deodorant n diaroglydd
depart vi ymadael; cychwyn
department n adran, dosbarth
department store n siop adrannol
departure n ymadawiad; cychwyniad
departure lounge n lolfa ymadael
depend vi dibynnu
dependable adj dibynadwy
dependant n dibynnydd
dependent adj dibynnol
depict vt darlunio
deplete vt gwacáu, gwagu, hysbyddu
depopulate vt diboblogi
deport vt alltudio
deportation n alltudiaeth
deportment n ymddygiad, ymarweddiad
deposit vt dodi i lawr; adneuo; gwaddodi ▷ n adnau, blaendal; gwaddod; **deposit account** cyfrif cadw
depot n storfa; gorsaf
depreciate vb dibrisio

depredation n anrheithiad
depress vt gostwng, iselu; digalonni
depressed adj digalon, iselfryd
depressing adj trist
depression n iselder (ysbryd); dibwysiant (tywydd); pant; dirwasgiad (diwydiant)
deprivation n enbydrwydd, amddifadedd, colled
deprive vt amddifadu
deprived adj amddifadus
depth n dyfnder
deputation n dirprwyaeth
deputise vt dirprwyo
deputy n dirprwy
derail vb taflu oddi ar gledrau
derelict adj wedi ei adael, diberchen, diffaith
deride vt gwatwar, gwawdio
derision n gwatwar, gwawd, dirmyg
derive vb derbyn, cael; tarddu, deillio
derogatory adj amharchus, difrïol, dilornus, gwawdus
descant vi desgant, cyfalaw
descend vi disgyn
descent n disgyniad, disgynfa; hil, ach
describe vt disgrifio, darlunio
description n disgrifiad, darluniad
desecrate vt digysegru, halogi
desert n haeddiant
desert adj diffaith, anial ▷ n diffeithwch
desert vb gadael, cefnu ar; encilio
deserter n enciliwr, ffoadur
deserve vb haeddu, teilyngu
deserving adj haeddiannol, teilwng
design n arfaeth; cynllun ▷ vb arfaethu; cynllunio
designer n cynllunydd, dylunydd
desirable adj dymunol, dewisol

d

desire vb dymuno ▷ n dymuniad, chwant

desk n desg

desolate adj anghyfannedd, diffaith ▷ vt anghyfanheddu

despair n anobaith ▷ vi anobeithio

desperate adj diobaith, anobeithiol; gorffwyll

desperation n anobaith, enbydrwydd, gorffwylltra

despicable adj dirmygedig, ffiaidd

despise vt dirmygu, diystyru

despite prep er, er gwaethaf

despoil vt anrheithio, ysbeilio

despondent adj digalon, isel-ysbryd

despot n unben, gormeswr

dessert n pwdin, melysfwyd

destination n cyrchfan, pen y daith

destiny n tynged, tynghedfen

destitute adj anghenus, amddifad

destroy vt distrywio, difetha, dinistrio

destroyer n dinistrydd; distrywlong

destruction n distryw, dinistr

detach vt datod, gwahanu, dadgysylltu

detached adj ar wahân

detachment n adran; didoliad; mintai (o filwyr)

detail n manylyn ▷ vb manylu, neilltuo; **in detail** yn fanwl; **details** npl manylion

detain vt cadw, atal, caethiwo

detect vt canfod, darganfod, datgelu

detection n darganfyddiad, datgeliad

detective n cuddswyddog, ditectif; **detective story** stori dditectif

detention n carchariad, ataliad

deter vt cadw rhag, atal, rhwystro

detergent n golchydd

deteriorate vb dirywio, gwaethygu

determination n penderfyniad

determine vb penderfynu, pennu

determined adj penderfynol

deterrent n atalrym, ataliad

detest vt ffieiddio, casáu, atgasu

detour n cylch

detract vt tynnu oddi wrth, bychanu

detriment n colled, niwed, anfantais

detrimental adj niweidiol, colledus, o anfantais

devaluation n gwerthostyngiad, datbrisiad

devastate vt diffeithio, difrodi

devastating adj difrodus

develop vb datblygu

developing adj datblygol, ar ei brifiant

development n datblygiad

device n dyfais

devil n diafol, diawl, cythraul

devilish adj dieflig

devious adj diarffordd, troellog; cyfeiliornus

devise vt dyfeisio

devoid adj amddifad

devolution n datganoli

devote vt cysegru, cyflwyno, ymroddi

devoted adj ffyddlon, ymroddgar

devotion n defosiwn, ymroddiad

devour vt ysu, difa, traflyncu

devout adj duwiol, crefyddol, defosiynol

dew n gwlith ▷ vb gwlitho

diabetes n clefyd melys/siwgr

diabetic adj, n diabetig

diabolical adj dieflig

diagnosis n diagnosis

diagonal n croeslin ▷ adj croeslinol

diagram n darlun eglurhaol, diagram

dial n deial ▷ vb deialu

dialect n tafodiaith

dialogue n ymddiddan, deialog, sgwrs

diameter n tryfesur, diamedr

diamond n diemwnt

diaphragm n llengig; diaffram

diarrhoea n rhyddni, dolur rhydd

diary n dyddiadur, dyddlyfr

dice n dîs

dictate vb arddywedyd, gorchymyn

dictate n arch, galwad, gorchymyn

dictation n arddywediad

dictatorship n unbennaeth

dictionary n geiriadur

diddle vt twyllo, hocedu

die vi marw, trengi, trigo, darfod

diehard n un di-ildio

diesel n disel

diet n ymborth, lluniaeth, deiet

dietetics n deieteg

differ vi gwahaniaethu

difference n gwahaniaeth

different adj gwahanol

differentiate vb gwahaniaethu

difficult adj anodd, caled

difficulty n anhawster

diffident adj petrusgar, anhyderus

dig vb palu, cloddio, ceibio

digest vb treulio, toddi; cymathu

digest n crynhoad

digestion n treuliad, traul

digit n digid, bys

digital adj digidol

digital camera n camera digidol

dignified adj urddasol

dignify vt anrhydeddu, urddasu

dignity n urddas, teilyngdod

digress vi gwyro, crwydro

dike, dyke n clawdd, ffos; argae

dilapidate vb adfeilio, malurio

dilapidated adj adfeiliedig

dilemma n dilema

diligence n diwydrwydd, dyfalwch

diligent adj diwyd, dyfal

dilute vt cymysgu â dwfr, teneuo, gwanhau

dim adj pŵl, aneglur ▷ vb tywyllu, cymylu

dimension n mesur, maintioli, dimensiwn

diminish vb lleihau, prinhau

diminutive adj bychan; bachigol ▷ n bachigyn

dimmer n pylydd

dimple n pannwl, pant ▷ vb panylu

din n twrf, dadwrdd, mwstwr

dine vi ciniawa

diner n ciniawr

dinghy n dingi

dingle n cwm, glyn, pant

dingy adj tywyll, dilewyrch; tlodaidd

dining room n ystafell fwyta

dinner n cinio

dinner jacket n cot ginio, cot giniawa

dinner party n cinio gwadd

dint n tolc; grym ▷ vt tolcio

diocesan adj esgobaethol ▷ n esgob

diocese n esgobaeth

dioxide n deuocsid

dip vb trochi, gwlychu; gostwng ▷ n trochfa

diphthong n deusain, dipton

diploma n tystysgrif, diploma

diplomacy n diplomyddiaeth

diplomat n diplomydd

diplomatic adj diplomyddol

dire adj dygn, arswydus, echryslon

direct adj union, uniongyrchol ▷ vt cyfarwyddo, cyfeirio

direction n cyfarwyddyd; cyfeiriad

directly adv yn union, yn ddi-oed

director n cyfarwyddwr

directory n cyfarwyddiadur

dirge n galarnad, marwnad

dirt n baw, llaid, llaca

dirty adj budr, brwnt ▷ vt budro, diwyno, maeddu

disability n anabledd
disable vt analluogi
disabled adj anabl
disadvantage n anfantais
disagree vi anghytuno
disagreeable adj annymunol, cas
disappear vi diflannu
disappearance n diflaniad
disappoint vt siomi
disappointed adj siomedig
disappointing adj siomedig
disappointment n siomedigaeth
disapprove vb anghymeradwyo
disarm vb diarfogi
disarmament n diarfogiad
disarray n anhrefn ▷ vb anrhefnu
disaster n trychineb, aflwydd
disband vb dadfyddino; gwasgaru
disbelief n anghrediniaeth, angoel
disc n disg(en)
discard vt rhoi heibio, gwrthod
discern vt canfod, dirnad
discerning adj deallus, craff
discharge vb dadlwytho, rhyddhau
  ▷ n gollyngdod, rhyddhad, gollwng
discipline n disgyblaeth ▷ vt
  disgyblu
disclaim vt diarddel, gwadu
disclose vt dadlennu, datguddio
disclosure n datguddiad, dadleniad
disco n disgo
discomfit vt gorchfygu,
  dymchwelyd
discomfort vt anghysuro ▷ n
  anghysur
discompose vt aflonyddu, cyffroi
disconcert vt aflonyddu, cyffroi,
  tarfu
disconnect vb datgysylltu
disconsolate adj digysur, anniddan,
  galarus
discontent n anfodlonrwydd
discontented adj anfodlon

discontinue vb torri, atal
discord n anghytgord
discount n disgownt
discourage vt digalonni
discourteous adj anghwrtais
discover vt darganfod, canfod
discovery n darganfyddiad
discredit n anfri, anghlod, amarch
  ▷ vt anghoelio; amau, difrio
discreet adj call, synhwyrol,
  pwyllog
discrepancy n anghysondeb
discretion n barn, pwyll, synnwyr
discriminate vb gwahaniaethu
discrimination n gwahaniaethu,
  rhagfarn, anffafriaeth
discursive adj crwydrol,
  anghysylltiol
discuss vt trin, trafod
discussion n trafodaeth, sgwrs
disdain vb diystyru, dirmygu,
  diystyrwch ▷ n dirmyg
disease n afiechyd, clefyd, clwyf
disembark vb glanio
disengage vb datgyweddu,
  rhyddhau
disentangle vb datod, datrys
disestablish vt datgysylltu
disfigure vt anffurfio, anharddu,
  hagru
disgrace vt gwaradwyddo ▷ n
  gwaradwydd, gwarth
disgraceful adj gwaradwyddus,
  gwarthus
disguise vt dieithrio, ffugio,
  lledrithio ▷ n rhith, dieithrwch
disgust n diflastod, ffieidd-dod ▷ vt
  diflasu, ffieiddio
disgusting adj ffiaidd, brwnt,
  gwrthun
dish n dysgl; dysglaid
dishcloth n cadach llestri
dishearten vt digalonni

dishevelled *adj* anhrefnus, aflêr, anniben
dishonest *adj* anonest
dishonour *n* amarch, gwarth ▷ *vb* amharchu
dishwasher *n* peiriant golchi llestri
disillusion *vb* dadrithio
disincentive *n* gwrthgymhelliant
disinfect *vb* diheintio
disinfectant *n* diheintydd
disintegrate *vb* datod, chwalu
disinterested *adj* heb ddiddordeb, diduedd
disjointed *adj* datgymalog
disk *n* disg(en)
disk drive *n* gyriant disg
dislike *vt* casáu ▷ *n* casineb
dislocate *vt* rhoi o'i le, datgymalu
dislodge *vt* symud, syflyd, gwared
dismal *adj* tywyll, dilewyrch, digalon
dismay *vt* brawychu, siomi, digalonni ▷ *n* braw, siom, chwithdod
dismiss *vt* gollwng; diswyddo
dismount *vb* disgyn, dymchwelyd
disobedience *n* anufudd-dod
disobedient *adj* anufudd
disobey *vb* anufuddhau
disorder *n* anhrefn; anhwyldeb ▷ *vt* anhrefnu
disorderly *adj* afreolus, anniben
disown *vt* gwadu, diarddel
disparage *vt* amharchu, bychanu, difrïo
disparaging *adj* amharchus, gwaradwyddus
disparity *n* anghyfartaledd, rhagor
dispatch *vb* anfon; diweddu ▷ *n* neges
dispel *vt* chwalu, gwasgaru
dispensary *n* fferyllfa
dispense *vb* rhannu; gweinyddu; hepgor

disperse *vb* gwasgaru, chwalu, taenu
dispirit *vt* digalonni, llwfrhau
dispirited *adj* digalon, gwangalon
display *vt* arddangos ▷ *n* arddangosiad
displease *vt* anfodloni, anfoddio, digio
displeasure *n* anfodlonrwydd, dicter
disposable nappies *npl* clytiau untro
dispose *vt* hepgor, gwaredu
disposition *n* anianawd
disprove *vt* gwrthbrofi
dispute *vb* dadlau, ymryson ▷ *n* dadl
disqualify *vb* difreinio, atal
disquiet *vb* anesmwytho
disregard *vt* diystyru, esgeuluso ▷ *n* diystyrwch, esgeulustra
disreputable *adj* gwarthus, amharchus
disrespect *n* amarch
disrupt *vb* rhwygo, amharu ar
dissatisfaction *n* anfodlonrwydd
dissatisfy *vt* anfodloni
dissect *vb* difynio, trychu; dadansoddi
disseminate *vt* hau, taenu, lledaenu
dissent *vi* anghytuno ▷ *n* anghytundeb; ymneilltuaeth
dissertation *n* traethawd
dissimilar *adj* annhebyg, gwahanol
dissipate *vt* chwalu, gwasgaru, afradloni
dissociate *vt* anghysylltu, gwahanu, dialelodi
dissolute *adj* afradlon, ofer
dissolution *n* ymddatodiad, datodiad, diddymiad
dissolve *vb* toddi, datod; datgorffori, diddymu

distance n pellter
distant adj pell, pellennig, oeraidd
distaste n difiastod, cas
distend vt estyn, lledu, chwyddo
distil vb distyllu, dihidlo
distillery n distyllty
distinct adj gwahanol; eglur
distinction n arbenigrwydd, rhagoriaeth, gwahaniaeth
distinctive adj gwahanredol, arbennig
distinguish vb gwahaniaethu; hynodi
distinguished adj enwog, amlwg
distort vt ystumio, anffurfio, gwyrdroi
distract vb tynnu ymaith, drysu, mwydro
distraction n dryswch, diffyg sylw
distress n cyfyngder, ing, trallod
distressing adj trallodus, blin, poenus
distribute vt rhannu, dosbarthu
distribution n dosbarthiad, rhaniad
distributor n dosbarthydd, dosbarthwr
district n dosbarth, ardal, rhandir; **district council** cyngor dosbarth
distrust n drwgdybiaeth ▷ vb drwgdybio
disturb vt aflonyddu, cyffroi
disturbance n aflonyddwch, cyffro, terfysg
disturbed adj blinderus, cynhyrfus
ditch n ffos
ditto adv eto, yr un, yr un peth
dive vi ymsuddo, deifio
diverse adj gwahanol; annhebyg
diversion n difyrrwch, adloniant; dargyfeiriad
divert vt dargyfeirio, difyrru
divide vb rhannu, dosbarthu, gwahanu ▷ n gwahanfa

divided adj rhanedig
dividend n buddran; difidend
divine adj dwyfol ▷ n diwinydd ▷ vb dewinio, dyfalu
divinity n duwdod; diwinyddiaeth
division n rhan, rhaniad; cyfraniaeth; **long division** rhannu hir
divorce vt ysgar(u) ▷ n ysgariad
divorced adj wedi ysgaru
divulge vt datguddio, dadlennu
DIY n abbr (= do-it-yourself) crefftau'r cartref, DIY
dizzy adj penysgafn, pensyfrdan
DJ n troellwr
do vb gwneud, gwneuthur
docile adj dof, hywedd, hydrin
dock n (dail) tafol
dock vt tocio, cwtogi
dock n doc, porthladd ▷ vt docio; cwtogi
dockyard n iard longau
doctor n doctor, meddyg; doethor, doethur
doctrine n athrawiaeth
document n ysgrif, gweithred, dogfen
documentary adj dogfennol
dodge vb osgoi, twyllo ▷ n cast, ystryw
doe n ewig
dog n ci ▷ vb dal i ddilyn
dogged adj cyndyn, ystyfnig
dogmatic adj athrawiaethol; awdurdodol, pendant
do-it-yourself n crefftau'r cartref, DIY
dole n dôl, dogn ▷ vt dogni, rhannu; **on the dole** yn ddi-waith, ar y clwt
doleful adj trist, prudd, galarus
doll n dol, doli
dollar n doler
dolphin n dolffin

domain n tiriogaeth, maes
dome n cromen, cryndo
domestic adj teuluaidd, cartrefol; gwâr, dof
dominant adj trech
dominate vb dominyddu
dominion n rheolaeth; dominiwn, tiriogaeth
don vt gwisgo (dilledyn) ▷ n athro (coleg)
donate vb rhoddi
donation n rhodd
donkey n asyn, mul
donor n rhoddwr
doodle vb dwdlan
doom n dedfryd, barn, tynged ▷ vt dedfrydu, tynghedu, collfarnu
doomsday n dydd barn
door n drws, dôr, porth
doorkeeper n porthor
door-step n rhiniog, trothwy
doorway n porth, drws
dope n cyffur ▷ vb rhoi cyffur
dormant adj ynghwsg; di-rym
dormitory n ystafell gysgu, hundy
dose n dogn ▷ vt dogni
dot n dot ▷ vb dotio
dote vi dotio, gwirioni, ffoli, dylu
double adj, n dwbl ▷ vb dyblu, plygu; **double flat** meddalnod dwbl
double-bass n bas dwbl
double-click vi clicio dwywaith
double-dealing n twyll
double glazing n gwydro dwbl, ffenestri dwbl
doubt vb amau, petruso ▷ n amheuaeth
doubtful adj amheus, petrus
doubtless adv yn ddiamau, diau
dough n toes
doughnut n toesen
douse vb trochi; diffodd
dove n colomen

dowdy adj aflêr, anniben
down n manblu
down n gwaun, rhos, mynydd-dir
down adv i lawr, i waered; **down and out** digalon, truenus
downcast adj digalon, prudd
downfall n cwymp, codwm, dinistr
download vt lawrlwytho, dadlwytho
downpour n tywalltiad, pistylliad ▷ vb tywallt, pistyllio
downright adj diamheuol
Down's syndrome n syndrom Down
downstairs n y llawr ▷ adv ar y llawr
downwards adv i lawr, i waered
dowry n gwaddol
doze vi hepian ▷ n cyntun
dozen n deuddeg, dwsin
drab adj llwydaidd, salw
draft n drafft, braslun ▷ vb drafftio braslunio
drag vb llusgo ▷ n car llusg
dragon n draig
dragon-fly n gwas y neidr
drain n traen, carthffos
drain vb draenio, diferu, yfed; **draining board** bwrdd diferu
drainage n draeniad; **drainage basin** dalgylch afon
drake n ceiliog hwyad, meilart
drama n drama
dramatic adj dramatig
dramatise vb dramadeiddio, dramodi
dramatist n dramodydd
drape vt gwisgo, gorchuddio
draper n dilledydd
drastic adj cryf, llym, trwyadl
draught n dracht, llymaid, drafft(en); tynfa (llong)
draughts npl drafftiau

draughtsman n drafftsmon, lluniedydd

draw n atyniad, tynfa ▷ vb tynnu, llusgo; lluniadu, darlunio; **draw to scale** graddluniadu; **drawn game** gêm gyfartal

drawback n anfantais

drawer n drâr, drôr

drawing n lluniad, llun

drawing room n ystafell groeso

drawl vb llusgo (geiriau)

dread vb ofni, arswydo ▷ n ofn, arswyd

dreadful adj ofnadwy

dream vb breuddwydio ▷ n breuddwyd

dreamy adj breuddwydiol

dreary adj llwm, diflas, digysur

dredge vb glanhau

dregs npl gwaddod, gwaelodion, gwehilion

drench vt gwlychu; drensio

dress vb gwisgo, dilladu ▷ n gwisg

dresser n dreser, gwisgwr

dressing n dresin; **salad dressing** dresin salad; **dressing gown** gŵn gwisgo

dressmaker n gwniadwraig

dressmaking n gwniadwaith ▷ vb gwneud dillad

dribble n dribl(ad), drefl ▷ vb driblo, dreflu, glafoerio

drier n peiriant sychu

drift n drifft, lluwch; tuedd ▷ vb drifftio, lluwchio

drill vb drilio ▷ n dril

drink vb yfed ▷ n diod, llymaid

drink-driving n gyrru tra'n feddw

drinker n yfwr, diotwr

drinking water n dŵr yfed

drip vb diferu, defnynnu ▷ n diferiad

dripping adj diferol ▷ n toddion, saim

drive n dreif, gyriant, cymhelliad ▷ vb

dreifio, gyrru

drivel vi glafoerio, driflan, dreflu ▷ n glafoerion

driver n gyrrwr

driving adj trwm, â grym y tu ôl iddo, grymus ▷ n gyrru

driving instructor n hyfforddwr gyrru

driving lesson n gwers gyrru

driving licence n trwydded gyrru

driving test n prawf gyrru

drizzle vb briwlan ▷ n glaw mân

droll adj digrif, ysmala

drone n gwenynen ormes; diogyn

droop vi llaesu, ymollwng; nychu

drop n diferyn, dafn, cwympiad ▷ vb diferu, cwympo, gollwng; **drop goal** gôl adlam

drought n tywydd sych, sychder, sychdwr

drover n porthmon, gyrrwr

drown vb boddi

drowsy adj cysglyd, marwaidd, swrth

drudgery n caledwaith, slafdod

drug n cyffur

drug addict n caeth i gyffuriau

drug dealer n gwerthwr cyffuriau

druid n derwydd

drum n tabwrdd, drwm ▷ vb tabyrddu

drummer n drymiwr

drunk adj meddw, brwysg

drunkard n meddwyn

dry adj sych, hysb, cras ▷ vb sychu

dry cleaner's n sych lanhawyr

dryness n sychder, craster

dry rot n sych-bydredd, tyllau pryfed

dual adj deuol; **dual carriageway** ffordd ddeuol

dub vt urddo, galw, llysenwi; dwbio, lleisio (ffilm)

dubious adj amheus, petrus

Dublin n Dulyn
duchess n duges
duchy n dugiaeth
duck n hwyad, hwyaden
duck vb trochi; gostwng pen, gwyro
duckling n cyw hwyaden
dud n ffugbeth
due adj dyledus, dyladwy ▷ n dyled,
  haeddiant
duel n gornest
duet n deuawd
duke n dug
dull adj dwl, hurt; marwaidd; diflas;
  cymylog; pŵl ▷ vb pylu, lleddfu
dumb adj mud
dumbfound vt syfrdanu, drysu
dummy n dymi; delw; ffug-bas
  (rygbi) ▷ vb ffug-basio
dump n dymp, storfa ▷ vb dympio
dumpling n tymplen, poten
dunce n hurtyn, twpsyn, penbwl
dune n twyn
dung n tom, tail
dungarees npl dyngarîs
dungeon n daeardy, daeargell,
  dwnsiwn
dupe n gwirionyn ▷ vt twyllo
duplex adj dwplecs
duplicate adj dyblyg ▷ n copi ▷ vt
  dyblygu
duplicity n dichell, rhagrith
durable adj parhaol, parhaus, cryf
duration n parhad
duress n gorfodaeth
during prep yn ystod
dusk n cyfnos, gwyll
dust n llwch ▷ vt taenu neu sychu
  llwch, dwstio
dustbin n bin sbwriel
duster n cadach, dwster
dustman n dyn lludw
dusty adj llychlyd
Dutch n Iseldireg

Dutchman n Iseldirwr
dutiful adj ufudd, ufuddgar
duty n dyletswydd; toll; **customs
  duty** tolldal; **import duty** toll
  fewnforio; **export duty** toll allforio
duvet n carthen blu
DVD n abbr DVD
DVD player n chwaraewr DVD
dwarf n cor, corrach ▷ adj
  corachaidd
dwell vi trigo, preswylio
dwelling n annedd, preswyl
dwindle vi darfod, lleihau, dirywio
dye vb lliwio, llifo ▷ n lliw, lliwur
dyke n morglawdd, cob
dynamic adj dynamig
dynamics n dynameg
dyslexic adj dyslecsig

each *adj, pron* pob, pob un; **each other** ei gilydd

eager *adj* awyddus, awchus

eagle *n* eryr

ear *n* clust, dolen; tywysen; **earache** clust dost

earl *n* iarll

early *adj* cynnar, bore, boreol ▷ *adv* yn fore

early retirement *n* ymddeoliad cynnar

earmark *n* clustnod, nod clust ▷ *vb* clustnodi, neilltuo

earn *vt* ennill, elwa

earnest *adj* difrif, difrifol, taer

earnest *n* ern, ernes ▷ *vb* gwystl

earnings *npl* enillion

earphone *n* ffôn clust

earring *n* clustlws

earshot *n* clyw

earth *n* daear, pridd ▷ *vt* priddo

earthenware *npl* llestri pridd

earthly *adj* daearol, ar wyneb daear

earthquake *n* daeargryn

ease *n* esmwythdra, esmwythyd; rhwyddineb ▷ *vb* esmwytho

easel *n* isl

east *n* dwyrain ▷ *adj* dwyreiniol; **East Germany** Dwyrain yr Almaen

Easter *n* y Pasg

eastern *adj* dwyreiniol

eastwards *adj, adv* tua'r dwyrain

easy *adj* hawdd, rhwydd

easy-chair *n* cadair esmwyth

easy-going *adj* didaro, di-hid

eat *vt* bwyta, ysu

eaves *npl* bargod, bondo

eavesdrop *vb* clustfeinio

ebb *n* trai ▷ *vi* treio

eccentric *adj* od, hynod; echreiddig

ecclesiastic *adj* eglwysig ▷ *n* clerigwr

echo *n* atsain, carreg ateb ▷ *vb* atseinio

eclipse *n* eclips, diffyg, clip ▷ *vb* tywyllu

ecological *adj* ecolegol

ecology *n* ecoleg

e-commerce *n* e-fasnach

economic *adj* economaidd

economical *adj* cynnil, darbodus

economics *n* economeg

economist *n* economegydd

economize *vb* cynilo

economy *n* cynildeb, darbodaeth, economi

ecstasy *n* gorfoledd, gorawen, hwyl

edge *n* min, ymyl ▷ *vb* minio, hogi; symud; **to be on edge** bod ar bigau'r drain

edible *adj* bwytadwy

edict *n* cyhoeddiad, gorchymyn

Edinburgh *n* Caeredin

edit *vt* golygu, paratoi i'r wasg

edition n argraffiad
editor n golygydd
editorial adj golygyddol
educate vt addysgu
education n addysg
educational adj addysgol
eel n llysywen
eerie adj iasol, annaearol
effect n effaith; canlyniad ▷ vt effeithio; **after-effects** sgil-effeithiau
effective adj effeithiol
effectiveness n effeithiolrwydd
effeminate adj merchetaidd
efficiency n effeithlonrwydd
efficient adj effeithiol, cymwys
effort n ymdrech, ymgais
effusive adj teimladol, arddangosiadol
e.g. abbr er enghraifft, e.e.
egg n wy; **scrambled egg** cymysgwy
egg vt annog, annos
egg cup n cwpan wy
egg shell n masgl/plisgyn wy
ego n ego, yr hunan
egoism n myfiaeth, egoistiaeth
egotism n hunanoldeb
egotist n un hunanol
Egypt n yr Aifft
eiderdown n cwrlid plu
eight adj, n wyth
eighteen adj, n deunaw, un deg wyth
eighth adj wythfed
eighty adj, n pedwar ugain, wyth deg
Eire n Iwerddon Rydd, Gweriniaeth Iwerddon
either adj un o'r ddau ▷ conj naill ai ▷ adv, conj na, nac, ychwaith
ejaculate vb saethu; gweiddi; ebychu
eject vt bwrw allan; diarddel

eke vt estyn allan; hel neu grafu
elaborate adj llafurfawr, manwl
elaborate vb manylu
elapse vi mynd heibio, treiglo
elastic adj hydwyth, ystwyth
elastic band n cylch lastig
elated adj gorawenus, calonnog
elation n gorawen
elbow n elin, penelin
elder n henuriad, hynafgwr ▷ adj hŷn
elderly adj oedrannus
eldest adj hynaf
elect vt ethol, dewis ▷ adj etholedig
election n etholiad; etholedigaeth
elector n etholwr
electorate n etholaeth
electric adj trydanol, electrig
electric blanket n blanced drydan
electric fire n tân trydan
electrician n trydanwr
electricity n trydan
electrify vt gwefreiddio, trydanu
electronic adj electronig
elegant adj cain, dillyn, lluniaidd
elegy n marwnad, galarnad
element n elfen
elementary adj elfennol
elephant n cawrfil, eliffant
elevate vt dyrchafu, codi
eleven adj, n un ar ddeg
eleventh adj unfed ar ddeg
elf (**elves**) n ellyll, coblyn
elicit vb mynnu gan
eligible adj cymwys, etholadwy, dewisol
eliminate vt dileu, deol
elm n llwyf, llwyfen
elongate vt hwyhau, estyn
elongated adj hirgul
eloquent adj huawdl
else adv arall, amgen, pe amgen
elsewhere adv mewn lle arall

e

elude vt osgoi
elusive adj di-ddal, gwibiog, ansafadwy
emaciate vt teneuo, culhau, curio
emaciated adj tenau, curiedig
email n ebost ▷ vt ebostio
email address n cyfeiriad ebost
emanate vi deillio, tarddu, llifo
emancipate vt rhyddfreinio, rhyddhau
embankment n clawdd, cob
embargo n gwaharddiad
embark vb mynd neu osod ar long; hwylio; **to embark on** ymgymryd â, dechrau
embarrass vt rhwystro, drysu
embarrassed adj mewn penbleth, trafferthus
embarrassing adj dyrys, anffodus
embarrassment n chwithedd, embaras
embassy n llysgenhadaeth
embed vb mewnosod
embers npl marwor, marwydos
embezzle vt celcio, darnguddio, lladrata
embitter vt chwerwi
emblem n arwyddlun
embody vt corffori
emboss vt boglynnu
embrace vt cofleidio; cynnwys ▷ n cofleidiad
embroider vt brodio
embroidery n brodwaith
embryo n cynelwad, embryo
emend vt cywiro, diwygio
emerald n emrallt
emerge vi dyfod allan, dyfod i'r golwg, ymddangos
emergence n ymddangosiad
emergency n cyfyngder, taro, argyfwng; **in an emergency** mewn taro

emigrate vi allfudo, ymfudo
eminent adj enwog, amlwg, o fri
emissions npl gollyngiadau
emit vt rhoddi neu fwrw allan
emotion n cyffro, teimlad, emosiwn
emotional adj emosiynol
empathy n empathi
emperor n ymerawdwr, ymherodr
emphasis n pwys, pwyslais
emphasize vt pwysleisio
emphatic adj pwysleisiol, pendant
empire n ymerodraeth
empirical adj empeiraidd
employ vt cyflogi; arfer, defnyddio ▷ n gwasanaeth
employee n gŵr cyflog
employer n cyflogwr
employment n cyflogaeth, gwaith
empower vt awdurdodi, galluogi
empress n ymerodres
empty adj gwag, coeg ▷ vb gwagu, arllwys, gwacáu, dihysbyddu
empty-handed adj gwaglaw
emulate vt ymgystadlu â; efelychu
emulsion n emwlsiwn
enable vt galluogi
enact vt deddfu, ordeinio; cyflawni
enchant vt swyno, cyfareddu, hudo
enclose vt amgáu
enclosed adj amgaeëdig
enclosure n lle caeëdig, lloc
encompass vt amgylchu, cylchynu
encore n encôr ▷ adv eto
encounter vt cyfarfod, taro ar ▷ n ymgyfarfod, brwydr
encourage vt cefnogi, calonogi, annog
encouragement n cefnogaeth, calondid, anogaeth
encroach vi llechfeddiannu
encyclopaedia n gwyddoniadur
end n diwedd; diben ▷ vb diweddu, dibennu, terfynu; **end point** pwynt

terfyn; **from end to end** o ben bwy gilydd

endanger vt peryglu

endear vt anwylo

endeavour vi ymdrechu ▷ n ymdrech

ending n diwedd, dibeniad, terfyniad

endless adj diddiwedd

endorse vt cefnogi, arnodi, ardystio

endorsement n arnodiad, ardystiad

endow vt gwaddoli, cynysgaeddu, donio

endowment n gwaddol, cynhysgaeth

endurance n dycnwch

endure vb parhau; dioddef, goddef

enemy n gelyn

energetic adj grymus, egnïol

energy n ynni, egni

enforce vt gorfodi

enforcement n gorfodaeth

engage vb ymrwymo, dyweddïo; cyflogi; ymladd

engaged adj ymrwymedig, wedi dyweddïo; prysur

engagement n ymrwymiad, dyweddïad; brwydr

engaging adj deniadol

engender vt achosi, peri

engine n peiriant, injan

engineer n peiriannydd

engineering n peirianneg

England n Lloegr

English adj Saesneg, Seisnig ▷ n Saesneg; **English Channel** Môr Udd

Englishman (**-men**) n Sais

Englishwoman (**-women**) n Saesnes

engrave vt ysgythru

engraving n ysgythrad

engulf vt llyncu

enhance vb chwanegu, mwyhau, chwyddo, hyrwyddo

enjoy vt mwynhau; meddu

enjoyable adj pleserus

enjoyment n mwynhad

enkindle vt ennyn

enlarge vt ehangu, helaethu

enlighten vt goleuo; hysbysu

enlightened adj goleuedig; golau

enlist vb ymrestru, listio; ennill

enmity n gelyniaeth

enormity n anfadrwydd, ysgelerder

enormous adj dirfawr, anferth, enfawr

enough adj, n, adv digon

enquire vb ymofyn, ymholi, gofyn, holi

enquiry n ymholiad

enrage vt ffyrnigo, cynddeiriogi

enrich vt cyfoethogi

enrol vt cofrestru

enrolment n cofrestrad

ensign n lluman, baner; llumanwr

enslave vt caethiwo

ensue vi dilyn, canlyn

ensure vt diogelu, sicrhau

entail vt gorfodi, gofyn

entangle vt drysu, maglu, rhwydo

enter vb mynd i mewn, treiddio; cofnodi

enterprise n anturiaeth, menter

enterprising adj anturiaethus, mentrus

entertain vt difyrru, adlonni; croesawu

entertainer n difyrrwr, diddanwr

entertaining adj difyrrus, diddan

entertainment n difyrrwch, adloniant

enthrall vb swyno

enthrone vt gorseddu

enthusiasm n brwdfrydedd

enthusiastic adj brwdfrydig, eiddgar

entice vb hudo, denu, llithio

entire adj cyfan, hollol, llwyr

entirely adv yn gyfan gwbl, yn llwyr

entirety n cyfanrwydd

entrails npl perfedd, ymysgaroedd

entrance n mynediad, mynedfa;
   entrance examination arholiad
   mynediad; **entrance fee** tâl
   mynediad

entrance vt swyno

entreat vt erfyn, ymbil, deisyf

entrust vt ymddiried

entry n mynediad, mynedfa;
   cofnodiad

envelop vt amgáu

envelope n amlen

envious adj cenfigennus

environment n amgylchedd,
   amgylchfyd

environmental adj amgylchol

environmentally adv yn
   amgylcheddol; **environmentally
   friendly** yn amgylcheddol garedig

envisage vb rhagweld

envoy n cennad, negesydd

envy n cenfigen, eiddigedd ▷ vt
   cenfigennu, eiddigeddu

epic adj arwrol, arwraidd ▷ n
   arwrgerdd, epig

epidemic adj heintus ▷ n haint

epiglottis n epiglotis

epilepsy n epilepsi

Epiphany n Yr Ystwyll

episcopate n esgobaeth

episode n digwyddiad, gogyfran,
   episôd

epistle n epistol, llythyr

epitaph n beddargraff

epitome n crynodeb, talfyriad

equable adj gwastad, cyson, tawel

equal adj cyfartal ▷ n cydradd ▷ vt
   bod yn gyfartal; **without equal** heb
   ei ail

equality n cydraddoldeb,
   cyfartaledd

equalize vb cydraddoli, cyfartalu

equally adv yn ogystal â, yn llawn,
   yn gyfartal

equanimity n tawelwch, anghyffro

equate vt cyfartalu, cymharu

equation n hafaliad; **simple
   equation** hafaliad syml; **quadratic
   equation** hafaliad dwyradd;
   simultaneous equation hafaliad
   cydamserol

equator n y cyhydedd

equatorial adj cyhydeddol

equestrian adj marchogol ▷ n
   marchog

equilateral adj hafalochrog

equilibrium n cydbwysedd,
   cymantoledd

equip vt taclu, paratoi, cymhwyso,
   cyfarparu

equipment n cyfarpar, offer

equipoise n cydbwysedd

equivalent adj cyfwerth, cyfartal

equivocal adj amwys

era n cyfnod

eradicate vt difodi, difa

erase vt dileu, rhwbio allan

eraser n dilëydd, rwber

erect adj syth, unionsyth ▷ vt codi,
   adeiladu

ermine n carlwm

erode vb ysu, treulio, erydu

erosion n erydiad

erotic adj serchol, nwydol, erotig

err vi cyfeiliorni

errand n neges, cenadwri

erratic adj ansefydlog, crwydraidd

error n cyfeiliornad, camgymeriad;
   bai, gwall; **in error** ar gam

erupt vb echdorri, torri allan

eruption n echdoriad, tarddiad

escalator n escaladur

escapade n pranc, direidi
escape vb dianc, osgoi ▷ n dihangfa
escort vt hebrwng ▷ n gosgordd
especial adj arbennig, neilltuol
especially adv yn arbennig, yn enwedig
espionage n ysbïaeth
esquire n yswain, ysgwier
essay n ymgais; traethawd, ysgrif
essay vt profi, ymgeisio
essence n hanfod; rhinflas
essential adj hanfodol, anhepgor ▷ n hanfod, anghenraid
essentially adv yn hanfodol
essentials npl hanfodion, anhepgorion
establish vt sefydlu
establishment n sefydliad
estate n stad, ystad, eiddo; **industrial estate** stad ddiwydiannol
estate agent n gwerthwr eiddo
esteem vt parchu, edmygu, cyfrif ▷ n parch, bri
estimate vt, n amcangyfrif
estimation n amcangyfrif, parch, bri
estrange vt dieithrio
estuary n aber
et cetera adv ac yn y blaen
eternal adj tragwyddol, bythol
eternally adv yn dragwyddol, yn oes oesoedd, byth bythoedd
eternity n tragwyddoldeb
ethical adj moesegol
ethics npl moeseg
Ethiopia n Ethiopia
ethnic adj ethnig, cenhedlig
ethos n ethos, naws, natur
e-ticket n e-diced
etiquette n moesau, arfer
etymology n geirdarddiad
EU n abbr UE

eucharist n cymun, cymundeb
euro n ewro
Europe n Ewrob, Ewrop
European adj Ewropeaidd ▷ n Ewropead
European Union n Undeb Ewropeaidd
evacuate vt ymgilio, ymadael (â)
evade vt gochelyd, osgoi
evangelical adj efengylaidd
evangelist n efengylydd
evangelize vt efengylu
evaporate vb ymageru, anweddu
evaporated milk n llaeth anwedd(og)
evasion n osgoad, gocheliad
eve n min nos, noswyl
even adj gwastad, llyfn; cyfartal ▷ adv hyd yn oed; **even number** eilrif
evening n noswaith, yr hwyr, min nos
evening class n dosbarth nos
evening dress n gwisg ffurfiol
evensong n prynhawnol weddi, gosber
event n digwyddiad; **in the event of** os bydd
eventful adj llawn digwyddiadau
eventuality n achlysur, digwyddiad posibl
eventually adv o'r diwedd
ever adv bob amser, erioed, byth; **ever and anon** byth a hefyd
evergreen n, adj bythwyrdd, anwyw
everlasting adj tragwyddol, bythol
evermore adv byth, byth bythoedd
every adj pob
everybody pron pawb, pob un
everyday adj bob dydd, beunyddiol
everyone pron pawb, pob un
everything pron popeth
everywhere adv ym mhobman
evict vt troi allan, dadfeddiannu
evidence n tystiolaeth, prawf

evident *adj* amlwg, eglur
evil *adj* drwg, drygionus ▷ *n* drwg, drygioni
evoke *vt* galw neu dynnu allan; gwysio
evolution *n* esblygiad
evolve *vb* datblygu; esblygu
ewe *n* dafad, mamog
ex *n* ex; **my ex** fy ex
ex- *prefix* allan o; cyn-
exact *adj* manwl, cywir, union
exact *vt* hawlio, mynnu
exacting *adj* manwl, gorthrymus
exactly *adv* yn union, i'r dim
exaggerate *vt* chwyddo, gorliwio
exaggeration *n* gormodiaith, gorliwiad
exalt *vt* dyrchafu, mawrygu
examination *n* arholiad, archwiliad
examine *vt* arholi, archwilio
examiner *n* arholwr, archwiliwr
example *n* esiampl, enghraifft
exasperate *vt* llidio, cythruddo
exasperation *n* llid, cythrudd
excavate *vt* cloddio
exceed *vt* rhagori ar, bod yn fwy na
exceedingly *adv* tros ben, tra
excel *vb* rhagori
excellent *adj* rhagorol, ardderchog, godidog, campus
except *prep* ac eithrio, eithr, namyn, oddieithr, heblaw
exception *n* eithriad
exceptional *adj* eithriadol
excerpt *n* dyfyniad, detholiad
excess *n* gormod, gormodedd
excessive *adj* gormodol, eithafol
exchange *vt* cyfnewid, ffeirio ▷ *n* cyfnewid, cyfnewidfa; **exchange rate** cyfradd cyfnewid
exchequer *n* trysorlys
excise *n* toll ▷ *vt* gosod toll
excite *vt* cynhyrfu, cyffroi

excited *adj* cynhyrfus
excitement *n* cynnwrf
exciting *adj* cyffrous
exclaim *vt* llefain, gweiddi, bloeddio, ebychu
exclamation *n* llef, gwaedd, ebychiad; **exclamation mark** ebychnod
exclude *vt* cau allan, bwrw allan
exclusion *n* gwaharddiad, gwrthodiad
exclusive *adj* cyfyngedig
excommunicate *vt* esgymuno
excrement *n* carth, tom, baw
excrete *vt* ysgarthu
excruciating *adj* dirdynnol
excursion *n* gwibdaith, pleserdaith
excuse *vt* esgusodi ▷ *n* esgus
execute *vt* cyflawni, gweithredu; dienyddio
execution *n* cyflawniad, dienyddiad
executioner *n* dienyddiwr
executive *adj* gweithiol, gweithredol ▷ *n* gweithredwr; **executive committee** pwyllgor gwaith
executor *n* ysgutor
exemplify *vt* egluro, dangos, enghreifftio
exempt *adj* rhydd, esgusodol ▷ *vt* rhyddhau, esgusodi
exercise *n* ymarfer, ymarferiad ▷ *vb* ymarfer; **exercise book** llyfr ysgrifennu, ymarfer
exert *vt* ymegnïo, ymdrechu
exertion *n* ymdrech, ymroddiad
exhale *vb* anadlu allan
exhaust *vt* disbyddu, diffygio, gwacáu ▷ *n* disbyddwr, gwacäwr
exhausted *adj* lluddedig, blin, disbyddedig, wedi ymlâdd
exhaustion *n* gorludded
exhaustive *adj* trwyadl

exhaust pipe n pibell nwyon
exhibit vt dangos, arddangos
exhibition n arddangosfa;
ysgoloriaeth
exhilarate vt llonni, sirioli, bywiogi
exile n alltud; alltudiaeth ▷ vt
alltudio
exist vi bod, bodoli
existence n bod(olaeth), hanfod; **in
existence** mewn bod, ar glawr
exit n allanfa ▷ vb mynd allan,
ymadael
exodus n ymadawiad
exonerate vt esgusodi
exorbitant adj afresymol, gormodol
exotic adj estron, egsotig
expand vb lledu, ehangu, datblygu
expanse n ehangder
expansion n ehangiad, ymlediad
expect vt disgwyl
expectancy n disgwyliad
expectation n disgwyliad
expediency n hwylustod
expedient adj hwylus, cyfleus ▷ n
ystryw
expedite vt hyrwyddo, hwyluso
expedition n ymgyrch, alldaith
expel vt bwrw allan, diarddel
expend vt gwario, treulio
expenditure n gwariant
expense n traul, cost
expenses npl treuliau
expensive adj drud, costus
experience n profiad ▷ vt profi
experienced adj profiadol
experiment n arbrawf ▷ vi arbrofi
expert n arbenigwr ▷ adj medrus,
deheuig
expertise n medr, dawn,
arbenigaeth
expire vb anadlu allan; darfod,
marw
expiry n diwedd, terfyn

explain vt egluro, esbonio
explanation n eglurhad, esboniad
explanatory adj eglurhaol,
esboniadol
explicit adj eglur, manwl, echblyg
explode vb ffrwydro, chwalu
exploit n camp, gorchest ▷ vt
gweithio, gwneud elw o, ymelwa ar
exploitation n ymelwad
explore vt fforio, chwilio
explorer n fforiwr
explosion n ffrwydriad; tanchwa
explosive n ffrwydrydd/yn ▷ adj
ffrwydrol
exponent n esboniwr, dehonglwr
export vt allforio ▷ n allforyn
exporter n allforiwr
expose vt amlygu, dinoethi
expound vt esbonio
express vt mynegi, datgan ▷ adj
cyflym, clir ▷ n trên cyflym
expression n mynegiant
expressly adv yn unig swydd, yn
benodol
expulsion n diarddeliad
exquisite adj odiaeth, rhagorol;
coeth
extempore adv, adj byrfyfyr, o'r frest
extend vb estyn, ymestyn; ehangu
extension n helaethiad, ehangiad,
(ym)estyniad
extensive adj ymestynnol, helaeth
extent n ehangder, maint, hyd,
mesur; **to some extent** i raddau
extenuate vt lleihau, lleddfu;
esgusodi
exterior adj allanol ▷ n tu allan
exterminate vt difodi, dileu
external adj allanol
extinct adj wedi diffodd, wedi
darfod, diflanedig
extinguish vt diffodd; diddymu,
dileu

e

extinguisher *n* diffoddwr
extol *vt* moli, moliannu, clodfori
extort *vt* cribddeilio, gwasgu
extortionate *adj* gormodol
extra *adj* ychwanegol ▷ *adv* tu hwnt,
  dros ben ▷ *n* peth dros ben,
  ychwanegiad
extract *vt* echdynnu, tynnu;
  dyfynnu, rhinio ▷ *n* echdyniad;
  dyfyniad; rhin, darn
extracurricular *adj* allgyrsiol
extramural *adj* allanol
extraordinary *adj* hynod,
  anghyffredin
extravagant *adj* gwastraffus,
  afradlon
extreme *adj* i'r eithaf, eithafol ▷ *n*
  eithaf
extremely *adv* dros ben, gor-
extremist *adj* eithafol ▷ *n* eithafwr
extremity *n* pen, eithaf; cyfyngder
extrovert *adj* allblyg, alltro ▷ *n*
  alltröedydd, person allblyg
eye *n* llygad; crau; dolen ▷ *vt*
  llygadu, sylwi ar, gwylio
eyeball *n* cannwyll y llygad
eyebrow *n* ael
eyelashes *npl* blew yr amrant
eye-level *n* llinell orwel
eyelid *n* amrant
eye-opener *n* agoriad llygad
eyesight *n* golwg
eyesore *n* hyllbeth
eyewitness *n* llygad-dyst

fable *n* chwedl, dameg; anwiredd
fabric *n* adail, adeilad, defnydd
fabricate *vt* llunio, dyfeisio, ffugio
fabrication *n* ffug, anwiredd
fabulous *adj* chwedlonol, diarhebol
face *n* wyneb, wynepryd ▷ *vb*
  wynebu
face cloth *n* clwtyn ymolchi; **face
  value** arwynebwerth
facilitate *vt* hwyluso, hyrwyddo
facility *n* hwylustod, cyfleustra,
  rhwyddineb
fact *n* ffaith, gwirionedd; **as a
  matter of fact** mewn gwirionedd
factor *n* ffactor, elfen, nodwedd;
  prime factor ffactor cysefin
factory *n* ffatri
factual *adj* ffeithiol
faculty *n* cynneddf; cyfadran
fad *n* mympwy, chwilen
fade *vb* diflannu, gwywo; colli ei liw

fag vb slafio, ymlâdd, blino ▷ n caledwaith, lludded; gwas bach

fail vi ffaelu, methu, pallu, diffygio; **without fail** yn ddi-ffael

failure n methiant, pall, aflwyddiant

faint adj llesmeiriol, gwan, llesg ▷ vi llewygu ▷ n llesmair, llewyg

fair n ffair

fair adj teg, glân; gweddol; golau

fairly adv yn deg/lân, yn weddol

fairness n glendid, tegwch

fair trade n masnach deg

fairy n un o'r tylwyth teg

fairy-tale n stori hud, chwedl werin

faith n ffydd, cred, coel

faithful adj ffyddlon, cywir

faithfully adv yn ffyddlon, yn gywir; **yours faithfully** yr eiddoch yn gywir

fake n ffug ▷ vb ffugio

falcon n hebog, curyll

fall vi cwympo, syrthio ▷ n cwymp; **fall out** cweryla; **fall through** methu

fallacy n cyfeiliornad, gwall

fallow n braenar ▷ vt braenaru

false adj gau, ffug, ffals, twyllodrus; **false teeth** dannedd gosod/dodi

falter vb petruso, methu, pallu

fame n enwogrwydd, clod, bri

familiar adj cynefin, cyfarwydd

familiarity n cynefindra

family n teulu, tylwyth

famine n newyn

famish vb newynu, llwgu

famous adj enwog

fan n gwyntyll; ffan ▷ vt gwyntyllio, chwythu

fanatic n penboethyn, ffanatig

fanaticism n penboethni, ffanatigiaeth

fanciful adj ffansïol

fancy n dychymyg, ffansi, serch ▷ vt dychmygu, ffansïo, serchu; **fancy dress** gwisg ffansi

fang n ysgithr, dant, pig, blaen

fantastic adj ffantastig, rhyfeddol

fantasy n ffantasi

far adj pell(ennig) ▷ adv ymhell; **as far as** hyd at

farce n ffars

fare n cost, pris; ymborth ▷ vi bod, dod ymlaen, byw

farewell excl yn iach, ffarwel ▷ n ffarwel; **to bid farewell** canu'n iach

farm n fferm ▷ vt amaethu, ffarmio

farmer n ffarmwr, ffermwr, amaethwr; **Young Farmers' Club** Clwb y Ffermwyr Ifainc

farmhouse n ffermdy

farming n ffermio; **intensive farming** ffermio dwys

farmyard n buarth, clos

fascinate vt hudo, swyno

fascinating adj hudol, swynol

fascism n ffasgaeth

fashion n ffasiwn, arfer, dull ▷ vt llunio, gwneud

fashionable adj ffasiynol

fast vi ymprydio ▷ n ympryd

fast adj tyn, sownd; buan, cyflym, clau

fasten vb sicrhau, cau, clymu, ffasno

fastener n ffasnydd

fastening n ffasnin

fast food n bwyd sydyn

fastidious adj cysetlyd

fat adj tew, bras ▷ n braster, bloneg, saim

fatal adj angheuol, marwol; andwyol

fatality n trychineb, marwolaeth

fate n tynged, ffawd ▷ vt tynghedu

fateful adj tyngedfennol

father n tad ▷ vt tadogi

Father Christmas n Siôn Corn

father-in-law n tad-yng-nghyfraith

fatherly adj tadol
fathom n gwryd ▷ vt plymio
fatigue n lludded, blinder ▷ vt lluddedu, blino
fatten vb tewhau, pesgi
fatty adj seimlyd, brasterog
fatuous adj ynfyd, ffôl
fault n bai, diffyg, nam, anaf; **at fault** ar fai
faultless adj di-fai, perffaith
faulty adj gwallus, diffygiol
favour n ffafr, cymwynas ▷ vt ffafrio; **in favour of** o blaid
favourable adj ffafriol
favourite adj, n ffefryn ▷ adj hoff
fawn n elain ▷ adj llwyd
fawn vi cynffonna, gwenieithio
fear n ofn, braw, arswyd ▷ vb ofni, arswydo
fearful adj ofnus, brawychus, arswydus
feasible adj dichonadwy
feast n gwledd, gŵyl ▷ vb gwledda
feat n camp, gorchest
feather n pluen, plufyn ▷ vt pluo, plufio
feature n arwedd, nodwedd
February n Chwefror, Mis Bach
federal adj cynghreiriol, ffederal
fed up adj wedi cael llond bol
fee n ffi, tâl, cyflog
feeble adj gwan, eiddil
feed vb porthi, ymborthi, bwydo ▷ n porthiant, ffîd, ymborth, gwledd
feedback n adborth, ymateb ▷ vb adborthi
feel vb teimlo, clywed, profi
feeler n teimlydd; ymchwiliad
feeling n teimlad, synhwyriad
feign vb cymryd arno, ffugio
fell vb cwympo, cymynu ▷ n croen; ffridd, rhos
fellow n cymar; cymrawd ▷ prefix cyd-

fellowship n cymdeithas, cyfeillach; cymrodoriaeth
felt n ffelt ▷ vb ffeltio
felt-tip pen n pin blaen ffelt
female adj, n benyw
feminine adj benywaidd, benywol
feminist n ffeminist
femur n ffemwr
fence n clawdd, ffens ▷ vb cau, amgáu
fencing n ffensio, cleddyfaeth
fend vb cadw draw; ymdaro, ymdopi
ferment n eples, cynnwrf ▷ vb eplesu, cynhyrfu
fermentation n eplesiad
fern n rhedynen, rhedyn
ferocious adj ffyrnig, gwyllt, milain
ferret n ffured ▷ vt ffuredu, chwilota
ferry n porth, fferi ▷ vb cludo dros
ferry-boat n ysgraff
fertile adj ffrwythlon, toreithiog
fertilisation n ffrwythloniad
fertility n ffrwythlonder
fertilize vb ffrwythloni; gwrteithio
fertilizer n gwrtaith
fervent adj brwd, gwresog, tanbaid, taer
fester vi crawni, gori, crynhoi
festival n gŵyl, dydd gŵyl; **singing festival** cymanfa ganu
festive adj llawen, llon
festivity n rhialtwch, miri, ysbleddach
fetch vt cyrchu, hôl, ymofyn, nôl
fête n gŵyl, miri ▷ vi gwledda
feud n cynnen, ffiwd
feudal adj ffiwdal
feudalism n ffiwdaliaeth
fever n twymyn, clefyd, gwres
feverish adj â thwymyn
few adj ychydig, prin, anaml
fiancé n darpar-ŵr

fiancée n darpar-wraig

fib n anwiredd, celwydd

fibre n edefyn, ffibr

fibreglass n ffibr gwydrog

fickle adj anwadal, oriog, gwamal

fiction n ffuglen

fictitious adj ffug, ffugiol

fiddle n ffidil, crwth ▷ vi canu'r ffidl; ffidlan

fidelity n ffyddlondeb, cywirdeb

fidget vt ffwdanu, aflonyddu ▷ n un ffwdanus, un aflonydd

field n cae, maes ▷ vb maesu

field marshal n maeslywydd

field work n gwaith maes

fiend n cythraul, ellyll, ysbryd drwg

fierce adj ffyrnig, milain; tanbaid

fiery adj tanllyd, tanbaid

fifteen adj, n pymtheg

fifth adj, n pumed

fifty adj, n hanner cant, deg a deugain

fig n ffigysen

fight vb ymladd, cwffio, brwydro, rhyfela ▷ n ymladdfa, brwydr

fighter n ymladdwr, brwydrwr

fighting n ymladd

figment n creadigaeth (y dychymyg)

figurative adj ffigurol, cyffelybiaethol

figure n ffigur; llun, ffurf ▷ vb cyfrif; llunio; ymddangos; **figure of speech** troad ymadrodd

figurehead n arweinydd (mewn enw)

file n ffeil, rhathell; rhes ▷ vb ffeilio, rhathu

filing cabinet n cwpwrdd ffeilio

fill vb llenwi ▷ n llenwad, llonaid, gwala

fill in vt (hole) llenwi

fillet n llain, ffiled

fillet steak n stêc ffiled

filling n llenwad, mewnyn

filly n eboles

film n pilen, caenen; ffilm ▷ vb ffilmio, gwneud ffilm

film star n seren ffilmiau

film strip n stribed ffilm

filter n hidl, hidlydd ▷ vb hidlo, ffiltro

filter tip n hidl difaco

filth n brynti, budreddi, baw

filthy adj brwnt, budr, aflan

filtrate n hidlif ▷ vb hidlo

fin n adain, asgell, ffin

final adj terfynol, olaf; **semi-final** cynderfynol

finale n ffinale, diweddglo

finally adv o'r diwedd, yn olaf

finance n cyllid ▷ vb cyllido, codi arian

financial adj cyllidol, ariannol

find vt darganfod ▷ n darganfyddiad

find out vb darganfod

finding n darganfyddiad, dedfryd

fine adj main; mân; gwych; braf

fine n dirwy ▷ vt dirwyo

finery n gwychder

finger n bys ▷ vt bysio, bodio; **little finger** bys bach; **third finger** bys y fodrwy; **middle finger** y bys canol

fingerprint n bysbrint, ôl bys

finicky adj cysetlyd, gorfanwl

finish vb diweddu, gorffen, cwblhau ▷ n diwedd; gorffeniad

finished adj gorffenedig

finite adj meidrol

Finland n y Ffindir

fir n ffynidwydden

fire n tân ▷ vb tanio, ennyn; **wild fire** tân gwyllt; **fire precautions** rhagodion tân

firearm n arf-tân

fire brigade n brigâd dân

fire engine n peiriant tân

fire escape n grisiau tân

fire-extinguisher n diffoddydd tân
fireguard n sgrin dân
fireman n taniwr, diffoddwr tân
fireplace n lle tân
fireside n aelwyd
fire station n gorsaf dân
firewood n coed tân, cynnud
fireworks npl tân gwyllt
firm n cwmni, ffyrm ▷ adj cadarn, diysgog
firmly adv yn gadarn, yn ddiysgog
first adj cyntaf, blaenaf, prif ▷ adv yn gyntaf
first aid n cymorth cyntaf
first class adj dosbarth cyntaf
first floor n llawr cyntaf
first-hand adj o lygad y ffynnon
first name n enw bedydd
first-rate adj campus, ardderchog, rhagorol
fish n pysgodyn, pysgod ▷ vb pysgota; **fish and chips** pysgodyn a sglodion
fisherman n pysgotwr
fish fingers npl sglodion pysgod
fishing n pysgota
fishing rod n genwair, gwialen bysgota
fishmonger n gwerthwr pysgod
fishy adj amheus; pysgodol
fist n dwrn
fit n llewyg, ffit, mesur
fit adj ffit, addas, cymwys, gweddus; abl, iach ▷ vb ffitio, gweddu, taro
fitful adj anwadal, gwamal
fitment n cynhalydd
fitness n ffitrwydd, addasrwydd
fitter n ffitiwr
fitting n ffitiad ▷ vb ffitio ▷ adj priodol, gweddus, addas; **fittings** npl mân daclau, ffitiadau
five adj pum ▷ n pump
fix vb sicrhau, sefydlu, gosod ▷ n cyfyngder, cyfyng-gyngor

fixation n sefydlogiad, sefydledd
fixed n sefydlog
fixture n gosodyn, peniant (byd chwarae)
fizz vi sïo
fizzle vb hisian, sïo
fizzy adj byrlymog
flabbergast vt synnu, syfrdanu
flabby adj llipa, llac, llaes
flag n baner, lluman; fflagen ▷ vb llumanu; llaesu
flake n fflaw, caenen; pluen (eira)
flamboyant adj coegwych
flame n fflam ▷ vi fflamio, ffaglu
flame-resistant adj gwrthfflam
flan n fflan
flank n ystlys, ochr ▷ vb ymylu, ystlysu
flannel n gwlanen
flap n llabed, fflap ▷ vb fflapio
flare vb fflêr, fflach; fflerio, fflachio
flash vb fflachio ▷ n fflach
flashback n ôl-fflach
flashlight n fflachlamp
flashy adj gorwych
flask n costrel, fflasg
flat n fflat, gwastad; meddalnod ▷ adj fflat, gwastad, lleddf ▷ vb fflatio
flatten vb gwastatáu
flatter vt gwenieithio
flattery n gweniaith
flatulence n gwynt (yn y cylla)
flaunt vb fflawntio, rhodresa
flavour n blas, cyflas ▷ vt blasu, cyflasu
flavouring n cyflasyn
flaw n bai, diffyg, nam
flax n llin
flaxen adj golau, o lin
flay vt blingo
flea n chwannen
flee vb ffoi, cilio, dianc, diflannu

fleece n cnu ▷ vt cneifio; ysbeilio
fleet n llynges, fflyd ▷ adj cyflym, buan
fleeting adj diflanedig
flesh n cig, cnawd; **flesh and blood** cig a gwaed; **flesh and bones** cnawd ac esgyrn
flex n fflecs
flexible adj hyblyg, ystwyth
flexitime, flextime n oriau hyblyg
flick vt cyffwrdd â blaen chwip, cnithio
flier n ehedwr
flight n hediad, ffo, rhes
flighty adj gwamal, penchwiban
flimsy adj tenau, simsan, bregus
flinch vi cilio yn ôl, gwingo, llwfrhau
fling vt taflu, bwrw, lluchio ▷ n rhwysg, tafliad
flint n callestr, carreg dân, fflint
flip vb cnithio ▷ n cnith
flippant adj tafodrydd, gwamal
flipper n asgell
flirt vb cellwair caru, fflyrtan ▷ n fflyrten, fflyrtyn
flit vi gwibio
float n arnofyn, fflôt, trol ▷ vb arnofio
flock n diadell, praidd ▷ vi heidio
flog vt fflangellu, chwipio
flood n llif, dilyw, cenllif ▷ vt llifo, gorlifo
flooding n llifogydd
floodlight n llifolau ▷ vb llifoleuo
floor n llawr ▷ vt llorio; methu; **ground floor** daearlawr; **first floor** llawr cyntaf
flop n methiant, ymollwng
flora n fflora, planhigion
floral adj fflurol
florid adj blodeuog
florist n tyfwr neu werthwr blodau
flounce vi swalpio, ysboncio ▷ n llam, ysbonc

flounder n lleden fach ▷ vb ymdrybaeddu, ffwndro
flour n blawd, can
flourish vb blodeuo; ffynnu; ysgwyd ▷ n rhwysg; cân cyrn
flout vb gwawdio, wfftio, diystyru
flow vi llifo, llifeirio ▷ n llif, llanw
flow chart n siart rhediad
flower n blodeuyn, blodyn ▷ vi blodeuo; **flowerpot** pot blodau
flowery adj blodeuog
flu n ffliw, anwydwst
fluctuate vi codi a gostwng, amrywio, anwadalu
flue n pibell simnai, ffliw
fluency n huodledd, llithrigrwydd
fluent adj llithrig, rhugl
fluff n fflwcs, fflwff ▷ vb bwnglera, methu
fluid adj hylif, llifol ▷ n hylif, llifydd
fluke n pry'r afu; ffliwc, lwc
fluoride n ffliworid
flurry n cyffro, ffwdan
flush n gwrid; rhuthr dŵr ▷ adj cyfwyneb, gorlawn ▷ vb gwrido, cochi; gorlifo
fluster vb ffwdanu, cyffroi ▷ n ffwdan, cyffro
flute n ffliwt
flutter vb dychlamu, siffrwd ▷ n dychlamiad, siffrwd
fly n gwybedyn, cleren, pryf
fly vb ehedeg, ehedfan; ffoi ▷ n pryf, cleren, copis; **fly into a passion** ymwylltio, gwylltu
flying adj hedegog, cyflym
flyover n pontffordd, trosffordd
foal n ebol, eboles ▷ vb bwrw ebol; **in foal** cyfebol
foam n ewyn ▷ vi ewynnu, glafoerio
focus n canolbwynt, ffocws ▷ vb canolbwyntio

f

fodder n porthiant, ebran
foe n gelyn
fog n niwl
foggy adj niwlog
foil vt rhwystro, trechu ▷ n ffoil, ffwyl, dalen
fold n plyg; corlan ▷ vb plygu, corlannu
folder n plygell
folding n plygiant
foliage n dail, deiliant
folio n ffolio
folk npl pobl, gwerin
folklore n llên gwerin
folk song n cân werin
follow vb canlyn, dilyn
follower n dilynwr, canlynwr
following adj dilynol, canlynol ▷ n dilyniad, canlynwyr
folly n ffolineb, ynfydrwydd
fond adj hoff, annwyl
fondle vt anwylo, anwesu
font n bedyddfaen
food n bwyd, ymborth, lluniaeth; **tinned food** bwyd tun
food poisoning n gwenwyn bwyd
fool n ffŵl, ynfytyn ▷ vb ynfydu, twyllo
foolhardy adj rhyfygus
foolish adj ffôl, ynfyd, annoeth
foot (feet) n troed; troedfedd ▷ vb troedio
foot and mouth disease n clwyf y traed a'r genau
football n pêl-droed
footballer n peldroediwr
footbrake n brêc troed
footbridge n pont gerdded, pompren
foothold n gafael troed, troedle
footing n sylfaen, safle
footlights npl golau'r godre
footman n gwas (â lifrai)

footmark n ôl troed
footnote n troednodiad
footpath n llwybr troed
footprint n ôl troed
footstep n cam, ôl troed
footway n troedffordd
footwear n troedwisg
for prep i, at, am, dros, er ▷ conj canys, oblegid, oherwydd, gan, achos
forage n bwyd (anifail), porthiant ▷ vb chwilio am fwyd
forasmuch conj yn gymaint ag, am, gan, oherwydd
foray n cyrch, rhuthr ▷ vb gwneud cyrch, rhuthro
forbid vt gwahardd, gwarafun, gomedd
forbidden adj gwaharddedig
force n grym; trais ▷ vt gorfodi; **centrifugal force** grym allgyrchol; **centripetal force** grym mewngyrchol; **the forces** y lluoedd arfog
forceful adj grymus, egnïol
forceps n gefel fain
forcible adj nerthol, effeithiol
ford n rhyd ▷ vt rhydio
fore adj blaen, blaenaf ▷ adv ymlaen ▷ prefix cyn-, rhag-, blaen-; **to the fore** amlwg, blaenllaw
forearm n elin ▷ vb rhagarfogi
forebode vt rhagargoeli, rhagarwyddo, darogan
foreboding n rhagargoel
forecast n rhagolygon, rhagolwg ▷ vb rhagddweud, darogan
forefather n cyndad
forefinger n mynegfys
forefront n lle blaen ▷ adj blaen
forego vb hepgor; **foregone conclusion** penderfyniad ymlaen llaw

foreground n blaendir
forehead n talcen
foreign adj estron, tramor; **foreign affairs** materion tramor
foreigner n estron, tramorwr
foreman n fforman
foremost adj blaenaf ▷ adv ym mlaenaf
forensic adj fforensig
forerunner n rhagredegydd
foresee vt rhagweld, rhagwybod
foreseeable adj rhagweladwy
foreshadow vb rhagarwyddo, rhagargoeli
foresight n rhagwelediad
forest n coedwig, fforest ▷ vt coedwigo, fforestu
forestall vt achub y blaen
forestry n coedwigaeth; **forestry commission** Comiswn Coedwigo
foretaste n rhagflas ▷ vb rhagbrofi
foretell vt rhagfynegi, darogan
forever adv am byth
foreword n rhagair, rhagymadrodd
forfeit n fforffed ▷ vt fforffedu, colli
forge n gefail, ffwrn ▷ vb gofannu; ffugio
forget vt anghofio
forgetful adj anghofus
forgive vt maddau
forgiveness n maddeuant
forgo vt gadael, hepgor, mynd heb
fork n fforch, fforc ▷ vb fforchio
forlorn adj amddifad, truan, anobeithiol
form n ffurf; mainc; ffurflen ▷ vb ffurfio; **application form** ffurflen gais
formal adj ffurfiol, defodol
former adj blaenaf, blaenorol
formerly adv gynt, yn flaenorol
formidable adj arswydus, ofnadwy, grymus

formula n rheol, fformwla
forsake vt gadael, ymadael â, gwrthod, cefnu ar
fort n caer, castell, amddiffynfa
forte n cryfder ▷ adj uchel, cryf
forth adv allan, ymlaen; **and so forth** ac felly yn y blaen
forthcoming adj ar ddod, gerllaw
forthright adj union, plaen
forthwith adv yn ddioed, ar unwaith
fortify vt cadarnhau, cryfhau
fortitude n gwroldeb, dewrder
fortnight n pythefnos
fortnightly adj, adv bob pythefnos
fortress n amddiffynfa, caer, castell
fortunate adj ffodus, ffortunus
fortunately adv yn ffodus, yn lwcus
fortune n ffawd; ffortun
fortune teller n un sy'n dweud ffortun
forty adj, n deugain
forum n fforwm
forward n blaenwr ▷ adj eofn, hy; blaen ▷ adv ymlaen ▷ vb anfon ymlaen; hwyluso, hyrwyddo; **inside forward** mewnwr; **wing forward** blaenasgellwr
fossil n ffosil ▷ adj ffosilaidd
fossilise vb ffosileiddio
foster vt magu, meithrin, coleddu
foster-child n plentyn maeth
foster-mother n mamfaeth
foul adj aflan; annheg; afiach ▷ n ffowl(en) ▷ vb ffowlio, llychwino; **foul play** anfadwaith; **foul throw** camdafliad
found vt dechrau, sylfaenu, sefydlu
foundation n sail, sylfaen
founder vb ymddryllio, suddo ▷ n sylfaenydd
foundry n ffowndri, efail
fountain n ffynnon, ffynhonnell
four adj, n pedwar; pedair

foursome n pedwarawd
fourteen adj, n pedwar (pedair) ar ddeg
fourth adj pedwerydd; pedwaredd
four-wheel drive n (car) gyriant pedair-olwyn
fowl n dofedn, ffowlyn, ffowl
fox n cadno, llwynog
foyer n cyntedd
fraction n ffracsiwn; **improper fraction** ffracsiwn pendrwm; **vulgar fraction** ffracsiwn cyffredin; **proper fraction** ffracsiwn bondrwm
fracture n toriad, drylliad ▷ vt torri, dryllio
fragile adj brau, bregus
fragment n dryll, darn, briwsionyn
fragrance n perarogl, persawr
frail adj brau, bregus, gwan, eiddil
frame n ffrâm; agwedd ▷ vt fframio, llunio; **frame of mind** agwedd meddwl
framework n fframwaith
France n Ffrainc
franchise n etholfraint ▷ vb etholfreinio
frank adj didwyll, agored
frankincense n thus
frantic adj cyffrous, gwallgof
fraternal adj brawdol
fraternity n brawdoliaeth
fraud n twyll, hoced
fraudulent adj twyllodrus
fraught adj llwythog, llawn
fray n ymryson, ymgiprys, ffrae, rhaflad ▷ vb treulio, rhaflo
freak n mympwy, peth od
freckle n brych, brychni
free adj rhydd; hael; di-dâl, rhad ▷ vb rhyddhau
freedom n rhyddid, rhyddfraint
free expression n rhyddfynegiant
freehold adj rhydd-ddaliadol

free kick n cic rydd
freelance adj llawrydd ▷ adv yn llawrydd; **a freelance translator** cyfieithydd llawrydd
freely adv yn rhydd, yn hael
freemason n saer rhydd
free-range adj maes
free trade n masnach rydd
free verse n mesur rhydd, y wers rydd
free will n ewyllys rydd, o'i fodd
freeze vb rhewi, fferru
freeze-dry vb sychrewi
freezer n rhewgist, rhewgell
freezing point n rhewbwynt
freight n llwyth llong ▷ vt llwytho llong
French adj Ffrengig ▷ n Ffrangeg
French beans npl ffa Ffrengig
Frenchman n Ffrancwr
Frenchwoman n Ffrances
frenzy n gorffwylltra, cynddaredd
frequency n amlder, mynychder
frequent adj mynych, aml ▷ vt mynychu
frequently adv yn fynych, yn aml
fresh adj ffres, crai, cri, croyw, newydd
freshen vb ffresáu, ireiddio
freshness n ffresni, creider, irder
fret vb sorri, poeni ▷ n soriant, trallod, ffret
friar n brawd, mynach
friction n ffrithiant, ymrafael
Friday n dydd Gwener
fridge n oergell, rhewadur
friend n cyfaill, ffrind
friendly adj cyfeillgar
friendship n cyfeillgarwch
frieze n ffrîs
fright n dychryn, ofn, braw
frighten vb dychrynu, brawychu, codi ofn ar

frightened adj ofnus
frightful adj dychrynllyd, brawychus
frigid adj oer, rhewllyd; oeraidd, oerllyd
frigid zone n cylchfa rew
frill n ffril
fringe n ymyl, ymylwe, rhidens ▷ vb ymylu, rhidennu; **fringe benefits** cilfanteision
frisk vt prancio
fritter vt afradu, ofera, gwastraffu
frivolous adj gwamal; diystyr, disylwedd
frizzy adj crychlyd
fro adv: **to and fro** yn ôl ac ymlaen
frock n ffrog
frog n llyffant (melyn), broga; bywyn, ffroga
frolic vi prancio, campio ▷ n pranc
from prep o, oddi, oddi wrth, gan
front n wyneb, blaen, ffrynt, talcen ▷ vb wynebu ▷ adj blaen; **front door** drws ffrynt; **front page** tudalen flaen; **front room** ystafell (ffrynt)
frontier n ffin, terfyn, goror
frost n rhew
frostbite n ewinrhew
frosty adj rhewllyd
froth n ewyn ▷ vi ewynnu
frown vi cuchio, gwgu ▷ n cuwch, gwg
frozen adj wedi rhewi
frugal adj cynnil, darbodus
fruit n ffrwyth, ffrwythau; **fruit juice** sudd ffrwyth; **fruit salad** salad ffrwythau
fruiterer n gwerthwr ffrwythau
fruitful adj ffrwythlon, toreithiog
fruition n ffrwythloniad
frustrate vt rhwystro, llesteirio
frustration n llesteiriant
fry vb ffrio ▷ n afu, sil, silod; **small fry** pobl ddibwys

frying-pan n ffrimpan, padell ffrio
fudge n cyffug
fuel n tanwydd; cynnud; **fuel cell** cynudydd
fugitive adj ar ffo, diflanedig ▷ n ffoadur
fulfil vt cyflawni
fulfilment n cyflawniad
full adj llawn, cyflawn ▷ n llonaid
full-back n cefnwr
fuller n pannwr
full stop n atalnod
full-time adj amser llawn
fully adv yn gyfan gwbl, yn gyflawn, yn hollol
fulsome adj ffiaidd, diflas (am weniaith etc)
fumble vb palfalu, bwnglera
fume n tarth, mwg; llid ▷ vb mygu; llidio, sorri
fun n difyrrwch, digrifwch, hwyl
function n swydd, swyddogaeth; ffwythiant (mathemateg)
functional adj swyddogaethol, ffwythiannol, defnyddiol
fund n cronfa, trysorfa
fundamental adj sylfaenol
funeral n angladd, cynhebrwng, claddedigaeth
fungus n ffwng
funnel n twmffat, twndis, corn
funny adj digrif, ysmala; rhyfedd, hynod
fur n blew, ffwr; cen
fur coat n cot ffwr
furious adj cynddeiriog, ffyrnig, gwyllt
furlong n ystad, wythfed ran milltir
furnace n ffwrn, ffwrnais
furnish vt dodrefnu, rhoddi
furnishings npl dodrefn
furniture n dodrefn, celfi
furrow n cwys, rhych ▷ vt cwyso, rhychu

furry *adj* blewog
further *adj* pellach ▷ *adv* ymhellach
    ▷ *vt* hyrwyddo; **further education**
    addysg bellach
fury *n* cynddaredd, ffyrnigrwydd
fuse *n* ffiws, toddyn, diogelydd ▷ *vb*
    ffiwsio
fuss *n* ffwdan, helynt, stŵr ▷ *vb*
    ffwdanu
fussy *adj* ffwdanus
futile *adj* ofer, di-les
future *adj*, *n* dyfodol
fuzzy *adj* blewog, aneglur

gabble *vb* bregliach, clebran ▷ *n*
    cleber
gable *n* piniwn, talcen tŷ
gadget *n* dyfais
Gaelic *n* Gaeleg ▷ *adj* Gaelaidd
gaff *n* bach pysgota
gag *n* smaldod; safnglo ▷ *vb* smalio;
    safngloi, cau ceg
gaiety *n* llonder, difyrrwch, miri
gaily *adv* yn llawen
gain *vb* ennill, elwa ▷ *n* ennill, elw,
    budd
gait *n* cerddediad, osgo
gale *n* awel, gwynt cryf; tymestl
gall *n* bustl, chwydd ▷ *vb* dolurio,
    blino
gallant *adj* gwrol, dewr ▷ *n* carwr
gall bladder *n* coden y bustl
gallery *n* oriel, llofft
galley *n* rhwyflong; gali
gallon *n* galwyn

gallop n carlam ▷ vb carlamu
gallows n crocbren
gall stones npl cerrig y bustl
galore n, adv digonedd
galvanize vt galfaneiddio, galfanu; symbylu
gamble vb hapchwarae, gamblo ▷ n gambl
game n chwarae, camp; helwriaeth ▷ adj calonnog, dewr, glew
game-keeper n cipar
games console n consol gêmau
game show n sioe gêm, sioe gêmau
gammon n palfais (mochyn); ffwlbri, lol
gander n ceiliagwydd, clacwydd
gang n mintai, torf, haid, gang
gangster n troseddwr
gangway n tramwyfa, eil, ale; pont
gaol n carchar ▷ vt carcharu
gap n bwlch, adwy
gape vi rhythu, syllu ▷ n rhythiad
gap year n blwyddyn bwlch
garage n modurdy, garej
garbage n ysgarthion, ysbwriel, sothach
garble vt darnio, llurgunio
garden n gardd ▷ vi garddio
gardener n garddwr
gardening n garddwriaeth
gargle n golch gwddf ▷ vb golchi gwddf
garish adj coegwych
garland n coronbleth, garlant, talaith
garlic n garlleg
garment n dilledyn, gwisg
garnish vt addurno, harddu
garrison n gwarchodlu, garsiwn
garrulous adj tafodrydd, siaradus
garter n gardas, gardys ▷ vb gardysu
gas n nwy ▷ vb gwenwyno â nwy; **gas cooker** ffwrn nwy; **gas fire** tân nwy; **gas ring** cylch nwy

gash n archoll, hollt, hac ▷ vt archolli, hacio
gasket n gasged
gas-mask n mwgwd nwy
gasometer n tanc nwy
gasp vb ebychu, anadlu'n drwm
gate n porth, llidiart, clwyd, gât, iet ▷ vb porthio, porthellu
gate-crasher n ymyrrwr
gatehouse n porthordy
gateway n mynedfa
gather vb casglu, cynnull, crynhoi, hel
gathering n casgliad, cynulliad
gaudy adj coegwych, gorwych
gauge n mesur; lled; meidrydd ▷ vt mesur, meidryddu
Gaul n Gâl
Gaulish n Galeg
gaunt adj llwm, tenau
gauntlet n dyrnfol, maneg ddur; **to throw down the gauntlet** herio
gauze n rhwyllen, gaws, meinwe
gay adj llon, bywiog, ofer, hoyw
gaze vi edrych, syllu, tremio ▷ n golwg, trem
gazette n newyddiadur (swyddogol)
gazetteer n geiriadur daearyddol
GCSE n abbr TGAU = Tystysgrif Gyffredin Addysg Uwchradd
gear n gêr, offer, taclau ▷ vb taclu, harneisio
gearbox n gergist, blwch gêr, gerbocs
gelignite n geligneit
gem n glain, gem, tlws
Gemini n yr Efeilliaid
gender n cenedl
gene n genyn
genealogy n achau; achyddiaeth
general adj cyffredin, cyffredinol ▷ n cadfridog

general election n etholiad cyffredinol
generalize vb cyffredinoli
generally adv yn gyffredinol
general practitioner n meddyg teulu
generate vt cenhedlu, cynhyrchu, generadu
generation n cenhedliad; cenhedlaeth, to
generator n cynhyrchydd; generadur
generosity n haelioni
generous adj hael, haelionus, haelfrydig
genetic adj genetig
genetically modified adj: **genetically modified food** bwyd a addaswyd yn enynnol
genetics n geneteg
Geneva n Genefa
genial adj hynaws, rhadlon, tyner, tirion
genital adj cenhedlol; **genitals** npl organau cenhedlu
genius n athrylith
genteel adj bonheddig, boneddigaidd
gentle adj bonheddig; mwyn, tyner
gentleman n gŵr bonheddig
gently adv yn dyner, addfwyn; gan bwyll
gentry npl bonedd
gents npl toiledau dynion
genuine adj dilys, diffuant, pur
geography n daearyddiaeth
geology n daeareg
geometry n geometreg
geriatrics n geriatreg
germ n hedyn, eginyn, germ
German adj Almaenaidd ▷ n Almaenwr; Almaeneg; **German measles** y frech Almeinig

Germany n yr Almaen
germinate vi egino, atyfu
germination n eginiad, atyfiant
gesture n ystum, arwydd, mosiwn
get vb cael, caffael, ennill; **to get on with it** bwrw arni, bwrw iddi
get back vi (return) cyrraedd
get off vt disgyn oddi ar ▷ vi disgyn
get up vi codi
geyser n geyser
Ghana n Ghana
ghastly adj erchyll, gwelw
gherkin n gercin
ghost n ysbryd, drychiolaeth, bwgan
giant n cawr ▷ adj cawraidd
gibberish n cleber, baldordd
gibe vb gwawdio ▷ n gwawd
giblets npl giblets, syrth gŵydd
Gibraltar n Gibraltar
giddiness n pendro
giddy adj penfeddw, penchwiban
gift n rhodd, dawn, anrheg, gwobr
gifted adj dawnus, talentog
gig n (concert) gig
gigantic adj cawraidd, dirfawr, anferth
giggle vb lledchwerthin, giglan
gill n tagell; gil, chwarter peint
gimmick n gimig
gin n jin; hoenyn
ginger n sinsir
gingerly adj, adv gochelgar, gwyliadwrus
gipsy, gy- n sipsi
giraffe n siráff
girder n trawst
girdle n gwregys, rhwymyn ▷ vt gwregysu
girl n merch, geneth, hogen
girlfriend n cariadferch, anwylyd
girth n cengl; cylchfesur, cwmpas
gist n cnewyllyn pwnc, ergyd, sylwedd

give vb rhoddi, rhoi
give back vt rhoi nôl
give in vi ildio
give up vb rhoi'r gorau i
glacier n rhewlif, iäen, glasier
glad adj llawen, llon, balch
gladiator n cleddyfwr, ymladdwr
gladly adv yn llawen, â phleser
glamorous adj swynol, cyfareddol, hudol
glamour n swyn, cyfaredd, hud
glance vb ciledrych, tremio ▷ n cipolwg, trem, cip
gland n chwarren, cilchwyrnen, gland
glare vb disgleirio; rhythu ▷ n disgleirdeb, tanbeidrwydd
glass n gwydr; gwydraid ▷ npl gwydrau, sbectol
glassy adj gloyw, pŵl
glaze vt gwydro; sgleinio ▷ n sglein, gwydredd
glazier n gwydrwr
gleam n pelydryn, llewyrch ▷ vi pelydru, llewyrchu
glean vb lloffa
glebe n clastir, tir eglwys
glee n llonder, hoen; rhangan
glen n glyn, cwm, dyffryn
glib adj llyfn, llithrig, rhugl, ffraeth
glide vi llithro, llifo ▷ n llithr, llithrad
gliding n, vb llithran
glimmer vi llewyrchu'n wan ▷ n llewyrchyn, llygedyn
glimpse n trem, cipolwg
glint vb fflachio ▷ n fflach, llewyrch
glisten vi disgleirio
glitter vi tywynnu, pelydru ▷ n pelydriad
gloat vb llawenhau
global adj hollfydol, cyffredinol
globalization n y globaleiddio
global warming n cynhesu byd-eang

globe n pêl, pelen
gloom n caddug, prudd-der, tywyllwch
gloomy adj prudd, digalon, tywyll
glorify vt gogoneddu
glorious adj gogoneddus
glory n gogoniant ▷ vi ymffrostio, gorfoleddu
gloss n disgleirdeb arwynebol, sglein; glòs, esboniad
glossary n geirfa
glossy adj llathraidd
glove n maneg
glow vi twymo, gwrido ▷ n gwres, gwrid
glower vi cuchio, gwgu
glue n glud ▷ vt gludio, asio
glum adj prudd, digalon, trist
glut vt gorlenwi, glythu ▷ n gormodedd, gorlawnder
glutton n glwth
gluttony n glythineb
GM abbr: **GM food** bwyd a addaswyd yn enynnol
gnarled adj cnotiog, ceinciog, garw
gnat n gwybedyn, cylionen
gnaw vb cnoi, deintio, cnewian
gnome n gwireb; ysbryd, coblyn
go vi mynd, cerdded, rhodio ▷ n tro
go on vi (happen) digwydd; **to go on doing sth** dal i wneud rhywbeth
goad n swmbwl ▷ vt symbylu
goal n gôl, nod, bwriad
goalkeeper n golgeidwad, golwr
goal posts npl pyst gôl
goat n gafr
goblin n ellyll, coblyn, bwgan
god n duw; **God** Duw
godchild n mab bedydd, merch fedydd
goddess n duwies
godfather n tad bedydd
godhead n duwdod

g

godly adj duwiol
godmother adj mam fedydd
godsend n caffaeliad
goggles npl gwydrau
gold n aur ▷ adj aur, euraid
golden adj euraid
goldfish npl eurbysg, pysgod aur
goldsmith n gof aur, eurych
golf n golff; **golf links** maes golff
golf course n maes golffio
golfer n golffwr
gong n gong, cloch fwyd
good adj da, daionus; cryn ▷ n da,
daioni, lles; **good morning** bore da;
good afternoon prynhawn da;
good evening noswaith dda;
good night nos da; **good enough**
digon da; **no good** dim gwerth,
da i ddim; **Good Friday** Dydd
Gwener y Groglith; **good humour**
natur dda
good-bye excl, n da bo chi, yn iach!
ffarwel
good-looking adj golygus
goodly adj hardd, teg
good-natured adj hynaws, rhadlon
goodness n daioni
goods npl nwyddau, eiddo
goodwill n ewyllys da; braint
(masnachol)
goose (**geese**) n gŵydd
gooseberry n eirinen Fair,
gwsbersen
gooseflesh n croen gŵydd
gore n gwaed, gôr ▷ vb cornio
gorge n hafn, ceunant ▷ vb safnio,
traflyncu
gorgeous adj ysblennydd, gwych
gorilla n gorila
gorse n eithin
gory adj gwaedlyd
gosling n cyw gŵydd
gospel n efengyl

gossip n clec, clonc, clebryn, clebran
▷ vb clebran, clecian, hel straeon
gout n gowt, cymalwst
govern vb llywodraethu, rheoli,
llywio
governess n athrawes
government n llywodraeth
governor n llywodraethwr
gown n gŵn
GP n abbr meddyg teulu
grab vb crafangu, cipio ▷ n gwanc,
crap
grace n gras, rhad, graslonrwydd;
gosgeiddrwydd ▷ vt harddu,
prydferthu, addurno
graceful adj graslon, rhadlon;
gosgeiddig, lluniaidd
gracious adj graslon, grasol,
rhadlon, hynaws
grade n gradd, safon ▷ vb graddio
gradient n graddiant
gradual adj graddol
gradually adv yn raddol
graduate vb graddio, graddoli ▷ n
gŵr gradd, graddedig
graduation n graddedigaeth,
graddnod
graffiti n graffiti
graft n impyn, hunan-les ▷ vt impio,
grafftio
grain n grawn, gronyn; mymryn;
graen ▷ vb graenu, graenio
gram n gram
grammar n gramadeg
grammar school n ysgol ramadeg
grammatical adj gramadegol
granary n ysgubor
grand adj mawreddog, ardderchog,
crand; prif, uchel
grandchild n ŵyr, wyres
granddaughter n wyres
grandfather n taid, tad-cu
grandmother n nain, mam-gu

grandson n ŵyr
granite n gwenithfaen, ithfaen
grant vt rhoddi, caniatáu ▷ n rhodd, grant; **to take for granted** cymryd yn ganiataol
granulated adj gronynnog
granule n gronynnell
grapefruit n grawnffrwyth
grapes n grawnwin
graph n graff
graphic adj graffig; byw
graphics npl graffigwaith, graffeg
grapple n gafl, gafaelfach ▷ vb gafaelyd, mynd i'r afael â
grasp vb gafael; amgyffred ▷ n gafael, amgyffrediad
grasping adj trachwantus
grass n glaswellt, porfa
grasshopper n ceiliog y rhedyn, sioncyn y gwair
grate n grat ▷ vb rhygnu, crafellu; merwino
grateful adj diolchgar; dymunol
grater n grater, crafellydd
gratify vt boddio, boddhau
grating adj garw, cras ▷ n gratin
gratitude n diolchgarwch
gratuity n cildwrn, rhodd
grave adj difrifol, dwys
grave n bedd, beddrod
gravel n graean, gro, grafel
gravestone n beddfaen, carreg fedd
graveyard n mynwent
gravitate vi disgyrchu, treiglo
gravity n disgyrchiant; pwysigrwydd; **centre of gravity** craidd disgyrchiant
gravy n grefi, isgell, sew
graze vb pori; crafu, rhwbio, ysgythru
grease n saim, iraid ▷ vt iro, seimio
greaseproof adj gwrthsaim
greasy adj seimllyd, ireidlyd

great adj mawr; **a great many** llawer iawn
Great Britain n Prydain Fawr
great grandchild n gorwyr(es)
great grandfather n hen daid, hen-dad-cu
greatly adv yn fawr
Greece n Groeg
greed n trachwant, gwanc
greedy adj barus, trachwantus, gwancus
Greek n Groeg; Groegwr ▷ adj Groegaidd
green adj gwyrdd, glas, ir ▷ vb glasu
greenery n gwyrddlesni
greengrocer n grîngroser, gwerthwr llysiau
greenhouse n tŷ gwydr
greenhouse gas n nwy tŷ gwydr
Greenland n Grønland
greet vt annerch, cyfarch
greeting n cyfarchiad
grenade n grenâd
grey adj llwyd, llwydwyn, glas
greyhound n milgi
grid n grid, alch; **grid reference** cyfeirnod grid
grief n gofid, galar, hiraeth
grievance n cwyn
grieve vb gofidio, galaru, hiraethu
grievous adj gofidus, poenus, blin, difrifol
grill n gril, gridyll ▷ vb grilio, gridyllu; **mixed grill** gril cymysg
grille n gril, dellt
grim adj sarrug, milain, difrifol
grimace n ystum ▷ vi ystumio
grimy adj budr, brwnt, diraen
grin vb lledwenu ▷ n gwên
grind vb malu (ŷd etc), llifo (arf), llifanu
grip vb gafael, gwasgu ▷ n gafael, crap

grisly *adj* erch, erchyll, hyll, milain
gristle *n* madruddyn, gwythi
grit *n* grit, grud, graean; pybyrwch
groan *vi*, *n* griddfan
grocer *n* groser
groceries *npl* nwyddau
groin *n* cesail morddwyd, gwerddyr
groom *n* priodfab; gwastrawd ▷ *vb* trwsio
groove *n* rhigol, rhych ▷ *vt* rhigoli, rhychu
grope *vi* ymbalfalu
gross *n* gros; crynswth ▷ *adj* bras, aflednais; **gross profit** elw gros
grotto *n* groto
ground *n* llawr, daear, tir; sail; gwaelod ▷ *vt* daearu, llorio
ground floor *n* daearlawr
groundless *adj* di-sail
groundwork *n* sylfaen, sail
group *n* grŵp, twr, bagad ▷ *vt* grwpio; **discussion group** cylch trafod
grouse *n* grugiar ▷ *vb* grwgnach
grove *n* llwyn, celli
grovel *vi* ymgreinio
grow *vb* tyfu, prifio, cynyddu, codi
grow up *vi* tyfu i fyny, tyfu lan
grower *n* tyfwr
growing *adj* yn tyfu
growl *vi* chwyrnu
grown-up *n* rhywun mewn oed, oedolyn
growth *n* twf, tyfiant, cynnydd
grub *n* pryf, cynrhonyn; bwyd ▷ *vb* dadwreiddio
grubby *adj* budr, brwnt
grudge *vt* gwarafun, grwgnach ▷ *n* dig, cenfigen, cas
gruesome *adj* erchyll, hyll, ffiaidd
gruff *adj* sarrug, garw, swta
grumble *vi* grwgnach, tuchan
grumpy *adj* sarrug, diserch

grunt *vi* rhochian ▷ *n* rhoch
guarantee *n* gwarant, ernes ▷ *vt* gwarantu, mechnïo
guard *n* gard, gwarchodydd; sgrin ▷ *vb* gwarchod
guarded *adj* gwyliadurus, gofalus
guardian *n* gwarcheidwad
guerilla *n* herfilwr
guess *vb* dyfalu, dyfeisio ▷ *n* amcan
guesswork *n* dyfaliad
guest *n* gwestai, gŵr/gwraig (g) wadd
guffaw *n* crechwen ▷ *vb* crechwenu
guidance *n* cyfarwyddyd
guide *n* arweinydd ▷ *vt* arwain, cyfarwyddo
guide book *n* teithlyfr
guide-dog *n* arweingi
guide-lines *npl* canllawiau
guild *n* cymdeithas, corfforaeth, urdd
guile *n* twyll, dichell, ystryw
guillotine *n* gilotîn
guilt *n* euogrwydd, bai
guilty *adj* euog
guinea pig *n* mochyn cwta
guise *n* dull, modd, rhith, diwyg
guitar *n* gitâr
guitarist *n* gitarydd
gulf *n* gwlff, geneufor; gagendor
gull *n* gwylan; gwirionyn ▷ *vt* twyllo
gullet *n* corn gwddf, sefnig
gullible *adj* hygoelus
gully *n* rhigol, ffos
gulp *vt* llawcian, traflyncu ▷ *n* llawc, traflwnc
gum *n* gwm, glud ▷ *vt* gymio, gludio
gumboots *npl* esgidiau rwber
gums *npl* cig y dannedd, gorcharfanau, crib y dannedd, gorfant
gun *n* gwn, dryll
gunner *n* gynnwr

gunpowder *n* powdr gwn
gunshot *n* ergyd gwn
gunsmith *n* gof gynnau (bach)
gurgle *vi* byrlymu
gush *vb* ffrydio, llifeirio ▷ *n* ffrwd,
  hyrddwynt
gust *n* chwythwm
gusto *n* awch, blas, sêl
gut *n* perfeddyn, coluddyn ▷ *vt*
  diberfeddu; difrodi, ysbeilio
gutter *n* ffos, cwter, cafn
guttural *adj* gyddfol
guzzle *vb* llawcio, traflyncu
gym *n* campfa
gymnasium *n* gymnasiwm, campfa
gymnast *n* mabolgampwr
gynaecologist *n* gynaecolegydd
gynaecology *n* gynaecoleg
gypsy *n* sipsi
gyrate *vi* troi, chwyrlio

ha *excl* ha!
haberdashery *n* dilladach, siop
  ddillad
habit *n* arferiad; anian; gwisg ▷ *vt*
  gwisgo, dilladu
habitable *adj* cyfannedd,
  cyfanheddol
habitat *n* cartref, cynefin
habitation *n* trigfa, preswylfa
habitual *adj* arferol, cyson
habituate *vt* arfer, cynefino
hack *vb* hacio, torri ▷ *n* hac
hack *n* hurfarch; cystog, slâf
hacker *n* (*computing*) haciwr
hackneyed *adj* ystrydebol, cyffredin
haddock *n* corbenfras, hadog
hades *n* annwfn
haemorrhage *n* gwaedlif
haemorrhoids *npl* clwyf y
  marchogion
haft *n* carn

hag n gwrach, gwiddon

haggard adj gwyllt, curiedig

haggle vi bargeinio'n daer

hail n cenllysg, cesair ▷ vb bwrw cesair

hail excl henffych well ▷ vb cyfarch, galw

hair n gwallt, blew, rhawn; **hair's breadth** trwch y blewyn; **hair splitting** hollti blew

hairbrush n brws gwallt

haircut n triniaeth gwallt, toriad, crop

hairdo n steil gwallt

hairdresser n triniwr gwallt

hair dryer n sychwr gwallt

hair gel n jel gwallt

hair spray n chwistrelliad gwallt; chwistrellydd gwallt

hairy adj blewog

hake n cegddu

hale adj iach, cryf, hoenus

half (**halves**) n hanner

half-back n hanerwr

half-breed adj cymysgryw

half-dead adj lledfyw

half fare n hanner pris

half-hearted adj diawydd, llugoer

halfpenny n dimai

half term n (school) hanner tymor

halfway adv: **halfway (to)** hanner ffordd (i)

halibut n halibwt

hall n llys, neuadd, plas; cyntedd

hallmark n dilysnod

hallo excl helô

hallow vt cysegru, sancteiddio

Halloween n nos Galangaeaf

hallucination n geuddrych, rhithwelediad

halo n corongylch, gogoniant, halo, lleugylch

halt vb sefyll ▷ n safiad; gorsaf, arosfa

halter n cebystr, tennyn

halve vt haneru

ham n morddwyd, ham

hames npl mynci

hamlet n pentref

hammer n morthwyl, mwrthwl, gordd ▷ vb morthwylio

hammock n hamog, gwely crog

hamper vt rhwystro, llesteirio

hamstring n llinyn y gar

hand n llaw; (of clock) bys ▷ vt estyn, trosglwyddo; **to be on hand** bod with law

handbag n bag llaw

handbook n llawlyfr

handbrake n brec llaw

handcuff n gefyn llaw

handful n dyrnaid, llond llaw

handicap n rhwystr, llestair, anfantais; blaen; **handicapped children** plant dan anfantais

handicraft n crefft

handiwork n gwaith llaw

handkerchief n cadach poced, hances, macyn, neisied

handle n carn, coes, troed, dolen, clust, dwrn ▷ vt trin, trafod; **to fly off the handle** colli tymer

handlebars npl cyrn

handmade adj wedi ei wneud â llaw

handmaid, handmaiden n llawforwyn

hand-off n hwp llaw

handrail n canllaw

hands-free adj heb afael; **hands-free kit** teclyn heb afael

handsome adj golygus, hardd, prydferth; hael

handwriting n llawysgrifen

handy adj hylaw, deheuig, cyfleus

hang vb crogi, hongian, dibynnu

hangar n awyrendy
hang-gliding vb barcuta
hangover n blinder ddoe, pen mawr
hank n cengl
hanker vi blysio, crefu, dyheu, hiraethu
hanky-panky n twyll, dichell ▷ adj twyllodrus, dichellgar
hap n hap, damwain
haphazard adj, adv damweiniol, ar siawns
happen vi digwydd
happily adv yn hapus
happiness n dedwyddwch, hapusrwydd
happy adj dedwydd, hapus
happy-go-lucky adj didaro, di-hid
harangue n araith, arawd ▷ vb areithio
harass vt poeni, blino, gofidio
harassment n poen, blinder
harbour n porthladd, harbwr ▷ vb llochesu
hard adj caled, anodd; **hard of hearing** trwm ei glyw; **to be hard done by** cael cam; **hard headed** hirben
hardboard n caledfwrdd
hard disk n (computing) disgen galed, disg caled
harden vb caledu
hardener n caledwr
hardness n caledwch
hardship n caledi
hard shoulder n llain galed
hard-up adj prin o arian
hardware n nwyddau metel
hardwood n pren caled
hard-working adj gweithgar, diwyd
hardy adj caled, cryf, gwydn; hy, eofn
hare n ysgyfarnog, ceinach
harebrained adj byrbwyll, gwyllt
harelip n bylchfin, gwefus fylchog

hark excl gwrando! clyw!; **hark back** dychwelyd
harlot n putain
harm n niwed, drwg, cam ▷ vt niweidio, drygu
harmful adj niweidiol
harmless adj diniwed, diddrwg
harmonious adj cytûn
harmonise vb cytgordio, cytuno
harmony n harmoni, cynghanedd
harness n harnais, gêr ▷ vt harneisio
harp n telyn ▷ vi canu'r delyn
harpoon n tryfer ▷ vt tryferu
harrow n og ▷ vt llyfnu; rhwygo, dryllio
harrowing adj dychrynllyd, ofnadwy, deifiol
harry vt difrodi, blino
harsh adj garw, gerwin, aflafar
harshness n craster, gerwindeb
hart n hydd
harvest n cynhaeaf ▷ vt cynaeafu
harvester n cynaeafwr; **combine harvester** combein
hash n briwgig; cymysgfa, cybolfa
hasp n hesben
hassle n helynt, trafferth
haste n brys, hast ▷ vi brysio, prysuro
hasten vb brysio, prysuro, hastu
hastily adv yn frysiog
hasty adj brysiog, byrbwyll
hat n het
hatch vb deor, gori ▷ n deoriad
hatch n gorddrws, rhagddor, dôr
hatchback n car cefn codi
hatchery n deorfa
hatchet n bwyell (fach)
hate vt casáu ▷ n cas, casineb
hateful adj cas, atgas
hatred n cas, casineb, digasedd
haughtiness n balchder, traha, ffroenucheledd

h

haughty adj balch, ffroenuchel, trahaus
haul vb tynnu, llusgo, halio ▷ n dalfa
haulage n cludiad, cludiant
haulier n haliwr
haunch n morddwyd, pedrain
haunt vt cyniwair, mynychu; trwblu, aflonyddu ▷ n cyniweirfa, cynefin, cyrchfa
have vt cael, meddu; **I have blue eyes** mae llygaid glas gennyf; **I have a cold** mae annwyd arnaf
haven n hafan, porthladd
haversack n ysgrepan
havoc n hafog, difrod
hawk n hebog, cudyll, curyll ▷ vb heboca
hawk vt gwerthu o dŷ i dŷ, pedlera
haws npl crawel y moch, criafol y moch
hawthorn n draenen wen
hay n gwair
hay fever n y dwymyn wair, clefyd y gwair
hayrick n tas wair
hazard n perygl, llestair, antur ▷ vt anturio, peryglu
hazardous adj peryglus, enbydus
haze n niwl, tarth, tawch
hazel n collen ▷ adj gwinau golau
haziness n aneglurder
hazy adj aneglur, niwlog
he pron ef, efe; efo, fo, o
head n pen ▷ vb blaenori, penio
headache n dolur (cur) yn y pen, pen tost
header n peniad
headgear n penffest, penwisg
heading n pennawd
headlamp n lamp fawr
headland n pentir, penrhyn; talar
headline n pennawd, teitl, hedin
headlong adv pendramwnwgl

headmaster n prifathro
headmistress n prifathrawes
headphones npl ffonau clust
headquarters npl pencadlys
headstrong adj cyndyn
headway n cynnydd
heal vb iacháu, meddyginiaethu
health n iechyd
health centre n canolfan iechyd
health food shop n siop bwyd iach
Health Service n y Gwasanaeth Iechyd
healthy adj iach, iachus
heap n crug, pentwr ▷ vt crugio, pentyrru
hear vb clywed
hearing n clyw
hearing aid n cymorth clywed
hearken vi gwrando, clustfeinio
hearsay n sôn, siarad ▷ adj o ben i ben, ail-law
hearse n hers
heart n calon
heart-ache n ing, dolur calon
heart attack n trawiad y galon
heartburn n dŵr poeth
heart disease n clefyd y galon
hearten vb calonogi
hearth n aelwyd
heartland n perfeddwlad
hearty adj calonnog, cynnes
heat n gwres, poethder; (in sport) rhagras ▷ vb twymo, poethi
heater n gwresogydd
heath n rhos, rhostir
heathen adj paganaidd ▷ n pagan
heather n grug
heating n gwres
heave vb codi, dyrchafu; chwyddo; taflu ▷ n hwb
heaven n nef, nefoedd
heavenly adj nefol, nefolaidd

heavily *adv* yn drwm, yn drymaidd

heavy *adj* trwm, trymaidd, trymllyd

heavyweight *n* pwysau trwm

Hebrew *n* Hebrëwr; Hebraeg ▷ *adj* Hebraeg; Hebreig

heckle *vb* ymyrryd

hectare *n* hectar

hectic *adj* prysur

hedge *n* clawdd, gwrych, perth

hedgehog *n* draenog

heed *vt* ystyried, talu sylw ▷ *n* ystyriaeth

heel *n* sawdl ▷ *vb* sodli

heifer *n* anner, heffer, treisiad

height *n* uchder, uchelder, taldra

heinous *adj* dybryd, anfad, ysgeler

heir *n* etifedd, aer

heiress *n* etifeddes, aeres

helicopter *n* hofrennydd

hell *n* uffern

hellish *adj* uffernol

hello *excl* helô!, hylô!, clyw!, gwrando!

helm *n* llyw; llywyddiaeth

helmet *n* helm

help *vt* helpu, cymorth, cynorthwyo ▷ *n* help, cymorth, cynhorthwy

helper *n* cynorthwywr, helpwr

helpful *adj* defnyddiol, cymwynasgar, gwasanaethgar, buddiol

helping *n* dogn, cyfran (o fwyd)

helpless *adj* diymadferth

helpline *n* llinell gymorth

helter-skelter *adv* blith-draphlith

hem *n* hem, ymyl ▷ *vt* hemio

hemi- *prefix* hanner

hemisphere *n* hemisffer

hemlock *n* cegid

hemp *n* cywarch

hen *n* iâr

hence *adv* oddi yma ▷ *excl* ymaith!

henceforth, henceforward *adv* rhag llaw, mwyach, o hyn ymlaen

henchman *n* gwas, canlynwr, cefnogydd

hen night, hen party *n* noson merched (cyn priodas)

hepatitis *n* hepatitis

her *pron* ei, hi, hithau

herald *n* herald ▷ *vt* cyhoeddi; rhagflaenu

herb *n* llysieuyn, sawr-lysieuyn

herbal *adj* llysieuol

herbal tea *n* te llysieuol

herbicide *n* llysleiddiad

herd *n* gyr, cenfaint, gre ▷ *vb* heidio

here *adv* yma

hereditary *adj* etifeddol

heredity *n* etifeddeg

heresy *n* heresi, gau athrawiaeth

heretic *n* heretic, camgredwr

heritage *n* etifeddiaeth, treftadaeth

hermit *n* meudwy

hernia *n* bors, hernia, torllengig

hero *n* arwr, gwron

heroic *adj* arwrol

heroin *n* heroin

heroine *n* arwres

heron *n* crëyr, crychydd

herring *n* pennog, ysgadenyn

hesitant *adj* petrusgar

hesitate *vi* petruso

hesitation *n* petruster

heterodox *adj* anuniongred

heterodoxy *n* anuniongrededd

heterogeneous *adj* anghydryw, afryw, heterogenus

heterosexual *n* anghyfunryw

hew *vt* naddu, torri, cymynu

hewer *n* cymynwr, torrwr

hexa- *prefix* chwech

heyday *n* anterth

hiatus *n* hiatws

hibernate *vi* gaeafu

hiccup *n* yr ig ▷ *vi* igian

hide *vb* cuddio, celu, ymguddio

h

hide n croen
hide-and-seek n chwarae mig
hideous adj hyll, erchyll
hiding place n cuddfan, lloches
hierarchy n gradd, offeiriadaeth
higgle vi taeru, bargenna
high adj uchel; mawr; cryf; llawn
highbrow adj uchel-ael
high chair n cadair ar gyfer plentyn
higher education n addysg uwch
highland n ucheldir
highlight vt pwysleisio ▷ n uchelbwynt; **highlights** npl aroleuadau (gwallt)
highlighter n (pen) aroleuydd
highly adv yn fawr, yn uchel
highness n uchelder
high-priest n archoffeiriad
high-spirited adj calonnog, nwyfus
high street n stryd fawr
high water n pen llanw
highway n priffordd, ffordd fawr
highwayman n lleidr penffordd
hijack vb cipio
hijacker n herwgipiwr
hike vb crwydro ▷ n taith gerdded
hilarious adj llawen, llon, siriol, hoenus
hill n bryn, allt, gorifyny
hillock n bryncyn, ponc, twmpath
hilly adj bryniog, mynyddig
hilt n carn cleddyf
him pron ef, efe, yntau
hind adj ôl
hind n ewig
hinder vt rhwystro, atal, lluddias, llesteirio
hindrance n rhwystr, llestair, lludd
Hindu n Hindw ▷ adj Hindwaidd
hinge n colyn drws ▷ vb troi, dibynnu
hint n awgrym ▷ vt awgrymu
hinterland n cefnwlad

hip n clun, pen uchaf y glun
hippie n hipi
hips npl egroes
hire vt cyflogi, hurio, llogi ▷ n cyflog, hur
hire car n car llog
hire purchase n hurbwrcas
hiss vb chwythu, sïo, hysio, hisian
historian n hanesydd
historic adj hanesyddol
historical adj hanesyddol
history n hanes
hit vb taro ▷ n ergyd, trawiad
hitch vb bachu ▷ n cwlwm; atalfa, rhwystr
hitchhike vb bodio
hitchhiker n bodiwr
hither adv yma, hyd yma, tuag yma
hitherto adv hyd yma, hyd yn hyn
HIV n abbr HIV; **HIV-negative/positive** HIV negyddol/positif
hive n cwch gwenyn
hive off vb rhannu, trosglwyddo, newid
hoar adj llwyd, penllwyd ▷ n llwydrew, barrug
hoard n cronfa, cuddfa ▷ vt cronni
hoarfrost n barrug, llwydrew
hoarse adj cryg, cryglyd
hoax vt twyllo ▷ n cast, tric, twyll
hob n pentan
hobble vb hercian
hobby n difyrwaith, hobi
hobby horse n ceffyl pren; hoff beth
hobgoblin n bwbach, bwci, bwgan
hockey n hoci
hoe n hof ▷ vb hofio
hog n mochyn
hoist vt codi, dyrchafu
hold vb dal, credu; atal; cadw ▷ n gafael, dalfa
hold n ceudod llong, howld
holdall n celsach

holding n deiliadaeth; tyddyn
hold up n (*robbery*) lladrad arfog;
(*in traffic*) rhwystr
hole n twll, ffau
holiday n gŵyl, dygwyl
holiness n sancteiddrwydd
Holland n Isalmaen
hollow adj cau, gwag ▷ n ceudod,
pant ▷ vt tyllu, cafnio
holly n celyn, celynnen
holocaust n lladdfa
holster n gwain
holy adj sanctaidd, glân
Holy Ghost/Spirit n Ysbryd Glân
homage n gwrogaeth
home n, adj cartref ▷ adv adref;
at home gartref
homeland n mamwlad
homeless adj digartref
homely adj cartrefol
home-made adj cartref
homeopathy n homeopatheg
home page n (*internet*) tudalen
gartref, tudalen hafan
home rule n ymreolaeth,
hunan-lywodraeth
homesick adj hiraethus
homestead n tyddyn
homework n gwaith cartref
homicide n dynleiddiad,
llofruddiaeth
homily n pregeth, homili
homogeneous adj cydryw,
homogenus
homosexual n gwrywgydiwr
homosexuality n gwrywgydiaeth
hone n carreg hogi, hôn ▷ vb hogi
honest adj (g)onest, didwyll
honesty n (g)onestrwydd
honey n mêl
honeycomb n dil mêl, crwybr ▷ vt
tyllu, britho
honeymoon n mis mêl

honeysuckle n gwyddfid
honorary adj mygedol
honour n anrhydedd ▷ vt anrhydeddu
honourable adj anrhydeddus
hood n cwfl, cwcwll
hoodie n (*hooded top*) hwdi
hoodwink vt dallu, twyllo
hoof n carn
hook n bach; cryman ▷ vb bachu
hooker n bachwr
hooligan n adyn, dihiryn
hoop n cylch, cant ▷ vt cylchu, cantio
hoot vb hwtian, hwtio ▷ n hŵt
hop vb hercian ▷ n llam, herc
hope n gobaith ▷ vb gobeithio
hopeless adj anobeithiol
horde n torf, haid, mintai
horizon n gorwel
horizontal adj llorwedd
hormone n hormon
horn n corn ▷ vt cornio, twlcio
horned adj corniog
hornet n gwenynen feirch, cacynen
horoscope n horosgôp
horrible adj erchyll, ofnadwy
horrid adj erchyll, echrydus, anferth
horrify vt brawychu
horror n arswyd, erchylltod
horse n march, ceffyl
horsehair n rhawn
horseman n marchog
horsemanship n marchogaeth
horseplay n direidi
horseshoe n pedol
horticultural adj garddwriaethol
horticulture n garddwriaeth
horticulturist n garddwriaethwr
hose (**hose**) n hosan
hose (**hoses**) n pibell ddŵr
hospitable adj lletygar, croesawus
hospital n ysbyty
hospitality n lletygarwch, croeso
host n llu, byddin

h

host n lletywr, gwesteiwr
hostage n gwystl
hostel n llety efrydwyr, neuadd breswyl
hostess n croesawferch
hostile adj gelyniaethus
hot adj poeth, twym, brwd, gwresog
hotbed n magwrfa
hotch-potch n cymysgfa, cybolfa
hotel n gwesty
hotelier n gwestywr
hot-headed adj penboeth, byrbwyll
hot-water bottle n jar/potel dŵr twym
hound n bytheiad, helgi ▷ vt hela, erlid, annos
hour n awr
house n tŷ, annedd ▷ vb lletya
household n teulu, tylwyth
householder n deiliad tŷ
housekeeper n gofalyddes
housewife n gwraig tŷ
housing n tai
hovel n penty, hofel
hover vi hofran
hovercraft n hofrenfad
how adv pa mor, pa fodd, pa sut, sut
howbeit adv er hynny
however adv pa fodd bynnag, sut bynnag
howl vi udo, oernadu ▷ n udiad, oernad
hoyden n rhampen, hoeden
hub n both olwyn; canolbwynt
hubbub n mwstwr
huddle vb tyrru, gwthio
hue n gwawr
huff vb sorri, tramgwyddo ▷ n soriant
hug vt cofleidio, gwasgu
huge adj anferth, enfawr, dirfawr
hulk n corff llong, llong foel, hwlc
hull n corff llong; cibyn, plisgyn

hullabaloo n dadwrdd, helynt, halibalŵ
hum vb mwmian ▷ n si, sibrwd
human adj dynol
humane adj tirion, tosturiol, trugarog
humanism n dyneiddiaeth
humanist n dyneiddiwr
humanistic adj dyneiddiol
humanitarian n dyngarwr
humanitarianism n dyngaroldeb
humanity n dynoliaeth, dynolryw
humble adj gostyngedig, ufudd ▷ vt darostwng
humble-bee n cacynen
humbug n twyll, ffug, hoced; twyllwr ▷ vt twyllo
humdrum adj diflas
humid adj llaith
humiliate vt bychanu, gwaradwyddo, darostwng, iselu
humiliation n darostyngiad
humility n gostyngeiddrwydd
humour n hwyl, donioldeb ▷ vt boddio
hump n crwmach, crwmp, crwb
hunch n syniad, tybiaeth
hunch backed adj cefngrwm
hundred adj cant, can ▷ n cant; cantref
Hungary n Hwngari
hunger n newyn, chwant bwyd ▷ vi newynu
hungry adj newynog
hunk n cwlff(yn)
hunt vb hela, erlid ▷ n helwriaeth, hela
hunter n heliwr; ceffyl hela
hunting n hela
hurdle n clwyd
hurl vt hyrddio
hurly-burly n hwrli-bwrli, dwndwr
hurricane n corwynt
hurried adj brysiog
hurry vb brysio ▷ n brys

hurt vb niweidio, dolurio, brifo ▷ n niwed, dolur
hurtful adj niweidiol
hurtle vb gwrthdaro, chwyrlïo
husband n gŵr, priod ▷ vt cynilo
husbandry n amaethyddiaeth, hwsmonaeth
hush excl ust ▷ vb distewi ▷ n distawrwydd
husk n plisgyn, cibyn ▷ vt plisgo
husky adj sych, cryglyd
hussy n maeden
hustings n hwstyng, llwyfan etholiad
hustle vb gwthio, prysuro
hut n bwth, caban, cwt
hutch n cwt cwningen, cwb
hyacinth n croeso haf
hybrid adj croesryw
hydration n hydradiad
hydraulic adj hydrolig
hydraulics n hydroleg
hydro- prefix dwfr
hydroelectric adj hydroelectrig
hydrophobia n hydroffobia
hygiene n iechydaeth, gwyddor glendid
hymn n emyn ▷ vb emynu
hyper- prefix gor-, tra-
hyperbole n gormodiaith
hypermarket n archfarchnad
hyphen n cyplysnod, cysylltnod (-)
hypnotism n swyngwsg, hypnotiaeth
hypnotize vt swyno, rheibio
hypochondria n pruddglwyf, y felan
hypocrisy n rhagrith
hypocrite n rhagrithiwr
hypothesis (**-theses**) n damcaniaeth
hyssop n isop
hysteria n y famwst, hysteria
hysterical adj hysterig

I pron mi, myfi; fi, i; minnau, innau
ice n iâ, rhew ▷ vt taenu (megis) â rhew
iceberg n mynydd rhew
ice cream n hufen iâ
Iceland n Gwlad yr Iâ
ice lolly n loli iâ
ice rink n llain iâ
icicle n clöyn iâ, cloch iâ, pibonwy
icing n eising
icon n eicon
icy adj rhewllyd
ID card n cerdyn adnabod
idea n drychfeddwl, syniad
ideal adj delfrydol, ideal ▷ n delfryd
idealism n delfrydiaeth
idealist n delfrydiwr
idealistic adj delfrydol
idealize vb delfrydu
identical adj yr un (yn union)
identify vt adnabod (fel yr un un); uniaethu

identikit, identikit picture n
tebyglun

identity n unfathiant, hunaniaeth

idiocy n gwiriondeb, penwendid

idiom n priod-ddull, idiom

idiosyncrasy n tymer, anianawd

idiot n gwirionyn, hurtyn

idle adj segur, ofer ▷ vb segura, ofera

idleness n segurdod, diogi

idol n eilun

idolater n eilunaddolwr

idolatry n eilunaddoliaeth

idolise vb addoli, gwirioni

idyll n bugeilgerdd; canig

if conj os, pe

igloo n iglw

ignite vb ennyn, tanio, cynnau

ignition n taniad

ignoble adj anenwog, isel, gwael, salw

ignominious adj gwarthus, gwaradwyddus

ignorance n anwybodaeth

ignorant adj anwybodus

ignore vt anwybyddu, diystyru

il- prefix di-, an-

ill adj drwg; gwael, claf ▷ adv yn ddrwg ▷ n drwg, niwed

ill-advised adj annoeth, ffôl

illegal adj anghyfreithlon

illegible adj annarllenadwy, aneglur

illegitimate, illicit adj anghyfreithlon

illiterate adj anllythrennog

illness n afiechyd, anhwylder, anhwyldeb

illogical adj afresymegol

ill-timed adj anamserol

ill-treat vb camdrin

illuminate vt goleuo, addurno

illumination n golau, esboniad

illusion n rhith, lledrith, rhithganfyddiad

illustrate vt egluro; darlunio

illustration n eglureb; darlun

illustrative adj darluniol, eglurhaol

illustrious adj enwog, hyglod

ill-will n gelyniaeth, casineb

im- prefix di, an-

image n delw, llun; delwedd

imagery n delweddaeth

imaginary adj dychmygol

imagination n dychymyg, darfelydd

imaginative adj dychmygus

imagine vt dychmygu, tybio

imbalance n anghydbwysedd

imbecile adj, n (un) penwan

imbue vt trwytho

imitate vt dynwared, efelychu

immaculate adj difrycheulyd, pur, glân

immaterial adj dibwys

immature adj anaeddfed

immediate adj agos, presennol

immediately adv ar unwaith

immemorial adj er cyn cof

immense adj anferth, eang, dirfawr

immerse vt trochi, suddo

immigrant n mewnfudwr

immigrate vi mewnfudo

imminent adj gerllaw, agos, wrth y drws

immobile adj diymod, disymud

immoral adj anfoesol

immortal adj anfarwol

immortality n anfarwoldeb

immortalize vb anfarwoli

immovable adj diysgog, ansymudol

immune adj rhydd rhag

immunization n gwrth-heintiad

immunize vb gwrtheintio

immure vt caethiwo, carcharu

immutable adj anghyfnewidiol, digyfnewid

imp n dieflyn, cenau

impact n ardrawiad, gwrthdrawiad

impair vt amharu

impale vt trywanu

impart vt cyfrannu, rhoddi

impartial adj diduedd, amhleidiol, teg

impassable adj na ellir mynd heibio iddo

impasse n ataliad, pen draw

impassioned adj brwd, hwyliog, cyffrous

impassive adj digyffro, didaro

impatient adj diamynedd

impeach vt cyhuddo, cwyno yn erbyn, uchelgyhuddo

impeccable adj di-fai

impede vt atal, rhwystro, llesteirio

impediment n atalfa, rhwystr, nam

impel vt gyrru, hyrddio, cymell

impending adj agos, gerllaw

imperative n gorchymyn ▷ adj gorchmynnol, gorfodol

imperfect adj amherffaith

imperial adj ymerodrol

imperil vt peryglu

imperious adj awdurdodol, trahaus

impermeable adj anathraidd

impersonal adj amhersonol

impersonate vt personoli, cynrychioli; portreadu

impertinent adj amherthnasol; digywilydd

imperturbable adj tawel, digyffro

impervious adj na ellir ei dreiddio, anhydraidd

impetuous adj byrbwyll, nwydwyllt

impetus n cymhelliad, symbyliad

impinge vi taro yn erbyn, gwrthdaro, cyffwrdd â

impious adj annuwiol, diras

implacable adj anghymodlon

implant vt plannu, gwreiddio

implement n offeryn, arf ▷ vb gweithredu

implication n ymhlygiad, goblygiad

implicit adj dealledig; ymhlyg, goblygedig

implore vt atolygu, ymbil, erfyn, crefu

imply vt arwyddo, awgrymu

impolite adj anfoesgar

import vt mewnforio ▷ n mewnforyn; arwyddocâd; pwys

importance n pwys, pwysigrwydd

important adj pwysig

importer n mewnforiwr

importune vt dyfal geisio, taer erfyn

impose vb gosod ar; twyllo

imposing adj llethol, mawreddog

impossibility n amhosibilrwydd

impossible adj amhosibl

impostor n twyllwr

imposture n twyll, hoced

impotence n anallu, analluedd

impotent adj di-rym, analluog

impound vi ffaldio; atafaelu

impoverish vt tlodi, llymhau

impracticable adj anymarferol

imprecate vt rhegi, melltithio

impregnable adj cadarn, di-syfl

impregnate vt ffrwythloni; trwytho

impress vt argraffu, pwyso, dylanwadu ▷ n argraffiad

impression n argraff

impressionable adj hawdd ei argyhoeddi

impressive adj trawiadol

imprint vt argraffu ▷ n argraff, delw

imprison vt carcharu

improbable adj annhebygol

impromptu adj, adv ar y pryd, byrfyfyr

improper adj anweddus

improve vb gwella, diwygio

improvement n gwelliant

improvise vb addasu ar y pryd

i

impudent *adj* digywilydd, haerllug
impulse *n* cymhelliad, ysgogiad
impulsive *adj* byrbwyll
impunity *n* bod heb gosb; **with impunity** yn ddi-gosb
impure *adj* amhur, aflan
impute *vt* cyfrif i; priodoli; bwrw ar
in *prep* yn, mewn, i mewn, o fewn
in- *prefix* di-, an-
inability *n* anallu
inaccessible *n* anhygyrch
inaccurate *adj* anghywir, anfanwl
inaction *n* segurdod
inadequate *adj* annigonol
inadmissible *adj* annerbyniol
inadvertent *adj* anfwriadol, amryfus
inane *adj* gwag, gwageddus, ofer
inanimate *adj* difywyd, dienaid
inappropriate *adj* anaddas
inasmuch *adv* yn gymaint (â)
inaudible *adj* anhyglyw, na ellir ei glywed
inaugurate *vt* urddo, cysegru, agor, dechrau
inauguration *n* agoriad, dechreuad
inborn *adj* cynhenid, greddfol
inbreed *vb* mewnfrido
incandescent *adj* gwynias
incantation *n* swyn, swyngyfaredd
incapability *n* anallu
incapable *adj* analluog
incapacitate *vt* anghymhwyso, analluogi
incarcerate *vt* carcharu
incarnation *n* ymgnawdoliad
incendiary *adj* llosg ▷ *n* bom tân
incense *n* arogldarth
incense *vt* llidio, cythruddo
incentive *adj* cymelliadol ▷ *n* cymhelliad
inception *n* dechreuad, agoriad
incessant *adj* di-baid, di-dor

incest *n* llosgach
inch *n* modfedd
incident *n* digwyddiad
incidental *adj* digwyddiadol, achlysurol
incidentally *adv* gyda llaw
incinerate *vb* llosgi'n ulw
incineration *n* llosgiad llwyr
incinerator *n* llosgydd, ffwrnais
incipient *adj* dechreuol
incise *vt* torri, trychu
incisive *adj* llym, miniog
incite *vt* annog, cyffroi, annos
inclement *adj* gerwin, garw, drycinog
inclination *n* tuedd, gogwydd
incline *vb* tueddu, gogwyddo ▷ *n* llethr
include *vt* cynnwys
including *prep* gan gynnwys
inclusive *adj* cynwysedig, gan gynnwys
incognito *adj* yn ddirgel, dan ffugenw
incoherent *adj* digyswllt, anghysylltus
income *n* incwm; **income tax** treth incwm
incompatible *adj* anghytûn
incompetent *n* anghymwys
incomplete *adj* anghyflawn
incomprehensible *adj* annealladwy
incongruous *adj* anghydweddol, anaddas
inconsistency *n* anghysondeb
inconsistent *adj* anghyson
inconspicuous *adj* anamlwg
incontestable *adj* diymwad, diamheuol
inconvenience *n* anghyfleustra
inconvenient *adj* anghyfleus
incorporate *vb* corffori, ymgorffori

incorporated adj corfforedig

incorrect adj anghywir

incorrigible adj anwelladwy

increase vb cynyddu ▷ n cynnydd

incredible adj anhygoel, anghredadwy

incredulity n anghrediniaeth

incredulous adj anghrediniol

increment n cynnydd, ychwanegiad

incriminate vt cyhuddo, euogi

incubate vb gori, deor

incubator n deorydd

incumbent adj rhwymedig ar ▷ n periglor, offeiriad, clerigwr

incur vt rhedeg i ddyled; achosi

incursion n cyrch

indebted adj dyledus

indecent adj anweddus

indecision n petruster

indecisive adj amhendant

indeed adv yn wir; iawn, dros ben

indefatigable adj diflin, dyfal

indefinite adj amhenodol, amhendant

indelible adj annileadwy

indelicate adj aflednais

indemnify vb digolledu

indemnity n iawn

indented adj bylchog, danheddus

indenture n cytundeb, cyfamod

independence n annibyniaeth

independent adj annibynnol ▷ n annibynnwr

indescribable adj annisgrifiadwy

indeterminate adj amhenodol, penagored

index n mynegai; mynegfys

India n India

Indian adj Indiaidd ▷ n Indiad

indicate vt dangos, arwyddo

indicative adj arwyddol, mynegol

indicator n dangosydd

indict vt cyhuddo

indifference n difaterwch, difrawder

indifferent adj difater; dibwys

indigenous adj cynhenid

indigent adj anghenus, tlawd, rheidus

indigestion n diffyg traul, camdreuliad

indignant adj dig, digofus, dicllon

indignation n dig, digofaint, llid

indignity n amarch, sarhad, anfri

indirect adj anuniongyrchol

indiscreet adj annoeth

indiscriminate adj diwahaniaeth

indispensable adj anhepgorol

indisposed adj anhwylus

indisputable adj diamheuol

indissoluble adj annatod

indistinct adj aneglur, anhyglyw, bloesg

indite vt cyfansoddi, traethu

individual adj unigol ▷ n un, unigolyn

indoctrinate vb trwytho (ag athrawiaeth), credorfodi

indoctrination n credorfodaeth

indolence n seguryd, syrthni

indolent adj segur, swrth, dioglyd

indomitable adj anorchfygol, di-ildio

Indonesia n Indonesia

indoor adj, adv dan do

indubitable adj diamheuol

induce vt darbwyllo, denu, cymell

inducement n anogiad

induct vt sefydlu; anwytho

induction n anwythiad

indulge vb boddio; maldodi

indulgence n ymfoddhad; maldod

indulgent adj ffafriol, maldodus

industrial adj diwydiannol, gweithfaol

industrial estate n stad ddiwydiannol

industrialize vb diwydiannu
industrious adj diwyd, dyfal, gweithgar
industry n diwydrwydd; diwydiant
inebriate vt meddwi ▷ n meddwyn
inedible adj anfwytadwy
ineffable adj anhraethol, anhraethadwy
ineffective adj aneffeithiol
inefficiency n anallu
inefficient adj annalluog
ineligible adj anghymwys
inept adj heb fod yn taro, gwrthun, gwirion
inequality n anghysondeb
inert adj swrth, diynni, diegni
inertia n anegni, inertia
inestimable adj amhrisiadwy
inevitable adj anochel, anesgorol
inexhaustible adj dihysbydd
inexorable adj di-ildio, anhyblyg
inexpensive adj rhad
inexperience n diffyg profiad
inexperienced adj amhrofiadol, dibrofiad
infallibility n anffaeledigrwydd
infallible adj anffaeledig
infamous adj gwaradwyddus, gwarthus
infancy n mabandod, mebyd, maboed
infant n maban, baban; un dan oed
infantry n gwŷr traed, milwyr traed
infant school n ysgol fach
infatuate vt gwirioni, ffoli, dwlu
infatuated adj wedi ffoli, wedi gwirioni
infect vt heintio, llygru
infection n haint
infectious adj heintus
infer vt casglu
inferior adj is, israddol ▷ n isradd
inferiority n israddoldeb

inferiority complex n cymhleth y taeog
infernal adj uffernol, dieflig
infertile adj anffrwythlon
infertility n anffrwythlondeb
infest vt bod yn bla, heigiannu
infidel n anffyddiwr
infidelity n anffyddlondeb
infield adj mewnfaes
infinite adj anfeidrol
infinitesimal adj anfeidrol fach, gorfychan
infinitive adj annherfynol ▷ n berfenw
infirm adj egwan, gwan, gwanllyd
infirmary n ysbyty, clafdy
infirmity n gwendid, llesgedd
inflame vb ennyn, cyffroi, llidio
inflamed adj llidus
inflammable adj hylosg, hyfflam
inflammation n enyniad, enynfa, llid
inflatable adj y gellir ei chwyddo neu ei chwythu
inflate vt chwyddo
inflation n chwyddiant
inflect vt ffurfdroi; treiglo
inflexibility n anhyblygrwydd
inflexible adj anhyblyg
inflict vt peri, gweinyddu (cosb, poen etc)
influence n dylanwad ▷ vt dylanwadu
influenza n ffliw
influx n dylifiad
inform vb hysbysu
informal adj anffurfiol
information n gwybodaeth, hysbysrwydd
information technology n technoleg gwybodaeth
infra- prefix is-
infra-red adj is-goch

infrastructure n seilwaith
infrequent adj anaml
infringe vt torri, troseddu
infuriate vt ffyrnigo, cynddeiriogi
infuse vt tywallt, arllwys; trwytho
infusion n trwyth, hydreiddiad
ingenious adj medrus, cywrain, celfydd
ingenuous adj didwyll, diddichell
ingenuousness n didwylledd, diffuantrwydd
ingrained adj wedi greddfu; cynhenid
ingratiate vt ennill ffafr
ingratitude n anniolchgarwch
ingredients npl cynhwysion, defnyddiau
inhabit vt cyfaneddu, trigo, preswylio
inhabitable adj cyfannedd, trigadwy
inhabitant n preswyliwr
inhale vt anadlu
inhaler n anadlydd
inhere vi glynu, ymlynu, bod
inherent adj cynhenid, greddfol
inherit vt etifeddu
inheritance n etifeddiaeth
inheritor n etifedd, etifeddwr
inhibit vt gwahardd, atal
inhibition n ataliad, atalnwyd
inhibitor n atalydd
inhuman adj annynol, creulon
inimical adj gelyniaethus
inimitable adj digyffelyb
iniquitous adj drwg, traws
iniquity n anwiredd, camwedd
initial adj dechreuol ▷ n llythyren gyntaf
initiate vt egwyddori; derbyn; dechrau
initiative n cynhoredd, menter
inject vt chwistrellu

injection n chwistrelliad, pigiad
injunction n gorchymyn, gwaharddiad
injure vt niweidio, anafu
injury n niwed, cam, anaf
injustice n anghyfiawnder, cam
ink n inc ▷ vt incio
inkling n awgrym, arwydd
inland adj canoldirol ▷ n canoldir
Inland Revenue n Cyllid y Wlad
in-laws npl teulu-yng-nghyfraith
inlet n cilfach, bae
inmate n trigiannydd, preswylydd
inmost adj nesaf i mewn, dyfnaf
inn n tafarn, tafarndy, gwesty
innate adj cynhenid, cynhwynol, greddfol
inner adj mewnol
innings npl batiad
innkeeper n tafarnwr
innocence n diniweidrwydd
innocent adj diniwed, gwirion, dieuog
innocuous adj diniwed, diberygl
innovate vi newid, cyflwyno
innovation n newyddbeth
innuendo n ensyniad
innumerable adj aneirif, afrifed, dirifedi, di-rif
inoculate vt brechu
inoculation n brechiad
inoffensive adj di-ddrwg
inordinate adj anghymedrol, di-rôl
inorganic adj anorganig
input n mewnbwn, cyfraniad
inquest n cwest; trengholiad
inquire vb ymofyn, ymholi, gofyn, holi
inquiry n ymholiad
inquisition n ymchwiliad; chwil-lys
inquisitive adj ymofyngar, holgar
in-road n cyrch
insane adj gwallgof, gorffwyll, ynfyd

insanitary adj afiachus, brwnt
insatiable adj anniwall
inscribe vt arysgrifio
inscription n arysgrif
inscrutable adj anolrheiniadwy, anchwiliadwy
insect n pryf, trychfil
insensibility n dideimladrwydd
insensible adj dideimlad
insert vb mewnosod
in-service adj mewn swydd
inside n tu mewn ▷ adj mewnol ▷ prep y tu mewn i ▷ adv i mewn, o fewn
inside-forward n mewnwr
inside-half n mewnwr
inside-out adv o chwith
inside-right n mewnwr de
insidious adj llechwraidd
insight n mewnwelediad
insignificance n dinodedd
insignificant adj di-nod, distadl, dibwys
insincere adj annidwyll, ffuantus, rhagrithiol
insincerity n annidwylledd
insinuate vb ensynio
insipid adj diflas, merfaidd
insist vi mynnu
insolence n haerllugrwydd
insolent adj haerllug
insolvent adj methdalus, wedi torri
insomnia n anhunedd
inspect vt arolygu, archwilio
inspection n archwiliad, arolygiad
inspector n arolygwr
inspiration n ysbrydoliaeth
inspire vb ysbrydoli
instability n ansadrwydd
install vt sefydlu, gorseddu
instalment n cyfran, rhandal
instance n enghraifft ▷ vt enwi, nodi

instant adj taer, ebrwydd ▷ n eiliad, moment
instantaneous adj yn y fan; disymwth
instant coffee n coffi powdr
instantly adv ar drawiad
instead adv yn lle
instep n mwnwgl troed, cefn troed
instigate vt annog, cymell
instil vt argymell
instinct n greddf
institute n athrofa
institution n sefydliad
instruct vt hyfforddi
instruction n hyfforddiant
instructor n hyfforddwr
instrument n offeryn
insubordinate adj anufudd, gwrthryfelgar
insufferable adj annioddefol
insufficient adj annigonol
insular adj ynysol, cul
insulate vt ynysu, inswleiddio
insult vt sarhau ▷ n sarhad
insuperable adj anorfod, anorchfygol
insurance n yswiriant
insurance policy n polisi yswiriant
insure vb yswirio
insurgent adj gwrthryfelgar ▷ n gwrthryfelwr
insurrection n terfysg, gwrthryfel
intact adj cyfan, dianaf
integral adj cyfan, cyflawn
integrate vb cyfannu
integrity n cywirdeb, gonestrwydd
intellect n deall
intellectual n deallusyn ▷ adj deallus, deallgar
intelligence n deallgarwch, deallusrwydd; hysbysrwydd
intelligent adj deallus
intelligible adj dealladwy

intend *vt* bwriadu, amcanu, golygu

intense *adj* angerddol, dwys

intensive care unit *n* unedgofal arbennig

intent *adj* dyfal, diwyd, astud

intent *n* bwriad, amcan; ystyr; diben

intention *n* bwriad

intentional *adj* bwriadol

inter *vt* claddu, daearu

inter- *prefix* rhwng, cyd

interaction *n* rhyngweithiad

interactive *adj* rhyngweithiol

interbreed *vb* rhyngfridio

intercede *vi* cyfryngu, eiriol

intercept *vt* rhyng-gipio, rhwystro, rhagod

intercession *n* cyfryngdod, eiriolaeth

interchange *vt* cyfnewid, ymgyfnewid

intercourse *n* cyfathrach

interdict *vt* gwahardd ▷ *n* gwaharddiad

interest *n* budd, buddiant; diddordeb; llog ▷ *vt* diddori

interested *adj* â chanddo ddidordeb

interesting *adj* diddorol

interest rate *n* cyfradd llog

interests *npl* diddordebau

interface *n* cydwyneb

interfere *vt* cyfryngu, ymyrryd, ymhél

interference *n* ymyrraeth

interim *adj* dros dro ▷ *n* cyfamser

interior *adj* mewnol ▷ *n* tu mewn, canol, perfeddwlad

interject *vt* ebychu

interlock *vb* cyd-gloi

interloper *n* ymwthiwr, ymyrrwr

interlude *n* egwyl; anterliwt

intermediary *n* canolwr, cyfryngwr

intermediate *adj* canol, canolradd

intern *vt* carcharu

internal *adj* mewnol

international *adj* cydwladol, rhyngwladol

internet *n* rhyngrwyd; **internet café** caffi rhyngrwyd, caffe rhyngrwyd

interpolate *vt* dodi i mewn, rhyngosod

interpolation *n* rhyngosodiad

interpose *vb* gosod rhwng, cyfryngu, rhyngwthio

interpret *vt* dehongli; cyfieithu

interpretation *n* dehongliad; cyfieithiad

interpreter *n* lladmerydd, cyfieithydd

interrelation *n* cydberthynas

interrogate *vt* holi

interrogative *adj* gofynnol

interrupt *vt* torri ar, torri ar draws, ymyrryd

intersect *vb* croesi ei gilydd; croesdorri

intersection *n* croesdoriad

intersperse *vb* gwasgaru, britho

interval *n* egwyl, saib

intervene *vi* ymyrryd

interview *n* cyfweliad ▷ *vb* cyfweld

interviewer *n* cyfwelydd

intestines *npl* perfedd, coluddion

intimacy *n* agosatrwydd

intimate *adj* cyfarwydd, agos ▷ *n* cydnabod

intimate *vt* arwyddo, hysbysu

intimidate *vt* dychrynu, brawychu

into *prep* i, i mewn i

intolerable *adj* annioddefol

intonation *n* tonyddiaeth, goslef

intone *vt* llafarganu

intoxicate *vt* meddwi

intoxication *n* meddwdod

intractable *adj* anhydrin, afreolus

intranet n intranet, mewnrwyd
intransitive adj cyflawn (gramadeg)
intrepid adj di-ofn, diarswyd, gwrol, dewr
intricate adj dyrys, cymhleth, astrus
intrigue vi, n cynllwyn
intrinsic adj priodol, hanfodol
introduce vt cyflwyno
introduction n cyflwyniad, rhagarweiniad
introductory adj dechreuol, agoriadol, rhagarweiniol
introspection n mewnsylliad
introvert adj mewnblyg
intrude vb ymyrryd
intruder n ymyrrwr, ymwthiwr
intrusion n ymwthiad, ymyrraeth
intuition n sythwelediad
inundate vt gorlifo, boddi
inundation n gorlifiad
inure vt cyfarwyddo, caledu
invade vt goresgyn
invalid adj di-rym, annilys
invalid n un afiach, un methedig
invaluable adj amhrisiadwy
invariable adj gwastad, dieithriad
invariably adv yn ddieithriad
invasion n goresgyniad
invective n difrïaeth, cabledd
invent vt dyfeisio, dychmygu
invention n dyfais
inventory n rhestr, stocrestr
inverse adj (yn y) gwrthwyneb, yn groes
inversion n gwrthdro
invert vt troi wyneb i waered, gwrthdroi
inverted commas npl dyfynodau
invest vt buddsoddi; arwisgo
investigate vt chwilio, archwilio, ymchwilio

investigation n ymchwiliad
investigator n ymchwiliwr
investiture n arwisgiad
investment n buddsoddiad
investor n buddsoddwr
invidious adj annymunol
invigilate vb arolygu
invigilator n arolygwr, gwyliwr
invigorate vt cryfhau, grymuso
invincible adj anorchfygol
inviolable adj dihalog, cysegredig
invisible adj anweledig, anweladwy
invitation n gwahoddiad
invite vt gwahodd
invoice n anfoneb
involuntary adj o anfodd, anfwriadol
involve vt drysu; cynnwys, ymwneud
involvement n ymwneud, ymglymiad
inward adj mewnol
iodine n ïodin
ion n ïon
ionisation n ïoneiddiad
ionise vb ïoneiddio
iota n mymryn, iod, gronyn
IQ n abbr IQ, CD, cyniferydd deallusrwydd
ir- prefix di-, an-
Iran n Iran
Iraq n Iraq
irate adj dig, llidiog
Ireland n Iwerddon
iris n enfys; elestr
Irish adj Gwyddelig ▷ n Gwyddeleg
Irishman (**-men**) n Gwyddel
Irishwoman (**-women**) n Gwyddeles
irksome adj blin, trafferthus, diflas
iron n, adj haearn ▷ vt smwddio
ironic adj eironig
ironing board n bwrdd smwddio

ironmonger n gwerthwr nwyddau haearn
irony n eironi
irradiate vt arbelydru
irradiation n arbelydredd
irrational adj direswm, afresymol
irreconcilable adj anghymodlon
irrefutable adj anatebadwy
irregular adj afreolaidd
irregularity n afreoleidd-dra
irrelevant adj amherthnasol
irreparable adj anadferadwy
irreproachable adj diargyhoedd, di-fai
irresistible adj anorchfygol
irretrievable adj anadferadwy
irrevocable adj di-alw-yn-ôl
irrigate vt dyfrhau
irritable n croendenau, anniddig, llidiog
irritate vt blino, poeni, cythruddo
is vi mae, sydd, yw, ydy(w), oes
Islamic adj Islamaidd
island, isle n ynys
islet n ynysig
isolate vt neilltuo, gwahanu
isolated adj wedi ei neilltuo, wedi ei wahanu
isolation n neilltuaeth, arwahanrwydd
ISP n abbr (= Internet Service Provider) ISP, Darparydd Gwasanaeth Rhyngrwyd
Israel n Israel
Israelite n Israeliad
issue n llif; agorfa, arllwysfa; hilogaeth, plant; canlyniad, pwnc mewn dadl ▷ vb tarddu, deillio; rhoi allan, cyhoeddi
isthmus n culdir
IT n abbr (= information technology) TG, technoleg gwybodaeth
it pron efe, fe, ef, efo, fo, o; hi

Italian adj Eidalaidd ▷ n Eidalwr; (language) Eidaleg
italic adj italig
italicize vb italeiddio
italics npl llythrennau italaidd
Italy n Yr Eidal
itch vi ysu, cosi ▷ n y crafu, ysfa
item n peth, pwnc, darn, tamaid
iterate vt ailadrodd
itinerant adj teithiol
itinerary n taith, teithlyfr
itinerate vi teithio, cylchdeithio
itself pron ei hun, ei hunan
ivory n ifori
ivy n eiddew, iorwg

i

J

jab *n* jab, pigiad ▷ *vb* procio, gwanu

jabber *vi* bragawthan, clebran ▷ *n* clebar

jack *n* jac

jackass *n* asyn gwryw; hurtyn

jackdaw *n* corfran, jac-y-do

jacket *n* siaced

jade *vt* blino, lluddedu

jagged *adj* danheddog, ysgithrog

jail *n* carchar

jam *n* jam; tagfa

jam *vt* jamio, tagu

Jamaica *n* Jamaica

jangle *vi* clochdar

janitor *n* porthor

January *n* Ionawr

Japan *n* Nihon, Japán, Siapán

Japanese *adj* Siapaneaidd ▷ *n* Siapanead; (*language*) Siapaneg

jar *n* anghytsain; anghydfod ▷ *vb* rhygnu

jar *n* jar

jargon *n* ffregod, bregiaith, jargon

jaundice *n* y clefyd melyn

jaunt *vi* gwibio, rhodio ▷ *n* gwibdaith

jaunty *adj* llon, bywiog, talog

javelin *n* picell, gwaywffon

jaw *n* gên, cern; **jaws** safn

jay *n* sgrech y coed

jazz *n* jas

jealous *adj* eiddigus, cenfigennus, gwenwynllyd

jealousy *n* cenfigen, eiddigedd

jeans *n* jîns

Jeep® *n* jîp

jeer *vb* gwawdio, gwatwar

jelly *n* jeli

jellyfish *n* slefren fôr

jeopardy *n* perygl, enbydrwydd

jerk *n* plwc, ysgytiad ▷ *vb* plycio, ysgytio

jerkin *n* siercyn, siaced

jersey *n* siersi

Jerusalem *n* Caersalem, Jerwsalem

jest *n* cellwair, ysmaldod ▷ *vi* cellwair, ysmalio

Jesus *n* Iesu

jet *n* ffrwd, jet; muchudd ▷ *vb* ffrydio, pistyllio

jet-ski *n* jet-sgi ▷ *vi* jet-sgïo

jettison *vt* taflu (llwyth) dros y bwrdd

jetty *n* jeti, glanfa

Jew *n* Iddew

jewel *n* gem, tlws

jeweller *n* gemydd

jewellery *n* gemwaith, gemau

Jewish *adj* Iddewig

jib *n* hwyl flaen llong, jib

jib *vi* nogio, strancio

jig *n* dawns fywiog, jig

jig-saw *n* jig-so

jilt *vt* siomi cariad

jingle n rhigwm, tinc ▷ vb tincial
job n tasg, gorchwyl, gwaith
Job Centre n Canolfan Gwaith
jobless adj diwaith
jockey n joci
jocose adj cellweirus, direidus, ysmala
jocular adj ffraeth, ysmala
jog vb loncian
jogger n lonciwr
jogging n loncian
join vb cydio, cysylltu, uno, ymuno, asio
joiner n asiedydd, saer coed
joint n cyswllt, cymal ▷ adj cyd;
  joint of meat darn o gig
joist n dist, trawst
joke n cellwair, maldod ▷ vb cellwair, ysmalio
jolly adj braf, difyr, llawen
jolt n ysgytiad ▷ vb ysgytio
Jordan n Iorddonen
jostle n hergwd ▷ vb gwthio
jot n iod, tipyn ▷ vt nodi
jotter n nodlyfr
journal n newyddiadur
journalism n newyddiaduraeth
journalist n newyddiadurwr
journey n taith, siwrnai ▷ vt teithio
jovial adj llon, llawen
joy n llawenydd, gorfoledd
joyful adj llon, llawen, gorfoleddus
JP n abbr (= justice of the peace) ynad heddwch
jubilant adj gorfoleddus
jubilee n jiwbili
Judaism n Iddewaeth
judge n barnwr, beirniad ▷ vb barnu, beirniadu
judgement, judgment n barn, brawd, dyfarniad; dedfryd
judicial adj barnwrol, ynadol
judiciary n barnwyr gwlad, barnwriaeth

judicious adj call, synhwyrol, doeth
jug n jwg
juggle vb siwglo
juggler n siwglwr
juice n sug, sugn, sudd, nodd
juicy adj llawn sudd
July n Gorffennaf
jumble vb cymysgu, cyboli ▷ n cymysgfa, cybolfa
jumble sale n ffair sborion
jump vb neidio, llamu ▷ n naid, llam
jumper n neidiwr; siwmper
jumpy adj ofnus
junction n cydiad; uniad; cyffordd
juncture n cyfwng, cyswllt
June n Mehefin
jungle n jyngl, coedwig; drysi
junior adj iau, ieuengach; ieuaf
junior school n ysgol iau
junk n sothach
junk food n bwyd sothach
junk mail n post sothach
jurisdiction n awdurdod
juror n rheithiwr
jury n rheithgor
just adj cyfiawn, uniawn, teg ▷ adv
  yn union; prin, braidd; newydd; **just now** gynnau(fach)
justice n cyfiawnder; ynad, ustus
justice of the peace n ynad heddwch
justify vt cyfiawnhau
jut vi taflu allan, ymwthio
juvenile adj ieuanc

kale *n* cêl, celys
kangaroo *n* cangarŵ
keel *n* gwaelod llong, trumbren, cilbren
keen *adj* craff, llym, awchus, brwd
keep *vb* cadw, cynnal ▷ *n* cadw; amddiffynfa
keeper *n* ceidwad
keep-fit *n* cadw'n heini
keepsake *n* cofrodd
kennel *n* cenel, cwb ci, cwt ci
Kenya *n* Cenia
kerb *n* cwrbyn
kerchief *n* cadach, neisied, hances, macyn
kernel *n* cnewyllyn
kestrel *n* cudyll
kettle *n* tegell
kettle-drum *n* tympan
key *n* agoriad, allwedd; cywair
keyboard *n* allweddell

keyhole *n* twll clo
key ring *n* cylch allweddi
key worker *n* gweithiwr allweddol
khaki *adj*, *n* caci
kick *vb* cicio, gwingo ▷ *n* cic
kick-off *n* cic gychwyn
kid *n* myn; hogyn, plentyn, crwt
kidnap *vt* herwgipio
kidney *n* aren
kidney beans *npl* ffa dringo, cidnebêns
kill *vt* lladd
killer *n* lladdwr
killing *n* lladd
kiln *n* odyn
kilo *n* cilo
kilogram *n* cilogram
kilometre *n* cilomedr
kilowatt *n* cilowat
kin *n* perthynas, tras, carennydd
kind *n* rhyw, rhywogaeth, math
kind *adj* caredig
kindergarten *n* ysgol feithrin
kindle *vb* ennyn, cynnau
kindly *adj* caredig, hynaws, tirion
kindness *n* caredigrwydd
kindred *n* perthynas; perthynasau ▷ *adj* perthynol
king *n* brenin
kingdom *n* teyrnas
kingfisher *n* glas y dorlan
kink *n* cinc
kiosk *n* ciosg, bwth
kipper *n* ciper, ysgadenyn hallt (neu sych)
kirk *n* eglwys (Albanaidd)
kiss *vt* cusanu ▷ *n* cusan
kit *n* cit, pac
kitchen *n* cegin
kitchenette *n* cegin fach
kitchen garden *n* gardd lysiau
kite *n* barcut
kitten *n* cath fach ▷ *vb* bwrw cathod

kleptomania *n* ysfa ladrata
knack *n* cnac, medr
knacker *n* prynwr hen geffylau, nacer
knapsack *n* ysgrepan
knave *n* cnaf, dihiryn
knead *vt* tylino
knee *n* glin, pen-lin, pen-glin
kneel *vi* penlinio
knell *n* cnul
knickers *npl* nicers
knife (**knives**) *n* cyllell
knight *n* marchog ▷ *vt* urddo yn farchog
knighthood *n* urdd marchog
knit *vb* gwau; clymu
knitting needle *n* gwaell
knob *n* cnap, cnwc; dwrn
knock *vb* cnocio, taro, curo ▷ *n* cnoc, ergyd
knot *n* cwlwm; cymal, cwgn, cainc ▷ *vt* clymu
know *vb* gwybod, adnabod
knowing *adj* gwybodus
knowingly *adv* yn fwriadol
knowledge *n* gwybodaeth
knowledgeable *adj* gwybodus
knuckle *n* cymal, migwrn, cwgn
Korea *n* Corea
Kosovo *n* Cosofo
Kuwait *n* Kuwait, Coweit

label *n* llabed, label ▷ *vt* llabedu, enwi
labial *adj* gwefusol
labialize *vb* gwefusoli
laboratory *n* labordy
laborious *adj* llafurus
labour *n* llafur; gwewyr esgor ▷ *vb* llafurio; **the Labour Party** Y Blaid Lafur
labourer *n* gweithiwr, labrwr
labour force *n* llafurlu
labyrinth *n* drysfa
lace *n* las, les; carrai ▷ *vb* cau (esgidiau)
lacerate *vt* rhwygo, llarpio, dryllio darnio
lack *n* eisiau, diffyg, gwall ▷ *vb* bod mewn eisiau
lackadaisical *adj* diynni, llipa
laconic *adj* byreiriog, byr, cwta
lacquer *n* lacer ▷ *vb* lacro

lad *n* bachgen, hogyn, llanc
ladder *n* ysgol; rhwyg (mewn hosan)
lade *vt* llwytho
ladies *npl* toiledau merched
ladle *n* lletwad, llwy
lady *n* arglwyddes; boneddiges, bonesig
ladybird *n* buwch goch gota
lag *vi* llusgo ar ôl, ymdroi, llercian
lagging *n* ynysydd, lagin
lagoon *n* morlyn, lagŵn
lair *n* gwâl, lloches, ffau
laity *n* lleygwyr
lake *n* llyn
lamb *n* oen ▷ *vb* bwrw ŵyn, wyna
lame *n* cloff ▷ *vt* cloffi
lament *vb* galaru, cwynfan, cwyno
lamentation *n* galar, galarnad
laminate *adj* haenog ▷ *vb* haenogi, lamineiddio, laminadu
lamp *n* lamp, llusern
lampoon *n* dychangerdd, gogangerdd ▷ *vb* dychanu
lamppost *n* polyn lamp
lampshade *n* lamplen
lance *n* gwaywffon, picell ▷ *vt* lansio, agor dolur
lance corporal *n* is-gorpral
land *n* tir, gwlad ▷ *vb* tirio, glanio
landing *n* glaniad, glanio; glanfa; pen y grisiau
landlady *n* perchennog llety, gwraig llety
landlord *n* meistr tir; lletywr, tafarnwr
landscape *n* tirlun
lane *n* lôn, wtre, beidr
language *n* iaith
language laboratory *n* labordy iaith
languid *adj* egwan, llesg
languish *vi* nychu, dihoeni, llesgáu
languor *n* llesgedd, nychdod

lank *adj* cul, tenau, main, llipa
lanky *adj* meindal
lantern *n* llusern
lap *n* arffed, glin
lap *vb* plygu, lapio ▷ *n* plyg, tro, cylch
lap *vb* llepian, lleibio
lapel *n* llabed
lapse *n* cwymp, methiant, gwall ▷ *vi* llithro, cwympo, methu
laptop, laptop computer *n* gliniadur
larceny *n* lladrad
larch *n* llarwydden
lard *n* bloneg ▷ *vt* blonegu
larder *n* bwtri, pantri
large *adj* mawr, helaeth, eang, maith
largely *adv* gan mwyaf
lark *n* ehedydd
lark *n* sbort, difyrrwch, miri ▷ *vi* cellwair, prancio
larva (**-ae**) *n* cynrhonyn, larfa
laryngitis *n* gwddf tost, laringitis
larynx *n* afalfreuant, bocs llais
lasagne *n* lasagne
lascivious *adj* anllad, trythyll, anniwair
laser *n* laser
lash *n* llach, fflangell ▷ *vb* llachio, fflangellu; rhwymo
lass *n* llances
lasso *n* dolenraff, lasŵ ▷ *vt* dolenraffu
last *adj* olaf, diwethaf ▷ *adv* yn olaf, yn ddiwetha; **at last** o'r diwedd; **last night** neithiwr; **last week** yr wythnos ddiwethaf
last *vi* parhau, para
latch *n* cliced ▷ *vt* clicedu
late *adj* hwyr, diweddar; **late developers** plant hwyrgynnydd
lately *adv* yn ddiweddar
latent *adj* dirgel, cudd

later adv wedyn, eto, yn ddiweddarach

lateral adj ochrol

latest adj diweddaraf

lath n eisen, dellten

lathe n turn

lather n trochion ▷ vb seboni, trochioni; golchi

Latin adj, n Lladin

Latin America n America Ladin

latitude n lledred; penrhyddid

latter adj diwethaf

lattice n dellt, rhwyllwaith

laud vt canmol, clodfori, moli

laudable adj canmoladwy

laugh vb chwerthin ▷ n chwerthiniad

laugh at vt (joke, situation) chwerthin am; (person) chwerthin am ben

laughable adj chwerthinllyd, digrif

laughing stock n cyff gwawd

laughter n chwerthin

launch vb lansio

Launderette® n landret, golchdy

laundry n golchdy; dillad golch

laureate adj llawryfog

laurel n llawryf

lavatory n tŷ bach, ymolchfa, ystafell ymolchi

lavender n lafant

lavish adj hael, afradlon, gwastraffus ▷ vb afradu, gwastraffu

lavishness n haelioni, afradlonedd

law n cyfraith, deddf; **law and order** cyfraith a threfn; **law of the land** cyfraith gwlad

lawful adj cyfreithlon

lawgiver adj deddfroddwr

lawless adj digyfraith

lawlessness n anghyfraith

lawn n lawnt, llannerch

lawnmower n peiriant torri porfa

lawn tennis n tenis (lawnt)

lawsuit n cyngaws, cyfraith

lawyer n cyfreithiwr, twrnai

lax adj llac, esgeulus, diofal

laxative n carthlyn

lay n cân, cerdd

lay vt gosod, dodi; dodwy

lay adj lleyg

layby n gorffwysfan

layer n haen

laze vb diogi, segura

laziness n diogi

lazy adj diog, dioglyd

lea n doldir, dôl

lead n plwm

lead vb arwain, tywys ▷ n blaenoriaeth

leader n arweinydd; erthygl flaen

leadership n arweinyddiaeth

leaf (**leaves**) n deilen, dalen

leaflet n taflen

league n cynghrair ▷ vi cynghreirio

leak n agen, coll ▷ vi gollwng, diferu, colli

lean adj main, tenau, cul ▷ n cig coch

lean vb pwyso, gogwyddo

leap vb neidio, llamu ▷ n naid, llam

leapfrog n chwarae naid

leap year n blwyddyn naid

learn vb dysgu

learned adj dysgedig, hyddysg

learner n dysgwr

learning n dysg, dysgeidiaeth

lease n prydles ▷ vt prydlesu

leasehold n prydles

leash n cynllyfan, tennyn ▷ vt cynllyfanu

least adj lleiaf; **at last** o leiaf

leather n lledr

leave n cennad, caniatâd

leave vb gadael, ymadael

leaven n lefain ▷ vt lefeinio

Lebanon n Libanus

lecherous *adj* trythyll, anllad
lechery *n* trythyllwch, anlladrwydd
lectern *n* darllenfa
lecture *n* darlith ▷ *vb* darlithio
lecturer *n* darlithydd
lecture theatre *n* darlithfa
ledge *n* silff, ysgafell; crib
ledger *n* llyfr cyfrifon
lee *n* ochr gysgodol, cysgod gwynt
leech *n* gelen
leek *n* cenhinen
leer *vi* cilwenu
lees *npl* gwaddod, gwaelodion
left *adj* aswy, chwith
left-handed *adj* llawchwith
left-handedness *n* llawchwithedd
left luggage *n* lle cadw bagiau
leg *n* coes
legacy *n* etîfeddiaeth, cymynrodd
legal *adj* cyfreithiol, cyfreithlon
legalize *vb* cyfreithloni
legation *n* llysgenhadaeth
legend *n* chwedl
legible *adj* darllenadwy, eglur
legion *n* lleng, llu
legislate *vi* deddfu
legislation *n* deddfwriaeth
legislative *adj* deddfwriaethol
legitimate *adj* cyfreithlon
leisure *n* hamdden
leisurely *adj* hamddenol
lemon *n* lemwn
lemonade *n* diod lemwn, lemonêd
lend *vt* benthyca, rhoi benthyg
length *n* hyd, meithder
lengthen *vb* estyn, hwyhau
lengthy *adj* hir, maith
leniency *n* tiriondeb, tynerwch
lens *n* lens; **concave lens** lens ceugrwm; **convex lens** lens amgrwm
Lent *n* y Grawys
lentil *n* corbysen, lentil

Leo *n* y Llew
leonine *adj* llewaidd
leopard *n* llewpart
leper *n* dyn gwahanglwyfus, gwahanglaf
leprosy *n* gwahanglwyf
lesbian *n* lesbiad ▷ *adj* lesbiaidd
less *adj*, *adv* llai
lessee *n* prydlesai
lessen *vb* lleihau
lesson *n* gwers; llith
lest *conj* rhag, rhag ofn, fel na
let *vt* gadael, goddef; gollwng; gosod, rhentu
let down *vt* gollwng; siomi
lethal *adj* marwol, angheuol
lethargy *n* cysgadrwydd, syrthni
letter *n* llythyren; llythyr
letterbox *n* bocs llythyrau
lettering *n* llythreniad
lettuce *n* letysen
level *n*, *adj* lefel, gwastad ▷ *vt* lefelu, gwastatáu; **spirit level** lefelydd
level crossing *n* croesfan
level-headed *adj* pwyllog
lever *n* trosol
leveret *n* ysgyfarnog ieuanc, lefren
Levite *n* Lefiad
levity *n* ysgafnder, gwamalrwydd
levy *vt* codi, trethu ▷ *n* treth
lewd *adj* anllad, anweddus
lexicographer *n* geiriadurwr
lexicon *n* geiriadur
liability *n* cyfrifoldeb, rhwymedigaeth
liable *adj* atebol
liaison *n* cyswllt
liar *n* gŵr celwyddog, celwyddgi
libel *n* athrod, enllib ▷ *vt* athrodi, enllibio
liberal *adj* hael, rhyddfrydig, rhyddfrydol ▷ *n* rhyddfrydwr
liberate *vt* rhyddhau

liberation n rhyddhad
liberty n rhyddid
Libra n y Fantol
librarian n llyfrgellydd
library n llyfrgell
Libya n Libya
licence n trwydded; penrhyddid; **driving licence** trwydded yrru
license vt trwyddedu
licensed adj trwyddedig
licentious adj penrhydd, ofer, anllad
lick vt llyfu, llyo; curo
lid n caead, clawr
lie n celwydd, anwiredd ▷ vi dweud celwydd
lie vi gorwedd
lie down vi gorwedd i lawr
liege adj ffyddlon, ufudd
lieutenant n is-gapten; rhaglaw
life (**lives**) n bywyd, einioes, oes, buchedd, hoedl
lifebelt n nofdorch, gwregys achub
lifeboat n bad achub
lifeguard n achubwr
life insurance n yswiriant bywyd
life jacket n siaced achub
lifeless adj difywyd, marw(aidd)
lifestyle n ffordd o fyw
lifetime n oes, einioes, hoedl
lift vt codi, dyrchafu ▷ n codiad; lifft
ligament n giewyn, gewyn
light n golau, goleuni ▷ adj golau ▷ vb goleuo, cynnau
light adj ysgafn
light bulb n bwlb golau
lighter n goleuydd, taniwr
light-footed adj ysgafndroed
light-headed adj penchwiban
light-hearted adj ysgafnfryd
lighthouse n goleudy
lightning n mellt, lluched
lightning conductor n cludydd mellt

lightship n goleulong
like adj tebyg, cyffelyb
like vb caru, hoffi
likeable adj hoffus; dymunol
likelihood n tebygolrwydd
likely adj, adv tebygol, tebyg
liken vt cyffelybu
likeness n tebygrwydd
likewise adv yn gyffelyb, yn yr un modd
lilac n lelog
lily n lili, alaw
lily-of-the-valley n lili'r dyffrynnoedd
limb n aelod, cainc
lime n calch
limekiln n odyn galch
limelight n amlygrwydd
limestone n carreg galch
limit n terfyn, ffin ▷ vt cyfyngu
limited adj cyfyngedig
limousine n limwsîn
limp adj llipa, ystwyth, hyblyg
limp vi hercian, cloffi
limpet n brenigen, llygad maharen
line n llin, llinell, lein, rhes; llinach ▷ vt llinellu, rhesu
lineage n ach, llinach
linear adj llinellog, llinellaidd, llinol, unionlin; **linear equation** hafaliad llinol
linen n lliain
line-out n lein, llinell
liner n leiner
linesman n llumanwr
linger vb ymdroi, aros
lingo n iaith ddieithr, cleber
linguist n ieithydd
linguistics n ieithyddiaeth
liniment n ennaint, eli
lining n leinin
link n dolen, cyswllt ▷ vb cydio, cysylltu

linnet n llinos
lino n leino
linseed n had llin, llinad
lintel n capan drws, lintel
lion n llew
lip n gwefus, min, gwefl
lipstick n minlliw
liquid n llyn, hylif ▷ adj gwlyb, hylif
liquidate vb talu, clirio (dyled),
   dirwyn i ben, diddymu, dileu
liquidize vb hylifo
liquor n diod, gwirod
lisp n bloesgni ▷ vb siarad yn floesg
list n rhestr, llechres ▷ vt rhestru
list n gogwydd, goledd ▷ vi pwyso,
   gwyro, gogwyddo
listen vi gwrando
listener n gwrandawr
listless adj llesg, diynni
listlessness n llesgedd
litany n litani
literacy n llythrennedd
literal adj llythrennol
literary adj llenyddol
literature n llenyddiaeth
lithe, lithesome adj ystwyth, hyblyg
lithograph n lithograff
litigate vb cyfreithio
litmus n litmws
litre n litr
litter n elorwely; ysbwriel, gwasarn;
   torllwyth, tor
litter bin n bin sbwriel
little adj bach, bychan; mân, ychydig
   ▷ n ychydig, tipyn
liturgy n litwrgi
live adj byw, bywiol, bywiog
live vi byw
livelihood n bywoliaeth
livelong adj maith, hirfaith
lively adj bywiog, hoyw, heini, sionc
liven vb bywiogi
liver n iau, afu

livery n lifrai
living n bywoliaeth; personiaeth
living room n ystafell fyw
lizard n madfall, modrchwilen
load n llwyth ▷ vb llwytho
loaf(loaves) n torth
loaf vb ystelcian, sefyllian, diogi
loafer n diogyn, segurwr
loam n tywotglai, marl, priddglai
loan n benthyg, benthyciad
loathe vt ffieiddio, casáu
loath, loth adj anewyllysgar,
   anfodlon
loathsome adj atgas, ffiaidd
lobby n cyntedd, porth, lobi
lobster n cimwch
local adj lleol
local government n llywodraeth
   leol
locality n lle, safle, ardal, cymdogaeth
locate vt lleoli, sefydlu, gosod
location n lleoliad
loch n llyn
lock n clo; llifddor ▷ vb cloi, cau
lock n cudyn; **locks** (hair) gwallt
locked adj ar glo, ynghlo, dan glo
locker n cwpwrdd clo
locomotion n ymsymudiad
locomotive adj ymsymudol ▷ n
   peiriant rheilffordd
locust n locust
lodge n lluest, llety; cyfrinfa ▷ vb
   lletya
lodger n lletywr
lodging n, **lodgings** npl llety
loft n taflod, llofft
lofty adj uchel, aruchel, dyrchafedig
log n cyff, boncyff, pren
loggerheads npl benben
logic n rhesymeg
logical adj rhesymegol
log in, log on vi (computing)
   mewngofnodi

log off, log out vi (computing) allgofnodi
loin n llwyn, lwyn
loiter vi ymdroi, loetran, sefyllian
loll vi gorweddian, diogi
lollipop n lolipop
London n Llundain
loneliness n unigrwydd
lonely adj unig
long adj, adv hir, maith, llaes
long vi hiraethu, dyheu
longevity n hirhoedledd, hiroes
long-headed adj call, hirben
longing n hireath, dyhead
longitude n hydred
longitudinal adj hydredol
long sight n golwg hir
long-suffering adj hirymarhous ▷ n hirymaros
long-term adj yn y tymor hir
long-winded adj hirwyntog
look vb edrych, syllu ▷ n edrychiad, golwg
look after vt gwarchod, gofalu (am), amddiffyn
look at vt edrych ar
look for vt chwilio am
looking-glass n drych
lookout n gwyliwr
loom n gwŷdd
loom vi ymrithio, ymddangos
loon n gwirionyn, dihiryn
loop n dolen ▷ vb dolennu
loophole n dihangdwll
loose adj rhydd, llac ▷ vt gollwng
loosen vb rhyddhau, llacio
loot n anrhaith, ysbail ▷ vb ysbeilio, anrheithio
looter n ysbeiliwr, anrheithiwr
lop vt tocio
lopsided adj unochrog, anghymesur, anghyfartal
lord n arglwydd ▷ vb arglwyddiaethu

lord mayor n arglwydd faer
lordship n arglwyddiaeth
lore n dysg, llên, traddodiad
lorry n lori
lorry driver n gyrrwr lori
lose vb colli
loss n colled
lost property office n swyddfa eiddo coll
lot n coelbren, rhan, tynged; **a lot** llawer
lotion n golchdrwyth, eli
lottery n hapchwarae, raffl
lotus n alaw'r dŵr
loud adj uchel, croch
loud speaker n corn siarad
lounge n lolfa ▷ vi segura, gorweddian
louse (**lice**) n lleuen
lousy adj lleuog, brwnt
lout n lleban, llabwst, delff
love n cariad, serch ▷ vt caru
loveliness n prydferthwch
lovely adj hawddgar, teg, hyfryd
lover n cariad, carwr
loving adj cariadus, serchog
loving-kindness n trugaredd, cariad
low adj isel
low vi brefu ▷ n bref (buwch)
lower vb gostwng, darostwng, iselu
lower vi gwgu, duo, hel cymylau
lowliness n gostyngeiddrwydd
lowly adj isel, iselfrydig, gostyngedig
low tide n llanw isel; trai
low water n trai, distyll
loyal adj teyrngar
loyalty n teyrngarwch, ffyddlondeb
lozenge n losin
lubricate vt iro, llithrigo, seimio
lucid adj eglur, clir
luck n lwc, damwain, hap, ffawd
lucky adj ffodus, lwcus**

ludicrous *adj* chwerthinllyd, gwrthun
lug *vb* llusgo, tynnu
luggage *n* clud, bagiau, celfi
luggage rack *n* silff eiddo
lukewarm *adj* claear, llugoer
lull *vt* suo, gostegu ▷ *n* gosteg
lullaby *n* hwiangerdd
lumbago *n* llwynwst
lumber *n* llanastr, anialwch
lumber *vb* pentyrru; llusgo
luminous *adj* golau, disglair, llachar
lump *n* lwmp, clamp, clap, talp;
  lump sum cyfandaliad
lunacy *n* lloerigrwydd,
  gwallgofrwydd
lunatic *n* lloerig, gwallgofddyn
lunch *vb* ciniawa (ganol dydd)
lunch, luncheon *n* byrbryd, cinio
  canol dydd
lung *n* ysgyfaint
lunge *n* hergwd, gwth, rhuthr
lurch *n* cyfyngder, dryswch, trybini
  ▷ *vi* gwegian
lure *n* hud ▷ *vt* hudo, denu
lurid *adj* erchyll, erchliw, fflamgoch
lurk *vi* llercian, llechu
luscious *adj* melys
lush *adj* toreithiog, ffrwythlon
lust *n* chwant, trachwant ▷ *vi*
  trachwantu
lustre *n* gloywder, disgleirdeb,
  llewyrch
lusty *adj* heini, cryf, pybyr, grymus
Luxembourg *n* Luxembourg
luxuriant *adj* toreithiog, bras,
  ffrwythlon
luxurious *adj* moethus
luxury *n* moeth, moethusrwydd,
  amheuthun
lying *adj* celwyddog
lyre *n* telyn gron
lyric *adj* telynegol ▷ *n* telyneg

mace *n* brysgyll, byrllysg
macerate *vb* meddalu, mwydo;
  nychu, curio
machine *n* peiriant
machinery *n* peiriannau
mackerel *n* macrell
mackintosh *n* cot law
mad *adj* cynddeiriog, gwallgof,
  gwyllt, ynfyd
madden *vb* gwallgofi, ffyrnigo
made-to-measure *adj* wedi ei dorri
  gan deiliwr
madman *n* ynfytyn, gwallgofddyn
madness *n* ynfydrwydd,
  gwallgofrwydd
madrigal *n* madrigal
magazine *n* ystorfa, arfdy;
  cylchgrawn
maggot *n* cynrhonyn
magic *adj* cyfareddol ▷ *n* hud,
  dewiniaeth, swyngyfaredd

magician n swynwr, dewin
magistrate n ynad
magnanimous adj mawrfrydig
magnet n magned
magnetic n magnetig
magnificent adj gwych, ysblennydd
magnify vt mawrhau, mwyhau, chwyddo
magnifying-glass n chwyddwydr
magnitude n maint, maintioli
magpie n pi, pia, pioden, piogen
maid n merch, morwyn
maiden name n enw morwynol
mail n y post
mail n arfwisg
mailbox n blwch postio
maim vt anafu, anffurfio, llurgunio
main n prif bibell; prif gebl; cefnfor;
   in the main yn bennaf, gan mwyaf
main adj pennaf, prif, mwyaf
main course n prif gwrs
mainland n y tir mawr
mainly adv yn bennaf
main road n priffordd, ffordd fawr
mainstay n prif gynhaliaeth
maintain vt dal, cynnal, maentumio
maintenance n cynhaliaeth, gofalaeth
maize n indrawn, injan corn
majestic adj mawreddog, urddasol
majesty n mawrhydi, mawredd
major adj mwy, mwyaf, pennaf ▷ n uwchgapten
Majorca n Maiorca, Mallorca
majority n mwyafrif; oedran llawn
make vt gwneud, gwneuthur, peri ▷ n gwneuthuriad
make up vt (invent) dyfeisio;
   (constitute) gwneud; **to be made up of** cynnwys
maker n gwneuthurwr, creawdwr
make-up n colur
making n gwneuthuriad, ffurfiad

malady n drwg, anhwyldeb, dolur
Malaysia n Maleisia
male n, adj gwryw
malevolence n malais
malevolent adj drygnaws, maleisus
malformation n camffurfiad
malice n malais
malign vt enllibio, difrïo, pardduo
malignant adj llidiog, adwythig, gwyllt
mallet n gordd
malnutrition n gwallfaethiad, camluniaeth
malt n brag ▷ vb bragu
Malta n Malta
maltreat vb cam-drin
maltreatment n camdriniaeth
mammal n mamal
mammoth n mamoth ▷ adj anferth
man (men) n dyn, gŵr
manacle n gefyn ▷ vt gefynnu
manage vb trin, llywodraethu, rheoli; ymdaro, ymdopi, llwyddo
manageable adj hydrin
management n rheolaeth, goruchwyliaeth
manager n goruchwyliwr, rheolwr
mandate n gorchymyn, arch
mane n mwng
mange n clafr, clefri, brech y cŵn
manger n mansier, preseb
mangle vt llurgunio
mangle n mangl
manhood n dyndod
mania n gwallgofrwydd, gorawydd
maniac n gwallgofddyn
manifest adj amlwg ▷ vt amlygu, dangos
manifesto n datganiad, maniffesto
manifold adj amryw, amrywiol
manipulate vt trin, trafod
mankind n dynolryw
manly adj dynol, gwrol

m

manner n modd; moes
mannerism n dullwedd
mannerly adj boneddigaidd, moesgar
manners npl moesau
manor n maenor, maenol
manse n tŷ gweinidog, mans
manservant n gwas
mansion house n trigfan y maer
manslaughter n dynladdiad
mantelpiece n silff ben tân
mantle n mantell ▷ vt mantellu
manual adj perthynol i'r llaw ▷ n llawlyfr
manufacture n gwaith, nwydd ▷ vt gwneuthur, gwneud
manure n tail, gwrtaith, achles ▷ vt teilo, gwrteithio, achlesu
manuscript n llawysgrif
many adj aml, sawl, llawer; **as many** cymaint, cynifer; **how many** sawl
map n map
maple n masarnen
mar vt difetha, andwyo, hagru
marathon n marathon
maraud vb ysbeilio, anrheithio
marble n marmor, mynor; marblen
March n (mis) Mawrth
march vb ymdeithio ▷ n ymdaith
march n mers, goror, cyffin
marchioness n ardalyddes
mare n caseg
margarine n margarîn
margin n ymyl, cwr, goror
marigold n gold Mair, gold
marine adj morol ▷ n môr-filwr; llynges
mariner n morwr, llongwr, mordwywr
marital n priodasol
maritime adj morol, arforol
mark n nod, marc ▷ vt nodi, marcio, craffu, sylwi

market n marchnad ▷ vb marchnata
maroon vb rhoi a gadael ar ynys anial ▷ adj coch tywyll
marquis n ardalydd
marriage n priodas
married adj priod
marrow n mêr; **vegetable marrow** pwmpen
marry vb priodi
Mars n Mawrth
marsh n morfa, cors, mignen
marshal n cadlywydd, marsialydd ▷ vt byddino, trefnu
mart n mart
martial adj milwraidd, milwrol
martinet n disgyblwr llym
martyr n merthyr ▷ vt merthyru
martyrdom n merthyrdod
marvel n rhyfeddod ▷ vi rhyfeddu, synnu
marvellous adj rhyfeddol, gwych
marxism n marcsiaeth
marxist adj marcsaidd
mascara n masgara, colur llygaid
masculine adj gwryw, gwrywaidd
mash n cymysg, stwns ▷ vt stwnsio
mask n mwgwd ▷ vt mygydu, cuddio
mason n saer maen, masiwn, meiswn
mass n pentwr, talp, crynswth, mas; **the masses** y werin
mass n offeren
massacre n cyflafan ▷ vt cyflafanu
massive adj anferth
mast n hwylbren
master n meistr, athro, capten (llong) ▷ vt meistroli
masterpiece n campwaith, gorchest
mastery n meistrolaeth, goruchafiaeth
masticate vt cnoi, malu

mastiff n gafaelgi, cystowci, catgi

mat n mat ▷ vt matio, plethu

match n matsen

match n cymar; priodas; ymrysonfa, gêm ▷ vb cystadlu; cyfateb

matchless n digymar, digyffelyb

mate n cymar, cydymaith; mêt ▷ vt cymharu

material adj materol; o bwys ▷ n defnydd

materialism n materoliaeth

maternal adj mamol; o du'r fam

maternity n mamolaeth

mathematics npl mathemateg

maths n mathemateg

matins npl boreol weddi, plygain

matriculate vb ymaelodi mewn prifysgol, matricwleiddio

matrimony n priodas

matron n gwraig briod, meistres, matron, modron

matter n mater; crawn ▷ vi bod o bwys

mattock n caib, matog

mattress n matras

mature adj aeddfed; mewn oed ▷ vb aeddfedu

mature student n myfyriwr hŷn

maturity n aeddfedrwydd

maul vt baeddu, pwyo ▷ n sgarmes

mauve n lliw porffor, piws

maxim n dihareb, gwireb, rheol

maximum n uchafswm, uchafrif, uchafbwynt

May n Mai

may n blodau drain gwynion

maybe adv efallai, hwyrach, dichon

May Day n Calan Mai

mayor n maer

mayoress n maeres

me pron myfi, mi, fi, i; minnau

mead n medd

meadow n dôl, gwaun, gweirglodd

meagre adj cul, tenau, prin, tlodaidd, llwm

meal n blawd

meal n pryd o fwyd

meals on wheels npl pryd ar glud

mean n cyfrwng, modd; canol; cymedr

mean vt meddwl, golygu, bwriadu

mean adj gwael, isel, crintach, iselwael

meander n ystum (afon) ▷ vi dolennu, troelli, ymdroelli

meaning n ystyr, meddwl

meanness n cybydd-dod, crintachrwydd

means npl cyfrwng, modd(ion), cyfoeth; **by all means** ar bob cyfrif, wrth gwrs

meantime, meanwhile adv yn y cyfamser

measles npl y frech goch

measure vt, n mesur

measurement n mesur, mesuriad

meat n ymborth, bwyd; cig

mechanic n peiriannydd

mechanical adj peiriannol, peirianyddol, mecanyddol

mechanics npl mecaneg

mechanism n peirianwaith

medal n bathodyn, medal

meddle vi ymyrryd, busnesa, ymhél

media npl cyfryngau

mediaeval adj canoloesol

medial adj canol, canolog

mediate vi canoli, cyfryngu

medical adj meddygol

medication n meddyginiaeth

medicine n meddyginiaeth; ffisig, moddion

mediocre adj canolig, cyffredin

meditate vb myfyrio

meditation n myfyrdod

Mediterranean n: **the Mediterranean** y Môr Canoldir

m

medium n canol; cyfrwng ▷ adj
canol, canolig
medley n cymysgfa, cybolfa;
cymysgedd, cadwyn o alawon
meek adj llariaidd, addfwyn
meekness n addfwynder
meet vb cyfarfod, cwrdd ▷ adj addas
meeting n cyfarfod, cyfarfyddiad
melancholy adj prudd,
pruddglwyfus ▷ n pruddglwyf, y
felan
mêlée n ymgiprys, ysgarmes
mellifluous adj melyslais, melysber
mellow adj aeddfed, meddal ▷ vb
aeddfedu
melody n peroriaeth, melodi
melt vb toddi, ymdoddi
member n aelod
Member of Parliament n Aelod
Seneddol
membership n aelodaeth
membrane n pilen, croenyn
memento n cofarwydd
memoir n cofiant
memorable adj cofiadwy,
bythgofiadwy
memorandum n cofnod, cofnodiad
memorial adj coffadwriaethol ▷ n
coffadwriaeth; cofeb; deiseb
memorise vt dysgu ar gof
memory n cof; coffadwriaeth
memory card n cerdyn cof,
cof-gerdyn
memory stick n cofbin
menace n bygythiad ▷ vt bygwth
menagerie n milodfa, sioe (siew)
anifeiliaid
mend vb gwella, cyweirio, trwsio,
helpu
mendacity n anwiredd, celwydd
mendicant adj cardotaidd,
cardotlyd ▷ n cardotyn
menial adj gwasaidd, isel ▷ n gwas

meningitis n llid yr ymennydd
menstruation n y misglwyf
mensuration n mesureg
mental adj meddyliol
mental hospital n ysbyty'r meddwl
mention vt crybwyll, sôn ▷ n
crybwylliad
mentor n cynghorwr, cyfarwyddwr
menu n bwydlen, arlwy
mercantile adj marchnadol,
masnachol
mercenary adj ariangar, chwannog
i elw ▷ n huriwr, milwr cyflog
merchandise n marsiandïaeth
merchant n masnachwr,
marsiandwr
merciful adj trugarog, tosturiol
mercifully adv drwy drugaredd
merciless adj didrugaredd
mercuric adj mercurig
mercury n arian byw, mercwri
mercy n trugaredd
mere adj unig, pur, moel, noeth,
hollol
mere n llyn, llwch
merge vb soddi, suddo, colli, ymgolli,
uno
merger n ymsoddiad, cyfuniad,
ymdoddiad, uniad
meridian n nawn; cyhydedd;
anterth
merit n haeddiant, teilyngdod ▷ vt
haeddu, teilyngu
mermaid n môr-forwyn
merriment n digrifwch, difyrrwch
merry adj llawen, llon
merry-go-round n ceffylau bach
mesh n masgl, magl, rhwydwaith
mess n saig; llanastr, annibendod
▷ vb bwyta; ymhél; maeddu
message n cenadwri, neges
messenger n cennad, negesydd
messieurs (**Messrs**) npl meistri

metabolism n metaboleg, metabolaeth

metal n metel ▷ adj metelaidd

metamorphosis (**-ses**) n trawsffurfiad, metamorffosis

metaphor n trosiad

metaphysics n metaffiseg

mete vb mesur

meteor n seren wib

meter n mesurydd; medr

method n trefn, method, dull

meticulous adj gorfanwl

metonymy n trawsenwad

metre n mesur, mydr

metric adj metrig

metrical adj mydryddol

metric system n system fedrig

metropolis n prifddinas

mettle n metel, anian, ysbryd

mew vi mewian

Mexico n México

miasma n tawch heintus

Michaelmas n gŵyl Fihangel

microbe n trychfilyn, meicrob

micro-chip n meicro-sglodyn

microphone n meicroffon, meic

microscope n chwyddwydr, meicrosgop

microwave n meicrodon; **microwave oven** ffwrn meicrodon, popty ping

mid adj canol

midday n canol dydd, hanner dydd

middle n, adj canol

middle-aged adj canol oed

middle school n ysgol ganolraddol

middling adj canolig, gweddol, symol

midge n gwybedyn

midget n corrach

midnight n canol nos, hanner nos

midriff n llengig

midst n canol, plith

midsummer n canol haf

Midsummer Day n gŵyl Ifan

midwife (**-wives**) n bydwraig

mien n golwg, pryd, gwedd, agwedd

might n nerth, cadernid, gallu

mighty adj cadarn, galluog, nerthol

migraine n meigryn

migrant n mudwr, ymfudwr, crwydrwr ▷ adj mudol, crwydrol

migrate vi symud, mudo

migration n mudiad, ymfudiad

milch adj blith, llaethog

mild adj tyner, tirion, mwyn; gwan, ysgafn

mildew n llwydi, llwydni

mildness n tynerwch, tiriondeb, mwynder

mile n milltir

mileage n milltiredd

milestone n carreg filltir

militant adj milwriaethus

military adj milwrol

militate vi milwrio

milk n llaeth, llefrith ▷ vt godro

milkman n dyn llaeth

milkshake n ysgytlaeth, llaeth 'di guro

Milky Way n: **the Milky Way** Y Llwybr Llaethog, Caer Wydion

mill n melin ▷ vt melino, malu

millennium n mil blynyddoedd

miller n melinydd

millimetre n milimedr

milliner n hetwraig

million n miliwn

millionaire n miliynydd

millstone n maen melin

mime n meim

mimic vt dynwared, gwatwar

mimicry n dynwarededd

mince vt malu ▷ n briwgig, briwfwyd

mind n meddwl, bryd, cof ▷ vb gofalu, cofio

mine n mwynglawdd, pwll
miner n mwynwr, glöwr
mineral adj mwynol ▷ n mwyn
mineral water n dŵr pistyll
mingle vb cymysgu, britho
mingy adj cybyddlyd, crintach
miniature n mân ddarlun ▷ adj bychan
minibus n bws mini, minibws
minimize vt lleihau, bychanu
minimum n lleiafswm, isafrif
mining n mwyngloddiaeth;
  opencast mining mwyngloddio brig
minister n gweinidog ▷ vb gwasanaethu, gweinidogaethu
ministry n gweinidogaeth, gweinyddiaeth, gwasanaeth
minnow n pilcodyn, pilcyn, sildyn, silcyn
minor adj llai, lleiaf, lleddf; un dan oed
minority n maboed, mebyd; lleiafrif
minster n mynachlog; eglwys gadeiriol
minstrel n clerwr, cerddor
mint n bathdy ▷ vt bathu
mint n mintys
minus adj, pron llai, heb, yn fyr o ▷ n minws
minute adj bach, bychan, mân; manwl
minute n munud; cofnod
minute book n llyfr cofnodion
minx n coegen, mursen, maeden
miracle n gwyrth
miraculous adj gwyrthiol
mirage n rhithlun, lleurith
mire n llaid, llaca, tom, baw
mirror n drych ▷ vt adlewyrchu
mirth n llawenydd, digrifwch, afiaith
mis- prefix cam-

misadventure n anffawd, damwain
misanthropist n dyngasáwr
misapprehension n camddealltwriaeth
misbehave vi camymddwyn
misbehaviour n camymddygiad
miscarriage n erthyliad
miscarriage of justice n aflwyddo cyfiawnder
miscarry vi erthylu; aflwyddo; colli
miscellaneous adj amrywiol
mischance n anffawd, damwain
mischief n drwg, drygioni, direidi
mischievous adj drygionus, direidus
misconception n camsyniad, cam-dyb
misconduct n camymddygiad ▷ vb camymddwyn
misdeed n drwgweithred, camwedd
misdemeanour n camwedd, trosedd
miser n cybydd
miserable adj truenus, gresynus, anhapus
misery n trueni, gresyni, adfyd
misfortune n anffawd, aflwydd
misgivings npl amheuon, ofnau
misguide vb camarwain
mishandle vb cam-drin
mishap n anap, anffawd, aflwydd
misinterpret vb camesbonio
misjudge vb camfarnu, camddeall
mislead vb camarwain, twyllo
misnomer n camenw
misprint n cambrint ▷ vb camargraffu
misread vb camddarllen
misrepresent vt camddarlunio, camliwio
miss vt methu, ffaelu, colli ▷ n meth
missal n llyfr offeren

missile n saethyn, taflegryn

missing adj yn eisiau, yngh120ll, ar goll

mission n cenhadaeth

missionary n cenhadwr ▷ adj cenhadol

missive n llythyr

misspell vb camsillafu

mist n niwl, nudden; tarth; caddug

mistake vt camgymryd, methu ▷ n camgymeriad, gwall

mistletoe n uchelwydd

mistress n meistres; athrawes; Mrs

mistrust vt drwgdybio, amau

misty adj niwlog

misunderstand vt camddeall

misunderstanding n camddealltwriaeth

mite n hatling; mymryn, tamaid

mitigate vt lleddfu, lliniaru, lleihau

mitre n meitr

mix vb cymysgu

mixture n cymysgedd, cymysgfa

moan n, vb ochain, griddfan, udo

moat n ffos (castell)

mob n torf, tyrfa, haid ▷ vt ymosod ar, baeddu

mobile adj symudol, symudadwy; mudol (cemeg)

mobile home n cartref symudol

mobile phone n ffôn symudol

mobilize vt dygyfor, byddino

mock vb gwatwar ▷ adj gau, ffug

mockery n gwatwar; ffug

mode n modd, dull

model n cynllun, patrwm ▷ vt llunio

moderate adj cymedrol ▷ vt cymedroli

moderation n cymedroldeb

modern adj modern, diweddar

modernize vb moderneiddio

modest adj gwylaidd; diymhongar

modesty n gwylder, gwyleidd-dra

modify vt newid, lleddfu

modulate vb cyweirio neu reoli llais

module n modiwl

moiety n hanner, hanereg

moist adj llaith, gwlyb

moisture n lleithder, gwlybaniaeth, gwlybwr

moisturizer n lleithydd

molar n cilddant

mole n man geni

mole n gwadd, twrch daear

mole n morglawdd

molecule n molecwl ▷ adj molecylig

molehill n pridd y wadd

molest vt molestu, aflonyddu, blino

mollify vt meddalu, tyneru, dyhuddo

mollycoddle vb maldodi

molten adj tawdd

moment n moment; pwys, pwysigrwydd

momentum n momentwm

monarch n brenin, teyrn, penadur

monarchy n brenhiniaeth

monastery n mynachlog, mynachdy

monastic adj mynachaidd

Monday n dydd Llun

monetary adj ariannol

money n arian, pres

mongrel adj cymysgryw ▷ n mwngrel

monitor n monitor

monk n mynach

monkey n mwnci

mono- prefix un-

monogamy n unwreigiaeth

monoglot adj uniaith ▷ n person uniaith

monolith n maen hir

monologue n ymson

monopoly n monopoli

monosyllable n gair unsill

monotheism n undduwiaeth

monotone adj, n unsain, un-dôn

m

monotonous adj undonog
monotony n undonedd, unrhywiaeth
monsoon n monsŵn
monster n anghenfil; clamp ▷ adj anferth
monstrous adj angenfilaidd, anferth, gwrthun
month n mis
monthly adj misol ▷ n misolyn
monument n cofadail, cofgolofn
mood n hwyl, tymer; modd
moody adj oriog, cyfnewidiol
moon n lleuad, lloer; **harvest moon** lleuad fedi
moonlight n golau leuad
moonshine n ffiloreg, ffwlbri, lol
moor n morfa, rhos, gwaun
moor vt angori, bachu, sicrhau
moorhen n iâr fach y dŵr
moorland n rhostir, gweundir
mop n mop ▷ vt mopio, sychu
mope vi pendrymu, delwi
moraine n marian
moral adj moesol ▷ n moeswers, addysg
morality n moesoldeb
morals npl moesau
morass n cors, mignen
morbid adj afiach
mordant adj brathog, llym
more adj mwy, ychwaneg, rhagor ▷ adv mwy, mwyach
moreover adv heblaw hynny, hefyd
moribund adj ar farw, ar dranc
morning n bore ▷ adj bore, boreol
Morocco n Moroco
morose adj sur, sarrug, afrywiog, blwng
morphology n ffurfianneg, morffoleg
morrow n trannoeth
morsel n tamaid, tameidyn

mortal adj marwol, angheuol ▷ n dyn marwol
mortar n cymrwd, morter; breuan, morter
mortgage n morgais, arwystl ▷ vt morgeisio, arwystlo
mortify vb marwhau; blino, siomi
mortise n mortais ▷ vt morteisio
mortuary n marwdy
mosaic adj brith, amryliw ▷ n brithwaith, mosaig
Moscow n Moscow
Moslem n, adj = **Muslim**
mosque n mosg
moss n mwswgl, mwsogl
most adj mwyaf, amlaf
mostly adv gan mwyaf, fynychaf
mote n brycheuyn, llychyn
moth n gwyfyn
mother n mam
mother-in-law n mam yng nghyfraith, chwegr
motion n symudiad, ysgogiad; cynigiad
motivate vt ysgogi, cymell
motive adj symudol, ysgogol ▷ n cymhelliad, amcan, motif
motley adj brith, cymysg
motor n modur
motorbike n beic modur
motorcycle n beic modur
motorcyclist n beicwr (modur)
motorist n modurwr
motorway n traffordd
mottle vt britho, brychu
motto n arwyddair
mould n pridd, daear, gweryd ▷ vt priddo
mould n mold; delw ▷ vt moldio, llunio, delweddu
mould n llwydni, llwydi
moulder vi malurio, adfeilio
moult vb bwrw plu, mudo

mound n twmpath, clawdd, crug
mount n mynydd, bryn
mount vb esgyn, dringo, codi, mynd ar gefn; gosod
mountain n mynydd
mountain bike n beic mynydd
mountaineer n mynyddwr
mountaineering n mynydda
mourn vb galaru
mournful adj galarus, dolefus, alaethus
mourning n galar; galarwisg
mouse (**mice**) n llygoden ▷ vb llygota
moustache n trawswch, mwstas
mouth n genau, safn, ceg ▷ vb cegu, safnu
move vb symud, syflyd; cymell; cynnig; cyffroi
movement n symudiad; ysgogiad
mow vt lladd (gwair) ▷ n mwdwl, medel
MP n abbr AS (aelod seneddol)
MP3 n MP3
MP3 player n peiriant MP3
much adj llawer ▷ adv yn fawr
mucilage n glud, llys, llysnafedd
muck n tail, tom, baw ▷ vt tomi, baeddu
mucus n llys, llysnafedd
mud n mwd, llaid, llaca, baw
muddle vi drysu ▷ n dryswch
mug n cwpan, godart
mulberry n morwydden
mule n mul, bastart mul
mullion n post ffenestr
multi- prefix aml, lluosog
multifarious n amryfath, lluosog
multiple adj amryfal ▷ n cynhwysrif, lluosrif
multiple choice n amlddewis, dewis lluosog
multiplicand n lluosrif, lluosyn

multiplication n amlhad, lluosogiad, lluosiad
multiplicity n lluosowgrwydd
multiply vb amlhau, lluosogi, lluosi
multitude n lliaws, tyrfa
mum n mam
mumble vb grymial, myngial
mummy n mwmi
mumps n clwy'r pennau, y dwymyn doben
munch vt cnoi
mundane adj bydol, daearol
municipal adj dinesig, bwrdeisiol
munificent adj hael, haelionus
munitions npl arfau neu offer rhyfel
mural adj murol ▷ n murlun
murder vt llofruddio ▷ n llofruddiaeth
murderer n llofrudd
murky adj tywyll, cymylog, dudew
murmur vb, n murmur, grwgnach
muscle n cyhyr, cyhyryn
muscular adj cyhyrog
muse n awen, awenydd
muse vi myfyrio, synfyfyrio
museum n amgueddfa
mushroom n madarch
music n miwsig, cerdd, cerddoriaeth, peroriaeth
musical adj cerddorol
musical instrument n offeryn cerdd
musician n cerddor
Muslim adj Moslemaidd, Mwslimaidd ▷ n Moslem, Mwslim
mussel n misglen; **mussels** npl cregyn gleision
must vb def rhaid
mustard n mwstart
muster vb casglu, cynnull, byddino ▷ n cynulliad, mwstwr
musty adj wedi llwydo, hendrwm, mws

m

mutable *adj* anwadal, cyfnewidiol
mutate *vb* treiglo (llythrennau)
mutation *n* cyfnewidiad, treiglad
mute *adj* mud ▷ *n* mudan
muteness *n* mudandod
mutilate *vt* anafu, hagru, llurgunio
mutiny *n* terfysg, gwrthryfel
mutter *vb* myngial, grymial, mwmian
mutton *n* cig dafad, cig mollt, cig gwedder
mutual *adj* cyd, o boptu, y naill a'r llall
muzzle *n* genau, ffroen; pennor ▷ *vt* cau safn, rhoi taw ar
my *pron* fy
myriad *n* myrdd
myrrh *n* myrr
myrtle *n* myrtwydd
myself *pron* myfi fy hun
mysterious *adj* dirgel, rhyfedd, dirgelaidd
mystery *n* dirgelwch
mystic *n* cyfriniwr, cyfrinydd
mystify *vt* synnu, syfrdanu
myth *n* dameg, chwedl, myth
mythology *n* chwedloniaeth

nab *vb* cipio, dal
nadir *n* isafbwynt, ory
nag *vb* cecru, ffraeo, cadw sŵn ▷ *n* ceffyl
nail *n* hoel, hoelen; ewin ▷ *vt* hoelio
nail file *n* ffeil/rhathell ewinedd
naïve *adj* diniwed, diddichell, gwirion
naked *adj* noeth
namby-pamby *adj* merf, merfaidd, llipa
name *n* enw ▷ *vt* enwi, galw
namely *adv* sef, nid amgen
namesake *n* cyfenw
nanny *n* nani
nap *vi* cysgu, pendwmpian ▷ *n* cyntun
nape *n* gwar, gwegil
napkin *n* napcyn, cadach, cewyn
nappy *n* cewyn, clwt
narcotic *adj* narcotig ▷ *n* moddion cwsg

narrate *vt* adrodd (hanes)
narrative *n* hanes, chwedl, stori
narrow *adj* cul, cyfyng ▷ *vb* culhau, cyfyngu
nasal *adj* trwynol
nasty *adj* cas, brwnt, budr, ffiaidd
natal *adj* genedigol
nation *n* cenedl
national *adj* cenedlaethol
nationalism *n* cenedlaetholdeb
nationalist *n* cenedlaetholwr
nationality *n* cenedl, cenedligrwydd
nationalization *n* gwladoliad
nationalize *vb* gwladoli, cenedlaetholi
national park *n* parc cenedlaethol
native *n* brodor ▷ *adj* brodorol; cynhenid
nativity *n* genedigaeth
natural *adj* anianol, naturiol
naturalist *n* naturiaethwr
naturalize *vb* naturioli, breinio, cywladu, brodori
nature *n* anian, natur; naturiaeth
nature reserve *n* gwarchodfa natur
naught *n* dim
naughtiness *n* drygioni, direidi
naughty *adj* drwg, drygionus
nausea *n* clefyd y môr; cyfog; ffieidd-dod
nauseous *adj* cyfoglyd, ffiaidd, atgas
nautical *adj* morwrol, mordwyol
naval *adj* llyngesol, morol
nave *n* corff eglwys
nave *n* both, bŵl
navel *n* bogail
navigate *vt* morio, mordwyo, llywio
navvy *n* cloddiwr, ceibiwr
navy *n* llynges
navy blue *n*, *adj* nefi-blw

nay *adv* na, nage; nid hynny yn unig
neap *adj*, *n*: **neap tide** nêp, llanw isel
near *adj*, *adv*, *prep* agos, ger, gerllaw ▷ *vb* agosáu, nesu
nearby *adv* gerllaw, yn ymyl
nearly *adv* bron
nearness *n* agosrwydd
neat *adj* del, destlus, twt, trefnus; pur
nebula (**-ae**) *n* niwlen; niwl sêr
nebulous *adj* niwlog
necessarily *adv* o angenrheidrwydd
necessary *adj* angenrheidiol
necessitate *vt* gorfodi, gwneud yn angenrheidiol
necessitous *adj* anghenus, rheidus
necessity *n* angen, anghenraid, rhaid
neck *n* gwddf, mwnwgl, gwar
necklace *n* mwclis
necromancy *n* dewiniaeth
nectar *n* neithdar
need *n*, *vb* (bod mewn) angen, eisiau
needful *adj* rheidiol, angenrheidiol
needle *n* nodwydd; gwaell
needless *adj* afreidiol, dianghenraid
needlework *n* gwniadwaith
nefarious *adj* anfad, drygionus, ysgeler
negation *n* nacâd, gwadiad, negyddiad
negative *adj* nacaol, negyddol
neglect *vt* esgeuluso ▷ *n* esgeulustra
negligence *n* esgeulustod
negligent *adj* esgeulus
negotiate *vb* trafod, trefnu, negodi
negotiation *n* trafodaeth, cyd-drafodaeth
negro *n* dyn du, negro
neigh *vi* gweryru ▷ *n* gweryriad
neighbour *n* cymydog**

neighbourhood *n* cymdogaeth
neither *conj* na, nac, ychwaith ▷ *adj*, *pron* na'r naill na'r llall, nid yr un o'r ddau
Nemesis *n* dialedd
neo- *prefix* newydd, diweddar
nephew *n* nai
nepotism *n* neigaredd
nerve *n* giewyn, gewyn, nerf ▷ *vt* gwroli
nervous *adj* gieuol; nerfus, ofnus
nest *n* nyth ▷ *vb* nythu
nestle *vb* nythu, gwasgu'n glos at
nestling *n* aderyn bach, cyw
Net *n*: **the Net** (*internet*) y Rhyngrwyd
net *n* rhwyd, rhwyden
net *adj* union, cywir, net ▷ *vt* rhwydo
netball *n* pêl rwyd
nether *adj* isaf
Netherlands *npl*: **the Netherlands** yr Iseldiroedd
nettle *n* danadl ▷ *vt* pigo; llidio
network *n* rhwydwaith
networking *n* rhwydweithio; **social networking** rhwydweithio cymdeithasol
neuralgia *n* gieuwst
neurasthenia *n* nerfwst
neuritis *n* newritis
neurosis *n* newrosis
neuter *adj* diryw
neutral *adj* amhleidiol ▷ *n* amhleidydd
neutrality *n* newtraliaeth, amhleidiaeth
neutralize *vt* dieffeithio, dirymu
never *adv* ni … erioed, ni … byth
nevertheless *adv*, *conj* eto, er hynny
new *adj* newydd
newcomer *n* newydd-ddyfodiad
newness *n* newydd-deb
news *n* newydd, newyddion, hanes

newsagent *n* gwerthwr papurau newyddion
newspaper *n* papur newydd, newyddiadur
newt *n* madfall, genau-goeg, modrchwilen
New Year *n* Y Calan, Y Flwyddyn Newydd
New Year's Eve *n* Nos Galan
New York *n* Efrog Newydd
New Zealand *n* Seland Newydd
next *adj* nesaf ▷ *adv* yn nesaf
nib *n* blaen, nib
nibble *vb* deintio, cnoi
nice *adj* neis, hardd, tlws; manwl, cynnil
niche *n* cloer, cilfach
nickname *n* llysenw ▷ *vt* llysenwi
niece *n* nith
Nigeria *n* Nigeria
niggard *n* cybydd ▷ *adj* cybyddlyd, crintach
nigger *n* dyn du (mewn dirmyg)
nigh *adj*, *adv* agos
night *n* nos; noson, noswaith; **by night** liw nos
night club *n* clwb nos
nightdress *n* gŵn nos, coban
nightfall *n* y cyfnos, yr hwyr
nightingale *n* eos
nightmare *n* hunllef
nil *n* dim
nimble *adj* gwisgi, heini, sionc
nimbleness *n* sioncrwydd
nincompoop *n* penbwl, gwirionyn
nine *adj*, *n* naw
nineteen *adj*, *n* pedwar (pedair) ar bymtheg, un deg naw
ninety *adj*, *n* deg a phedwar ugain, naw deg
ninth *adj* nawfed
nip *vb* brathu, cnoi; deifio
nipple *n* diden, teth, tethan

nit n nedden
nitrate n nitrad
nitre n neitr
nitrogen n nitrogen
nitrous n nitrus
no adj ni … neb, dim ▷ adv ni etc, dim; nac oes, nage, naddo
nobility n bonedd, urddas, mawredd
noble adj ardderchog, urddasol, pendefigaidd ▷ n pendefig
nobleman n pendefig
nobody n neb
nocturnal adj nosol, gyda'r nos
nod vb amneidio; pendrymu ▷ n amnaid
noise n sŵn, twrf, trwst
noisome adj niweidiol, atgas, ffiaidd
noisy adj swnllyd
nomad n nomad, crwydrwr ▷ adj crwydrol
nom de plume n ffugenw
nomenclature n cyfundrefn enwau
nominal adj enwol, mewn enw
nominate vt enwi, enwebu
nomination n enwebiad
nominative adj enwol
non- prefix an-, di-
nonagenarian n un deng mlwydd a phedwar ugain
non-alcoholic adj di-alcohol
nonce n: **for the nonce** am y tro
nonchalance n difrawder, difaterwch
nonchalant adj didaro, difater
nonconformist n anghydffurfiwr, ymneilltuwr
nonconformity n anghydffurfiaeth, ymneilltuaeth
nondescript adj anodd ei ddarlunio, od
none pron neb, dim, dim un
nonentity n dyn dibwys, neb
nonplus vt drysu, dymchwelyd

nonsense n lol, dyli, gwiriondeb
non-violence n didreisedd
non-violent adj di-drais, didrais
noodle n gwirionyn, ffwlcyn; nwdl
nook n congl, cornel, cilfach
noon n nawn, hanner dydd, canol dydd
no-one pron neb
noose n cwlwm rhedeg, magl
nor conj na, nac
normal adj rheolaidd, cyffredin, safonol
normality n normalrwydd
north n gogledd ▷ adj gogleddol
northern adj gogleddol
Northern Ireland n Gogledd Iwerddon
North Pole n Pegwn y Gogledd
North Sea n Môr y Gogledd
Norway n Norwy
nose n trwyn ▷ vb trwyno, ffroeni, gwyntio
nosebleed n gwaedlif o'r trwyn
nosegay n blodeuglwm, pwysi
nostalgia n hiraeth
nostril n ffroen
not adv na, nac, nad, ni, nid
notable adj nodedig, hynod, enwog
notary n nodiadur, nodiedydd
notation n nodiant
notch n rhic, bwlch, hecyn, rhwgn, rhint
note n nod, nodyn ▷ vt nodi, sylwi
notebook n llyfr nodiadau, nodlyfr
noted adj nodedig, hynod, enwog
note pad n pad ysgrifennu
notepaper n papur ysgrifennu
noteworthy adj nodedig
nothing n dim; **nothing at all** dim byd, dim byd o gwbl
notice n sylw, rhybudd ▷ vt sylwi
noticeboard n hysbysfwrdd
notify vt hysbysu, rhoi rhybudd

n

notion *n* tyb, amcan, syniad
notoriety *n* enw gwael
notorious *adj* hynod, carn, rhemp
notwithstanding *conj* er ▷ *prep* er, er gwaethaf
nought *n* dim; gwagnod (o)
noun *n* enw
nourish *vt* maethu, meithrin
nourishing *adj* maethlon
nourishment *n* maeth
novel *adj* newydd ▷ *n* nofel
novelist *n* nofelydd
November *n* Tachwedd
novice *n* newyddian, nofis
now *adv, conj, n* yn awr, yr awron, yrŵan, weithian, bellach; **just now** gynnau; **now and then** yn awr ac yn y man
nowadays *adv* yn y dyddiau hyn
nowhere *adv* dim yn unlle
noxious *adj* niweidiol, afiach
nozzle *n* ffroenell
nuclear *adj* niwclear
nucleus *n* cnewyllyn, bywyn
nude *adj* noeth, noeth lymun
nudge *vt* pwnio, penelino
nugatory *adj* ofer, disylwedd, dirym
nugget *n* clap aur
nuisance *n* pla, poendod, budreddi
null *adj* diddim, dirym, ofer
numb *adj* diffrwyth, cwsg ▷ *vt* fferru, merwino
number *n* nifer, rhif, rhifedi; rhifyn ▷ *vt* rhifo, cyfrif
number plate *n* plat rhif car, plat cofrestru
numeral *n* rhifol, rhifnod
numeration *n* cyfrifiad
numerator *n* rhifiadur
numerical *adj* rhifiadol
numerous *adj* niferog, lluosog, aml
nun *n* lleian, mynaches

nurse *n* mamaeth, gweinyddes, nyrs ▷ *vt* magu, meithrin, nyrsio
nursery *n* magwrfa, meithrinfa
nursery school *n* ysgol feithrin
nurture *n* maeth, magwraeth, meithriniad ▷ *vt* maethu, meithrin
nut *n* cneuen; gwain, gweinell
nutcracker *n* gefel gnau
nutriment *n* maeth
nutrition *n* maeth, maethiad
nutritious *adj* maethlon
nutshell *n* plisgyn (masgl) cneuen
nuzzle *vb* trwyno, turio, ymwasgu
nylon *n* neilon

O

oaf n delff, hurtyn, awff, llabwst
oak n derwen; derw
oakum n carth, breisgion
oar n rhwyf
oatcake n bara ceirch, teisen geirch
oath n llw
oatmeal n blawd ceirch
oats npl ceirchen, ceirch
obdurate adj caled, cyndyn, ystyfnig, anhyblyg
obedience n ufudd-dod
obedient adj ufudd
obese adj tew, corffol
obesity n gor-dewdra
obey vb ufuddhau
obituary n marwgoffa
object n gwrthrych; amcan ▷ vb gwrthwynebu
objection n gwrthwynebiad
objectionable adj annymunol

objective adj gwrthrychol ▷ n amcan, nod
obligation n dyled, rhwymau
oblige vt rhwymo; boddio; gorfodi
obliging adj caredig, cymwynasgar
oblique adj lleddf, gŵyr, ar osgo
obliterate vt dileu
oblivion n angof, ebargofiant
oblong adj hirgul ▷ n oblong
obnoxious adj atgas, ffiaidd
obscene adj serth, anllad, anniwair, brwnt
obscure adj tywyll; anhysbys ▷ vt tywyllu
obsequious adj gwasaidd, cynffongar
observation n sylw; sylwadaeth
observatory n arsyllfa
observe vb sylwi, arsyllu; cadw
observer n sylwedydd, arsyllwr
obsolete adj anarferedig, ansathredig
obstacle n rhwystr, atalfa
obstinate adj cyndyn, ystyfnig, gwrthnysig
obstreperous adj trystiog, afreolus
obstruct vt cau, tagu; rhwystro, lluddio
obtain vt cael, caffael, ennill
obtrude vb gwthio ar, ymwthio
obtrusive adj ymwthgar
obtuse adj pŵl, di-fin, hurt; **obtuse angle** ongl aflem
obvious adj eglur, amlwg
occasion n achlysur ▷ vt achlysuro
occasional adj achlysurol, anaml
occidental adj gorllewinol
occult adj cudd, dirgel, cêl, cyfrin
occupation n gwaith, galwedigaeth; meddiant
occupy vt meddu, meddiannu; llenwi; dal
occur vi digwydd; taro i'r meddwl
occurrence n digwyddiad

o

ocean n môr, cefnfor, cyfanfor, eigion
o'clock adv o'r gloch
octagon n wythongl
octave n wythawd, octef
octavo adj wythblyg ▷ n llyfr wythblyg
October n Hydref
octogenarian n gŵr pedwar ugain mlwydd oed
odd adj od, hynod; **odd number** odrif
odds npl ots, gwahaniaeth; mantais
ode n awdl
odious adj atgas, cas, ffiaidd
odium n atgasrwydd; gwaradwydd; bai
odour n arogl, aroglau, sawr
of prep o; gan; am; ynghylch; **of course** wrth gwrs
off adv ymaith, i ffwrdd ▷ prep oddi, oddi wrth, oddi ar; **off and on** yn awr ac yn y man
offal n syrth, gwehilion, perfedd
offence n tramgwydd, trosedd, camwedd
offend vb tramgwyddo, troseddu, pechu; digio
offender n troseddwr
offensive adj tramgwyddus, atgas, ffiaidd; ymosodol
offer vb cynnig, cyflwyno; offrymu ▷ n cynnig
offering n offrwm, aberth
office n swydd; swyddfa
office block n bloc swyddfeydd
officer n swyddog, swyddwr
official adj swyddogol ▷ n swyddog
officiate vi gweinyddu
officious adj ymyrgar, busneslyd
offside n camochr, camsefyll ▷ vb camochri, camsefyll
offspring n hiliogaeth, epil, hil, plant
often adv yn aml, yn fynych
ogle vb cilwenu, ciledrych

ogre n anghenfil, bwystfil, cawr
oh excl O!
oil n olew, oel ▷ vt iro, oelio
oil rig n llwyfan olew
ointment n ennaint, eli
okay excl popeth yn iawn
old adj hen, oedrannus; **of old** gynt; **old age** henaint, henoed; **old and infirm** hen a methedig
old-fashioned adj henffasiwn
old people's home n cartref henoed
old stager n hen law
olive n olewydden
Olympic adj Olympaidd; **the Olympic Games**, **the Olympics** y Chwaraeon Olympaidd
omelette n crempog wyau
omen n argoel, arwydd, rhagarwydd
ominous adj argoelus, bygythiol
omission n gwall
omit vt gadael allan, esgeuluso
on prep ar, ar warthaf ▷ adv ymlaen
once adv unwaith; gynt
one adj, n un
one-way adj unffordd
onion n wynwynyn, wnionyn
online adj, adv ar lein
only adj unig ▷ adv yn unig; ond
onset n ymosodiad, cyrch; cychwyn
onslaught n ymosodiad, rhuthr, cyrch
onus n baich, dyletswydd, cyfrifoldeb
onward adj, adv, **onwards** adv ymlaen
ooze n llaid, llysnafedd ▷ vi chwysu
opaque adj afloyw, tywyll
open adj agored ▷ vb agor, ymagor
open-air n, adj awyr agored
opencast n (coal) (glo) brig
opening n agoriad, agorfa
operate vb gweithredu, gweithio
operation n gweithrediad; gweithred, triniaeth lawfeddygol

operator n gweithredydd, trafodwr
opiate n cysglyn
opinion n tyb, meddwl, barn, opiniwn
opponent n gwrthwynebydd
opportune adj amserol, cyfleus
opportunity n cyfle, egwyl
oppose vt gwrthwynebu, cyferbynnu
opposite adj, adv, prep gwrthwyneb, cyferbyn
opposition n gwrthwynebiad, gwrthblaid
oppress vt gorthrymu, llethu
optician n optegydd
optimism n optimistiaeth
optimist n optimist
option n dewisiad, dewis
optional adj dewisol
or conj neu, ai, ynteu, naill ai
oracle n oracl
oral adj geneuol, llafar, anysgrifenedig
orally adv ar lafar
orange n oren, oraens ▷ adj melyngoch
oration n araith, anerchiad
orator n areithiwr, areithydd
orb n pêl, pelen, pellen; y llygad
orbit n rhod, tro, cylchdro, chwyldro
orchard n perllan
orchestra n cerddorfa
ordain vt ordeinio, urddo
ordeal n prawf llym
order n trefn; gorchymyn, archeb; urdd ▷ vb ordeinio, trefnu, gorchymyn; archebu; urddo; **in order to** er mwyn
orderly adj trefnus ▷ n gwas milwr
ordinal adj trefnol
ordinarily adv fel rheol
ordinary adj cyffredin, arferol
ordination n ordeiniad, urddiad

ore n mwyn
organ n organ, offeryn
organic adj organaidd
organist n organydd
organization n trefn; cyfundrefn; trefniadaeth
organize vb trefnu
organized adj trefnus
organizer n trefnydd
orgy n gloddest, cyfeddach
oriental adj dwyreiniol ▷ n dwyreiniwr
orientate vb cyfeirio
orifice n genau, ceg, agorfa
origin n dechreuad, tarddiad
original adj, n gwreiddiol
originality n gwreiddioldeb
originate vb dechrau, tarddu
ornament n addurn ▷ vt addurno
ornate adj addurnedig, mawrwych
ornithology n adaryddiaeth, adareg
orphan adj, n amddifad
orthodox adj uniongred
orthography n orgraff
oscillate vb siglo, dirgrynu, osgiladu
ostensible adj ymddangosiadol, proffesedig
ostentation n rhodres
ostentatious adj rhodresgar
osteopath n osteopath
ostracize vt diarddel, alltudio
ostrich n estrys
other adj, pron arall, llall, amgen
otherwise adv amgen, fel arall
otter n dyfrgi, dwrgi
ought vb: **I ought to do it** dylwn i ei wneud **she ought to win** dylai hi ennill
ounce n owns
our pron ein, ein … ni
oust vt disodli

out *adv* allan, i maes; **out of date**
(*passport, ticket*) â'r dyddiad wedi
mynd heibio
outcast *n* alltud, digartref,
gwrthodedig
outcome *n* canlyniad, ffrwyth
outcrop *n* brig, cribell ▷ *vb* brigo
outcry *n* gwaedd; dadrwdd;
gwrthdystiad
outdo *vt* rhagori ar, trechu
outdoor *adj* yn yr awyr agored
outer *adj* allanol, nesaf allan, cyrion
outing *n* pleserdaith, gwibdaith
outlandish *adj* dieithr, estronol,
anghysbell, diarffordd
outlast *vb* goroesi
outlaw *n* herwr
outlay *n* traul, cost
outlet *n* allfa
outline *n* amlinelliad, braslun;
amlinell ▷ *vb* amlinellu
outlive *vb* goroesi
outlook *n* rhagolwg, argoel;
golygfa
outrageous *adj* gwarthus;
beiddgar, cywilyddus
outset *n* dechrau, dechreuad
outside *n* tu allan, tu faes ▷ *adj, adv*
allan(ol), oddi allan ▷ *prep* tu allan i,
tu faes i
outside-forward *n* blaenwr mas
outside-half *n* maswr
outside-left *n* asgellwr chwith
outside-right *n* asgellwr de
outskirts *npl* cyrrau, maestrefi
outstanding *adj* amlwg; dyledus
outward *adj* allanol
outwards *adv* tuag allan
outweigh *vt* gorbwyso
oval *adj* hirgrwn
ovary *n* wygell, wyfa, ofari
ovation *n* cymeradwyaeth
oven *n* ffwrn, popty

over *prep* uwch, tros ▷ *adv* gor, rhy,
tra
overall *adj* o ben i ben ▷ *n* troswisg
overbearing *adj* gormesol
overcast *adj* cymylog
overcharge *vt* gorbrisio, codi
gormod
overcoat *n* cot fawr/uchaf
overcome *vt* gorchfygu, trechu, cael
y gorau ar
overdo *vb* gorwneud
overdose *n* gor-ddogn
overflow *n* gorlif(iad) ▷ *vb* gorlifo
overhead *adj, adv* uwchben
overheat *vi* gorboethi
overload *vb* gorlwytho
overlook *vb* edrych dros; esgeuluso
overnight *adv* dros nos
overpopulate *vb* gorboblogi
overpower *vb* trechu
overrun *vb* goresgyn
overseas *adv* tramor, dros y môr
overtake *vt* goddiweddyd
overthrow *n* dymchweliad ▷ *vt*
dymchwelyd
overtime *n* goramser, oriau
ychwanegol
overture *n* cynnig; agorawd
overturn *vt* troi, dymchwelyd
overwhelm *vt* llethu, gorlethu
overwork *vb* gorweithio
owe *vb* bod mewn dyled
owing to *prep* oherwydd
owl *n* tylluan, gwdihŵ
own *adj* eiddo dyn ei hun, priod ▷ *vt*
meddu; arddel, addef
owner *n* perchen, perchennog
ox(-en) *n* ych, eidion
oxide *n* ocsid
oxygen *n* ocsigen
oyster *n* llymarch, wystrysen
ozone layer *n* haen osôn

p

pace n cam, camre; cyflymdra ▷ vb camu, cerdded
pacemaker n (device) rheoliadur y galon, rheoliadur calon
pacific adj heddychol, tawel
Pacific Ocean n Môr Tawel
pacifism n heddychiaeth
pacifist n heddychwr
pacify vt heddychu, tawelu
pack n pac, swp, pwn ▷ vb pacio, pynio
package n pecyn, bwndel, sypyn
packaging n deunydd lapio
packed adj (crowded) gorlawn
packed lunch n tocyn, pryd wedi ei bacio
packet n sypyn, paced
pact n cyfamod, cynghrair
pad n pad ▷ vt padio
paddle n padl, rhodl, rhwyf ▷ vb rhodli, padlo

paddling pool n pwll padlo
paddock n marchgae, cae bach
padlock n clo clap, clo clwt, clo egwyd
paedophile n pedoffeil, pedoffilydd
pagan n pagan ▷ adj paganaidd
page n tudalen
pageant n pasiant
pail n ystwc, crwc, bwced
pain n poen, gwayw, dolur ▷ vt poeni
painful adj poenus
painkiller n lleddfydd poen, lladdwr poen, dofydd poen
painstaking adj gofalus, trylwyr, diwyd
paint n paent, lliw ▷ vt peintio, lliwio
painter n peintiwr; arlunydd
painting n llun, darlun
pair n pâr, dau, cwpl ▷ vb paru
Pakistan n Pakistan
palace n plas, palas, palasty
palaeo-, paleo- prefix hen, hynafol
palatable adj archwaethus, blasus
palate n taflod y genau; blas, archwaeth
palatial adj palasaidd, gwych
palaver n cleber, baldordd ▷ vb clebran, baldorddi
pale adj gwelw, llwyd, glas, gwelwlas ▷ vb gwelwi
pale n pawl, cledr; clawdd, ffin
Palestine n Palestina
palisade n palis, gwalc
pall vb diflasu
pallet n gwely gwellt, matras
pallid adj gwelw, llwyd
pallor n gwelwedd
palm n palf, cledr llaw ▷ vt palfu
palm n palmwydden; **Palm Sunday** Sul y Blodau
palpable adj amlwg, dybryd, teimladwy
palpitate vi curo, dychlamu

palsy n parlys ▷ vt parlysu, diffrwytho
paltry adj distadl, gwael, pitw
pamper vt mwytho, maldodi
pamphlet n pamffled, llyfryn
pan n padell
pan- prefix oll-
pancake n crempog, cramwythen, ffroisen
pandemonium n dadwrdd, terfysg, mwstwr
pander vb porthi, gweini
pane n cwar, cwarel, paen
panegyric n molawd
panel n panel
pang n gloes, gwasgfa, brath, gwayw
panic n dychryn, panig
pansy n trilliw, llysiau'r Drindod
pant vi dyheu
pantaloons npl llodrau
panties npl pantos
pantomime n pantomeim
pantry n bwtri, pantri
pants npl pants
papacy n pabaeth
papal adj pabaidd
paper n papur **blotting paper** papur sugno; **brown paper** n papur llwyd; **tissue paper** papur sidan ▷ vb papuro
paperback n llyfr clawr meddal
paperclip n clip papur
papist n pabydd
papyrus(**-i**) n papurfrwyn
par n cyfartaledd, llawn werth
parable n dameg
parachute n parasiwt
parade n rhodfa; rhodres, rhwysg
paradise n paradwys, gwynfa, gwynfyd
paradox n gwrthddywediad, paradocs

paradoxical adj paradocsaidd
paradoxically adv yn baradocsaidd
paraffin n paraffin
paragraph n paragraff
parallel adj cyfochrog, cyflin, paralel
paralysis n parlys
paralytic adj, n claf o'r parlys
paralyze vt parlysu, diffrwytho
paramedic n parafeddyg
paramount adj pen, pennaf, prif
paramour n gordderch
parapet n canllaw, rhagfur
paraphernalia npl meddiannau, taclau, celfi, petheuach
paraphrase n aralleiriad ▷ vt aralleirio
parasite n un yn byw ar gefn un arall, cynffonnwr
parcel n parsel, swp, sypyn
parch vb crasu, deifio, golosgi, sychu
parched adj cras, crasboeth
parchment n memrwn
pardon n maddeuant, pardwn ▷ vt maddau, pardynu
parent n tad neu fam; **parents** rhieni
parenthesis(**-ses**) n sangiad, ymadrodd rhwng cromfachau
pariah n dyn ysgymun
parings npl pilion, creifion
Paris n Paris
parish n plwyf ▷ adj plwyf, plwyfol
parishioner n plwyfolyn
parity n cydraddoldeb, cyfartaledd
park n parc, cae, coetgae ▷ vb parcio
parking meter n amserydd parcio, rheolydd parcio
parking ticket n tocyn parcio
parlance n ymadrodd, iaith
parliament n senedd
parliamentary adj seneddol
parlour n parlwr
parochial adj plwyfol

parody n parodi ▷ vb gwatwar, dynwared

parole n gair, addewid, parôl

parricide n tadladdiad; tadleiddiad

parrot n parot, perot

parry vt osgoi, gochelyd, troi heibio

parse vt dosbarthu

parsimonious adj crintach, cybyddlyd

parsimony n crintachrwydd

parsley n persli

parsnip n panasen

parson n person, offeiriad

part n rhan; parth; plaid ▷ vb rhannu, parthu; gwahanu; ymadael

partake vb cyfrannu, cyfranogi

partial adj rhannol; pleidiol, tueddol

participate vb cyfranogi

participle n rhangymeriad

particle n mymryn, gronyn; geiryn

particular adj neilltuol, penodol; manwl ▷ n pwnc; **particulars** manylion

parting n ymadael

partisan n pleidiwr

partition n canolfur, gwahanfur, palis

partly adv mewn rhan, yn rhannol

partner n partner; cymar

partridge n petrisen

part-time adj rhan amser

party n plaid; parti, mintai

pass vb myned heibio, llwyddo, pasio; treulio, bwrw ▷ n cyflwr, sefyllfa; bwlch; trwydded; pas

pass away vi marw

passable adj y gellir mynd heibio iddo; purion

passage n tramwyfa; mordaith; cyfran

passenger n teithiwr

passing n ymadawiad, tranc, pasio ▷ adj yn pasio, diflannol

passion n dioddefaint; gwŷn, nwyd

passionate adj angerddol, nwydwyllt

passive adj goddefol

Passover n y Pasg

passport n trwydded deithio, pasbort

password n cyfrinair

past adj, n gorffennol ▷ prep wedi ▷ adv heibio

paste n past ▷ vt pastio, gludio

pastern n egwyd

pasteurize vb pasteureiddio

pasteurized adj wedi ei basteureiddio

pastime n difyrrwch, adloniant

pastor n bugail (eglwys), gweinidog

pastoral adj bugeiliol ▷ n bugeilgerdd

pastry n pasteiod, pasteiaeth, tarten; crwst

pasture n porfa ▷ vb porfelu, pori

pasty n pastai

pat vt patio, pratio, canmol ▷ adj parod, cymwys, priodol

patch n clwt, darn ▷ vt clytio

patchwork n clytwaith

paten n plat cymundeb

patent adj agored, cyhoedd, amlwg; breintiedig ▷ n breintlythyr

paternal adj tadol

paternoster n pader

path n llwybr

pathetic adj gresynus, pathetig

pathological adj patholegol

pathos n teimlad, dwyster

patience n amynedd

patient adj amyneddgar, dioddefus ▷ n dioddefydd, claf

patriarch n patriarch

patrimony n treftadaeth; gwaddol

patriot n gwladgarwr

patriotic adj gwladgarol

P

patrol *n* gwyliadwriaeth, gwylfa, patrôl
patron *n* noddwr
patronage *n* nawdd, nawddogaeth
patronize *vt* noddi, nawddogi
patronizing *adj* nawddogol
patronymic *n* tadenw
patter *vb* curo (fel glaw ar ffenestr)
patter *vb* padera ▷ *n* clebar, siaradach
pattern *n* patrwm, cynllun
paucity *n* prinder
paunch *n* bol, cest
pauper *n* dyn tlawd, tlotyn
pause *n* saib, seibiant, hoe ▷ *vi* aros, sefyll, ymbwyllo
pave *vt* palmantu
pavement *n* palmant, pafin
pavilion *n* pabell, pafiliwn
paw *n* palf, pawen ▷ *vb* palfu, pawennu
pawky *adj* direidus
pawn *n* gwystl; (*in chess*) gwerinwr ▷ *vt* gwystlo
pay *vb* talu ▷ *n* tâl, cyflog, pae, hur;
  back pay ôl-dâl
pay-as-you-go *adj* talu-wrth-ddefnyddio
payment *n* taliad, tâl
PC *n abbr* (= *personal computer*) PC, cyfrifiadur personol; (= *police constable*) cwnstabl (heddlu) ▷ *abbr* (= *politically correct*) PC, gwleidyddol-gywir
PE *n abbr* = *physical education*) addysg gorfforol
pea *n* pysen
peace *n* heddwch, tangnefedd ▷ *excl* gosteg!, ust!
peaceful *adj* heddychol, tangnefeddus, llonydd
peach *n* eirinen wlanog
peacock *n* paun

peak *n* pig; crib, copa; uchafbwynt
peal *n* sain clychau; twrf (taran) ▷ *vb* canu
peanut *n* cneuen ddaear
pear *n* gellygen
pearl *n* perl
peasant *n* gwladwr, gwerinwr
peasantry *n* gwerin
peat *n* mawn
pebble *n* carreg lefn, cerrigyn, gröyn
peck *vb* pigo, cnocellu ▷ *n* cnoc, pigiad
peculiar *adj* priod, priodol; hynod
peculiarity *n* hynodrwydd
pecuniary *adj* ariannol
pedagogue *n* athro plant, ysgolfeistr
pedal *n* pedal ▷ *vb* pedalu
pedant *n* pedant
pedantic *adj* pedantig
peddle *vb* pedlera
pedestal *n* troed, bôn, gwaelod
pedestrian *adj* ar draed, pedestrig ▷ *n* gŵr traed, cerddwr
pedestrian crossing *n* croesfan
pedigree *n* ach, achau, bonedd
pedlar *n* pedler
pee *n* pisiad ▷ *vb* pisio
peel *n* pil, croen, rhisgl ▷ *vb* pilio, plicio, crafu
peep *vi* cipedrych, sbïo ▷ *n* cipolwg, cip
peer *vi* ciledrych, syllu
peer *n* gogyfurdd, cydradd; pendefig
peevish *adj* anniddig, blin, piwis
peg *n* hoel bren, peg ▷ *vt* pegio
Peking *n* Peking
pelf *n* golud
pellet *n* peled, pelen, haelsen
pelt *vt* lluchio, taflu, peledu, baeddu
pelvis *n* pelfis
pen *n* pin, ysgrifbin ▷ *vt* ysgrifennu

pen n lloc, ffald, cwt ▷ vt ffaldio, llocio

penal adj penydiol

penalize vb cosbi

penalty n cosb, cosbedigaeth

penalty (kick) n cic gosb

penance n penyd

pence npl ceiniogau, pres

pencil n pwyntil, pensel, pensil

pencil sharpener n naddwr pensiliau

pendant n tlws

pending prep hyd, nes, yn ystod

pen drive n (computing) cofbin

pendulous adj yn hongian, yn siglo

pendulum n pendil

penetrate vb treiddio; dirnad

penfriend n cyfaill llythyru

penguin n pengwin

penicillin n penisilin

peninsula n gorynys

penis n cala, pidyn

penitence n edifeirwch

penitent adj edifar, edifarus, edifeiriol

penitentiary n carchar

penknife (-knives) n cyllell boced

pen name n ffug enw

pennant, pennon n penwn, baner

penniless adj heb geiniog

penny (pence, pennies) n ceiniog

pension n blwydd-dal, pensiwn

pensioner n pensiynwr

pensive adj synfyfyriol, meddylgar

pent adj wedi ei gau i mewn, caeth

Pentateuch n pumllyfr Moses

penult n goben

people n pobl, gwerin ▷ vt pobli, poblogi

pepper n pupur

peppermint n mintys poethion; botwm gwyn

per prep trwy, wrth, yn ôl

peradventure adv efallai

perceive vt canfod, gweld, dirnad, deall

per cent adv y cant

percentage n canran

perceptible adj canfyddadwy

perception n canfyddiad, canfod

perceptive adj yn gallu dirnad

perch n perc; clwyd ▷ vb clwydo

perchance adv efallai, hwyrach

percolate vb hidlo, diferu

percussion n trawiad, gwrthdrawiad; **percussion band** seindorf daro

peremptory adj pendant, awdurdodol

perennial adj drwy'r flwyddyn; bythol, lluosflwydd

perfect adj perffaith ▷ vt perffeithio

perfection n perffeithrwydd

perfectly adv yn berffaith

perfervid adj brwd, tanbaid

perfidy n brad, dichell, ffalster

perforate vt tyllu

perforated adj tyllog

perforation n twll

perforce adv o orfod, drwy drais

perform vb cyflawni; chwarae, perfformio

performance n perfformiad

performer n perfformiwr

perfume n perarogl, persawr ▷ vt perarogli

perfunctory adj o raid, diofal, esgeulus

perhaps adv efallai, hwyrach, ond odid, dichon

peril n perygl, enbydrwydd

perimeter n amfesur, perimedr

period n cyfnod; cyfadran (miwsig); diweddnod; misglwyf

periodic adj cyfnodol

P

periodical n cyfnodolyn
peripatetic adj crwydrol, cylchynol, peripatetig
peripheral adj ymylol
periphery n ymylon, cylchfesur
periphrastic adj cwmpasog
perish vi colli, trengi, marw, darfod; llygru
periwinkle n gwichiad
perjure vt: **perjure oneself** tyngu anudon
perjury n anudon, anudoniaeth
perk n mantais
perky adj bywiog, eofn, hyf
permanent adj parhaol, arhosol, sefydlog
permeate vt treiddio, trwytho
permissible adj wedi ei ganiatáu
permission n caniatâd, cennad
permissive adj goddefol; **the permissive society** y gymdeithas oddefol
permit vb caniatáu ▷ n trwydded
peroration n diweddglo araith, perorasiwn
perpendicular adj syth, unionsyth
perpetrate vt cyflawni (rhyw ddrwg)
perpetual adj parhaol, parhaus, bythol
perpetuate vt parhau, anfarwoli
perplex vt drysu, cythryblu, trallodi
persecute vt erlid
persevere vi dyfalbarhau
persist vi dal ati; mynnu, taeru, dyfalbarhau
persistent adj dyfal, taer, cyndyn, parhaus
person n person
personable adj golygus, prydweddol, hawddgar
personal adj personol
personal assistant n cynorthwyydd personol

personality n personoliaeth
personally adv yn bersonol
perspective n persbectif, safbwynt
perspiration n chwys
perspire vb chwysu
persuade vt darbwyllo, perswadio
pert adj eofn, tafodrydd
pertain vi perthyn
pertinent adj perthynol, cymwys
perturb vt cyffroi, aflonyddu, cythruddo
peruse vt darllen, chwilio
pervade vt treiddio, trwytho
perverse adj gwrthnysig, trofaus, croes
pervert vt gwyrdoi, llygru, camdroi ▷ n cyfeiliornwr
pessimism n pesimistiaeth
pessimist n pesimist
pest n pla, haint, poendod
pester vt blino, aflonyddu, poeni
pestilence n haint, pla
pet n anwylyn, ffafryn ▷ adj llywaeth, swci ▷ vt anwesu, canmol
petal n petal
petite adj bychan
petition n deisyfiad; deiseb, petisiwn
petitioner n deisebwr
petrel n aderyn drycin
petrified adj stond
petrify vb parlysu
petroleum n petroliwm
petrol pump n pwmp petrol
petrol station n gorsaf betrol
petticoat n pais
petty adj bach, bychan, mân, gwael
petulant adj annidig, anfoddog, anynad
pew n eisteddle, côr, sedd
pewit, peewit n cornicyll, cornchwiglen
pewter n piwter

phantom n rhith, drychiolaeth
Pharisee n Pharisead
pharmacy n fferylliaeth; fferyllfa
pharynx n sefnig
phase n golwg, gwedd, agwedd; tro
pheasant n ceiliog coed, coediar, ffesant
phenomenon (**-na**) n ffenomen; rhyfeddod
phial n ffiol
philander vi gwamalio caru
philanthropist n dyngarwr
philanthropy n dyngarwch
Philippines n Pilipinas
Philistine n Philistiad
philology n ieitheg
philosopher n athronydd
philosophical adj athronyddol
philosophy n athroniaeth
phlegm n cornboer, llysnafedd, fflem
phlegmatic adj difraw, digyffro, difywyd
phobia n ffobia
phone n ffôn, teleffon ▷ vb ffonio
phone book n cyfeiriadur ffôn
phone box n caban ffôn
phone call n galwad ffôn
phonetic adj seinegol
phonetician n seinegydd
phonetics n seineg
phoney adj ffug
phonology n ffonoleg
phosphorus n ffosfforws
photocopier n llungopïydd
photocopy n llungopi ▷ vb llungopïo
photograph n llun, ffotograff
photographer n ffotograffydd
photography n ffotograffiaeth
phrase n ymadrodd; cymal ▷ vt geirio
phraseology n geiriad, geirweddiad
physical adj corfforol, materol; ffisegol

physical education n addysg gorfforol
physician n meddyg, ffisigwr
physicist n ffisegydd/wr
physics n ffiseg
physiology n ffisioleg
physiotherapy n ffisiotherapi
physique n corffolaeth, cyfansoddiad
piano n piano
pick n caib ▷ vb ceibio
pick vb pigo, dewis, dethol ▷ n dewis
pickaxe n caib
picket n polyn, cledren; gwyliwr, gwyliadwriaeth, picedwr ▷ vb picedu
pickle n picl, heli ▷ vt piclo, halltu
pickpocket n pigwr pocedi, codleidr
picnic n picnic
pictorial adj darluniadol
picture n llun, darlun, pictiwr;
picture book llyfr lluniau
picturesque adj darluniaidd, gwych, byw
pie n pastai
piebald adj brith; brithryw
piece n darn, dryll, rhan ▷ vt clytio, asio, uno
piecemeal adv bob yn damaid
pie chart n siart olwyn
pied adj brith, brithliw
pier n piler; pier
pierce vb brathu, gwanu, trywanu
piety n duwioldeb
piffle n lol, oferedd, gwegi
pig n mochyn ▷ vb porchellu, bwrw perchyll
pigeon n colomen
pigeonhole n cloer
pigeon-house n colomendy
piggy bank n cadw-mi-gei, blwch cynilo

P

pig-headed adj pendew, ystyfnig
pigment n paent, lliw
pigsty n twlc mochyn
pigtail n pleth
pike n gwaywffon; penhwyad
pile n crug, pentwr ▷ vt pentyrru
pile n pawl, cledr
pile n blew, ceden
piles npl clwyf y marchogion
pilfer vb chwiwladrata
pilgrim n pererin
pilgrimage n pererindod
pill n pelen, pilsen
pillage n ysbail, anrhaith ▷ vt ysbeilio, anrheithio
pillar n colofn, piler
pillar box n bocs postio
pillion n sgil
pillory n rhigod, pilwri
pillow n gobennydd, clustog
pillow case n cas gobennydd
pilot n cyfarwyddwr llongau, peilot
pimple n ploryn, tosyn
pin n pin ▷ vt pinio, hoelio
pinafore n brat, piner
pincers npl gefel, pinsiwrn
pinch vb pinsio, gwasgu; cynilo ▷ n pins, pinsiad; gwasgfa, cyfyngder
pincushion n pincas, pincws
pine n pinwydden
pine vi dihoeni, nychu, curio
pineapple n afal pîn
pinion n asgell, adain ▷ vt torri esgyll
pink adj, n pinc
pinpoint vb pinbwyntio
pint n peint
pioneer n arloeswr, arloesydd
pious adj duwiol, duwiolfrydig, crefyddol
pip n hedyn afal etc
pipe n pib, pibell ▷ vb canu pibell
piping adj: **piping hot** chwilboeth
piquant adj pigog, llym, tost

pique vt llidio, cyffroi; ymfalchïo ▷ n soriant
pirate n môr-leidr
piss vb pisio
pissed adj meddw
pistol n llawddryll, pistol
pit n pwll, pydew ▷ vt pyllu; **coal pit** pwll glo
pitch n pyg ▷ vt pygu
pitch vb bwrw; gosod; taro (tôn) ▷ n gradd, mesur, traw
pitcher n piser, ystên, cawg
pitchfork n picfforch, picwarch; seinfforch
piteous adj truenus, gresynus
pitfall n magl, perygl
pith n bywyn; mwydion; mêr; grym, sylwedd
pithy adj cryno, cynhwysfawr
pitiful adj truenus, tosturiol
pitiless adj didostur, didrugaredd
pittance n dogn, cyfran (annigonol)
pity n tosturi, trueni, gresyn ▷ vt tosturio, gresynu
pivot n colyn, pegwn
placable adj cymodlon, hynaws
placard n murlen, hysbyslen
placate vt cymodi, heddychu, dyhuddo
place n lle, man, mangre ▷ vt cyfleu, gosod; **to take place** digwydd; **in the first place** yn y lle cyntaf
placid adj araf, tawel, llonydd
plagiary n llên-ladrad; llên-leidr
plague n pla, haint ▷ vt poeni, blino
plaice n lleden
plaid n plod
plain adj plaen, eglur ▷ n gwastadedd
plaintiff n achwynwr, hawlydd
plait n pleth ▷ vt plethu
plan n cynllun, plan ▷ vt cynllunio, planio

plane adj, n gwastad, lefel
plane n plaen; awyren ▷ vt plaenio
planet n planed
plank n astell, estyllen, planc
planning n cynllunio
planning permission n caniatâd cynllunio
plant n planhigyn, llysieuyn; offer; ffatri ▷ vt plannu
plaster n plaster ▷ vt plastro
plastic n, adj plastig; **plastic bag** cwdyn plastig
plat n darn o dir, clwt, lawnt
plate n plat; llestri aur etc ▷ vt golchi â metel
plateau n gwastatir uchel
platform n llwyfan, esgynlawr
platitude n sylw hen a diflas, gwireb
platoon n platŵn
platter n plat, dysgl, noe
plaudit n banllef o gymeradwyaeth
plausible adj teg neu resymol yr olwg, ffals
play vb chwarae; canu (offeryn) ▷ n chwarae
player n chwaraewr
playful adj chwareus
playground n chwaraele
playgroup n grŵp chwarae
playing field n maes chwarae
plaything n tegan
playwright n dramodydd
plea n ple, dadl, hawl; esgus
plead vb pledio, dadlau, eiriol, ymbil
pleasant adj hyfryd, pleserus, difyr, siriol
please vb boddhau, boddio, rhyngu bodd; **if you please** os gwelwch yn dda
pleased adj boddhaus, bodlon, hapus; **pleased to meet you** mae'n dda gen i gwrdd â chi
pleasing adj dymunol

pleasure n pleser, hyfrydwch
pleat n plet, pleten ▷ vt pletio
plebeian n gwerinwr, gwrêng
plebiscite n pleidlais y bobl
pledge n gwystl, ernes ▷ vt gwystlo
plenary adj llawn, cyflawn, diamodol
plenty n digon, helaethrwydd
plethora n gorgyflawnder
pleurisy n eisglwyf, plewrisi
pliable, pliant adj ystwyth, hyblyg
pliers npl gefel fechan
plight n cyflwr, drych, anghyflwr
plight vt addo, gwystlo
plod vb troedio, ymlafnio, llafurio, slafio
plot n darn o dir; brad, cynllwyn; cynllun, plot, ystofiad ▷ vb cynllwyn; cynllunio
plotter n cynllwynwr
plough n aradr, gwŷdd ▷ vb aredig, troi
ploy n cynllun, strategiaeth
pluck vt tynnu; pluo ▷ n glewder
plucky adj dewr, gwrol, glew
plug n topyn, plwg ▷ vt topio, plygio
plum n eirinen
plumage n plu
plumber n plymwr
plumbing n gwaith plymwr
plume n pluen, plufyn ▷ vt pluo, plufio
plummet n plymen
plump adj tew, llyfndew, graenus ▷ vb pleidleisio i un (yn unig)
plunder n ysbail, anrhaith ▷ vt ysbeilio, anrheithio
plunge n plymiad ▷ vb plymio, trochi, bwrw
pluperfect adj gorberffaith
plural adj lluosog
plus n plws, ychwaneg ▷ prep, adj ychwanegol

p

plush n plwsh
ply vb arfer, defnyddio, gyrru; poeni
plywood n pren haenog (tair-haen, pum-haen)
pneumatic adj â'i lond o wynt, awyrog
pneumonia n llid yr ysgyfaint, niwmonia
poach vb herwhela, potsio
poach vt berwi (wy) heb ei blisg
poacher n herwheliwr, potsiwr
pock n brech, ôl brech
pocket n poced, llogell ▷ vt pocedu; **pocket knife** cyllell boced; **pocket money** arian poced
pod n coden, plisgyn, masgl, cibyn
podgy adj byrdew
poem n cerdd, cân
poet n bardd, prydydd
poetry n barddoniaeth, prydyddiaeth
poignant adj llym, tost, ingol, aethus, awchlym
point n pwynt; man; blaen ▷ vb pwyntio; blaenllymu; dangos; **to be on the point of doing sth** bod ar fin gwneud rhywbeth; **to get the point** deall; **there's no point (in doing)** does dim diben (gwneud)
point out vt nodi
pointed adj pigfain
pointedly adv yn llym
pointer n cyfeirydd; mynegfys
pointless adj dibwynt, diystyr, gwag
point of view n safbwynt
poise vb mantoli; hofran ▷ n ystum, osgo
poison n gwenwyn ▷ vt gwenwyno
poisoning n gwenwyno
poisonous adj gwenwynig
poke vb gwthio, pwnio, procio
poker n pocer

poky adj cyfyng, gwael
polar adj pegynol
pole n pawl, polyn; pegwn
polemic adj dadleuol ▷ n dadl
police n heddlu
police car n car heddlu
policeman n heddwas, heddgeidwad, plismon
police station n gorsaf heddlu
policewoman n heddferch, plismones
policy n polisi
polish vb cwyro, caboli, gloywi, llathru ▷ n cwyr
polite adj moesgar, boneddigaidd
politic adj call, cyfrwys, doeth, buddiol
political adj gwleidyddol
politician n gwleidydd, gwleidyddwr
politics n gwleidyddiaeth
poll n pen, copa; pôl ▷ vb cneifio; pleidleisio, polio; **poll tax** treth y pen
pollen n paill
polling booth n bwth pleidleisio
polling day n dydd pleidleisio
polling station n gorsaf bleidleisio
pollute vt halogi, difwyno, llygru
pollution n llygredd
polo neck n jersi polo
polygamy n amlwreiciaeth
polysyllable n gair lluosill
polytechnic n polytechnig
pomegranate n pomgranad
pomp n rhwysg
pompous adj rhwysgfawr, balch
pond n llyn, pwll
ponder vb ystyried, myfyrio, pwyso
ponderous adj pwysfawr, trwm
pong n drewdod
pontiff n archoffeiriad; y Pab
pontoon n ysgraff

pony n merlyn, poni, merlen; **pony trekking** merlota

pooh excl pw!

pool n pwll, llyn

pool n cronfa; pwll ▷ vt cydgyfrannu

poor adj tlawd, truan, gwael, sâl

poorly adj sâl, gwael, claf

pop vb ffrwydro, ysgortio; picio, plannu, taro

pope n pab

popery n pabyddiaeth

pop-gun n gwn clats

poplar n poplysen

poppy n pabi (coch), llygad y bwgan

populace n gwerin, gwerinos

popular adj poblogaidd

population n poblogaeth

populous adj poblog

porcelain n porslen

porch n porth, cyntedd

porcine adj mochaidd

porcupine n ballasg

pore n twll chwys

pore vi astudio, myfyrio, synfyfyrio

pork n cig moch, porc

porker n mochyn, porcyn

pornography n pornograffi

porous adj tyllog

porpoise n llamhidydd

porridge n uwd

port n porth, porthfa, porthladd

port n ochr aswy llong wrth edrych ymlaen

port n gwin Oporto, gwin coch

portable adj cludadwy

portcullis n porthcwlis

portent n argoel; rhyfeddod, gwyrth

porter n porthor

portfolio n cas papurau, portffolio; swydd

porthole n ffenestr llong; gyndwll

portion n rhan, cyfran, gwaddol

portly adj tew, corffol

portrait n llun, darlun

portray vt portreadu, darlunio

Portugal n Portiwgal

pose vb sefyll, ymddangos, cymryd ar ▷ n ystum, rhodres

posh adj hardd, coeth

position n safle, sefyllfa, swydd

positive adj cadarnhaol, pendant, posidiol

posse n mintai, torf

possess vt meddu, meddiannu

possession n meddiant

possessor n perchen, perchennog

possibility n posibilrwydd

possible adj posibl, dichonadwy

possibly adv dichon, efallai

post n post, cledr ▷ vt gosod, cyhoeddi

post n post, llythyrfa; safle, swydd ▷ vb postio

post- prefix wedi, ar ôl

postage n cludiad (llythyr, etc.)

postal adj post

postal order n archeb bost

postbox n bocs postio

postcard n cerdyn post

postcode n côd post

poster n hysbyslen, poster

posterior adj ar ôl, ôl

posterity n cenedlaethau'r dyfodol, hiliogaeth

postgraduate adj graddedig

posthumous adj ar ôl marw

postman n postmon

postmark n postfarc

postmaster n postfeistr

post office n llythyrdy, swyddfa'r post

postpone vt gohirio, oedi

postscript n ôl-ysgrif

posture n agwedd, ystum, osgo

postwar adj ar ôl y rhyfel

P

posy n blodeuglwm, pwysi
pot n pot, potyn; crochan ▷ vb potio
potato (**-oes**) n taten, pytaten
potency n nerth, grym
potent adj cryf, galluog, grymus, nerthol
potential adj dichonadwy, dichonol ▷ n potensial
pothole n ceubwll
potion n dogn, llymaid, llwnc
pottage n cawl, potes
potter n crochenydd
potter vb diogi, ymdroi, sefyllian, swmera
pottery n llestri pridd; gwaith llestri pridd; priddweithfa
potty n pot
pouch n cod, coden, cwd ▷ vb cydu
poultice n powltis
poultry n dofednod, ffowls
pounce vb disgyn ar, dyfod ar warthaf
pound n pwys; punt
pound n ffald ▷ vt ffaldio
pound vb pwyo, pwnio, malu, malurio
pour vb tywallt, arllwys; bwrw
pout vi pwdu, sorri, terru, monni
poverty n tlodi
poverty-stricken adj tlawd, llwm
powder n powdr, llwch, pylor ▷ vt powdro
powdered milk n llaeth powdr
powder room n ystafell bincio
power n gallu, nerth, grym, awdurdod; pŵer
power cut n toriad yn y cyflenwad
power failure n pall ar y cyflenwad
powerful adj nerthol, grymus
powerless adj dirym
power station n pŵerdy
pox n brech
PR n abbr (= public relations) PR, cysylltiadau cyhoeddus

practicable adj dichonadwy
practical adj ymarferol
practically adv (almost) bron;
    practically certain bron yn sicr
practice n arfer, arferiad, ymarferiad
practise vb arfer, ymarfer
practising adj ymarferol; yn dilyn ei swydd
practitioner n meddyg; cyfreithiwr
prairie n gwastatir, gweundir, paith
praise vt canmol, moli ▷ n canmoliaeth, mawl
pram n coets, pram
prance vi prancio
prank n cast, ystranc, pranc
prawn n corgimwch
pray vb gweddïo; **I pray thee** atolwg
prayer n gweddi
pre- prefix cyn-, rhag-, blaen-
preach vb pregethu
preacher n pregethwr
preamble n rhagymadrodd, rhaglith
precarious adj ansicr, peryglus, enbyd
precaution n rhagofal, rhagocheliad, gofal
precede vb blaenori, blaenu, rhagflaenu
precedence n blaenoriaeth
precedent n cynsail
precentor n arweinydd y gân, codwr canu
preceptor n athro, hyfforddwr
precinct n cyffin, rhodfa
precious adj gwerthfawr, prid, drud
precipice n dibyn, diffwys, clogwyn
precipitate vt bwrw, hyrddio ▷ vi gwaddodi, gwaelodi ▷ adj byrbwyll, anystyriol
précis n crynodeb
precise adj penodol, manwl
preclude vt cau allan, atal, rhwystro

precocious adj hen o'i oed, henaidd, henffel

precondition n rhagamod

precursor n rhagredegydd, rhagflaenydd

predatory adj anrheithgar, ysglyfaethus

predecessor n rhagflaenydd

predestination n rhagarfaethiad

predicament n cyflwr, helynt, sefyllfa

predicate vt haeru, honni ▷ n traethiad

predict vt rhagfynegi, rhagddywedyd, proffwydo

predilection n hoffter, tuedd, tueddfryd

predominate vi bod yn bennaf neu yn fwyaf, arglwyddiaethu, rhagori

pre-eminent adj ar y blaen i bawb

preen vb pincio, harddu

preface n rhagymadrodd, rhaglith

prefect n rhaglaw; swyddog

prefer vt dewis yn hytrach, bod yn well gan

preferable adj gwell

preference n dewis, hoffter, ffafraeth, blaenoriaeth

preferential adj ffafriol

preferment n dyrchafiad, codiad

prefix vt rhagddodi ▷ n rhagddodiad

pregnancy n beichiogaeth

pregnant adj beichiog, llawn

prehistoric adj cynhanesiol

prejudice n rhagfarn; niwed ▷ vt rhagfarnu, niweidio

prejudiced adj rhagfarnllyd

prelate n esgob, prelad

preliminary adj arweiniol, rhagarweiniol

prelude n rhagarweiniad; preliwd

premarital adj cyn priodi

premature adj anaeddfed, cynamserol

premier adj blaenaf, pennaf, prif ▷ n prifweinidog

première n blaenberfformiad

premise n rhagosodiad ▷ vt rhagosod; **premises** npl adeiladau

premium n gwobr, tâl, taliad

preoccupied adj wedi ymgolli

preoccupy vt rhagfeddiannu; llenwi, ymgolli

prepaid adj wedi ei dalu ymlaen llaw, rhagdalwyd

preparation n paratoad, darpariaeth

preparatory adj rhagbaratoawl

prepare vb paratoi, darparu, darbod, arlwyo

prepared adj parod; effro

preposition n arddodiad

preposterous adj afresymol, gwrthun

prerequisite n rhaganghenraid

prerogative n braint, rhagorfraint

presage n argoel, rhagargoel ▷ vt argoeli

presbyter n henuriad, offeiriad

Presbyterian adj Henadurol, Presbyteraidd ▷ n Presbyteriad

presbytery n henaduriaeth; tŷ offeiriad Pabyddol

prescience n rhagwybodaeth

prescribe vb gorchymyn, cyfarwyddo

prescription n cyngor, cyfarwyddyd, presgripsiwn

presence n gŵydd, presenoldeb

present adj, n presennol

present n anrheg ▷ vt anrhegu; cyflwyno; dangos

presentation n cyflwyniad

presentiment n rhagargoel

presently adv yn fuan

preserve vt cadw, diogelu ▷ n jam

preside vi llywyddu

P

president n llywydd, arlywydd
press vb gwasgu ▷ n gwasg; gwrŷf; cwpwrdd
pressing adj taer, dwys
pressure n gwasgiad, gwasgfa, pwys
prestige n bri, dylanwad, braint
presumable adj y gellir ei dybio
presumably adv yn ôl pob tebyg, gellid tybio
presume vb tybio, tebygu; beiddio, rhyfygu
presumption n rhyfyg; tyb
presumptuous adj rhyfygus
pretence n rhith, esgus, ffug
pretend vb ffugio, cymryd ar, cogio; proffesu; honni hawl
pretension n honiad, hawl
preter- prefix tu hwnt i, mwy na
pretext n esgus, cochl
pretty adj tlws, del, pert ▷ adv cryn, go
prevail vi tycio, ffynnu; gorfod, trechu
prevalent adj cyffredin; nerthol
prevent vt rhagflaenu; atal, rhwystro
preview n rhagolwg
previous adj blaenorol, cynt
prey n ysglyfaeth, aberth ▷ vi ysglyfaethu
price n pris, gwerth ▷ vt prisio
price list n rhestr prisiau, taflen brisiau; telerau
prick n pigyn, swmbwl ▷ vb pigo; picio, codi
prickle n draen ▷ vb pigo, tymhigo
pride n balchder ▷ vt balchïo, ymfalchïo
priest n offeiriad
priesthood n offeiriadaeth
prig n sychfoesolyn, mursennwr, coethyn

prim adj cymen, cymhenllyd
primary adj prif, cyntaf, cysefin; cynradd
primary school n ysgol gynradd
primate n archesgob
prime adj prif, cyntaf; gorau ▷ n anterth
prime vt llwytho, llenwi, cyflenwi
primer n llyfr cyntaf, cynlyfr
primeval adj cynoesol, cyntefig
primitive adj cyntefig; garw, amrwd
primordial adj cyntefig, cysefin
primrose n briallen
prince n tywysog
princess n tywysoges; **Princess Anne** y Dywysoges Anne
principal adj prif ▷ n pen; prifathro; corff
principality n tywysogaeth
principle n egwyddor, elfen
print n argraff, print, ôl ▷ vb argraffu, printio
printed adj argraffedig, wedi ei argraffu
printer n argraffydd
printer's n argraffdy
printout n allbrint
prior adj cynt, blaenorol ▷ n prior, priol
priority n blaenoriaeth
priory n priordy, mynachdy
prise, prize vt dryllio'n agored â throsol
prism n prism
prison n carchar, carchardy
prisoner n carcharor
pristine adj hen, cyntefig, cysefin
private adj preifat, cyfrinachol, personol
private enterprise n ymroddiad unigol
privation n amddifadrwydd, diffyg
privilege n braint, rhagorfraint

privy adj dirgel, cudd, cyfrin ▷ n geudy
prize n gwobr ▷ vt prisio, gwerthfawrogi
prize n ysbail, caffaeliad, gwobr
pro- prefix am, yn lle; o blaid
probability n tebygolrwydd
probable adj tebygol, tebyg
probably adv mae'n debyg, yn ôl pob tebyg; **it will probably be all right** bydd hi'n iawn, mae'n debyg or yn ôl pob tebyg
probate n prawf ewyllys
probation n prawf
probe n profiedydd ▷ vt profi, chwilio
probity n uniondeb, cywirdeb
problem n pwnc, drysbwnc, problem
procedure n trefn, arfer, defod, dull
proceed vi myned, deillio, tarddu; erlyn
proceeds npl enillion, elw
process n gweithrediad, goruchwyliaeth, dull
procession n gorymdaith; deilliad
proclaim vt cyhoeddi, datgan
proclamation n cyhoeddiad, proclamasiwn
proclivity n gogwydd, tuedd
proconsul n rhaglaw
procrastinate vi oedi, gohirio
procreate vt cenhedlu
procure vb ceisio, caffael, cael
prod vt procio, pwnio, symbylu
prodigal adj afradlon, hael
prodigious adj aruthrol, anferth
prodigy n rhyfeddod, gwyrth
produce vt cynhyrchu, epilio; dwyn ▷ n cynnyrch, ffrwyth
product n cynnyrch, ffrwyth
production n cynhyrchiad
profane adj anghysegredig,

halogedig ▷ vt anghysegru, halogi
profess vb proffesu, arddel
profession n proffes, galwedigaeth
professional adj proffesiynol
professor n proffeswr; athro
proffer vt, n cynnig
proficient adj hyddysg, cyfarwydd
profile n ystlyslun, cernlun
profit n budd, lles, elw, proffid ▷ vb llesáu, proffidio
profitable adj (financially) proffidiol, yn dwyn elw; (advantageous) proffidiol, manteisiol
profiteer vi gwneud elw
profligate adj afradlon, ofer
profound adj dwfn, dwys, angerddol
profundity n dyfnder
profuse adj hael, helaeth, toreithiog
progenitor n cyndad
progeny n hil, epil, hiliogaeth
prognostic n argoel, rhagarwydd
program n rhaglen ▷ vb rhaglennu
programme n rhaglen
programmer n rhaglennydd
progress n cynnydd; taith ▷ vi cynyddu
progressive adj cynyddgar, progresif
prohibit vt gwahardd
project n bwriad, cynllun; project
project vb bwrw; bwriadu; ymestyn; taflunio
projectile n teflyn
projector n taflunydd
proletariat n gwerin, gwrêng
prolific adj epiliog, ffrwythlon, toreithiog
prolix adj maith, amleiriog
prologue n rhagair, prolog
prolong vt hwyhau, estyn
promenade n rhodfa ▷ vb rhodianna
prominent adj yn sefyll allan, amlwg

P

promise n addewid ▷ vb addo, argoeli

promissory adj addewidiol

promontory n pentir, penrhyn

promote vt hyrwyddo, meithrin, dyrchafu

promoter n hyrwyddwr

promotion n (at work) dyrchafiad; (of event) hyrwyddiad

prompt adj parod, buan ▷ vt cofweini; cymell

promptitude n parodrwydd

promulgate vt cyhoeddi, lledaenu

prone adj â'i wyneb i waered; tueddol

prong n fforch, pig fforch

pronominal adj rhagenwol

pronoun n rhagenw

pronounce vb cynanu, yngan; cyhoeddi, datgan

pronunciation n cynaniad

proof n prawf; proflen

prop n ateg, post, prop ▷ vt ategu

propaganda n propaganda

propagate vt epilio, cenhedlu; lledaenu

propel vt gyrru ymlaen, gwthio

propensity n tuedd, tueddfryd, gogwydd

proper adj priod, priodol, gweddus

property n priodoledd; eiddo; priodwedd (cemeg)

prophecy n proffwydoliaeth

prophesy vb proffwydo

prophet n proffwyd

propinquity n agosrwydd, cyfnesafrwydd

propitiate vt cymodi, dyhuddo

propitiation n cymod, iawn

propitious adj tirion, ffafriol

proportion n cyfartaledd, cyfrannedd

proportional adj cyfrannol

proportionate adj cymesur

proposal n cynnig

propose vb cynnig, bwriadu

proposition n cynigiad; gosodiad

propound vt cynnig, gosod gerbron

proprietor n perchen, perchennog

propriety n priodoldeb, gwedduster

propulsion n gwthiad, gyriad

prorogue vt gohirio

prosaic adj rhyddieithol, cyffredin

proscribe vt deol, diarddel, gwahardd

prose n rhyddiaith

prosecute vt erlyn, dilyn, dwyn ymlaen

prosecutor n erlynydd

proselyte n proselyt

prosody n mydryddiaeth

prospect n rhagolwg, golwg, golygfa

prospectus n rhaglen, hysbyslen, prosbectws

prosper vb llwyddo, tycio, ffynnu

prosperity n llwyddiant, hawddfyd, ffyniant

prostitute n putain ▷ vt darostwng

prostrate adj yn gorwedd ar ei wyneb; ar lawr yn lân ▷ vt bwrw i lawr; ymgrymu

protect vt amddiffyn, noddi

protection n amddiffyn, nawdd, diogelwch

protective adj amddiffynnol

protector n amddiffynnydd

protest vb gwrthdystio ▷ n gwrthdystiad

prototype n cynddelw, cynllun

protract vt estyn, hwyhau

protrude vb gwthio allan

protuberance n chwydd

proud adj balch

prove vb profi

provender n ebran, gogor, porthiant

proverb n dihareb

provide *vt* darparu
providence *n* rhagluniaeth, darbodaeth
provident *adj* darbodus
providential *adj* rhagluniaethol
province *n* talaith, tiriogaeth; cylch, maes
provision *n* darpariaeth; **provisions** *npl* darbodion; ymborth
proviso *n* amod
provocation *n* anogaeth, cyffroad, cythrudd
provoke *vt* annog, cyffroi, cythruddo, profocio
provost *n* maer, profost
prow *n* pen blaen bad neu long
prowess *n* dewrder, glewder, grymuster
prowl *vi* ysglyfaetha, prowlan
proximate *adj* nesaf, agos at; agos
proximity *n* agosrwydd
proxy *n* dirprwy
prude *n* mursen, coegen
prudence *n* pwyll, synnwyr, callineb
prudent *adj* pwyllog, synhwyrol, call, doeth
prune *n* eirinen sech
Prussia *n* Prwsia
pry *vi* chwilota, chwilenna
psalm *n* salm
psalmody *n* caniadaeth y cysegr, salmyddiaeth
psalter *n* llyfr salmau, sallwyr
pseudo- *prefix* gau, ffug
pseudonym *n* ffugenw
pshaw *excl* wfft, pw, och, ffei
psychiatrist *n* seiciatrydd
psychological *adj* seicolegol, meddyliol
psychologist *n* seicolegydd
psychology *n* seicoleg
puberty *n* aeddfedrwydd oed, blaenlencyndod, puberdod

public *adj* cyhoeddus ▷ *n* y cyhoedd
publican *n* publican; tafarnwr
public house *n* tŷ tafarn
publicity *n* cyhoeddusrwydd
public library *n* llyfrgell gyhoeddus
public relations *npl* cysylltiadau cyhoeddus
public school *n* ysgol fonedd
publish *vt* cyhoeddi
pucker *vb* crychu, crybachu
pudding *n* pwdin
puddle *n* corbwll; pydew, llaca
puerile *adj* bachgennaidd, plentynnaidd
puff *n* pwff, chwa, chwyth ▷ *vb* pwffio, chwythu
pugilist *n* paffiwr, ymladdwr
pugnacious *adj* ymladdgar, cwerylgar
puissant *adj* galluog, grymus, nerthol
pull *vt* tynnu ▷ *n* tynfa, tyniad
pullet *n* cywen
pulley *n* chwerfan, troell, pwli
pullover *n* gwasgod wlân
pulmonary *adj* ysgyfeiniol
pulp *n* bywyn, mwydion
pulpit *n* pulpud
pulsate *vb* curo (megis y galon)
pulse *n* curiad y galon, curiad y gwaed
pulse *n* pys, ffa *etc*
pulverize *vt* malu yn llwch, chwilfriwio
pummel *vt* pwnio, dyrnodio, curo
pump *n* sugnedydd, pwmp ▷ *vb* pwmpio
pumpkin *n* pwmpen
pun *n* gair mwys, mwysair
punch *n* pwns; dyrnod ▷ *vb* pwnsio, dyrnodio
punch-up *n* ysgarmes
punctilious *adj* cysetlyd, gorfanwl**

P

punctual adj prydlon
punctuate vt atalnodi
puncture n twll ▷ vt tyllu
pundit n ysgolhaig, doethwr
pungent adj llym, llymdost, siarp
punish vt cosbi, ceryddu; poeni
punishment n cosb, cosbedigaeth
punitive adj cosbol
puny adj eiddil, bychan, tila, pitw
pupil n ysgolhaig, ysgolor, disgybl;
cannwyll llygad
puppet n delw, dol, pyped; gwas
puppy n ci bach
purblind adj cibddall, coegddall
purchase vt prynu, pwrcasu ▷ n
pryniant, pwrcas
pure adj pur, noeth
purgative adj carthol ▷ n carthlyn
purgatory n purdan
purge vt puro, glanhau, carthu,
coethi ▷ n carthlyn
purification n puredigaeth
purify vt puro, coethi, glanhau
Puritan n Piwritan
purity n purdeb
purl vi crychleisio, byrlymu
purlieu n cyffin, ffin, cymdogaeth
purloin vt lladrata, dwyn
purple adj, n porffor
purport n ystyr, rhediad, ergyd ▷ vt
arwyddo, proffesu, honni
purpose n pwrpas, bwriad, arfaeth
▷ vt bwriadu, arfaethu
purr vb canu crwth, grwnan
purse n pwrs, cod ▷ vb crychu
pursue vb dilyn, erlyn, erlid, ymlid
pursuit n ymlidiad; ymchwil,
gorchwyl
purulent adj crawnllyd, gorllyd
purvey vb darparu lluniaeth,
darmerth
purview n amcan, maes, cylch
pus n crawn, gôr

push vb gwthio ▷ n gwth, ysgŵd;
ymdrech
pushchair n coets
puss n titw, pws; ysgyfarnog
pustule n ploryn, llinoryn
put vb gosod, dodi, rhoddi, rhoi
put back vt (replace) rhoi yn ôl;
(postpone) gohirio
put off vt (postpone) gohirio;
(discourage) digalonni; (switch off)
diffodd
put on vt gwisgo; troi ymlaen;
to put on weight enill pwysau
putative adj tybiedig, cyfrifedig
putrefaction n pydredd, madredd
putrefy vb pydru, madru
putrid adj pwdr, mall
putty n pwti ▷ vt pwtio
puzzle n dryswch, penbleth, pos ▷ vb
drysu, pyslo
pygmy n corrach
pyjamas npl gwisg nos, gŵn nos
pyramid n pyramid, bera
pyre n cynnau angladdol, coelcerth
pyrotechnic adj, n (o natur) tân
gwyllt

q

quack n crachfeddyg, cwac
quack vi cwacian
quadrangle n pedrongl
quadrant n cwadrant
quadruped n pedwarcarnol
quadruple adj pedwarplyg
quadruplet n pedrybled
quaff vb drachtio, cofftio, yfed
quagmire n siglen, cors, mignen, sybwll
quail n sofliar
quaint adj od, henffasiwn
quake vi crynu
Quaker n Crynwr
qualification n cymhwyster; cymhwysiad
qualified adj cymwys
qualify vt cymhwyso, cyfaddasu
quality n ansawdd, rhinwedd
qualm n petruster, amheuaeth
quandary n penbleth, cyfyng-gyngor

quantity n swm, maint, mesur
quarantine n cwarant, neilltuaeth
quarrel n ymrafael, ffrae, cweryl
▷ vi ffraeo
quarry n chwarel, cloddfa, cwar
▷ vb cloddio
quarry n ysglyfaeth
quart n chwart, cwart
quarter n chwarter; man; trugaredd; **a quarter of an hour** chwarter awr; **quarter final** rownd gogynderfynol
quarters npl llety
quarter-sessions n llys chwarter
quartet, quartette n pedwarawd
quarto adj, n (llyfr) pedwarplyg
quartz n creigrisial, cwarts
quash vt diddymu, dirymu
quaver vi cwafrio, crynu ▷ n cwafer
quay n cei
queen n brenhines
queer adj od, hynod, digrif, ysmala
quell vt llonyddu, gostegu, darostwng
quench vt diffodd, dofi, torri
quern n llawfelin, breuan
querulous adj cwynfanllyd, blin
query n holiad, gofyniad ▷ vb holi, amau
quest n ymchwil, ymchwiliad, cwest
question n gofyniad, cwestiwn ▷ vt holi, amau
questionable adj amheus
question mark n gofynnod
questionnaire n holiadur
queue n cynffon, cwt, ciw
quibble n geirddadl, mân-ddadl ▷ vi geirddadlau, mân-ddadlau, hollti blew
quick adj byw; buan, cyflym, clau; **to the quick** i'r byw
quicken vb cyflymu
quicksilver n arian byw**

quid *n* punt
quiescent *adj* distaw, llonydd, digyffro
quiet *adj* llonydd, tawel, distaw ▷ *n* llonyddwch, tawelwch ▷ *vt* llonyddu, tawelu
quill *n* pluen, plufyn, cwilsyn
quilt *n* cwilt, cwrlid ▷ *vt* cwiltio
quintet *n* pumawd
quintuplet *n* pumled
quip *n* gair ffraeth, ateb parod
quirky *adj* od, hynod
quit *vt* gadael, symud ▷ *adj* rhydd
quite *adv* cwbl, llwyr, hollol
quits *adj* yn gyfartal
quiver *n* cawell saethau
quiver *vi* crynu, dirgrynu
quixotic *adj* mympwyol, gwyllt
quiz *vt* holi, pyslo, profocio
quoit *n* coeten, coetan
quondam *adj* wedi bod, gynt, hen
quorum *n* nifer gofynnol, corwm
quota *n* rhan, cyfran, dogn, cwota
quotation *n* dyfyniad; prisiant
quote *vt* dyfynnu; nodi (prisiau)
quoth *vt* meddai, ebe

rabbi *n* rabi
rabbit *n* cwningen
rabble *n* ciwed, tyrfa ddireol
rabid *adj* cynddeiriog
rabies *n* y gynddaredd
race *n* ras, gyrfa, rhedfa ▷ *vi* rasio
race *n* hil
racial *adj* hiliol
racism *n* hiliaeth
racist *adj* hiliol ▷ *n* hilydd, hiliwr
rack *n* rac, clwyd, rhestl; arteithglwyd ▷ *vt* arteithio, dirdynnu
racket *n* twrf, mwstwr; (*for tennis etc*) raced
racy *adj* blasus; arab, ffraeth
radiant *adj* disglair, llachar, tanbaid
radiate *vb* pelydru, rheiddio
radiation *n* ymbelydredd
radiator *n* rheiddiadur

radical *adj* gwreiddiol, cynhenid; trylwyr ▷ *n* rhyddfrydwr, radical
radio *n* radio
radioactive *adj* ymbelydrol
radio station *n* gorsaf radio
radish *n* rhuddygl, radis
radius (-ii) *n* cylch; radius
raffle *n* raffl
raft *n* cludair, ysgraff, rafft
rafter *n* tulath, ceibren, trawst
rag *n* carp, clwt
rag doll *n* doli glwt
rage *n* cynddaredd ▷ *vi* terfysgu, cynddeiriogi
ragged *adj* carpiog, bratiog
raid *n* rhuthr, cyrch ▷ *vb* anrheithio, ysbeilio
rail *n* canllaw, cledren, rheilen ▷ *vb* cledru
rail *vi* difrïo, difenwi, cablu
raillery *n* difyrrwch, cellwair
railway *n* rheilffordd
railway station *n* gorsaf reilffordd
raiment *n* dillad, gwisg
rain *n* glaw ▷ *vb* glawio, bwrw glaw
rainbow *n* enfys
raincoat *n* cot law
rainforest *n* fforest law
rainy *adj* glawog
raise *vt* codi, cyfodi, dyrchafu
raisin *n* rhesinen
rake *n* cribin, rhaca ▷ *vb* cribinio, crafu, rhacanu
rally *vb* atgynnull; adgyfnerthu, gwella ▷ *n* cynulliad
ram *n* hwrdd, maharen ▷ *vt* hyrddio, pwnio
ramble *vi* gwibio, crwydro ▷ *n* gwib
rambler *n* crwydrwr
rampant *adj* uchel ei ben, rhonc
rampart *n* caer, rhagfur, gwrthglawdd
ramshackle *adj* bregus, candryll

rancid *adj* â blas cryf arno, drewllyd
rancour *n* digasedd, chwerwder
random *n* antur, siawns, damwain ▷ *adj* damweiniol
range *n* amrediad; cwmpas; ystod; lle tân â ffwrn ▷ *vb* rhestru, cyfleu; crwydro
ranger *n* coedwigwr, ceidwad parc
rank *n* rheng, gradd ▷ *vb* rhestru; **the rank and file** y bobl gyffredin
rank *adj* mws; gwyllt; bras; rhonc, noeth
rankle *vi* gori, madru; cnoi, llidio
ransack *vt* chwilio, chwilota, ysbeilio
ransom *n* pridwerth ▷ *vt* prynu, gwaredu
rant *vi* bragaldian, brygawthan
rap *n* cnoc, ergyd ▷ *vt* cnocio, curo
rap *n* gronyn, mymryn, blewyn
rapacious *adj* rheibus, ysglyfaethus
rape *vt* treisio ▷ *n* trais
rapid *adj* cyflym, buan, chwyrn, gwyllt
rapist *n* treisiwr
rapture *n* perlewyg, gorawen, afiaith
rare *adj* anaml, prin; godidog; tenau
rascal *n* dihiryn, cnaf, gwalch, cenau
rash *adj* byrbwyll, rhyfygus, anystyriol
rash *n* brech, tarddiant
rasher *n* ysglisen, sleisen, tafell, golwyth
rasp *vb* rhasglio, crafu, rhygnu
raspberry *n* afanen, mafonen
rat *n* llygoden fawr, llygoden ffrengig ▷ *vi* llygota
rate *vt* ffraeo, dwrdio, dweud y drefn
rate *n* cyflymder; treth; (*of interest*) cyfradd
rateable value *n* gwerth trethiannol
ratepayer *n* trethdalwr**

rather *adv* braidd, hytrach, go, lled
ratify *vt* cadarnhau
ratio *n* cyfartaledd; cymhareb
ration *n* dogn, saig ▷ *vt* dogni
rational *adj* rhesymol
rationale *n* rhesymwaith
rationalization *n* rhesymoliad
rationalize *vb* rhesymoli
rattle *vb* rhuglo, trystio ▷ *n* rhugl,
 rhwnc
raucous *adj* cryg, garw, aflafar
ravage *vt* anrheithio, diffeithio,
 difrodi
rave *vi* gwallgofi, ynfydu, gwynfydu
ravel *vb* drysu; dad-weu, datod
raven *n* cigfran
ravenous *adj* rheibus, gwancus
ravine *n* hafn, ceunant
raving *adj* ynfyd, dwl, gwallgof
ravish *vt* treisio, cipio; swyno, hudo
ravishing *adj* deniadol iawn
raw *adj* amrwd; crai, cri; noeth,
 dolurus, garw; dibrofiad ▷ *n* cig
 noeth, dolur
ray *n* paladr, pelydryn
ray *n* cath fôr
raze *vt* llwyr ddymchwelyd, dileu
razor *n* ellyn, rasal ▷ *vt* eillio
razor blade *n* llafn ellyn
re *prep* ym mater, mewn perthynas â
re- *prefix* ad-, ail-
reach *vb* cyrraedd, estyn ▷ *n* cyrraedd
react *vi* adweithio
reaction *n* adwaith
reactionary *adj* adweithiol
reactor *n* adweithydd
read *vb* darllen
readable *adj* darllenadwy
reader *n* darllenydd
readily *adv* yn barod, yn ddiffwdan
reading *n* darllen
readjustment *n* atgywiriad,
 addasiad

ready *adj* parod, rhwydd
reafforestation *n* ailfforestiad
real *adj* gwir, real, go-iawn
realistic *adj* realistig, realaidd
reality *n* gwirionedd, sylwedd;
 dirwedd, realiti
realize *vt* sylweddoli; troi yn arian
really *adv* gwir, hollol, mewn difrif
realm *n* teyrnas, gwlad, bro
reap *vb* medi
reappear *vb* ailymddangos
rear *n* cefn, pen ôl, ôl
rear *vb* codi, magu; codi ar ei draed ôl
reason *n* rheswm ▷ *vb* rhesymu
reasonable *adj* rhesymol
reassurance *n* calondid
reassure *vt* calonogi, cysuro
rebate *n* ad-daliad
rebel *vi* gwrthryfela ▷ *n*
 gwrthryfelwr
rebellion *n* gwrthryfel
rebound *vi* adlamu ▷ *n* adlam
rebuff *n* nacâd, sen ▷ *vt* nacáu,
 sennu
rebuke *vt* ceryddu ▷ *n* cerydd, sen
rebut *vt* gwrthbrofi,
 gwrthddywedyd
recall *vt* galw yn ôl; galw i gof, cofio
recant *vb* datgyffesu
recapitulate *vt* ailadrodd (yn gryno)
recede *vi* encilio, cilio yn ôl
receipt *n* derbyniad; derbynneb
receive *vt* derbyn
receiver *n* derbynnydd
recent *adj* diweddar
receptacle *n* llestr; cynheiliad
 (llysieueg)
reception *n* derbyniad, croeso
reception desk *n* man croeso, man
 derbyn
receptionist *n* croesawferch,
 croesawydd
recess *n* cil, encil; cilfach; gwyliau

recessional *adj, n* (emyn) ymadawol
recharge *vt* aildrydanu
recipe *n* cyfarwyddyd; rysáit
recipient *n* derbyniwr, derbynnydd
reciprocal *adj* cilyddol
reciprocate *vb* talu'n ôl,
   cydgyfnewid; cilyddu
recital *n* adroddiad, datganiad
recitation *n* adroddiad
recite *vb* adrodd
reck *vb* gofalu, ystyried
reckless *adj* anystyriol, rhyfygus,
   dibris
reckon *vb* cyfrif, barnu, bwrw
reclaim *vt* adennill, diwygio
recline *vb* lledorwedd, gorwedd,
   gorffwys
recluse *n* meudwy, ancr
recognition *n* adnabyddiaeth,
   cydnabyddiaeth
recognize *vt* adnabod, cydnabod
recoil *vi* adlamu, gwrthneidio, cilio
recollect *vt* galw i gof, atgofio, cofio
recommend *vt* cymeradwyo,
   argymell
recommendation *n*
   cymeradwyaeth
recompense *vt* ad-dalu, gwobrwyo,
   talu
reconcile *vt* cymodi, cysoni
recondite *adj* dwfn, cudd, cêl,
   tywyll
recondition *vt* atgyflyru, ail-wneud
reconnaissance *n* rhagchwiliad
reconnoitre *vt* chwilio, archwilio
record *vt* cofnodi, recordio ▷ *n*
   cofnod, record
recorder *n* cofiadur; (*musical
   instrument*) recordydd
recording *n* recordiad
recount *vt* adrodd
re-count *vb* ailgyfrif
recoup *vb* digolledu

recourse *n* cyrchfa; **to have
   recourse to** mynd at, defnyddio
recover *vb* cael yn ôl, adennill;
   ymadfer; adferiad
recreation *n* difyrrwch, adloniant
recruit *n* recriwt; newyddian ▷ *vt*
   codi gwŷr; adennill
rectangle *n* petryal
rectangular *adj* petryalog
rectify *vt* unioni, cywiro; puro,
   coethi
rectilinear *adj* unionlin
rector *n* rheithor
rectory *n* rheithoriaeth; rheithordy
recuperate *vb* adfer, ymadfer,
   cryfhau, gwella
recur *vi* ailddigwydd, dychwelyd
recurrence *n* ail-ddigwyddiad,
   ail-ymddangosiad
recurring *adj* cylchol
recusant *n* anghydffurfiwr
recycle *vb* ailgylchu
recycling *n* ailgylchu
red *adj, n* coch, rhudd
redeem *vt* prynu (yn ôl), gwaredu
redemption *n* prynedigaeth
redeploy *vb* adleoli
redeployment *n* adleoliad,
   trawsgyflogaeth
red herring *n* (met) ysgyfarnog
redirect *vb* ailgyfeirio
redo *vb* ail-wneud
redolent *adj* yn sawru o
redoubtable *adj* i'w ofni; pybyr
redress *vt* unioni ▷ *n* iawn (am gam)
Red Sea ; **the Red Sea** y Môr Coch
reduce *vt* lleihau, gostwng;
   rhydwytho
reduced *adj* gostyngol
reduction *n* lleihad, gostyngiad
redundancy *n* anghyflogaeth
redundant *adj* gormodol;
   anghyflog, digyflog

r

reed n cawnen, corsen, calaf; pibell
reef n plyg hwyl, rîff ▷ vt plygu hwyl
reef n creigle (yn y môr), creigfa, rîff
reek n mwg, tarth, drewdod ▷ vb mygu, drewi
reel n ril ▷ vb dirwyn
reel vi troi, chwyldroi ▷ n dawns
refectory n ffreutur
refer vb cyfeirio, cyfarwyddo
referee n dyfarnwr; canolwr ▷ vt dyfarnu
reference n cyfeiriad; geirda
refill n adlenwad ▷ vt adlenwi
refine vb puro, coethi
reflect vb adlewyrchu; myfyrio
reflection n adlewyrchiad, myfyrdod, ailfeddwl
reflex n adweithred, atgyrch
reflexive adj atblygol
reform vb diwygio, gwella ▷ n diwygiad
reformation n diwygiad
reformatory n ysgol ddiwygio
refrain vb ymatal
refrain n byrdwn
refresh vt adfywio, dadebru, adlonni
refresher course n cwrs adolygu
refreshing adj adfywiol
refreshments npl ymborth, lluniaeth
refrigerate vt rheweiddio, cadw'n oer
refrigerator n rhewgell, oergell
refuge n noddfa, lloches
refugee n ffoadur
refund n ad-daliad ▷ vb ad-dalu
refurbish vb adnewyddu
refusal n gwrthodiad, nacâd
refuse vb gwrthod
refuse n ysbwriel, gwehilion, sothach
refute vt gwrthbrofi, datbrofi
regal adj brenhinol

regard vt edrych ar, ystyried ▷ n sylw, parch, hoffter
regarding prep ynglŷn â, ynghylch
regardless adj heb ofal, diofal
regenerate vt aileni
régime n trefn, cyfundrefn
regiment n catrawd
region n ardal, bro, gwlad
regional adj rhanbarthol
register n cofrestr ▷ vt cofrestru
registered adj cofrestredig
registrar n cofrestrydd
registration n cofrestriad
registration number n rhif cofrestru, rhif trethiant
registry n cofrestrfa
regret vt gofidio, edifaru ▷ n gofid
regular adj rheolaidd, cyson
regularly adv yn rheolaidd
regulate vt rheoleiddio, llywio, rheoli
regulation n rheol, trefniant
rehabilitate vt adfer i fri neu fraint, ailsefydlu
rehabilitation n adferiad
rehearsal n rihyrsal, practis
rehearse vt adrodd; ymarfer ymlaen llaw
reign vi teyrnasu ▷ n teyrnasiad
reimburse vt talu yn ôl, ad-dalu
rein n afwyn, awen ▷ vt ffrwyno
reindeer n carw
reinforce vt atgyfnerthu
reinstate vt adfer i safle neu fraint
reiterate vt ailadrodd, mynychu
reject vt gwrthod, bwrw ymaith
rejection n gwrthodiad
rejoice vb llawenhau, gorfoleddu
rejoin vb ateb, gwrthateb
rejoinder n ateb, gwrthateb
rejuvenate vb adfywiogi, adnewyddu
relapse vi ailglafychu, ailymhoelyd, atglafychu

relate vb adrodd, mynegi; perthyn

related adj yn perthyn; wedi ei ddweud

relating to prep yn ymwneud â

relation n adroddiad; perthynas

relationship n perthynas

relative adj perthnasol ▷ n perthynas; **relative pronoun** rhagenw perthynol

relax vb llacio, llaesu, ymollwng

relaxing adj ymlaciol

relay n cyflenwad newydd, cyfnewid; darlledu ▷ vb ailosod

relay race n ras gyfnewid

release vt rhyddhau, gollwng ▷ n rhyddhad

relegate vt alltudio, deol, darostwng

relent vi tyneru, tirioni, llaesu

relevant adj perthnasol

reliable adj y gellir dibynnu arno, dibynadwy

reliance n ymddiried, dibyniaeth, hyder, pwys

relic n crair; gweddillion

relief n cynhorthwy; gollyngdod, ymwared; tirwedd

relieve vt cynorthwyo; esmwytho, ysgafnhau; rhyddhau, gollwng

religion n crefydd

religious adj crefyddol

relinquish vt gollwng, gildio, gwadu

relish n blas; enllyn, mwyniant ▷ vb blasio, hoffi

reluctance n amharodrwydd, anfodlonrwydd

reluctant adj anfodlon, anewyllysgar

rely vi hyderu, ymddiried, dibynnu

remain vi aros, parhau, gorffwys

remainder n gweddill, rhelyw

remains npl olion, gweddillion

remand vt aildraddodi

remand home n cartref i droseddwyr ifanc

remark vb sylwi ▷ n sylw

remarkable adj nodedig, hynod, rhyfedd, syn

remarry vi ailbriodi

remedial n adferol; meddyginiaethol

remedy n meddyginiaeth ▷ vt meddyginiaethu, gwella

remember vt cofio

remembrance n cof, coffa, coffadwriaeth

remind vt atgofio, atgoffa, cofio

reminiscence n atgof

remiss adj esgeulus, diofal, llac

remission n maddeuant

remit vb maddau; arafu, peidio; anfon

remittance n taliad

remnant n gweddill, gwarged

remonstrance n cwyn, gwrthdystiad

remonstrate vi ymliw, gwrthdystio

remorse n edifeirwch, gofid, atgno

remote adj pell, pellennig, anghysbell

remote control n rheolaeth bell

remotely adv o bell

removable adj symudadwy, y gellir ei symud

removal n symudiad, diswyddiad

remove vb symud, dileu; mudo

remunerate vt talu, gwobrwyo

renaissance n dadeni

rend vb rhwygo, dryllio, llarpio

render vb talu; datgan; gwneud; troi, cyfieithu

rendezvous n cyrchfa, man cyfarfod

renegade n gwrthgiliwr

renew vt adnewyddu

renounce vt ymwrthod, ymwadu, gwadu

r

renovate vt adnewyddu
renown n clod, bri, enwogrwydd
rent n rhwyg
rent n ardreth, rhent ▷ vt ardrethu, rhentu
rental n rent
repair vi cyrchu, mynd
repair vi atgyweirio, trwsio ▷ n cywair
reparation n iawn, ad-daliad
repartee n ateb parod
repatriate vb adfer i'w wlad ei hun
repeal vt diddymu ▷ n diddymiad
repeat vb ailadrodd, ailgyflawni
repel vt bwrw yn ôl
repent vb edifarhau, edifaru
repentance n edifeirwch
repetition n ailadroddiad
repetitive adj ailadroddus
replace vb ailosod, dodi'n ôl; cymryd lle (arall)
replacement n un sy'n cymryd lle arall
replay vb ailchwarae
replenish vt ail-lenwi, diwallu
replete adj llawn, cyflawn, gorlawn
replica n copi cywir, cyflun
reply vi ateb ▷ n ateb, atebiad
report vt adrodd, hysbysu ▷ n adroddiad; sŵn ergyd
reporter n gohebydd
repose vb gorffwys ▷ n gorffwys
repository n ystorfa, trysorfa
reprehend vt ceryddu, argyhoeddi
represent vt portreadu; cynrychioli
representative adj yn cynrychioli ▷ n cynrychiolydd
repress vt atal, gostegu, llethu
repression n ataliad, darostyngiad, gwrthodiad
reprimand n cerydd ▷ vt ceryddu
reprisal n dial

reproach vt ceryddu, gwaradwyddo, edliw ▷ n gwaradwydd
reproduce vt atgynhyrchu, epilio
reproduction n atgynhyrchiad, copi; epiliad
reproof n cerydd
reprove vt ceryddu, argyhoeddi
reptile n ymlusgiad
republic n gweriniaeth, gwerinlywodraeth
repudiate vt diarddel, diarddelwi, gwadu
repugnant adj croes, atgas, gwrthun
repulse vt bwrw'n ôl; nacáu ▷ n gwrthergyd
repulsion n gwrthnysedd
repulsive adj atgas, ffiaidd
reputable adj parchus, cyfrifol
reputation n gair, cymeriad, enw da
repute vt cyfrif, tybied ▷ n parch, bri
request n cais ▷ vt ceisio, gofyn
requiem n offeren dros y meirw; galargerdd
require vt gofyn, mynnu
requisite adj gofynnol, angenrheidiol
requisition n archeb ▷ vb hawlio
requite vt talu, gwobrwyo, talu'r pwyth
rescind vt diddymu, dirymu
rescue vt achub ▷ n achubiad
research n ymchwil, ymchwiliad ▷ vb ymchwilio
resemblance n tebygrwydd
resemble vt tebygu i
resent vt tramgwyddo, digio, cymryd yn chwith
resentful adj digofus, llidiog
resentment n dig, dicter
reservation n cadw, cadfa

reserve vt cadw yn ôl, cadw wrth gefn ▷ n yr hyn a gedwir, cronfa; swildod

reserved adj swil; wedi ei gadw; **reserved seat** sedd gadw

reservoir n cronfa, llyn

reshuffle vb aildrefnu

reside vi preswylio

residential adj preswyl

residue n gweddill

resign vb rhoi i fyny, ymddiswyddo, ymddeol

resignation n ymddiswyddiad; ymostyngiad

resilience n hydwythder, ystwythder

resilient adj hydwyth, ystwyth

resin n ystor, rhwsin

resist vb gwrthsefyll, gwrthwynebu

resistance n gwrthwynebiad, gwrthsafiad

resit vt (exam) ailsefyll ▷ n ailarholiad, ailgynnig

resolute adj penderfynol

resolution n penderfyniad

resolve vb penderfynu ▷ n penderfyniad

resonant adj atseiniol

resort vi cyrchu ▷ n cyrchfa; ymwared

resound vb atseinio, diasbedain

resource n sgil, dyfais; **resources** npl adnoddau

respect vt parch ▷ n golwg; parch

respectable adj parchus

respectful adj boneddigaidd, yn dangos parch

respective adj priodol, ar wahân

respite n oediad, saib, seibiant, hamdden

resplendent adj disglair, ysblennydd

respond vi ateb, ymateb; porthi

response n ateb, atebiad

responsibility n cyfrifoldeb

responsible adj atebol, cyfrifol

responsive adj ymatebol

rest n, vb gorffwys ▷ n (in music) tawnod

rest vi aros, parhau ▷ n gweddill

restaurant n tŷ bwyta, bwyty

restful adj tawel, llonydd, esmwyth

restitution n adferiad; iawn

restive adj ystyfnig, ystranclyd, noglyd, diamynedd

restless adj aflonydd, rhwyfus

restore vt adfer; atgyweirio

restrain vt atal, ffrwyno

restrained adj cynnil, gochelgar, cymhedrol

restraint n atalfa, ffrwyn, caethiwed

restrict vt cyfyngu, caethiwo

restriction n cyfyngiad

result vi deillio, canlyn ▷ n canlyniad

resume vt ailddechrau

résumé n crynodeb

resumption n ailddechreuad

resurgent adj yn ailgodi, yn ailfyw

resurrection n atgyfodiad

resuscitate vb adfywhau, dadebru

retail vt manwerthu, adwerthu ▷ n adwerth

retailer n mân-werthwr

retain vb cadw, dal; llogi

retaliate vb talu'n ôl, talu'r pwyth, dial

retaliation n dial

retard vb rhwystro, oedi

retch vi cyfogi, chwydu

retentive adj yn dal heb ollwng; gafaelgar

reticent adj tawedog, distaw

retina n rhwyden y llygad, retina

retinue n gosgordd, gosgorddlu

retire vi ymneilltuo, encilio, cilio, ymddeol

r

retired adj wedi ymddeol
retirement n ymddeoliad
retiring adj swil
retort vb gwrthwynebu ▷ n ateb parod; ritort (cemeg)
retrace vb mynd yn ôl dros yr un ffordd, dychwelyd
retract vb tynnu'n ôl
retrain vb ailhyfforddi
retreat vi cilio, encilio, ffoi ▷ n encil, ffo
retrench vb cwtogi, cynilo
retribution n ad-daledigaeth, cosb, dial
retrieve vt olrhain; adennill, adfer
retrogress vi mynd yn ôl, dirywio
retrospect n ad-drem, adolwg
return vb dychwelyd ▷ n dychweliad; elw, enillion
return (ticket) n tocyn dwyffordd
reveal vt datguddio, amlygu, dangos
revel vi gloddesta; ymhyfrydu ▷ n gloddest
revelry n miri
revenge vb, n dial
revenue n cyllid, enillion, incwm
reverberate vb taro'n ôl; atseinio
revere vt parchu, anrhydeddu
reverence n parch, parchedigaeth
reverend adj parchedig
reverent adj parchus, gŵyl, gwylaidd
reversal n dymchweliad, cwymp
reverse adj gwrthwyneb, chwith ▷ vb troi, gwrthdroi ▷ n gwrthdro, aflwydd
reverse charge call n galwad y telir amdani'r pen arall
reverse (gear) n gêr ôl
revert vb troi yn ôl, dychwelyd
review vt adolygu ▷ n adolygiad
reviewer n adolygydd
revile vt difenwi, cablu, gwaradwyddo

revise vt cywiro, diwygio
revision n cywiriad; adolygiad
revival n adfywiad, diwygiad
revive vb adfywio, adnewyddu
revoke vb galw yn ôl, diddymu, dirymu
revolt vb gwrthryfela ▷ n gwrthryfel
revolting adj gwrthnaws, atgas, ffiaidd
revolution n chwyldro, chwyldroad
revolutionary adj chwildroadol ▷ n chwildrowr
revolve vb troi, amdroi, cylchdroi
revolver n llawddryll
revulsion n atgasedd
reward n gwobr ▷ vt gwobrwyo
reword vb ailysgrifennu, ailddweud
rhapsody n hwyl, ymfflamychiad
rhetoric n rhetoreg, rhethreg
rheumatism n cryd cymalau, gwynegon
rhinoceros n rhinoseros
rhombus n rhombws
rhubarb n rhiwbob
rhyme n odl, rhigwm ▷ vb odli, rhigymu
rhythm n rhythm, rhediad
rib n asen, eisen
ribald n masweddwr ▷ adj masweddol
ribbon n rhuban, ysnoden
rice n reis
rich adj cyfoethog, goludog, bras
riches npl cyfoeth, golud
richness n cyfoethogrwydd, braster, ffrwythlonrwydd
rick n tas
rickets npl y llech(au)
rickety adj simsan, bregus
rid vt gwared
riddle n dychymyg, pos
riddle n rhidyll ▷ vt rhidyllio, gogrwn
ride vb marchogaeth, marchocáu

rider n marchogwr; atodiad
ridge n grwn, trum, cefn, crib
ridicule n gwawd ▷ vt gwawdio, chwerthin am ben
ridiculous adj chwerthinllyd
riding n marchogaeth
riding school n ysgol farchogaeth
rife adj aml, cyffredin, rhemp
riff-raff n gwehilion y bobl, dihirod
rifle vt anrheithio, ysbeilio
rifle n dryll, reiffl
rift n agen, hollt, rhwyg
rig vb rigio, taclu ▷ n rig
right adj iawn, uniawn; deau ▷ adv yn iawn ▷ vt unioni, cywiro ▷ n iawnder, hawl; **rights and customs** braint a defod; **right wing** (politics) asgell dde
right angle n ongl sgwâr
righteous adj cyfiawn
righteousness n cyfiawnder
rightful adj cyfreithlon, iawn, teg
rigid adj anhyblyg, manwl, caeth
rigmarole n ffregod, rhibidirês
rigour n llymder
rile vt cythruddo, ffyrnigo, llidio
rim n ymyl, cylch, cant
rind n pil, croen, crawen, rhisgl
ring n modrwy, cylch ▷ vb modrwyo
ring vb canu cloch, atseinio; modrwyo ▷ n sŵn cloch, tinc
wedding ring n modrwy briodas
ring road n cylchffordd
ring tone n tôn ffôn
rinse vt golchi, trochi
riot n terfysg, gloddest ▷ vi terfysgu
rip vb rhipio, rhwygo, datod ▷ n rhwyg
ripe adj aeddfed
rip-off n lladrad amlwg
ripple n crych ▷ vb crychu
rise vi codi, cyfodi ▷ n codiad
risk n perygl, enbydrwydd ▷ vt

peryglu, anturio, mentro
rite n defod
ritual adj defodol ▷ n defod
rival n cydymgeisydd ▷ vb cystadlu
river n afon
rivet n rhybed, hem, rifet ▷ vb rhybedu, hemio, rifetio
rivulet n afonig, nant, cornant
road n ffordd, heol; angorfa
road map n map ffyrdd, map moduro
road sign n arwydd ffordd
road tax n treth ffordd
road works n gwaith cynnal y ffordd
roam vi crwydro, gwibio
roar vi rhuo ▷ n rhu, rhuad
roast vb rhostio, crasu, pobi, digoni
rob vt lladrata, ysbeilio
robber n lleidr, ysbeiliwr
robbery n lladrad
robe n gwisg, gŵn
robin n brongoch
robust adj cadarn, cryf, grymus
rock vb siglo
rock n craig
rockery n gardd gerrig
rocket n roced
rocky adj creigiog; sigledig
rod n gwialen, llath
rodent n cnofil
roe n iyrches, ewig
roe n grawn pysgod, gronell
roebuck n iwrch
rogue n gwalch, cnaf
role n rhan, tasg, cymeriad
roll vb rholio, treiglo ▷ n rhòl
roll call n galw enwau (ar restr)
rolling adj tonnog
rolling pin n rholbren
rolling stock n rholstoc
Roman n Rhufeiniwr ▷ adj Rhufeinaidd, Rhufeinig
Roman Catholic n Pabydd

r

romance n rhamant ▷ vi rhamantu
Romania n România
romantic adj rhamantus
Rome n Rhufain
romp vi rhampio ▷ n rhamp; rhampen
rood n rhwd; y grog, y groes
roof n to, nen ▷ vt toi
rook n ydfran, brân
room n lle; ystafell
roommate n cydletywr
room service n gwasanaeth ystafell
roomy adj helaeth, eang
roost n clwyd ▷ vi clwydo
rooster n ceiliog
root n gwraidd, gwreiddyn ▷ vb
  gwreiddio; diwreiddio
rope n rhaff ▷ vt rhaffu, rhwymo
rosary n paderau, llaswyr
rose n rhosyn
rose hips npl egroes
rosette n ysnoden
rostrum n llwyfan, areithfa
rosy adj rhosynnaidd, gwritgoch,
  disglair
rot vb pydru, braenu ▷ n pydredd; lol
rota n rhod, trefn
rotate vi troi, cylchdroi, chwyldroi
rote n tafod-leferydd
rotten adj pwdr, pydredig, sâl
rouge n lliw coch, gruddliw
rough adj garw, gerwin, bras
round adj crwn ▷ n crwn, cylch, tro,
  rownd ▷ adv, prep o glych, o amgylch
  ▷ vb crynio, rowndio
roundabout n cylchdro, cylchfan,
  cylch ogylch; ceffylau bach ▷ adj o
  amgylch, cwmpasog
rouse vb dihuno, deffroi, cyffroi
rout n rhawt; ffo, dymchweliad ▷ vb
  ymlid, dymchwelyd
route n ffordd, llwybr, hynt
routine n defod, arfer
rove vb crwydro, gwibio

roving adj crwydrol
row n rhes, rhestr
row vb rhwyfo
row n terfysg, cythrwfl, ffrae
rowan n criafol
rowdy adj trystiog, afreolus
rowel n troell ysbardun, rhywel
rowing boat n cwch rhwyfo
royal adj brenhinol
royalty n brenhiniaeth; toll, tâl,
  breindal
rub vb rhwbio, rhathu, iro, crafu
rub out vt rhwbio allan, dileu
rubber n rwber
rubbish n ysbwriel, sothach; lol
rubbish bin n bin ysbwriel
rubbish dump n tomen ysbwriel
rubble n rhwbel
ruby n rhuddem ▷ adj coch, rhudd
ruck n pentwr, crynswth, haid,
  ysgarmes
rucksack n rhychsach
ruction n helynt, terfysg
rudder n llyw
ruddy adj coch, gwridog, gwritgoch
rude adj anfoesgar; anghelfydd,
  garw
rudiment n egwyddor, elfen
rue vt galaru, gofidio, edifaru
rueful adj trist, truenus, gresynus
ruffian n adyn, anfadyn, dihiryn
ruffle vb crychu, cyffroi, aflonyddu
rug n hugan
rugby n rygbi
rugged adj garw, gerwin, clogyrnog
ruin n distryw, dinistr; adfail ▷ vb
  difetha, andwyo
rule n rheol, llywodraeth; riwl ▷ vb
  rheoli, llywodraethu; llinellu
ruler n llywodraethwr; pren mesur,
  rhiwl
ruling n dyfarniad, barn ▷ adj
  llywodraethol, mewn grym

rum *n* rym ▷ *adj* od, rhyfedd
Rumania *n* Rwmania
rumble *vi* trystio, tyrfu, godyrfu
rummage *vb* chwalu a chwilio,
  chwilota
rumour *n* chwedl, gair, sôn, achlust
rump *n* tin, bôn, cwman, cloren
rumple *vt* crychu, sybachu
rumpus *n* helynt, terfysg
run *vb* rhedeg, llifo ▷ *n* rhediad,
  rhedfa; **in the long run** yn y pen
  draw
run away *vi* ffoi, rhedeg ymaeth,
  rhedeg i ffwrdd
run out of *vt* rhedeg allan o
rung *n* ffon ysgol
rupture *n* rhwyg; tor llengig ▷ *vb*
  rhwygo
rural *adj* gwledig, gwladaidd
ruse *n* ystryw, dichell
rush *n* brwynen, pabwyryn
rush *vb* rhuthro ▷ *n* rhuthr
rush hour *n* awr brysur
russet *adj* llwytgoch
Russia *n* Rwsia
rust *n* rhwd ▷ *vb* rhydu
rustic *adj* gwladaidd, gwledig ▷ *n*
  gwladwr
rusticate *vt* anfon adref am dymor
rustle *vi* siffrwd, chwithrwd, rhuglo
rusty *adj* rhydlyd
rut *n* rhych, rhigol
ruthless *adj* didostur, diarbed,
  creulon
rye *n* rhyg

S

Sabbath *n* Sabath, Saboth
sabotage *n* difrod bwriadol ▷ *vb*
  difrodi
sacerdotal *adj* offeiriadol
sack *n* sach, ffetan ▷ *vt* sachu;
  difrodi; diswyddo
sackcloth *n* sachlen, sachliain
sacrament *n* sacrament, ordinhad
sacred *adj* cysegredig, glân,
  sanctaidd
sacrifice *n* aberth, offrwm ▷ *vb*
  aberthu
sacrilege *n* halogiad,
  cysegr-ysbeiliad
sad *adj* trist, athrist, prudd, digalon
saddle *n* cyfrwy ▷ *vt* cyfrwyo;
  beichio
saddler *n* cyfrwywr
sadness *n* tristwch, prudd-der
safe *adj* diogel, dihangol, saff ▷ *n*
  cell, cist, cloer

safety n diogelwch; **safety belt** gwregys diogelwch; **safety pin** pin cau

saffron n saffrwm ▷ adj melyn

sag vb segio, segian, sagio, ymollwng

sage adj doeth ▷ n gŵr doeth

sage n saets

Sagittarius n y Saethydd

Sahara n Sahara

sail n hwyl ▷ vb hwylio, morio, mordwyo

sailing n hwylio

sailing boat n llong hwylio

sailor n morwr, llongwr

saint n sant

sake n mwyn; **for the sake of** er mwyn

salad n salad

salary n cyflog

sale n gwerth, gwerthiant, arwerthiant

salient adj amlwg

saline adj heliaidd, hallt ▷ n heli

saliva n haliw, poer, dŵr anadl

sallow adj melyn afiach

salmon n eog, gleisiad, samwn

saloon n neuadd, salŵn

salt n halen, halwyn (cemeg) ▷ adj hallt ▷ vt halltu

salt cellar n llestr halen

salt water n dŵr hallt, dŵr y môr

salty adj hallt

salute vt cyfarch; saliwtio ▷ n cyfarchiad; saliwt

salvation n iachawdwriaeth; **Salvation Army** Byddin yr Iachawdwriaeth

salve n eli, ennaint ▷ vt elïo, lleddfu; achub

same adj yr un, yr unrhyw, yr un fath

sample n sampl, enghraifft ▷ vt samplu, samplo

sanctify vt sancteiddio

sanctimonious adj ffug-sanctaidd, sych-dduwiol

sanction n caniatâd; cosb; sancsiwn (moeseg) ▷ vt caniatáu; cosbi

sanctity n sancteiddrwydd

sanctuary n cysegr; noddfa, nawdd

sand n tywod ▷ vt tywodi

sandal n sandal

sand castle n castell tywod

sandpaper n papur gwydrog

sandpit n pwll tywod

sandwich n brechdan

sandy adj tywodlyd; melyngoch

sane adj iach, call, synhwyrol

sanitary adj iechydol

sanitary towel n tywel misglwyf, tywel iechydol

sanitation n iechydaeth

sanity n iechyd meddwl, iawn bwyll

Santa Claus n Siôn Corn

sap n nodd, sudd, sugn ▷ vt sugno, hysbyddu

sap vb tangloddio, diseilio

sapling n pren ieuanc

sapphire n saffir ▷ adj glas

sarcasm n gwawdiaith, coegni, gair du

sarcastic adj gwawdlym, coeglyd, brathog

sardine n sardîn

sash n gwregys; ffrâm ffenestr

satchel n sachell, cod lyfrau

sate vt digoni, llenwi, diwallu

satellite n canlynwr, cynffonnwr; lleuad; lloeren

satellite dish n dysgl loeren, soser lloeren

satiate vt digoni, diwallu, syrffedu

satin n satin, pali

satire n dychan, gogan

satirize vb dychan, goganu

satisfaction n bodlonrwydd; iawn

satisfactory adj boddhaol; iawnol
satisfy vt bodloni, diwallu, digoni
saturate vt trwytho, mwydo
Saturday n dydd Sadwrn
sauce n saws; haerllugrwydd
saucepan n sosban
saucer n soser
saucy adj digywilydd, haerllug
Saudi Arabia n Saudi Arabia, Sawdi Arabia
saunter vi rhodianna, ymdroi, swmera
sausage n selsig, selsigen
savage adj gwyllt, ffyrnig, milain, anwar ▷ n dyn gwyllt, anwariad, anwarddyn
save vb achub, arbed, gwaredu; cynilo ▷ prep oddieithr, ond
saving adj achubol, darbodus
savings npl cynilion
saviour n achubwr, gwaredwr, iachawdwr
savour n sawr, blas ▷ vb sawru
savoury n blasusfwyd ▷ adj sawrus
saw n llif ▷ vb llifio
sawdust n blawd llif
sawmill n melin lifio
say vb dywedyd, dweud
saying n dywediad, ymadrodd, gair
scab n crachen, cramen; clafr
scabies n y crafu
scaffold n ysgaffald; dienyddle
scald vt ysgaldio, sgaldan(u) ▷ n ysgaldiad
scale n clorian, tafol, mantol
scale n graddfa ▷ vb dringo
scale n cen ▷ vb cennu; digennu, pilio
scallop n cylfragen; gwlf ▷ vt gylfu, minfylchu
scalp n copa, croen y pen ▷ vt penflingo
scam n sgam

scammer n sgamiwr
scamp n cnaf, gwalch, dihiryn
scamper vi ffoi, carlamu, brasgamu
scan vb corfannu; sganio, edrych, chwilio
scandal n tramgwydd, gwarth, enllib
Scandinavia n Llychlyn
scanner n sganydd; sganiwr; **virus scanner** sganiwr feirws
scant, scanty adj prin
scapegoat n bwch dihangol
scapegrace n dyn diras, oferwr, dihiryn
scar n craith ▷ vt creithio
scarce adj, adv prin
scarcely adv prin, braidd, odid, nemor
scare vt brawychu, tarfu ▷ n dychryn
scared adj wedi cael ofn, wedi rhuso, wedi brawychu
scarf n crafat, sgarff
scarlatina n y dwymyn goch
scarlet adj ysgarlad
scarp n llethr
scary adj sgêri
scathe vt deifio, anafu, niweidio
scathing adj deifiol, miniog
scatter vb gwasgaru, chwalu, taenu
scavenger n carthwr, carthydd
scene n lle; golwg, golygfa
scenery n golygfa
scenic adj hardd, golygfaol
scent n arogl, aroglau, trywydd; perarogl ▷ vt arogli
sceptic n amheuwr
sceptical adj amheugar
sceptre n teyrnwialen
schedule n atodlen, cofrestr, taflen
scheme n cynllun; cynllwyn ▷ vb cynllunio
schism n rhwyg, ymraniad, sism
scholar n ysgolhaig, ysgolor

s

scholarly *adj* ysgolheigaidd
scholarship *n* ysgolheictod;
ysgoloriaeth
scholastic *adj* athrofaol
school *n* ysgol, ysgoldy ▷ *vt* disgyblu
schoolbook *n* llyfr ysgol
schoolboy *n* bachgen ysgol
schoolchildren *npl* plant ysgol
schooldays *npl* dyddiau ysgol
schoolgirl *n* merch ysgol
schoolmaster *n* athro
schoolmistress *n* athrawes
schooner *n* ysgwner
sciatica *n* clunwst
science *n* gwyddor, gwyddoniaeth
science fiction *n* ffuglen wyddonol
scientific *adj* gwyddonol
scientist *n* gwyddonydd
scissors *npl* siswrn
scoff *n* gwawd ▷ *vi* gwawdio,
gwatwar
scold *vb* dwrdio, tafodi, ceryddu,
cymhennu ▷ *n* cecren
scone *n* sgon
scoop *n* lletwad ▷ *vt* cafnu, cafnio
scooter *n* sgwter
scope *n* ergyd, bwriad; cylch,
cwmpas, lle
scorch *vb* deifio, llosgi, greidio,
rhuddo
score *n* hac, rhic; cyfrif, dyled; sgôr;
ugain
score *vb* rhicio, cyfrif, sgori(o)
scorn *n* dirmyg ▷ *vb* dirmygu,
gwatwar
Scorpio *n* y Sgorpion
scorpion *n* ysgorpion
Scot *n* Ysgotyn, Albanwr
Scotch *adj* Ysgotaidd, Albanaidd
scotch *vt* hacio, darnio, trychu
scot-free *adj* croeniach, dianaf
Scotland *n* Yr Alban
Scottish *adj* Albanaidd

scoundrel *n* cnaf, dihiryn
scour *vt* carthu, ysgwrio
scour *vb* rhedeg; chwilio
scourge *n* fflangell, pla ▷ *vt*
fflangellu
scout *n* sgowt, ysbïwr ▷ *vt* sgowta,
ysbïo
scowl *vb* cuchio, gwgu ▷ *n* cilwg,
gwg
scraggy *adj* esgyrnog, tenau, cul,
salw
scramble *vi, n* ciprys, ymgiprys
scrambled egg *n* cymysgwy
scrap *n* tamaid, tameidyn, dernyn
scrapbook *n* llyfr lloffion
scrape *vb* crafu ▷ *n* helynt, helbul,
crafiad
scratch *vb* crafu, cripio
scratch card *n* cerdyn crafu
scrawl *vb* ysgriblo, ysgriblan
scream *vi* ysgrechain ▷ *n* ysgrech,
gwawch
screech *vi* ysgrechain ▷ *n* ysgrech
screen *n* llen, cysgod; sgrin ▷ *vt*
cysgodi
screen saver *n* arbedwr sgrin
screw *n* sgriw, hoel dro ▷ *vb* ysgriwio
screwdriver *n* tyrnsgriw
scribble *n* ysgribl ▷ *vb* ysgriblo,
ysgriblan
script *n* llawysgrif, ysgrif, sgript
scripture *n* ysgrythur
scroll *n* rhòl, plyg llyfr
scrub *n* prysgwydd; ysgwrfa ▷ *vt*
ysgwrio
scruff *n* gwar, gwegil
scrum, scrummage *n* sgrym,
ysgarmes
scruple *n* petruster (moesol) ▷ *vi*
petruso
scrupulous *adj* gwyliadwrus,
manwl
scrutinize *vt* chwilio, archwilio

scrutiny n archwiliad
scuffle vi, n ymgiprys, ymryson
scull n rhwyf unllaw, rhodl ▷ vb rhodli
scullery n cegin fach, cegin gefn
sculptor n cerflunydd
sculpture n cerfluniaeth; cerflun ▷ vb cerfio, torri
scum n sgum; gwehilion, sorod
scurf n cen, mardon
scurrilous adj bustlaidd, brwnt, difriol
scurry vi ffrystio ▷ n ffrwst, ffwdan
scurvy adj crachlyd, crach ▷ n llwg
scutter vi ffoi, diengyd
scuttle n llestr glo
scuttle vt tyllu llong i'w suddo
scuttle vi heglu ffoi, dianc
scythe n pladur
sea n môr, cefnfor; moryn
seaboard n morlan, glan y môr
seafood n bwyd môr
seagull n gwylan
seal n morlo
seal n sêl, insel ▷ vt selio
sea level n lefel y môr
seam n gwnïad, gwrym; haen, gwythïen; craith
seaman n morwr, llongwr
seamstress n gwniadwraig, gwniadyddes
seamy adj annymunol
seance n seawns
seaplane n awyren fôr
sear adj sych, crin, gwyw ▷ vt serio, deifio
search vb chwilio, profi ▷ n ymchwil
search engine n peiriant chwilio, chwiliadur
seashore n glan y môr
seasick adj sâl môr; **to be seasick** dioddef o salwch môr
seasickness n salwch y môr

seaside n glan y môr
season n tymor, amser, pryd, adeg ▷ vb tymheru; halltu; **high/low season** tymor prysur/llac
seasonal adj tymhorol
season ticket n tocyn tymor
seat n sedd, sêt, eisteddle ▷ vi eistedd
seat belt n gwregys diogelwch
sea water n dŵr y môr
seaweed n gwymon, gwmon
seaworthy adj addas i'r môr, diogel
secede vi ymneilltuo, encilio; torri'n rhydd, ymwahanu
secession n ymneilltuad, enciliad; ymwahaniad
seclude vt cau allan, neilltuo
second adj ail ▷ n ail; eiliad ▷ vt eilio
secondary adj eilradd, uwchradd
secondary school n ysgol uwchradd
second class adj ail ddosbarth, isradd
second-hand adj ail-law
secret adj dirgel, cyfrinachol ▷ n cyfrinach
secretary n ysgrifennydd
Secretary of State n Ysgrifennydd Gwladol
secretive adj yn celu, tawedog
sect n sect, enwad
sectarian adj enwadol, cul
section n toriad, trychiad; rhan, adran
sector n sector
secular adj bydol; lleygol; seciwlar
secure adj sicr, diogel ▷ vt sicrhau, diogelu
security n diogelwch, sicrwydd, gwystl
security guard n gwarchodwr
sedate adj tawel, digyffro ▷ vb rhoi i gysgu, tawelu

S

sedative *adj* lleddfol, lliniarol
sedge *n* hesg
sediment *n* gwaelodion, gwaddod
sedition *n* terfysg, brad, gwrthryfel
seduce *vt* llithio, hudo, twyllo
seductive *adj* llithiol, deniadol
see *n* esgobaeth
see *vb* gweld, canfod
seed *n* had, hedyn ▷ *vb* hadu, hedeg
seedy *adj* hadog; salw; sâl,
  anhwylus
seek *vb* ceisio, ymofyn, chwilio
seem *vi* ymddangos
seemly *adj* gweddus, gweddaidd,
  addas
seep *vb* diferu, gollwng
seer *n* gweledydd
seesaw *n* siglenydd
seethe *vb* berwi, byrlymu
segment *n* darn, rhan, segment
segregate *vt* didoli, neilltuo,
  gwahanu
seize *vb* gafael mewn, atafaelu, dal,
  achub
seizure *n* daliad; strôc
seldom *adv* anfynych, anaml
select *vt* dewis, dethol
self (**selves**) *n* hun, hunan
self- *prefix* hunan-, ym-
self-catering *adj* hunan arlwy
self-confident *adj* hunanhyderus
self-conscious *adj*
  hunanymwybodol, swil
self-contained *adj* annibynnol, ar
  wahân
self-control *n* hunanlywodraeth
self-employed *adj*
  hunangyflogedig
self-evident *adj* amlwg, eglur
self-government *n* ymreolaeth
self-interest *n* hunan-les
selfish *adj* hunanol
self-possessed *adj* hunanfeddiannol

self-respect *n* hunan-barch
self-sacrifice *n* hunanaberth
selfsame *adj* yr un, yr unrhyw
self-satisfied *adj* hunanddigonol
self-service *n* hunanwasanaeth
self-sufficient *adj* hunanddigonol,
  hy
sell *vb* gwerthu; siomi ▷ *n* siom
seller *n* gwerthwr
Sellotape® *n* selotâp
semblance *n* tebygrwydd, rhith
semi- *prefix* hanner, lled, go
semicolon *n* gwahannod
semidetached (house) *n* tŷ pâr
seminar *n* seminar
seminary *n* athrofa, ysgol
semi-skimmed *adj* hanner-sgim
sempiternal *adj* bythol, tragwyddol
senate *n* senedd
send *vt* anfon, danfon, gyrru
senile *adj* hen a methedig,
  heneiddiol
senior *adj* hŷn ▷ *n* hynaf
seniority *n* blaenoriaeth
sensation *n* ymdeimlad, teimlad;
  cyffro, ias, syndod
sensational *adj* iasol, cyffrous
sense *n* synnwyr, pwyll, ystyr;
  sense of humour synnwyr
  digrifwch
senseless *adj* dienaid, disynnwyr,
  hurt
sensible *adj* synhwyrol; teimladwy
sensitive *adj* teimladwy,
  croendenau; hydeiml
sensual *adj* cnawdol; trythyll,
  chwantus
sensuous *adj* teimladol, synhwyrus
sentence *n* brawddeg; barn,
  dedfryd ▷ *vt* dedfrydu
sententious *adj* doetheiriog
sentiment *n* syniad, teimlad
sentry *n* gwyliwr, gwyliedydd

separate adj ar wahân ▷ vb gwahanu, neilltuo, ysgar; ymwahanu

separation n gwahaniad

sept- prefix saith, seith-

September n Medi

septic adj braenol, pydrol, madreddol

sepulchre n bedd, beddrod

sequel n canlyniad

sequence n trefn, dilyniad

sequester vt neilltuo; atafaelu

Serbia n Serbia

serenade n hwyrgan, nosgan ▷ vt hwyrganu

serene adj teg; tawel, digynnwrf

sergeant n rhingyll, sarsiant

serial adj cyfresol, bob yn rhifyn ▷ n stori gyfres

serial killer n llofrudd cyfresol

series n rhes, cyfres

serious adj difrifol

seriously adv yn ddifrifol

sermon n pregeth

serpent n sarff

serrated adj danheddog

serum n serwm

servant n gwas; morwyn

serve vb gwasanaethu, gweini

server n gweinydd

service n gwasanaeth, oedfa; llestri

serviceable adj gwasanaethgar, defnyddiol

service charge n tâl am wasanaeth

serviette n napcyn

servile adj gwasaidd

session n eisteddiad; sesiwn; tymor

set vb gosod, dodi; plannu; sadio; sefydlu; machlud ▷ n set; impyn, planhigyn

settee, settle n sgiw, setl

setting n lleoliad, safle; machludiad

settle vb sefydlu; penderfynu; cytuno, setlo; plwyfo; talu

settlement n cytundeb; gwladfa

seven adj, n saith

seventeen adj, n dau (dwy) ar bymtheg, un deg saith

seventh adj seithfed

seventy adj, n deg a thrigain, saith deg

sever vb gwahanu, datod, torri

several adj amryw; gwahanol

severance n gwahaniad, datgysylltiad

severe adj caled, tost, llym, gerwin

severity n llymder, gerwindeb

sew vb gwnïo, pwytho

sewage n carthffosiaeth, carthion

sewer n ceuffos, carthffos

sewing machine n peiriant gwnïo

sex n rhyw

sex education n addysg ryw

sexism n rhywiaeth

sexist adj rhywiaethol, secsist

sextet n chwechawd

sexton n clochydd; torrwr beddau

sexual adj rhywiol

shabby adj carpiog, gwael, aflêr

shack n caban

shackle n hual, gefyn, llyffethair

shade n cysgod; ysbryd ▷ vt cysgodi

shadow n cysgod ▷ vt cysgodi

shadowy adj cysgodol, rhithiol

shady adj cysgodol; amheus

shaft n paladr, saeth; llorp, braich; pwll; gwerthyd

shaggy adj cedenog, blewog

shake vb ysgwyd, siglo, crynu

shaky adj ansad, crynedig

shallow adj bas ▷ n basle, beisle

sham vb ffugio ▷ adj ffug, gau, coeg ▷ n ffug, ffugbeth

shambles npl galanastra

S

shame n cywilydd, gwaradwydd, gwarth ▷ vb cywilyddio, gwaradwyddo
shamefaced n swil, gwylaidd
shameful adj cywilyddus, gwarthus
shampoo vt golchi pen ▷ n siampŵ
shank n coes, gar, esgair; paladr
shanty n caban, bwthyn, penty
shape n siâp, llun ▷ vt siapio, llunio
shapeless adj afluniaidd, di-lun
shapely adj siapus, lluniaidd, gosgeiddig
share n rhan, cyfran ▷ vb rhannu; cyfranogi
share n swch aradr
shareholder n cyfranddaliwr
shark n siarc, morgi; twyllwr
sharp adj siarp, llym, miniog ▷ n llonnod (cerdd)
sharpen vb hogi, minio, awchlymu
sharpener n naddwr
sharper n siarpwr
sharply adv yn sydyn
shatter vb dryllio, chwilfriwio; ysigo
shattered adj wedi dryllio; drylliedig; wedi blino'n lân
shave vb eillio, torri barf; rhasglio
shavings npl naddion
shawl n siôl
she pron hi ▷ adj, prefix benyw
sheaf (**sheaves**) n ysgub
shear vt cneifio; siero
shears npl gwellau
sheath n gwain; (contraceptive) maneg atal cenhedlu
sheathe vt gweinio
shed n penty, sied
shed vt tywallt; gollwng; colli; dihidlo, bwrw
sheen n disgleirdeb, llewyrch, gwawr
sheep (**sheep**) n dafad
sheer vi gwyro o'r ffordd, cilio

sheer adj pur, glân, noeth, syth, serth
sheet n llen; cynfas; hwylraff; taflen
shekel n sicl
shelf (**shelves**) n silff, astell
shell n cragen; plisgyn, masgl; tân-belen
shellfish npl cregynbysg
shelter n cysgod, lloches ▷ vb cysgodi, llochesu; ymochel; llechu
shelve vi llechweddu, llethru
shelve vt gosod naill ochr, troi o'r neilltu
shepherd n bugail ▷ vt bugeilio
sheriff n sirydd, siryf
sherry n sieri
Shetland n Shetland
shield n tarian ▷ vt cysgodi, amddiffyn
shift vb newid, symud; ymdaro ▷ n newid; tro, stem, shifft
shilling n swllt
shilly-shally n anwadalwch
shimmer vi tywynnu, caneitio, rhithio
shin n crimog, crimp coes
shindy n helynt, ffrwgwd, terfysg
shine vb disgleirio, llewyrchu, tywynnu ▷ n disgleirdeb, sglein, llewyrch
shingle n graean, gro
shingle n peithynen; estyllen
shingles npl yr eryr, yr eryrod
shiny adj gloyw, disglair
ship n llong ▷ vt trosglwyddo
shipping n llongau (gwlad)
shipshape adj, adv taclus, trefnus, twt
shipwreck n llongddrylliad
shire n sir
shirk vt gochel, osgoi
shirt n crys
shiver vi crynu

shiver vb dryllio, chwilfriwio

shoal n haig ▷ vi heigio

shoal n basle, beisle

shock n sioc, ergyd, ysgytiad ▷ vt ysgytio; tramgwyddo

shocking adj arswydus, ysgytiol

shoddy n brethyn eilban ▷ adj ffug, gwael

shoe n esgid; pedol ▷ vt pedoli

shoehorn n seisbin, siasbi

shoelace n carrai/lasen esgid

shoemaker n crydd

shoe shop n siop esgidiau

shoot vb tarddu, blaguro; saethu ▷ n ysbrigyn, blaguryn

shooting n saethu

shop n masnachdy, siop ▷ vb siopa

shop assistant n dyn siop; merch siop

shopkeeper n siopwr

shoplifting n siopladrad

shopper n prynwr

shopping n siopa

shore n glan, traeth

short adj byr, cwta, prin

shortage n prinder, diffyg

short circuit n cylchedd byr

shortcoming n diffyg, bai

short cut n llwybr tarw, llwybr llygad, ffordd fer

shorthand n llaw-fer

shorts npl trowsus cwta

shot n ergyd; saethwr

shoulder n ysgwydd, palfais ▷ vt ysgwyddo

shoulder blade n sgapwla, pont yr ysgwydd

shout vb bloeddio, gweiddi ▷ n bloedd, gwaedd

shove vb gwthio

shovel n llwyarn ▷ vt rhofio

show vb dangos, arddangos ▷ n arddangosfa, sioe, siew

show off vi tynnu sylw atoch eich hun ▷ vt (display) arddangos

shower n cawod, cawad ▷ vb cawodi, bwrw

shower gel n gel cawod

shred n llarp, cerpyn ▷ vb rhwygo, torri'n fân

shrew n cecren, gwraig anynad; llyg

shrewd adj ffel, craff, call, cyfrwys

shriek vb ysgrechian ▷ n ysgrech

shrill adj llym, main, meinllais

shrimp n berdysen ▷ vi berdysa

shrine n ysgrîn; creirfa; cysegr, seintwar

shrink vb crebachu, tynnu ato, cilio

shrivel vb crychu, crebachu

shroud n amdo, amwisg ▷ vt amdoi, cuddio, celu

Shrove Tuesday n Mawrth Ynyd

shrub n prysgwydden, llwyn

shrug vb codi'r ysgwyddau

shudder n crynfa, echryd, arswyd ▷ vi crynu, arswydo

shuffle vb siffrwd; llusgo; gwingo, gwamalu

shun vt gochelyd, osgoi

shunt vb troi o'r neilltu, symud o'r ffordd, siyntio

shut vb cau ▷ adj caeëdig

shutter n caead, clawr, gwerchyr

shuttle n gwennol (gwëydd)

shuttlecock n gwennol

shy adj swil ▷ vi osgoi, rhusio

siblings npl plant

sick adj claf; yn chwydu, â chyfog arno; wedi diflasu

sickbay n canolfan iechyd

sickening adj atgas, diflas, cyfoglyd

sickle n cryman

sick leave n seibiant salwch

sickly adj afiach, nychlyd

side n ochr, ystlys; tu, plaid ▷ vi ochri

sidestep vb ochrgamu

S

sidetrack vb troi o'r neilltu
sideways adv tua'r ochr, yn wysg ei ochr
sidle vi cerdded yn wysg ei ochr, gwyro
siege n gwarchae
sieve n gogr, gwagr, rhidyll, sife
sift vt gogrwn, nithio, hidlo, rhidyllio
sigh vb ochneidio ▷ n ochenaid
sight n golwg, golygfa ▷ vt gweld
sightseeing n taith i weld y wlad
sign n arwydd, argoel ▷ vb arwyddo, llofnodi
signal adj hynod ▷ n arwydd
signatory adj arwyddol ▷ n arwyddwr
signature n llofnod
significance n arwyddocâd, ystyr
significant adj arwyddocaol; o bwys
signify vb arwyddo, arwyddocáu
signpost n mynegbost, arwyddbost
silence n taw, distawrwydd ▷ vt rhoi taw ar
silent adj distaw, tawedog, mud
silhouette n llun du, cysgodlun, silŵet
silicon n silicon; **silicon chip** sglodyn silicon
silk n sidan
silky adj sidanaidd
sill n sil
silly adj gwirion, ffôl, disynnwyr
silt n gwaelodion, llaid ▷ vb gwaelodi, tagu
silver n arian ▷ vt ariannu
silver paper n papur arian
silversmith n gof arian
silvery adj ariannaid(d)
similar adj tebyg, cyffelyb
simile n cyffelybiaeth, cymhariaeth
simmer vi lledferwi, goferwi
simper vi cilwenu, glaswenu

simple adj syml, unplyg; gwirion, diniwed
simplicity n symlrwydd, unplygrwydd
simplify vt symleiddio
simply adv yn syml; yn ddi-lol; yn wirioneddol
simulate vt ffugio, dynwared
simultaneous adj cyfamserol, ar y pryd
sin n pechod ▷ vb pechu
since conj gan, yn gymaint ▷ prep er, er pan
sincere adj diffuant, didwyll, pur
sincerely adv yn ddiffuant; **Yours sincerely** yr eiddoch yn gywir
sinew n gewyn, giewyn
sing vb canu
singe vt deifio
singer n canwr, cantwr, cantores
singing n canu
single adj sengl, dibriod, gweddw
single bed n gwely sengl
single-minded adj unplyg, cywir
single parent n rhiant sengl
single room n ystafell sengl
singlet n gwasgod wlanen, crys isaf
singular adj unigol; hynod
sinister adj ysgeler; chwithig
sink vb soddi, suddo ▷ n sinc
sinner n pechadur
sinuous adj dolennog, troellog
sip vt llymeitian ▷ n llymaid, llymeidyn
siphon n siffon
sir n syr
siren n corn, seiren
sirloin n llwyn eidion
sissy n cadi(ffan)
sister n chwaer
sister-in-law n chwaer yng nghyfraith
sit vb eistedd
site n safle, lle ▷ vb lleoli

sitting n eisteddiad

sitting room n parlwr, lolfa, ystafell fyw

situated adj yn sefyll, wedi ei leoli

situation n lle, safle; sefyllfa

six adj, n chwech

sixteen adj, n un ar bymtheg, un deg chwech

sixth adj chweched

sixth form n chweched dosbarth

sixth-form college n coleg chweched dosbarth

sixty adj, n trigain, chwe deg

sizable adj gweddol fawr

size n maint, maintioli

sizzle vb ffrio

skate n cath fôr

skate n sgêt ▷ vb ysglefrio

skateboard n bwrdd sglefrio

skein n cengl, sgain

skeleton n ysgerbwd; amlinelliad

sketch n llun, braslun ▷ vb braslunio, tynnu

skewer n gwaell, gwachell

ski n sgi ▷ vb sgïo

skid vb llithro (naill ochr)

skier n sgïwr

skiff n ysgafnfad, ceubal, sgiff

skill n medr, medrusrwydd

skilled adj medrus, crefftus

skim vb tynnu, codi (hufen)

skimmed milk n llaeth glas, llaeth sgim

skimp vb crintachu, cybydda

skimpy adj crintach

skin n croen ▷ vb blingo

skinny adj tenau; prin, crintach

skip vi llamu, sgipio

skipper n capten llong

skipping rope n rhaff sgipio

skirmish n ysgarmes

skirt n godre, sgyrt ▷ vt dilyn gyda godre

skit n gogan

skittish adj nwyfus, gwantan, anwadal

skittles npl ceilys

skulk vi llechu, techu

skull n penglog

skunk n drewgi

sky n wybren, wybr, awyr

skylark n ehedydd

skylight n ffenestr do

slab n llech

slack adj llac, diofal, esgeulus ▷ n glo mân

slacken vb llacio, llaesu

slag n sorod, slag

slake vt torri (syched), slecio

slam vb cau yn glats, clepian

slander n enllib ▷ vt enllibio

slang n iaith sathredig, slang ▷ vt difrïo

slant vb gwyro, gogwyddo ▷ n gogwydd

slanting adj ar oledd/osgo

slap vt clewtian ▷ n clewt(en), palfod

slapdash adj ffwrdd-â-hi, rhywsut-rywfodd

slash n slaes, hac ▷ vt slasio, chwipio

slate n llech, llechen

slate vt sennu, difrïo

slattern n slwt, slebog, sopen

slaughter n lladdedigaeth, lladdfa ▷ vt lladd

slaughterhouse n lladd-dy

slave n slaf, caethwas ▷ vi slafio

slavery n caethiwed, caethwasanaeth

slay vt lladd

sled, sledge, sleigh n car llusg, sled

sledgehammer n gordd

sleek adj llyfn, llyfndew, graenus

sleep vb cysgu, huno ▷ n cwsg, hun

s

sleeper n (*person*) cysgwr; pren neu ddefnydd arall i ddal y cledrau
sleeping bag n sach gysgu
sleeping pill n pilsen gysgu
sleepy adj cysglyd
sleet n eirlaw
sleeve n llawes
sleight n deheurwydd, cyfrwystra, dichell
slender adj main, eiddil, prin
slice n tafell, ysglisen ▷ vt tafellu, ysglisio
slick adj llyfn, tafodrydd, slic
slide vb llithro, sglefrio ▷ n llithren, sleid
slight adj ysgafn, eiddil, prin ▷ vt diystyru ▷ n diystyrwch, sarhad
slightly adj yn fain; ychydig
slim adj main, eiddil
slime n llaid, llaca; llys, llysnafedd
slimming n colli pwysau
sling vt taflu, lluchio ▷ n ffon dafl
slip vb llithro, dianc; gollwng ▷ n slip
slipper n llopan, sliper
slippery adj llithrig, diafael, di-ddal
slipshod adj anniben
slipway n llithrfa
slit vb hollti, agennu, rhwygo ▷ n hollt
slither vb ymlusgo, llithro
slobber vb glafoerio, slobran
sloe n eirinen ddu fach, draenen ddu
slog vb gweithio'n galed
sloop n slŵp
slop vb gwlychu, trochi
slope n llethr, gogwydd ▷ vb gogwyddo
sloppy adj lleidiog, tomlyd; meddal, masw; anniben
slops npl golchion
slot n agen, twll
sloth n diogi, seguryd, syrthni
slouch vb llaesu, ymollwng; cerdded yn aflêr

Slovakia n Slofacia
sloven n dyn aflêr, slebog
Slovenia n Slofenia
slovenly adj anniben
slow adj araf, hwyrfrydig, hwyrdrwm ▷ vb arafu
slowly adj yn araf (deg)
sludge n llaid, llaca
slug n gwlithen, malwoden
sluggish adj diog, dioglyd, swrth
sluice n llifddor
slum n slym
slumber vb hepian, cysgu ▷ n cwsg
slump n cwymp, gostyngiad; dirwasgiad
slur vb difrïo ▷ n llithriad, cyflusg (cerdd.); anfri
slush n llaid, llaca, eira gwlyb
slut n slwt, slebog
sly adj cyfrwys, ffals, dichellgar, tan din
smack n blas ▷ vi blasu, blasio, archwaethu
smack n smac, palfod ▷ vb smacio, chwipio
smack n llongan, smac
small adj bach, bychan, mân, main
smallholder n tyddynnwr
small-pox n y frech wen
smart vi gwynio, dolurio, llosgi ▷ n gwŷn, dolur ▷ adj llym, bywiog; ffel, ffraeth; crand
smash vb torri, malu, chwilfriwio
smattering n gwybodaeth fas, crap
smear vt iro, dwbio
smell n arogl, aroglau ▷ vb arogli
smile vb gwenu ▷ n gwên
smirch vt llychwino, difwyno
smirk vi cilwenu, glaswenu ▷ n cilwen
smith n gof
smithy n gefail (gof)
smog n smog, mwgwl

smoke n mwg ▷ vb mygu, ysmygu, smocio
smoke alarm n larwm mwg, larwm fwg
smoked adj wedi ei fygu
smoky adj myglyd
smooth adj llyfn, esmwyth ▷ vt llyfnhau
smother vb mygu, llethu
smoulder vi mudlosgi
SMS message n neges SMS
smudge n baw, staen, smotyn ▷ vb difwyno, trochi
smug adj hunanol, cysetlyd
smuggle vt smyglio
smut n parddu, huddygl, smotyn; siarad aflan
smutty adj aflan, brwnt
snack n tamaid, byrbryd
snack bar n lle am damaid
snag n rhwystr, maen tramgwydd
snail n malwoden, malwen
snake n neidr
snap vb clecian, torri'n glats; tynnu llun ▷ n clec
snare n magl, croglath ▷ vt maglu, rhwydo
snarl vi ysgyrnygu, chwyrnu
snatch vb cipio ▷ n cip, crap; tamaid
sneak vi llechian ▷ n llechgi
sneaking adj llechwraidd, cachgïaidd
sneer vb gwawdio, glaswenu ▷ n gwawd, glaswen
sneeze vi tisian
sniff vb ffroeni, gwyntio
snigger vb glaschwerthin
snip vb torri, cynhinio ▷ n demyn, toriad
snipe n giach
snippet n tamaid, cynhinyn
snob n crechyn, snob

snobbish adj crachaidd, snoblyd
snooker n snwcer
snooze vb hepian ▷ n cyntun
snore vi chwyrnu
snort vi ffroeni, ffroenochi
snotty adj cas
snout n trwyn anifail, duryn
snow n eira, ôd ▷ vb bwrw eira, odi
snowball n pelen eira
snowdrift n lluwch
snowflake n pluen eira
snow plough n aradr eira
snub vt sennu ▷ n sen
snub adj pwt, smwt
snub-nosed adj trwyn smwt
snuff vb ffroeni, snwffian ▷ n trwynlwch, snisyn
snug adj cryno, clyd, diddos
snuggle vb ymwasgu at; llochi, anwesu
so adv, conj fel, felly; mor, cyn
soak vb mwydo, sucio; slotian
soap n sebon ▷ vb seboni
soap opera n opera sebon
soap powder n powdr golchi
soapy adj sebonllyd
soar vi ehedeg, esgyn
sob vi igian, beichio ▷ n ig, ebwch
sober adj sobr, sad ▷ vb sobri
sobriety n sobrwydd
so-called adj dywededig
soccer n pêl-droed, y bêl gron
sociable adj cymdeithasgar
social adj cymdeithasol
social club n clwb cymdeithasol
socialism n sosialaeth
socialist n sosialydd
socialize vi cymdeithasu
social networking n rhwydweithio cymdeithasol
social security n nawdd cymdeithasol
social work n gwaith cymdeithasol

S

social worker n gweithiwr cymdeithasol
society n cymdeithas, cyfeillach
sociology n cymdeithaseg
sock n hosan
socket n twll, crau, soced
sod n tywarchen
soda water n dŵr soda
sodden adj wedi mwydo, soeglyd
sofa n glwth, esmwythfainc, soffa
soft adj meddal, tyner; distaw; gwirion
soft drink n diod ysgafn
software n meddalwedd
soggy adj gwlyb, lleidiog
soil n pridd, daear, gweryd
soil vt difwyno, baeddu ▷ n baw, tom
solace n cysur, diddanwch ▷ vt cysuro, diddanu
solar adj heulog, solar
solar power n ynni'r haul, ynni haul
solder n sawdring, sawdur, sodr ▷ vt asio, sawdurio, sodro
soldier n milwr
sole adj unig, unigol, un
sole n gwadn ▷ vt gwadnu
sole n (fish) lleden chwithig
solemn adj difrifol, dwys
sol-fa n sol-ffa ▷ vb solffeuo
solicit vt erfyn, ymofyn; llithio
solicitor n cyfreithiwr
solid adj caled, sylweddol, solet, cadarn
solid n solid
solidarity n undod
solitary adj unig; anghyfannedd
solitude n unigedd
solo n unawd
soloist n unawdydd
soluble adj toddadwy, hydawdd
solution n dehongliad, esboniad; toddiant
solve vt datrys, dehongli

solvent adj yn gallu talu, di-ddyled ▷ n toddfa
sombre adj tywyll, prudd
some adj rhai, rhyw, peth, ychydig ▷ pron rhywrai, rhywfaint ▷ adv ynghylch, tua, rhyw
somebody pron = **someone**
somehow adv rywfodd, rhywsut
someone pron rhywun
somersault n trosben ▷ vb troi tin tros ben, pen dra mwnwgl
something n rhywbeth
sometime adv rywbryd, gynt
sometimes adv weithiau, ar brydiau, ambell waith
somewhat adv go, lled, braidd
somewhere adv (yn) rhywle
son n mab
song n cân, cathl, cerdd
sonic adj sonig
son-in-law n mab yng nghyfraith
sonnet n soned
soon adv buan, ebrwydd, clau
sooner adv (time) ynghynt, yn gynt; **I would sooner do** (preference) byddai'n well gennyf wneud; **sooner or later** yn hwyr neu'n hwyrach
soot n huddygl, parddu
soothe vt lliniaru, lleddfu, dofi, tawelu
sop n tamaid (wedi ei wlychu)
sophism n soffyddiaeth
sophist n soffydd
sophistical adj soffyddol
sophisticated adj soffistigedig
sopping adj gwlyb diferu
soppy adj teimladol; mwydlyd
soprano n soprano
sorcerer n swynwr, dewin
sorcery n swyngyfaredd, dewiniaeth
sordid adj brwnt, cybyddlyd, gwael
sore adj tost, blin, dolurus ▷ n dolur

sorrow n tristwch, gofid, galar ▷ vi tristáu, gofidio
sorry adj drwg gan, edifar; salw
sort n modd; math, bath ▷ vt trefnu, dosbarthu
sortie n cyrch
sorting office n swyddfa ddosbarthu
so-so adv gweddol
sot n diotyn, meddwyn
soul n enaid
soul-destroying adj yn fwrn llethol
sound n sain, sŵn, trwst ▷ vb seinio
sound vb plymio, chwilio
sound n culfor, swnt
sound adj iach, iachus, dianaf, cyfan, dilys
soundboard n seinfwrdd
sound effects npl effeithiau sain
soundly adv yn drwm, yn llwyr
soundproof adj yn gwrthsefyll sŵn
soup n potes, cawl
sour adj sur ▷ vb suro
source n ffynhonnell, tarddiad
south n deau, de
South Africa n De Affrica
southern adj deheuol
souvenir n cofrodd
sovereign adj pen ▷ n penadur; sofren
Soviet adj Sofietaidd
Soviet Union n: **the Soviet Union** yr Undeb Sofietaidd
sow n hwch
sow vt hau
soya n soya
soya beans npl ffa soya
space n lle, gwagle, gofod, encyd, ysbaid
spaceman n gofodwr
spaceship n llong ofod
spacious adj eang, helaeth
spade n rhaw, pâl

Spain n Hisbaen
spam n sbam ▷ vt sbamio
spammer n sbamiwr
span n rhychwant ▷ vt rhychwantu
spaniel n adargi, sbaniel
Spanish adj Sbaenaidd ▷ n Sbaeneg
spank vt slapio, smacio, palfodi, chwipio tin
spanner n sbaner
spar vi cwffio, paffio
spar n polyn, cledren, ceibren
spare adj prin; tenau; sbâr ▷ vt arbed; hepgor
spare rib n sbarib, asen-frân
spare time n oriau hamdden, amser sbâr
sparing adj cynnil, prin
spark n gwreichionen
sparkle vi gwreichioni, serennu, pefrio
sparkling adj gloyw, llachar; byrlymog
sparrow n aderyn y to
sparse adj tenau, prin, gwasgarog
spasm n pwl, gwayw, brath
spate n llifeiriant sydyn
spatter vb tasgu
spawn n grawn, gronell; grifft; sil ▷ vb silio, bwrw grawn
speak vb llefaru, siarad
speaker n llefarydd, siaradwr
spear n gwaywffon, picell ▷ vt trywanu
special adj neilltuol, arbennig
special effects npl effeithiau arbennig
specialist n arbenigwr
speciality n arbenigrwydd
specialize vi arbenigo
special needs npl anghenion arbennig
species (**species**) n rhywogaeth
specific adj priodol, penodol, pendant

specify vt enwi, penodi
specimen n enghraifft, cynllun
specious adj teg yr olwg, rhithiol
speck n brycheuyn, ysmotyn
speckle vt britho, brychu
spectacle n drych, golygfa
spectacles npl sbectol
spectacular adj ysblennydd, trawiadol
spectator n edrychwr, gwyliwr
spectre n drychiolaeth
spectrum (-ra) n spectrwm
speculate vi dyfalu; anturio, mentro
speculation n dyfaliad; antur, menter
speech n llafar, lleferydd, parabl, ymadrodd; araith
speed n cyflymder, buander ▷ vb prysuro, cyflymu
speeding n goryrru, gyrru'n rhy gyflym
speed limit n ataliad cyflymder
speedometer n mesurydd cyflymdra
spell n cyfaredd, swyn
spell n sbel, hoe, ysbaid
spell vt sillafu
spellchecker n gwiriwr sillafu
spend vb treulio, gwario, bwrw
spendthrift n afradwr, oferwr, gwastraffwr
sperm n had
spew vb chwydu
sphere n cronnell, sffêr, pêl; cylch, maes
spice n perlysiau, peraroglau, sbeis
spick-and-span adj fel y pin
spicy adj blasus; ffraeth, diddorol; coch
spider n cor, corryn, pryf copyn
spike n pig, hoel, cethren
spikenard n ysbignard, nard

spill vb colli, tywallt
spin vb nyddu, troi, troelli
spinach n pigoglys, sbinais
spindle n gwerthyd; echel
spin-dryer n trowasgwr
spine n asgwrn cefn; draen, pigyn
spinner n nyddwr
spinning top n top tro
spinning-wheel n troell
spin-off n mantais
spinster n merch ddibriod, hen ferch
spiral adj fel cogwrn tro, troellog
spirant adj llaes ▷ npl llaesion
spire n meindwr, pigwrn, pigdwr
spirit n ysbryd; gwirod
spirited adj calonnog, nwyfus, ysbrydol
spiritual adj ysbrydol
spiritualist n ysbrydegydd
spit n bêr
spit vb poeri
spite n sbeit, malais ▷ vt sbeitio
spiteful adj maleisus, sbeitlyd
spittle n poer, poeryn
spittoon n llestr poeri
splash vb sblasio, tasgu
spleen n y ddueg; pruddglwyf; natur ddrwg, gwenwyn
splendid adj ysblennydd, gwych, campus
splendour n ysblander, gwychder
splint n dellten, ysgyren, sblint
splinter vb ysgyrioni ▷ n ysgyren, fflaw
split vb hollti, rhannu, gwahanu
spoil n ysbail, anrhaith ▷ vb ysbeilio, ysbwylio, difetha
spoke n adain olwyn, sbogen, braich
spokesman n llefarwr, llefarydd
spoliation n ysbeiliad, ysbwyliad
sponge n sbwng ▷ vb ysbyngu
sponsor n mach, hyrwyddwr, noddwr; tad bedydd, mam fedydd

spontaneous adj gwirfoddol, digymell

spook n ysbryd, bwgan, bwci

spool n gwerthyd

spoon n llwy ▷ vb llwyo; caru

spoonful n llwyaid

spoor n brisg, ôl

sporadic adj achlysurol, gwasgarog

spore n had (rhedyn etc)

sport n sbort, chwarae, difyrrwch, cellwair, hwyl

sportive adj chwareus, nwyfus

sports npl mabolgampau, chwaraeon

sports centre n canolfan chwaraeon

spot n man, lle, llecyn; brycheuyn, ysmotyn ▷ vt mannu, brychu, ysmotio ▷ adj ar y pryd

spotless adj difrycheulyd, glân

spotted adj brith, brych

spouse n priod

spout vt pistyllio, ffrydio ▷ n pistyll

sprain vt ysigo

sprawl vi ymdaenu, ymdreiglo, ymrwyfo

spray n gwlith, tawch, trochion ▷ vt taenellu; chwistrellu

spray n ysbrigyn, cainc; chwystrellydd

spread vb lledu, taenu, lledaenu, gwasgaru

spreadsheet n taenlen

spree n sbri

sprig n brigyn, ysbrigyn

sprightly adj bywiog, hoenus, nwyfus

spring vb tarddu, codi, deillio; llamu, neidio ▷ n ffynnon; llam; sbring; gwanwyn

spring-clean n glanhau'r gwanwyn

springy adj sbringar

sprinkle vb taenellu, ysgeintio

sprint vb gwibio

sprinter n gwibiwr

sprit n sbryd

sprite n ysbryd, bwgan, bwci

sprout vb tarddu, egino, glasu

sprouts npl (Brussels) ysgewyll Brysel

spruce adj twt, taclus, smart, crand ▷ n pyrwydden

spry adj sionc, heini, hoyw

spur n ysbardun, swmbwl ▷ vb ysbarduno, symbylu

spurious adj ffug, gau, annilys

spurn vb cicio, dirmygu, tremygu

spurt n ysbonc

sputter vb poeri siarad, baldorddi

spy n ysbïwr ▷ vb ysbïo

squabble vi cweryla, ffraeo ▷ n ffrwgwd, ffrae

squad n carfan, mintai

squadron n sgwadron

squalid adj brwnt, bawlyd, budr

squall vi ysgrechain ▷ n gwawch; storm o wynt

squalor n brynti

squander vt gwastraffu, afradu

square adj, n sgwâr, petryal

squash vt gwasgu, llethu ▷ n sboncen; **orange squash** sudd oren

squat vi swatio, cyrcydu

squawk vi gwawchio ▷ n gwawch

squeak vi gwichian ▷ n gwich

squeal vi gwichian

squeamish adj dicra, misi

squeeze vb gwasgu

squelch vt llethu, gostegu, rhoi taw ar

squib n tanen wyllt, fflachen; gogan, dychan

squint vb ciledrych, cibedrych ▷ n llygaid croes

squire n ysgweier, yswain

squirm vb gwingo

S

squirrel *n* gwiwer

squirt *vb* chwistrellu, tasgu ▷ *n* chwistrell, gwn dŵr

stab *vb* brathu, gwanu, trywanu

stable *n* ystabl

stable *adj* diysgog, sefydlog, safadwy, sad

stack *n* tas, bera; corn simnai, stac

staff *n* ffon; erwydd; staff

stag *n* carw, hydd

stage *n* pwynt; gradd, lefel; llwyfan

stage-coach *n* y goets fawr

stagger *vb* honclan, gwegian; syfrdanu

stagnant *adj* llonydd, marw

stagnate *vi* cronni, sefyll

stag night, stag party *n* noson stag

staid *adj* sad, sobr

stain *vb* ystaenio, llychwino ▷ *n* staen

stained glass window *n* ffenestr liw

stainless *adj* difrycheulyd, gloyw

stair *n* gris, staer

stake *n* polyn, pawl, ystanc; cyngwystl

stale *adj* hen, hendrwm; diflas, mws

stalk *vb* torsythu, rhodio'n benuchel, mynd ar drywydd

stalk *n* paladr, gwelltyn, coes

stall *n* côr, stondin; talcen glo ▷ *vb* stolio

stallion *n* march, stalwyn

stalls *npl* (*in cinema, theatre*) seddau; stondinau

stalwart *adj* cadarn, pybyr, dewr

stamen *n* brigeryn

stamina *n* saf, ynni

stammer *vb* bloesgi, siarad ag atal arno

stamp *n* stamp, delw, argraff ▷ *vb* stampio; curo traed

stampede *n* chwalfa, rhuthr

stanch *vt* atal, sychu (gwaed)

stanchion *n* annel, ateg, post, gwanas

stand *vb* sefyll, bod, aros ▷ *n* safiad; eisteddle; stondyn

standard *n* lluman, baner; post; safon

standard of living *n* safon byw

stanza *n* pennill

staple *n* prif nwydd; edefyn (gwlân *etc*)

staple *n* ystwffwl, stapal

stapler *n* styffylwr

star *n* seren ▷ *vb* serennu

starch *n* starts

stare *vb* llygadrythu, synnu

stark *adj* syth, moel, rhonc ▷ *adv* hollol

starling *n* aderyn drudwy, drudwen, aderyn yr eira

starry *adj* serennog

start *vb* dechrau, cychwyn, codi, rhusio, tasgu

startle *vt* brawychu, dychrynu, rhusio

starvation *n* newyn

starve *vb* newynu; fferru, rhynnu

state *n* ystad, cyflwr, ansawdd; rhwysg; gwladwriaeth; talaith

state *vt* mynegi, datgan; penodi

stately *adj* urddasol, mawreddog

statement *n* mynegiad, datganiad, haeriad

statesman (**men**) *n* gwladweinydd

station *n* gorsaf, stesion; safle, sefyllfa

stationary *adj* sefydlog

stationer *n* gwerthwr papurau

stationer's *n* (*shop*) siop bapurau

stationmaster *n* gorsaf-feistr

statistics *npl* ystadegau

statue *n* delw, cerfddelw, cerflun

stature n uchder, taldra, corffolaeth

status n safle, braint, statws

statute n deddf, cyfraith, ystatud

staunch adj pybyr, cywir

stave n estyllen, erwydd ▷ vt astellu; dryllio; **stave off** cadw draw

stay vb aros; ategu; atal ▷ n arhosiad; ateg

stay behind vi aros ar ôl

stay in vi (at home) aros gartref

stead n lle

steadfast adj diysgog

steadily adv yn bwyllog, yn gyson

steady adj sad, diysgog; cyson, gwastad

steak n golwyth, stec

steal vb dwyn, lladrata, cipio

stealth n lladrad; **by stealth** yn ddistaw bach

stealthy adj lladradaidd

steam n ager, anwedd, stêm, tarth ▷ vb ageru

steamer n agerlong, stemar

steed n march, ceffyl

steel n dur ▷ vt caledu

steelworks n gwaith dur

steep adj serth ▷ n dibyn, clogwyn, llethr

steep vt rhoi yng ngwlych, mwydo, sucio

steeple n clochdy

steer n bustach

steer vb llywio; cyfeirio

steering n llywio

steering wheel n llyw

stem n paladr, corsen, coes, bôn; ach; pen blaen

stem vt gwrthsefyll, gwrthladd, atal

stench n drewdod, drycsawr

stenography n llaw-fer

step vi camu; cerdded ▷ n cam; gris

step- prefix llys-

stepbrother n llysfrawd

stepdaughter n llysferch

stepfather n llystad

stepmother n llysfam, mam wen

stepsister n llyschwaer

stepson n llysfab

stereotype n ystrydeb ▷ vt ystrydebu

sterile adj diffrwyth, sych

sterilize vb diffrwythloni, diheintio

sterling adj ysterling; diledryw, diffuant

stern adj llym, penderfynol

stern n starn, pen ôl llong

stethoscope n corn meddyg

stevedore n llwythwr a dadlwythwr llongau

stew vb araf ferwi, stiwio ▷ n stiw

steward n stiward, goruchwyliwr, distain

stick n pren, ffon, pric, gwialen

stick vb glynu; gwanu, brathu

sticky adj gludiog, glynol; anodd

stiff adj syth, anystwyth, anhyblyg, ystyfnig

stiffen vb sythu, ystyfnigo

stifle vt mygu, tagu, diffodd

stigma n gwarthnod, stigma

stile n camfa, sticil, sticill

still n distyllfa, stil

still adj llonydd; marw ▷ vb llonyddu

still adv eto, er hynny; byth

stilt n ystudfach

stilted adj annaturiol; mawreddog

stimulant n symbylydd; gwirod

stimulate vt symbylu

stimulus (-li) n symbyliad, swmbwl

sting vb pigo, brathu, colynnu ▷ n colyn

stingy adj crintach, cybyddlyd

stink vi, n drewi

stinking adj drewllyd

stint vt cynilo, cybydda ▷ n prinder

S

stipend n cyflog, tâl
stipulate vb amodi, mynnu
stir vb cyffroi, cynhyrfu, symud ▷ n stŵr, cynnwrf
stirrup n gwarthol
stitch n pwyth; gwayw, pigyn ▷ vt pwytho, gwnïo
stoat n carlwm
stock n cyff; stoc, ystôr; **stocks** npl cyffion
stock exchange n cyfnewidfa stoc
stocking n hosan
stocky adj cadarn, cryf, cydnerth
stodgy adj toeslyd, trymllyd, diflas
stoke vb edrych ar ôl tân, tanio
stole n ystola
stolid adj swrth, digyffro
stomach n cylla, stumog
stone n carreg, maen ▷ vt llabyddio
stool n ystôl
stoop vb plygu, crymu, gwargrymu, ymostwng
stop vb atal, rhwystro; stopio, cau; aros, sefyll ▷ n atalfa; atalnod
stoppage n (pay) ataliad; (strike) streic
stopper n topyn, caead
storage n stôr, storfa
store n ystôr, ystorfa ▷ vt ystorio
storey, story n uchdwr, llofft, llawr
stork n ciconia, chwibon
storm n (y)storm, tymestl
stormy adj stormus, tymhestlog, garw
story n hanes, chwedl, stori; celwydd
stout adj tew, ffyrf; pybyr, gwrol, glew
stove n stof, ffwrn
stow vt pacio, dodi o'r neilltu
stowaway n teithiwr cudd
straddle vi bongamu, lledu'r traed
straggle vi crwydro, gwasgaru

straggler n crwydryn
straight adj union, syth
straighten vb unioni
straightforward adj syml; didwyll, gonest
straightway adv yn y fan, yn syth
strain vb straenio, streifio, ysigo; tynhau; hidlo ▷ n straen
strainer n hidl(en)
strait adj cyfyng, cul, caeth ▷ n cyfyngder; culfor
strand n traeth, traethell, tywyn
strand n cainc (rhaff), edau
strange adj dieithr, estronol, rhyfedd
stranger n dyn dieithr, estron
strangle vt tagu, llindagu
strap n strap, cengl
strategic adj strategol
strategy n strategaeth
stratum (**-ta**) n haen
straw n gwellt; gwelltyn, blewyn
strawberry n mefysen, syfïen
stray vi crwydro, cyfeiliorni
streak n llinell, rhes, rhesen; stremp ▷ vb gwibio
stream n ffrwd ▷ vb ffrydio, llifo
streamer n rhuban, baner
street n heol, ystryd
strength n cryfder, nerth, grym
strengthen vb cryfhau, nerthu
strenuous adj egnïol, ymdrechgar
stress n pwys, straen, caledi
stretch vb estyn, tynhau ▷ n estyniad
stretcher n trestl, stretsier
strew vt gwasgaru, sarnu, chwalu, taenu
strict adj cyfyng, caeth, llym
stricture n cyfyngiad; cerydd, sen
stride vb camu, brasgamu ▷ n cam
strife n cynnen, ymryson, ymrafael
strike vb taro; gostwng ▷ n taro, streic

striker n streiciwr
striking adj trawiadol, hynod
string n llinyn, tant, cortyn
stringent adj caeth, llym, tyn
strip n llain, llafn, llefnyn; **film strip** striplun, stribed ffilm
strip vb diosg, ymddiosg, ymddihatru
stripe n rhes, rhesen; gwialennod
striped adj rhengog, rhesenog; â llinellau amliw ar hyd-ddo
stripling n glaslanc, llanc, llencyn
strive vi ymdrechu; ymryson
stroke n dyrnod, ergyd, trawiad; llinell
stroke vt llochi, dylofi, pratio, canmol
stroll vi crwydro, rhodianna
strong adj cryf, grymus, cadarn
stronghold n amddiffynfa, cadarnle
structure n adail, adeilad, saernïaeth, adeiledd, strwythur
struggle vi gwingo; ymdrechu ▷ n ymdrech
strut vi torsythu
stub n bonyn
stubble n sofl
stubborn adj cyndyn, ystyfnig
stuck-up adj ffroenuchel
stud n boglwm, boglyn, styden
stud n gre
student n myfyriwr, efrydydd
studio n stiwdio
study n astudiaeth, efrydiaeth ▷ npl efrydiau; myfyrgell, stydi ▷ vb myfyrio, efrydu, astudio
stuff n defnydd, stwff ▷ vb stwffio, gwthio
stuffing n stwffin
stuffy adj myglyd, trymllyd, trymaidd
stumble vb tramgwyddo, baglu, syrthio

stump n bonyn, boncyff
stun vt syfrdanu, byddaru, hurtio
stunt vt crabio
stunted adj crablyd
stupefy vt syfrdanu, hurtio
stupendous adj aruthrol
stupid adj hurt, pendew, dwl, twp
stupor n syfrdandod, syrthni
sturdy adj talgryf, pybyr, cadarn, cryf
stutter vi siarad ag atal arno, bloesgi
sty n cwt, cut, twlc
style n dull, arddull; cyfenw, teitl ▷ vt cyfenwi
stylish adj dillyn, trwsiadus
stylus n (of record player) nodwydd
suave adj mwyn, tirion, hynaws, rhadlon
sub- prefix tan-, is-, go-
subconscious n isymwybod ▷ adj isymwybodol
subdue vt darostwng; lleddfu
subject adj darostyngedig; caeth; ufudd ▷ n deiliad; pwnc, testun; goddrych
subject vt darostwng, dwyn dan
subjective adj goddrychol
subjugate vt darostwng
subjunctive adj dibynnol
sublime adj aruchel, arddunol
submarine adj tanforol ▷ n llong danfor
submerge vb soddi, suddo
submission n ymostyngiad; ufudd-dod; cyflwyniad
submissive adj gostyngedig, ufudd
submit vb ymostwng, ymddarostwng; datgan barn; cyflwyno
subnormal adj isnormal
subordinate adj israddol ▷ vt darostwng
subpoena n gŵys
subscribe vb tanysgrifio, cyfrannu

s

subscription n tanysgrifiad, cyfraniad
subsequent adj canlynol, dilynol
subsequently adv wedyn, ar ôl hynny
subside vi soddi, ymollwng; darfod
subsidiary adj israddol; ychwanegol, atodol
subsidy n arian cymorth, cymhorthdal
subsist vb byw, bod, bodoli, ymgynnal
subsistence n cynhaliaeth
subsoil n isbridd
substance n sylwedd, defnydd; da
substantial adj sylweddol
substantiate vt profi, gwirio
substitute n eilydd, dirprwy, un yn lle arall ▷ vt rhoi yn lle
subterfuge n ystryw, cast
subterranean adj tanddaearol
subtitles npl is-deitlau
subtle adj cyfrwys, craff
subtract vt tynnu ymaith
suburb n maestref
subvert vt dymchwelyd, gwyrdroi
subway n isffordd
succeed vb dilyn, canlyn, llwyddo, ffynnu
success n llwyddiant, llwydd, ffyniant
successful adj llwyddiannus
successfully adv yn llwyddiannus
succession n dilyniad, olyniaeth
successive adj dilynol, olynol
succinct adj byr, cryno
succour vt swcro, ymgeleddu ▷ n swcr, ymgeledd
succulent adj ir, iraidd, noddlyd
succumb vi ymollwng dan, ildio, marw
such adj cyfryw, y fath, cyffelyb
suck vb sugno, dyfnu; llyncu, yfed

suckle vt rhoi bron, sugno
suction n sugn, sugniad, sugndyniad
sudden adj sydyn, disymwth, disyfyd
suddenly adv yn sydyn
suds npl trochion sebon, sucion
sue vb erlyn; erfyn, deisyf
suede n swêd
suet n gwêr, swyf, siwed
suffer vb goddef, dioddef, gadael
sufferer n dioddefydd
suffering n dioddef
suffice vb bod yn ddigon, digoni
sufficient adj digon, digonol
suffix n olddodiad
suffocate vb mygu, tagu
suffrage n pleidlais
suffuse vt taenu, gwasgaru, ymledu
sugar n siwgr ▷ vt siwgro
suggest vt awgrymu
suggestion n awgrym, awgrymiad
suicide n hunanladdiad
suicide bomber n bomiwr hunanleiddiol
suit n cwyn, cyngaws, hawl; deisyfiad, cais; siwt, pâr ▷ vb ateb, siwtio, gweddu, taro
suitable adj addas, cyfaddas, cymwys
suitably adv yn addas
suitcase n bag dillad
suite n cyfres; gosgordd, nifer
suitor n cwynwr; cariadfab
sulk vi sorri, pwdu, mulo
sullen adj sarrug, cuchiog, blwng
sully vt difwyno, llychwino
sulphur n sylffwr
sultan n swltan
sultry adj mwrn, mwll, clòs
sum n swm ▷ vt crynhoi, symio
summarize vb crynhoi
summary adj byr, cryno ▷ n crynodeb
summer n haf

summerhouse n tŷ haf
summit n pen, copa, crib
summon vt gwysio, dyfynnu
summons n gwŷs, dyfyn
sump n swmp
sumptuous adj moethus
sun n haul ▷ vt heulo
sunbathe vb torheulo, bolaheulo
sunbeam n pelydryn
sunbed n gwely haul
sunburn n llosg haul
Sunday n dydd Sul
sunder vt ysgaru, gwahanu
sundry adj armryw, amrywiol
sunflower n blodyn yr haul
sunglasses npl sbectol haul
sunny adj heulog
sunset n machlud haul
sunshine n heulwen
sunstroke n ergyd (yr) haul
suntan n lliw haul
sup vb llymeitian; swpera, swperu
  ▷ n llymaid
super- prefix uwch, goruwch, gor-,
  tra-, ar-
superannuation n ymddeolaeth,
  pensiwn
superb adj ysblennydd, godidog
supercilious adj balch, ffroenuchel
superficial adj arwynebol, bas
superfine adj coeth
superfluous adj gormodol, afreidiol
superintend vt arolygu
superintendent n arolygwr,
  arolygydd
superior adj uwch, gwell,
  rhagorach; uwchraddol ▷ n
  uchafiad, uwchradd
superiority n rhagoriaeth
superlative adj uchaf; eithaf
supermarket n archfarchnad
supernatural adj goruwchnaturiol
supersede vt disodli

superstition n coelgrefydd,
  ofergoeliaeth
superstitious adj coelgrefyddol,
  ofergoelus
supervene vi digwydd
supervise vt arolygu
supervision n arolygiaeth
supervisor n goruchwyliwr,
  arolygydd
supine adj diofal, didaro, swrth
supper n swper
supplant vt disodli
supple adj ystwyth, hyblyg
supplement n atodiad ▷ vt atodi
supplementary adj atodol,
  ychwanegol
suppliant n ymbiliwr, erfyniwr
supplicate vb erfyn, ymbil, deisyf
supplier n cyflenwr, cyflenwydd
supply vt cyflenwi, cyflawni ▷ n
  cyflenwad
support vt cynnal ▷ n cynhaliaeth
supporter n cefnogwr, cefnogydd
suppose vt tybio, tybied, bwrw
suppository n tawddgyffur
suppress vt llethu, gostegu; atal;
  celu
suppurate vi crawni, gori
supreme adj goruchaf, prif, pennaf
sur- prefix gor-
surcharge n gordal, gordoll ▷ vb
  codi gormod
sure adj, adv siwr, sicr; diamau, diau
surely adv yn sicr, yn ddiau
surety n mach, meichiau, gwystl
surf n traethfor, beiston; gorewyn
  ▷ vb brigo, brigdonni
surface n wyneb, arwynebedd, caen
surfeit n syrffed ▷ vb alaru, syrffedu
surge vi ymchwyddo ▷ n ymchwydd
surgeon n llawfeddyg
surgery n llawfeddygaeth;
  meddygfa, llys meddyg

s

surgical *adj* llawfeddygol
surly *adj* sarrug, afrywiog
surmise *n* tyb ▷ *vt* tybied, amau
surmount *vt* mynd dros, gorchfygu, trechu
surname *n* cyfenw ▷ *vt* cyfenwi
surpass *vt* rhagori ar, trechu
surplice *n* gwenwisg
surplus *n* gweddill, gormod, gwarged
surprise *n* syndod ▷ *vt* synnu
surprised *adj* syn, wedi synnu
surprising *adj* syn, rhyfedd
surrender *vb* traddodi, ildio
surreptitious *adj* lladradaidd, llechwraidd
surrogate *n* dirprwy, rhaglaw esgob
surround *vt* amgylchu, amgylchynu
surroundings *npl* amgylchoedd
surveillance *n* arolygiaeth, gwyliadwriaeth
survey *vt* edrych, arolygu; mesur ▷ *n* arolwg
survival *n* goroesiad
survive *vb* goroesi
survivor *n* goroeswr
susceptible *adj* parod i, tueddol i
suspect *vt* drwgdybio, amau ▷ *n* un a ddrwgdybir
suspend *vt* crogi; gohirio, atal
suspended sentence *n* dedfryd wedi'i gohirio
suspense *n* pryder, petruster, oediad
suspension *n* ataliad
suspension bridge *n* pont grog
suspicion *n* drwgdybiaeth, amheuaeth
suspicious *adj* drwgdybus, amheus
sustain *vt* cynnal; dioddef, goddef
sustained *adj* parhaus, cyson
sustenance *n* cynhaliaeth, ymborth, bwyd

swagger *vb* rhodresa, torsythu, swagro
swallow *n* gwennol
swallow *vt* llyncu ▷ *n* llwnc
swamp *n* cors ▷ *vt* gorlifo, boddi
swan *n* alarch
swank *vi* bocsachu, rhodresa ▷ *n* bocsach
swap *vb* ffeirio
swarm *n* haid ▷ *vi* heidio, heigio
swarm *vb* dringo
swarthy *adj* melynddu, croenddu, tywyll
swat *vb* taro
swathe *vt* rhwymo, rhwymynnu
sway *vb* siglo, gwegian; llywio ▷ *n* llywodraeth, swae
swear *vb* tyngu, rhegi
swearword *n* rheg
sweat *n* chwys ▷ *vb* chwysu
sweater *n* cot wlan, sweter
sweatshirt *n* crys chwys
sweaty *adj* chwyslyd
Swede *n* Swediad
swede *n* rwden, sweden
Sweden *n* Sweden
Swedish *adj* Swedaidd
sweep *vb* ysgubo ▷ *n* ysgubiad; ysgubwr
sweeping *adj* ysgubol
sweet *adj* melys, pêr, peraidd ▷ *n* pwdin
sweeten *vb* melysu; pereiddio
sweetheart *n* cariad
sweetmeat *n* fferin, melysyn
swell *vb* chwyddo ▷ *n* chwydd, ymchwydd; gŵr mawr
swelling *n* chwydd(i)
swelter *vi* crasu; lluddedu, dyddfu
sweltering *adj* llethol, tesog
swerve *vi* gwyro, osgoi, cilio, troi
swift *adj* cyflym, buan, chwyrn, clau
swift *n* gwennol ddu

swig n llymaid, dracht ▷ vb drachtio
swill n golchion; bwyd sur ▷ vb golchi; slotian
swim vb nofio ▷ n nawf
swimmer n nofiwr
swimming n nofio
swimmingly adv yn braf, yn hwylus
swimming pool n pwll nofio
swimming trunks npl trowsus nofio
swimsuit n dillad nofio, gwisg nofio
swindle vb twyllo, hocedu ▷ n twyll
swine (swine) n mochyn
swing vb siglo ▷ n sigl, siglen, swing
swinge vt llachio, baeddu
swipe card n cerdyn sweip
swirl vb troi, chwyldroi, chwyrndroi
swish vb chwipio
switch n swits, botwm ▷ vb troi, newid
switch off vt diffodd
switch on vt dodi, troi ymlaen; cychwyn
switchboard n switsfwrdd
Switzerland n y Swistir
swivel n bwylltid ▷ vb troi
swollen adj chwyddedig, wedi chwyddo
swoon vt llewygu, llesmeirio ▷ n llewyg
swoop vb dyfod ar warthaf, disgyn
swop vt cyfnewid, ffeirio
sword n cleddyf, cleddau, cledd
sycamore n sycamorwydden
syllable n sillaf
syllabus n rhaglen, maes llafur
syllogism n cyfresymiad
symbol n arwyddlun, symbol, symlen (estheteg)
symbolism n symboliaeth
symmetrical adj cymesur
symmetry n cymesuredd
sympathetic adj cydymdeimladol

sympathize vi cydymdeimlo
sympathy n cydymdeimlad
symphony n symffoni
symposium (-ia) n trafodaeth, cynhadledd
symptom n arwydd
synagogue n synagog
synchronize vb cyfamseru, cydamseru
syncopation n trawsacen (cerdd)
syncope n marwlewyg; syncopé
syndicate n cwmni
synod n cymanfa, senedd, synod
synonym n (gair) cyfystyr
synopsis (-ses) n cyfolwg; crynodeb
syntax n cystrawen
synthesis (-ses) n cyfosodiad, synthesis
Syria n Syria
syringe n chwistrell ▷ vt chwistrellu
syrup n sudd; triagl (melyn)
system n cyfundrefn; trefn, system
systematic adj cyfundrefnol
systematize vb cyfundrefnu

s

tab *n* tafod, llabed
tabby *n* cath frech, cath fenyw
tabernacle *n* tabernacl, pabell
table *n* bwrdd, bord; tabl, taflen
tableau *n* golygfa (ddramatig)
table-cloth *n* lliain bord (bwrdd)
tableful *n* bordaid, byrddaid
tablespoon *n* llwy fwrdd
tablet *n* llechen, llech; tabled
table tennis *n* tennis bwrdd, ping
  pong
taboo *n* ysgymunbeth;
  gwaharddiad, tabŵ
tabular *adj* taflennol
tabulate *vt* tablu, taflennu
tacit *adj* dealledig (ond heb ei grybwyll)
taciturn *adj* tawedog
tack *n* tac, pwyth, brasbwyth ▷ *vb*
  tacio
tackle *n* taclau, offer, tacl (mewn
  rygbi), taclad ▷ *vb* ymosod ar, taclo

tackler *n* taclwr
tact *n* tact, callineb, doethineb
tactful *adj* doeth, pwyllog,
  synhwyrol
tactician *n* tactegydd
tactics *npl* cynlluniau, tactegau
tactile *adj* cyffyrddol
tactless *adj* di-dact, annoeth
tadpole *n* penbwl, penbwla
tag *n* pwyntl; clust, dolen
tail *n* cynffon, llosgwrn, cwt
tailback *n* cwt, tagfa
tailor *n* teiliwr
taint *vb* llygru, heintio, difwyno ▷ *n*
  llwgr, ystaen, mefl
take *vb* cymryd, derbyn, cael
take off *vi* (*plane*) esgyn, mynd i'r
  awyr ▷ *vt* (*remove*) tynnu
talcum *n* talcwm
tale *n* chwedl, hanes, stori, clec, clep
talent *n* talent
talisman *n* swynbeth, swyn,
  cyfaredd
talk *vb, n* siarad
talkative *adj* siaradus
tall *adj* tal, hir, uchel
tallness *n* taldra
tallow *n* gwêr
tally *n* cyfrif ▷ *vb* cyfateb, cytuno
talon *n* ewin, crafanc (aderyn)
tambourine *n* tambwrîn
tame *adj* dof, gwâr ▷ *vt* dofi
tamper *vi* ymhél(â), ymyrryd(â)
tampon *n* tampwn
tan *vb* trin lledr; llosgi, melynu
tangent *n* tangiad, llinell gyffwrdd
tangible *adj* cyffyrddadwy,
  sylweddol
tangle *vb* drysu, cymysgu ▷ *n*
  dryswch, cymhlethdod
tank *n* dyfrgist, tanc
tankard *n* diodlestr, tancr
tanker *n* tancer, llong olew

tannery n barcerdy, crwynfa, tanerdy
tantalize vt poeni, poenydio, pryfocio
tantamount adj cyfwerth, cyfystyr
tantrums npl stranciau, nwydau
Tanzania n Tansania
tap vb taro yn ysgafn
tap n tap, feis ▷ vt tapio, gollwng
tape n tâp, incil
tape measure n tâp mesur
taper n cannwyll gŵyr, tapr ▷ vb meinhau, tapro
tape recorder n recordydd tâp, peiriant recordio, arnodydd
tapestry n tapestri
tapeworm n llyngeren
tapioca n tapioca
tar n tar; llongwr, morwr
tardy adj hwyrfrydig, araf, diweddar, ymarhous
target n nod, targed
tariff n toll; rhestr taliadau, rhestr prisiau
tarmac n tarmac
tarnish vb pylu, cymylu, llychwino
tarpaulin n tarpolin
tarry vb aros, oedi, tario; trigo, preswylio
tart n tarten, pastai
tart adj sur, surllyd
tartan n brithwe, plod
task n gorchwyl, tasg ▷ vt rhoi tasg, trethu, llethu
tassel n tusw, tasel
taste vb chwaethu, blasu, profi ▷ n blas; chwaeth
tatter n rhecsyn, cerpyn
tattered adj carpiog
tattle vb clebran, clegar ▷ n cleber, baldordd
tattoo n tatŵ ▷ vb torri llun (yn y croen)

taunt vt edliw, dannod, gwatwar ▷ n gwaradwydd, sen
Taurus n y Tarw
taut adj tyn
tautologous adj ailadroddol, cyfystyrol
tautology n tawtologaeth, ailadrodd, cyfystyredd
tavern n tafarn, tafarndy, tŷ tafarn
tawdry adj coegwych
tawny n melynddu, melyn
tax n treth ▷ vt trethu; cyhuddo
taxi n tacsi
taxidermist n stwffiwr anifeiliaid
taxi driver n gyrrwr tacsi
taxi rank n lloc dacsi
tea n te
tea bag n bag te, cwdyn te
teach vt dysgu, addysgu
teacher n athro
teaching n dysgeidiaeth; dysgu
teacup n disgl de, cwpan te
teak n tîc
tea leaves n dail te
team n gwedd, pâr, tîm
tea party n teparti
teapot n tebot
tear n deigryn, deigr
tear vb rhwygo, llarpio ▷ n rhwyg
tearful adj dagreuol
tease vt pryfocio, plagio, poeni
teaser n poenwr, poenydiwr
teaspoon n llwy de
teaspoonful n llond llwy de
teat n teth, diden, bron
technical adj technegol
technician n technegydd
technique n techneg
technological adj technolegol
technology n technoleg
teddy, teddy bear n arth anwes, tedi
tedious adj blin, anniben, poenus

tedium n diflastod, blinder
teem vb epilio, hilio, heigio
teenager n un yn yr arddegau
teens n arddegau
teethe vi torri dannedd
teetotaller n llwyrymwrthodwr, titotal
telecast n telediad
telecommunication n cysylltiad trwy'r teliffon, telegyfathrebaeth
telegram n teligram
telegraph n teligraff ▷ vb teligraffio
teleology n dibenyddiaeth
telepathy n telepathi
telephone n teliffon, ffôn
telephone box n bocs ffonio
telephone call n galwad ffôn
telephone directory n cyfeirlyfr ffôn
telescope n ysbienddrych, telisgob
televise vb teledu
television n teledu
tell vb dweud, traethu, adrodd, mynegi; cyfrif, rhifo
tell off vt dweud y drefn wrth, cystwyo
telltale n clepgi, clepiwr, clepwraig
temerity n rhyfyg, hyfdra
temper n tymer, naws ▷ vt tymheru
temperament n anianawd
temperamental adj gwamal, oriog, di-ddal
temperance n dirwest
temperate adj cymedrol; tymherus
temperature n tymheredd
tempest n tymestl
tempestuous adj tymhestlog
temple n teml
temple n arlais
temporal adj tymhorol
temporary adj dros amser, tymhoroi
temporize vi oedi, anwadalu

tempt vt temtio, profi
temptation n temtiad, temtasiwn
tempter n temtiwr
ten adj, n deg
tenable adj daliadwy, y gellir ei ddal; diffynadwy
tenacious adj tyn ei afael, gwydn, gludiog, cyndyn
tenacity n cyndynrwydd
tenant n deiliad, tenant
tench n tens
tend vb tendio, gweini
tend vi tueddu, cyfeirio, symud
tendance n sylw, gofal, tendans
tendency n tuedd, gogwydd
tendentious adj pleidiol, pleidgar
tender adj tyner, tirion, mwyn; meddal
tender vb cynnig, cyflwyno ▷ n cynnig
tenderness n tynerwch
tendon n gewyn
tendril n tendril
tenement n annedd, rhandy
tenet n daliad, barn, tyb
tenfold adj dengwaith
tennis n tennis
tennis ball n pêl dennis
tennis court n cwrt tennis
tennis racket n raced tennis
tenon n tyno
tenor n cyfeiriad, tuedd, rhediad; tenor
tense adj tyn, dirdynnol, dwys, angerddol
tense n amser (berf)
tension n tyndra, pwys, tyniant
tent n pabell
tentacle n tentacl, braich
tentative adj arbrofiadol, dros dro; ansicr
tenter-hook n bach deintur; **on tenter-hooks** ar bigau'r drain

tenth adj degfed
tenuous adj tenau, main, prin
tenure n deiliadaeth
tepid adj claear
tercentenary n trichanmlwyddiant
term n terfyn; term; teler, amod; tymor ▷ vt galw, enwi
terminal adj terfynol, termol
terminate vb terfynu
termination n terfyniad
terminology n termynoleg
terminus n terfyn
termites npl morgrug gwynion
tern n môr-wennol
terrace n rhes dai, teras
terrain n tir, bro, ardal
terrestrial adj daearol
terrible adj dychrynllyd, ofnadwy, arswydus
terrier n daeargi
terrific adj dychrynllyd, arswydus
terrify vt brawychu, dychrynu
terrifying adj brawychus, dychrynllyd
territorial adj tiriogaethol
territory n tir, tiriogaeth
terror n dychryn, braw, arswyd, ofn
terrorise vb dychrynu, brawychu
terrorism n terfysgaeth
terrorist n terfysgwr, brawychwr
terror-stricken adj wedi ei ddychrynu
terse adj byr a chryno
terseness n byrdra
test n prawf ▷ vt profi
testament n testament, cyfamod, ewyllys
testator n cymynnwr
tester n profwr
testicle n caill, carreg
testify vb tystio
testimonial n tysteb, tystlythyr
testimony n tystiolaeth; profiad

testy adj afrywiog, ffrom, croes
tetanus n gên glo, tetanws
tether n rhaff, tennyn ▷ vt clymu
text n testun, adnod
text vt tecstio
textbook n gwerslyfr
textile adj gweol
text message n neges destun
textual adj testunol
texture n gwe, gwead, cyfansoddiad
Thailand n Gwlad Thai
than conj na, nag
thank vt, n diolch
thankful adj diolchgar
thankless adj diddiolch
thanks npl diolch, diolchiadau
thanksgiving n diolchgarwch
that pron dem hwn (hon) yna (acw), hwnnw, honno, hynny ▷ pron rel a, y(r) ▷ adj hwn, hon, yma, yna, acw ▷ conj mai, taw
thatch n to, to gwellt ▷ vt toi
thatcher n töwr (to gwellt)
thaw vb dadlaith, dadmer, meirioli, toddi
the adj yr, y
theatre n theatr, chwaraedy; maes, golygfa
theatrical adj theatraidd
thee pron ti, tydi, tithau
theft n lladrad
their pron eu
theirs pron yr eiddynt, eiddynt hwy
theism n duwiaeth, theistiaeth
theist n un sy'n credu yn Nuw
them pron hwy, hwynt, hwythau
theme n testun, pwnc, thema
themselves pron eu hunain
then adv y pryd hwnnw, yna ▷ conj yna
thence adv oddi yno, o hynny
thenceforth adv o'r amser hwnnw ymlaen

theocracy n theocratiaeth
theologian n diwinydd
theological adj diwinyddol
theology n diwinyddiaeth
theorem n theorem
theoretical adj damcaniaethol,
mewn theori
theorise vb damcaniaethu
theory n damcaniaeth, tyb
therapeutic adj iachaol, meddygol
therapy n therapi
there adv yna, yno, acw; dyna, dacw
thereafter adv wedyn
thereat adv ar hynny, yna
thereby adv trwy hynny
therefore conj gan hynny, am hynny
therefrom adv oddi yno
therein adv yno, ynddo
thereupon adv ar hynny
therewith adv gyda hynny
thermal adj thermol, gwresol, brwd
thermometer n thermomedr,
mesurydd gwres
these adj pl y rhai hyn, y rhai yma
thesis (-**ses**) n gosodiad; traethawd,
thesis
they pron hwy, hwynt, hwynt-hwy
thick adj tew, praff, trwchus
thicken vb tewhau, tewychu
thicket n prysglwyn, llwyn
thick-headed adj pendew, hurt,
twp
thickness n trwch, tewder
thick-skinned adj croendew
thief (**thieves**) n lleidr
thieve vi lladrata, dwyn
thigh n clun, morddwyd
thimble n gwniadur
thin adj tenau, cul, main; anaml, prin
▷ vb teneuo
thine pron eiddot ti; dy
thing n peth, dim
think vb meddwl

thinker n meddyliwr
third adj trydydd, trydedd
thirst n syched ▷ vi sychedu
thirsty adj sychedig; **I am thirsty**
mae syched arna i
thirteen adj, n tri (tair) ar ddeg, un
deg tri (tair)
thirty adj, n deg ar hugain, tri deg
this adj, pron hwn, hon, hyn
thistle n ysgallen
thither adv yno, tuag yno
thong n carrai
thorax n y ddwyfron, y frest, thoracs
thorn n draen, draenen; pigyn,
swmbwl
thorny adj dreiniog, pigog
thorough adj trwyadl, trylwyr
thoroughbred adj tryryw, o
rywogaeth dda
thoroughfare n tramwyfa
thorough-going adj trwyadl
thoroughness n trylwyredd
those adj pl y rhai hynny, y rhai yna
thou pron ti, tydi, tithau
though conj er, pe, cyd
thought n meddwl
thoughtful adj meddylgar, ystyriol
thoughtless adj difeddwl,
anystyriol
thousand adj, n mil
thraldom n caethiwed
thrall n caethwr, caethwas
thrash vt dyrnu, ffusto, curo
thread n edau, edefyn
threadbare adj llwm, treuliedig,
wedi treulio
threat n bygwth, bygythiad
threaten vt bygwth
threatening adj bygythiol
three adj, n tri, tair
three-cornered adj trichornel
threefold adj triphlyg
three-legged adj teircoes

threepence n tair ceiniog, pisyn tair
thresh vt dyrnu, ffusto
thresher n dyrnwr, ffustwr
threshold n trothwy, rhiniog, hiniog
thrice adv teirgwaith
thrift n darbodaeth, cynildeb
thriftless adj gwastraffus
thrifty adj darbodus, cynnil,
 diwastraff
thrill vb gwefreiddio ▷ n ias, gwefr
thriller n stori iasoer
thrilling adj cyffrous, gwefreiddiol
thrive vi llwyddo, ffynnu; prifio
throat n gwddf
throb vi dychlamu, curo
throe n dolur, poen, gloes, gwewyr
thrombosis n clot mewn gwythïen,
 thrombosis
throne n gorsedd, gorseddfainc
throng n tyrfa, torf ▷ vb tyrru, heidio
throstle n bronfraith
throttle n corn gwynt, corn gwddf,
 sbardun ▷ vt llindagu
through prep trwy ▷ adv trwodd
throughout prep trwy, trwy gydol
 ▷ adv trwodd
throw n tafliad ▷ vb taflu, bwrw,
 lluchio
throw away vt taflu, lluchio
thrower n taflwr
thrush n bronfraith
thrush n llindag, gân
thrust vb gwthio, gwanu, brathu ▷ n
 gwth
thud n twrf, sŵn trwm
thug n llindagwr, dihiryn
thumb n bawd ▷ vt bodio
thump vb dyrnodio, pwnio, dulio
thumping adj aruthrol
thunder n taran(au), tyrfau, trystau
 ▷ vb taranu
thunderbolt n llucheden
thunderstorm n storm dyrfau

Thursday n dydd Iau
thus adv fel hyn, felly
thwart vt croesi, gwrthwynebu
thwart vb rhwystro
thy pron dy, 'th
thyme n teim
thyroid n thiroid
tiara n talaith, coron, coronig
tibia n asgwrn y grimog
tick vi tipian, ticio ▷ n tipian, tic
tick vt marcio, ticio ▷ n nod, marc, tic
tick n lliain gwely, tic
ticket n tocyn, ticed
ticket collector n tocynnwr
ticket office n swyddfa docynnau
tickle vb goglais, gogleisio ▷ n
 goglais
ticklish n gogleisiol; anodd, dyrys
tide n llanw, teid; amser, pryd;
 high tide penllanw; **low tide** trai
tidiness n taclusrwydd
tidings npl newyddion, chwedlau
tidy adj taclus, twt, trefnus, destlus
tie vt clymu, rhwymo ▷ n cwlwm,
 cadach
tier n rhes, rheng
tiff n ffrae fach
tiger n teigr, dywalgi
tight adj tyn, cryno, twt; cyfyng
tighten vb tynhau
tightness n tyndra
tights npl teits
tigress n teigres
tile n priddlech, teilsen
till prep, conj hyd
till vt trin, amaethu, llafurio
tiller n coes llyw; llafurwr, triniwr
tilt vb gogwyddo; gosod (â gwayw)
tilth n triniaeth tir, âr
timber n coed, pren
time n amser ▷ vt amseru
timely adj amserol, prydlon
timepiece n cloc, wats

t

timetable n amserlen

timid adj ofnus, ofnog, llwfr

timidity n ofnusrwydd

timing n amseriad

timorous adj ofnus, ofnog

tin n alcam, tun

tincture n lliw

tinfoil n ffoel alcam

tinge vt lliwio, arlliwio ▷ n arlliw, gwawr

tingle vi ysu, llosgi, merwino

tinker n tincer; eurych ▷ vb tincera

tinkle vb tincian

tinned adj mewn tun, tun

tint n lliw, arlliw, gwawr ▷ vt lliwio

tinted adj wedi ei liwio

tinworker n gweithiwr tun, gweithiwr alcam

tiny adj bychan, bach, pitw

tip n blaen, pen ▷ vt blaenu

tip vb troi, dymchwelyd; gwobrwyo ▷ n tip, tomen; cyngor; gwobr, cil-dwrn

tipple vb llymeitian, diota

tippler n diotwr, meddwyn

tipsy adj meddw, penfeddw, brwysg

tiptoe n: **on tiptoe** ar flaenau ei draed

tip-top adj campus, penigamp

tirade n araith lem

tire vb blino, lluddedu, diffygio

tire, tyre n cant, cylch, teiar

tired adj blinedig

tiredness n blinder

tireless adj diflino

tiresome adj blin, diflas, plagus

tiro, tyro n newyddian, dechreuwr

tissue n gwe, meinwe; defnydd cnawd

tissue paper n papur sidan

titanic adj cawraidd, anferth, aruthrol

titbit n tamaid blasus, amheuthun

tithe n degwm ▷ vt degymu

titivate vb pincio, ymbincio

title n teitl, hawl, hawlfraint

titled adj â theitl

title-deed n dogfen hawlfraint

title-page n wyneb-ddalen

titmouse n gwas y dryw, yswidw

titter vi cilchwerthin, chwerthinial

tittle n gronyn, mymryn, tipyn

tittle-tattle n cleber

titular adj yn rhinwedd teitl; mewn enw

to prep i, at, hyd, er mwyn, wrth, yn

toad n llyffant du dafadennog

toadstool n caws llyffant, bwyd y boda, madarch

toady n cynffonnwr ▷ vt cynffonna

toast n tost; llwncdestun ▷ vb tostio, crasu

toaster n tostiwr

tobacco n tybaco, baco

tobacconist n gwerthwr tybaco

toboggan n tybogan, sled fach, car llusg

today adv heddiw

toddle vi cropian

toddler n plentyn bach

toe n bys troed; blaen carn ceffyl

toe-cap n blaen esgid

toffee n taffi, cyflaith

together adv ynghyd, gyda'i gilydd

toil vi llafurio, poeni ▷ n llafur

toilet n trwsiad, gwisgiad; ystafell ymolchi, tŷ bach

toilet paper n papur tŷ bach

toilet roll n rholyn toiled, rholyn tŷ bach

toilet water n dŵr Groeg

token n arwydd, argoel; tocyn

tolerable adj goddefol; gweddol, symol, cymhedrol

tolerant adj goddefgar

tolerate vt goddef

toleration n goddefgarwch

toll n toll, treth

toll vb canu (cloch, cnul)

tollbooth n tollfa

tomato n tomato

tomb n bedd, beddrod

tomboy n hoeden, rhampen

tom-cat n gwrcath, cwrcyn

tome n cyfrol (fawr)

tomfool n ynfytyn, pen-ffŵl

tomfoolery n ynfydrwydd, ffwlbri

tomorrow adv yfory

tomtit n gwas y dryw, yswidw

ton n tunnell

tonality n tonyddiaeth

tone n tôn, oslef ▷ vb tyneru, lleddfu

tongs npl gefel

tongue n tafod; tafodiaith, iaith

tonic n meddyginiaeth gryfhaol, tonic

tonic water n dŵr tonig

tonight adv heno

tonnage n pwysau llwyth (llong); toll

tonsil n tonsil

tonsillitis n llid y tonsil

tonsure n corun, tonsur

too adv rhy; hefyd; **too much** gormod

tool n arf, erfyn

toot vb canu corn

tooth (**teeth**) n dant

toothache n dannoedd

toothbrush n brws dannedd

toothed adj danheddog

toothless adj diddanedd, mantach

toothpaste n sebon dannedd, past dannedd

toothpick n pic dannedd

toothsome adj danteithiol, blasus

top n cogwrn, top

top n pen, brig, copa ▷ vt tocio; rhagori ar

top up vt ail-lenwi; **to top up one's mobile (phone)** rhoi credyd ar eich ffôn symudol

to perk up vb bywhau, adfywio

top-heavy adj pendrwm

topic n pwnc

topical adj amserol

topography n daearyddiaeth leol

topple vb syrthio, cwympo, dymchwel

topsy-turvy adv wyneb i waered, yn bendramwnwgl

torch n fflach, tors, ffagl

torch-light n golau tors

torment n poen, poenedigaeth ▷ vt poeni, poenydio

tormentor n poenydiwr

torn adj wedi ei rwygo, rhwygedig

tornado n hyrddwynt, corwynt

torpedo n torpedo

torpid adj marwaidd, cysglyd, swrth

torrent n cenllif, llifeiriant, rhyferthwy

torrential adj llifeiriol, trwm

torrid adj poeth, crasboeth

torso n corff (heb y pen a'r aelodau), torso

tortoise n crwban

tortoise-shell n cragen crwban, trilliw (am gath)

tortuous adj troellog, trofaus

torture n dirboen, artaith ▷ vt arteithio

torturer n arteithiwr

tory n tori, ceidwadwr ▷ adj torïaidd

toryism n torïaeth

toss vb taflu, lluchio, bwrw

total adj hollol, cyflawn ▷ n cyfan, cyfanswm

totalitarian adj totalitaraidd

totalitarianism n totalitariaeth

totality n cyfanrwydd

totally adv yn llwyr, yn gyfan, yn ei grynswth

totter vi honcian, siglo, gwegian

touch vb teimlo, cyffwrdd ▷ n teimlad

touched adj dan deimlad

touching adj teimladwy

touch-line n yr ystlys

touchstone n maen prawf, safon

touchy adj croendenau

tough adj gwydn, caled, cyndyn

toughen vb gwneud yn wydn, cryfhau

tour n tro, taith

tourism n twristiaeth

tourist n teithiwr, ymwelydd, twrist

tourist office n swyddfa twristiaid

tournament n twrnamaint

tourniquet n offeryn i atal gwaed

tousle vt dragio, anhrefnu

tousled adj anniben

tout vi poeni pobl am archebion, gwasgu ar

tow n carth

tow vt llusgo, tynnu

toward, towards prep tua, tuag at

towel n lliain sychu, tywel

tower n twr ▷ vi esgyn, ymgodi, sefyll yn uchel

town n tref

town centre n canol(y) dref

town clerk n clerc y dref

town council n cyngor y dref

town hall n neuadd y dref

township n trefgordd

toxic adj gwenwynig

toy n tegan ▷ vi chwarae, maldodi

trace n tres; ôl, trywydd

trace vt olrhain, dilyn ▷ n ôl

tracery n rhwyllwaith (maen etc)

trachea n breuant, corn gwynt, pibell wynt

track n ôl, brisg; llwybr ▷ vt olrhain

tracksuit n tracwisg

tract n ardal, rhandir

tract n traethodyn

tractable adj hydyn, hydrin, hywedd

traction n tyniad, tyniant, llusgiad

tractor n tractor

trade n masnach; crefft ▷ vb masnachu

trade-mark n nod masnach

trader n masnachwr

trade-union n undeb llafur

trade-wind n gwynt y dwyrain, cylchwynt

tradition n traddodiad

traditional adj traddodiadol

traduce vt cablu, difenwi, enllibio

traffic vb masnachu, trafnidio ▷ n masnach, trafnidiaeth

traffic jam n tagfa

traffic lights npl goleuadau traffig

traffic warden n warden traffig

tragedy n trasiedi, trychineb

tragic adj trychinebus, alaethus

trail n llusg, brisg, ôl ▷ vb llusgo

trailer n ôl-gerbyd, ôl-gart, cart; rhaglun (ffilm)

train vb hyfforddi, ymarfer ▷ n gosgordd; godre; trên, cerbydres

trained adj hyfforddedig, cymwys, wedi ei hyfforddi

trainee adj, n hyfforddedig

trainer n hyfforddwr

trainers npl esgidiau ymarfer, treners, trenars

training n hyfforddiant, disgyblaeth

training course n cwrs hyfforddiant

training shoes npl esgidiau ymarfer

trait n nodwedd

traitor n bradwr, teyrnfradwr

trajectory n taflwybr

trammel n rhwyd; hual ▷ vt llyffetheirio, hualu

tramp vb crwydro, trampio ▷ n crwydryn
trample vb sathru, sangu, mathru
trampoline n trampolîn
trance n llewyg, llesmair, perlewyg
tranquil adj tawel, llonydd, digyffro
tranquility n tawelwch, llonyddwch
tranquillizer n tawelyn, tawelydd
trans-, tran-, tra- prefix tros-, tra-
transact vt trafod, gwneud, trin
transaction n trafodaeth
transactions n trafodion
transcend vt rhagori ar, trarhagori
transcendent adj tra-rhagorol
transcendental adj trosgynnol
transcribe vt copïo
transcriber n adysgrifiwr, copïwr, copïydd
transcript n copi, adysgrifiad
transept n croes (eglwys)
transfer vt trosglwyddo ▷ n trosglwyddiad
transference n trosglwyddiad
transfiguration n gweddnewidiad
transfigure vt gweddnewid
transfix vt trywanu, gwanu
transform vt trawsffurfio
transformation n trawsffurfiad
transformer n newidydd
transfusion n trosglwyddiad (gwaed), trallwysiad (gwaed)
transgress vt troseddu
transgression n trosedd, camwedd
transgressor n troseddwr
transient adj diflanedig, darfodedig
transit n mynediad dros, trosiad
transition n trosiad, trawsgyweiriad
transitional adj ar newid, tros dro
transitive adj anghyflawn
transitory adj diflanedig, darfodedig
translate vt cyfieithu

translation n cyfieithiad
translator n cyfieithydd
transliterate vt trawslythrennu
translucent adj tryloyw
transmigrate vi trawsfudo
transmission n trosglwyddiad
transmit vt anfon, trosglwyddo
transmitter n trosglwyddydd
transmitting-station n gorsaf drosglwyddo
transmute vt trawsnewid
transparency n tryloywder
transparent adj tryloyw
transpire vb dyfod yn hysbys, digwydd
transplant vt trawsblannu
transport vt trosglwyddo; alltudio ▷ n trosglwyddiad; cludiant; perlewyg, gorawen
transpose vt trawsddodi, trawsgyweirio
transubstantiation n traws-sylweddiad
transverse adj croes, traws
trap n trap, magl; car bach ▷ vt dal, maglu
trapeze n trapîs
trappings npl harnais, gêr
trash n sothach, gwehilion, ffwlbri, ysbwriel
travail vi trafaelu ▷ n trafael, llafur
travel vb teithio, trafaelio ▷ n teithio
travel agent n asiant teithio
traveller n teithiwr, trafaeliwr
traveller's cheque n siec deithio
travelling adj teithiol
traverse vb mynd ar draws, croesi
travesty n parodi
trawl vb llusgrwydo ▷ n llusgrwyd
trawler n llong bysgota
tray n hambwrdd
treacherous adj twyllodrus
treachery n brad, bradwriaeth

treacle n triagl
tread vb sathru, sengi, troedio ▷ n sang
treadmill n troell droed
treason n brad, bradwriaeth
treasonable adj bradwrus
treasure n trysor ▷ vt trysori
treasurer n trysorydd
treasury n trysorfa, trysordy, y Trysorlys
treat vb trin; tretio; traethu ▷ n gwledd, amheuthun
treatise n traethawd
treatment n triniaeth, ymdriniaeth
treaty n cyfamod, cytundeb
treble adj triphlyg ▷ n trebl ▷ vb treblu
tree n pren, coeden
trefoil n meillionen, meillion
trek vi mudo ▷ n mud, mudo
trellis n delltwaith
tremble vi crynu, echrydu, arswydo
tremendous adj dychrynllyd, ofnadwy, anferth
tremor n crynfa, cryndod, ias
tremulous adj crynedig
trench n ffos, rhigol, rhych ▷ vb ffosi
trenchant adj llym, miniog
trencher n trensiwr, treinsiwr, plat
trend vi tueddu ▷ n tuedd, gogwydd
trepidation n cryndod, ofn, dychryn
trespass vi troseddu ▷ n trosedd
trespasser n tresmaswr
tress n cudyn gwallt, tres
trestle n trestl
tri- prefix tri
triads npl trioedd
trial n prawf, profedigaeth, treial
trial period n cyfnod prawf
triangle n triongl
triangular adj trionglog
tribal adj llwythol
tribe n llwyth, tylwyth, gwehelyth

tribulation n trallod, cystudd
tribunal n brawdle, llys, tribiwnlys
tributary adj dan deyrnged ▷ n rhagafon, isafon, cainc
tribute n teyrnged, treth
trice n munudyn, chwinciad
trick n tric, cast, ystryw ▷ vt castio
trickery n dichell, twyll, ystryw
trickle vi diferu, diferynnu
trickster n twyllwr, castiwr
tricky adj ystrywgar; anodd
tricycle n treisigl
trident n tryfer
triennial adj bob tair blynedd
trifle n gronyn, mymryn; gwaelbeth ▷ vt ofera, cellwair
trifling adj diwerth, dibwys
trigger n cliced, triger
trigonometry n trigonomeg
trill vb crychleisio, cwafrio ▷ n crychlais
trillion n triliwn
trilogy n cyfres o dair (nofel, drama etc)
trim adj taclus, twt, del ▷ vb taclu, trwsio ▷ n diwyg, trefn
trinity n trindod
trinket n tegan, tlws
trio n triawd
trioxide n triocsid
trip vb tripio, maglu; disodli ▷ n trip, tro
tripartite adj teiran
tripe n tripa
triple adj triphlyg
triplet n tripled
tripod n trybedd
trite adj cyffredin, sathredig
triumph n gorfoledd, buddugoliaeth ▷ vi gorfoleddu; buddugoliaethu
triumphal adj buddugol
triumphant adj buddugoliaethus
triumvirate n llywodraeth tri (Rhufain)

trivet n trybedd

trivial adj distadl, dibwys, diwerth

trolley, trolly n troli

troop n byddin, torf, mintai ▷ vb tyrru; **troops** npl lluoedd, minteioedd

trooper n milwr (ar farch)

trophy n gwobr, tlws

tropic n trofan

tropical adj trofannol

trot vb tuthio, trotian ▷ n tuth, trot

troubadour n trwbadŵr, bardd telynegol

trouble vt blino, trafferthu ▷ n blinder, trallod, helbul, trafferth

troubled adj aflonydd, anesmwyth, pryderus, ofnus, dyrys

troubles npl trafferthion, helbulon, pryderon, ofnau

troublesome adj blinderus, trafferthus

trough n cafn

trounce vt ffonodio, cystwyo, baeddu

troupe n mintai o berfformwyr

trousers npl llodrau, trowsus, trwser

trousseau n dillad priodasferch

trout n brithyll

trow vb tybied, meddylied, credu

trowel n trywel

truant n triawnt, mitsiwr

truce n cadoediad

truck n trwc, gwagen

truck vb cyfnewid, ffeirio

truckle vi plygu, ymostwng, ymgreinio

truculent adj ffyrnig, milain

trudge vb cerdded yn ffwdanus, trwmgerdded

true adj gwir, cywir

truism n gwireb, gwiredd

truly adv yn wir, yn ddiau, yn gywir

trump vb utganu; twyllo, ffugio ▷ n trwmp

trumpery n sothach, ffwlbri ▷ adj coeg, gwacsaw

trumpet n utgorn, corn, trwmped

truncheon n pastwn, trensiwn

trundle vb treiglo, rholio

trunk n cyff, cist; corff; duryn, trwnc

trunks npl trons

truss vb gwneud bwndel; gwaellu (ffowlyn)

trust n ymddiried, ymddiriedaeth, coel; ymddiriedolaeth ▷ vb hyderu, ymddiried, coelio

trustee n ymddiriedolwr

trusteeship n ymddiriedolaeth

trustworthy adj y gellir dibynnu arno

trusty adj ffyddlon, cywir, teyrngar

truth n gwir, gwirionedd

truthful adj geirwir

truthfulness n geirwiredd

try vb profi, cynnig, ceisio, treio

trying adj poenus, anodd, blin

tryst n oed

T-shirt n crys-T

tub n twba, twb, baddon

tuba n tiwba

tube n pib, pibell, tiwb, corn

tuber n cloronen, taten

tuberculosis n darfodedigaeth, dicáu, dicléin

tubular adj tiwbaidd; **tubular bridge** ceubont

tuck vt cwtogi, plygu ▷ n plyg, twc

Tuesday n dydd Mawrth

tuft n cogyn, tusw, cudyn

tug vb llusgo, tynnu

tuition n addysg, hyfforddiant

tulip n tiwlip

tumble vb cwympo ▷ n codwm, cwymp

tumbler n gwydryn

t

tumid adj chwyddedig
tummy n bola
tumour n chwydd, casgliad, cornwyd
tumult n terfysg, cynnwrf
tumultuous adj terfysglyd
tuna n tiwna
tune n tôn, tiwn, cywair ▷ vb cyweirio
tuneful adj soniarus
tunic n crysbais, siaced
Tunisia n Tunisia
tunnel n ceuffordd, twnnel
turban n twrban
turbid adj afloyw, cymysglyd, lleidiog
turbine n twrbin
turbot n twrbot
turbulence n terfysg, cynnwrf
turbulent adj terfysglyd, afreolus
turf n tywarchen
turgid adj chwyddedig
Turk n Twrc
Turkey n Twrci
turkey n twrci
Turkish adj Twrcaidd
turmoil n trafferth, ffwdan, berw
turn vb troi ▷ n tro, trofa
turncoat n gwrthgiliwr
turner n turniwr
turning n tro; tröedigaeth
turning point n trobwynt
turnip n erfinen, meipen
turnout n cynulliad
turnover n cyfanswm busnes
turnpike n tollborth, tyrpeg
turnstile n camfa dro
turntable n trofwrdd
turpentine n twrpant, turpant
turpitude n gwarth, ysgelerder
turquoise n maen glas (gwerthfawr)
turret n twred, tyryn
turtle n crwban môr

turtle dove n turtur
tusk n ysgithrddant, ysgithr
tussle n ymgiprys, ysgarmes
tut excl twt!
tutelage n hyfforddiant, nawdd
tutor n athro, hyfforddwr ▷ vt hyfforddi
tutorial adj tiwtorial
TV n abbr teledu
twaddle n lol, ffiloreg
twang vb clecian, swnio ▷ n sŵn, llediaith
tweed n brethyn gwlân, twid
tweezers n gefel fach
twelfth adj deuddegfed
twelve adj, n deuddeg, un deg dau
twentieth adj ugeinfed
twenty adj, n ugain
twice adv dwywaith
twiddle vt chwarae bodiau, cellwair
twig n brigyn, ysbrigyn, impyn
twilight n cyfnos, cyfddydd
twill n brethyn caerog
twin n gefell
twine n llinyn ▷ vb cyfrodeddu, cordeddu
twinge n cnofa, brath, gwayw
twinkle vi serennu, pefrio
twinkling n chwinciad, amrantiad
twirl vb chwyrndroi, chwyldroi, nydd-droi
twist vb nyddu, nydd-droi, cyfrodeddu; troi, gwyrdroi ▷ n tro; edau gyfrodedd
twit n dannod, edliw; un ffôl
twitch vb tymhigo, brathgnoi ▷ n tymig
twitch n gwayw, brath, plwc ▷ vb brathu, tynnu'n sydyn, plycio
twitter vi trydar
two adj, n dau, dwy
two-faced adj dauwynebog
twofold adv deublyg

two piece *n* deuddarn
tympan *n* tabwrdd, tympan
type *n* math, teip
typescript *n* teipysgrif
typewriter *n* teipiadur, peiriant teipio
typhoid *n* twymyn yr ymysgaroedd
typhoon *n* corwynt
typhus *n* twymyn heintus, teiffws
typical *adj* arwyddol, nodweddiadol
typify *vt* arwyddo, nodweddu
typist *n* teipydd
typographical *adj* argraffyddol
typography *n* argraffwaith
tyrannize *vb* gormesu, treisio
tyranny *n* tra-arglwyddiaeth, gormes
tyrant *n* gormesteyrn, gormeswr
tyre *n* teiar
tyro *n* newyddian, dechreuwr

ubiquitous *adj* hollbresennol
udder *n* pwrs, cadair, piw
Uganda *n* Uganda, Iwganda
ugh *excl* ach!, ych y fi!
ugliness *n* hagrwch, hylldra
ugly *adj* hagr, hyll
UK *n abbr* DU, Deyrnas Unedig
ulcer *n* casgliad, cornwyd, wlser
Ulster *n* Ulster
ulterior *adj* tu draw i, tu hwnt i, pellach; cudd
ultimate *adj* diwethaf, olaf, eithaf
ultimately *adv* o'r diwedd
ultimatum *n* y gair olaf, y rhybudd olaf
ultra *adj* eithafol ▷ *prefix* tu hwnt i, gor-
ultramodern *adj* modern iawn
umbrage *n* tramgwydd
umbrella *n* ymbrelo, brela, ambarél, ymbarél
umpire *n* dyfarnwr, canolwr**

un- *prefix* an-, am-, ang-, af-, di-, heb
unable *adj* analluog
unaccented *adj* diacen
unacceptable *adj* anghymeradwy,
annerbyniol
unaccompanied *adj* heb gwmni;
heb gyfeiliant
unaccountable *adj* anesboniadwy
unaccustomed *adj* anghyfarwydd,
anghynefin
unacquainted *adj* anghyfarwydd
unadulterated *adj* pur, digymysg
unaffected *adj* naturiol; heb ei
effeithio gan
unanimity *n* unfrydedd
unanimous *adj* unfrydol
unanimously *adv* yn unfryd
unarmed *adj* diamddiffyn, heb
arfau
unassailable *adj* diysgog
unassuming *adj* diymhongar
unattainable *adj* anghyraeddadwy
unavoidable *adj* anorfod
unaware *adj* anymwybodol
unawares *adv* yn ddiarwybod
unbearable *adj* annioddefol
unbecoming *adj* anweddus,
anweddaidd
unbeliever *n* anghredadun,
anffyddiwr
unbelieving *adj* anghrediniol
unbiassed *adj* diduedd
unblemished *adj* di-nam, dinam
unbounded *adj* diderfyn
unbridled *adj* heb ei ffrwyno
unbroken *adj* di-dor
unbutton *vb* datod, datfotymu
uncalled-for *adj* di-alw-amdano
uncanny *adj* rhyfedd, dieithr,
annaearol
uncle *n* ewythr
unclean *adj* brwnt, aflan
uncomfortable *adj* anghysurus

uncommon *adj* anghyffredin
uncompromising *adj* di-ildio,
digyfaddawd, cyndyn
unconcerned *adj* difater, didaro
unconditional *adj* diamod
unconfirmed *adj* heb ei gadarnhau
unconquerable *adj* anorchfygol
unconscionable *adj* digydwybod,
afresymol
unconscious *adj* anymwybodol
unconstitutional *adj*
anghyfansoddiadol
uncontaminated *adj* di-lwgr, pur
uncontrollable *adj* aflywodraethus
unconventional *adj*
anghonfensiynol
uncouth *adj* trwsgl, lletchwith,
garw, amrwd
uncover *vb* datguddio
unction *n* eli; eneiniad, arddeliad,
hwyl
unctuous *adj* seimlyd; rhagrithiol
uncultivated *adj* heb ei feithrin
undamaged *adj* heb ei niweidio
undecided *adj* petrus, mewn
penbleth
undefended *adj* diamddiffyn
undefiled *adj* dihalog, pur
undefined *adj* amhenodol,
annelwig
undeniable *adj* anwadadwy
under *prep* tan, is, islaw ▷ *adv*
tanodd, oddi tanodd ▷ *prefix* is-, tan-
undercurrent *n* islif
underestimate *vb* prisio'n rhy isel
undergraduate *n* myfyriwr
israddedig
underground *adj* tanddaearol
underhand *adj* llechwraidd, tan din
underline *vb* tanlinellu, pwysleisio
undermine *vb* tanseilio
underneath *adv* oddi tanodd ▷ *prep*
tan

underpass n ffordd danddaearol, tanffordd
underrate vb tanbrisio, iselbrisio
understand vt deall, dirnad
understanding n amgyffred, dealltwriaeth
understatement n tanosodiad
undertake vb ymgymryd
undertaker n ymgymerydd; saer (coffinau)
undertaking adj ymrwymiad
undertone n islais
underwear n dillad isaf
underworld n annwn
undeserved adj anhaeddiannol
undesirable adj annymunol
undeveloped adj heb ei ddatblygu
undeviating adj diwyro
undignified adj anurddasol, diurddas
undisciplined adj diddisgyblaeth
undisputed adj diamheuol
undisturbed adj llonydd, tawel, digyffro
undo vt dadwneud; datod; andwyo, difetha
undoing n distryw, dinistr
undoubted adj diamheuol
undress vb dadwisgo
undue adj amhriodol
undulate vi tonni
unearned adj heb ei ennill
unearthly adj annaearol
uneasiness n anesmwythder, pryder
uneasy adj anesmwyth, aflonydd, pryderus
unedifying adj di-fudd, anadeiladol
uneducated adj annysgedig
unemployed adj di-waith, segur
unemployment n diweithdra, anghyflogaeth
unending adj diddiwedd

unendurable adj annioddefol
unequal adj anghyfartal
unequalled adj digymar, dihafal
unequivocal adj diamwys
unerring adj sicr
uneven adj anwastad
uneventful adj diddigwyddiad
unexpected adj annisgwyliadwy
unfailing adj di-feth
unfair adj annheg
unfairness n annhegwch
unfaithful adj anffyddlon
unfamiliar adj anghyfarwydd
unfasten vb datod
unfathomable adj annealladwy
unfavourable adj anffafriol
unfeeling adj dideimlad
unfettered adj dilyffethair
unfinished adj anorffenedig
unfit adj anghymwys; afiach
unfitting adj amhriodol
unflinching adj diysgog, dewr
unfold vb datblygu
unforeseen adj heb ei ragweld
unforgiving adj anfaddeugar
unfortunate adj anffodus
unfortunately adj yn anffodus
unfounded adj di-sail
unfrequented adj anhygyrch, unig
unfriendly adj anghyfeillgar
unfrock vb diarddel
unfulfilled adj heb ei gyflawni
unfurnished adj diddodrefn
ungainly adv afrosgo, trwsgl
ungentlemanly adj anfoneddigaidd
ungodly adj annuwiol, drwg
ungrammatical adj anramadegol
ungrateful adj anniolchgar
unguarded adj ar awr wan
unguent n ennaint, eli
unhallowed adj halogedig
unhappiness n anhapusrwydd

u

unhappy adj anhapus
unharmed adj dianaf
unhealthy adj afiach
unheeding adj diofal
unhesitating adj dibetrus
unhorse vb taflu oddi ar geffyl
unicorn n uncorn, unicorn
unification n uniad
uniform adj unffurf ▷ n gwisg swyddogol
uniformity n unffurfiaeth
unify vt unoli, uno
unilateral adj unochrog
unimpaired adj dianaf
unimpeded adj dirwystr
unimportant adj dibwys
uninspired adj diawen
unintelligent adj anneallus
unintelligible adj annealladwy
unintentional adj anfwriadol
uninteresting adj anniddorol
union n undeb; uniad
unionism n undebaeth
unionist n undebwr; unoliaethwr (Iwerddon)
unique adj dihafal, digymar
unison n unsain, unseinedd
unit n un, rhif un; uned; undod
Unitarian n Undodwr ▷ adj Undodaidd
Unitarianism n Undodiaeth
unite vb uno, cyfuno, cyduno, cydio
united adj, n unol, unedig; **the United Kingdom** y Deyrnas Unedig; **the United States** yr Unol Daleithiau
unity n undod
universal adj cyffredinol
universe n bydysawd
university n prifysgol
unjust adj anghyfiawn, annheg
unjustly adv ar gam
unkempt adj heb ei gribo, aflêr, anniben

unkind adj angharedig
unknown adj anadnabyddus, anenwog
unlace vb datod
unlawful adj anghyfreithlon
unlearned adj annysgedig
unless conj oni, onid
unlettered adj anllythrennog
unlike adj annhebyg
unlikely adj annhebygol
unlimited adj diderfyn
unload vb dadlwytho
unlock vb datgloi
unlucky adj anlwcus
unmanageable adj aflywodraethus
unmannerly adj anfoesgar
unmarried adj dibriod
unmask vb dinoethi
unmatched adj digymar
unmerciful adj didrugaredd
unmistakable adj digamsyniol
unmixed adj digymysg
unnatural adj annaturiol
unnecessary adj dianghenraid
unobserved adj heb ei weld
unobtrusive adj anymwthiol
unoccupied adj gwag
unopened adj heb ei agor
unopposed adj yn ddiwrthwynebiad
unorthodox adj anarferol, anuniongred
unpack vb dadbacio
unpaid adj di-dâl, didal
unparalleled adj digyffelyb
unpardonable adj anfaddeuol
unpatriotic adj anwlatgar
unpleasant adj annymunol
unpolluted adj dihalog, pur
unpopular adj amhoblogaidd
unpopularity n amhoblogrwydd
unpractical adj anymarferol
unprejudiced adj diragfarn

unprepared *adj* amharod
unprincipled *adj* diegwyddor
unprofitable *adj* amhroffidiol
unprotected *adj* diamddiffyn
unpublished *adj* anghyhoeddedig
unqualified *adj* heb gymhwyster
unquestionable *adj* diamheuol
unready *adj* amharod
unrealistic *adj* afrealaidd, afrealistig
unreasonable *adj* afresymol
unrelated *adj* amherthnasol; heb berthyn
unremitting *adj* dyfal
unrestrained *adj* dilywodraeth
unripe *adj* anaeddfed
unrivalled *adj* digymar
unruffled *adj* tawel
unruly *adj* afreolus
unsafe *adj* anniogel
unsatisfactory *adj* anfoddhaol
unsatisfied *adj* anfodlon
unsatisfying *adj* annigonol
unscathed *adj* dianaf
unscrew *vt* agor; llacio; datroi
unscrupulous *adj* diegwyddor
unseasonable *adj* annhymorol
unseat *vb* troi o'i swydd; taflu (ceffyl)
unseemly *adj* anweddaidd
unseen *adj* anweledig
unsettled *adj* ansefydlog
unshaken *adj* diysgog, cadarn
unsighted *adj* heb allu gweld
unsightly *adj* diolwg, blêr
unskilful *adj* anfedrus
unskilled *adj* anghelfydd
unsociable *adj* anghymdeithasgar
unsolicited *adj* heb ei ofyn
unsound *adj* diffygiol, cyfeiliornus
unsparing *adj* diarbed, hael
unspeakable *adj* anhraethol
unstable *adj* ansefydlog
unstained *adj* dilychwin
unsteadiness *n* ansadrwydd

unsteady *adj* ansefydlog
unsubstantial *adj* ansylweddol
unsuccessful *adj* aflwyddiannus
unsuitable *adj* anaddas
unsullied *adj* dilychwin
unsurmountable *adj* anorchfygol
unsurpassed *adj* diguro
unsuspecting *adj* heb amau dim
untainted *adj* di-lwgr, pur
untangle *vb* datrys
unthankful *adj* anniolchgar
unthinking *adj* difeddwl
untidy *adj* anniben
untie *vb* datod
until *prep*, *conj* hyd, hyd oni, nes, tan
untimely *adj* anamserol
untiring *adj* diflino
unto *prep* i, at, hyd at, wrth
untold *adj* di-ben-draw
untoward *adj* anffodus, cyndyn
untrodden *adj* disathr
untrue *adj* celwyddog
unusual *adj* anarferol, anghynefin; anghyffredin; newydd; dieithr
unutterable *adj* anhraethadwy
unvarying *adj* digyfnewid, cyson
unveil *vb* dadorchuddio
unversed *adj* anhyddysg
unwarranted *adj* heb ei warantu
unwary *adj* diofal
unwell *adj* anhwylus
unwholesome *adj* afiach
unwieldy *adj* afrosgo
unwilling *adj* anfodlon, amharod
unwise *adj* annoeth
unwittingly *adv* yn ddiarwybod
unworthiness *n* annheilyngdod
unworthy *adj* annheilwng
unwounded *adj* dianaf, cyfan
unyielding *adj* di-ildio
up *adj*, *prep* i fyny, (i'r) lan
upbringing *n* magwraeth

u

upheaval n cyffro, terfysg
uphill adj i fyny
uphold vb cynnal
upholsterer n dodrefnwr, clustogwr
upkeep n cynhaliaeth
upland n ucheldir, blaenau
uplifting adj dyrchafol
upload vt llwytho i fyny
upon prep ar, ar warthaf, ar uchaf
upper adj uwch, uchaf
uppermost adj, adv uchaf
upright adj syth, union, unionsyth
uprising n terfysg, gwrthryfel
uproar n terfysg, cythrwfl, dadwrdd
uproot vt diwreiddio
upset vb troi, dymchwelyd, cyffroi, gofidio
upshot n swm, canlyniad, diwedd
upside-down adj, adv (â'i) wyneb i waered
upstairs n llofft
upstart n crach fonheddwr
up-to-date adj cyfoes
upward adj, adv, **upwards** adv i fyny
uranium n wraniwm
urban adj dinasol, dinesig
urbane adj hynaws, mwyn, boneddigaidd
urbanize vb gwneud yn drefol
urchin n draenog; crwtyn
urethra n pibell ddŵr o'r bledren
urge vt cymell, annog
urgency n brys
urgent adj taer, pwysig, yn gofyn brys
urine n troeth, trwnc, piso
urn n wrn
US n abbr UD, Unol Daleithiau
us pron ni, nyni, ninnau; 'n
USA n abbr UDA, Unol Daleithiau America
usage n arfer, defod, triniaeth

use n iws, arfer, defnydd, gwasanaeth, diben ▷ vb iwsio, arfer, defnyddio
use up vt defnyddio'r cyfan o, defnyddio'r cwbl o
used adj arferedig, mewn arfer, cynefin; (car) ail-law
useful adj defnyddiol
useless adj diwerth
user n defnyddiwr
user-friendly adj hawdd ei drin
usher n rhingyll; isathro; tywysydd ▷ vt arwain i mewn, dwyn ymlaen
usual adj arferol, cynefin
usually adv fel arfer, fel rheol
usurer n usuriwr
usurp vt trawsfeddiannu
usurper n trawsfeddiannwr
usury n usuriaeth, ocraeth
utensil n offeryn, llestr
uterus n croth, bru
utilitarian adj defnyddiol
utilitarianism n llesyddiaeth
utility n defnyddioldeb, budd, lles
utilization n defnydd
utilize vt defnyddio
utmost adj eithaf, pellaf
utopia n gwlad ddelfrydol (ddychmygol)
utopian adj defrydol, anymarferol
utter adj eithaf, pellaf; hollol, llwyr
utter vt yngan, traethu, dywedyd
utterance n parabl, ymadrodd, lleferydd
uttermost adj eithaf, pellaf
U-turn n tro pedol
uvula n tafod bach, tafodig
uvular adj tafodigol

V

vacancy *n* lle gwag, swydd wag, gwacter
vacant *adj* gwag; syn, synfyfyriol, hurt
vacate *vt* ymadael â, gadael yn wag
vacation *n* seibiant, gwyliau
vaccinate *vt* brechu, bufrechu, torri'r frech
vaccination *n* y frech, brechiad
vaccine *n* brech
vacillate *vi* anwadalu, bwhwman
vacuous *adj* gwg, syn, hurt
vacuum *n* gwag, gwagle, gwactod
vacuum cleaner *n* sugnydd llwch
vacuum flask *n* thermos, jac
vagabond *n* crwydryn, dihiryn
vagary *n* mympwy
vagrancy *n* crwydro
vagrant *adj* crwydrol ▷ *n* crwydryn
vague *adj* amwys, amhenodol
vagueness *n* amwysedd

vain *adj* balch, coegfalch; ofer
vale *n* dyffryn, glyn, bro, cwm, ystrad
valediction *n* ffarwel
valentine *n* falant, folant
Valentine's Day *n* Dydd Sant Ffolant
valet *n* gwas
valiant *adj* dewr, dewrwych, gwrol, glew
valid *adj* digonol, dilys, cyfreithlon, iawn
validate *vb* cadarnhau, dilysu
validity *n* dilysrwydd
valley *n* dyffryn, cwm, glyn
valour *n* dewrder, gwroldeb, glewder
valuable *adj* gwerthfawr
valuation *n* prisiad
value *n* gwerth ▷ *vt* gwerthfawrogi, prisio
valuer *n* prisiwr
valve *n* falf
vampire *n* sugnwr gwaed
van *n* blaen cad, y rheng flaenaf
van *n* men, fan
vandal *n* fandal
vandalism *n* fandaliaeth
vandalize *vt* fandaleiddio
vane *n* ceiliog gwynt
vanguard *n* blaen cad, blaenfyddin
vanilla *n* fanila
vanish *vi* diflannu, darfod
vanity *n* gwagedd, gwegi, coegfalchder
vanquish *vt* gorchfygu, trechu
vanquisher *n* gorchfygwr
vantage *n* mantais
vapid *adj* diflas, merf, marwaidd, egr
vaporize *vb* anweddu
vaporous *adj* llawn tarth
vapour *n* tawch, tarth, ager, anwedd
variable *adj* cyfnewidiol, anwadal, oriog

V

variable n newidyn (rhifyddiaeth)
variance n anghytundeb, anghydfod, amrywioldeb
variant n amrywiad
variation n amrywiad
varicose adj chwyddedig (am wythiennau)
varied adj amrywiol
variegated adj brith, brithliw
variety n amrywiaeth
various adj gwahanol, amrywiol
varnish n barnais, farnais ▷ vt barneisio, farneisio
varnisher n farneisiwr
vary vb amrywio; newid
vase n cwpan, cawg
Vaseline® n faselin, eli
vassal n caethddeiliad, taeog, aillt, deiliad
vast adj dirfawr, anferth
vastness n mawredd, ehangder
vat n cerwyn
Vatican n plas y Pab
vaticinate vb proffwydo, darogan
vaticination n proffwydoliaeth, darogan
vault n daeargell, claddgell; cromen ▷ vb neidio, llamu
vaulted adj bwaog
vaunt vb ymffrostio, bostio, brolio
veal n cig llo
vector n fector
veer vb troi, cylchdroi; trawshwylio
vegan adj feganaidd, figanaidd ▷ n fegan, figan
vegetable adj llysieuol ▷ n llysieuyn ymborth
vegetarian n llysieuwr
vegetate vi tarddu, tyfu; ofera
vegetation n tyfiant llysiau, llystyfiant
vehemence n angerdd
vehement adj angerddol, tanbaid

vehicle n cerbyd; cyfrwng, moddion
veil n gorchudd, llen ▷ vt gorchuddio
vein n gwythïen
velar adj felar
veldt n anialdir, maestir
vellum n memrwn
velocity n buander, cyflymder, buanedd (mathemateg)
velvet n melfed
venal adj llygredig, anonest
vend vt gwerthu
vendor n gwerthwr
veneer n argaen, wynebiad; rhith, ffug
venerable adj hybarch
venerate vt parchu, anrhydeddu
venereal adj gwenerol
Venetian blind n llen Fenis
vengeance n dial, dialedd
vengeful adj dialgar
venial adj maddeuadwy, esgusodol
venison n cig carw, fenswn
venom n gwenwyn
venomous adj gwenwynig
venous adj gwythennol
vent n agorfa, twll, arllwysfa ▷ vt arllwys, gollwng
ventilate vt awyru, gwyntyllu
ventilation n awyriad, gwyntylliad
ventilator n awyrydd, gwyntyllydd
ventricle n bolgell y galon, fentrigl
ventriloquism n tafleisiaeth
venture n anturiaeth, mentr ▷ vb anturio, mentro
venturesome adj mentrus, anturus
venue n man cyfarfod
Venus n Gwener, duwies serch
veracious adj cywir, geirwir, gwir
veracity n geirwiredd
verandah n feranda
verb n berf
verbal adj berfol; geiriol

verbally adv mewn geiriau, gair am air

verbatim adv air am air, air yng ngair

verbiage n amleiriaeth, geiriogrwydd

verb-noun n berfenw

verbose adj amleiriog

verbosity n geiriogrwydd

verdant adj gwyrddlas, gwyrdd

verdict n dyfarniad, dedfryd, rheithfarn

verdure n gwyrddlesni

verge n min, ymyl ▷ vi ymylu

verger n byrllysgydd, eglwyswas

verification n gwireddiad

verify vt gwiro, gwireddu

verily adv yn wir, yn ddiau

verisimilitude n tebygolrwydd

veritable adj gwirioneddol

verity n gwir, gwirionedd

vermilion n fermiliwn, lliw cochlyd

vermin npl pryfed, pryfetach; llygod etc

vernacular adj cynhenid, brodorol ▷ n iaith y wlad

vernal adj gwanwynol

veronica n feronica, llysiau Llywelyn

versatile adj amryddawn

versatility n amlochredd

verse n gwers, adnod, pennill; prydyddiaeth

versed adj cyfarwydd, hyddysg

versify vb mydru, prydyddu, prydu

version n cyfieithiad, trosiad; esboniad

vers libre n gwers rydd

versus prep yn erbyn

vertebra (**-brae**) n un o gymalau'r asgwrn cefn

vertebrate n anifail ag asgwrn cefn

vertex (**-tices**) n pen, crib, copa

vertical adj syth, unionsyth, plwm

vertigo n y bendro, y ddot

vervain n llysiau hudol, y ferfain

verve n bywyd, egni, asbri

very adj, adv iawn, pur, tra; diamheuol

vespers npl gosber

vessel n llestr

vest n gwasgod, crys isaf ▷ vb arwisgo, cynysgaeddu

vestal adj gwyryfol ▷ n lleian, gwyry

vested adj yn ymwneud ag eiddo

vestibule n porth, cyntedd

vestige n ôl, ôl troed, brisg

vestigial adj gweddilliol, ôl

vestment n gwisg, defodwisg

vestry n festri

vesture n gwisg, dilledyn, dillad

vet vb arholi, archwilio ▷ n meddyg anifeiliaid

vetch n pys llygod

veteran n un hen a chyfarwydd

veterinary adj milfeddygol;
veterinary surgeon meddyg anifeiliaid, milfeddyg

veto (**-oes**) n gwaharddiad ▷ vt gwahardd

vex vt blino, poeni, poenydio, cythruddo

vexation n blinder, gofid

vexed adj blin, dig

vexing adj blin, plagus

via prep trwy, ar hyd

viable adj abl i fodoli, dichonadwy

viaduct n pontffordd, fforddbont

vial n ffiol

viand n bwyd, ymborth

vibrant adj dirgrynol

vibrate vb crynu, dirgrynu

vibration n dirgryniad

vicar n ficer

vicarage n ficeriaeth; ficerdy

vicarious adj dirprwyol, mechnïol

vice n drygioni, drygedd, bai, gwŷd

vice n gwasg, feis

V

vice- *prefix* rhag-, is-
vice-admiral *n* is-lyngesydd
vice-chairman *n* is-gadeirydd
vice-chancellor *n* is-ganghellor
vice-president *n* is-lywydd
viceroy *n* rhaglaw
vice-versa *adv* i'r gwrthwyneb
vicinity *n* cymdogaeth
vicious *adj* drygionus, gwydus
viciousness *n* drygioni, sbeit
vicissitude *n* cyfnewidiad, tro
victim *n* aberth, ysglyfaeth
victimise *vb* erlid, gormesu
victor *n* gorchfygwr
victorious *adj* buddugol,
  buddugoliaethus
victory *n* buddugoliaeth
victual *vt* bwydo
victualler *n* gwerthwr bwyd
victuals *npl* bwyd, lluniaeth
vide *vb* gwêl
videlicet (viz) *adv* sef, h.y.
video *n* fideo
video camera *n* camera fideo
video game *n* gêm fideo
vie *vi* cystadlu, cydymgais
Vienna *n* Fienna
Vietnam *n* Fietnam
view *n* golygfa, barn ▷ *vt* edrych
viewer *n* gwyliwr (teledu)
viewpoint *n* safbwynt
vigil *n* noswyl, gwylnos
vigilant *adj* gwyliadwrus
vignette *n* addurn, llun
vigorous *adj* grymus, egnïol
vigour *n* grym, nerth, egni, ynni
viking *n* môr-leidr (o Lychlyn gynt)
vile *adj* gwael, brwnt
vileness *n* brynti
vilify *vt* pardduo, difrïo
villa *n* fila
village *n* pentref
villager *n* pentrefwr

villain *n* cnaf, adyn, dihiryn
villainous *adj* anfad, ysgeler
villainy *n* anfadwaith
vim *n* grym, ynni
vindicate *vt* amddiffyn, cyfiawnhau
vindication *n* cyfiawnhad
vindictive *adj* dialgar
vindictiveness *n* dialedd
vine *n* gwinwydden
vinegar *n* finegr
vineyard *n* gwinllan
vintage *n* cynhaeaf gwin
vintner *n* gwinwr, gwinydd
viola *n* fiola
violate *vt* torri, troseddu, treisio,
  trochi
violation *n* treisiad, trosedd
violence *n* ffyrnigrwydd, trais
violent *adj* gwyllt, tanbaid,
  angerddol
violet *n* fioled, crinllys
violin *n* ffidil
violinist *n* feiolinydd, ffidler
violoncello *n* basgrwth
viper *n* gwiber
viper's bugloss *n* tafod y bwch
virago *n* cecren
virgin *n* gwyry, morwyn
virginal *n* fyrginal ▷ *adj* gwyryfol,
  morwynol
Virgo *n* y Forwyn, y Wyryf
virile *adj* gwrol, egnïol
virility *n* gwrolaeth, gwroldeb
virtual *adj* rhinweddol
virtually *adv* i bob pwrpas
virtue *n* rhinwedd
virtuoso *n* un celfydd, carwr
  celfyddyd
virulence *n* gwenwyn, caseineb
virulent *adj* gwenwynig, ffyrnig
virus *n* gôr, crawn; gwenwyn, firws
visa *n* fisa
visage *n* wyneb, wynepryd

vis-à-vis adv wyneb yn wyneb, gyferbyn

viscid adj gwydn, gludiog

viscount n is-iarll

visible adj gweladwy, gweledig

vision n gweledigaeth; golwg, gweled

visionary n breuddwydiwr ▷ adj breuddwydiol

visit vt ymweld, gofwyo ▷ n ymweliad

visitation n ymweliad, archwiliad

visitor n ymwelwr, ymwelydd

visitor centre n canolfan ymwelwyr

visor n miswrn, mwgwd

vista n golygfa

visual adj gweledol, golygol; **visual aids** cyfarpar gweld

visualise vb gwneud yn weledig, disgrifio, dychmygu

vital adj bywiol, bywydol, hanfodol

vitality n bywyd, bywiogrwydd

vitalize vb bywiocáu, bywiogi

vitamin n fitamin

vitiate vt llygru, difetha, dirymu

vitreous adj gwydrol, gwydraidd

vitriol n fitriol, asid sylffurig

vitriolic adj fitriolaidd, atgas, chwerw

vituperate vt cablu, difenwi, difrïo

vituperative adj difrïol

vivacious adj bywiog, heini, nwyfus

vivacity n hoen, nwyf

viva voce adv ar lafar

vivid adj byw, clir, llachar, tanbaid

vividness n eglurder

vivify vt bywhau, bywiocáu

vivisection n bywdrychiad, bywddifyniad

vixen n cadnawes, llwynoges

viz. adv sef (talfyriad o videlicet)

vizier n swyddog gwlad (Mohametanaidd)

vocable n gair

vocabulary n geirfa

vocal adj lleisiol, llafarol, llafar

vocalist n lleisiwr, cantor

vocalize vt llafarseinio; llafarogi

vocally adv â'r llais

vocation n galwad, galwedigaeth

vocational adj galwedigaethol, gyrfaol

vocative adj cyfarchol

vociferate vb crochlefain, gweiddi

vodka n fodca

vogue n arfer, ffasiwn, bri

voice n llais, lleferydd; (grammar) stad

voiced adj llafarog, lleisiol

voiceless adj dilais, mud

voicemail n (message) neges lais

void adj gwag; ofer, di-rym ▷ n gwagle ▷ vt gwagu, gollwng; gwacau

volatile adj hedegog, anwadal, gwamal, ysgafn, cyfnewidiol

volcanic adj folcanig

volcano n llosgfynydd, mynydd tân

vole n llygoden y maes

volition n ewyllysiad, ewyllys

volley n cawod o ergydion; taro pêl yn yr awyr

volt n uned grym trydan, folt

voltage n grym trydan

voluble adj rhugl, ymadroddus

volume n cyfrol; swm, crynswth, folum (cemeg), cyfaint (matemateg)

voluminous adj mawr, helaeth

voluntary adj gwirfoddol

volunteer n gwirfoddolwr ▷ vb gwirfoddoli

voluptuary n pleserwr, glythwr

voluptuous adj glwth, trythyll

V

voluptuousness *n* trythyllwch
vomit *vb* chwydu, cyfogi
voracious *adj* gwancus, rheibus
vortex *n* trobwll, chwyldro
votary *n* addunwr, diofrydwr; pleidiwr
vote *n* pleidlais ▷ *vb* pleidleisio
voter *n* pleidleisiwr
votive *adj* addunedol, addunol
vouch *vb* gwirio, gwarantu
vouchsafe *vt* caniatáu, rhoddi
vow *n* adduned, diofryd ▷ *vb* addunedu
vowel *n* llafariad; **vowel affection** affeithiad; **vowel mutation** gwyriad
voyage *n* mordaith ▷ *vb* mordeithio, mordwyo
voyager *n* mordeithiwr
vulcanize *vb* caledu rwber
vulgar *adj* cyffredin; isel, di-foes, aflednais
vulgarism *n* ymadrodd aflednais
vulgarity *n* diffyg moes
Vulgate *n* Y Fwlgat
vulnerable *adj* archolladwy, hyglwyf, hawdd ei niweidio
vulture *n* fwltur

wad *n* sypyn, wad
wadding *n* wadin
waddle *vi* siglo, honcian
wade *vb* beisio, rhydio
wader *n* rhydiwr
wadi *n* gwely afon (sy'n dueddol i sychu)
wafer *n* afrlladen
waft *vt* chwifio, cludo, dygludo
wag *vb* ysgwyd, siglo, honcian
wag *n* cellweiriwr, wag
wage *vt* gwneuthur, dwyn ymlaen
wage *n* cyflog, hur
wager *n* cyngwystl ▷ *vt* cyngwystlo
waggish *adj* cellweirus
waggle *vb* siglo
wagon *n* men, gwagen
wagtail *n* sigl-i-gwt
waif *n* plentyn digartref
wail *vb* cwynfan, wylofain, udo
wainscot *n* palis

waist n gwasg, canol
waistcoat n gwasgod
wait vb aros; gweini ▷ n arhosiad
waiter n gweinydd
waiting n aros, sefyll
waiting room n ystafell aros
waitress n gweinyddes
wake vb deffro ▷ n gwylmabsant;
gwylnos
wake n ôl, brisg
wakefulness n anhunedd
waken vb deffro, dihuno
Wales n Cymru
walk vb cerdded, rhodio ▷ n rhodfa;
tro
walker n cerddwr
walkie-talkie n set radio symud a
siarad
walking n cerddediad; cerdded;
walking stick ffon gerdded
walkover n goruchafiaeth hawdd,
digystadleuaeth
wall n mur, gwal, pared ▷ vt murio
wallaby n cangarŵ bach
wall-cress n berwr y fagwyr
wallet n ysgrepan, gwaled
wallflower n llysiau'r fagwyr,
blodau'r fagwyr, blodau mamgu
wallop vt curo, llachio, wado
wallow vi ymdreiglo, ymdrybaeddu
wallpaper n papur wal
walnut n cneuen Ffrengig
walrus n morfarch
waltz n wols
wan adj gwelw, gwelwlas, llwyd
wand n gwialen, llath, hudlath
wander vb crwydro, gwibio,
cyfeiliorni
wanderer n crwydryn
wandering adj ar grwydr
wanderlust n elfen grwydro
wane vi darfod, treio, cilio, lleihau
wangle vb dyfeisio

want n angen, eisiau, diffyg ▷ vb bod
mewn angen
wanting adj yn eisiau
wanton adj anllad, trythyll; diachos
wantonness n anlladrwydd
war n rhyfel ▷ vb rhyfela
warble vb telori
warbler n telor
ward n gwart, gward;
gwarchodaeth ▷ vt gwarchod,
amddiffyn
warden n gwarden, gwarcheidwad
wardenship n gwardeniaeth
warder n gwarchodwr, gwyliwr
wardrobe n cwpwrdd dillad,
gwardrob
ware n nwydd; llestri, wâr
warehouse n ystordy, ystorfa,
warws
warfare n milwriaeth, rhyfel
wariness n pwyll, gwyliadwriaeth
warlike adj rhyfelgar, milwraidd,
milwrol
warm adj cynnes ▷ vb cynhesu
warmonger n rhyfelgi
warmth n cynhesrwydd
warn vt rhybuddio
warning n rhybudd
warp n ystof, dylif ▷ vb gwyro,
lleddfu
warrant n gwarant, awdurdod ▷ vt
gwarantu, cyfreithloni
warrantor n gwarantydd
warren n cwningar, parc cwningod
warrior n rhyfelwr
warship n llong rhyfel
wart n dafad, dafaden
wary adj gwyliadwrus, gochelgar
was vi oedd, bu
wash vb golchi ▷ n golchiad,
golchfa; golchion
washable adj golchadwy
washing n golch

washing machine *n* peiriant golchi
washing powder *n* powdr golchi
washing-up liquid *n* sebon golchi llestri
wasp *n* cacynen, gwenynen feirch
wassail *n* gwasael
waste *vb* difrodi, gwastraffu, treulio ▷ *n* gwastraff, traul
wasteful *adj* gwastraffus
wastepaper basket *n* basged sbwriel
wastrel *n* oferwr, oferddyn
watch *vb* gwylio, gwylied, gwarchod ▷ *n* gwyliadwriaeth; oriawr, oriadur, wats
watchful *adj* gwyliadwrus
watchmaker *n* oriadurwr, trwsiwr watsys
watchman *n* gwyliwr
watch-night *n* gwylnos
watchword *n* arwyddair, cyswynair
water *n* dwfr, dŵr ▷ *vb* dyfrhau
water-cock *n* tap
watercolour *n* paent (i'w gymysgu â dŵr); dyfrlliw
watercress *n* berwr dŵr
waterfall *n* rhaeadr, pistyll, cwymp dŵr, sgwd
waterhen *n* iâr fach y dŵr
watering place *n* lle i anifeiliaid gael dŵr; tref ffynhonnau
waterlogged *adj* llawn dŵr
watermark *n* dyfrnod
waterproof *adj* diddos
watershed *n* trum, gwahanfa ddŵr
water skiing *n* sglefrio ar ddŵr
watertight *adj* diddos, heb ollwng dŵr neu leithder
water wagtail *n* sigwti fach y dŵr
watt *n* wat, uned pŵer trydan
wattle *n* clwyd, pleiden; tagell ceiliog
wave *vb* chwifio; tonni ▷ *n* ton

waver *vi* anwadalu, petruso, gwamalu
wax *n* cwyr ▷ *vt* cwyro
wax *vi* cynyddu, tyfu
wax-candle *n* cannwyll gŵyr
waxworks *npl* arddangosfa delwau cwyr
way *n* ffordd, modd, arfer
wayfarer *n* fforddolyn, teithiwr, tramwywr
wayfaring tree *n* ysgawen y gors
waylay *vt* cynllwyn, rhagod
wayside *n* ymyl y ffordd
wayward *adj* cyndyn, ystyfnig, gwrthnysig
we *pron* ni, nyni, ninnau
weak *adj* gwan, egwan
weaken *vb* gwanhau, gwanychu
weakling *n* un gwan, edlych, ewach
weakly *adj* gwanllyd
weak-minded *adj* diniwed, gwirion
weakness *n* gwendid
weal *n* llwydd, llwyddiant, lles
weald *n* fforest; gwlad agored
wealth *n* golud, cyfoeth, da
wealthy *adj* cyfoethog
wean *vt* diddyfnu
weapon *n* arf
wear *vb* gwisgo, treulio ▷ *n* traul; gwisg
weariness *n* blinder
weary *adj* blin, blinedig ▷ *vb* blino
weasel *n* gwenci, bronwen
weather *n* tywydd, hin ▷ *vt* dal, dioddef
weather-beaten *adj* ag ôl y tywydd arno
weather forecast *n* rhagolygon y tywydd
weatherglass *n* baromedr
weather vane *n* ceiliog gwynt
weave *vb* gwau, gweu
weave (**wove, woven**) *vb* gwehyddu; plethu

weaver n gwehydd
web n gwe; **the (World-Wide) Web** y We (Fyd-Eang)
web address n cyfeiriad gwe
webbing n webin
webcam n gwe-gamera
web-footed adj â thraed gweog
web page n tudalen we
website n gwefan, safle gwe
wed vb priodi, ymbriodi
wedding n priodas
wedge n cŷn, gaing, lletem ▷ vt cynio; gwthio i mewn
wedlock n ystad priodas, priodas
Wednesday n dydd Mercher
wee adj bach, bychan, pitw
weed n chwynnyn, chwyn ▷ vb chwynnu
week n wythnos
weekday n diwrnod gwaith
weekend n dros y Sul, penwythnos
weekly n wythnosolyn (cylchgrawn) ▷ adj wythnosol ▷ adv yn wythnosol
weep vb wylo, wylofain, llefain
weevil n gwyfyn yr ŷd
weft n anwe
weigh vb pwyso; codi (angor)
weight n pwys, pwysau
weighty adj pwysig, trwm
weir n cored
weird adj annaearol, iasol
welcome excl, n croeso ▷ vt croesawu ▷ adj derbyniol, dymunol
weld vt asio
welfare n llwydd, lles
welfare state n gwladwriaeth les
well adv yn dda ▷ adj da, iach ▷ excl wel
well n ffynnon, pydew
well-balanced adj cytbwys
wellbeing n lles, budd
well-bred adj boneddigaidd
well-fed adj mewn cas cadw da

wellingtons npl esgidiau glaw
well-known adj (person) adnabyddus; (fact) tra hysbys
well-off adj cefnog, da ei fyd
well-paid adj â chyflog da
Welsh adj Cymreig; Cymraeg ▷ n Cymraeg
Welshman n Cymro
Welshwoman n Cymraes
welt n gwald, gwaldas
welter vi ymdrybaeddu
wen n wen
wench n geneth, llances
wend vt mynd, cerdded
werewolf n bleidd-ddyn
Wesleyan adj Wesleaidd
west n gorllewin ▷ adj gorllewinol
westerly adj gorllewinol, o'r gorllewin
western adj gorllewinol
West Germany n Gorllewin yr Almaen
West Indies npl: **the West Indies** India'r Gorllewin
westwards adv tua'r gorllewin
wet adj gwlyb ▷ vt gwlychu ▷ n gwlybaniaeth
wether n mollt, gwedder
wetness n gwlybaniaeth
wetting n gwlychfa
whack vb llachio, baeddu, ffonodio
whale n morfil
wharf n porthfa, llwythfa
what adj, pron yr hyn; pa beth, pa faint
whatever pron beth bynnag
whatsoever pron pa beth bynnag
wheat n gwenith
wheedle vt denu, hudo, llithio, truthio
wheel n olwyn, rhod, troell ▷ vt olwyno, powlio
wheelbarrow n berfa (drol), whilber

W

wheelchair n cadair olwyn
wheelwright n saer troliau
wheeze vi gwichian ▷ n gwich
wheezy adj gwichlyd
whelk n chwalc, gwalc
whelp n cenau
when adv pan, pa bryd
whence adv o ba le, o ba un
whenever adv pa bryd bynnag
where adv ym mha le; yn y lle, lle
whereabouts adv ymhle
whereas conj gan, yn gymaint â
whereby adv trwy yr hyn
wherefore adv paham, am hynny
wherein adv yn yr hyn
whereof adv y ... amdano
whereon adv ar yr hwn
wheresoever, wherever adv pa le
bynnag
whereto adv y ... iddo
whereupon adv ar hynny
wherewithal n modd, arian
wherry n ysgraff, ceubal, porthfad
whet vt hogi, minio, awchlymu
whether conj ai, pa un ai
whetstone n carreg hogi, hogfaen,
agalen
whey n maidd, gleision
which pron pa un, pa rai; a ▷ adj pa
whichever pron, adj pa un bynnag
whiff n chwiff, pwff, chwyth, chwa
Whig n Chwig, Rhyddfrydwr
while n ennyd, talm, amser ▷ vt
treulio ▷ adv cyhyd, tra
whilst adv cyhyd, tra
whim n mympwy, chwim
whimper vb swnian crio
whimsical adj ysmala, mympwyol
whimsicality n bod yn fympwyol
whin n eithin
whinchat n clochdar yr eithin
whine vb swnian crio, cwynfan
whinny vi gweryru

whip vb chwipio, ffrewyllu, fflangellu
▷ n chwip, ffrewyll, fflangell
whip hand n llaw uchaf
whippet n corfilgi
whipping n chwipiad, fflangelliad
whir vi chwyrndroi, chwyrnu
whirl vb chwyrlïo, chwyrnellu,
chwyrndroi
whirligig n chwyrligwgan,
chwyrnell
whirlpool n pwll tro, trobwll
whirlwind n trowynt, corwynt
whisk n tusw ▷ vb ysgubo; chwyrlïo
whiskered adj blewog, barfog
whiskers npl blew, barf
whisky n chwisgi
whisper vb, n sibrwd, sisial
whist n chwist
whistle vb chwibanu ▷ n chwiban,
chwibanogl, chwît
whit n tipyn, gronyn, mymryn
white adj gwyn, can, cannaid
whiten vb gwynnu, cannu
whiteness n gwynder, gwyndra
whitewash n gwyngalch ▷ vb
gwyngalchu
whither adv i ba le
whiting n gwyniad
whitlow n ffelwm, ffalwm, ewinor,
bystwn
whitlow grass n llysiau'r bystwn
Whit Monday n Llungwyn
Whitsun, Whitsunday n Sulgwyn
Whitsuntide n dros y Sulgwyn
whittle vt naddu, lleihau
whiz vi sïo, chwyrnellu, chwyrlïo
who pron a, pwy
whoever pron pwy bynnag
whole adj cyfan, holl; iach, holliach
▷ n cyfan
wholehearted adj â'i holl galon
wholemeal adj â'r grawn cyfan,
cyflawn

wholeness n cyfanrwydd
wholesale n cyfanwerth ▷ adj yn y crynswth
wholesaler n cyfanwerthwr
wholesome adj iach, iachus, iachusol
wholly adv yn hollol, yn gyfan gwbl, yn llwyr
whom pron a (y, yr)
whomsoever pron pwy bynnag
whoop vi bloeddio, banllefain ▷ n bloedd
whooping cough n pas
whop vt ffusto, baeddu
whopper n un mawr
whopping adj mawr iawn
whore n putain, hŵr
whorl n tro, troell, sidell
whortleberry n llus, llusi duon bach
whose pron y ... ei, eiddo pwy? pwy biau?
whosoever pron pwy bynnag
why adv paham, pam
wick n pabwyr, pabwyryn, wic
wicked adj drwg, drygionus, ysgeler
wickedness n drygioni
wicker n gwaith gwiail
wickerwork n plethwaith, basgedwaith
wicket n wiced, clwyd, llidiart
wide adj llydan, eang, helaeth; rhwth
wide-awake adj effro, ar ddihun
widely adj yn eang
widen vb lledu, llydanu
widespread adj cyffredinol
widgeon n wiwell
widow adj gweddw ▷ n gwraig weddw, gwidw
widowed adj gweddw
widower n gwidman
widowhood n gweddwdod
width n lled, ehangder

wield vt llywio, rheoli; ysgwyd, arfer, trin
wife (**wives**) n gwraig, gwraig briod, priod
wig n gwallt gosod, perwig, wig
wigging n cerydd
wild adj gwyllt ▷ n diffeithle
wilderness n anialwch
wildfire n tân gwyllt
wildlife n bywyd gwyllt
wildness n gwylltineb
wile n dichell, ystryw, cast
wilful adj gwirfoddol, bwriadol; ystyfnig
wilfully adj o fwriad
wilfulness n ystyfnigrwydd
wiliness n dichell, cyfrwystra
will vt ewyllysio, mynnu ▷ n ewyllys
willing adj ewyllysgar, bodlon
willingly adj o wirfodd
willingness n parodrwydd
will-o'-the-wisp n jacolantern
willow n helygen, pren helyg
willowherb n helyglys
willowy adj helygaidd, gosgeiddig
willpower n grym ewyllys
willy-nilly adv bodlon neu beidio, o fodd neu anfodd
wily adj cyfrwys, dichellgar
wimple n gwempl
win vb ennill
wince vi gwingo
winch n wins
wind n gwynt
wind vb dirwyn, troi
windbag n clebryn
windfall n lwc, ffawd dda
windflower n anemoni, blodyn y gwynt
windless adj di-wynt, llonydd
windmill n melin wynt
window n ffenestr
windowpane n cwarel

w

windpipe *n* breuant, y bibell wynt
windscreen *n* ffenestr flaen
windscreen wiper *n* braich law
windsurfing *n* bordhwylio
windward *adj* tua'r gwynt
windy *adj* gwyntog
wine *n* gwin
wineglass *n* gwydr gwin
wing *n* adain, asgell; asgellwr (rygbi)
wing-commander *n*
asgell-gomander
winged *adj* adeiniog
wing-forward *n* blaenasgellwr
wink *vb* wincio, cau llygad ▷ *n* winc;
hunell
winner *n* enillydd
winning *adj* enillgar, deniadol
winnings *npl* enillion
winnow *vt* nithio, gwyntyllio
winnower *n* nithiwr
winsome *adj* serchog, deniadol
winter *n* gaeaf ▷ *vb* gaeafu
winter sports *npl* chwaraeon y
gaeaf
wintertime *n* tymor y gaeaf
wintry *adj* gaeafol
wipe *vt* sychu
wire *n* gwifr, gwifren
wireless *n* radio ▷ *adj* di-wifr;
wireless network rhwydwaith
di-wifr
wirepulling *n* cynllwyn, dylanwadu,
'tynnu gwifrau'
wiring *n* weiro
wiry *adj* gwydn, caled
wisdom *n* doethineb
wise *adj* doeth
wiseacre *n* doethyn, ffwlcyn
wish *vb* dymuno, chwennych ▷ *n*
dymuniad
wishbone *n* asgwrn tynnu
wishful *adj* awyddus; **wishful
thinking** breuddwyd gwrach

wishy-washy *adj* gwan,
di-asgwrn-cefn
wisp *n* tusw
wistful *adj* awyddus, hiraethus
wit *vb*: **to wit** sef, hynny yw, nid
amgen
wit *n* synnwyr; arabedd; gŵr ffraeth
witch *n* dewines, gwrach
witchcraft *n* dewiniaeth
with *prep* â, ag, gyda, gydag, efo,
gan
withdraw *vb* tynnu yn ôl, encilio;
codi arian
withdrawal *n* enciliad
withe *n* gwden, gwialen helyg
wither *vb* gwywo, crino
withering *adj* gwywol, crin
withers *npl* ysgwydd march
withhold *vt* atal, cadw yn ôl
within *adv, n, prep* i mewn, o fewn
without *prep* heb, di- ▷ *adv, n* tu
allan
withstand *vt* gwrthsefyll
witless *adj* disynnwyr, ynfyd, ffôl
witness *n* tyst; tystiolaeth ▷ *vb*
tystio
wits *npl* synhwyrau
witticism *n* ffraethair, ffraetheb
wittiness *n* ffraethineb
wittingly *adv* trwy wybod, yn
fwriadol
witty *adj* arab, arabus, ffraeth
wizard *n* swynwr, dewin
wizardry *n* dewiniaeth, hud
wizened *adj* gwyw, crin, sybachog
woad *n* glaslys
wobble *vi* siglo, honcian, anwadalu
wobbly *adj* sigledig
woe *n* gwae
woebegone *adj* athrist
wolf (**wolves**) *n* blaidd
wolfsbane *n* llysiau'r blaidd
woman (**women**) *n* gwraig, merch

womanliness n rhinweddau benywaidd

womanly adj gwreigaidd, benywaidd

womb n croth, bru

wonder n rhyfeddod, syndod ▷ vi rhyfeddu, synnu

wonderful, wondrous adj rhyfeddol

wont vb, n arfer ▷ adj arferol

woo vt caru; deisyf

wood n coed, coedwig; pren

woodbine n gwyddfid

woodcock n cyffylog

woodcutter n torrwr coed

wooded adj coedog

wooden adj o goed, o bren; trwsgl, trwstan

woodland n coetir

woodlark n ehedydd y coed

wood-louse (-lice) n gwrach y lludw, mochyn y coed, tyrchyn llwyd

woodpecker n taradr y coed

wood-pigeon n ysguthan

wood sage n chwerwlys yr eithin, saets gwyllt

wood sorrel n surran y coed

woodwind npl chwythoffer pren

woodwork n gwaith coed, gwaith saer

woof n anwe

wool n gwlân

woollen adj gwlanog, gwlân

woolly adj gwlanog

woolsack n sedd yr Arglwydd Ganghellor

word n gair ▷ vt geirio

wording n geiriad

word processing n prosesu geiriau, geirbrosesu

wordy adj geiriog, amleiriog

work n gwaith, gweithred, gorchwyl ▷ vb gweithio

worker n gweithiwr

work experience n profiad gwaith

workhouse n tloty, wyrcws

working adj yn gweithio, gwaith

workman n gweithiwr

workmanlike n gweithgar, diwyd

workmanship n saernïaeth, crefft

workout n sesiwn ymarfer

worksheet n taflen waith

workshop n gweithdy

world n byd

worldly adj bydol

worldwide adj byd-eang

worm n pryf, abwydyn; llyngyren ▷ vb ymnyddu

wormwood n wermod

worn-out adj wedi blino; wedi treulio

worried adj pryderus, gofidus

worry vb cnoi, baeddu, blino, poeni, poenydio ▷ n pryder, blinder

worse adj gwaeth

worsen vb gwaethygu

worship n addoliad ▷ vb addoli

worshipper n addolwr

worst vt gorchfygu, trechu

worsted n edafedd hirwlan, wstid

worth n gwerth, teilyngdod

worthless adj diwerth

worthy adj teilwng ▷ n gŵr o fri

wound n archoll, clwyf ▷ vt archolli, clwyfo

wraith n cyhiraeth, cyheuraeth

wrangle vb cecru, cweryla, ffraeo ▷ n ffrae, ymryson

wrap vt plygu, amdoi, lapio

wrapping paper n papur lapio

wrasse n gwrachen y môr

wrath n llid, digofaint, soriant

wrathful adj digofus, llidiog, dig

wreak vt tywallt, dial (llid)

wreath n torch

wreck n llongddrylliad ▷ vb llongddryllio

w

wren *n* dryw, dryw bach
wrench *vt* rhwygo ymaith, tyndroi
  ▷ *n* tyndro
wrestle *vi* ymgodymu, ymaflyd
  codwm
wrestler *n* ymgodymwr, taflwr
  codwm
wretch *n* adyn, truan; gwalch,
  dihiryn
wretched *adj* truan, truenus,
  gresynus
wriggle *vb* gwingo, ymnyddu
wright *n* saer
wring *vt* troi, gwasgu
wrinkle *n* crych, crychni ▷ *vb* crychu
wrinkle *n* awgrym, hysbysrwydd
wrinkled *n* crychiog
wrist *n* arddwrn
wristband *n* rhwymyn llawes
wristwatch *n* wats arddwrn, wats
  fraich, oriawr
writ *n*: **Holy Writ** yr Ysgrythur Lân
write *vb* ysgrifennu
writer *n* ysgrifennwr, awdur
writhe *vb* ymnyddu, gwingo
writing *n* ysgrifen; ysgrifennu
writing paper *n* papur ysgrifennu
wrong *adj* cyfeiliornus, cam,
  anghywir, o'i le ▷ *n* cam ▷ *vt*
  gwneud cam â, niweidio, drygu
wrongdoing *n* trosedd, camwedd
wrongful *adj* anghyfiawn, ar gam
wroth *adj* dig, dicllon, digofus, llidiog
wrought *adj*: **wrought iron** haearn
  gyr
wry *adj* cam, gwyrgam

xenophobia *n* senoffobia
X-rays *npl* pelydrau X
xylophone *n* seiloffon